Destination Hig

A Motorcycle Enthusiast's Guide to the Best 334 Roads in Northern California

By Brian Bosworth and Michael Sanders

Twisted Edge Publishing Inc.
Suite 194 - 1857 West 4th Avenue
Vancouver, BC, Canada
V6J 1M4

Phone: 604.721.5001 (toll free: 877.655.5006)
Fax: 604.721.5002 (toll free: 877.655.5007)
Website: destinationhighways.com
Email: info@destinationhighways.com

OREGON
NEVADA
CALIFORNIA
MEXICO
PACIFIC OCEAN
WILD RIVER
REDWOODS
INTER-MOUNTAIN
RUSSIAN COAST
FOREST REGION
WINE COUNTRY
GOLD COUNTRY
HIGH SIERRA
BAY AREA-SANTA CRUZ MTNS
YOSEMITE
BORDERLAND
CVA I
CVA II
CVA III
CVA IV
CVA V
Donut Hole
Crescent City
Yreka
Weed
Eureka
Alturas
Redding
Leggett
Red Bluff
Susanville
Fort Bragg
Chico
Quincy
Ukiah
Nevada City
Reno
Jenner
Santa Rosa
Sacramento
Placerville
South Lake Tahoe
Markleeville
San Francisco
Oakland
Stockton
Modesto
San Jose
Turlock
Lee Vining
Santa Cruz
Mammoth Lakes
Oakhurst
Bishop
Fresno
Bakersfield
Las Vegas
Santa Barbara
Los Angeles
Fauquier
Needles
Palm Springs
San Diego
Tijuana
Yuma
N
40 km
40 miles

DEDICATED TO:

MARK TWAIN
(1835 - 1910)

"I cannot call to mind a single instance where I have ever been irreverent, except toward the things which were sacred to other people."

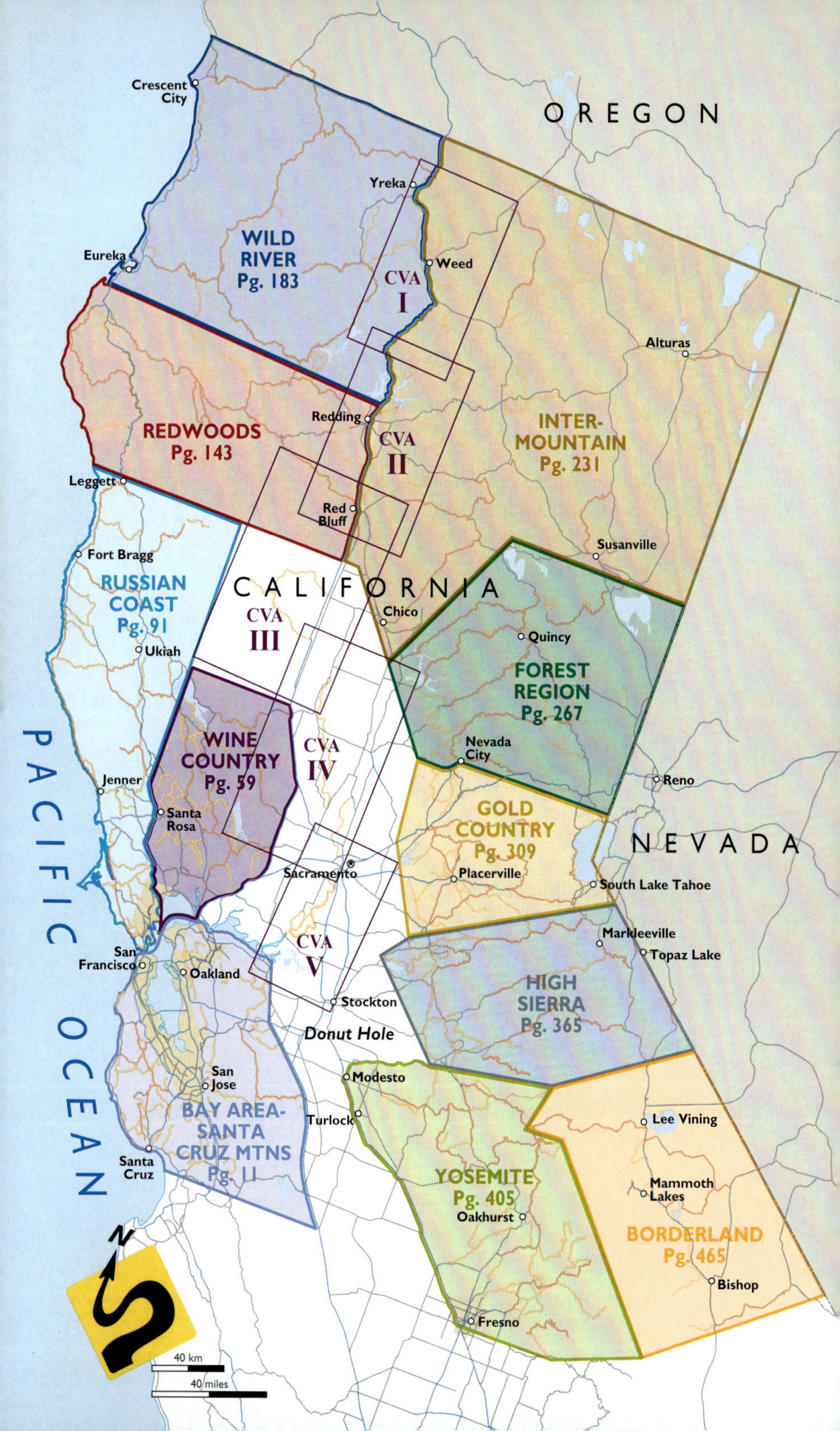

OREGON
CALIFORNIA
NEVADA
PACIFIC OCEAN
Crescent City
Eureka
Yreka
Weed
WILD RIVER Pg. 183
CVA I
Alturas
Redding
REDWOODS Pg. 143
CVA II
INTER-MOUNTAIN Pg. 231
Leggett
Red Bluff
Susanville
Fort Bragg
RUSSIAN COAST Pg. 91
CVA III
Chico
Ukiah
Quincy
FOREST REGION Pg. 267
WINE COUNTRY Pg. 59
CVA IV
Nevada City
Reno
Jenner
Santa Rosa
GOLD COUNTRY Pg. 309
Sacramento
Placerville
South Lake Tahoe
Markleeville
Topaz Lake
San Francisco
Oakland
CVA V
HIGH SIERRA Pg. 365
Stockton
Donut Hole
San Jose
Modesto
Turlock
BAY AREA-SANTA CRUZ MTNS Pg. 11
Santa Cruz
Lee Vining
Mammoth Lakes
YOSEMITE Pg. 405
Oakhurst
BORDERLAND Pg. 465
Bishop
Fresno
N
40 km
40 miles

"There is no room in the brain for idle thought (except on the highway, when idle thoughts appear and float and reconfigure in endless array), and a biker can go for miles and miles without waking up to any sudden realization, including the one that nothing at all has been thought for miles and miles. The faster you ride, the more closed the circuit becomes, deleting everything but this second and the next, which are hurriedly merging. Having no past to regret and no future to await, the rider feels free."

OREGON
CALIFORNIA
PACIFIC OCEAN
WILD RIVER
Pg. 183
REDWOODS
Pg. 143
RUSSIAN COAST
Pg. 91
INTER-MOUNTAIN
Pg. 231
WINE COUNTRY
CVA I
CVA II
CVA III
O'Brien
Crescent City
Klamath
Happy Camp
Yreka
Fort Jones
Gazelle
Weed
Macdoel
Callaghan
Mount Shasta
McCloud
Cecilville
McKinleyville
Blue Lake
Arcata
Eureka
Willow Creek
Weaverville
Ferndale
Fortuna
Rio Dell
Hyampom
Douglas City
Hayfork
Shasta
Redding
Mad River
Anderson
Triangle Jct
Weott
Phillipsville
Redway
Garberville
Shelter Cove
Dales
Red Bluff
Corning
Orland
Willows
Leggett
Covelo
Laytonville
Longvale Jct
Cleone
Fort Bragg
Willits
Mendocino
Albion
Navarro
Elk
Ukiah
Colusa
199
48
96
101
3
97
17
93
89
5
1
299
301
36
44
511
501
A8
99
A9
162
45
20

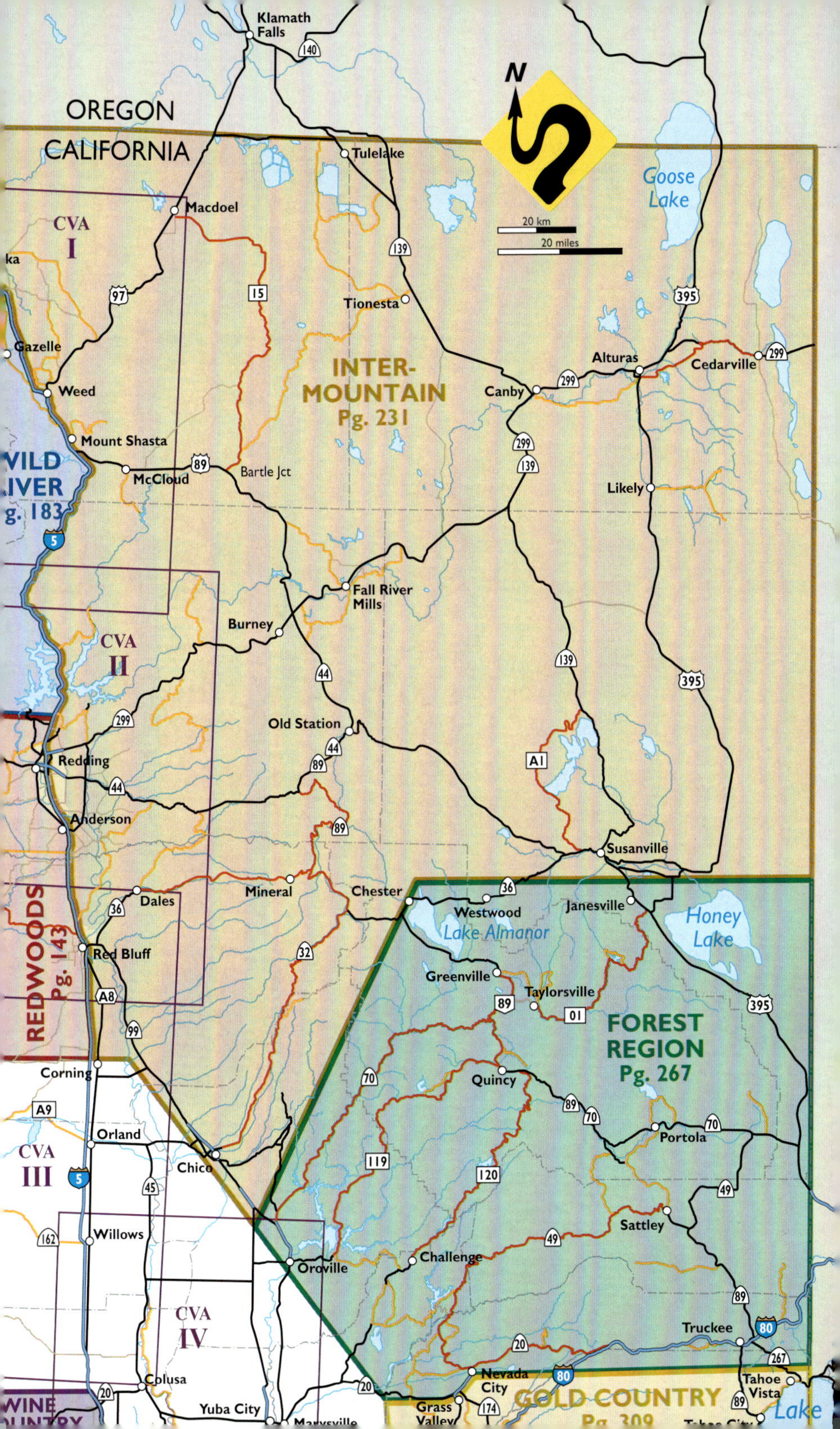

OREGON
CALIFORNIA
Klamath Falls
Tulelake
Macdoel
CVA I
Gazelle
Weed
Mount Shasta
McCloud
Bartle Jct
Tionesta
INTER-MOUNTAIN Pg. 231
Goose Lake
20 km
20 miles
Alturas
Cedarville
Canby
Likely
WILD RIVER Pg. 183
Fall River Mills
Burney
CVA II
Old Station
Redding
Anderson
Susanville
Mineral
Chester
Westwood
Janesville
Honey Lake
Lake Almanor
Dales
Red Bluff
REDWOODS Pg. 143
Greenville
Taylorsville
FOREST REGION Pg. 267
Corning
Quincy
Portola
Orland
CVA III
Chico
Sattley
Willows
Oroville
Challenge
CVA IV
Truckee
Nevada City
Colusa
Yuba City
Grass Valley
Tahoe Vista
GOLD COUNTRY

RUSSIAN COAST
Pg. 91
CVA III
CVA IV
PORES REGIO
Pg. 26
WINE COUNTRY
Pg. 59
CVA V
SACRAMENTO
OAKLAND
SAN FRANCISCO
SAN FRANCISCO BAY
SAN JOSE
BAY AREA SANTA CRU MTNS
Pg. 11
PACIFIC OCEAN
Cleone
Fort Bragg
Willits
Mendocino
Albion
Navarro
Elk
Ukiah
Boonville
Manchester
Point Arena
Lakeport
Clear Lake
Old Hopland
Kelseyville
Clearlake
Lower Lake
Cloverdale
Gualala
Middletown
Stewart Point
Healdsburg
Fort Ross
Guerneville
Calistoga
Jenner
Santa Rosa
Sebastopol
St. Helena
Rutherford
Bodega Bay
Tomales
Sonoma
Napa
Petaluma
Point Reyes Station
Novato
Vallejo
Crockett
Mill Bay
Tamalpais Valley
Willows
Colusa
Williams
Yuba City
Oroville
Marysville
Capay
Woodland
Roseville
Lake Berryessa
Winters
Vacaville
Fairfield
Rio Vista
Antioch
Walnut Creek
Stockt
Tracy
Livermore
Pacifica
Half Moon Bay
Woodside
Sky Londa
San Gregorio
Pescadero
Saratoga
Los Gatos
Boulder Creek
Morgan Hill
Davenport
Santa Cruz
Capitola
Aptos
Gilroy
Watsonville
Hollister
20 km
20 miles
N

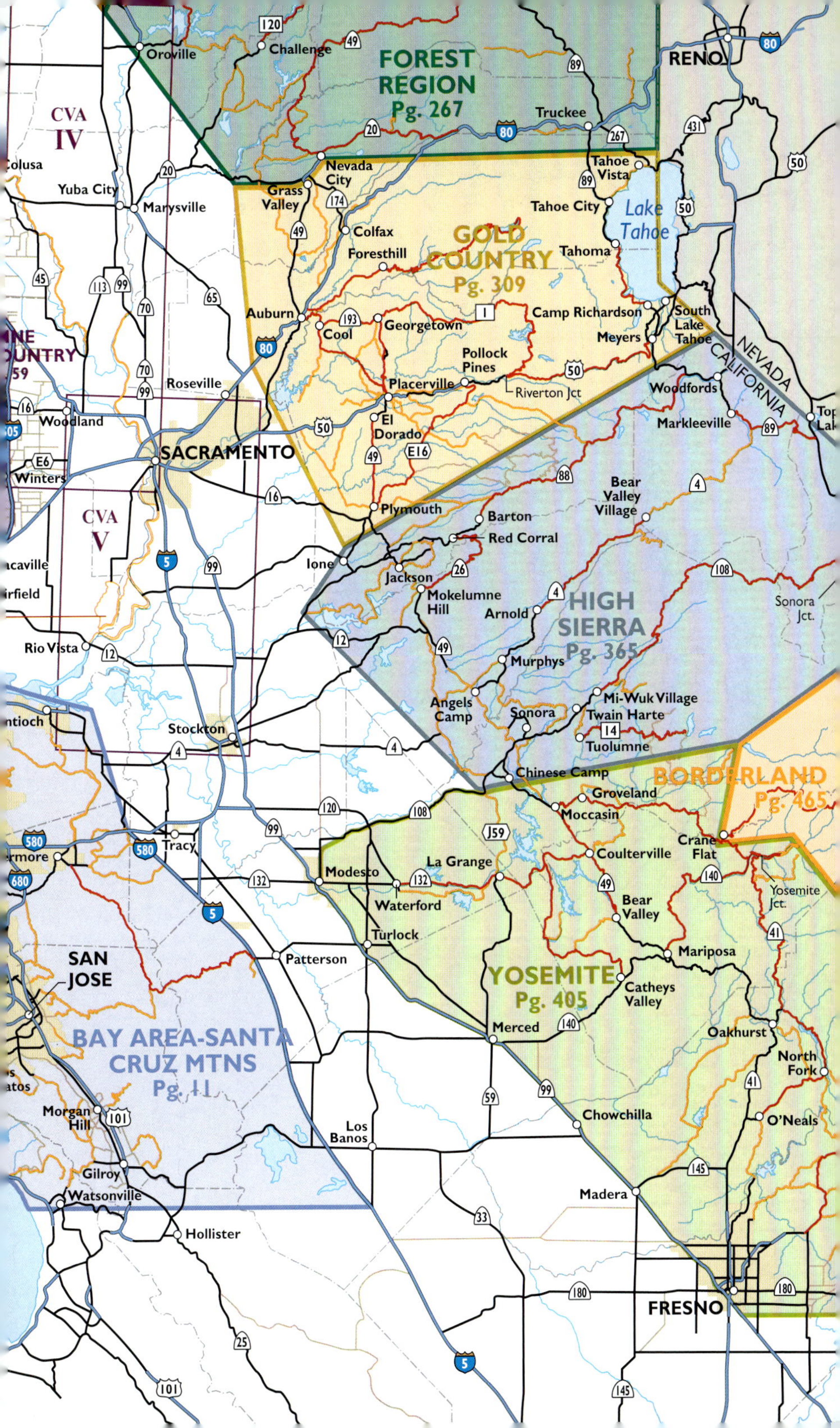

FOREST REGION Pg. 267
GOLD COUNTRY Pg. 309
HIGH SIERRA Pg. 365
BORDERLAND Pg. 465
YOSEMITE Pg. 405
BAY AREA-SANTA CRUZ MTNS Pg. 11
CVA IV
CVA V
RENO
SACRAMENTO
SAN JOSE
FRESNO
Lake Tahoe
NEVADA
CALIFORNIA
Oroville
Challenge
Truckee
Nevada City
Grass Valley
Colfax
Foresthill
Auburn
Cool
Georgetown
Pollock Pines
Placerville
Riverton Jct
El Dorado
Plymouth
Tahoe Vista
Tahoe City
Tahoma
Camp Richardson
South Lake Tahoe
Meyers
Woodfords
Markleeville
Colusa
Yuba City
Marysville
Roseville
Woodland
Winters
Barton
Red Corral
Bear Valley Village
Ione
Jackson
Mokelumne Hill
Arnold
Murphys
Angels Camp
Sonora
Mi-Wuk Village
Twain Harte
Tuolumne
Sonora Jct.
Rio Vista
Stockton
Chinese Camp
Groveland
Moccasin
Crane Flat
Coulterville
Tracy
Modesto
La Grange
Waterford
Turlock
Bear Valley
Mariposa
Yosemite Jct.
Patterson
Catheys Valley
Merced
Oakhurst
North Fork
O'Neals
Chowchilla
Los Banos
Madera
Morgan Hill
Gilroy
Watsonville
Hollister

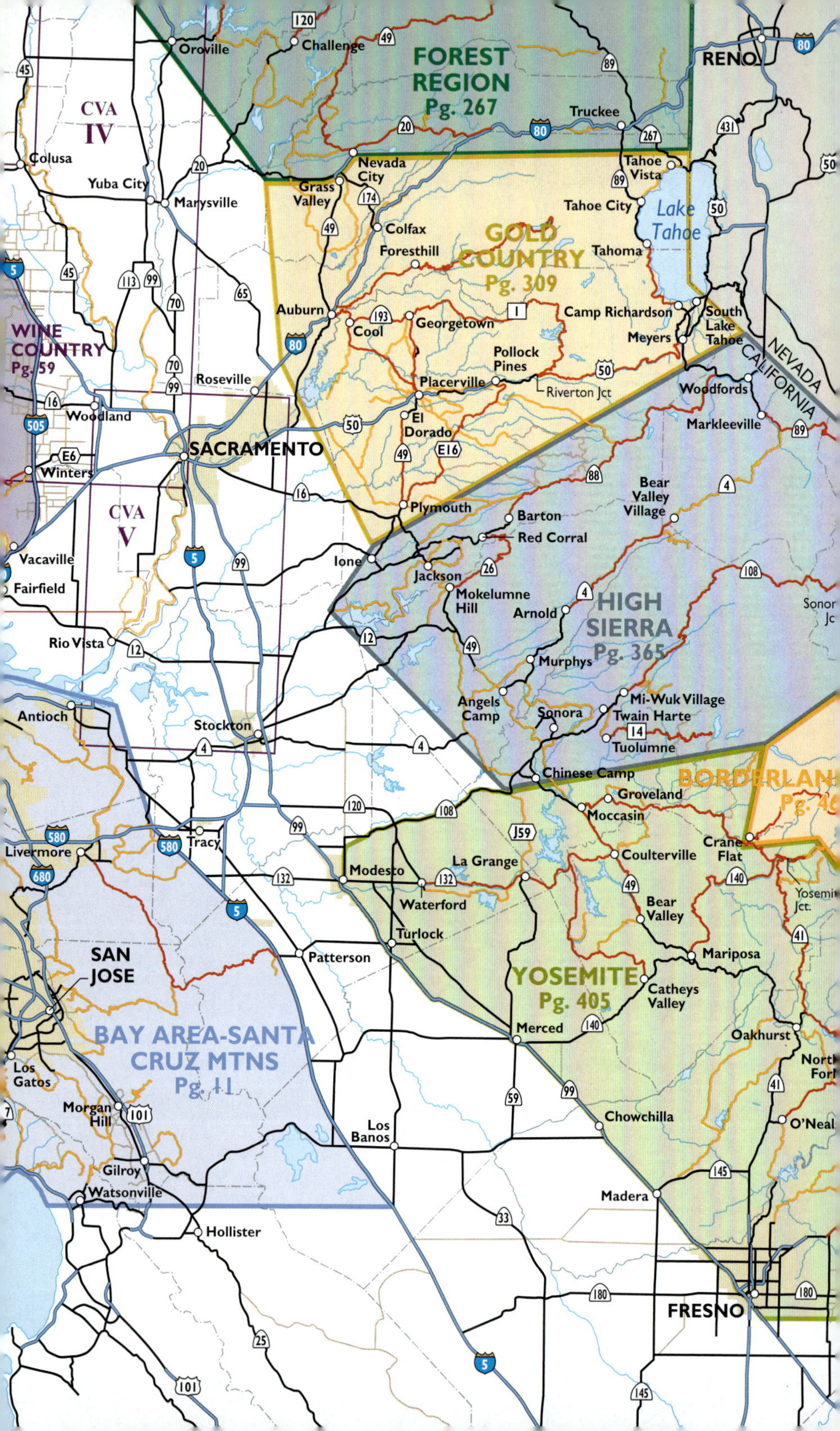

FOREST REGION Pg. 267
GOLD COUNTRY Pg. 309
HIGH SIERRA Pg. 365
YOSEMITE Pg. 405
BAY AREA-SANTA CRUZ MTNS Pg. 11
WINE COUNTRY Pg. 59
CVA IV
CVA V
RENO
SACRAMENTO
SAN JOSE
FRESNO
Lake Tahoe
NEVADA
CALIFORNIA
Oroville
Challenge
Truckee
Colusa
Yuba City
Marysville
Nevada City
Grass Valley
Tahoe Vista
Tahoe City
Colfax
Foresthill
Tahoma
Auburn
Cool
Georgetown
Camp Richardson
South Lake Tahoe
Meyers
Pollock Pines
Placerville
Riverton Jct
Roseville
Woodland
Winters
El Dorado
Woodfords
Markleeville
Plymouth
Bear Valley Village
Barton
Red Corral
Vacaville
Fairfield
Ione
Jackson
Mokelumne Hill
Arnold
Rio Vista
Murphys
Angels Camp
Sonora
Mi-Wuk Village
Twain Harte
Tuolumne
Antioch
Stockton
Chinese Camp
Groveland
Moccasin
Tracy
Livermore
Crane Flat
Coulterville
La Grange
Modesto
Waterford
Bear Valley
Turlock
Mariposa
Patterson
Catheys Valley
Merced
Oakhurst
Los Gatos
Morgan Hill
Chowchilla
Los Banos
Gilroy
Watsonville
Madera
Hollister

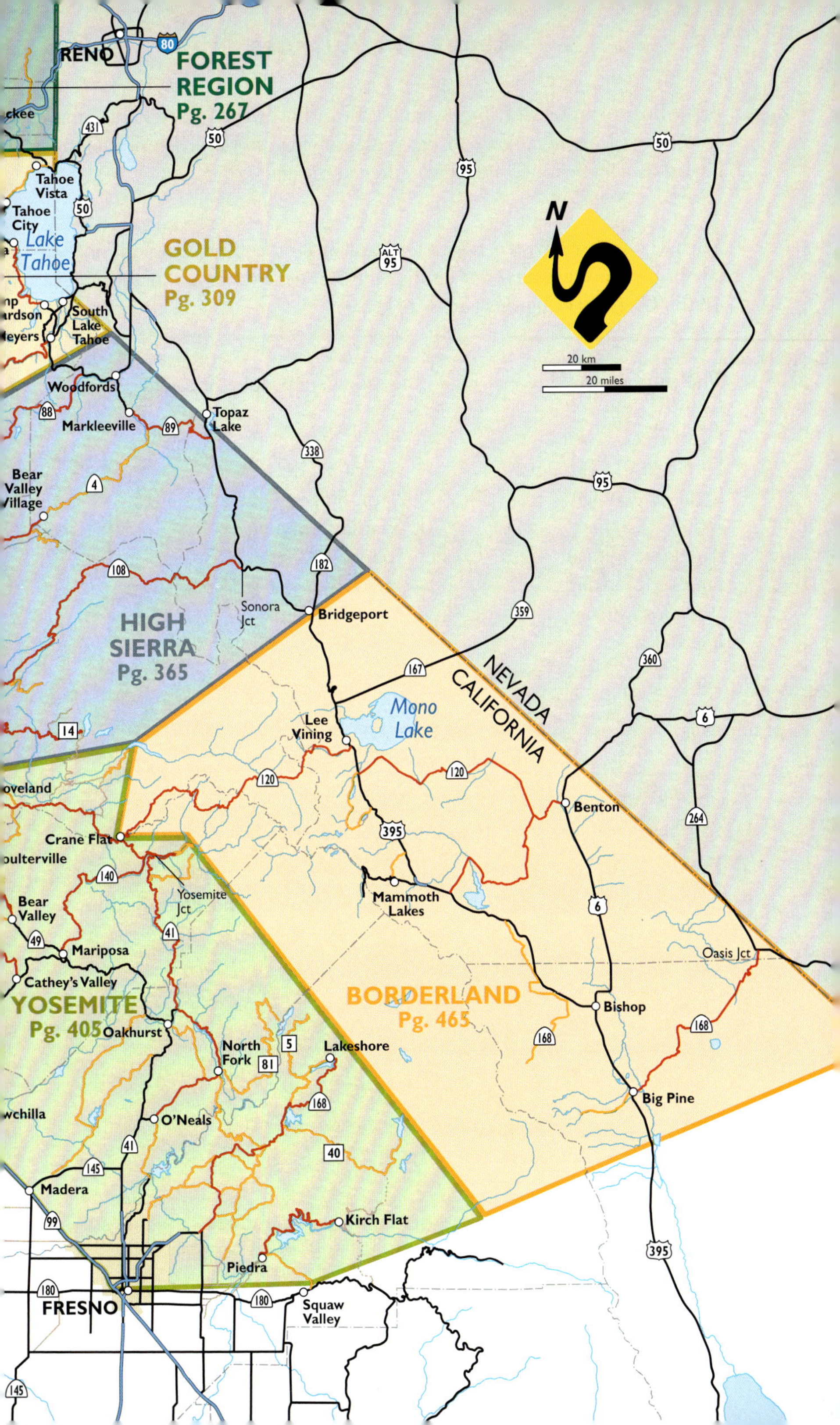

FOREST REGION Pg. 267
GOLD COUNTRY Pg. 309
HIGH SIERRA Pg. 365
YOSEMITE Pg. 405
BORDERLAND Pg. 465
NEVADA
CALIFORNIA
N
20 km
20 miles
RENO
Tahoe Vista
Tahoe City
Lake Tahoe
South Lake Tahoe
Woodfords
Markleeville
Topaz Lake
Bear Valley Village
Sonora Jct
Bridgeport
Mono Lake
Lee Vining
Benton
Crane Flat
Yosemite Jct
Mammoth Lakes
Oasis Jct
Bishop
Big Pine
Bear Valley
Mariposa
Cathey's Valley
Oakhurst
North Fork
Lakeshore
O'Neals
Madera
Kirch Flat
Piedra
FRESNO
Squaw Valley

About The Authors

Brian Bosworth, Chief Motorcycling Officer for Twisted Edge Publishing, co-owns Videomatica, Vancouver's specialty video store. When not biking, he can usually be found in some darkened theater.

Michael Sanders, Twisted Edge's Director of Protocol, practices criminal law in Vancouver. When not on his bike, he spends far too much time in Traffic Court fighting Bosworth's tickets.

The authors would like to thank the following people for their contributions:

Heather Anderson
Don and Cat Bosworth
Lynn M. Coolen
John O. Cooper
Cheramie Johnson
James McFadyen
Veronica Murray
Joel Ritch
Dr. & Mrs. H.D. Sanders
Jessica Sanders
Dani Singer
Mariko Summers
John D. Whyte, Esq
Heinz Woodendunk
Stephanie Yank

Chief Aviator: Don Bosworth

Editor: Caroline Wiggins

Senior Manager Statistics and Cartography: Heidi Windebank

Executive Assistants Cartography Research: Jennifer Jarvis, Jessica Selzer

Maps and Design: Dennis & Struthers Visual Communications Inc.

Published in Canada by Twisted Edge Publishing Inc.

Suite 194 - 1857 West 4th Avenue, Vancouver, British Columbia, Canada, V6J 1M4

ISBN 0-9684328-2-4

Table of Contents

What is Destination Highways Northern California?

A Destination Highway is usually not a major route and often not even a secondary one. It's the kind of road you'd travel to, to journey on – it *is* the destination. And *Destination Highways Northern California* is the most comprehensive guidebook ever produced for the motorcycle enthusiast touring Northern California. Using **TIRES**, or the **Total Integrated Road Evaluation System**, paved roads are rated from a street motorcyclist's unique perspective. TIRES identifies and evaluates elements – some obvious, some not – that together determine if a road is good enough to be called a Destination Highway.

In technically evaluating a road, TIRES counts and categorizes every curve for **Twistiness**, classifies every mile (1.6 km) of a road's surface for **Pavement**, and assesses lane width, shoulder width, sightlines and camber for **Engineering**. It also rates **Scenery** and **Remoteness** according to specific criteria. A road's **Character** is determined by how the other five components blend together, reflecting the overall quality of the riding experience – that "feeling" you only get aboard a bike on a good road. You know the one.

A higher number of points is assigned to those TIRES components that more directly result in a better motorcycle road. The total number of points determines a road's TIRES rating out of 100. With this, the road earns its DH number – its ranking among Northern California's 74 Destination Highways.

While the total rating of every Destination Highway shows how one DH compares to another overall, that isn't always enough. Two roads with close, or even identical total ratings may offer entirely different experiences, depending on how they score their points. So the important thing is to zero in on the TIRES components that most appeal to you. Do you seek twisties above all? Is it that remote, biking experience you prefer? Or are you a stickler for smooth pavement? Once you ride a few roads, you'll get a comparative feel for the numbers and be able to use TIRES to find the roads you like, according to what you like.

However, even TIRES doesn't tell the whole story. The numeric ratings are complemented by written descriptions of the unique riding adventure each Destination Highway offers. **At A Glance** gives you a short summary of the DH's most noteworthy features. **Access** gets you there. For those who want more detail, **On The Road** provides an in-depth, corner-by-corner chronicle. And if you're looking for more, you can always check out the video of each DH at **destinationhighways.com**.

What about those roads you wouldn't "travel to, to journey on" but are worth checking out if you happen to be in the neighborhood? In addition to the 74 Destination Highways, *DH NorCal* guides you to 260 **Twisted Edges**. Described in a single paragraph, TEs may be quiet bypass routes that offer alternatives to major highways, access roads to out-of-the-way lakes, parks or tourist attractions, links to other DHs or TEs or simply winding dead-enders that gravel out in the middle of nowhere. In other words, they're all those little side roads you tend to pass up because you don't know whether the time spent going down them will be well spent or wasted. Not any more.

Of course, there's more to motorcycling than smooth, twisty, traffic-free roads. Your baby needs fuel and maintenance. And these can be a hassle to find, especially in more remote areas. Where's the nearest gas when you're hitting reserve? Where's the most convenient bike shop to arrange that new back tire that you're going to need in two days? Or that just went flat.

And what about you? Maybe you're wondering if there's a nice pub on the water nearby. Or perhaps it's just getting late on a beautiful afternoon, you're having a great day and want to keep going for an hour or two but you've just hit a town and the "where am I going to eat/sleep" thoughts start to nag. You don't want to be riding tired and hungry four hours from now, so you stop. Or get into an argument about whether or not to stop. With the detailed LO-LITE maps, you can easily confirm what service options are down the road, call ahead if you want to and get back on the road, worry free.

Northern California has been subdivided into eleven regions, each with between four and nine Destination Highways. Regional maps show how all the good roads in a given area fit together while the Local maps for each DH (and affiliated TEs) focus in on specific rides. And there's no need to try to pre-plan your whole trip. As you enter a new region, you can make choices quickly and easily to ensure you won't miss any roads that appeal to you.

Spiral bound for longevity and sized to fit a standard tank bag map window, *DH NorCal* is designed so that you'll spend your valuable time, rubber and gas on good roads rather than mediocre ones. For the price of just two or three fill ups, you'll possess the kind of knowledge that is normally acquired only after riding a given area for years. Even if you've never ridden here before, *Destination Highways Northern California* turns you into a "local" wherever you are, while helping you find and enjoy *your* favorite Destination Highway.

Map Icons, Abbreviations & Legend

Destination Highways Northern California maps include thousands of services. None of these businesses has paid any fee for inclusion and they are listed for your convenience. Unless they have been identified as "Recommended" – a designation based on first hand experience – we don't vouch for their quality. But then, finding that out is part of the journey, too.

BLUE icons
Location has three or more of the service. Where icon is blue, specific businesses are not listed.

RED icons
Services offering a discount to holders of a DH book. Just show 'em your copy, and ask for their discount. You will find more not listed in the book at "DH Rider Discounts" on destinationhighways.com

Police
"**L**" (Local/Municipal) "**C**" (County Sheriff) "**S**" (State Patrol).

Bike Shop
Motorcycle Dealer. Brands carried are abbreviated after name e.g. (DUC/YAM)

Accommodations
Maps generally do not list specific accommodation within 10 mi (16 km) of a town with a blue accommodation icon (see BLUE icons)

Pub
Place where you can buy alcohol for on-premises consumption with out also purchasing food. "Lounge" means hard liquor is available. "Tavern" generally means beer and wine only.

Campground
CG Campground with some amenities including flush toilets
BCG Backcountry Campground. Rustic camping. Vault or pit toilets.

Grocery Store
SM Supermarket offering meat, fish, poultry and produce.

Restaurant
Restaurant open for dinner. Fully licensed restaurants and those licensed to sell beer and wine only are not distinguished.
NL Not licensed to serve any alcohol.

Cafe
Not open for dinner. If licensed, will usually be beer and wine only.
NL Not licensed to serve any alcohol.

Gas Station
Many have small convenience stores. These are not specified.

Wineries
Wineries that have tasting rooms.

Tourist Info Centre
May be open seasonally. In smaller centers, this service is often provided by the local chamber of commerce. Many are closed week ends. Hours vary.

Abbreviations

APR	Aprilia
B&B	Bed and Breakfast
BCG	Backcountry Campground
BMW	Hmm
BUE	Buell
C	County Sheriff
CG	Campground
CP	City or County Park
D-	Dealer
DH	Destination Highway
DUC	Ducati
GC	Golf Course
GS	General Store
HD	Harley-Davidson
HON	Honda
JPN	Japanese Motorcycles
KTM	Hmm
KAW	Kawasaki
L	Local/Municipal
MG	Moto Guzzi
MW	Motorworks
MS	Motorsports
NF	National Forest
NL	Not licensed
NP	National Park
NRA	National Recreation Area
PS	Power Sports
Rest	Restaurant
RA	Recreation Area
RP	Regional Park
RS	Recreational Site
S	State Patrol
S-	Service Shop
SM	Supermarket
SP	State Park
SUZ	Suzuki
TE	Twisted Edge
TRI	Triumph
VIC	Victory
YAM	Yamaha

Map Legend

Featured DH

Featured TE

Non-Featured DH

Non-Featured TE

Interstate/Divided Highway

Major Highway/Access To DH

Gravel Highway/Connector

Minor Paved Road

Gravel/Dirt Road

How To Use Our Maps

Although they might look complicated at first, *Destination Highways* maps are actually quite easy to navigate.

In addition to a map showing the whole state and one just showing Northern California, there are three basic types: Overall, Regional and Local. Start with the maps located at the front of the book. They show Northern California's eleven regions. When you turn to the page indicated for any region, you'll find a Regional map showing all of the Destination Highways within the region. On the facing page, a puzzle map shows where the featured region fits in context with the other regions.

Now, turn to the Local map for a specific Destination Highway that interests you. Be sure to check the compass arrow; to increase the scale, some Local maps don't have north at the top of the page. The featured DH is shown in RED and any featured TEs are shown in ORANGE. Non-featured DHs/TEs appear in DARK GREEN/PALE GREEN. Should you wish to navigate to a non-featured DH map, use the DH tabs that run down the side of the facing page. If a non-featured DH is in another region, a page number is indicated.

Central Valley (CVA) TEs and Bay Area (BAY) TEs are not associated with a particular Destination Highway. The CVA TE maps are therefore set out in a separate collection of maps in a stand-alone section after the last region. The BAY TE maps are at the end of the Bay Area – Santa Cruz Mountains Region.

Our book is not an atlas and therefore our Local maps only cover those parts of Northern California where good motorcycle roads are found. Therefore, the next map to the north, south, east or west may or may not be contiguous. To navigate to the next Local map, look for the white navigation arrows where roads go off the edge of the Local Map. These will indicate the next DH map or relevant CVA TE map. When more than one DH is listed, the one nearest geographically is listed first. Again, page numbers are only given for DHs in another region. If no DH or map is indicated, that means there is no Local map for a significant distance. For information in that direction go back to the Regional or Overall maps.

Touring Northern California — What You Should Know

Required Documents

You must carry a valid driver's license and proof of insurance from your home state or country. The minimum age for drivers is 16 with training. 18 without. And 50 if you're riding a trike.

Drinking and Driving

It is illegal (not too mention ill advised) to ride your ZX14 with a blood alcohol level of 08% or higher. If stopped, you may have to submit to a breath and possibly a blood test to determine this. Sobriety checkpoints are used in California.

Helmet Requirement

'Fraid so.

Lane Splitting

In the interests of making motorcycle travel more challenging and fun, California gives its motorcyclists a choice: you can either join the lines of pylons sitting for endless hours in stop-and-go freeway traffic or you can aim your bike between the lanes and scoot right up the middle. It doesn't matter if the traffic's moving; the only legal limitation is that it "must be done in a safe and prudent manner." Start slow.

Sidewalk Parking

It seems to be acceptable (if technically illegal) in San Francisco to park a motorcycle, European style, on public sidewalks. With parking becoming harder to find in increasingly congested cities, this is a reasonable custom that deserves to spread far and wide, no?

Speed Tax Collection in California

To serve and collect. California's monetary approach to "traffic safety" is pretty much indistinguishable from other American jurisdictions. And with so many different types of speed tax collectors, every piece of road seems to be on somebody's patrol route. Having said this, most of the STC hot spots seem to lie on busy parts of the interstates and inside the city limits of small towns. Fortunately, many California officers are motorcyclists themselves and as a result, may cut you a little slack as long as you're properly dressed and not behaving like a total squid. Though red light cameras are used, photo radar is otherwise banned. Thus, a combination of sanity, open eyes, a good LASER/radar detector and some police discretion (more likely the more remote the area) should keep you on the road. Here's who to look out for.

California Highway Patrol

Forget about the warm, fuzzy "Chippies" you see on TV. While these highwaymen normally restrict themselves to state highways and interstates, they've been known to make special appearances in certain "trouble spots". They also make unsporting use of airborne units, so when you see the speed limit painted in very large numbers on the asphalt, keep an eye on the sky. Apart from stationary LASER, airborne radar and VASCAR, they use moving radar as well. Reports are the CHP has pretty much abandoned X band in favor of Ka and K band units. Ticket still costs the same, though.

County Sheriffs
These good ol' boys and gals generally have better things to do than patrol quiet county roads issuing tickets to clean cut motorcyclists out for a little fun. That said, they tend to specialize in coming over the next rise just when you least expect them.

Municipal and Local Police
The kids who never left home. Not bright enough to go to college, not dumb enough to get into fast food management training, these valued civil servants get a cut of whatever they contribute to the local economy. Or maybe it just seems that way.

National and State Park Rangers
Yes, they have the power to issue speeding tickets. And yes, they sometimes use radar. And yes, that infinitesimal number is actually the park speed limit.

Countermeasures

Radar and Laser Detectors
Legal to own and operate in California.

Laser Jammers
These devices are illegal in California. Does that mean they actually work?

Radar Jammers
These devices are also illegal in California.

Reciprocity

California driving records are available to other states and Canadian provinces. You'll have to check with your state or provincial department of motor vehicles to see how a California traffic infraction might affect your driving record and insurance rates. California, however, is one of only six states that have not signed the "Non-Resident Violator Compact". Therefore, your local jurisdiction will not suspend your license for failure to pay or answer a California ticket. Of course, your drivers license may ultimately be suspended in California. Which is only a problem if you ever plan on coming back.

Accidents

If you're involved in an accident where anyone is injured or killed, or if more than $500 in damage is incurred, you must report the accident to the Department of Motor Vehicles (800.777.0133).

Road Conditions

These can be confirmed for any major highway by calling 800.427.ROAD or 916.445.1534.

Gravel Roads

Though we at *Destination Highways* are strictly pavement, many of our readers actually like riding on gravel (aka "maxburning"). So *DH NorCal's* maps include gravel connections as options to doubling back on dead-enders. As for the quality of the gravel roads? Sorry, wrong book.

Motorcycle Dealers

Destination Highways endeavors to list 'em all in the Bike Shop Index and show their locations on our Local and Regional maps. The question is, why is it still so tough to find one open on Sundays or Mondays in the peak of riding season?

Accommodation in Northern California

Looking for a place to stay the night? Wondering if there even is a place to stay? *Destination Highways NorCal* maps provide detailed information about accommodation for less populated areas. Hotels, motels, B&Bs, resorts and even guest ranches are included. Local Tourist Info offices, or Chambers of Commerce provide the most comprehensive information on accommodation in any given area. They're also a good place to call when you're really stuck.

Camping in Northern California

There are many different organizations offering camping in Northern California. Apart from private campgrounds, you'll find State Park, National Park, National Forest, National Rec Area, County Park and so on. And let's not forget the Army Corps of Engineers. But really, if your idea of roughing it consists of carrying the topbox into the Best Western, you probably have one question when it comes to campgrounds: Do they or do they not have flush toilets? *Destination Highways* understands. A **CG** designation means it has flush toilets. A **BCG** (Backcountry Campground) means it doesn't. In the case of a CG, private campgrounds simply bear the campground name (ie Beaver Valley CG). If it is a government campground, CG will have a prefix (ie Beaver Valley SP CG). Many parks, forests and recreational areas have more than a single campground. For that reason, the name of the park, forest or rec area generally do not appear. Instead you'll see the name of the specific campground within the park, forest or recreation area.

State Park Reservations

Some of Northern California's state parks accept reservations. The reservation -by-phone number is 800.444.PARK (7275) or punch **www.parks.ca.gov** into your Blackberry. A non-refundable reservation fee will be charged to your credit card.

National Park Reservations

The only national park in Northern California that accepts reservations is Yosemite, and only for some of its campgrounds. Phone 800.436.PARK (7275) or go online to **reservations.nps.gov**.

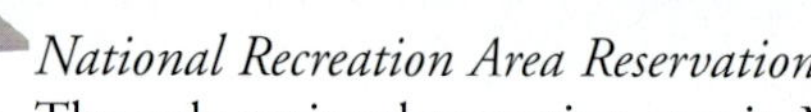

National Recreation Area Reservations
The only national recreation area in Northern California that accepts reservations is the Whiskeytown National Recreation Area. 800.365.CAMP (2267) or **reservations.nps.gov**.

Private Campgrounds
Private campgrounds are shown on the maps with a phone number. Naturally, reservation policies will vary.

Dining in Northern California

Our definition of a café/restaurant does not include fast food joints and their ilk (eg. Dennys). Even "In N Out", no matter how the locals rave about their burgers and fries. And if you're in a place that is large enough to have fast food emporiums, you generally have other options anyway. Unless you're in downtown Fresno.

Wineries in Northern California

What's a road trip to California without a little wine tasting? *Destination Highways* lists wineries that offer drop-in wine tasting and that appear on or near our featured roads. If you want more detail, free regional guides are abundant and available at any tourist info office. Oh, and don't forget to spit (see *Drinking and Driving* above).

When You Should Ride

With its long riding season, the question in Northern California is really when not to ride. Two things are relatively certain: it never rains in the summer and July and August are hellishly hot, especially inland and at lower elevations. If you ride in high summer, extreme temperatures may mandate riding near the Pacific, with its frequent fog, or in the mountains. Winter brings snow to the Cascades/Sierra Nevada and can block some of the higher elevation roads as late as May/June. Temperature is more moderate and uniform from day to day and from season to season on the ocean side of the Coast Range and in coastal valleys, though winters are cooler and wetter the farther north and closer to the ocean you are.

Warning

Although the descriptions in this book are based on actual riding experiences, riding conditions on any given road are constantly changing. Weather, pavement damage, traffic and development can all create unforeseen hazards. Always wear protective riding gear and observe local traffic laws.

Riding motorcycles is exhilarating, partially due to the fact that you risk injury or death while doing it. The authors and Twisted Edge Publishing Inc. accept no responsibility for your individual application of the contents of this book which might result in any harm, injury or property damage to yourself or others.

SACRAMENTO
Berryessa
Winters
St. Helena
Rutherford
WINE COUNTRY Pg. 59
Dixon
Vacaville
Elk Grove
Sonoma
Napa
Fairfield
Suisun City
CVA V
Rio Vista
Lodi
RUSSIAN COAST Pg. 91
BAY I
Grizzly Bay
SAN PABLO BAY
Vallejo
Crockett
Pittsburg
Oakley
Concord
Antioch
BAY II
Stockton
Corte Madera
Walnut Creek
Berkeley
OAKLAND
SAN FRANCISCO
San Ramon
Manteca
Daly City
SAN FRANCISCO BAY
San Leandro
Tracy
Hayward
Livermore
Pacifica
Burlingame
Half Moon Bay
San Mateo
Redwood City
Fremont
BAY III
BAY AREA-SANTA CRUZ MTNS
DH55
Woodside
Milpitas
DH47
Mountain View
Sunnyvale
Sky Londa
DH28
SAN JOSE
Santa Clara
San Gregorio
Saratoga
Pescadero
DH39
Los Gatos
Boulder Creek
DH74
Morgan Hill
BAY V
BAY IV
San Luis Res.
Davenport
Aptos
Gilroy
Capitola
Santa Cruz
Watsonville
Hollister
PACIFIC OCEAN
DH34
(D-HON)
(D-POL)
(D-BUE/HD)
(D-HON/KAW/SUZ)
(D-HD)
(D-KAW/YAM)
(D-YAM)
(D-APR/DUC/KAW/SUZ)
(D-KAW)
(D-POL/TRI)
(D-SUZ/YAM)
(D-HON)
(D-HD)
(D-KTM)
(D-DUC/TRI YAM)
(D-BUE/HD)
(D-HON/KTM/YAM)
(D-KAW/SUZ)
(D-HON/SUZ)
(D-SUZ/YAM)
(D-BMW)
(D-HON/SUZ)
(D-KAW/YAM)
(D-BUE/HD)
(D-SUZ)
(D-BUE/HD)
(D-HON/YAM)
(D-KAW/SUZ)
(D-APR/BIM/KTM/VIC)
(D-AUG/DUC/MG/TRI)
(D-BMW)
(D-BUE/HD)
(D-HON/KAW/SUZ/YAM)
(D-HON/YAM)
(D-BMW/KAW)
(D-BUE/HD)
(D-APR)
(D-DUC/KTM/TRI)
(D-HD)
(D-HON/KAW)
(D-SUZ)
(D-BUE/HD)
(D-HD)
(D-HON/KAW/SUZ/YAM)
(D-HON YAM)
(D-HON/KAW/YAM)
(D-BUE/HD)
(D-HON/KAW/KTM/SUZ)
(D-BUE/HD)
(D-HON/KAW)
(D-APR/KTM/MG)
(D-HON)
(D-KAW/SUZ/YAM)
(D-YAM)
(D-BMW)
(D-HD)
(D-YAM)
(D-HON/SUZ)
(D-APR/MG/TRI)
(D-HON/SUZ/YAM)
(D-BMW/TRI)
(D-HD)
(D-DUC/HON)
(D-KAW/SUZ)
(D-HON/KAW/SUZ/YAM)
(D-VIC)
(D-BUE/HD)
(D-HON/KAW/SUZ)
(D-KTM)
(D-APR/DUC/MG)
(D-KAW)
(D-BUE/HD)
(D-BMW/YAM)
N
10 km
10 miles

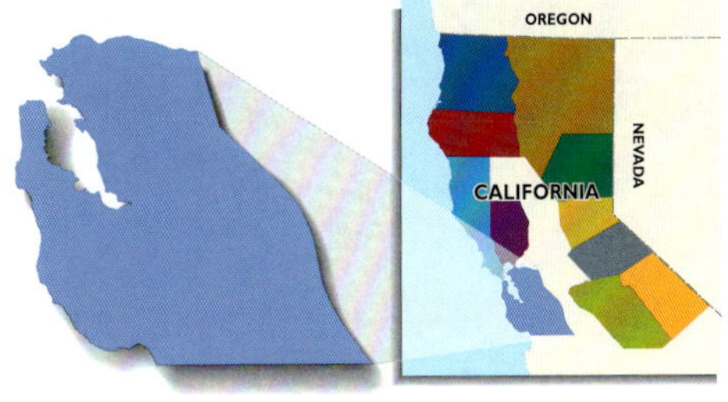
OREGON
NEVADA
CALIFORNIA

To San Francisco
To DH37 Pg. 93
Mission St.
To San Francisco
Daly City
South San Francisco
225 Rockaway Beach Ave 650.355.4122
Mission Motorcycles (HON/KAW/YAM) 6232 Mission 650.992.1234
To Oakland
To San Jose
San Bruno
Seal Cove Inn B&B 650.728.4114
Moss Beach Distillery 650.728.5595
Chevron
Coastside Market SM
Pizzeria Del Sol Café 650.728.5151
Bay Area Yamaha (YAM) 1601 Adrian 650.343.9750
San Mateo Bridge (Toll)
For East Bay Bike Shops see Pg. 532
SAN FRANCISCO BAY
Pacifica
Andreas Lake
Millbrae
Burlingame
Hillsborough
Hillside Blvd.
Honda-Suzuki San Mateo (HON/SUZ) 101 E 25th Ave 650.341.5867
San Mateo
Foster City
Peninsula HD (BUE/HD) 380 Convention 650.568.0800
Redwood City Honda (HON/KAW/KTM/SUZ) 890 2nd Ave 650.364.1104
Montara
Moss Beach
MONTARA MTN.
El Granada
Lower Crystal Springs Res.
Belmont
San Carlos
Dumbarton Bridge
Veterans Blvd.
To BAY III Pg. 50
Whipple Ave.
Redwood City
Bay Rd.
Half Moon Bay
Harbor Bar
Skyline Blvd.
Upper Crystal Springs Res.
Edgewood Rd.
Farm Hill Blvd.
Middlefield Rd.
Palo Alto
Half Moon Bay State Beach CG
Higgins Purisima Rd.
KINGS MTN.
DH28 TE-A
Woodside
5th Ave.
Marsh Rd.
King's Mountain Country Store
Purisima Creek
Purisima Creek Rd.
Lobitos Creek Rd.
Kings Mtn. Rd.
MORENA SIERRA
Sand Hill Rd.
Alpine Rd.
To Saratoga & DH39
To San Jose
Portola Valley
Los Altos
S. El Monte Ave.
Tunitas Creek
Tunitas Creek Rd.
Star Hill Rd.
Bear Gulch Rd.
W. Bear Gulch Rd.
Sky Londa
TE-B
Moody Rd.
Page Mill Rd.
El Monte Rd.
The Mountain House 650.851.8541
Skywood Trading Post
Alice's Rest 650.851.0303
SANTA CRUZ
La Honda Rd.
TE-B ALT
BLACK MTN.
San Gregorio
San Gregorio Creek
DH28
La Honda
MINDEGO
Alpine Rd.
DH55
SAN ANDREAS FAULT ZONE
Goose & Turrets B&B 650.728.5451
Farallone Inn 650.728.8200
Montera Beach Outrigger 650.728.7366
Fog City Pizza 650.728.5672
Neighborhood Mart
Pompinios Cr. Rd.
DH28 TE-C
DH28 TE-B
Pescadero Rd.
Portola Creek County Park
TE-A
Stage Rd.
North St.
Pescadero Cr. Rd.
Loma Mar
Pescadero Creek
State Park Rd.
MTNS.
Pescadero
Bean Hollow Rd.
Butano Cutoff Rd.
Cloverdale Rd.
Canyon Rd.
Butano Creek
Portola Redwoods SP CG
DH39
Pescadero Cr. Rd.
Gazos Grill
SAN MATEO
SANTA CRUZ
San Lorenzo River
DH28 TE-D
Gazos Cr. Rd.
Gazos Creek
DH39 TE-C
BIG BASIN REDWOODS STATE PARK
DH39 TE-A
PINE MTN.
DH74
To Santa Cruz
To BAY IV Pg. 52
To Santa Cruz
To BAY IV Pg. 52
Empire Grade Rd.
Boulder Creek
2 km
2 miles

DH55 Saratoga Gap – Hwy 35/Hwy 92 Jct

Skyline Blvd (Hwy 35)

Distance:	26.2 mi / 42.2 km	Traffic:	Light

At a Glance

This road is called the Alice's Restaurant road, though it's not about Alice and the restaurant, so it's not the real name of the road, that's just the name of the restaurant but that's why we called it the Alice's Restaurant road. Now it all started many years ago when riders went up along the spine of the Santa Cruz Mountains for the good Pavement and Twistiness and to get away from the traffic and the crowds and the heat of the Bayatopolis metropolitan area. And ridin' along like that, they'd get some decent Scenery when they get up there, though sometimes all you can see are trees. 'Course it bein' so close to a great urban conglomeration and all, that kinda weighs on the feeling of Remoteness. And maybe they'd be a tad disappointed that the Engineering and Character aren't perfect, not that they aren't pretty good but some might think they could be better. Now friends, you gotta remember that there's lots of fast ridin' goin' on up here and you just know that kind of thing attracts Officer Obie and, well, he might put you in the back of his patrol car and take you down to the police officer station for bein' so brave and honest about how fast you were goin'. So, be careful you don't find yourself in a pickle. 'Cuz you always want to ride on your motorsickle.

TIRES	
Twistiness	24.7/30
Pavement	14.9/20
Engineering	6.0/10
Remoteness	4.3/10
Scenery	9.2/15
Character	4.2/15
Total	**63.3**

Access

From mid-DH40 Boulder Creek – Saratoga (San Jose) (Hwy 9)

Turn north at the Saratoga Gap four-way junction of Hwy 9 with 35. You is on the road.

From Hwy 35/Hwy 92 Jct

Turn south on Hwy 35. You's on the road.

On The Road

It all starts at Saratoga Gap where Hwy 35 heads north from its junction with Hwy 9. See that deer sign? That might be worth paying attention to. The smooth, immediately curving asphalt slices through a grassy cut and heads into some overhanging deciduous trees. And when they're not overhanging the road, they are perilously close to it. But on the other hand, isn't this asphalt nice?

Glimpses of the dense urbania east of the San Andreas Fault Zone appears through and between the trees on the right. Through and between those on the left, you might see Butano Ridge lighting up the rolling Santa Cruz topography.

At 1.6 mi (2.6 km), you apex gracefully right into a more open area, at least on your left side, where you can see some nearby, tree-covered hills. Then you're curving back among dark woods before re-emerging alongside some generic vineyard to your right. An incongruous Palo Alto city limit sign flashes by at 3.3 mi (5.3 km). Seems awfully aggressive of PA to be staking its claim for future sprawl up here but, fortunately, there's no evidence of that actually happening. At least so far.

The pretty, open area continues for a while but you inevitably return to the enclosure of the forest. Triffid-like greenery makes it hard to see around some of the continuing corners. At 5.2 mi (8.4 km), you're again out in the open on an actual straight, more or less the first one you've experienced. Then, you're back in the bush.

Alpine Rd (**TE-A**) and Page Mill Rd (**TE-B**) junction left and right respectively at 6.4 mi (10.3 km). Right after that, another long straight out in the open allows you to dispense with any pylonic blockage. But surprisingly, the traffic may be so light that you don't have to.

A vista point at 7.5 mi (12.1 km) offers a sweeping view over the south Bay Area. Its quality, however, depends entirely on the quantity of the air pollution. Just as the quality of the curves seems to depend on the quantity of trees. The more you're in the forest, the tighter it is. And when the terrain opens up, the road tends to be straighter. When you are out in the open, it's easy to see you are running along the Santa Cruz crest, as the topography falls away quite steeply either side.

Great views spread out from atop the crest. At 10.8 mi (17.4 km), a northwest vista of staggered ridges drops Pacificward, stretching blue into the distance. By contrast, the stuff on the right is mostly urban.

So much for the great sights and sightlines. Before long you're back curving in the forest on a slight downhill slope and then junctioning with mid-**DH28 Woodside – San Gregorio** in Sky Londa at 13.7 mi (22.0 km). Lots of choices here. Might be time to set a spell at Alice's and figure out which scene you want to make.

Staying with the DH, you are quickly out of Londaland. Initially, it's straight but it's not long before you're twisting back and forth and climbing through more forest. This is the tightest section of the DH; you may be forced to cut back your speed on the blind but nicely banked corners.

You turn eastward to round the unseen peak of Morena Sierra. The turnoff for the Skeggs viewpoint comes up in your right at 17.9 mi (28.8 km). You can't see the view here without actually turning off; the woods are too thick. But there's no missing the low-speed advisories along here. You should be going slowly enough not to miss Kings Mtn Rd (**DH28TE-A**), junctioning right at 19.3 mi (31.1 km). Should you be aiming for it.

Hmm, might be wishing you took that TE. As you carry on, there's starting to be quite a few buildings sprouting up in the trees. Always hate to see that. Mind you, the forest is so thick here on Kings Mtn, it tends to do a pretty good job of hiding 'em.

At 22.8 mi (36.7 km), three things happen. You exit the deep forest pretty much for the last time, the curves relax considerably and the pavement assumes a downward cant. When the last tight curves arrive at 24.9 mi (40.1 km), there is a good perspective on the Upper Crystal Springs Reservoir down and over to your right in the middle distance. Beyond that, up ahead on your left, is a good view of the lowly but very green Montera Mtn, though most of the terrain on this side of the road drops away steeply down to Half Moon Bay rather than up. The remainder of your ride sweeps back and forth as it clings to the top of the ridge. The DH ends by T-boning Hwy 92 at 26.2 mi (42.2 km).

Twisted Edges

TE-A Alpine Rd (7.5 mi / 12.1 km)

Don't mind narrow and bumpy as long as you get some remote and scenic? That's what you find on this, the roughest Santa Cruz TE. It winds through mostly undeveloped countryside and forest on the Santa Cruz' Pacific-side slope.

ROUTING OPTION: If you're looking for more back-country stuff, this one hooks up with the whole lot smoother ***DH28TE-B Pescadero Rd-Pescadero Cr Rd***

TE-B Page Mill Rd (8.6 mi / 13.8 km)

Pretty clean pavement on this constantly curving route off I-280 up to Skyline helps gets you quickly out of the west Bay Area's urban morass. It's not that there's no suburbia on the lower part, but the curves help distract you. Some rougher, narrower asphalt on the higher bits, but there's some pretty Santa Cruz scenery up here as well. You may experience a fair number of stretchy-panted lowlanders peddling up and zipping down this one.

TE-B ALT El Monte Rd - Moody Rd (3.2 mi / 5.2 km)

Another urban escape route via the next I-280 exit south of the one for TE-B. Though it's not exactly free from houses or spandex either, there are lots of curves and pretty swell pavement.

TE-C Montara – Pacifica (Hwy 1) (3.8 mi / 6.1 km)

It's really hard to believe that CalTrans engineers managed to put their helmets together and punch a road through one of Northern California's most rugged sections of coastline. This dramatic piece of road is literally sculpted into the steep, solid cones of red-brown rock that soar vertically above the crashing surf south of Pacifica. But after spending a gazillion dollars per mile to create this short, but scenic and curving masterpiece, why can't they budget for a fresh patina of pavement every now and then? Kinda leaves you scratchin' your Shoei.

RIDER'S LOG: **DATE RIDDEN:** **YOUR RATING: /10**

Just what is an "STC" or "maxburner" anyway?
Check out these and other Twisted Terms in the Glossary at p.549

MONTARA MTN.
To San Francisco To DH37 Pg. 93
To San Francisco & DH37 Pg. 93
Lower Crystal Springs Res.
To BAY I Pg. 44
Belmont
To San Francisco
San Carlos
Peninsula HD (BUE/HD) 380 Convention 650.568.0800
Redwood City Honda (HON/KAW/KTM/SUZ) 890 2nd Ave 650.364.1104
Veterans Blvd.
Whipple Ave.
Redwood City
Edgewood Rd.
Bay Rd.
Middlefield Rd.
Marsh Rd.
5th Ave.
To BAY III Pg. 50
Palo Alto
Farm Hill Blvd.
37°30'
Half Moon Bay Rd.
Half Moon Bay
Upper Crystal Springs Res.
Higgins Purisima Rd.
Skyline Blvd.
KINGS MTN.
TE-A
Woodside
Kings Mtn. Rd.
Purisima Creek Rd.
Purisima Creek
Lobitos Creek Rd.
Star Hill Rd.
SANTA
MORENA SIERRA
Bear Gulch Rd.
Sand Hill Rd.
To San Jose To Saratoga & DH39
Tunitas Creek Rd.
Tunitas Creek
PACIFIC
Pioneer Village Pub
Robert's Mkt
Chevron
W. Bear Gulch Rd.
Sky Londa
Portola Rd.
Alpine Rd.
DH55 TE-B
Page Mill Rd.
Moody Rd.
Skyline
CRUZ
La Honda Rd.
DH55
SAN ANDREAS FAULT ZONE
DH55 TE-B ALT
37°20'
BLACK MTN.
San Gregorio
San Gregorio GS
Blvd.
San Gregorio Creek
La Honda
Pescadero Rd.
MTNS.
MINDEGO
Pompinios Cr. Rd.
DH28
Alpine Rd.
DH55 TE-A
OCEAN
TE-C
TE-B
Memorial CP CG
Loma Mkt
Stage Rd.
Pescadero Cr. Rd.
Loma Mar
Creek
State Park Rd.
North St.
Pescadero
Pescadero Cr. Rd.
Pescadero
BUTANO RIDGE
Skywood Trading Post
Alice's Rest 650.851.0303
DH39
Bean Hollow Rd.
Butano Cutoff Rd.
Cloverdale Rd.
Butano Creek
Canyon Rd.
SAN MATEO
SANTA CRUZ
Butano SP CG
Creek
TE-D
Gazos Grill
Gazos Cr. Rd.
Gazos
BIG BASIN REDWOODS STATE PARK
DH39 TE-A
Apple Jacks Inn
Pioneer Mkt
La Honda House 650.747.0312
37°10'
Rossi Rd.
CHALK MTN.
PINE MTN.
EAGLE ROCK
Costanoa 877.262.7848
Pescadero Creek Inn B&B 650.879.1898
Pecadero Creekside Barn 650.879.0868
Duarte's Tavern 650.879.0464
Muzzi's Mkt & Deli
Arcangeli Country Bakery
Empire Grade Rd.
DH74
To Santa Cruz To BAY IV Pg. 52
Scott Creek
N
Ano Nuevo Bay
DH74 TE-E
2 km
2 miles
122°20'
To Santa Cruz & DH 74
Swanton Rd.
122°10'

DH28 Woodside – San Gregorio

Highway 84

Distance:	19.4 mi / 31.2 km	Traffic:	Moderate

At a Glance

Rides Like Teen Spirit

Load up on gas and bring your friends
It's fun to ride, not to pretend
On Pavement overboard and self assured
Oh no, this li'l DH is no dirty word
Hello, hello, hello, how low
Hello, hello, hello, can you go?

With your lights on
The woods're less dangerous
Uphill tight curves, entertain us
Don't get stupid, it's contagious
Here's more curves now, entertain us
A Gixxer and a Ninja to Sky Londa and
La Honda, Yeh!

Named for a bike, it's great at its best
And for this gift you'll feel blessed
Your riding group has always been
And always will until the end
Hello, hello, hello, how low?
Hello, hello, hello, can you go?

With your lights on, it's less dangerous
Downhill curves now, entertain us
STCs, they're outrageous
Lots more curves now, entertain us
A Ducati and Aprilia to Sky Londa and La Honda, Yeh!

TIRES	
Twistiness	29.4/30
Pavement	17.0/20
Engineering	6.3/10
Remoteness	3.7/10
Scenery	8.5/15
Character	8.0/15
Total	**72.9**

Access

From Woodside

On Hwy 84

Head west on 84. Once you pass King's Mtn Rd (**TE-A**), you're on the road.

From I-280

Via Hwy 84

Take Exit 25 west to Woodside. Stay on 84 through town and once past King's Mtn Rd (**TE-A**) you're on the road.

From San Gregorio

On Hwy 84

Head east on 84. You're on the road.

On The Road

The curve right off the top as you leave the junction with Kings Mtn Rd (**TE-A**) is an overture for the music to come. Unfortunately, the speed limit of 25 mph (40 kmh) also portends; it don't get much higher on this climb. As if that wasn't sufficiently dissonant, there are *two* 20-mph (30-kmh) advisories for the same corner. By the time you see the warning for the next "killer" curve, you're immune to such fooleries. Unless you're on a Rune.

Forget about the signs. The frequent driveways, access roads and vegetation pressing right up to the road edge should counsel prudence... as should the bus filling up the opposite lane. Narrow road? Yeah, you could say that.

At 0.8 mi (1.3 km), things begin to look up as the speed limit rises to a lofty 35 mph (55 km). You'd tap your toes for glee, but there are no corners and a pylon is blocking the way ahead... not any more, he's not.

The straight ends at 1.6 mi (2.6 km), where Portola Rd junctions left. The DH angles right in another suggested 20-mph (30-kmh) curve. Surely, the deer warning sign isn't serious either. Wouldn't the buses take care of that particular problem?

Ah, a welcome sign – one promising twisties for 3 mi (5 km). And sure enough, the tango begins immediately. The low-speed advisories kind of make sense here; the curves are tight and linked, there's little or no shoulder and the thick bush/slope/rock wall begins right at the road's edge.

It's dark in here as well. The forest is thick and tall, forming a canopy that keeps out much of the daylight, even on a bright day. But your main problem is likely to be that single pylon from Arizona crawling along in front of you. There's no place for him to pull over even if he were so inclined and there's no way you can get past him on these tight corners. Seems ya gotta get up early to beat the traffic around here. Like 4am.

At least you're back in the daylight at 2.5 mi (4.0 km), though there is still not much freeboard beyond the white edge line. The asphalt between the white lines is nice though. You've probably got enough time to admire its smooth, fine-grained quality. Not to mention the high view over urbania to your left at 3.4 mi (5.5 km). It shows how high you've come already.

Truth be told, you wouldn't be going much faster even if there were no one in front of you. You're in and out of dark forest and when you're in it, it's as dark as night. The slow-speed corners are continuous almost right up until you hit the stop sign at 5.1 mi (8.2 km), marking the four-way junction on the crest of the Santa Cruz Mtns with mid-**DH55 Saratoga Gap – Hwy 35/Hwy 92 Jct.**

You can stop for refreshment, chat or just ogle all the bikes parked in Sky Londa. Or you can motor across Hwy 35 and get on La Honda Rd, Hwy 84's alias on the west side of the Santa Cruz Mountains. With the name like that, can the road be anything but good?

The speed limit leaps to a bracing 40 mph (65 kmh), though you are also warned that your rate of progress will be, ahem, "checked by radar." Back in the deep dark forest, the ubiquitous low-speed advisory precedes the first corner, which could contain a bicycle towing a trailer. If you happen to be pylon-free, you can still really enjoy these continuous, provocatively banked, slightly downhill curves. Because the pavement remains as smooth and sweet as Charlize Theron playing Britt Ekland in *The Life and Death of Peter Sellers.*

Before too long, the forest canopy opens and you're in sunlight. At 7.7 mi (12.4 km), there is even a view to the right just before Old La Honda Rd junctions left. Forget it – despite the views of the Vintage Japanese Motorcycle Club, an old Honda can't compare with a new one.

Mini fields and such appear amid the still-predominant forest. The curves relax. At the same time, more and more vistas of the surrounding hilly countryside can be seen. At least until 9.5 mi (15.3 km), when the vegetation presses in once more, the semidarkness returns and tight, numerous corners return. Your Honda's in La Honda at 11.1 mi (17.9 km).

Stop for a photo op? Maybe not. The curves keep it up past town to the junction with Pescadero Rd (**TE-B**) left, at 11.9 mi (19.2 km). And they continue as you cross La Honda Creek and begin to track the San Gregorio Creek and its valley. The roadway is thick with trees and low-speed advisories now, but as the landscape flattens out, it's definitely not as narrow. There's even sometimes a shoulder. Great, but what happened to the quality pavement?

The curves decrease in both frequency and intensity by 13.7 mi (22.0 km) as the valley widens, opens up and straightens. Dotted yellow shows up. By 16.1 mi (25.9 km), the surrounding hills are pretty much bare on both sides of the still-expanding valley. Despite the fact that the terrain gets flatter as you approach the coast, curves continue to make regular appearances, all the way up to the end of the DH at 19.4 mi (31.2 km) in San Gregorio.

Twisted Edges

TE-A King's Mtn Rd (5.1 mi / 8.2 km)
A lesser-trafficked, narrow, hairpinny, darkness-enshrouded alternative from the west Bay Area urban flat up to Hwy 35. The pavement, great up to Huddart Park, is not so good past it.

TE-B Pescadero Rd-Pescadero Cr Rd (12.8 mi / 20.6 km)
Baptists and beer trucks? A church camp attracts the former to this road but it's hard to figure out what draws not one but *two* beer trucks. Maybe they handle curves better than you'd think. Other pylon traffic is light on this mostly well-paved twister through the lower Santa Cruz Mountains and the forest along Pescadero Creek's valley. It's probably the best Santa Cruz TE, all things considered. Deserves to be famous. Do it.

TOUR NOTE: If you have a beer at Duarte's Tavern in Pescatown, you might want to know its artichoke soup deserves almost as much fame as the TE. Mmm, mmm good.

TE-C Stage Rd (7.0 mi / 11.3 km)
The mediocre-to-poor, narrow and patchy pavement shouldn't dissuade you from doing this better option to parallel, boring coastal Hwy 1. Especially if you're Scottish and are pinin' to be windin' in the Highlands. Probably the most remote-feeling Santa Cruz TE. Whether you enter Stage left or right.

TE-D Cloverdale Rd - Gazos Creek Rd (7.6 mi / 12.2 km)
The first half of Cloverdale has good pavement and is straight enough that it can be ridden as fast as Hwy 1. The rest curves but has inferior pavement, though not as bad as that on **TE-C**. The Gazos part is also narrow, so keep an eye out for beer (or UPS) trucks trying to deliver you to the next world.

RIDER'S LOG: **DATE RIDDEN:** **YOUR RATING: /10**

How does this book work again? RTFM. "What is Destination Highways Northern California?" and "How to Use Our Maps" appear at the front of the book.

To DH28
To San Francisco
SAN JOSE
DH55
DH28
Skyline Blvd.
SAN ANDREAS FAULT ZONE
Stevens Crk. Blvd.
Foothill Blvd.
Stevens Crk. Blvd.
N Bascom Ave.
W San Carlos St
Flagg Ave.
Cupertino
Pescadero Rd.
Alpine Rd.
Pescadero Cr. Rd.
DH55 TE-A
Stevens Creek Res.
Stevens Cyn. Rd.
TE-D
Mt. Eden Rd.
Pierce Rd.
Saratoga-Sunnyvale Rd.
Saratoga Ave.
To BAY III Pg. 50
To Oakland
DH28 TE-B
Portola Creek County Park
State Park Rd.
Pescadero Creek
Savannah Chanelle
408.741.2934
Redwood Gulch Rd.
Saratoga Gap
Camden Ave.
Saratoga
Los Gatos Blvd.
Union Ave.
White Cockade Rest
831.338.4148
DH39
SANTA CRUZ MTNS.
Ahlgren
831.338.6071
Los Gatos
Shannon Rd.
SAN MATEO
SANTA CRUZ
MT. BIELAWSKI
Skyline Blvd.
TE-C
Black Rd.
Montevina Rd.
TE-E ALT
Hicks Rd.
BAY TE-Z
2 km
2 miles
San Lorenzo River
Kings Creek Rd.
Alma Bridge Rd.
Lexington Res.
To BAY IV Pg. 52
BIG BASIN REDWOODS STATE PARK
Bear Crk. Rd.
TE-A
TE-B
Creek
Two Bar Rd.
Bear Creek Rd.
Bear Creek
SANTA CLARA
SANTA CRUZ
Aldercroft Hts. Rd.
Old Santa Cruz Hwy.
PINE MTN.
Jamison Crk. Rd.
Big Basin Redwoods SP CG
EAGLE ROCK
TE-E
Patchen Pass (1800ft/545m)
Summit Rd.
Boulder Creek
Boulder Creek GC
831.338.2111
Empire Grade Rd.
Brookdale
E. Zayante Rd.
DH74 TE-F
West Branch
Soquel-San Jose Rd.
Alba Rd.
Ben Lomond
DH74 TE-G
Glenwood Dr.
DH74 TE-D
DH74 TE-B
Felton Empire Rd.
Bean Cr. Rd.
Vine Hill Rd.
Mtn. View Rd.
Laurel Glen Rd.
Swanton Rd.
Pine Flat Rd.
Scotts Valley
Ice Cream Grade Rd.
Fenton
Mt. Hermon Rd.
Granite Ck. Rd.
Soquel Creek
Bonny Doon
DH74 TE-E
DH74
Lockewood Ln.
Graham Hill Rd.
DH74 TE-G ALT
N
DH74 TE-C
Bonny Doon Rd.
Smith Grade Rd.
DH74 TE-A
Empire Grade Rd.
HENRY COWELL SP
Glen Cyn. Rd.
Rodeo Gulch Rd.
Branciforte Dr.
Davenport
San Lorenzo River Dr.
Porter St.
Kennedy Dr.
To Bay IV Pg. 52
To Monterrey
To SoCal
San Jose Bike Shops
1 GP Sports (HON/SUZ/YAM) 2020 Camden Ave 408.377.8780
2 Moto Italiano (APR/MG/TRI) 1425 W San Carlos 408.287.6680
3 San Jose BMW 1886 W San Carlos 408.295.0205
4 San Jose HD 1551 Parkmoor 408.998.1464
5 San Jose Yam 776 N 13th St 408.287.2946
WILDER RANCH SP
UCSC
Market St.
Soquel Dr.
Water St.
High St.
41 Ave.
Highland Ave.
Capitola
Bay Dr.
Western Dr.
Santa Cruz
Soquel Ave.
Brookdale Lodge
831.338.6433
Brookdale Grill
831.338.9529
Brookdale Market
Felton Crest Inn
831.335.4011
Fern River Resort Motel
831.335.4412
Moto Italiano (APR/DUC/MG) 200 Kennedy 831.476.3663
All American Honda Suzuki (HON/KAW/SUZ) 6990 Soquel Ave 831.476.8100
Boulder Creek Brewery
831.338.7882
Merrybrook Lodge
831.338.6813
Johnnie's Super
Texaco
Econo Lodge
831.336.2292
Jaye's Timberlane Resort
831.336.5479
Firehouse Tavern
Ben Lomond SM
Shell
SLC
1211 Ocean
800.833.3494
Santa Cruz HD (BUE/HD) 1148 Soquel Ave 831.421.9600
Moore & Sons MC (KTM) 2-1431 E Cliff 831.475.3619

DH39 Boulder Creek – Saratoga (San Jose)

Highway 9

Distance:	20.6 mi / 33.2 km	Traffic:	Moderate

At a Glance

TIRES	
Twistiness	30/30
Pavement	15.4/20
Engineering	5.4/10
Remoteness	4.0/10
Scenery	7.1/15
Character	8.1/15
Total	70.0

One of the problems on this constantly twisting road is that if you get stuck behind a single pylon, you can end up going about as fast as a Model-T. And given the generally great asphalt and lack of driveways east of the Hwy 236 Jct, if Henry J. Ford is out there, you're going to catch up to him. Until you encounter a horsepowerless carriage, however, you'll experience the unforgettable feeling of essing on smooth, climbing, well-engineered blacktop through a mature redwood forest that breaks only to offer you some panoramic southern views from the ridge atop Waterman Gap. When it drops down the Saratoga side, past the junction with DH55 Saratoga Gap – Hwy 35/Hwy 92 Jct, the road is bumpier, steeper and more erratically engineered. It's more erratically forested, too, as the solid redwoods give way to a mixed forest of alder, ash and pine. But whichever scenic section of this DH you're on, it's a great place to be laying on the throttle, getting down on your sliders and, if a Tin Lizzie appears, leaning on the horn. AAAOOOGAH!

Access

From Boulder Creek

On Hwy 9

Head north on Hwy 9. You're on the road.

From Saratoga

On Hwy 9 (Saratoga Ave/Big Basin Way)

Head west. You're on the road.

From DH55 Hwy 35/Hwy 92 Jct – Saratoga Gap (Hwy 35)

The south end of Hwy 35 junctions with the DH 13.6 mi (21.9 km) east of Boulder Creek, 7.0 mi (11.3 km) west of Saratoga.

On The Road

Departing Boulder Creek from the Bear Creek Rd (**TE-B**) junction, the DH curves northward through the last strands of development that impair

Hwy 9 all the way from Santa Cruz. Houses, summer camps and lots of driveways bask in the forest shade. The development doesn't relent until 4.1 mi (6.6 km).

Now the road begins to ess in earnest as it climbs slowly into thick forest and rough terrain. Excellent if slightly tar-stripped pavement comes together with beautifully banked engineering, increased remoteness and a dwindling number of driveways. The great thing is, there's lot more of this to come. The not-so-great thing? It's going to be a bitch to get past that logging truck. And you know he won't be using any of the pullouts.

The road enters Castle Rock State Park at 5.6 mi (9.0 km). Once it does, the redwoods get taller and the entire forest takes on a certain old-growth airiness. Low banks rise right, then left, then you're into a 15-mph (25-kmh) hairpin at 6.7 mi (10.8 km). This forest seems a funny place for a vineyard, but there is a marked turnoff for one at 6.9 mi (11.1 km).

You'll probably pass on the vino. Because the clenched, banked curves and great pavement through the trees just keep on going. You pass the turnoff left to Hwy 236 at 7.5 mi (12.7 km), though "highway" is a bit of a misnomer.

*TOUR NOTE: This alternate route back to Boulder Creek offers 8.3 mi (13.4 km) of steep, mainly one-lane crap pavement before it turns into a beautiful piece of asphalt (**TE-A**) at the state park's western entrance. See **TE-A** for more information about this section of road.*

Can it get better? Sure, this is a Destination Highway, after all. The smooth pavement gets even silkier past the junction. The redwoods get taller and the curves continue unrelentingly. They ease a little in tightness as you traverse Waterman Gap, where a gap in the trees lets you see Mt. Bielawski and myriad other Santa Cruz Mtns to the south. That's what happened when you spent 45 years working for the U.S. Land Office back in the 1880s. Instead of giving you a raise, they named a mountain after you.

And when you put TIRES elements together the way this road does, you get a DH named after you. This is one of the nicest little pieces of highway in Northern California. In fact, it bears a striking similarity to the much longer and more remote northern part of **DH5 Cleone (Ft Bragg) – Leggett**. Less traffic up there, to be sure, but it's a long way to go for a quick lunchtime ride.

Intermittent mountain views continue until 10.1 mi (16.3 km) but end when you enter a rare straightway. The corners resume at 10.6 mi (17.1 km), flicking back and forth atop a treed slope that angles down to the left. At 11.2 mi (18.0 km), there's a big view over Saratoga Gap through a momentary opening in the trees. Don't let your eyes linger too long over the scene; that's a pretty tight sweeper ahead.

You continue to see the drop-off view to the left through the trees as you ess past a vista point/day use area at 12.7 mi (20.4 km). As you descend from the DH's high point, there are places to stop, hang on the grass and admire the south-facing views from the top of this ridge. But why chill out when you've just gotten warmed up? There are more S-curves to take you to the stop-signed junction with Hwy 35 at 13.6 mi (21.9 km). Turning left here will put you on **DH55 Saratoga Gap – Hwy 35/92 Jct**. Turning right will put you on Skyline Blvd (**TE-C**). To stay on the DH all the way to Saratoga, **go straight**.

The S-curves continue as you cross Hwy 35 and drop down a steep grade through thick, jumbled, overhanging forest. Gone are the uniform redwoods. Trees from every genus in Linnaeus' *Systema Naturae* jostle along the roadside. Pavement's still all right but the engineering is not nearly as good as prior to the junction. Corkscrewing your way down, the corners come blind, extremely sharp and even U-shaped. This would be enough of a challenge going up, but it's coming down that really separates the six-hundreds from the twelves.

You curl past a brief, south-facing view at 15.9 mi (25.6 km) whereupon, apart from the hairpin at 16.3 mi (26.2 km), the curves loosen enough that you can accelerate more through the S-turns. They take on a much more steady rhythm as you coast down through the outskirts of Saratoga.

Saratoga's 30-mph (50-kmh) speed zone comes at 18.1 mi (29.1 km). You continue through the trees on tight, but beautifully sculpted turns that, if anything, get better as town approaches. Especially when the new pavement takes over at 18.8 mi (30.2 km). You cross a bridge and continue to ess tightly past a few side streets that duck into the trees including the poorly marked Pierce Rd (**TE-D**) that goes off left at 19.3 mi (31.1 km). The DH ends when you reach the town's 25-mph (40-kmh) speed zone at 20.6 mi (33.1 km).

Twisted Edges

TE-A Boulder Creek – Big Basin Redwoods SP (Hwy 236)

(9.0 mi / 14.5 km)

Why does this TE not follow Hwy 236 all the way to the northern junction with Hwy 9? Well, there's a reason. Up to its endpoint in Big Basin Redwoods State Park, it's a smoothly paved, winding and well-engineered climb up and into the park's enormous redwoods. Indeed, the section north of **DH74 Santa Cruz - Jamison Creek Rd/Hwy 236 Jct**, where Boulder Creek's sprawl ends, is very similar to Hwy 9, but with less traffic.

TOUR NOTE: Unfortunately, once you pass the park HQ at the end of the TE, Hwy 236 narrows for the remaining 8.3 mi (13.4 km). It starts as smooth, twisty one lane, becomes bumpy, twisty one lane, then steep and bumpy one lane and finishes with a final tidbit of two lanes.

TE-B Bear Creek Rd (9.3 mi / 15.0 km)

The many curves that scoot up from Boulder Creek to Skyline Rd at the top of the Santa Cruz range have great pavement and engineering. Even when the road narrows and roughens a bit toward the top, it offers more remoteness in compensation, as well as some views. Bottom line: it'll have you smiling for sure and that's the second best thing you can do with those lips.

TE-C Skyline Blvd - Black Rd (11.0 mi / 17.7 km)
The smooth pavement and engineering of Skyline Blvd's long, gentle sweepers and occasional tight curves contrast markedly with the steep, and bumpy ride you get on Black Rd's contorted one and two lanes down from the top of the ridge to Hwy 17.

NAVIGATION: To access Black Rd from Hwy 17, take the Bear Creek Rd exit off of Hwy 17. Then head slightly north following the marked signs to Black Rd.

TE-D Pierce Rd - Mt Eden Rd - Stevens Canyon Rd (6.4 mi / 10.3 km)
Large-lot development has spread up from the flatland to engulf the Pierce/Mt Eden area's vineyards. But at least these people demand good asphalt and the terrain is robust enough to ensure curves. The northern half around the reservoir is mostly protected from sprawl by the Stevens Creek County Park.

NAVIGATION: If you are coming from the south end, make sure you turn 90 degrees left at one mile onto Mt Eden from Pierce or you'll be sucked into the Saratogaville vortex.

North access is from Foothill Blvd (south from I-280) or via Stevens Cr Blvd (west from Hwy 85)

TE-E Old Santa Cruz Hwy (5.7 mi / 9.2 km)
Tired of the ratrace on Hwy 17 between Los Gatos and Santa Cruz? Then maybe it's time to quit working and check out the well-paved and continually S-curving old timer that was left in its dotage to toddle along quietly through the forest to Summit Rd. Ah… in your now much more relaxxxed mind, time will slowww… and distance will stretcchhh…. Just don't ruin your retirement by taking the other, crappy part of Old Santa Cruz from Summit back down to 17.

TE-E ALT Alma Bridge Rd - Aldercroft Heights Rd (5.1 mi / 8.2 km)
The same length as Old Santa Cruz, but this rougher, out-in-the-open twister around the Lexington Reservoir sure doesn't have as much *concorde*, as the French would say, as Old SC. Still beats 17, though.

*NAVIGATION: If you are coming south from Los Gatos on Hwy 17, you can only access this TE by taking the Bear Creek exit, doubling back along Montevina Rd past the left turn for Black Rd (**TE-C**) and then nipping east under 17.*

RIDER'S LOG: **DATE RIDDEN:** **YOUR RATING:** /10

Find more information about camping in Northern California, including how to make a reservation, in the "Touring Northern California – What You Should Know" section at the front of the book.

DH28
La Honda
Pescadero Rd.
Alpine
Pescadero Cr. Rd.
Portola Creek County Park
State Park Rd.
To San Gregorio & DH28 To San Francisco
Pescadero Creek
DH28 TE-B
Page Mill Rd.
Skyline Blvd.
DH55 TE-B
DH55 TE-A
DH55
SANTA
SAN ANDREAS FAULT ZONE
Redwood Gulch Rd.
Saratoga Gap
To DH28 To San Francisco
Stevens Crk. Blvd.
Foothill Blvd
Stevens Cyn. Rd.
Mt. Eden Rd.
DH39 TE-D
Cupertino
SAN JOSE
N Bascom Ave.
W San Carlos St.
Flagg Ave.
To BAY III Pg. 50 To Oakland
Saratoga-Sunnyvale Rd.
Saratoga Ave.
Pierce Rd.
Saratoga
Camden Ave.
Union Ave.
Los Gatos Blvd.
Los Gatos
Shannon Rd.
Hicks Rd.
To BAY IV Pg. 52
DH39
DH39 TE-C
DH39 TE-E ALT
MT. BIELAWSKI
Skyline
SAN MATEO
SANTA CRUZ
BIG BASIN REDWOODS STATE PARK
PINE MTN.
EAGLE ROCK
Jamison Crk. Rd.
DH39 TE-A
San Lorenzo River
Kings Creek Rd.
CRUZ
Creek
DH39 TE-B
Two Bar Rd.
Bear Creek Rd.
Bear
Montevina Rd.
Black Rd.
Bear Creek Rd.
Alma Bridge Rd.
Lexington Res.
Aldercroft Hts. Rd.
Old Santa Cruz Hwy.
SANTA CLARA
SANTA CRUZ
DH39 TE-E
BAY TE-Z
Burrell School Winery 408.353.6290
Casa Del 17 Country Store 408.353.1717
Patchen Pass 1800ft/545m)
Summit Rd.
Highland Wy.
TE-F
To San Gregorio & DH28 To San Francisco
Boulder Creek
Brookdale
TE-D
Empire Grade Rd.
Alba Rd.
For details see DH39
Ben Lomond
E. Zayante Rd.
MTNS.
TE-G
Glenwood Dr.
West Branch
Soquel-San Jose Rd.
Summit Market
Swanton Rd.
Pine Flat Rd.
DH74
Felton Empire Rd.
Bean Cr. Rd.
Scotts Valley
Vine Hill Rd.
Laurel Glen Rd.
Mtn. View Rd.
Ice Cream Grade Rd.
TE-E
Bonny Doon Rd.
Fenton
Mt. Hermon Rd.
TE-B
TE-A
TE-C
Davenport
Bonny Doon Rd.
Smith Grade Rd.
Empire Grade Rd.
Lockewood Ln.
HENRY COWELL SP
Graham Hill Rd.
TE-G ALT
Glen Cyn. Rd.
Granite Ck. Rd.
Branciforte Dr.
Rodeo Gulch Rd.
Soquel Creek
Casa Legno's
Porter St.
BAY TE-W
Aptos
Hallcrest Vineyards 831.335.4441
San Lorenzo River Dr.
UCSC
WILDER RANCH SP
Highland Ave.
Water St.
High St.
Bay Dr.
Market St.
Soquel Dr.
41 Ave.
Capitola
Santa Cruz
Western Dr.
Soquel Ave.
Kennedy Dr.
To BAY IV Pg. 52 To Monterrey To SoCal
37°20'
37°10'
37°00'
36°50'
122°10'
122°00'
2 km
2 miles
N
San Jose Bike Shops
1 GP Sports (HON/SUZ/YAM) 2020 Camden Ave 408.377.8780
2 Moto Italiano (APR/MG/TRI) 1425 W San Carlos 408.287.6680
3 San Jose BMW 1886 W San Carlos 408.295.0205
4 San Jose HD 1551 Parkmoor 408.998.1464
5 San Jose Yam 776 N 13th St 408.287.2946
Henry Cowell CG
Bonny Doon Winery 831.425.4518
Moore & Sons MC (KTM) 2-1431 E Cliff 831.475.3619
New Brighton State Beach CG
Seacliff State Beach CG
Hilton 831.440.1000
Best Western Inn 831.438.6666
Carbonero Creek RV CG 831.438.1288
Safeway SM
Shell/76
4 Camp Evers 831.438.1010
1211 Ocean 800.833.3494
New Davenport Inn B&B 831.425.1818
Whale City Bakery Bar & Grill 831.423.9803
Arrow Store
La Cabana Taqueria 831.425.7742
Moto Italiano (APR/DUC/MG) 200 Kennedy 831.476.3663
Santa Cruz HD (BUE/HD) 1148 Soquel Ave 831.421.9600
All American Honda Suzuki (HON/KAW/SUZ) 6990 Soquel Ave 831.476.8100

DH74 Santa Cruz – Jamison Creek Rd/Hwy 236 Jct

Empire Grade Rd / Jamison Creek Rd

Distance:	17.9 mi / 28.8 km	Traffic:	Moderate

At a Glance

TIRES	
Twistiness	22.5/ 30
Pavement	11.5/ 20
Engineering	5.5/ 10
Remoteness	3.8/ 10
Scenery	7.8/ 15
Character	3.9/ 15
Total	**55.0**

"Restrictions on homosexuality to be eased in Poland's penal code" read the sly San Francisco newspaper headline. No matter whether your preferred mount is a Junak or something else, riders of all proclivities can agree on the civil union of uninhibited TIRES components here that can be had right now in and out of the hunky Santa Cruz Mountains. One attraction is that the boys in blue are likely to be on the prowl for crotch rockets cruising the more radical DHs hereabouts. Another is the Kinkiness on this sometimes nicely cut curver. Empire Grade's Pavement and Engineering overall is more butch than femme. And you can expect some rough stuff on the Jamison Creek Rd north end part down to Hwy 236. If you prefer Remoteness when using your rubber, you won't find a lot here. Scenery's not overly cutiepie either; usually you're just stuck in random bush. Some will say this option has Character flaws but whether you're GLBT or straight, if you like to dress up in leather, you should at least once this short one. Because it ain't no Polish penile joke.

Access

From Santa Cruz

Via Hwy 1/Highland Ave

Hwy 1 (also called Mission St between Bay St and Highland Ave) is the major east-west route through Santa Cruz. Highland turns left after two blocks onto High St. High eventually becomes Empire Grade. After you pass the main turnoff to UC Santa Cruz, you are on the road.

Via Hwy 1/Bay St or Western Dr

You can take Bay St or Western Dr (west of Bay) off Hwy 1. Both will take you to High St. Turn left on High, which eventually becomes Empire Grade. After you pass the main turnoff to UC Santa Cruz, you are on the road.

From Hwy 236

Jamison Creek Rd junctions with Hwy 236 just south of the Boulder Creek Golf and Country Club. Take it. You're on the road.

On The Road

Coming off the green, open area fronting UC Santa Cruz, the road immediately narrows and plunges deeply and abruptly into dark forest. You want preliminaries? A deer warning sign along with a 25-mph (40-kmh) advisory precedes some multiple, linked corners. Just as you get used to working them, the road pops out into the open at 1.2 mi (1.9 km) and the lascivious curves back off. You're in a 25-mph (40-kmh) school zone. Hope school's out for summer.

Driveways lead to buildings tucked back just off the road. Soon these give way to open fields before loose bush begins to appear intermittently. By the time you skirt the edge of the Wilder Ranch State Park, however, trees dominate.

You're in the middle of a straight when you come upon Smith Grade Rd (**TE-A**), left at 3.7 mi (6.0 km). A sweeper starts off a series of good, linked curves. There's even an abrupt rockface tight to your right, sometimes matched by one to your left. The DH is nicely banked through here and there's even an occasional bit of a shoulder to give you extra leeway. The couple of tighter corners at a 5.1 mi (8.2 km) might surprise you. Hopefully, the return of the driveways won't.

You're back in brush until you reach the four-way junction with Felton Empire Rd (**TE-B**) right and Ice Cream Grade Rd left at 7.0 mi (11.3 km). (The latter may sound sweet but it's not.) From here, it's more of the same on the DH: medium-radius curves and miscellaneous vegetation. Some outright forest close to the road occasionally impairs the sight lines. This, together with random driveways, inhibit your faster-harder desires. Just as the curves recoil and enter another patch of thick, shadowy forest, the pavement gets a little rougher with you. But you're no candy ass.

At 8.9 mi (14.3 km), Pine Flat Rd (**TE-C**) hooks up left as the road briefly straightens in the open and smooths out. Then it's back in the trees. You'd think the ones on the right would be more impressive given they're part of Henry Cowell Redwoods State Park. In any case, Hank's efforts are quickly overtaken as you pass the park boundary and scattered development reappears.

More signs—one prescribing a 40-mph (65-kph) speed zone and another cautioning about the cloven-hooved ones. So where's the warning about the logging trucks? These pylons are the worst road flotsam of all because the drivers get paid by the load and they usually know the road. This makes 'em go faster than other pylons, which, of course, is still incredibly slow. And them suckers is *lonnggg*, so it's hard to get past them, especially in the tight stuff. You could turn right onto Alba Rd (**TE-D**) at 10.8 mi (17.4 km), but hang on, here's a bit of a straight. A quick move by your right hand excites your mount and... you're done with that guy.

If you're not paying too much attention to the left-handed sweeper along your own little ridge, check out the break in the forest at a 13.9 mi

(22.4 km). For a spell you can see the Santa Cruz Mtns to the east across the San Lorenzo River valley but it doesn't last long. Soon, all you can see again are trees either side of this tightly curving road. Life's tough.

Just when you're getting into a really good groove, you've got to slow down. If you don't, you'll miss Jamison Creek Rd, right angling at 14.8 mi (23.8 km). Empire Grade dead ends about a mile straight on. To stay on the DH, **turn right**.

Big breath. All right, everything just got a whole lot cruder now as you slide into an underworld of very dark forest. Probably the place that bears would hang out, if there were bears around here. The only thing that gets better is the remoteness. Yes, the curves are still tight and constant but the rough pavement, choppy engineering and steep descent prevent you from having a whole lot of fun with them.

At 17.1 mi (27.5 km), you're almost happy when the curves back off as the terrain flattens and buildings appear. You hit Hwy 236 and the end of the DH at 17.9 mi (28.8 km).

Twisted Edges

TE-A Smith Grade Rd (5.2 mi / 8.4 km)
This twisty and, at times narrow, strip of asphalt has you almost entirely in forest while climbing up from **TE-C**. And while you can't go fast on it, that just makes it last all the longer. The air is a lot fresher and sweeter up here. Much cooler, too, no matter how hot it is down below (unless the marine fog has moved in to cool the lowland). Bonus: the Pacific slope of the Santa Cruz Mtns is an area with less population and therefore fewer pylons.

TE-B Felton Empire Rd (3.7 mi / 6.0 km)
Stuck in the crowd on Hwy 9? You might escape by turning west on this smoothly paved squiggle up through the impressive, twilight-inducing climes of Henry Cowell Redwoods State Park. If there are any pylons in front of you, resign yourself to sucking on their exhaust pipe the rest of the way after you catch up to them.

TE-C Pine Flat Rd - Bonny Doon Rd (7.4 mi / 11.9 km)
Pine Flat's na quite so bonny as BDs drop steeply doon to the cool coast. Afore lang, ye'll no doubt be bendin' doon and crackin' on this 'un's weel-paved curves and caws. Och yes, mair… please mair…

TE-D Alba Rd (3.8 mi / 6.1 km)
Another narrow, twisty uphiller from Hwy 9 to the DH. Pavement's not as good as partner **TE-B**, especially on the upper half. And you could have a UPS experience on it. What can Brown do for you? Stop trying to kill you.

TE-E Swanton Rd (6.8 mi / 10.9 km)
If you want to swan out of the straight, coastal Hwy 1 closet, do this remote bypass. As long as you can handle the rougher treatment the pavement's going to mete out. But if you can take it, you'll find those curves you lust for. They're mostly in the forest, although on the southern, open

part, it might seem like you're riding them on a lonely, windswept Scottish moor. Especially when the fog banks roll in off the Pacific to cover-up your indiscretions.

TE-F Soquel-San Jose Rd (11.0 mi / 17.7 km)
This one's well known to local riders. Must have something to do with the abundance of good curves and great pavement that run through this woody terrain. It does have a fair bit of hard-to-pass traffic as well as more straights and development the farther south you go. Always preferable to Hwy 17, though.

TE-G West Vine Hill Rd - Vine Hill Rd - Branciforte Dr
(7.0 mi / 11.3 km)
Vine Hill coils tightly through the woods with less than perfect pavement. Branciforte has better pavement but a fair number of houses scattered among its trees. Less traffic than **TE-F**. Another route preferable to 17.

NAVIGATION: The Santa Cruz end of this TE is accessed from Market St, which turns into Branciforte. There is no access to Market directly from Hwy 1. From central SC, take Water St north from Ocean St to Market.

TE-G ALT Granite Creek Rd (2.7 mi / 4.3 km)
Much like **TE-G**'s Vine Hill part. Carries you to or from Scotts Valley without using Hwy 17.

TE-G ALT Glen Canyon Rd (3.0 mi / 4.8 km)
A somewhat better paved, less curvy variation on the Vine Hill theme.

NAVIGATION: You can't access this directly from Hwy 17 at the Scotts Valley end. Take the Mt Hermon Rd exit from 17 and then turn right on Glen Canyon. Once you cross over 17 and turn right, you'll be on the TE.

RIDER'S LOG: **DATE RIDDEN:** **YOUR RATING: /10**

DH55
DH28
DH39
DH74
DH47
BAY

Remember, you'll find video clips of all of Northern California's DHs at **destination highways.com.**

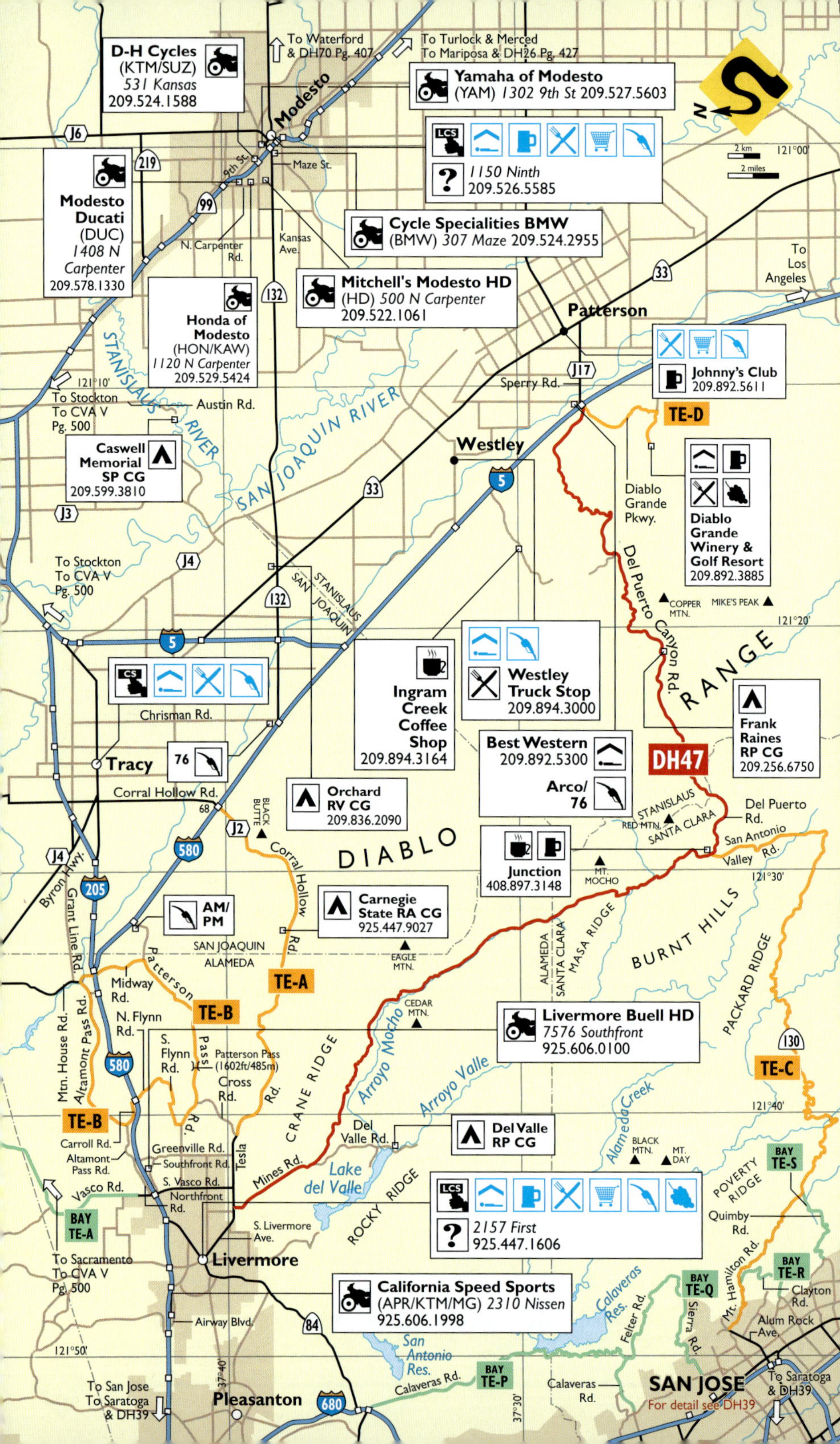

D-H Cycles
(KTM/SUZ)
531 Kansas
209.524.1588
To Waterford & DH70 Pg. 407
To Turlock & Merced
To Mariposa & DH26 Pg. 427
Yamaha of Modesto
(YAM) 1302 9th St 209.527.5603
Modesto
LCS
1150 Ninth
209.526.5585
Modesto Ducati
(DUC)
1408 N Carpenter
209.578.1330
Maze St.
9th St.
N. Carpenter Rd.
Kansas Ave.
Cycle Specialities BMW
(BMW) 307 Maze 209.524.2955
Honda of Modesto
(HON/KAW)
1120 N Carpenter
209.529.5424
Mitchell's Modesto HD
(HD) 500 N Carpenter
209.522.1061
To Los Angeles
Patterson
Johnny's Club
209.892.5611
Sperry Rd.
TE-D
To Stockton
To CVA V
Pg. 500
Austin Rd.
STANISLAUS RIVER
SAN JOAQUIN RIVER
Caswell Memorial SP CG
209.599.3810
Westley
Diablo Grande Pkwy.
Diablo Grande Winery & Golf Resort
209.892.3885
Del Puerto Canyon Rd.
COPPER MTN.
MIKE'S PEAK
To Stockton
To CVA V
Pg. 500
STANISLAUS
SAN JOAQUIN
RANGE
Chrisman Rd.
CS
Ingram Creek Coffee Shop
209.894.3164
Westley Truck Stop
209.894.3000
Frank Raines RP CG
209.256.6750
Tracy
76
Best Western
209.892.5300
Arco/ 76
DH47
Corral Hollow Rd.
BLACK BUTTE
Orchard RV CG
209.836.2090
STANISLAUS
SANTA CLARA
RED MTN.
Del Puerto Rd.
San Antonio Valley Rd.
DIABLO
Junction
408.897.3148
MT. MOCHO
Byron Hwy.
Grant Line Rd.
Corral Hollow Rd.
AM/ PM
Carnegie State RA CG
925.447.9027
SAN JOAQUIN
ALAMEDA
EAGLE MTN.
ALAMEDA
SANTA CLARA
MASA RIDGE
BURNT HILLS
PACKARD RIDGE
Patterson
Midway Rd.
N. Flynn Rd.
TE-B
TE-A
CEDAR MTN.
Livermore Buell HD
7576 Southfront
925.606.0100
S. Flynn Rd.
Pass
Patterson Pass (1602ft/485m)
Cross Rd.
CRANE RIDGE
Arroyo Mocho
Arroyo Valle
TE-C
Mtn. House Rd.
Altamont Pass Rd.
TE-B
Carroll Rd.
Altamont Pass Rd.
Greenville Rd.
Southfront Rd.
Tesla
Del Valle Rd.
Del Valle RP CG
Alameda Creek
BLACK MTN.
MT. DAY
BAY TE-S
Mines Rd.
Lake del Valle
ROCKY RIDGE
POVERTY RIDGE
Vasco Rd.
S. Vasco Rd.
Northfront Rd.
LCS
2157 First
925.447.1606
Quimby Rd.
BAY TE-A
S. Livermore Ave.
Livermore
To Sacramento
To CVA V
Pg. 500
California Speed Sports
(APR/KTM/MG) 2310 Nissen
925.606.1998
Calaveras Res.
Felter Rd.
BAY TE-Q
Sierra Rd.
Mt. Hamilton Rd.
BAY TE-R
Clayton Rd.
Alum Rock Ave.
Airway Blvd.
San Antonio Res.
Calaveras Rd.
BAY TE-P
Calaveras Rd.
To San Jose
To Saratoga & DH39
Pleasanton
SAN JOSE
For detail see DH39
To Saratoga & DH39
2 km
2 miles

DH47 Livermore – Patterson

Mines Rd / Del Puerto Canyon Rd

Distance:	52.9 mi / 85.1 km	Traffic:	Light

At a Glance

Evolution or Intelligent Design? Some believe that this DH evolved over the generations from old logging or gold trails, the naturally selected path through the Diablo Mtns. They point to the untamed Character and Stone Age Engineering of the northern half of this route, most evident in the primitive 8.5 miles (13.7 km) of precarious one-lane road that climbs off the wide, smoothly paved flat south of Livermore and adapts to the sharp, wavering lip of the deep trough of Arroyo Mocho. They say that this, along with the pleistocene Remoteness and dry, rugged, unblemished Scenery, is a glimpse of a DH in transition. Others dismiss these claims, arguing all you need to do is look at Del Puerto Canyon Rd, particularly the divinely paved and engineered canyon section that esses east of Frank Raines Regional Park, to see that this road is the obvious creation of some higher power. But whether you prefer your fish insignia with or without feet, there's one thing we should all remember: the importance of respecting and preserving this and all Destination Highways – and even Twisted Edges, for that matter – regardless of their origin. And isn't that really what we want our kids to learn at school?

TIRES	
Twistiness	30/30
Pavement	10.6/20
Engineering	3.8/10
Remoteness	5.8/10
Scenery	9.6/15
Character	7.3/15
Total	**67.1**

Access

From Livermore

On North or South Livermore Ave (J 2)

North Livermore turns into South Livermore, which ultimately turns into Tesla Rd. When it does, turn right onto Mines Rd. You're on the road.

From I-580

Take the North Livermore Ave exit. Head south on North Livermore Ave (J 2), following the directions above.

From Patterson

Via Sperry Ave (J 17)

Head out Sperry Ave (J 17). Pass under the I-5 and turn left onto Del Puerto Canyon Rd. You're on the road.

On The Road

Wide shoulders, good pavement and easy, well-engineered curves start you off out of Livermore. May as well enjoy the smooth, easy trek through the vineyards and hobby ranches because it doesn't last long. Rocky Ridge moves gradually in from the west. At 3.4 mi (5.5 km), you reach a junction. Going straight puts you on Del Valle Rd down to Lake Del Valle in Del Valle Regional Park. To continue on del DH, however, you **turn left**.

Pavement drops a grade after the turn, but it's still okay. The road is shoulderless as you ride straight toward the low, rounded hills ahead. It's a beautiful piece of the valley, though. Crane Ridge runs parallel to the road to the east. Its chalky grey rock looks like huge pieces of flint that have been chipped away to a glinting sharpness. Striking – almost as striking as the "Twisties Next 15 Miles" sign at 4.7 mi (7.6 km).

With the sign comes the climb. And as you rise, the deep trough of Arroyo Mocho yawns open to your right. The canyon is truly stunning to behold, especially the thick patches of forest that drape over the steep brown earth on the opposite side. The sharpness of the right edge dropoff is matched only by the sharpness of the esses. Guardrails? Who're you kidding? You're lucky it's two lanes.

Looks like your luck just ran out. At 11.4 mi (18.3 km), the two lanes narrow to one. And although the road moves off the gorge now and then to pass a small ranch, it can be particularly disconcerting to be on a thin trail of pavement when you're edging along a chasm. The narrowness of the road is exacerbated by the thick oaks that crowd and overhang it in spots. Not to mention the pylon coming round a blind corner the other way taking up more than their half.

The canyon walls remain steep but get shallower as you head south. At 13.0 mi (20.1 km), you actually catch a glimpse of the creek along the bottom, assuming it has any water in it. And by 13.7 mi (22.0 km), the creek is right beside the road. Don't get too excited when the road widens to two lanes for the bridges over the creek at 13.9 mi (22.4 km) and 15.1 mi (24.3 km). It's back to one before you can say "Daniel Woleesenbet".

You now enter a flatter section, shifting either side of a new creek bed – this one long dry – through a gulch full of bleached rock, burnt grass, young oaks and various mystery flora. The gulch widens at 17.3 mi (27.8 km) to make room for some spotty ranch houses and mobile homes well off the road. It eventually narrows again. If you want an idea of how long this part of the creek has been without water, pay attention at 19.0 mi (30.6 km). You'll note the creek bed stops on the right side of the road and continues on the left. No bridge required.

You see more bridgeless creek-bed crossings past 19.9 mi (32.0 km), when Santa Clara County takes over from Alameda and life has two lanes again. It's not just the engineering that changes after you pass the county line, the scenery does as well. At 22.8 mi (36.7 km), you climb and emerge from the scruffily forested creek valley into the rough hewn hills of Masa Ridge. It's a remote, almost otherworldly landscape blanketed with low, dark green, yellow-fingered brush.

Trees regain a foothold in the scene at 24.0 mi (38.6 km) but hints of the green moonscape continue as far as 25.7 mi (41.4 km), where the road drops down a slope, continuing its tight and twisting ways. Then, it's back into a mangy hollow full of shacks, old trailers and some mysterious offering called "Ruthie's Shopping Mall," unique among malls in that nothing actually appears to be for sale. The roadside junk collections disappear quickly and the hollow widens into a valley. The road straightens as it approaches the Sweetwater Jct, arriving at 28.1 mi (45.2 km). San Antonio Valley Rd (**TE-C**) goes straight here to San Jose. To stay on the DH, **go left**.

"No gas 25 miles" says the sign. Don't recall much gas the last 25 miles either. But at least if you're going on reserve, you can put it in neutral and coast since the road descends off the junction through shallow-walled Del Puerto Canyon. Curves are not quite as tight initially and there's even a short, breezy straight at 29.9 mi (48.1 km). Pavement has improved a bit, though whoever installed the frequent cattleguards had little regard for how far you might be into your turn at that particular point. At least none interfere with the sinuous section that approaches the Stanislaus County line, crossed at 31.0 mi (49.9 km).

The downgrade steepens, the road narrows and the pavement gets bumpy again as you cross into Stan's County. Nice welcome. In fairness, the terrain is much rougher here as the canyon narrows sharply and the road has to hug a steep crumbling slope. The canyon scenery and outlooks toward Copper Mtn and Mike's Peak (no relation) are gorgeous. That is if you can take your eyes off the upcoming corner long enough to look at it.

At 33.7 mi (54.2 km), the gorge's grip relaxes and the steep slopes gradually back away. The engineering improves and you no longer feel like you're trying to ride your bike on a wobbling tightrope. The pavement varies, improving from time to time and then degrading again. At 36.1 mi (58.1 km), you pass a barb-wired installation on your left. A California State penal institution? No, the Deer Creek Campground and picnic area. Guess they like you to stay more than one night.

The campground is followed immediately on the right by the oasis of Frank Raines Regional Park. Probably the better choice for a lunch break and a nap than Deer Creek. If only because it feels less like Dachau.

Rangeland opens up as you tour eastward from the park. The terrain's still rough and there's no shortage of corners, but they're not as sharp as before, at least until you enter the zigzag gorge at 39.4 mi (63.4 km). The only drawback to the dramatically shaped and contoured walls of this beautiful passage are the rocks you see on the road. Especially on the blind, right-hand corners when you don't see them at all.

But it's a great section. Sage grips the rust-colored slopes like algae in an undersea garden. Other times, the rock takes on the look of rotting stumps. The pavement and engineering in this section are superior to Stanislaus' first piece. It twists, turns and even sweeps as the canyon broadens again and the terrain gradually levels out down to the short straightaway at 42.7 mi (68.7 km).

At 43.3 mi (69.7 km), the road starts to curve again, wending through the valley along Del Puerto Creek, matching it bend for bend. At 45.4 mi (73.1 km), the dry surroundings take on an even drier countenance as a row of barren brown hills angle in from the north, folding one into the other.

Apart from a 20-mph sweeper at 46.2 mi (74.3 km), the curves are not too tight as you shift toward the base of the modest, but steep-walled hills that seem to explode out of the ground. Then, at 47.4 mi (76.3 km), you're amid them, picking your way through tight, contorting turns. It's scenic as well. Oaks begin to appear by the roadside, providing a dark green contrast to the otherwise overwhelming dryness. The bleached white of granite is exposed at the base of the left-hand slope. The scenery continues to impress as a huge, sculpted monolith emerges from the grass cover at 48.8 mi (78.5 km).

But it's nothing but brown again at 50.0 mi (80.5 km) as the terrain opens up into a huge, sweeping basin with nothing to interrupt it but a road, a low line of fencing and a track of powerlines. You steer your way past the rattlesnakes sunbathing on the straightening pavement to the stop sign at 52.9 mi (85.1 km). Left takes you down to the I-5 and, beyond that, into Patterson. Right puts you on the Diablo Grande Pkwy (**TE-D**).

Twisted Edges

TE-A Coral Hollow Rd (J 2) (16.2 mi / 26.1 km)
Good pavement and some curves on the high part make this a good route across the northern section of the dry Diablo Range between Livermore and the Great Central Valley. Seems Dale Carnegie was a maxburner; he apparently donated money not only to libraries but also to off road motorcycle parks. Public education indeed.

NAVIGATION: J 2 in Livermore is identified as Tesla Rd.

TE-B Livermore Loop (23.0 mi / 37.0 km) *Carroll Rd - N Flynn Rd - S Flynn Rd Rd - Patterson Pass Rd - Midway Rd - Altamont Pass Rd*
Going down to the Cross Rd just to find yourself the best ride do-do-do-de-do-do.... The truth is you can get on this not-too-twisty and sometimes-roughish mélange at many spots. The loop through dry, hilly terrain either side of I-580 does provides the best of what entertainment exists this close to Hepatitis-town, as long as you don't mind the narrower Patterson Pass piece. If you do, the smoother Altamont Pass part may make up for it.

TE-C San Antonio Valley Rd – Mt. Hamilton Rd (Hwy 130)
(37.0 mi / 59.5 km)

Do you know this TE from San Jose?
If you've been there long you've gone wrong and lost your way
Do you know this remote way to San Jose?

No point in going back to find some peace of mind in San Jose
SJ is a great big freeway
Put a thousand down and buy a Star
You don't need a week or two to ride this far
Tightly climbing up to many views, how quick you pass
All the SUVs you wish were never there
Slow as parked cars and sucking gas

Pavement and twistiness is a magnet
It can pull you far away from home
With this dream in your heart you're never alone
Dreams sometimes turn narrow and rough and blow you away
But there you are, this road's still your friend
So pack your Star and ride away

TE-D Diablo Grande Pkwy (9.4 mi / 15.3 km)
Nothing devilish about this deadender. Divinely paved and engineered, it winds gracefully from the Patterson start of the DH up into the Diablo Range foothills to a heavenly little valley complete with a housing development and golf resort.

RIDER'S LOG: **DATE RIDDEN:** **YOUR RATING: /10**

Vacaville
(D-HD)
(D-KAW/ YAM)
Grove
(D-HON)
(D-HD)
(D-KTM)
Sonoma
Napa
(D-BUE/HD)
(D-HON/KAW/SUZ)
(D-YAM)
Fairfield
Suisun City
WINE COUNTRY
Pg. 59
(D-DUC/TRI YAM)
(D-BUE/HD)
(D-HON/KTM/YAM)
(D-KAW/SUZ)
(D-HON/ SUZ)
Rio Vista
CVA V
BAY I
Grizzly Bay
RUSSIAN COAST
SAN PABLO BAY
Vallejo
Crockett
(D-HON/SUZ)
(D-KAW/YAM)
Pittsburg
(D-BUE/HD)
(D-SUZ)
Oakley
(D-BMW)
(D-APR)
Concord
Antioch
(D-APR/BIM/KTM/VIC)
(D-AUG/DUC/MG/TRI)
(D-BMW)
(D-BUE/HD)
(D-HON/KAW/SUZ/YAM)
Corte Madera
BAY II
Walnut Creek
(D-HON/YAM)
(D-BMW/KAW)
(D-BUE/HD)
Berkeley
OAKLAND
(D-HON/KAW/ SUZ/YAM)
(D-BUE/ HD)
SAN FRANCISCO
(D-DUC/ KTM/TRI)
(D-HD)
(D-HON/KAW)
(D-SUZ)
San Ramon
SAN FRANCISCO BAY
San Leandro
(D-HD)
Tracy
Daly City
(D-HON/ KAW/ YAM)
Hayward
Livermore
Pacifica
(D-BUE/HD)
(D-HON/KAW/ KTM/SUZ)
Burlingame
(D-APR/ KTM/MG)
San Mateo
Fremont
(D-BUE/HD)
(D-HON/KAW)
DH47
BAY III
(D-HON)
Redwood City
Half Moon Bay
DH55
(D-YAM)
(D-KAW/ SUZ/YAM)
BAY AREA-SANTA CRUZ MTNS
Woodside
Milpitas
(D-HON/ SUZ)
Mountain View
Sky Londa
Sunnyvale
(D-BMW)
(D-HD)
(D-YAM)
DH28
San Gregorio
Santa Clara
SAN JOSE
(D-APR/ MG/TRI)
Saratoga
Pescadero
(D-BMW/ TRI)
DH39
(D-HON/SUZ/YAM)
Los Gatos
(D-HD)
(D-DUC/HON)
(D-KAW/SUZ)
Boulder Creek
DH74
Morgan Hill
BAY V
BAY IV
(D-HON/K SUZ/YAM)
(D-VIC)
N
10 km
10 miles
Davenport
Santa Cruz
Aptos
Capitola
Gilroy
Watsonville
(D-BUE/HD)
(D-HON/KAW/SUZ)
(D-KTM)
(D-APR/ DUC/MG)
(D-KAW)
PACIFIC OCEAN
(D-BUE/HD)
(D-BMW/YAM)
Hollis

SERVICE NOTE: The only services shown on these roads are generally bike shops, more remote campgrounds and the odd winery. In this area, if you run out of gas, starve to death or can't find a place to stay, you really shouldn't be out in public without adult supervision anyway.

BAY TE-A Livermore – Byron (13.1 mi / 21.1 km) *Vasco Rd*

MAP II The local paper, *The Samantha Bee*, reports that state STCs pay particular attention – both on the ground and from the air – to this excellently paved and engineered road. No wonder. Despite the lack of legal passing opportunities, this yet-to-be suburbanized but heavily pyloned route seduces cock rockets from the bulging pocket of population nearby. So, as you arc through the dry countryside, remember: unless you're looking to become a Byronic speed tax hero, those large 55-mph (90-kmh) signs painted on the road aren't there for your benefit.

NAVIGATION: At the Livermore end, the TE starts when it passes Garaventa Ranch Rd, 0.8 mi (1.3 km) from I-580.

BAY TE-B Clayton – Byron (15.8 mi / 25.4 km) *Marsh Creek Rd - Camino Diablo Rd*

MAP II Shhhh… we won't tell anyone about this remarkably development-free marriage of pavement to rolling countryside north of Mt. Diablo, if you don't. Oh, sorry…

NAVIGATION: Clayton Rd crosses Ygnacio Valley Rd/Kirker Pass Rd in Clayton and will lead you to Marsh Creek Rd. If you're coming from this direction, slant right at 12.4 mi (20.0 km) off Marsh and onto Camino to stay on the TE.

BAY TE-C Deer Valley Rd - Empire Mine Rd (7.8 mi / 12.6 km)

MAP II Sprawl slopping up from the triburbs of Pittsburg, Antioch and Oakley menaces the north end of this otherwise pleasant wander across shallow, open Briones, Deer and Lone Tree valleys. The Antioch city limit notification way out at the south end of Empire is not a good sign in terms of continued urbanization. Hopefully, the collapse of the California real estate bubble will fix that.

*NAVIGATION: If you come from mid-**BAY TE-B**, make sure you take the 90° turn left off Deer Valley and onto Empire Mine at 4.4 mi (7.1 km). Unless you want to get to Antioch faster on the non-TE part of Deer Valley.*

To get on Empire Mine from Antioch, take Lone Tree Way south off Hwy 4. A little over a mile later, take Golf Course Way right. A few blocks later, turn right on Mesa Ridge Dr. Right on Empire Mine puts you on the TE. (If you get to Prewett Ranch Rd, you've gone too far on Mesa.)

BAY TE-D Danville – Walnut Creek (Mount Diablo) (9.1 mi / 14.5 km) *Mt Diablo Scenic Blvd - Jupiter Summit Rd - North Gate Rd*

MAP I/II Since most of this devilishly tight ride is protected by the Mount Diablo State Park, it should survive a lot longer than many BAY TEs. The

To Napa & DH34 Pg. 61
To Sacramento
To CVA IV Pg. 499/ CVA V Pg. 500
122°20'
122°10'
122°00'
38°10'
38°00'
37°50'
N
2 km
2 miles
NAPA
SOLANO
I
(II)
La Loma Ave.
Shasta Rd.
Grizzly Peak Blvd.
S. Park Dr.
BAY TE-J
Lomas Cantadas Rd.
Gayley Rd.
UC Berkeley
Centennial Dr.
Fish Ranch Rd.
BAY TE-K
Claremont Ave.
College Ave.
Bay Forest Dr.
Old Tunnel Rd.
Caldecott Ln.
Skyline Blvd.
BAY TE-L
Columbus Pkwy.
Sonoma Blvd.
Vallejo
(D-BUE/HD)
(D-HON/KTM/YAM)
(D-KAW/SUZ)
Lake Herman Rd.
SAN PABLO BAY
SOLANO
CONTRA COSTA
Crockett
BAY TE-F
Port Costa
Benicia
BAY TE-E ALT
Carquinez Scenic Dr.
Crockett Blvd.
Cummings Skyway
Ian McEwen Rd.
SUISUN BAY
Port Chicago Hwy
Waterfront Rd.
Martinez
Pacheco Blvd.
Concord Ave.
Willow Pass Rd.
Pinole
Hercules
Franklin Cyn. Rd.
BAY TE-E
FRANKLIN RIDGE
Alhambra Valley Rd.
Alhambra Ave.
Pacheco
East St.
Concord
Clayton Rd.
Concord Blvd.
El Sobrante
Pereira Rd.
Alhambra Valley Rd.
Castro Ranch Rd.
BAY TE-G
BRIONES
Reliez Valley Rd.
Taylor Blvd.
(D-HON/SUZ)
(D-KAW/YAM)
To Tamalpais Valley & DH37 Pg. 93
San Pablo Dam Rd.
BAY TE-H
Bear Creek Rd.
BRIONES REGIONAL PARK
Pleasant Hill
San Pablo Res.
Briones Res.
BAY TE-I
HILLS
(D-BMW/KAW)
(D-BUE/HD)
Pleasant Hill Rd.
Ygnacio Valley Rd.
Oak Grove Rd.
Diablo Ranch SP CG
El Cerrito
BAY TE-J
Bear Creek Rd.
Wildcat Cyn. Rd.
Walnut Creek
North Gate Rd.
SAN FRANCISCO BAY
Centennial Dr.
S. Park Dr.
Grizzly Peak Blvd.
Orinda
Lafayette
Berkeley
BAY TE-K
Grizzly Peak Blvd.
See Inset Above
Moraga Wy.
Moraga Rd.
St. Marys Rd.
BAY TE-D
Danville Blvd.
Mt. Diablo Scenic Blvd.
Alamo
(D-HON/YAM)
Skyline Blvd.
Diablo Rd.
Moraga
Canyon Rd.
Blackhawk Rd.
Camino Tassajara Rd.
BAY TE-L
BAY TE-K
Skyline Blvd.
Pinehurst Rd.
BAY TE-N ALT
LAS TRAMPAS RIDGE
Danville
(D-HD)
San Ramon
Bollinger Canyon Rd.
To San Francisco & DH37 Pg. 93
OAKLAND
(D-APR)
Redwood Rd.
CONTRA COSTA
ALAMEDA
Upper San Leandro Res.
BAY TE-N
Skyline Blvd.
BAY TE-M
S.F.-Oakland Bay Bridge (Toll)
Alameda
Keller Ave.
Grass Valley Rd.
Golf Links Rd.
98 Ave.
Norris Cyn. Rd.
Crow Canyon Rd.
CONTRA COSTA
ALAMEDA
San Leandro
BAY TE-N
Lake Chabot
(D-HON/KAW)
(D-HD)
(D-SUZ)
(D-DUC/KTM/TRI)
Anthony Chabot RP CG
Castro Valley Blvd.
Redwood Rd.
Castro Valley
SAN FRANCISCO BAY
To San Jose
To Saratoga & DH39
Paloverde Rd.
E. Castro Valley Blvd.
Palomares Rd.
BAY TE-O

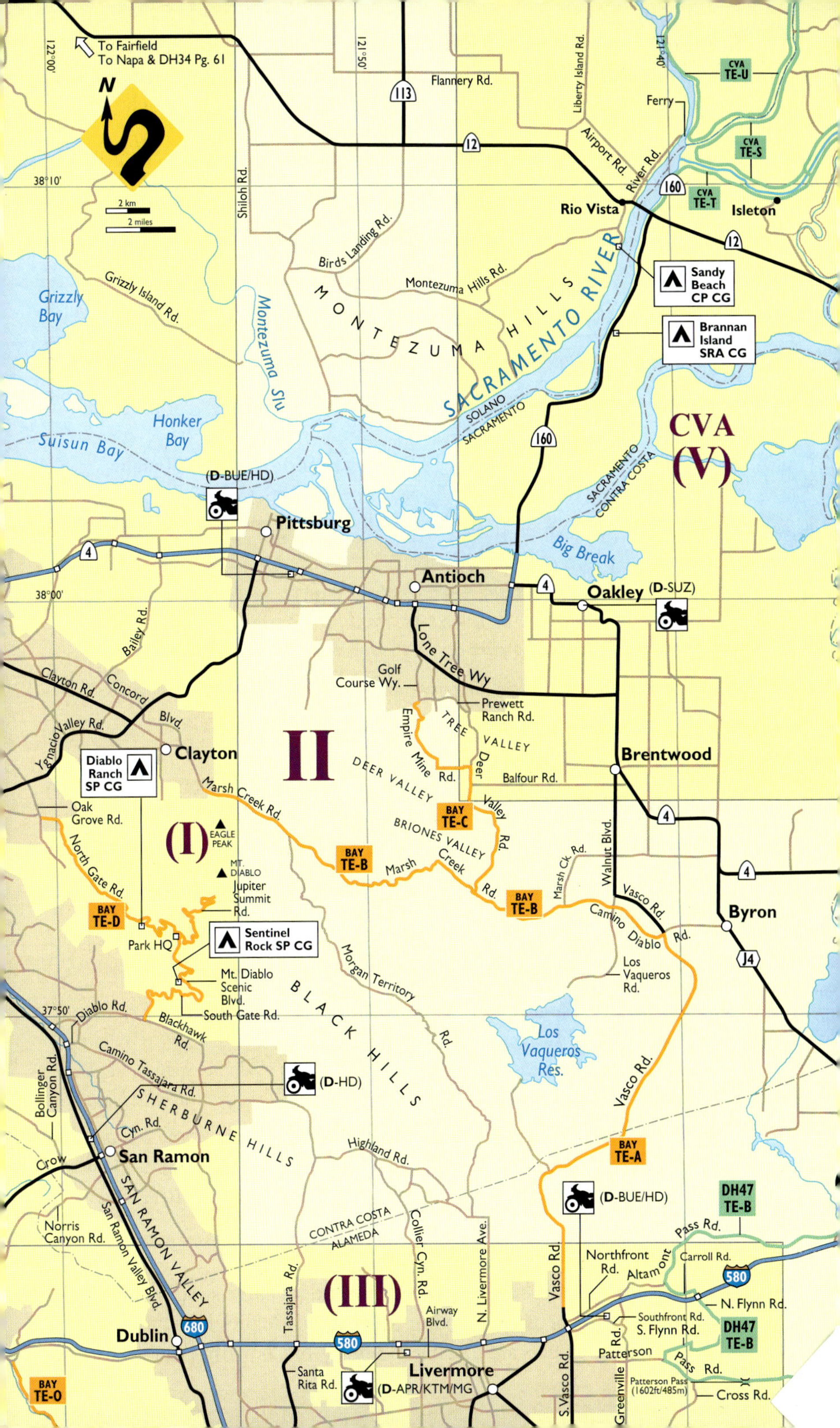

To Fairfield
To Napa & DH34 Pg. 61
122°00'
121°50'
121°40'
38°10'
38°00'
37°50'
N
2 km
2 miles
Flannery Rd.
Liberty Island Rd.
Airport Rd.
River Rd.
Ferry
CVA TE-U
CVA TE-S
CVA TE-T
Rio Vista
Isleton
Shiloh Rd.
Birds Landing Rd.
Montezuma Hills Rd.
MONTEZUMA HILLS
SACRAMENTO RIVER
Sandy Beach CP CG
Brannan Island SRA CG
Grizzly Bay
Grizzly Island Rd.
Montezuma Slu
Honker Bay
Suisun Bay
SOLANO
SACRAMENTO
CVA (V)
SACRAMENTO
CONTRA COSTA
(D-BUE/HD)
Pittsburg
Big Break
Antioch
Oakley
(D-SUZ)
Bailey Rd.
Clayton Rd.
Concord Blvd.
Ygnacio Valley Rd.
Clayton
Golf Course Wy.
Lone Tree Wy
Prewett Ranch Rd.
TREE VALLEY
Empire Mine Rd.
Deer Valley Rd.
Balfour Rd.
Brentwood
II
DEER VALLEY
Diablo Ranch SP CG
Oak Grove Rd.
Marsh Creek Rd.
BAY TE-C
BRIONES VALLEY
(I)
EAGLE PEAK
MT. DIABLO
North Gate Rd.
BAY TE-B
Marsh Creek Rd.
Jupiter Summit Rd.
BAY TE-B
Marsh Ck. Rd.
Walnut Blvd.
Vasco Rd.
Byron
BAY TE-D
Park HQ
Sentinel Rock SP CG
Camino Diablo Rd.
Los Vaqueros Rd.
Mt. Diablo Scenic Blvd.
South Gate Rd.
Morgan Territory Rd.
Diablo Rd.
Blackhawk Rd.
BLACK HILLS
Los Vaqueros Res.
Camino Tassajara Rd.
Bollinger Canyon Rd.
(D-HD)
SHERBURNE HILLS
Vasco Rd.
Crow Cyn. Rd.
San Ramon
Highland Rd.
BAY TE-A
SAN RAMON VALLEY
San Ramon Valley Blvd.
(D-BUE/HD)
DH47 TE-B
Norris Canyon Rd.
CONTRA COSTA
ALAMEDA
Collier Cyn. Rd.
N. Livermore Ave.
Vasco Rd.
Northfront Rd.
Altamont Pass Rd.
Carroll Rd.
Tassajara Rd.
(III)
Airway Blvd.
N. Flynn Rd.
Southfront Rd.
S. Flynn Rd.
DH47 TE-B
Dublin
Patterson Pass Rd.
Santa Rita Rd.
(D-APR/KTM/MG
Livermore
Patterson Pass (1602ft/485m)
Cross Rd.
BAY TE-O
S. Vasco Rd.
Greenville Rd.

(sort of) good news is that traffic's low since you do have to pay to ride in the park. The bad news is that they don't appear to spend much of the loot on pavement. The ranger beer fund is looking good, though.

NAVIGATION: From the Danville end, head east on Diablo Rd (I-680 Exit 39). It will swing north at its junction with Camino Tassajara and lead you to the junction with the Mt Diablo Scenic Blvd end of the TE.

From Walnut Creek, take Ygnacio Valley Rd. Turn south on Oak Grove Rd, where it crosses Ygnacio and takes you to the North Gate Rd end of the TE.

ROUTING OPTION: The extra Juniper Summit Rd (offering more of the same) up to the great panoramas over the surrounding TEs adds 8.6 mi (13.8 km) return. Might as well get your money's worth.

BAY TE-E Franklin Canyon Rd – Cummings Skyway (8.0 mi / 12.9 km)
MAP I Good primarily for Hwy 4/I-80 avoidance. Straight Franklin Canyon is fairly housey, especially at the beginning. Cummings has better, wider pavement as it drops down to I-80 outside Crocket but it's straight as well.

NAVIGATION: From Hwy 4 (south of Martinez), take the exit south onto Alhambra Ave and then turn west on Franklin Canyon. Hwy 4's Exit 5 splits the Franklin Canyon Rd part of the TE from the Cummings Skyway part.

To get on it from the other direction, take the I-80 exit onto Cummings Skyway.

BAY TE-E ALT Crockett Blvd (1.9 mi / 3.1 km)
MAP I The straight, short and well-paved way to insert your c-rocket into "historical and traditional" Crockett. Where you'll find gas, food, a beer and **BAY TE-F**.

BAY TE-F Carquinez Scenic Dr – Ian McEwen Rd (4.5 mi / 7.3 km)
MAP I You can no longer get through to Martinez on Carquinez, but McEwen up to Hwy 4 and mid-**BAY TE-E** isn't bad. The pavement isn't new but at least this quiet TE has some curves.

NAVIGATION: Pomona St becomes Carquinez at the eastern edge of Crockett.
– 0.4 mi (0.7 km) south of Port Costa, turn right on McEwen at the sign indicating the freeway. Carquinez, straight ahead, dead ends a mile later.

TOUR NOTE: The business district in passed-by-time Port Costa has been pretty much reduced to the biker-friendly Warehouse Café. It boasts 450 beers from all over the world but you can still get good 'ol American Babeweiser (and Babe Lite).

BAY TE-G Alhambra Valley Rd (7.6 mi / 12.2 km)
MAP I It's a little off camber in spots but it does curve sweetly, especially the piece wedged between Franklin Ridge and Brionnes Hills. Be warned, though, the developers are moving in on this one now that they've turned

Castro Ranch Rd into Castro Rancher Rd. And what's with that section of shoulder with the softball sized "gravel?"

*NAVIGATION: If you're coming from the north on **BAY TE-E** (or from Hwy 4) turn south on Alhambra Rd and then bear right on Alhambra Valley Rd when it splits off Alhambra. When Alhambra Valley turns ninety degrees east at its junction with (straight-ahead) Reliez Valley Rd, stay with A-Valley to begin the TE.*

If you're coming from the west off San Pablo Dam Rd, take Castro Ranch Rd east just past the north end of the San Pablo Reservoir. When Castro T-bones Alhambra Valley, turn right to start the TE.

BAY TE-H San Pablo Dam Rd (5.4 mi / 8.7 km)
MAP I Excellently paved and gently curved, Dam Rd (as it's known locally) has been preserved as a TE primarily because there's no room along it for development. Too dam bad about all the heavy local traffic.

BAY TE-I Bear Creek Rd (13.8 mi / 22.2 km)
MAP I A Chippie told us that you can safely do this road at 70-80 mph (110-130 kmh) in spite of the bootilicious (as defined by Beyonce Knowles: beautiful, bountiful and bouncible) pavement. The lack of curves is bullish for speed but you'll have to be the booty judge.

BAY TE-J Wildcat Canyon Rd - South Park Dr (5.1 mi / 8.2 km)
MAP I Wildcat is a clutter of wild corners clawing up San Pablo Ridge. Unlike its own namesake, mellow South Park runs along the ridge without offending any sensibilities at all. Your biggest problem is going to be finding a time to enjoy either part without the pylons bogging you down.

NAVIGATION: If you're coming up from the three-TE junction south of San Pablo Res, slant south off Wildcat and onto South Park at 3.7 mi (6.0 km). Staying on Wildcat will put you in urbania.

*There are gates at either end of South Park Dr. If you find them closed, there is a link between Wildcat and **BAY TE-K** slightly west of South Park made up of Shasta Rd – Golf Course Rd that'll run you up to the junction of Centennial Dr and Grizzly Peak Blvd.*

BAY TE-K Centennial Dr - Grizzly Peak Blvd - Skyline Blvd Part 1 (12.2 mi / 19.6 km)
MAP I In an America where you can get nearly two years of general college credits for attending McDonalds Hamburger U or receive a master's degree in "Student Activities", it only makes sense that you should be able get a degree in Twistology. And this radical course from UC Berkeley should be on every rider's syllabus. Centennial winds up past some university buildings, then tight Grizzly Peak wanders south along the top of San Pablo Ridge offering good views of the Bay Area before eventually changing its name to Skyline. The TE then edges along Redwood Regional Park before bisecting Joaquin Miller Park. Nice trip if the traffic doesn't bring you down, man.

NAVIGATION: At the Berkeley end, the TE starts at (unmarked) Centennial on the east side of the stadium. There's a gate at either end of Centennial, so it's reasonable to assume that it is sometimes used to close the road. If an administration lockdown stops your Berkeley Free Ride Movement, work your way northeast up from the uni on La Loma Ave-Shasta Rd until you hit Grizzly Peak Blvd. Turn right on Grizzly. Once you leave the development and pass the junction with Centennial (presumably also with its gate closed), you'll be on the rest of the TE. With a PhD in NAVIGATION.

BAY TE-L Caldecott Ln - Old Tunnel Rd - Skyline Blvd Part 2 (3.1 mi / 5.0 km)

MAP I This short, winding climb through housing gets you up from Hwy 13 to mid-**BAY TE-K**.

NAVIGATION: The turn onto Caldecott from Hwy 13 is a bit north of 13's junction with Hwy 24 (which occurs just after 24 emerges from the Caldecott Tunnel.) You can't get on to Caldecott if you're heading south on Hwy 13.

BAY TE-M Skyline Blvd Part 3 - Grass Valley Rd - Golf Links Rd (6.7 mi / 10.8 km)

MAP I Skyline is boulevarded into two lanes each way for the first 2.6 mi (4.2 km) as it slices through what one assumes is very expensive housing on the top of the ridge. The development thins out when the TE goes to one lane in either direction and Anthony Chabot Regional Park makes its presence felt, though some comes back when the TE morphs into Grass Valley Rd. A very relaxed, low-speed toodle.

NAVIGATION: From I-880, take the Golf Links Rd exit.

BAY TE-N Redwood Rd (10.7 mi / 17.2 km)

MAP I It's a whole lot more remote over here on this side of the San Pablo Ridge. Of course, that has a lot to do with the fact you're either in or near Redwood Regional Park, Anthony Chabot Regional Park and the unseen Upper San Leandro Reservoir. There are quite a few curves here, especially on the northern part. And the pavement and engineering are generally good enough to let you enjoy them. Light traffic but any you find can be tough to get by.

NAVIGATION: From the Castro Valley end, get to this TE by taking Exit 35 north off I-580.

*To get to the southern end of this TE from **BAY TE-O**, reverse the NAVIGATION for that TE. You can also take the I-580 route.*

*ROUTING OPTION: If you want to non-interstate it between Castro Valley and San Ramon (on I-680) or further on to **BAY TE-D***, you might be interested in the excellent pavement on Norris Canyon Rd, a better 6.3 mi (10.1 km) partial option to parallel, busier Crow Canyon Rd. Norris would be a TE, except it will probably soon be screwed by the cancerous growth around it.*

*To get to Norris Canyon Rd from the Castro Valley end of **BAY TE-N**, continue on Redwood Rd until it intersects Castro Valley Blvd. Turn east on Castro*

Valley until you turn north on Crow Canyon Rd. (Or you can hop on I-580 at the end of Redwood Rd, head east and take the next exit to get to Crow Canyon Rd.) After a few miles as the Crow flies, turn east on Norris Canyon.

To get to Norris Canyon Rd at the San Ramon end, turn south on Bollinger Canyon Rd from Crow Canyon Rd (just east of where Crow crosses I-680). Turn west on Norris a mile or so later.

The interstate-free way to get to **BAY TE-D from San Ramon: stay on Crow Canyon east over I-680 until you cross Camino Tassajara. You'll be on Blackhawk Rd, which will take you to the Mt Diablo Scenic Blvd start of **BAY TE-D.***

BAY TE-N ALT Pinehurst Rd (6.6 mi / 10.6 km)
MAP I Check out the sign promising twisties for 14 mi (22 km) at the **BAY TE-M** end of this one. Mind you, some of those curves are on **BAY TE-N.** Still, this ***ALT*** is curvier than the mother TE. Also narrower, rougher and less well engineered. As remote, though. And it's dark and cool down in the forest at its northern end.

BAY TE-O Palomares Rd (9.7 mi / 15.6 km)
MAP III "Deer Next 10 Miles" says the sign at the north end. Where's hunter/rocker Ted Nugent when you need him? Sheesh, a gazillion guns in America and no one hunts non-humans anymore. The next bad sign: "40 to 100 Acre Lots". Deer and development: the two damnable d's. Still, the mostly mellow curves on this north-south route along the heavily wooded Palomares Creek valley between Walpert and Sunol Ridges provide enjoyable and easy riding. At least until the first "d" nails you or the second one nails the road.

NAVIGATION: To get on this TE from the southern end of TE-N, continue on Redwood Rd until it intersects Castro Valley Blvd. Turn and stay east on Castro Valley until it crosses under I-580 and connects with the Paloverde Rd loop. Turn right on Paloverde and it will take you to Palomares Rd.

Prefer to go by faster interstate? Hop on I-580 at the end of Redwood Rd, head east and take the third exit to Paloverde and Palomares.

BAY TE-P Sunol – Milpitas (14.0 mi / 22.5 km) *Calaveras Rd Part 1*
MAP III The first 4.1 mi (6.6 km) from the I-680 Sunol Exit 21A is straight. But the rest is a just-slightly-wider-than-one-lane twistathon in forested hills and along the west side of the Calaveras Reservoir. Keep an eye out for UPS trucks taking up the whole road if you don't want to find out what Brown can do to you. In combination with whatever arm of **BAY TE-Q** you prefer, it's a great way to escape southern Bayatopolis.

BAY TE-Q San Jose – Milpitas (12.3 mi / 19.8 km) *Calaveras Rd Part 2 - Felter Rd - Sierra Rd*
MAP III Only got time for a quick fix out of San Jose? With its non-impoverished pavement and relatively high-speed curves, this loop through the open countryside between the Los Buellis Hills and Poverty Ridge should do the trick. Sierra is generally tighter than Felter, while Calaveras

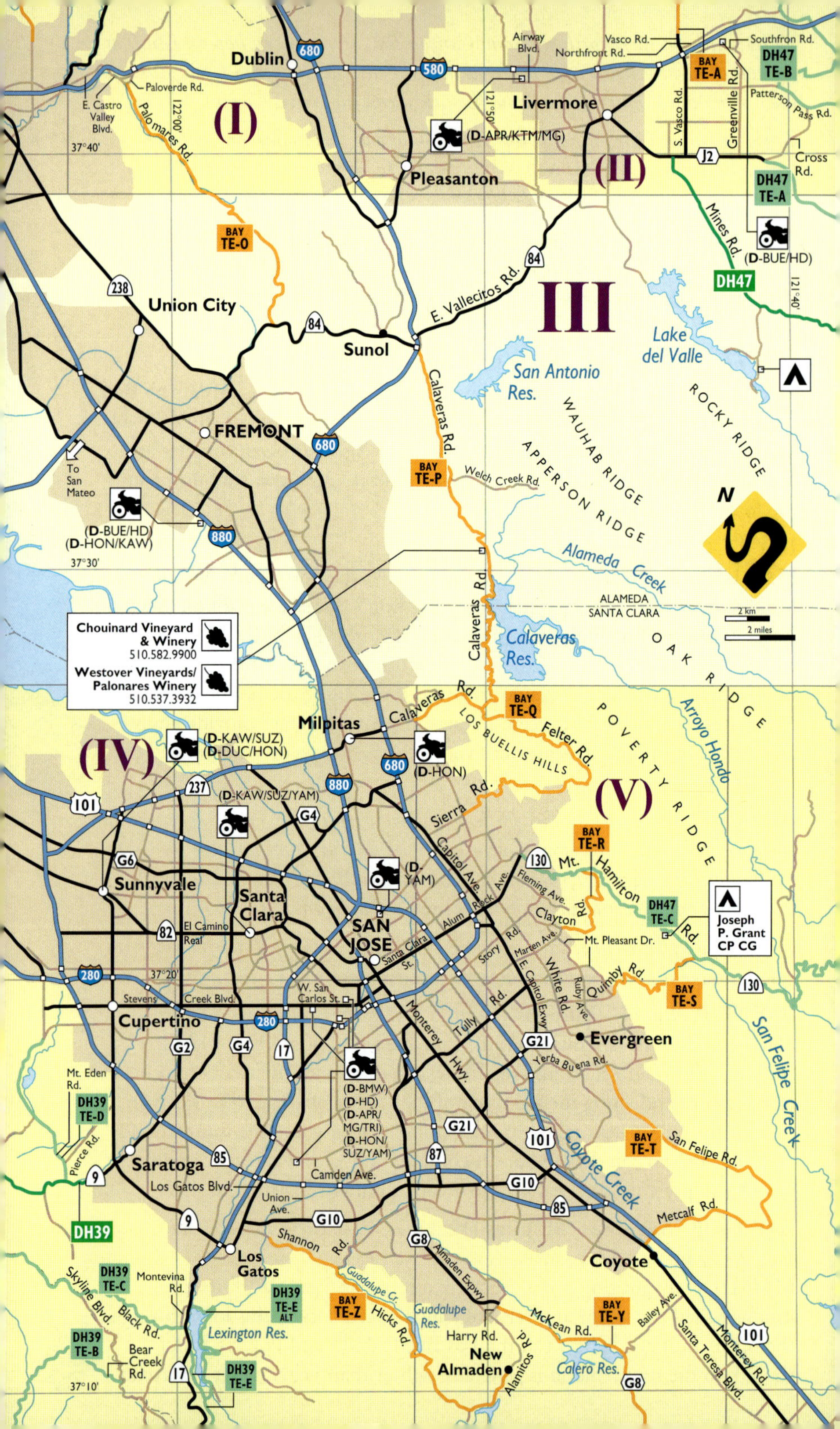

Dublin
Livermore
Pleasanton
Union City
Sunol
FREMONT
Milpitas
Sunnyvale
Santa Clara
SAN JOSE
Cupertino
Saratoga
Los Gatos
Evergreen
Coyote
New Almaden
(I)
(II)
III
(IV)
(V)
Lake del Valle
San Antonio Res.
Calaveras Res.
Lexington Res.
Guadalupe Res.
Calero Res.
ROCKY RIDGE
WAUHAB RIDGE
APPERSON RIDGE
OAK RIDGE
POVERTY RIDGE
LOS BUELLIS HILLS
Alameda Creek
Arroyo Hondo
San Felipe Creek
Coyote Creek
ALAMEDA
SANTA CLARA
Chouinard Vineyard & Winery 510.582.9900
Westover Vineyards/ Palonares Winery 510.537.3932
Joseph P. Grant CP CG
BAY TE-O
BAY TE-P
BAY TE-Q
BAY TE-R
BAY TE-S
BAY TE-T
BAY TE-Y
BAY TE-Z
BAY TE-A
DH47 TE-A
DH47 TE-B
DH47 TE-C
DH47
DH39
DH39 TE-B
DH39 TE-C
DH39 TE-D
DH39 TE-E
DH39 TE-E ALT
(D-APR/KTM/MG)
(D-BUE/HD)
(D-BUE/HD) (D-HON/KAW)
(D-KAW/SUZ) (D-DUC/HON)
(D-HON)
(D-KAW/SUZ/YAM)
(D-YAM)
(D-BMW) (D-HD) (D-APR/ MG/TRI) (D-HON/ SUZ/YAM)
To San Mateo
Paloverde Rd.
E. Castro Valley Blvd.
Palomares Rd.
Airway Blvd.
Vasco Rd.
Northfront Rd.
Southfron Rd.
Greenville Rd.
S. Vasco Rd.
Patterson Pass Rd.
Cross Rd.
Mines Rd.
E. Vallecitos Rd.
Calaveras Rd.
Welch Creek Rd.
Felter Rd.
Sierra Rd.
Capitol Ave.
Rock Ave.
Alum
Fleming Ave.
Mt. Hamilton Rd.
Clayton Rd.
Mt. Pleasant Dr.
Marten Ave.
Story Rd.
E. Capitol Expwy
White Rd.
Ruby Ave.
Quimby Rd.
Tully Rd.
Monterey Hwy.
Yerba Buena Rd.
San Felipe Rd.
Metcalf Rd.
Santa Clara St.
W. San Carlos St.
El Camino Real
Stevens Creek Blvd.
Mt. Eden Rd.
Pierce Rd.
Los Gatos Blvd.
Camden Ave.
Union Ave.
Shannon Rd.
Guadalupe Cr.
Hicks Rd.
Almaden Expwy
Harry Rd.
Alamitos Rd.
McKean Rd.
Bailey Ave.
Santa Teresa Blvd.
Monterey Rd.
Skyline Blvd.
Montevina Rd.
Black Rd.
Bear Creek Rd.
122°00'
121°50'
121°40'
37°40'
37°30'
37°20'
37°10'
2 km
2 miles
N

and has some one-lane stretches.

NAVIGATION: To get on the north arm of this TE from I-680, take the exit onto Calveras Rd.

To access the south arm from I-680, take Berryessa Rd to Capitol Av.

Turn left on Capitol then right on Sierra Rd.

ROUTING OPTION: Wanna loop-de-loop again? Piedmont Rd connects both ends of the TE.

BAY TE-R Clayton Rd (4.9 mi / 7.9 km)
MAP III Good pavement and nice curves on this little loop through widely spaced, large-lot suburban development below the south end of **DH47TE-C.**

NAVIGATION: To get to the south end of Clayton from I-680: take E Capitol Expy east. Capitol will swing south and intersect Story Rd after a few blocks. Turn left on Story until you can turn right on Clayton.

*If you want to get from the south end of **BAY TE-A** to the south end of **BAY TE-B** when you reach suburban hell: Turn left from Clayton onto Marten Ave, then left on Mt Pleasant Rd. Stay straight on Ruby Ave when Mt Pleasant splits off left. When you reach Quimby turn left.*

BAY TE-S Quimby Rd (5.1 mi / 8.2 km)
MAP III/V Once you escape from Jose's high-density suburban crap, this TE hairpins up through some more developed acreage to **DH47TE-C**. On the last 1.1 mi (1.8 km) one-lane piece, stay tucked to your side of the road and watch for Brown (or any other pylons for that matter) trying to do you.

NAVIGATION: To get to the south end of Quimby from Hwy 101 (south of I-280/680): Take Tully Rd east. A few blocks later, turn right on Quimby.

*If you want to get from the south end of **BAY TE-B** to the south end of **BAY TE-A**: Turn right off Quimby, when you hit Ruby Ave which will eventually angle right and become Mt Pleasant Rd. Stay on Mt Pleasant until you can turn right on Marten Ave. When you reach Clayton, turn right.*

BAY TE-T Evergreen – Coyote (9.7 mi / 15.6 km) *San Felipe Rd - Metcalf Rd*
MAP III/V It's a shame that suburbs continue to devour the San Felipe way from San Jose. Because once you finally reach the expanding edge of urbanity, you're on a fairly smooth ribbon of pavement, curving through a treed canyon. The asphalt on Metcalf is not as smooth as on San Felipe, but the terrain starts out similarly before opening up and allowing a bit of development. Including a Pratt and Whitney space program plant and a City of Santa Clara Motorcycle Park. Serious maxburners may want to stop and play – one assumes at the motorcycle park.

*NAVIGATION: If you want to get to the San Felipe end from **BAY TE-B**, stay on Quimby Rd until you can turn left on White Rd. A couple of miles later, White Rd will angle slightly left and become San Felipe.*

Mountain View
Sunnyvale
Santa Clara
SAN JOSE
Cupertino
Saratoga
Los Gatos
Evergreen
Coyote
New Almaden
Boulder Creek
Brookdale
Ben Lomond
Fenton
Scotts Valley
SANTA CRUZ
Capitola
Aptos
Corralitos
Watsonville
(D-DUC/HON)
(D-KAW/SUZ)
(D-KAW/SUZ/YAM)
(D-YAM)
(D-BMW/TRI)
(D-BMW)
(D-HD)
(D-APR/MG/TRI)
(D-HON/SUZ/YAM)
(D-BUE/HD)
(D-HON/KAW/SUZ)
(D-KTM)
(D-APR/DUC/MG)
(D-BMW/YAM)
(D-BUE/HD)
Joseph P. Grant CP CG
Uvas Canyon CP CG
Manresa SB CG
Santa Cruz KOA CG
831.722.0551
DH55 TE-B ALT
DH55
DH39 TE-D
DH39
DH39 TE-C
DH39 TE-B
DH39 TE-E ALT
DH39 TE-E
DH39 TE-A
DH74 TE-D
DH74 TE-C
DH74 TE-B
DH74
DH74 TE-A
DH74 TE-G ALT
DH74 TE-G
DH74 TE-F
DH47 TE-C
BAY TE-Q
BAY TE-R
BAY TE-S
BAY TE-T
BAY TE-Z
BAY TE-Y
BAY TE-W
(III)
IV
(V)
FOR AREA DETAIL SEE DH74
For services see DH74
SANTA TERESA HILLS
SANTA CRUZ MOUNTAINS
SANTA CLARA
SANTA CRUZ
MONTEREY BAY
Soquel Cove
Lexington Res.
Guadalupe Res.
Calero Res.
Guadalupe Cr.
EL SOMBOSO
MT. THAYER
MT. UMUNHUM
Feller Rd.
Sierra Rd.
Capitol Ave.
Alum Rock Ave.
Fleming Ave.
Clayton Rd.
Mt. Pleasant Dr.
Quimby Rd.
Marten Ave.
Story Rd.
White Rd.
Ruby Ave.
E. Capitol Expy.
Tully Rd.
Monterey Hwy.
Santa Clara St.
W. San Carlos St.
Stevens Creek Blvd.
Yerba Buena Rd.
San Felipe Rd.
Camden Ave.
Los Gatos Blvd.
Union Ave.
Shannon Rd.
Almaden Expwy
Hicks Rd.
Harry Rd.
McKean Rd.
Almaden Rd.
Stevens Canyon Rd.
Mt. Eden Rd.
Pierce Rd.
Skyline Blvd.
Montevina Rd.
Black Rd.
Bear Creek Rd.
Alma Bridge Rd.
Old Santa Cruz Hwy.
Aldercroft Hts. Rd.
Alba Rd.
Empire Grade Rd.
Pine Flat Rd.
Bonny Doon Rd.
Smith Grade Rd.
Empire Grade Rd.
Vine Hill Rd.
Soquel-San Jose Rd.
Granite Ck. Rd.
Glen Cyn. Rd.
Branciforte Dr.
Porter St.
Highland Way
Eureka Cyn. Rd.
Browns Valley Rd.
Hazel Dell Rd.
Green Valley Rd.
Day Valley Rd.
Trout Gulch Rd.
Valencia Rd.
Freedom Blvd.
Hawes Rd.
Mt. Madonna Rd.
Casserly Rd.
101
237
680
880
G4
G6
130
85
82
280
G2
17
9
35
G21
101
87
G10
G8
1
37°20'
37°10'
37°00'
122°00'
121°50'
N
2 km
2 miles

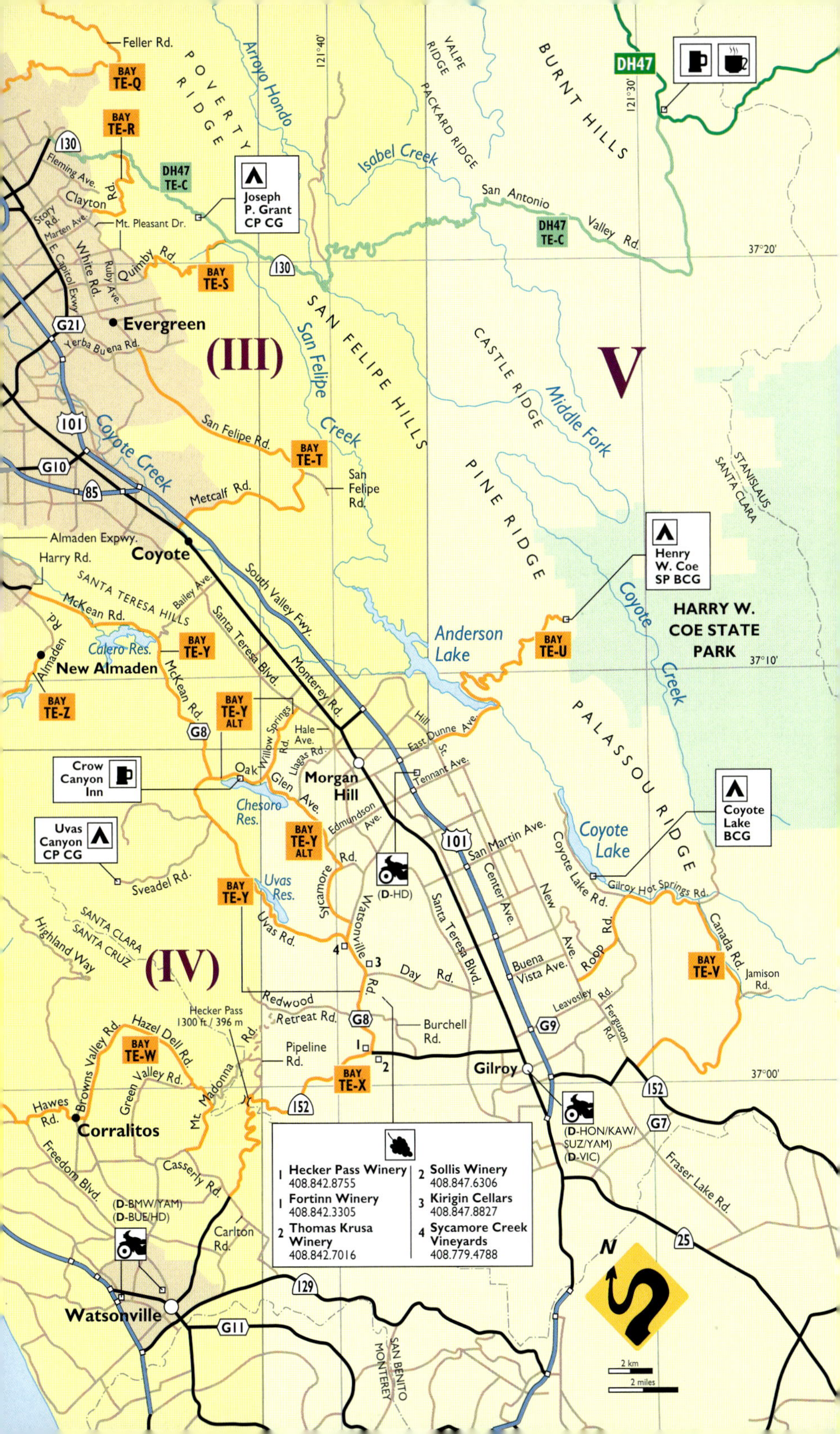

Feller Rd.
BAY TE-Q
BAY TE-R
POVERTY RIDGE
Arroyo Hondo
121°40'
VALPE RIDGE
PACKARD RIDGE
BURNT HILLS
DH47
121°30'
130
Fleming Ave.
Clayton Rd.
DH47 TE-C
Joseph P. Grant CP CG
Isabel Creek
San Antonio Valley Rd.
Story Rd.
Marten Ave.
Mt. Pleasant Dr.
DH47 TE-C
37°20'
E. Capitol Exwy.
White Rd.
Ruby Ave.
Quimby Rd.
BAY TE-S
SAN FELIPE HILLS
G21
Evergreen
Yerba Buena Rd.
(III)
San Felipe Creek
CASTLE RIDGE
V
Middle Fork
101
Coyote Creek
San Felipe Rd.
BAY TE-T
San Felipe Rd.
G10
85
Metcalf Rd.
PINE RIDGE
STANISLAUS
SANTA CLARA
Almaden Expwy.
Harry Rd.
Coyote
South Valley Fwy.
Henry W. Coe SP BCG
SANTA TERESA HILLS
Bailey Ave.
McKean Rd.
Santa Teresa Blvd.
Coyote Creek
HARRY W. COE STATE PARK
Almaden Rd.
Calero Res.
BAY TE-Y
Anderson Lake
BAY TE-U
New Almaden
Monterey Rd.
37°10'
BAY TE-Z
McKean Rd.
BAY TE-Y ALT
Willow Springs Rd.
Hale Ave.
Hill Rd.
PALASSOU RIDGE
G8
Llagas Rd.
East Dunne Ave.
St.
Crow Canyon Inn
Oak Glen Ave.
Morgan Hill
Tennant Ave.
Chesbro Res.
Edmundson Ave.
Coyote Lake BCG
Uvas Canyon CP CG
BAY TE-Y ALT
101
San Martin Ave.
Coyote Lake
Rd.
Coyote Lake Rd.
Sveadel Rd.
(D-HD)
Santa Teresa Blvd.
Center Ave.
New Ave.
Gilroy Hot Springs Rd.
BAY TE-Y
Uvas Res.
Sycamore Rd.
Watsonville Rd.
Roop Rd.
SANTA CLARA
SANTA CRUZ
Highland Way
Uvas Rd.
Canada Rd.
BAY TE-V
(IV)
Day Rd.
Buena Vista Ave.
Jamison Rd.
Redwood Retreat Rd.
Leavesley Rd.
Ferguson Rd.
Hecker Pass 1300 ft / 396 m
G8
Burchell Rd.
G9
Hazel Dell Rd.
BAY TE-W
Browns Valley Rd.
Pipeline Rd.
Gilroy
37°00'
Green Valley Rd.
BAY TE-X
152
Mt. Madonna Rd.
Hawes Rd.
152
Corralitos
(D-HON/KAW/SUZ/YAM)
(D-VIC)
G7
Freedom Blvd.
Casserly Rd.
Fraser Lake Rd.
1 Hecker Pass Winery 408.842.8755
1 Fortinn Winery 408.842.3305
2 Thomas Krusa Winery 408.842.7016
2 Sollis Winery 408.847.6306
3 Kirigin Cellars 408.847.8827
4 Sycamore Creek Vineyards 408.779.4788
(D-BMW/YAM)
(D-BUE/HD)
Carlton Rd.
25
N
129
Watsonville
G11
SAN BENITO
MONTEREY
2 km
2 miles

To get to the San Felipe end from San Jose, the fastest way is to use Hwy 101. Exit at Blossom Hill Rd/G 20 to the west, Silver Creek Valley Rd to the east. Follow Silver Creek Valley until you can turn right on Silver Creek Rd. The TE begins when you turn right on San Felipe.

You cannot get to the Metcalf Rd end of the TE directly off Hwy 101. From the north, you have to take Hwy 85 off Hwy 101 and then turn south on Monterey Rd (B 101). A couple of miles later, Metcalf junctions to the left.

From the south, take one of the Morgan Hill 101 Exits west to Monterey Rd (B 101). Take Monterey north 8 mi (13 km) or so to the junction right with Metcalf.

BAY TE-U Morgan Hill – Henry W Coe SP (10.1 mi / 16.3 km)
E Dunne St

MAP V This snake around sometimes skanky-smelling Anderson Lake becomes one lane and rough in spots while it climbs up to the state park on top of Pine Ridge. But even when the pavement is new, it's not that smooth. California used to spend 30 per cent of its budget on infrastructure and now spends only 1 per cent. And you can sure feel it here. Scenic and peaceful up on top, though.

NAVIGATION: E Dunne is a Hwy 101 marked exit at Morgan Hill.

BAY TE-V Canada Rd - Gilroy Hot Springs Rd - Roop Rd (14.6 mi / 23.5 km)

MAP V Yes, this loop into the hills east of Gilroy – part of the Juan Bautista D'Anza National Historic Trail – has a bit of the narrow, no center-line stuff. But, overall, the pavement's pretty good. The curves are more fun on Canada and Roop. And there's even some scenic variety: open rolling hills for Great White North and Roop; forested creek canyon on Gilroy HS.

TOUR NOTE: The hot springs are not open to the public. But, in this heat, who cares? And don't be thinking about a swim in Coyote Lake; you're not allowed in the water of this reservoir either.

BAY TE-W Trout Gulch Rd - Valencia Rd - Day Valley Rd - Freedom Blvd - Hawes Rd - Browns Valley Rd - Hazel Dell Rd - Mt Madonna Rd (15.1 mi / 24.3 km)

MAP IV/V You won't be a navigation virgin if you can follow this multi-road TE. And you'll have picked up the best of what curves remain to ride in this sometimes forested, sometimes open and occasionally populated area between the increasingly urban coastal strip and the crest of the south-western Santa Cruz Mtns. Just don't expect great pavement. It's restricted to Valencia and the miniscule piece of what used to be French Blvd.

NAVIGATION: Coming from the Aptos end, turn north from Soquol Dr and onto Trout Gulch Rd to start the TE. After about a mile, Trout Gulch turns left while you stay straight on Valencia.

- At 3.1 mi (5.0 km), turn left off Valencia and onto Day Valley.

- At 4.4 mi (7.1 km), turn left from Day Valley onto Freedom and then about a block later, left off Freedom and onto Hawes.

- At 5.1 mi (8.2 km), stay left on Hawes or you'll end up on Pleasant Valley Rd, which will take you back to the (non-TE part of) Freedom Blvd.

- Even if you're not naturally so inclined, stay straight at the four-way junction in Corralitos where Hawes butt ends Browns Valley.

ROUTING OPTION: From Corralitos, you can take Eureka Canyon Rd north up to the top of the Santa Cruz Mtns but we don't know why you'd want to. Even though it is paved – if you can call it that – it's very rough and no fun. The Harley on it was probably lost.

BAY TE-X Hecker Pass Hwy (Hwy 152) (9.7 mi / 15.6 km)
MAP V In spite of this TE's name, it can be hard to pass the freakin' heavy pylon parade, due to the scarcity of extra lanes or dotted yellow. So you may find it difficult to get much use out of the great curves and good pavement.

BAY TE-Y McKean Rd - Uvas Rd - Watsonville Rd Part 1
(19.7 mi / 31.7 km)
MAP V Not many curves, or surprisingly, traffic but there is excellent pavement on this meander through the pretty, low-hill country south of Greater San Jose's present extrusion. There's only large-lot development here for now but you can assume that SJ will keep marching relentlessly this way.

ROUTING OPTION: If you like this road, there's 4.0 mi (6.4 km) of similar stuff on Croy Rd about halfway along. Past no-service Syeadal, Croy turns to crap for the remaining mile to Uvas Canyon County Park CG.

BAY TE-Y ALT Oak Glen Ave - Sycamore Rd - Watsonville Rd Part 2
(8.3 mi / 13.4 km)
MAP V Watsonville is all straight. Sycamore is pretty straight. Oak Glenn curves slightly, and then a little more when it gets around Chesoro Reservoir. This *ALT* also has the added benefit of taking you to the motorcycle-friendly Crow Canyon Inn bar overlooking the Res. A sheriff was parked at the side of the road here. He must've just been chillin'.

NAVIGATION: Coming from the south at 0.5 mi (0.8 km), turn left off Watsonville and onto Sycamore. At 2.6 mi (4.2 km), make sure you 90° left off Sycamore and onto Oak Glen.

BAY TE-Y ALT2 Willow Springs Rd (2.5 mi / 4.0 km)
MAP V This is a short, sometimes curved option up and then down to Hale Ave just north of downtown Morgan Hill. And if you're in MH, it provides an alternate way to the Crow Canyon Inn.

ROUTING OPTION: About a mile south of Willow, Llagas Rd provides a shorter version of Willow from Oak Glen Ave to Morgan Hill.

BAY TE-Z Los Gatos – New Almaden (13.0 mi / 20.9 km) *Shannon Rd - Hicks Rd - Almaden Rd*
MAP III/IV/V This twisty surprise runs through rugged, heavily forested country along the northern edge of the Sierra Azul Preserve and beside the

Golden Gate Cycles
(HON/KAW/SUZ/YAM)
1540 Pine 415.771.4535
BMW of San Francisco
(BMW)
1675 Howard
415.551.4207
Treasure Island
Golden Gate Bridge
Golden Gate
Dudley Perkins Co.
(BUE/HD)
66 Page 415.703.9494
Scuderia West
(APR/BIM/KTM/VIC)
69 Duboce
415.621.7223
Munroe Motors
(AUG/DUC/MG/TRI)
412 Valencia
415.626.3496
Mission Motor Cycles
(HON/KAW/YAM)
6232 Mission
650.992.1234
Bay Area Yamaha
(YAM)
1601 Adrian
650.343.9750
SAN FRANCISCO
China Basin
PACIFIC OCEAN
SAN FRANCISCO BAY
Daly City
Brisbane
SAN BRUNO MTN.
South San Francisco
San Bruno
Millbrae
Pacifica
San Francisco International Airport
San Andreas Lake
SAN FRANCISCO
SAN MATEO
Lombard St.
Bay St.
Embarcadero
Broadway
California St.
Fillmore St.
Van Ness Ave.
Market St.
Howard St.
Geary Blvd.
Fulton St.
Union Wy.
Lincoln Wy.
Lincoln Blvd.
16th St.
Mission St.
Great Hwy.
Sunset Blvd.
Noriega St.
Taraval St.
Cesar Chavez St.
Portola Dr.
Stoat Blvd.
Ocean Ave.
Silver Ave.
Geneva Ave.
Lake Merced Blvd.
John Daly Blvd.
Guadalupe Cyn. Pkwy.
Bayshore Blvd.
Bayshore Fwy.
Hillside Blvd.
Sister Cities Blvd.
Junipero Serra Blvd.
Grand Ave.
Westborough Blvd.
Skyline Blvd.
Junipero Serra Fwy.
Bayshore Fwy.
E. Millbrae Ave.
Rollins Rd.
Adrian Rd.
101
80
280
1
35
82
380
37°40'
122°30'
N
2 km
2 miles
DH55
TE-C

Guadalupe Reservoir. Both should ensure a continued lack of development. Pavement can be bouncy-bouncy on Hicks.

NAVIGATION: From Los Gatos, Los Gatos Blvd runs parallel to and just east of Hwy 17. Take Shannon east off Los Gatos. The TE starts where Shannon Y's right at Short Rd.

RIDER'S LOG: **DATE RIDDEN:** **YOUR RATING: /10**

Map Tip: Services on non-featured DHs and TEs are generally shown as bare icon only and sometimes as no icon. For the full detail, just turn to the featured map.

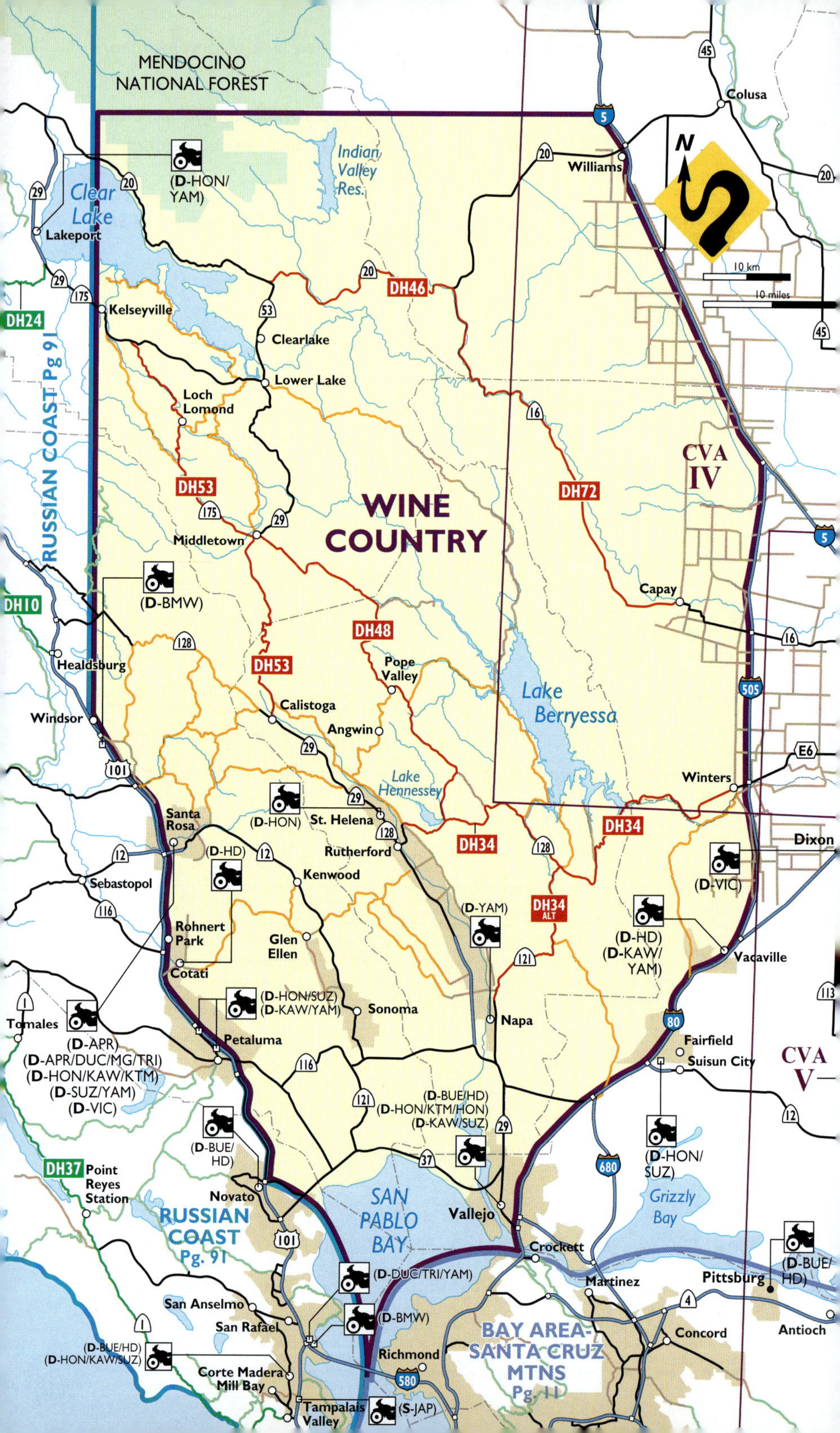
MENDOCINO NATIONAL FOREST
WINE COUNTRY
CVA IV
CVA V
RUSSIAN COAST Pg 91
RUSSIAN COAST Pg. 91
BAY AREA-SANTA CRUZ MTNS Pg. 11
10 km
10 miles
Clear Lake
Indian Valley Res.
Lake Berryessa
Lake Hennessey
San Pablo Bay
Grizzly Bay
DH24
DH10
DH37
DH46
DH53
DH72
DH48
DH34
DH34 ALT
Lakeport
Kelseyville
Clearlake
Lower Lake
Loch Lomond
Middletown
Williams
Colusa
Capay
Healdsburg
Windsor
Pope Valley
Calistoga
Angwin
Winters
Dixon
Santa Rosa
St. Helena
Rutherford
Kenwood
Sebastopol
Rohnert Park
Cotati
Glen Ellen
Sonoma
Napa
Vacaville
Fairfield
Suisun City
Tomales
Petaluma
Point Reyes Station
Novato
Vallejo
Crockett
Martinez
Pittsburg
Antioch
Concord
San Anselmo
San Rafael
Richmond
Corte Madera
Mill Bay
Tampalais Valley
(D-HON/YAM)
(D-BMW)
(D-HON)
(D-HD)
(D-YAM)
(D-VIC)
(D-HD)
(D-KAW/YAM)
(D-HON/SUZ)
(D-KAW/YAM)
(D-APR)
(D-APR/DUC/MG/TRI)
(D-HON/KAW/KTM)
(D-SUZ/YAM)
(D-VIC)
(D-BUE/HD)
(D-HON/KTM/HON)
(D-KAW/SUZ)
(D-BUE/HD)
(D-HON/SUZ)
(D-BUE/HD)
(D-DUC/TRI/YAM)
(D-BMW)
(D-BUE/HD)
(D-HON/KAW/SUZ)
(S-JAP)

WINE COUNTRY

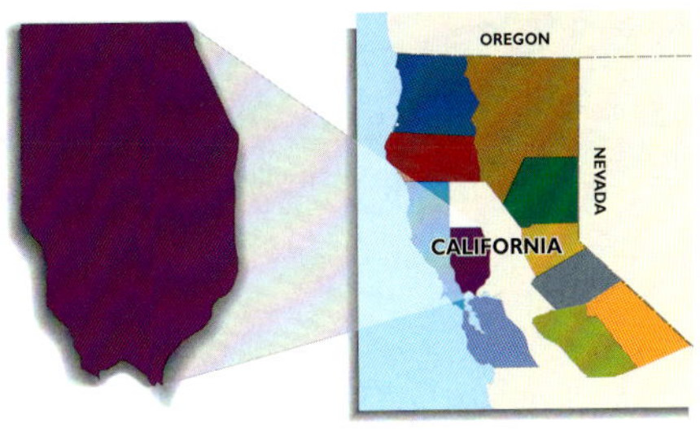

RANK DH#/74	TIRES Total/100	DESTINATION HIGHWAY	PAGE
DH34	71.2	Winters – Rutherford/Napa 35.0 mi / 56.3 km 30.0 mi / 48.3 km	61
DH48	66.4	Lake Hennessey – Middletown 30.8 mi / 49.6 km	69
DH53	65.0	Calistoga – Kelseyville 36.0 mi / 57.9 km	73
DH46	67.2	Clearlake – Hwy 16/Hwy 20 Jct 18.4 mi / 29.6 km	83
DH72	55.2	Capay – Hwy 16/Hwy 20 Jct 32.8 mi / 52.8 km	87

Creekside
Chevron
To Sacramento
To CVA IV Pg. 499
Chevron
Town & Country SM
Winters Store
Pisani
To CVA IV Pg. 499
Winters
To Capay & DH72
Midway RV Park CG 707.446.7679
Neil's Vineyard RV Park CG 707.447.8797
Oates
Vacaville
Fairfield
Pardehsa Store
TE-A
Lake Solano CP CG 530.795.2990
1111 Webster 707.425.4625
(II)
VACA MTNS.
Fairfield Cycle Center (HON/SUZ) 1800 West Texas 707.432.1660
Rockville
Lake Curry
TE-C
Wooden Valley Winery 707.864.0730
Rockville Inn 707.864.4325
Valley Café 707.864.2507
Tower
2 km
2 miles
To Livermore & DH47 Pg. 37
LAKE BERRYESSA
TE-B
MILLIKEN CYN.
DH34 ALT
1. Vacaville HD 100 Auto Center 707.455.7000
2. Vacaville Motorsports (KAW/YAM) 1385 E Monte Vista 707.469.7195
313 Parker 707.450.0500
Jimmy's Truck Stop
To Livermore & DH47 Pg. 37
DH48 TE-A
NON-FEATURED DH SERVICES NOT SHOWN
Napa
DH34
DH48
NAPA VALLEY
Yountville
TE-E
I
To Middleton & mid-DH53
TE-D
Oakville
Rutherford
TE-F
Angwin
DH48 TE-B
TE-G
Sonoma
St. Helena
To Tamalpais Valley & DH37 Pg. 93
Glen Ellen
TE-H ALT
Cycle West Honda Suzuki (HON/SUZ) 1375 Industrial 707.769.5240
To Middleton & DH48
Calistoga
DH53 TE-F
TE-H
G&B Kawasaki (KAW/YAM) 326 Petaluma Blvd N 707.763.4658
210 Lakeville 707.769.0429
To Tamalpais Valley & DH37 Pg. 93
DH53 TE-C
DH53 TE-E
Petaluma
DH37 TE-F
DH53 TE-D
For detail, see DH53
Santa Rosa
Rohnert Park
Cotati
DH37 TE-G
DH53 TE-C ALT
Mark West Springs
To Healdsburg & DH10 Pg. 137
To Sebastapol
To Jenner & DH29 Pg. 103
KOA CG 707.763.1492
To Tomales & DH37 Pg. 93

DH34 Winters – Rutherford / Napa

Hwy 128 / Hwy 121

Distance:	35.0 mi (56.3 km)/ 30.0 mi (48.3 km)	Traffic:	Moderate to Heavy

At a Glance

Tasting notes: This vintage, medium-paved '34 from the Napa Valley is a layered and complex DH with well-integrated oak Scenery and definite hints of Remoteness. Sipping it from Winters, you first taste a bland straightness and orchards more commonly associated with plonk from the San Joaquin Valley. But once into the hills, you detect intriguing notes of Twistiness along Putah Creek. They intensify as the road swirls westward, enhanced by the scenic flavors of Lakes Berryessa and Hennessey. The heavier concentration of S-curves on both tongues west of the Hwy 121 Jct has a slight Engineering acidity, notably on the *ALT* section to Napa where the steeply graded Twistiness is particularly robust. Because the traffic is sometimes hard to get by, particularly on the *ALT*, a lighter sportbike is an ideal pairing. But this adaptable DH goes surprisingly well with beefy cruisers, too. Can be ridden now or cellared for future touring.

TIRES	
Twistiness	30/30
Pavement	11.6/20
Engineering	5.3/10
Remoteness	4.0/10
Scenery	9.9/15
Character	10.4/15
Total	**71.2**

Access

From Winters

On Hwy 128

Head west. You're on the road.

From Rutherford

On Hwy 128/29

Follow Hwy 128 (also marked Rutherford Rd and later Conn Creek Rd) to the unmarked Silverado Trail. Here Hwy 128 does a little jog south. Once you follow the Hwy 128 signs left off Silverado Trail, you're on the road.

From Napa (*ALT*)

On Hwy 29

Take the Trancas St exit. Go east on Trancas. When Trancas turns into Monticello (Hwy 121) at the Silverado Trail, you're on the road.

N
2 km
2 miles
NON-FEATURED DH SERVICES NOT SHOWN
Putah Creek
38°30'
PLEASANTS RIDGE
Canyon Creek Resort CG 530.795.4133
Markley Cove Store
128
Mix Canyon
VACA MOUNTAINS
SOLANO
NAPA
38°20'
Vintage Café 707.425.3207
Pleasure Cove Resort CG 707.966.2172
MT. VACA
Gordon Valley Rd.
OKELL HILL
SUISUN VALLEY
Suisun Valley Rd.
Lambert Rd.
LEMON HILL
Lake Curry
Wooden Valley Cross Rd.
Wooden Valley Rd.
TE-C
122°10'
Wrag Cyn. Rd.
Pleasure Cove Resort GS
Steele Cyn. Rd.
TE-B
Capell Valley
LAKE BERRYESSA
MILLIKEN CYN.
DH34 ALT
MT. GEORGE
Yamaha of Napa (YAM) 459 S Soscol 707.254.7432
1310 Napa Town Centre 707.226.7459
Turtle Rock 707.966.2246
Capell Creek
Turtle Rock Motel 707.966.0389
Berryessa-Knoxville Rd.
DH48 TE-A
LITTLE SUGARLOAF PEAK
Four Corners GS
IRON MTN.
DH34
William Harrison 707.963.8271
1st Ave.
Soscol Ave.
221
Nichelini 707.963.0717 (Wknds only)
Rust Ridge Ranch 707.965.9353
Napa
Trancas Rd.
Lower Chiles Rd.
Ugly Corner Café 707.945.0975
II
Napa River
Brown Valley Rd.
Auberge de Soleil 707.963.1211
Chiles Pope Valley Rd.
Silverado Trail
NAPA VALLEY
Yountville Cross Rd.
Solano Ave.
Orchard Rd.
Creek Rd.
Redwood Rd.
122°20'
Buhman Rd.
DH48
Chiles Pope Valley Rd.
Hennessey Lake
Yountville
Dry
TE-E
Rd.
Shady Oaks Country Inn 707.963.1190
Oakville Cross Rd.
Exxon BP 6484 Washington 707.9440.0904
128
Oakville
Oakville Grade Rd.
Mt. Veeder
TE-G
Rutherford
Zinfindel Ln.
Chateau Potelle 707.255.9440
TE-F
Dry Creek Rd.
Howell Mtn. Rd.
Angwin
TE-D
29
DH48 TE-B
Pope St.
St. Helena
Kenwood Rest 707.833.6326
Kenwood Gas
NAPA SONOMA
TE-G
Sonoma
Above The Clouds B&B 800.736.7894
Trinity Rd.
Deer Park Rd.
Silverado Trail
Cavedale Rd.
Parriott Motors (HON) 1027 Pope 707.963.3190
Arnold Dr.
12
Valley Rd.
122°30'
VALLEY
NAPA
Spring Mtn. Rd.
Adobe Cyn. Rd.
453 E 1st 707.996.1090
TE-H ALT
Glen Ellen
Kenwood
Sugarloaf Ridge SPCG
Napa River
Warm Springs Rd.
Morton's Warm Springs
Jack London Lodge 707.938.8510
Gaige House Inn B&B 800.935.0237
DH53 TE-F
NON-FEATURED DH SERVICES NOT SHOWN
TE-H
Calistoga
Matanzas Creek 800.590.6464
Bennett Valley Rd.
Sonoma Mtn. Rd.
128
DH53 TE-A
Franz Valley School Rd.
St. Helena Rd.
Sonoma Hwy.
1 Brix 707.944.2749
2 Ugly Corner Café 707.945.0975
3 La Toque 707.963.9770
4 Rancho Caymus Inn 707.963.1777
5 Hotel D'Amici 707.942.1007
1458 Lincoln 707.942.6333
DH53 TE-C
Spring Lake RP CG 707.539.8092
Pressley Rd.
DH53 TE-E
Grange Rd.
Petrified Forest Rd.
Calistoga Rd.
Summerfield Rd.
Roberts Rd.
Montecito Blvd.
Petaluma Hill Rd.
122°40'
Wallace Rd.
DH53 TE-D
Rieblí Rd.
Brush Cr. Rd.
Los Alivos Ave.
Rohnert Park
For services, see DH53
Franz Valley Rd.
Porter Creek Rd.
Mark West Springs
Santa Rosa
Cotati
101
DH53 TE-C ALT
Mark West Springs Rd.
Redwood Dr.
116
Michael's HD 7601 Redwood 707.793.9180
To Healdsburg & DH10 Pg. 137
To Sebastapol To Jenner & DH29 Pg. 103

On The Road

The ride uncorks from Winters, pouring west through orchards on a wide-shouldered straightaway. The least complex part of the DH is over quickly, though. At 1.8 mi (2.9 km), a hard sweeper ricochets you left against the base of a gentle foothill and a few lazier curves take you to the junction with Pleasants Valley Rd at 3.1 mi (5.0 km). Turning south here puts you on mid-**TE-A** after about a mile. But you might not want to quit now.

You pick up Putah Creek past the junction and the flavor of the road changes instantly. The pavement loses its shoulders as it navigates the shoreline of the wide creek. To the right, steep grass slopes open from time to time, revealing their rocky underbellies. At 4.2 mi (6.8 km), you're off the creek and venturing through a broad basket of grassland toward some oak-encrusted hills. Angling back towards the creek, the right roadside rises to crowd the path even closer to the water than before. A solid section of curves ensues below the distinctive, heavily treed lines of Pleasants Ridge.

Road and river continue together through the lush landscape. Oak branches reach across the lanes from both right and left. The right-hand slope keeps prodding the road closer to the creek. Quite idyllic really, but for the yellow signs warning of possible deer attacks.

At 7.7 mi (12.4 km), you pass a café/store and campground and cross the southeast tip of Lake Berryessa, just below the dam. Not much development on this road, but when it's there, you'll usually find some service or another. You sweep right up a steep slope and enter Napa County at 8.5 mi (13.7 km). Jagged rock cliffs scale the sky on your left, mirroring the eye-catching view of the huge, tree- and grass-covered mass of rock that rises high above the north side of the dam.

Five S-curves take you up and off the reservoir into a much drier landscape of broom and other low-order vegetation. The terrain lushes up again quickly though, with the grand oaks making a strong comeback as the road revisits blue Lake Berryessa. You descend and pass the Markley Cove Marina, on the right at 10.7 mi (17.2 km).

The lake's gone for good as you climb again on a series of spaced, unexceptional curves through a landscape of bushy trees (or maybe treeish bushes). At 11.9 mi (19.2 km), the grade increases across dirt slopes as the corners tighten, condensing into a series of S-curves and sweepers that flip-flop you up to a low summit.

The curviness definitely eases as you peer over a valley stuffed with oaks toward the modest Vaca Range. The road descends and there are a couple of esses between 13.5 mi (21.7 km) and 14.1 mi (22.7 km). After that, it's more straight than not through an area that's flattened enough to accommodate a couple of small ranches. Then, at 15.6 mi (25.1 km), the road winds up enough to ess between the ridge to the right and the treed knob to the left. It then spits out into an oaky vale at 16.8 mi (27.0 km).

A rightward slope ends abruptly at 18.1 mi (29.1 km) where the terrain expands into a flat, grassy plateau. A minor collection of buildings flags the junction with Hwy 121 at 18.9 mi (30.4 km) and Steele Canyon Rd (**TE-B**). Here the DH splits, with the primary route continuing on Hwy 128 to Rutherford and the alternative going south on Hwy 121 to Napa*.

Hwy 128/121 Jct – Rutherford

As you go right from the junction, you'll notice that more businesses are closed than open in the no-name town located there. The road continues its new-found curvelessness with a long straightaway through the green fields and light population of the Capell Valley. The straightness continues even when the fields end and the terrain roughens at 22.2 mi (35.7 km). As you cross Capell Creek and climb, the green valley is rapidly transformed into a deep, narrow gorge. Still, it's not until 23.6 mi (38.0 km) that this promising topography coughs up any notable curves.

With the last few miles being so uneventful, you might be tempted to dump the DH and try the compelling **DH48TE-A Berryessa-Knoxville Rd - Pope Canyon Rd**, which junctions from the north at 23.9 mi (38.5 km). Go ahead. But just know you'll be missing out on one of this DH's best sections. Not to mention some wine-tasting rooms.

No, you won't regret finishing off the main route. Immediately after the junction, sweet S-curves slice up the slopes below Little Sugarloaf Peak. The plateauing of the terrain at 24.4 mi (39.3 km) makes no difference. This DH is on a roll. Almost like it's got something to prove.

The flatland widens at 25.8 mi (41.5 km) and the curves separate out a little. But when the pavement corners, it does it with gusto. At 26.7 mi (43.0 km), the road narrows and squiggles down across Sage Creek to the junction right with the forgettable Lower Chiles Rd right. Nothing hot there. Stay with the paint and **veer left**.

This tight, twisty and challenging section of the DH closely follows the path of Sage Creek. The curlicue of esses is intense all right, with a non-existent shoulder and sidecase-scraping overgrowth. But it's short, too, culminating at 27.5 mi (44.3 km) in a sudden straight. The curves that resume at 27.8 mi (44.7 km) aren't so tight but are far better sightlined, climbing predictably along a steep-rising, rock-hugging ledge. Nine linked S-curves in a row. Believe it, baby.

TOUR NOTE: The historic Nichelini Winery is tucked away in the heart of this very twisty section. So if you stop for a tasting (weekends only), you might want to spit rather than swallow. Or, if you'd rather not have wine dribbling down your chin, you can chill at the picnic tables and chuck a few balls on the bocce court before hopping back on your bike.

After a breath, another series of nine essess appears, this one running along the narrow ledge high above the creek. At 30.5 mi (49.1 km), the rock slope eases to layered, grass- and oak-covered banks. But the curves, though not so linked, are still deep and smooth. Water appears on the left

– the eastern end of Lake Hennessey. You reach the junction with **DH48 Lake Hennessey – Middletown** at 31.3 mi (50.4 km). To keep dancing with the DH that brung ya, **stay left**.

Across the causeway, tight, sweeping curves continue along the left side of the widening water. You stay pretty level with the lake as you dip and weave along its shoreline. The pavement quality takes a little dip in here as well but it's temporary. The road leaves the lake at 33.8 mi (54.4 km) and straightens. Tidbits of housing and other bits of man-made flotsam appear, but no sooner do you see them than you're at the junction with the Silverado Trail (**TE-D**), and the end of the road, at 35.0 mi (56.3 km).

*TOUR NOTE: To carry on to Rutherford, turn right on the unmarked Silverado Trail (**TE-D**), then left on Conn Creek Rd. Hwy 128 winds 2.7 mi (4.3 km) through the vineyards to the Rutherford Jct with Hwy 29. Beaulieu's tasting room is on your right.*

**DH ALT Hwy 128/121 Jct – Napa*

Where the main route takes its time in finding its twisty muse, Hwy 121 gets to the curvin' in a hurry. Turns, many of them tight, fill the steady climb into Milliken Canyon through the rolling fields and airy roadside stands of oak. By the time you're into the woods at 22.7 mi (36.5 km), you've already logged 39 curves. And that's just for starters.

With the woods come a short descent and some arboreal views to the far side of the canyon. At 23.8 mi (38.3 km), the terrain flattens into fields again, but this road just does not stop winding. If you want something milder, Wooden Valley Rd (**TE-C**) arrows left mid-sweeper at 24.4 mi (39.3 km).

The tightest, essiest section of Hwy 121 starts at 25.1 mi (40.4 km). A collection of 20-mph (30-kmh) advised curves edge up along the barrier of soil and rock that constitute the north side of Mt. George. And if you're going to catch up with a listless string of pylons, by George, this is probably one of the places it will happen.

You leave the ridge you've been climbing and flip across Mt. George at 26.4 mi (42.5 km). Congratulations – you are now officially in the Napa Valley. Don't crack open the bubbly right away, though. It's one steep pitch as you feel your way down the rocky and thick-treed east side of the valley through the tight curves. If you'd rather do this slope the other way, no problem. When you reach the end of the DH at 30.0 mi (48.3 km), at the junction with Silverado Trail (**TE-D**), you can turn around and do just that.

Twisted Edges

TE-A Winters – Vacaville (17.4 mi / 28.0 km)

Putah Creek Rd - Pleasants Valley Rd - Cherry Glen Rd

This pleasant TE between Winters and I-80 is sweetly paved and engineered along Putah Creek, though the asphalt averages out as the road spins up the pretty Vaca Valley between the Vaca Mtns and the English Hills. It's similar to **TE-C**, though nowhere near as twisty. So you won't have to use as much English.

NAVIGATION: Coming from the Vacaville end, you can vacate I-80 in favor of this TE at either of the two Cherry Glen Rd loop exits.

From the Winters end, look for Railroad Ave downtown, south off Hwy 128. Once you take it out of town and cross Putah Creek itself, look for the Putah Creek Rd turn off right (from Winters Rd straight ahead) just past the bar. On second thought…

TE-B Steele Canyon Rd (5.1 mi / 8.2 km)
Worn out by the Napa Valley heat? Steel yourself for smoothly forged pavement, solid engineering and frequent-if-not-radical curves (until the straight last mile or so) climbing up from the *DH ALT* junction to what is basically a suburb on cool Lake Berryessa.

TE-C Wooden Valley Rd - Suisun Valley Rd (12.3 mi / 19.8 km)
Given the throngs of humanity around here, this side road through the forest and fields of Wonder Valley, the vineyards of the Suisun Valley to the mapdot of Rockville is relatively remote. Twistiest on north Wooden, it's pretty much straight for the last third at the south end.

TE-D Conn Creek – Calistoga (13.3 mi / 21.4 km) *Silverado Trail*
Sorry, *mon ami*. If there are two things the new world might generally do better than the old, they're pavement and engineering. And this TE has some of the best. Some of the best wines in the world too, as countless vineyards populate this thoroughfare along the scenic eastern edge of the Napa Valley. Yes, the tasting rooms generate a lot of pylon dregs, but there are enough complex curves to make this *promenade des motocyclettes* worthwhile.

TE-E Dry Creek Rd Part 1 (6.8 mi / 11.0 km)
As you carve quietly through forest and the occasional vineyard up in the western hills parallel to the Napa Valley, it's hard to believe you're only a couple of miles away from Napa's Disneylandish zoo. While it's still too close to be completely exempt from traffic, bicyclists and development, it's far enough away to find signs warning you to look out for Bambi.

NAVIGATION: From Napa, take Redwood Rd west from its traffic light junction with Hwy 29/128 at the north end of town. About a mile later, turn north on Dry Creek Rd. The TE starts in a couple of miles when you pass the right-hand junction with Orchard Ave.

On the east side Hwy 29/128, Trancas St butt ends Redwood and will take you to/from the Silverado Trail start/finish of ***DH34 Winters – Napa****.*

TE-F Redwood Rd - Mt Veeder Rd (11.0 mi / 17.7 km)
Just slightly higher up in the hills than **TE-E**, this similar, parallel route through the Mt Veeder appellation has even more unceasing curviness and rural ambience. Feels like you've gone back in time to old California.

NAVIGATION: Redwood Rd connects with Hwy 29/128 at the north end of Napa. The TE starts a couple of miles west of this junction, once Redwood passes Browns Valley Rd and angles right.

On the east side of Hwy 29/128, Trancas St butt ends Redwood and will take you to/from the Silverado Trail start/finish of ***DH34 Winters – Napa****.*

TE-G Oakville – Glen Ellen (10.9 mi / 17.5 km) *Oakville Grade Rd - Dry Creek Rd Part 2 - Trinity Rd*
This quiet connector winds across the hills between the Napa Valley and the Valley of the Moon. Oakville Grade is a little more stretched out and relaxed compared to **TE-E** and **F** but Dry Creek Part 2 is similar to them. Trinity is a tight-turning drop down to Hwy 12 – a nice descent but it is tough to get by any pylons here. And take seriously the sharp curves sign on both approaches to the one-lane bridge.

TE-H Glen Ellen – Rohnert Park (12.5 mi / 20.1 km) *Warm Springs Rd Part 1 - Bennett Valley Rd - Sonoma Mtn Rd - Pressley Rd - Roberts Rd*
Not much winding on this one, especially on the busy Bennett Valley piece. But it does have an attractive, rural, winey ambience.

NAVIGATION: If you're heading to Rohnert Park and miss the 10-mph (15-kmh) advisory about a mile before the TE's end,, you could end up in someone's driveway. Or worse.

In Rohnert Park, take either Rohnert Park Exwy or Cotati Ave off Hwy 101 over to Petaluma Hill Rd. Turn south on Petaluma to the Roberts Rd start of the TE.

ROUTING OPTION: Headed to Santa Rosa? You can stay straight on Bennett Valley for a couple more miles to the junction of Hwy 12 rather than taking the Sonoma Mtn Rd part of the TE at the 6.1 mi (9.8 km) mark (from Glen Ellen).

TE-H ALT Warm Springs Rd Part 2 (2.7 mi / 4.4 km)
A short, straightish spur through more pretty wine countryside to the wineries at Kenwood.

RIDER'S LOG: **DATE RIDDEN:** **YOUR RATING:** **/10**

To Lakeport & DH24, Pg. 133
To Williams & I-5
To CVA IV Pg. 499
CACHE CREEK
WILDLIFE AREA
CORTINA RIDGE
Cache Creek
Bear Creek
Rocky Creek
Clearlake
Lower Lake
4700 Golf
707.994.3600
Shaw's Shady Acres CG
707.994.2236
Funtime RV CG
707.994.6267
Tower Mart
Susie's Grill
707.994.2328
Foster's Freeze
707.995.0685
Lower Lake Coffee Co
707.995.2558
Shell
DH46
DH72
DH53 TE-K
Morgan Valley Rd.
Spruce Grove Rd.
Rumsey
To Capay & I-5
To CVA IV Pg. 499
Ployez
707.994.2106
Hidden Valley Lake GC
707.987.3138
Hidden Valley Lake
Spanish Flat Resort CG
707.966.7700
Country Store &Deli
Cucina Italiana
707.966.2433
Eagle & Rose Inn
707.987.7330
Mount St Helena Brewing Co
Boar's Breath
707.987.9491
15500 Central Park
707.987.4270
Havy's Rest
707.987.8892
Lake Berryessa Marina Resort/CG
707.966.2161
Middletown
Guenoc & Langtry
707.987.2385
Stagecoach Mkt
707.965.1217
Putah Creek Resort
707.966.2116
DH48
DH53
College Mkt
Chevron
Aetna Springs
LAKE BERRYESSA RECREATION AREA
LAKE BERRYESSA WILDLIFE AREA
LAKE BERRYESSA
TE-A
Pope Valley
Pope Valley Market
Rancho Monticello Resort/CG
707.966.2188
Angwin
Calistoga
TE-B
Rust Ridge Ranch
707.965.9353
St. Helena
DH34
1458 Lincoln
707.942.6333
Parriott Motors
(HON) 1027 Pope
707.963.3190
Rutherford
To Winters & I-505
To CVA IV Pg. 499
To Santa Rosa
To Sonoma
To Napa & DH34
Sonoma Hwy.
DH34 ALT

DH48 Lake Hennessey – Middletown

Chiles-Pope Valley Rd / Pope Valley Rd / Butts Canyon Rd

Distance:	30.8 mi / 49.6 km	Traffic:	Light

At a Glance

TIRES	
Twistiness	26.5/ 30
Pavement	14.3/ 20
Engineering	6.1/ 10
Remoteness	5.1/ 10
Scenery	9.4/ 15
Character	5.0/ 15
Total	66.4

When people think of Napa County, they think of sweeping vineyards, lush hillsides, colorful flower gardens, stylish wineries, spas and gourmet dining. But the county ain't all Napa Valley chic. For those unafraid to witness the dark underbelly of wine country, this DH offers a glimpse of it just across the Pallisades, one valley to the east. While there's a bit of smooth Pavement corresponding with the road's tightest and twistiest sections – along Lake Hennessey, Chiles Creek and further north in the arid Butts Canyon – the rest is barely mid-grade. However, what's far more disturbing is seeing firsthand that much of the unkempt, third world farmland still hasn't been replaced with vineyards. In fact, some of the so-called Scenery is nothing more than rocks and scrub. As if this weren't shocking enough, there's nary a bistro in sight. Most pylons prefer to pretend this part of Napa County doesn't exist. As a result, few venture this way, especially north of the TE-B turnoff. But grittier motorcyclists should take this remote tour off the beaten track and see how the other half lives. If only to go back and tell the other folks back at the B&B in St. Helena.

Access

From mid-DH34 Winters – Rutherford (Hwy 128)

The turnoff north onto Chiles-Pope Valley Rd is 31.3 mi (50.4 km) west of Winters and 4.7 mi (7.6 km) east of the Silverado Trail junction (Conn Creek). If you're coming up from Napa via **DH34 ALT**, the turn is 12.4 mi (20.0 km) west of the junction of the ALT and the main DH.

From Middletown (mid-DH53 Calistoga – Kelseyville)

Via Hwy 29

Just north of Middletown, you'll see the signed turnoff for Butts Canyon Rd. Turn right. You're on the road.

On The Road

The road starts nicely from the south end, curving evenly on good pavement beside Lake Hennessey and then curling more tightly through the smooth corners that crisscross and run along Chiles Creek. Oaks fill the marshland and then mix with alder when some rockfaces come at 2.4 mi (3.9 km). The only problem can be the lack of passing lanes and pullouts to deal with the pylons. Because in here all it takes is one.

The great twisties continue past the junction with the forget-it Lower Chiles Rd at 3.6 mi (5.8 km) but loosen up at 4.2 mi (6.8 km) when you see your first in a series of small vineyards. This is not Napa's high rent district, however. The modest vineyards are separated by scrubby terrain. And the modest curves are separated by scrubby straightaways.

The scenery improves at 6.3 mi (10.1 km) but the general curvelessness continues. The vineyards look more typical now, surrounded by green pastures, rolling hillocks and treed slopes. The road starts to bend again at 7.9 mi (12.7 km), curving respectably despite the breadth of the valley. It gets even more respectable at 9.6 mi (15.5 km), where a series of S-curves slithers through a small stretch of forest.

You emerge from the esses in time to see Pope Canyon Rd (**TE-A**) come in from the right at 10.4 mi (16.7 km) – not a bad option if you want more of that well-paved, twisty lakeside stuff (on its second half, anyway). Carrying on north across an oak-clustered farming flat puts you in the townlet of Pope Valley – better known as the junction with Howell Mtn Rd (**TE-B**).

Minor development between the vineyards spoils the valley north of town. Though you have a soft spot for the guy with the hubcap collection covering his property at 14.4 mi (23.2 km). Is this an omen of some kind? Well, the DH's nicest stretch of pavement starts just beyond, if that means anything. It also corresponds with the esses of Butts Canyon that begin at 17.4 mi (28.0 km) as the last white fence ends.

This "rock slide area" is some section – as distinctive and memorable as the DH's fine southern end. Though that part had marshy, oak-filled wetlands, this is an arid canyon featuring a rugged hodgepodge of Gray Pines, brush and bleached rock. It's a dramatic shift from the farmland, too, as you climb up to a low pass. A brief view opens up to the northeast as you start the descent from the pass at 18.9 mi (30.4 km) and ride toward Adams Ridge, The Cedars and Goat Hill. At 21.0 mi (33.8 km), you cross from Napa into Lake County. And leave the good pavement behind.

The dust-colored landscape continues into Lake County, though the terrain flattens and becomes less rocky. Coming over a crest at 23.3 mi (37.5 km), you get a long view to the blue outlines of Harbin and Boggs Mtns. But scenery's about all you get as the curves dissipate in the unchallenging terrain.

At 25.7 mi (41.4 km), the road sweeps left around the end of the Detert Reservoir, then right into the straightness of Long Valley. In fact, this northern end of the road could just as easily be called Wide Flat Straight and Long Valley. Apart from a sweeper and a couple of curves squished in beside a farm at 28.7 mi (46.2 km), that's pretty much it for a DH that started with a bang but ends with a bit of a whimper at Hwy 29, just north of Middletown, at 30.8 mi (49.6 km).

Twisted Edges

TE-A Pope Canyon Rd - Berryessa-Knoxville Rd (22.3 mi / 35.9 km)

Pope Canyon Rd is hardly infallible, given that its catholic pavement shoots heretically straight across the Pope Valley. At least a benediction of plentiful, moderate, better-paved curves is offered along Pope Creek. The TE undergoes a reformation on the Berryessa-Knoxville piece, where predictable, well-engineered pavement twists along the edge of Lake Berryessa. Even John Knox would enjoy it.

TE-B Howell Mtn Rd - Deer Park Rd (8.0 mi / 12.9 km)

Before Angwin, Howell Mtn is a tightly coiled and well-paved little snake through the forest. A couple miles south of this tiny college town, the TE becomes Deer Park Rd and drops down the east side of the Napa Valley to the wine-tasting cornucopia known as Silverado Trail (**DH34TE-D**). The second half has pretty good pavement but is not nearly as curvy.

Rider's Log: **Date Ridden:** **Your Rating:** **/10**

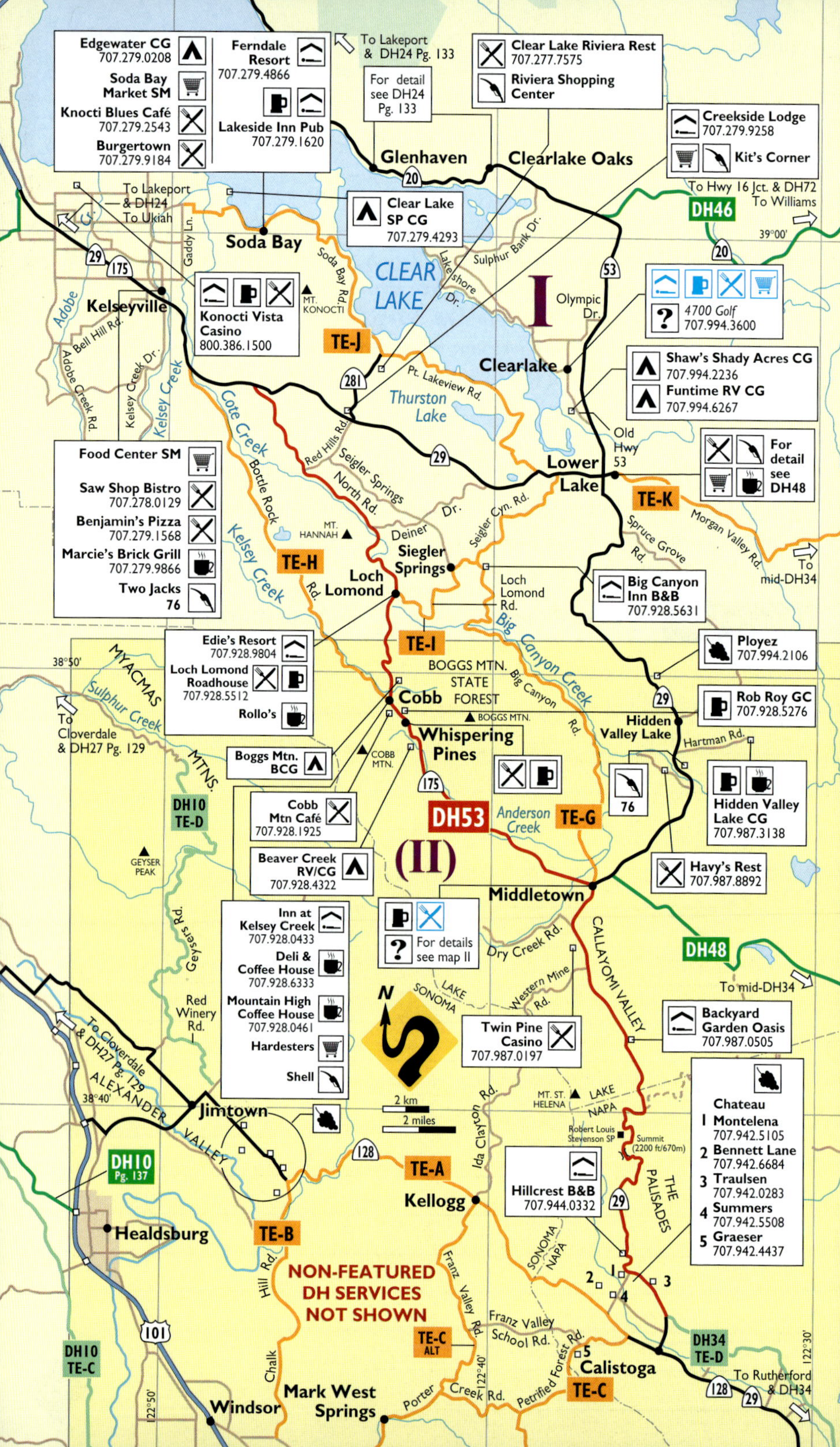

Edgewater CG 707.279.0208
Soda Bay Market SM
Knocti Blues Café 707.279.2543
Burgertown 707.279.9184
Ferndale Resort 707.279.4866
Lakeside Inn Pub 707.279.1620
To Lakeport & DH24 Pg. 133
For detail see DH24 Pg. 133
Clear Lake Riviera Rest 707.277.7575
Riviera Shopping Center
Creekside Lodge 707.279.9258
Kit's Corner
Glenhaven
Clearlake Oaks
To Hwy 16 Jct. & DH72 To Williams
DH46
To Lakeport & DH24 To Ukiah
Clear Lake SP CG 707.279.4293
Soda Bay
CLEAR LAKE
Kelseyville
Konocti Vista Casino 800.386.1500
MT. KONOCTI
TE-J
I
4700 Golf 707.994.3600
Clearlake
Shaw's Shady Acres CG 707.994.2236
Funtime RV CG 707.994.6267
Thurston Lake
Food Center SM
Saw Shop Bistro 707.278.0129
Benjamin's Pizza 707.279.1568
Marcie's Brick Grill 707.279.9866
Two Jacks 76
Lower Lake
For detail see DH48
TE-K
To mid-DH34
Cote Creek
Kelsey Creek
MT. HANNAH
TE-H
Loch Lomond
Siegler Springs
Big Canyon Inn B&B 707.928.5631
Edie's Resort 707.928.9804
Loch Lomond Roadhouse 707.928.5512
Rollo's
TE-I
Ployez 707.994.2106
Cobb
BOGGS MTN. STATE FOREST
Rob Roy GC 707.928.5276
To Cloverdale & DH27 Pg. 129
Whispering Pines
Hidden Valley Lake
Boggs Mtn. BCG
Cobb Mtn Café 707.928.1925
DH10 TE-D
DH53
Anderson Creek
TE-G
76
Hidden Valley Lake CG 707.987.3138
Beaver Creek RV/CG 707.928.4322
(II)
Havy's Rest 707.987.8892
Middletown
Inn at Kelsey Creek 707.928.0433
Deli & Coffee House 707.928.6333
Mountain High Coffee House 707.928.0461
Hardesters
Shell
For details see map II
DH48
To mid-DH34
Twin Pine Casino 707.987.0197
Backyard Garden Oasis 707.987.0505
To Cloverdale & DH27 Pg. 129
Jimtown
ALEXANDER VALLEY
DH10 Pg. 137
Chateau
1 Montelena 707.942.5105
2 Bennett Lane 707.942.6684
3 Traulsen 707.942.0283
4 Summers 707.942.5508
5 Graeser 707.942.4437
TE-A
Kellogg
Hillcrest B&B 707.944.0332
Healdsburg
TE-B
NON-FEATURED DH SERVICES NOT SHOWN
TE-C ALT
DH34 TE-D
Calistoga
TE-C
To Rutherford & DH34
DH10 TE-C
Windsor
Mark West Springs

DH53 Calistoga – Kelseyville
Hwy 29 / Hwy 175

Distance:	36.0 mi / 57.9 km	Traffic:	Heavy

At a Glance

TIRES	
Twistiness	26.3/ 30
Pavement	17.3/ 20
Engineering	6.0/ 10
Remoteness	2.6/ 10
Scenery	7.0/ 15
Character	5.8/ 15
Total	**65.0**

Well, CalTrans, you've blown it again. It's painfully obvious that whoever assigns your highway numbers is paying absolutely no attention to *Destination Highways'* TIRES system. Case in point: your numbering of Hwys 29 and 175 makes no sense and needs to be reversed. Consider Hwy 29. The steep, 11.1 mi (17.9 km) of winding passing lanes north of Calistoga through the overhanging forest on Hwy 29 are great. Then, you're faced with five boring miles through the flattening prairie-scape to Middletown. Fine, it happens. But at that point, there's a fork in the highway. So there's a decision to make. And what do you do? You number the straight, mind-numbing road to Lower Lake "29" and give the excellent, twisting climb up through the little towns in the Boggs Mountain State Forest a pathetically low number like "175"! True, the Engineering's not quite as good on Hwy 175 as Hwy 29, but what about the other five TIRES components? The fact is, your nonsensical highway numbering gives no guidance to the best motorcycling routes. Undoubtedly, you'll wish to remedy this situation now that it has been brought to your attention. A copy of *Destination Highways Northern California* is enclosed for your easy reference.

Access

From Calistoga

On Hwy 29

Head north on Hwy 29. You're on the road.

Coming in on TE-A Alexander Valley – Calistoga (Hwy 128)

For an easy short cut to the DH, instead of continuing on into Calistoga, turn left on Tubbs Lane and cut across to Hwy 29. Turn left. You're on the road.

From Kelseyville

Head south on Hwy 29/175. Turn left onto Hwy 175 when it splits south. You're on the road.

Cobb
Whispering Pines
Cobb Mtn Café 707.928.1925
Whispering Pines Tavern & Cocktails
Bruceski's Bar & Grill 707.928.5781
Beaver Creek RV CG 707.928.4322
Hidden Valley Lake
Rob Roy GC 707.928.5276
Hidden Valley Lake GC 707.987.3138
Havy's Rest 707.987.8892
76
Hartman Rd.
Canyon Creek
Big Canyon Rd.
Guenoc Ln.
Anderson Creek
175
29
TE-G
DH10 TE-D
Middletown
LONG VALLEY
DH48
2 km
2 miles
Butts Canyon Rd.
BUTTS CANYON
To Mid-DH34
(I)
CALLAYOMI VALLEY
DH53
Sausal 707.433.2285 1
White Oak 707.433.8429 2
Alexander Valley 707.433.7209 3
Hanna 707.431.7209 4
Field Stone 800.547.7273 5
Eagle & Rose Inn 707.987.7330
Mount St Helena Brewing Co
Boar's Breath 707.987.9491
15500 Central Park 707.987.4270
Dry Creek Rd.
Western Mine Rd.
LAKE SONOMA
LAKE NAPA
Backyard Garden Oasis 707.987.0505
NON-FEATURED DH SERVICES NOT SHOWN
Twin Pine Casino 707.987.0197
Geysers Rd.
Red Winery Rd.
Jimtown
38°40'
ALEXANDER VALLEY
Napa County Fairgrounds CG 707.942.5221
Ida Clayton Rd.
Robert Louis Stevenson SP
Summit (2200 ft 670m)
THE PALISADES
Chateau Montelena 707.942.5105 1
Bennett Lane 707.942.6684 2
Traulsen 707.942.0283 3
Summers 707.942.5508 4
Graeser 707.942.4437 5
TE-A
Kellogg
Spencer Ln.
Hillcrest B&B 707.944.0332
Markwest Lodge Bistro & Bar 707.528.9378
TE-B
Bear Flag Inn B&B 707.942.5534
Calistoga Country Lodge 707.942.5555
Home Plate Café 707.942.5646
Franz Valley Rd.
128
Tubbs Ln.
Bothe-Napa Valley SP CG 707.942.4575
Franz Valley School Rd.
Forest Rd.
DH34 TE-D
Chalk Hill Rd.
TE-C ALT
Calistoga
Napa River
NAPA VALLEY
Mark West Springs
Porter Creek Rd.
Petrified
TE-C
Windsor
To Cloverdale & DH27 Pg. 129
Pleasant Ave.
Mark West Cr.
NAPA SONOMA
Silverado Trail
Deer Park Rd.
DH48 TE-B
38°50'
Faught Rd.
Old Redwood
Mark West Springs Rd.
Foothill Ranch Rd.
Calistoga Rd.
TE-E
St. Helena Rd.
TE-F
Spring Mtn. Rd.
To Rutherford & DH34
Santa Rosa BMW 800 American Wy 707.838.9100
TE-D
Riebli Rd.
Wallace Rd.
Meadowlark B&B 707.942.5651
Arco
St. Helena
Mark West Cr.
River Rd.
101
Hwy.
Fountain Grove Pkwy.
Fulton Rd.
Brush Cr. Rd.
Montecito Blvd.
Mission Blvd.
Calistoga Rd.
Piner Rd.
Los Alivos Ave.
II
1458 Lincoln 707.942.6333
Guerneville Rd.
Santa Rosa
4th St.
Sonoma Hwy.
Santa Rosa Creek
Hall Rd.
To Jenner & DH29 Pg. 103
Spring Lake RP CG 707.539.8092
Parriott Motors (HON) 1027 Pope 707.963.3190
Occidental Rd.
12
DH34 TE-H ALT
Laguna
Kenwood
Morton's Warm Springs
NAPA SONOMA
Sebastopol
265 S Main 707.823.3032
Petaluma Hill Rd.
TAYLOR MTN.
Bennett Valley Rd.
Matanzas Creek
DH34 TE-H
DH34 TE-G
To Tomales & DH37 Pg. 93
116
de Santa Rosa
Stony Point Rd.
Grange Rd.
Sonoma Mtn. Rd.
Warm Springs Rd.
Glen Ellen
Trinity Rd.
Dry Creek Rd.
122°30'
Redwood Dr.
Rohnert Park
Rohnert Park Expy
Petaluma Hill
Pressley Rd.
Cavedale Rd.
Gravenstien Hwy.
Cotati
38°20'
E. Cotati Rd.
Michael's HD 7601 Redwood 707.793.9180
Roberts Rd.
Santa Rosa Vee Twin (VIC) 1240 Petaluma Hill 707.523.9696
Jim & Jim's of Santa Rosa (SUZ/YAM) 910 Santa Rosa 707.545.1672
Moto Mechanica (APR/DUC/MG/TRI) 1111 Petaluma Hill 707.578.6686
Northbay MS (HON/KAW/KTM) 2875 Santa Rosa 707.542.5355
Revolution Moto (APR) 301 D St. 707.523.2371
4795 Old Redwood Hwy 707.578.7975
For detail see DH34
To Napa & DH34
122°50'
To Tamalpais Valley & DH37 Pg. 93
To San Francisco
122°40'
Sonoma

On The Road

The quiet grassy landscape north of Calistoga belies the intensity to come. Brown and green hills beckon. Vineyards span the valley below them. The hills bring the first of the curves at 0.8 mi (1.3 km). If your tires aren't warm, they soon will be.

A climb starts immediately north of the Tubbs Lane junction, the handy connection to Hwy 128 (**TE-A**). The tight, essing, switchbacking hairpins are wide-shouldered, well-paved and offer views over the Pallisades to the right. Shoulders narrow as you ess into a stretch of tangled, leafy forest and dark brown, moss-covered cliffs. With the steep grade and tight curves, you're bound to catch up with some struggling pylons. At least you can get by a few of them on the short, winding passing lane at 2.5 mi (4.0 km).

The pavement could be better on the climb. But the scenery picks up some of the slack. Gaps in the right-side trees provide closer views of the Pallisades' fine features as you stay on a south-facing slope. At 3.8 mi (6.1 km) the trees clear and the terrain opens up enough for a longer passing lane where the left-side cliffs level into a short, grassy plateau. At 4.4 mi (7.1 km), this passing lane ends and the rockfaces return. So does the forest, thicker than ever.

Trees overhang both sides of the road to the point where you're winding through a tunnel of leaves. The deep, steep, hairpin S-curves return at 5.0 mi (8.0 km), as does a another short passing lane. When the road widens, there's another close sighting of the Pallisades' grand, Teton-like cliffs rising ahead out of the forest. The silhouetted pine tree at 7.3 mi (11.7 km) marks the end of the last switchbacking passing lane and the entrance to Robert Louis Stevenson Memorial State Park. The author of Dr. Jekyll and Mr. Hyde spent some time here in 1880. No doubt drawing inspiration for the latter from the local speed tax collectors.

You reach the (2200 ft/ 670 m) summit at 7.6 mi (12.2 km) and begin your descent. As is typically the case on the lee side of a climb, the passing lanes are now on the other side of the double yellow. That's bad enough, but then some barely-in-control pylon comes screaming around the corner in the middle lane just as you're reaching maximum lean. When he nears the apex, all you can do is hope he manages to stay in his lane.

The curves maintain their tight radius on the way down. In fact, they may be even tighter. Blind, 20-mph (30-kmh) hairpins are commonplace and with the steep grade, can challenge your riding skills. Not to mention your nerve.

At 9.4 mi (15.1 km), there's a short piece of passing lane. Ordinarily, good. But in this case, it's not really long enough to accomplish much. Worse, it marks a change in the road. S-curves loosen up. Terrain starts to level out. The cloistering forest, so lush and verdant up near the summit has become ratty.

There is an improvement in the pavement at 10.7 mi (17.2 km) when you cross the Lake County line. But it's just in time for the straight that will take you out of the dry foothills and across the farmland plain of the Collayomi Valley all the way to Middletown. You reach the junction with Hwy 175 (Main St) in the middle of Middletown at 16.2 mi (26.0 km). **Turn left**.

There's not much to Middletown; seems Napafication hasn't reached here yet. Its 45-mph (70-kmh) speed zone ends soon and you head straight toward Cobb Mtn through some farms and vineyards. Gentle curves come at 17.6 mi (28.3 km), followed by a longer, bolder sequence at 20.3 mi (32.7 km). Lots of trees and a creek along the roadside create an almost Constable-like impression. Relax, that's Constable as in the *artist*.

But if you truly want artistry, how about those S-curves that brush up the steady and steepening slope starting at 20.9 mi (33.6 km)? Or the classical composition of pavement and engineering beneath a delineation of solid leaves? Too bad the terrain opens up at 22.0 mi (35.0 km) and flattens to the point where a few structures can grab hold. Still, you do get a good glimpse to the east of the still life of Boggs Mtn State Forest.

Check out that huge block of rock to your left at 22.9 mi (36.8 km). More to the point, check out the much smaller ones tumbling off of it. The roughening landscape produces a tight, flicky little section cutting along a steep, east-facing slope. You scrape your pegs into the woodsy little hamlet of Whispering Pines at 23.5 mi (37.8 km).

Nothing like a tiny mountain lake shimmering in the trees to make you feel like you're getting away from it all. And nothing like a golf course and country club to put an end to that notion. A sort of mallish thing on the left follows and then you're in the 40-mph (60-kmh) town of Cobb. Bottle Rock Rd (**TE-H**) splits off left in the middle of town at 24.6 mi (39.6 km).

With the country club and mall experience behind you, it's actually quite scenic just north of Cobb. Twisting through the pines, both whispering and otherwise, you continue a shallow climb. There's more development at 25.6 mi (41.2 km) as you exit a 20-mph (30-kmh) corner. And you get back into the trees only to come around a corner and find something else entirely. Can you say hidden driveways? Better learn fast.

At 27.0 mi (43.4 km), the road begins to descend. And at 27.8 mi (44.7 km), you enter Loch Lomond, another nothing town. As is often the case, the real issue here is not the development but the traffic it can generate. If you get stuck behind some polyester papa in his Caddy, fresh from the 19th hole, you're not getting by him too easily. There are options, one being Loch Lomond Rd (**TE-I**), turning off right from the center of Loch Lomond at 28.0 mi (45.1 km).

Chances are if you stay on the DH, you'll be glad you took the high road. Despite the lack of remoteness, the pavement's good and the twisties are tight. And I'll still be in Kelseyville afore ye.

The curves ease a bit as you gun it downhill through the woods. And then you encounter the corner at 29.1 mi (46.8 km). The wide turnoff to the right at first looks like it's the way to go. It isn't. The DH is that decreasing radius number veering off to the left. Yeah, that one.

A field appears through the trees to the right at 29.3 mi (47.1 km). And where did that come from? It seems completely out of place on a steep, shady, mountain ride. Not surreal enough? Why not throw in a few Far Side cows.

The road levels through the valley. And with the leveling comes a further loosening up of the curves. The endless non-descript, low buildings are now nestled in redwoods rather than pines. At 31.4 mi (50.5 km), the highway actually straightens, coasting along the right edge of the marshy headwaters of Cote Creek.

The terrain is much flatter and more open. It's drier too – there's much more shrubbery and that sense of thick forest is gone. There are still some good curves to come, but if you want to take a short cut over to Soda Bay Rd (**TE-J**), turn right on Red Hills Rd at 33.1 mi (53.3 km).

*ROUTING OPTION: Red Hills Rd becomes Hwy 281 after crossing Hwy 29. 281 takes you to mid-**TE-J**.*

The landscape gives way to vineyards and orchards as the road starts to steadily curve again toward the green, lunar-pocked surface of Mt. Knocti. You knock about for a bit through a section of rougher-paved corners. Then the asphalt improves at 34.9 mi (56.2 km), providing a sweet finish to an unusual DH that ends at the junction with Hwy 29 at 36.0 mi (57.9 km).

Twisted Edges

TE-A Calistoga – Alexander Valley (Hwy 128) (12.0 mi / 19.3 km)
The uncurving Napa, Knights and Alexander Valleys may have their wineries, but the twisty sections of nouveau pavement stored in the American Oaks that separate the valleys is where you'll taste the really good stuff.

NAVIGATION: The north end of the TE is the junction with Chalk Hill Rd. It's the marked turnoff to Santa Rosa.

TE-B Alexander Valley – Santa Rosa (8.0 mi / 12.9 km) *Chalk Hill Rd*
Don't expect the great curves, pavement and engineering of **TE-A** to continue on the loop down to Santa Rosa. But don't expect much traffic, either as you meander down this county road through mixed forest, vineyards, rolling pastureland and some houses.

NAVIGATION: Southern access to Chalk Hill Rd is off Pleasant Ave, which turns off the Old Redwood Hwy just south of the Windsor exit..

TE-C Petrified Forest Rd - Porter Creek Rd - Mark West Springs Rd (12.3 mi / 19.8 km)

This cruiser's delight between the Sonoma and Napa Valleys can be quite refined in terms of sweepers, pavement and engineering on the suburban

Santa Rosa end and the touristy Calistoga end. Particularly on the latter when it plummets into an ocean of trees with the Pallisades rising behind. The less-trafficked middle of the TE has its more rustic moments when you ride through goat and sheep-filled pasture and drop into the bottom of two short, bumpy, but striking river canyons.

TE-C ALT Franz Valley Rd (7.4 mi / 11.9 km)
In contrast to the main TE, the southern half of Franz Valley Rd is a variably paved, one- to-one-and-a-half-lane trail with no centerline that climbs up and down the side of Chalk Hill, then settles into the trees, fields and vineyards of Franz Valley. What makes it worthwhile, apart from rural ambience, is having some curves to yourself when the route turns into a normal two-lane road east of the one-lane Franz Valley Schoolhouse Rd.

TE-D Wallace Rd - Riebli Rd (3.8 mi / 6.1 km)
If you're looking for something tighter, this reasonably paved combination dips and squiggles through the vineyards, farms and ranches on the edge of Santa Rosa's suburbia.

NAVIGATION: Riding south on Riebli Rd from the Markwest Springs Rd end, turn right on Wallace Rd at the stop sign at 2.5 mi (4.0 km).

From Santa Rosa, 4th Street heads east from downtown and turns into the Sonoma Hwy. Turn left on Los Alivos Ave and then veer right onto Brush Creek Rd. This green byway turns into Wallace Rd at the Santa Rosa city limit. Remember to turn left on Riebli Rd 2.4 mi (3.9 km) from the start of Brush Creek Rd or 1.3 mi (2.1 km) from the Santa Rosa city limit.

TE-E Calistoga Rd (7.1 mi / 11.4 km)
Sometimes good, sometimes rough, sometimes narrow, this decently engineered path from mid-**TE-C** curves on mixed pavement through scrubby oaklands down into Santa Rosa.

*NAVIGATION: Calistoga Rd turns off Montecito Ave. Montecito is an uncomplicated way to connect **TE-D** and **TE-E**.*

TE-F St Helena Rd - Spring Mtn Rd (11.8 mi / 19.0 km)
With its western half in Sonoma County and its eastern in Napa, this remote-feeling TE between St Helena and mid-**TE-E** shows how these two famous wine regions compare where it really counts – pavement. No surprise, Napa wins hands down. Asphaltophiles find the surface in Sonoma inconsistent, ranging from good to patchy to very patchy on the secluded, creekside ascent through thick mountain forest. In Napa, however, the fresh blacktop exhibits a forward, smooth, silky boldness on the steep descent through the mix of forest and vineyards.

NAVIGATION: From St Helena on Hwy 29 (Main St), turn south on Madrona. A few blocks later, turn onto Spring Mtn Rd.

TE-G Middletown – Siegler Springs (12.5 mi / 20.1 km) *Big Canyon Rd*
Big Canyon Rd is old and forgotten. Probably because apart from its

notable lack of traffic, it isn't much of a road. It follows the course of Big Canyon Creek (which isn't much of a creek) down Big Canyon (which isn't much of a canyon). It's not too curvy either, except for the one tight, twisty piece at the canyon's north end. How's the pavement? Let's just say if they could easily have named this road "Rough" instead of "Big."

NAVIGATION: In Middletown, Big Canyon starts out from Hwy 175 just west of the Hwy 29/175 junction as Barn St.

TE-H Cobb – Kelseyville (10.9 mi / 17.5 km) *Bottle Rock Rd*
You can really rocket on Bottle's many fine curves, courtesy of its good pavement and engineering. Especially further north when the development around Cobb finally disappears.

TE-I Loch Lomond – Lower Lake (8.0 mi / 12.9 km) *Loch Lomond Rd - Siegler Canyon Rd*
This quiet, generally well-paved rural router twists pretty much continuously, though some corners are a bit blind. More canyon-like on Siegler Canyon, woodsier on Loch Lomond.

TE-J Kelseyville – Lower Lake (16.5 mi / 26.5 km)
Soda Bay Rd - Pt Lakeview Rd
Might as well go for a ride along Soda Bay. Nobody hurts and nobody cries as you and your open pipes sweep, climb and drop along the Clear Lake shoreline. Except maybe the occupants of the houses that line parts of the mostly well-paved route.

NAVIGATION: From Kelseyville, Merritt Rd curls into Gaddy Lane which in turn T-junctions at Soda Bay Rd.

Riding the TE from the Kelseyville end, it's easy to miss the left turn onto Point Lakeview Rd at 9.7 mi (15.6 km). If you see the Riviera Shopping Center on Hwy 281, you passed the turn.

Riding from the Lower Lake end, you turn right off Hwy 29 onto Soda Bay Rd at 6.8 mi (10.9 km).

TE-K Morgan Valley Rd (16.8 mi / 27.0 km)
"A smooth, winding ridge run through a rolling, oak-filled landscape without a shred of traffic!" declares *American Motorcycle*. "A tour de force of curves, scenery, engineering and remoteness," exclaims *Modern Rider*. "It turns to one-lane crap pavement!" raves Tim Mayhew.

ROUTING OPTION: Yes, it does turn into a goat path at 16.8 mi (27.0 km). And from here, some will opt to brave the 14.3 mi (23.0 km) of lousy asphalt (sometimes dipping into waterways) to enjoy the remote, scenic trip through Eticuera Creek's marshy wetlands north of Lake Berryessa. Early in the year, the creek floods the road and may make the road impassable. Unless you carry a snorkel.

Rider's Log: **Date Ridden:** **Your Rating:** /10

Map Tip: To see the next good motorcycle road, look for the white navigation arrows at the edge of the Local maps.

N. Fork Cache Creek
Indian Valley Res.
CHOCOLATE PEAK
ROCKY RIDGE
S. Fork Wall Creek
Long Valley Creek
ROUND MTN.
BALDY MTN.
Mill Creek
BEAR VALLEY
Bear Valley Rd.
Leesville Rd.
THREE SISTERS
Old Wilbur Rd.
To Williams & I-5
To CVA IV Pg. 499
CORTINA RIDGE
BLUE RIDGE
Bear Creek
COLUSA
LAKE
4700 Golf
707.994.3600
To Lakeport & DH24 Pg. 133
Sweet Hollow Creek
Oasis Café
20
DH46
39°10'
39°00'
38°50'
53
BALD MTN.
BALLY PEAK
Olympic Dr.
Cache Creek
CACHE CREEK WILDLIFE AREA
Clearlake
Shaw's Shady Acres CG
707.994.2236
Funtime RV CG
707.994.6267
Old Hwy 53
Tower Mart
Susie's Grill
707.994.2328
Foster's Freeze
707.995.0685
Lower Lake Coffee Co
707.995.2558
Shell
Rocky Creek
CACHE CRK RIDGE
DH72
16
LAKE
NAPA
To Kelseyville & DH53
29
Lower Lake
BRUSHY SKY HIGH
Seigler Cyn. Rd.
DH53 TE-I
Morgan Valley Rd.
DH53 TE-K
MORGAN VALLEY
GRIZZLY PEAK
Reiff Rd.
LITTLE BLUE RIDGE
Davis Creek
LANGS PEAK
CR 40
To Capay
To I-505
To CVA IV Pg. 499
Spruce Grove Rd.
LITTLE HIGH VALLEY
YOLO
NAPA
Big Canyon Creek
Big Canyon Rd.
Soda Creek
Hartman Rd.
Berryessa-Knoxville Rd.
LAKE
NAPA
COYOTE VALLEY
DH53 TE-G
Dry Creek
To Kelseyville
175
LONG VALLEY
Middletown
DH53
DH48
Butts Canyon Rd.
Dry Crk Rd.
To Calistoga
122°30'
To Mid-DH34
To mid-DH34
N
2 km
2 miles
122°20'

DH46 Clearlake – Hwy 16/Hwy 20 Jct

Highway 20

Distance:	18.4 mi / 29.6 km	Traffic:	Heavy

At a Glance

TIRES

Twistiness	21.7/30
Pavement	16.6/20
Engineering	9.6/10
Remoteness	6.0/10
Scenery	10.4/15
Character	2.9/15

Total 67.2

The Iron Pigs are an obviously good-humored group of law enforcement officers from Kelseyville who like to get together and ride off duty. And why not, when there are options like this around? A short but excellently paved and engineered route through rolling hills that starts east of Clear Lake and ends at the approaches to the Central Valley, this is a wide-open sweepathon with lots of passing lanes. It's just the kind of road that might invite disdain for the double-nickel limit in spite of the large speed-enforced-by-aircraft sign. Problem is, it's also a fairly major highway with lots of traffic so, by definition, it's a perfect spot for a little serving and collecting. And because not every local officer is a motorcyclist, you can't count on getting a free ride. So, if you do get stopped here for a chat about throttle overindulgence, hope that it's by a fellow enthusiast with some understanding of your "safety fast" motto. Just put on a big smile and ask him good naturedly: "Hey bro, you a Pig?"

Access

From Clearlake

Via Hwy 53

Go north on Hwy 53 to its junction with Hwy 20. Turn east on Hwy 20. You're on the road.

From Hwy 16/Hwy 20 Jct

Coming in on DH72 Capay – Hwy 16/Hwy 20 Jct

Turn left on Hwy 20. You're on the road.

On The Road

Whether you're coming from Clearlake or Clear Lake, the first miles of this short DH aren't too eventful. You descend from the start, negotiating a short series of sweepers while overlooking the oak- and pine-filled Cache Creek Valley. You reach the valley bottom at 2.5 mi (4.0 km) and, at 3.2 mi (5.2 km), pick up Sweet Hollow Creek to the left. A chopped off hillside traces the creek. At 3.7 mi (6.0 km), there's a tree sticking up out of a little island in the water looking like a flagstick on an elevated green. Just roll on the throttle and yell "Fore!"

The creek soon disappears, crossing inconspicuously under the road and vanishing south into the Cache Creek Wildlife Area. Curves seem to have disappeared, too, on the DH's straightest, flattest section that bisects a wooded wildlife area left and a grassy plain right. At 6.5 mi (10.5 km), however, the left side plain hills up and the road starts bending to accommodate the rougher terrain. And when wide, smooth pavement like this starts bending, you start leaning. So much so, you may miss the mini-mountain with the deeply carved flanks off to the left at 8.0 mi (12.9 km).

Your deep carving opportunities would normally be curtailed when a road widens like this one does at 8.3 mi (13.4 km) to provide an east-bound passing lane. Not so this time. Three lanes of modestly climbing pavement sweep smoothly and, depending on your velocity, tightly through a shallow, but picturesque canyon.

It's amazing how many pylons like to hang out in the passing lane, twiddling their air-conditioning controls, DVD players and who knows what else. Still, the fact is traffic's a lot easier to get by when you have the extra lane to work with. Thanks CalTrans, keep up the good work. Of course, when you're stuck behind a Volkswagen van going 47 mph (76 kmh) while "passing" a semi, a second passing lane just for bikes would be nice.

TOUR NOTE: Watch out or you might miss the black and white hiding in the shade tree on the right around the shallow corner at 11.0 mi (18.0 km). Unfortunately, he won't miss you. Don't forget to ask if he's a heavy metal serofa domesticus.

The good work by CalTrans comes to an end at 12.2 mi (19.6 km) when the third lane shifts to the other side of the double yellow on a descent off a minor summit. So if you're stuck behind a pylon, you won't be able to get by it and enjoy the big, sinuous curves on the way down. But at 13.7 mi (22.0 km), CalTrans comes through with another passing lane, however it's brief. After only a few broad, shallow corners, you're again back to a single lane at 14.9 mi (24.0 km).

More long, respectably tight, sweeping corners follow as the left side of the road drops away and a deep ravine opens up. The big, long sweeper at 15.8 mi (25.4 km) is one of the road's best and it's followed by another big one at 16.8 mi (27.0 km). But that's about it for curves as the scene opens up into a broad, grassy valley backed by the dark green undulations of Cortina Ridge. You coast down to the junction with **DH72 Capay – Hwy 16/Hwy 20 Jct,** arriving at 18.4 mi (29.6 km).

RIDER'S LOG: **DATE RIDDEN:** **YOUR RATING:** /10

Don't forget to print the DH Rider Discount list of service providers from destinationhighways.com *and take it with you. Then, just show 'em your book and ask for the discount.*

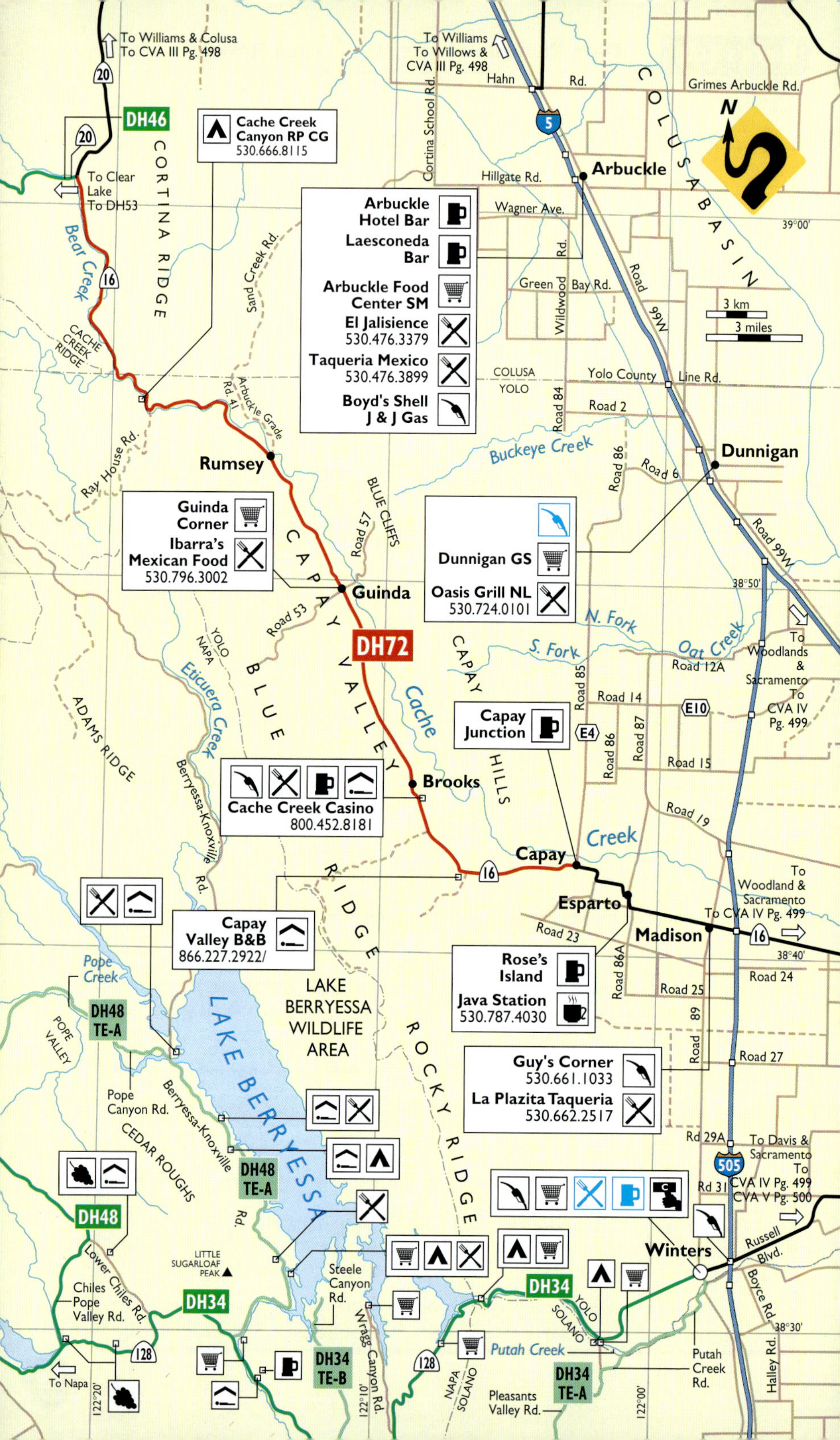

To Williams & Colusa
To CVA III Pg. 498
To Williams
To Willows &
CVA III Pg. 498
DH46
Cache Creek
Canyon RP CG
530.666.8115
CORTINA RIDGE
To Clear
Lake
To DH53
Bear Creek
CACHE CREEK RIDGE
Sand Creek Rd.
Cortina School Rd.
Hahn Rd.
Grimes Arbuckle Rd.
COLUSA BASIN
Arbuckle
Hillgate Rd.
Wagner Ave.
Arbuckle
Hotel Bar
Laesconeda
Bar
Arbuckle Food
Center SM
El Jalisience
530.476.3379
Taqueria Mexico
530.476.3899
Boyd's Shell
J & J Gas
Green Bay Rd.
Wildwood Rd.
Road 99W
39°00'
3 km
3 miles
COLUSA
YOLO
Yolo County Line Rd.
Road 84
Road 2
Arbuckle Grade
Rd. 41
Ray House Rd.
Rumsey
Buckeye Creek
Road 86
Road 6
Dunnigan
Dunnigan GS
Oasis Grill NL
530.724.0101
Road 99W
38°50'
Guinda
Corner
Ibarra's
Mexican Food
530.796.3002
CAPAY VALLEY
BLUE CLIFFS
Road 57
Guinda
Road 53
DH72
N. Fork
S. Fork
Oat Creek
To
Woodlands
&
Sacramento
To
CVA IV
Pg. 499
Road 12A
YOLO
NAPA
Eticuera Creek
BLUE
Cache
CAPAY
Road 85
Road 14
E10
ADAMS RIDGE
Capay
Junction
E4
Road 86
Road 87
HILLS
Road 15
Berryessa-Knoxville Rd.
Cache Creek Casino
800.452.8181
Brooks
Road 19
Creek
Capay
RIDGE
Esparto
To
Woodland &
Sacramento
To CVA IV Pg. 499
Capay
Valley B&B
866.227.2922/
Road 23
Madison
38°40'
Pope
Creek
LAKE
BERRYESSA
WILDLIFE
AREA
Rose's
Island
Java Station
530.787.4030
Road 86A
Road 24
Road 25
Road 89
DH48
TE-A
POPE VALLEY
LAKE BERRYESSA
ROCKY RIDGE
Road 27
Guy's Corner
530.661.1033
La Plazita Taqueria
530.662.2517
Pope
Canyon Rd.
CEDAR ROUGHS
Berryessa-Knoxville Rd.
DH48
TE-A
Rd 29A
To Davis &
Sacramento
505
To
CVA IV Pg. 499
CVA V Pg. 500
Rd 31
DH48
LITTLE
SUGARLOAF
PEAK
Lower Chiles Rd.
Chiles
Pope
Valley Rd.
DH34
Steele
Canyon
Rd.
Wragg Canyon Rd.
DH34
TE-B
DH34
YOLO
SOLANO
Winters
Russell
Blvd.
Boyce Rd.
38°30'
Putah Creek
Putah
Creek
Rd.
To Napa
122°20'
122°10'
NAPA
SOLANO
DH34
TE-A
Pleasants
Valley Rd.
122°00'
Halley Rd.

DH72 CAPAY – HWY 16/HWY 20 JCT

Highway 16

DISTANCE:	32.8 mi / 52.8 km	TRAFFIC:	Moderate

AT A GLANCE

Feel like doing a little gambling? Because unless you go all in and up your speed above the allowable 55 mph (90 kmh) house limit, the riding stakes on this DH might be too penny ante. Except if you're coming from the curve-washed-out Central Valley, in which case, the subtle bends in the shallow Capay Valley might make you feel like you just hit the jackpot. Going fast on a two-digit state highway can, of course, be risky to your bankroll. Especially when those black and whites flash snake eyes at you. You could play your cards close to your chest and just pass for the first two thirds of this route through farmland, then bet most of your chips on the sweepy Cache Creek Canyon section that makes up the northern third of the road. Or if this last 10 mi (16 km) of Twistiness doesn't give you enough action, you can always shoot some craps at the Indian casino south of Brooks. After all, baby can always use a new pair of tires

TIRES	
Twistiness	14.3/ 30
Pavement	14.0/ 20
Engineering	6.8/ 10
Remoteness	4.7/ 10
Scenery	10.1/ 15
Character	5.3/ 15
TOTAL	**55.2**

ACCESS

From Capay

On Hwy 16

Just stay on Hwy 16 west. Exit Capay and you're on the road.

From I-505

Take the Hwy 16 exit west through Madison, Esparto and Capay. Once out of the latter, you're on the road.

From Hwy 16/Hwy 20 Jct

Coming in on DH46 Clearlake – Hwy 16/Hwy 20 Jct (Hwy 20)

Turn south on Hwy 16 and you're on the road.

From I-5

Take the Hwy 20 exit (one north of the exit for Williams) west. When you get to the junction of Hwy 20 and Hwy 16, turn south. You're on the road.

DH34 DH48 DH53 DH46 DH72

On The Road

Madison, Esparto & Capay sounds like a law firm. And perhaps that's no coincidence. Because if you're not careful, you might need an attorney, as the smooth Hwy 16 west of Capay stretches out in a most alluring manner. There's not too much in the way of twisties to moderate your velocity. And with lots of dotted yellow, any traffic is easy to get by. But remember: contrary to urban legend, there's really no such plea as "guilty with an explanation."

Vineyards backed by the Capay Hills ripen on your right while the tree-covered lower part of the Blue Ridge/Rocky Ridge promontory takes up station to your left. A big, banked sweeper re-orients the road more to the north at 3.6 mi (5.8 km). Trees, some of them in orchards, move in on both sides of the road. But it's not long before the only trees left are the two solitary rows of sentinels some good citizen planted on both shoulders.

The sprawling complex of the Cache Creek Casino disfigures a large chunk of roadside at 5.6 mi (9.0 km). A couple of shallow curves deliver you to Brooks, where the elevation of 300 ft (92 m) is roughly triple the population. Even that estimate of the locals seems generous, given that the town's most notable feature is a bright-white, out-of-business gas station.

Ho-hum. A few orchards, a couple of buildings and very few curves. Still, the pavement's excellent as you sweep past the – gulp – county sheriff parked on the right side of the road. Either you are going slower than you thought, he's not a keen speed tax collector or he's a motorcyclist. Or maybe he's just there to alert you to the 35 mph (55 kmh) speed limit that marks the town of Guinda at 13.0 mi (20.9 km).

You're quickly back up to 55 mph (90 kmh). Just in time for a few curves plus a lovely single ess combination at 15.4 mi (24.8 km). Then it's pretty much straight to the clump of buildings that make up Rumsey at 18.1 mi (29.1 km). But there's reason to feel encouraged – you're rapidly running out of valley.

Hello. Would this be a side slope to your left at 19.5 mi (31.4 km)? You kind of forgot what those look like. Trees draw in to your right and the road starts to curve and climb. A mile later, a big left hook pulls you into the Cache Creek Canyon. The creek's on the right, leaving just enough room in here for the road to squeak through.

Despite the tight fit, the towering landscape remains more impressive than the curves. The latter improve when you cross the creek at 21.4 mi (34.4 km) and move over to climb the other side of the canyon. Even then, they consist mostly of relaxed but enjoyable sweepers. A brief widening in the canyon occurs at the Cache Creek Canyon Regional Park.

Cortina Ridge to the east and Cache Creek Ridge to the west pinch in at 24.2 mi (38.9 kmh), adding more curves to terrain that's becoming progressively drier. The steep incline on your right is unstable and has been known to spit some fairly large rocks onto the road. Good time to get out of Yolo and into Colusa County.

The sweepers carry on over the boundary. As you continue to climb, they increase in frequency and tighten up. Bear Creek crosses under the road at 28.4 mi (45.7 km), staying on your right until it flips back a mile later. You'll hardly notice because you're in the middle of the best piece of the DH, arcing easily on good pavement around continuous, relaxed and banked corners.

As is often the case, the best part seems all too short. By 31.0 mi (49.9 km), the terrain has mellowed and the curves have followed suit, disappearing as the valley widens. You arrive at the east end of **DH46 Hwy 16/ Hwy 20 Jct – Clearlake** and the end of this DH at 32.8 mi (52.8 km).

RIDER'S LOG: **DATE RIDDEN:** **YOUR RATING: /10**

What are the Top Ten Rides based on Twistiness, Pavement, Engineering, Remoteness, Scenery and Character? You'll find the answers in the TIRES Charts at the back of the book. The complete list of DHs by TIRES components is at **destinationhighways.com.**

REDWOODS Pg. 143
RUSSIAN COAST
CVA III
CVA IV
WINE COUNTRY Pg. 59
BAY AREA-SANTA CRUZ MTNS Pg. 11
PACIFIC OCEAN
SAN FRANCISCO
Leggett
Covelo
Laytonville
Longvale Junction
Cleone
Fort Bragg
Willits
Mendocino
Albion
Navarro
Elk
Ukiah
Clear Lake
Lakeport
Boonville
Manchester
Old Hopland
Kelseyville
Clearlake
Lower Lake
Point Arena
Gualala
Cloverdale
Middleton
Stewarts Point
Healdsburg
Calistoga
Windsor
Guerneville
Forestville
Jenner
Sebastopol
Santa Rosa
St. Helena
Rutherford
Bodega Bay
Cotati
Sonoma
Napa
Tomales
Petaluma
Novato
Vallejo
Point Reyes Station
San Rafael
Corte Madera
Mill Bay
Tamalpais Valley
DH5
DH15
DH32
DH22
DH24
DH27
DH29
DH10
DH37
DH46
DH72
DH53
DH48
DH34
101
162
20
253
128
29
1
175
53
12
116
121
37
580
A9
(D-HON/KAW)
(D-KTM)
(D-SUZ/YAM)
(D-BUE/HD)
(D-HON/YAM)
(D-BMW)
(D-HD)
(D-HON)
(D-HON/SUZ)
(D-KAW/YAM)
(D-BUE/HD)
(D-HON/KTM/YAM)
(D-KAW/SUZ)
(D-VIC)
(D-SUZ/YAM)
(D-APR/DUC/MG/TRI
(D-HON/KAW/KTM)
(D-APR)
(D-BUE/HD)
(D-DUC/TRI YAM)
(D-BMW)
(D-BUE/HD)
(D-HON/KAW/SUZ)
(D-APR/BIM/KTM/VIC)
(D-AUG/DUC/MG/DRI)
(D-BMW)
(D-BUE/HD)
(D-HON/KAW/SUZ/YAM
(S-JPN)
N
10 km
10 miles

Russian Coast

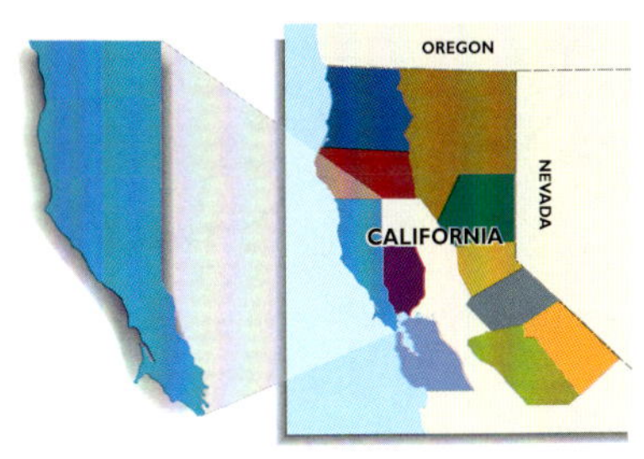

Valley Ford
Tony's Seafood Rest 415.663.1107
Marshall Store
To Santa Rosa
For detail, see DH34, Pg 61
Sonoma
To Napa & DH34 Pg. 61
Petaluma
Tomales
Dillon Beach
Tomales Bay B&B 415.663.9002
Marshall
POINT REYES NATIONAL SEASHORE
Port Reyes NS Visitors Center 415.464.5100
Inverness Store
Inverness
Point Reyes Station
Holly Tree B&B 415.663.1554
Novato
San Pablo Bay
Olema
Drakes Bay
Pt Reyes Vineyard Inn B&B 415.663.1011
Pt Reyes Country Inn B&B 415.663.9696
San Rafael
San Anselmo
Dogtown
Bolinas
Stinson Beach
Corte Madera
Mill Valley
Tamalpais Valley
Tiburon
Sausalito
Gulf of Farallones
San Francisco Bay
Golden Gate Bridge
Old Western Saloon
Palace Mkt SM
Green Bridge Gas & Auto
Olema Inn 415.663.9559
Point Reyes Seashore Lodge 415.663.9000
English Oak B&B 415.663.1500
Farm House 415.663.1264
Redwood Oil
Olema Ranch RV CG 415.663.8001
SAN FRANCISCO
(D-APR/BIM/KTM/VIC) (D-AUG/DUC/MG/DRI) (D-BMW) (D-BUE/HD) (D-HON/KAW/SUZ/YAM)
Daly City
D-HON/KAW/YAM
225 Rockaway Beach Ave 650.355.4122
Pacifica
PACIFIC OCEAN
DH55 TE-C
Montara
Moss Beach
El Granada
To DH55 Pg. 13
DH37
4 km
4 miles

DH37 Tamalpais Valley (San Francisco) – Tomales

Shoreline Highway (Hwy 1)

Distance:	43.2 mi / 69.5 km	Traffic:	Moderate

At a Glance

Riding Northern California just wouldn't be complete without a trip along the San Andreas Fault, America's most notorious earthquake zone. Leaving Tamalpais Valley, foreshocks of esses reverberate through the grassy hills and side-slip the treed gorges of the Golden Gate Rec Area. Pavement is tightly engineered and rock solid, except for the shaky bit north of Muir Valley, where some of it is so bumpy you could be forgiven for thinking it's 1906 all over again. Ironically, the section between Dogtown and Olema, where the DH directly tracks the fault line, shows minimal side-to-side asphalt movement – at least for now. But the dramatic scenic subduction points over Stinson Beach and beside the broad waterscapes of Tomales Bay more than make up for it. Funnily enough, the biggest peril on this DH isn't the pending quake. It's getting distracted by all the bikes displaced outside the saloons in the epicenter of Point Reyes Station. Because if you do, you'll miss the event that'll move you the most – the smooth, remote, essing tilt right along the water south of Tomales that's so hot, it's right off the TIRES scale. Might want to hurry up and ride here, though. Before the big one hits.

TIRES	
Twistiness	27.5/ 30
Pavement	15.1/ 20
Engineering	5.4/ 10
Remoteness	4.2/ 10
Scenery	9.6/ 15
Character	8.9/ 15
Total	**70.7**

Access

From San Francisco

Via Hwy 101

The exit for Hwy 1 is a few exits north of the Golden Gate. Follow Hwy 1 through Tamalpais Valley. Once you're out of town, you're on the road.

From Tomales

On Hwy 1

Go south on Hwy 1. You're on the road.

On The Road

"Larry Nager, Live to Ride" says the Adopt a Highway sign marking the southern end of this DH at the edge of the town of Tamalpais Valley. Better yet, it's followed by more signs that say "End 35-mph Limit" and "Twisties for the Next 10 Miles".

KOA CG
707.763.1492
G&B Kawasaki
(KAW/YAM)
326 Petaluma
707.763.4658
SONOMA
Ely Blvd.
McDowell
Blvd.
Bodega Ave.
Petaluma Blvd. N.
Petaluma
Western Ave.
Spring Hill Rd.
Petaluma River
116
210 Lakeville
707.769.0429
N
2 km
2 miles
SONOMA
MARIN
Chileno Valley Rd.
San Antonio
San Antonio Rd.
Creek
II
121
Wilson Hill Rd.
TE-G
Cycle West
(HON/SUZ)
1375 Industrial
707.769.5240
101
MTNS.
38°10'
Marshall
HAMMOCK HILL
Petaluma Rd.
Hicks Rd.
TE-F
Petaluma - Point Reyes Rd.
San Marin Dr.
807 DeLong
415.897.1164
Indian Valley GC
415.892.5885
Golden Gate
(BUE/HD)
7077 Redwood
415.878.4988
TE-I
HICKS MTN.
Novato Blvd.
Atherton Ave.
Novato
Stafford Lake
Rancho Nicasio
415.662.2219
SLC
San Anselmo
San Rafael
Kentfield
Larkspur
Corte Madera
Mill Valley
Tamalpais Valley
Sausalito
37
Two Bird Café & Lodging
415.488.0105
Samuel P. Taylor SP CG
Paper Mill Creek Saloon
Nicasio
TE-J
Nicasio Res.
Nicasio
China Camp SP CG
415.456.0766
Hattar MS
(DUC/TRI/YAM)
601 E Francisco
415.456.3345
Woodacre Mkt & Deli
Valley Rd.
Lucas Valley Rd.
Miller Creek
Marin BMW
(BMW)
30 Castro
415.454.2041
San Pablo Bay
TE-K
LOMA ALTA
San Geronimo
Lagunitas
Woodacre
N. San Pedro Rd.
TE-L
Mt Tamalpais Visitor's Center
38°00'
Francis Drake
Kent Lake
San Geronimo GC
415.488.5030
BOLINAS RIDGE
Shoreline Hwy.
1
SAN ANDREAS FAULT ZONE
San Rafael
Point San Pedro Rd.
San Anselmo
Yellow Door Café
415.488.0311
Lagunitas Grocery
Bon Temple Lake
Blvd.
Golden Gate
(BUE/HD)
13 San Clemente
415.927.4464
Marin Cycle Works
(HON/KAW/SUZ)
5776 Paradise
415.924.0327
POINT REYES NATIONAL SEASHORE
Fairfax-Bolinas Rd.
College Ave.
Magnolia Ave.
Kentfield
Dogtown
Pan Toll SP CG
Larkspur
Doherty Dr.
580
Mountain House Inn
415.381.9000
DH37
TE-D
Ridgecrest Rd.
MT. TAMALPAIS
Corte Madera
Tamalpais Dr.
Bolinas
TE-B
Sequoia Valley Rd.
E. Blithedale Ave.
Quality MC
(S-JPN)
235 Shoreline Hwy
415.381.5059
Panoramic Hwy.
Paradise Dr.
Stinson Beach
GOLDEN GATE NRA
Mill Valley
131
Gulf of Farallones
Muir Woods Rd.
Camino Alto Dr.
Tiburon Blvd.
TE-M
Tiburon
Miller Ave.
Tamalpais Valley
Beach Rd.
Smiley's
415.868.1311
MARIN PENINSULA
101
Sausalito
Steep Ravine BCG
415.388.2070
TE-C
Ft. Baker Rd.
Coast Café
415.868.2298
Bolinas SM
415.868.1441
Bunker Hill Rd.
TE-A ALT
San Francisco Bay
RODEO BEACH
Bunker Rd.
37°50'
Pelican Inn
415.383.6000
Tiburon Lodge
415.435.3133
Guaymas
415.435.6300
The Caprice
415.435.3400
Beckers Groceries SM
TE-A
Conzelman Rd.
Golden Gate Bridge
122°40'
122°30'

And so there are. Tight, blind, switchbacking curves contort up the steep slope through the sweet-smelling eucalyptus trees. But when the pavement is this good, blind and steep is okay. Your only concern on this essing climb is the threat of getting stuck behind a pylon. With virtually no chance of passing, one is all it takes. Hopefully, he'll choose the route you don't when you reach the turnoff right at 1.3 mi (2.1 km) for Panoramic Hwy (**TE-B**). To remain on the DH, **stay left**.

The grassy hills of the Golden Gate Recreational Area create some sense of openness as you drop down from the **TE-B** junction. The round hills to the right narrow to sharp, crumbling rockfaces as the road descends steeply into a green gulch. It's nice that CalTrans has had the foresight to carve out some pullouts. They give the pylons crawling along, distracted by the view of the road snaking down toward the ocean, somewhere to get out of the way. Especially when two-wheelers with bright headlights are on their bumpers.

At 3.7 mi (6.0 km), you reach bottom and arrive at a small settlement with signs pointing off left to Muir Beach. Just past the Pelican Inn, Muir Woods Rd (**TE-C**) junctions from the north. The DH continues, winding through some trees and emerging at the foot of the Muir Valley. Then it bumps upward along the ridge west of the valley on some of the DH's worst pavement. You reach the Muir Beach Overlook at 5.0 mi (8.0 km). To the left, you look over the ocean, to the right, **TE-C**. Looks pretty good from here. Might have to check **C** out after all.

At 5.7 mi (9.2 km), the road descends and you're now part of a gorgeous scene, riding a barren sage, rock and grass bluff down toward the ocean. It's remote. It's spectacular. It twists and turns. But what's with the crappy pavement?

You get your first view of the breakers creaming in on Stinson Beach at 9.3 mi (15.0 km) and, with it, your first sight of decent pavement in a while. You enter the busy beach town itself at 10.1 mi (16.3 km), leaving it – and most of the traffic – behind at 10.7 mi (17.2 km).

It's not nearly as corkscrewy north of Stinson Beach as it was coming in from the south. But the longer corners that sweep and ess right along the edge of Bolinas Lagoon are still plenty tight. And frankly, with the better pavement, they're a lot easier to appreciate.

TOUR NOTE: At 14.7 mi (23.7 km), there's the turnoff to the small, eclectic coastal village of Bolinas, site of the 150-year old Smiley's Bar. The turnoff may be unmarked, since locals tear down the sign every time it goes up. If that's the case, look for the road heading west toward the coast across from the Bolinas-Fairfax Rd (which comes in from the east).

Enormous eucalyptus trees tower above the road as it curves inland and traces the infamous San Andreas Fault. Bolinas Ridge rises to the west and the leaky, inland marsh of the Pt Reyes National Seashore squishes in on the left. The mapdot of Dogtown comes and goes at 16.0 mi (25.7 km), beyond which short, forested sections of moderate to sharp corners alternate with

38°40'
N
2 km
2 miles
To Cloverdale & DH27
To Mid-DH29
W. Dry Ck. Rd.
Dry Creek Rd.
Jimtown
Alexander Vly. Rd.
128
38°40'
101
Soda Rock Ln.
To Calistoga & DH53 Pg. 73
DH10
Dry Creek
Lambert Bridge Rd.
DH10 TE-B
LAGUNA WILDLIFE AREA
Healdsburg
217 Healdsburg 707.433.6935
Mill St.
Dry Creek Rd.
Dry Creek
III
DH10 TE-A
Westside Rd.
Santa Rosa BMW 800 American 707.838.9100
To mid-DH29
Fort Ross Rd.
Cazadero
Cazadero Hwy.
Austin
Armstrong Woods Rd.
Sweetwater Springs Rd.
Arata Rd.
Windsor
To Santa Rosa
Conde Ln.
Shiloh Rd.
Eastside Rd.
RUSSIAN RIVER VALLEY
Guerneville
GABES ROCK
38°30'
Hacienda
Creek
RUSSIAN RIVER
Odd Fellows Rd.
116
River Rd.
Mark West Creek
38°30'
To Santa Rosa
To DH34 Pg. 61
To DH53 Pg. 73
DH29 TE-C
Guerneville Rd.
Forestville
Hwy.
Vine Hill Rd.
Laguna Rd.
To Mendocino
Monte Rio
DH29 TE-A
Jenner
Duncans Mills
GREEN VALLEY
Green Valley Rd.
116
DH29
DH29 TE-B
Bohemian Hwy.
Rd.
Graton
Graton
1
Occidental
DH29 TE-B ALT
Laguna de Santa Rosa
12
To Santa Rosa
To DH34 Pg. 61
To DH53 Pg. 73
Coleman Valley Rd.
Occidental Rd.
Sebastopol
116
Freestone
IRISH HILL
265 S Main 707.823.3032
Salmon Creek
Bodega Hwy.
Valley Ford-Freestone Rd.
To San Francisco
Bodega Bay
38°20'
Valley Ford
Bodega Dunes CG 707.875.3483
Bodega Harbor
Valley Ford Estero Rd.
Petaluma - Valley Ford Rd.
Marsh Rd.
Franklin School Rd.
TE-H
(I)
122°50'
Westside RP CG
Doran RP CG
Sonoma Coast Villa Inn & Spa 888.404.2255
Fallon - Two Rock Rd.
Middle Rd.
1
Valley Ford Hotel 707.876.3600
Valley Ford Mkt SM
Dinucci's 707.876.3260
Route 1 Diner 707.876.9600
Bodega Bay Lodge & Spa 800.368.2468
Bodega Harbor GC 707.875.3538
Diekmann's SM
Texaco
Dillon Beach
Valley Ford Rd.
Tomales
Dillon Beach Rd.
SONOMA
MARIN
Dillon Beach Resort 707.878.2094
1
Continental Inn 707.878.2396
William Tell House 707.878.2403
DH37
Lawson's Landing CG 707.878.2443
PACIFIC OCEAN
123°00'

long, straighter sections along a rolling, grassy slope. Which of course, can crack open at any time swallowing you, your Goldwing and your trailer. If it happens, the best you can hope for is that it takes some pylons with you.

Who let the dogs out? You arrive in Olema at 23.9 mi (38.5 km) where you're joined by the stream of pylons bouncing along the busy and bumpy artery of Sir Francis Drake Blvd. Fortunately, most of them are headed out to explore Pt Reyes Beach.

*TOUR NOTE: If you're into a taste of la playa as well, the better option is to turn left out of Olema onto Bear Valley Rd and access Limantour Rd (**TE-E**) down to the quieter Limantour Beach.*

Only a handful of easy curves and golden, grassy hills separate Olema from the next town. In fact, no sooner are you out of Olema's speed zone than you're into another. You cross the old bridge and enter Pt Reyes Station, a popular stop for riders, at 26.1 mi (42.0 km).

Just north of Reyes, you climb briefly onto a flat plain, then wind tightly and steeply downward on a primo section of excellent, well-engineered pavement toward the coastline of Tomales Bay. The water comes into view at 28.1 mi (45.2 km) and you settle in alongside it at 30.4 mi (48.9 km), still smoothly carving turns. You wonder how many of those riders for beer you saw in Pt Reyes come up from the south, stop there and turn around. You won't make the same mistake.

The esses end when the road moves off the water at 31.2 mi (50.2 km) and beelines for a short bit across lightly treed grassland before turning back toward the bay. It shifts, bends, curves and occasionally sweeps en route to Marshall, where small, faded, ramshackle buildings spread out beside the water at 34.5 mi (55.5 km).

TOUR NOTE: If you want to get out into Tomales Bay and admire this DH from a different perspective, you can rent a kayak from Blue Waters Kayaking, beside the Marshall Store.... Okay, okay, it was just an idea.

For a place with a population of 50, Marshall's speed zone lasts waaay too long. It's irritating to have it contain the two good corners past the junction for the Marshall-Petaluma Rd (**TE-G**) at 36.5 mi (58.7 km). It remains as you go up and a little inland on a short, moderately curving rise above the water. And it's still there when you wind into yet another collection of buildings by the sea at 39.5 mi (63.6 km).

You're climbing off the water again through a stretch of eucalyptus at 39.7 mi (63.9 km), negotiating a couple of solid uphill turns. You finally see a 55-mph (90-kmh) speed sign beside Hamlet Acres at 40.0 mi (64.4 km). To observe it or not to observe it, that is the question.

The curtain opens on the DH's final act. And what an ending it is. Up on a low grass bench above the ocean, perfectly paved esses wind tightly through rough, green, rounded hills. Before you realize it, the road turns eastward along an arm of Tomales Bay at 41.6 mi (66.9 km). Suddenly, the scene transforms. One moment you were above the bay and the next, you're in this wide, windswept marshy delta with low, marine flora with no real idea of how you got there. But with the steady stream of exquisitely paved and marvelously engineered S-turns, you're undoubtedly loving this play.

At least that's how you feel until the lights come up. The storyline ends as suddenly as it began when the road leaves the water, shifts north and straightens. You blink and you're in the small, old town of Tomales, at 43.2 mi (69.5 km).

Twisted Edges

TE-A Conzelman Rd - McCullough Rd - Bunker Rd (4.2 mi / 6.8 km)
An instant nature experience, this TE through the Marin Headlands turns off Hwy 101 just north of the Golden Gate, tears up the green slopes with a series of sweepers on above-average pavement then winds out to the surf-dom of Rodeo Beach.

NAVIGATION: Conzelman shoots off the on-ramp of the first exit north of the Golden Gate Bridge. So if you are coming across the bridge, leave 101 at this exit and make as if you're heading back to San Francisco to access it. Conzelman will become McCullough. When you reach Bunker, turn left to go out to the beach.

TE-A ALT Bunker Hill Rd - Sausalito Lateral Rd - Ft Baker Rd
(2.0 mi / 3.2 km)
If you want to add an interesting tag to the main TE, try looping back along Bunker Hill Rd. Going east from the McCullough/Bunker Rd junction (see *NAVIGATION* above), you'll pass over the Fort Cronkhite speed bumps and enter a long, one-lane tunnel that routes deep under the 101. You'll then wind down through the gorgeous grounds of Fort Baker and end up in chichi Sausalito.

TE-B Panoramic Hwy (8.6 mi / 13.8 km)
Spectacular views, pavement that varies from great to so-so and tight S-curves are all featured on this fetching, ridge-running alternative to part of the DH. There's a residential area smothering the TE's south end but forest replaces the houses once you enter Mt Tamalpais State Park.

TE-C Muir Woods Rd (3.9 mi / 6.3 km)
Quiet roads can be hard to find in this area and Muir Woods Rd is pleasant enough as it winds through – what else? – Muir Woods before ascending sharply and tightly along a rising cliff up to the junction with **TE-B**.

TE-D Ridgecrest Rd (5.4 mi / 8.7 km)
Escape the madding crowds (if not the maddening cyclists) by checking out Ridgecrest Rd. Acceptably paved, more than acceptably curvy and incredibly scenic, this great trip over the Californian moors effectively dead ends at the junction of the Bolinas-Fairfax Rd.

ROUTING OPTION: Turning left at the north end of the TE puts you on a narrow, bumpy one-lane goat path out to the coast. Turning right puts you on a narrow, bumpy two-lane goat path to Fairfax. The latter is so steep you'll want to gear down from first to negotiate the downhill hairpins.

TOUR NOTE: For some unbelievable Bay Area views, take the 3.0 mi (4.8 km) side trip up Mt. Tamalpais from Ridgecrest Rd. Although the road is paved well enough, it's narrow and not that well engineered.

TE-E Limantour Rd (7.6 mi / 12.2 km)
A sweepy, surprisingly well-paved dead-ender out to a lonely piece of the Point Reyes National Seashore. This road is particularly inviting not only because of the great sweepers, but because the road comes out of the redwood forest, rises up and overlooks the coast before descending to the beachside parking lot.

NAVIGATION: From Hwy 1 just north of Olema and the Sir Francis Drake Blvd intersection, head west down Bear Valley Rd and turn left onto Limantour. If you reach the stop sign (at Sir Francis Drake again, it seems) you've gone too far and need to backtrack half a mile or so.

TE-F Petaluma – Point Reyes (18.7 mi / 30.1 km) *Petaluma-Point Reyes Rd*
The road from Petaluma ain't so young and lovely at times. In fact it's a bit old and rough in spots. Still, this generally smooth road unfolds beautifully riding west, mixing long sweepy sections, a few straights and a short, tightly curved segment in the hills just out of Flowertown. The section bisecting the Nicasio Reservoir is particularly sublime. And when you pass, each one you pass goes "a-a-ah."

NAVIGATION: From Petuluma, D Street turns into the Platform Bridge Rd. When you reach the stop sign about 15.4 mi (24.8 km) out of Petaluma, turn right to stay on the Petaluma-Point Reyes Rd.

TE-G Marshall – Petaluma (17.4 mi / 28.0 km) *Chileno Valley Rd - Wilson Hill Rd - Marshall-Petaluma Rd*
The frequent, though sometimes off-camber curves up mellow Verde Canyon are the real reason to do this TE. Wilson and Chileno Valley are similar mostly straight scoots through open, rolling countryside with Chileno being better paved and engineered.

NAVIGATION: If you're coming from downtown Petaluma, take Western Ave 1.9 mi (3.1 km) west where Western changes names to Spring Hill Rd at the same time as it junctions with Chileno Valley Rd. 3.8 mi (6.1 km) along Chileno, stay straight on Wilson Hill.

*ROUTING OPTION: About halfway along **TE-F**, you can take the Hicks Valley Rd loop around Hammock Hill west to the three-way junction with Marshall-Petaluma Rd and Wilson Hill Rd to get the best of **TE-G**, though you'll be doing it downhill.*

TE-H Tomales – Valley Ford (8.9 mi / 14.3 km) *Dillon Beach Rd - Valley Ford-Franklin School Rd - Valley Ford Estero Rd*
This moderately winding route through open, roller-coaster countryside is quite reminiscent of south-coastal England. Though that may just be

because of the marine fog. Always preferable to the straight part of Hwy 1 north of Tomales.

TE-I Novato Rd - Novato Blvd (6.0 mi / 9.7 km)
With its moderate curves and moderate pavement, this ride is quite similar to **TE-J**. But it's more scenic and interesting since you get not only the rolling California hills and a waterside traverse, but some rock faces as well. Not to mention an official spot to stop for a dip in Stafford Lake.

NAVIGATION: Forget about the long trip through suburban Novato. If you've ridden this TE north-south, turn up Santa Clara Blvd and head out to the 101. Heading east from Novato toward Napa or points beyond, the Atherton Ave connector is a no-brainer bypass to Hwy 37.

Coming from the south, reverse the directions above.

TE-J Nicasio Valley Rd (7.7 mi / 12.4 km)
This decently paved and well engineered TE packs a lot of variety into a short distance. Satisfying curves through a little canyon at the south end ease off as the valley widens and makes way for some white-fenced ranches in an idyllic, green-hilled setting. Above Nicasio, at the sweepy north end, the landscape takes on a more open, windswept feel, almost evoking a sense of northern Scotland. That is, if you can imagine that the body of water you see is Loch Ness instead of the Nicasio Reservoir.

TE-K Lucas Valley Rd (6.8 mi / 11.0 km)
With a lot of tight narrow curves through forest and some steep sections, this road could be a bad experience. But good pavement can make all the difference. And does it ever here. May be the best TE of the bunch.

TE-L Point San Pedro Rd - North San Pedro Rd (4.6 mi / 7.4 km)
Changes are often sudden in California; a single curve can move you from suburban sprawl into untouched hinterland. Like here. After slogging through the suburbs of San Rafael, you enter China Camp State Park and wind out onto the inter-tidal salt marshes aside San Pablo Bay.

NAVIGATION: For southern access to the TE off Hwy 101, take the Central San Raphael exit and head southwest on one-way 2nd Ave. After about a block, it merges into 3rd Ave, which, in turn, becomes Point San Pedro Rd. The TE begins when the suburbia finally fizzles out, 4.5 mi (7.2 km) from the interstate.

For northern access, take the North San Pedro Rd exit for Santa Venetia off Hwy 101.

TE-M Corte Madura – Tiburon (6.5 mi / 10.5 km) *Paradise Dr*
A tight and twisty cliffside drive to the funky little seaside town of Tiburon. Driveways, cyclists and overly conscientious pylons abiding by the 20-mph (30-kmh) advisories keep the speed down.

ROUTING OPTION: Luxurious houses and even more luxurious views populate the extremely winding and narrow, one-lane Beach Rd that extends out of Tiburon and comes back to meet Tiburon Blvd. Watch the blind turns if you want to avoid a head on with a Rolls Corniche.

Rider's Log: **Date Ridden:** **Your Rating:** /10

How do YOU rate Northern California's 74 Destination Highways? Go to destinationhighways.com *and let other riders know.*

Van Damme SP CG
To Fort Bragg & DH5/32
Mendocino
Heritage House 800.235.5885
Little River
Little River Airport Rd.
Comptche-Ukiah Rd.
Albion
Comptche
Albion River Inn 707.937.1919
Fensalden Inn B&B 800.959.3850
Navarro River Redwoods SP CG (Navarro Beach)
Little River Market
Albion River CG 707.937.0606
Albion Grocery
Ledford House 707.937.0282
Comptche Store 707.937.5637
Navarro River Redwoods SP CG (Dimmick)
Navarro Store
Floodgate Store & Deli
Hendy Woods SP CG
Jack's Valley Store
Elk
Elk Guest House 707.877.3308
Bridget Dolan's 707.877.1820
Inn at Victorian Gardens B&B 707.882.3606
Navarro
Philo
Boonville
For details see DH56
For detail see DH22
Manchester
Manchester Beach KOA CG 800.562.4188
Point Arena
Manchester SP BCG
Rollerville Junction CG 707.882.2440
Old House Cafe
Sjolund Square Country Mkt SM
Whale Watch Inn B&B 800.942.5342
Anchor Bay
Anchor Bay Store
Redwood Grill 707.884.1639
Anchor Bay CG 707.884.4222
Gualala
Gualala Point CP CG 707.565.2267
Gualala River Park CG 707.884.3533
Gualala SM
Chevron/ Pacific 76
Sea Shell Inn Motel 707.882.2000
Wharf Master's Inn 800.932.4031
Coast Guard House B&B 707.882.2442
Point Arena GS
Point Arena Garage
Sea Ranch Lodge 800.732.7262 (Recommended)
Stewarts Point
Stewart Point Store
Annapolis Winery 707.886.5460
PACIFIC
OCEAN
Salt Point SP CG
Ocean Cove CG 707.847.3422
Salt Point Lodge 800.956.3437
Stillwater Cove Ranch 707.847.3227
Stillwater Cove CP CG 707.565.2267
Fort Ross Ranch 707.847.3422
Timber Cove Inn 800.987.8319
Fort Ross
Timber Cove CG 707.847.3278
Cazadero
Fort Ross Lodge 707.847.3333
Fort Ross Store
Fort Ross Reef SP CG
River's End 707.865.2484
Jenner Inn B&B 800.732.2377
Fast & Easy 10439 Hwy 1 707.865.9757
Jenner
Guerneville
To Longvale Jct & DH15
Willits
NON-FEATURED DH SERVICES NOT SHOWN
4 km
4 miles
Ridgewood Summit (1953ft/592m)
LOUGHLIN RANGE
Redwood Hwy.
Orr Springs Rd.
Lake Mendocino
To Kelseyville & DH53 Pg. 73
Ukiah
Talmage
Robinson Creek
Ukiah Boonville Rd.
Motorsports of Ukiah (HON/KAW) 1850 N State 707.462.8653
Ukiah Cycle Center (KTM) 1420 S State 707.463.2424
Lost Coast MC of Ukiah (SUZ/YAM) 1125 S State 707.462.5160
Buell HD of Ukiah (BUE/HD) 2501 N State 707.462.1672
To Lakeport To Kelseyville & DH53 Pg. 73
Old Hopland
Hopland
Yorkville
Mtn. House Rd.
MENDOCINO
SONOMA
Cloverdale
Dutcher Cr. Rd.
Skaggs Springs Rd.
Fort Ross Rd.
Meyers Grade Rd.
King Ridge Rd.
Seaview Rd.
Timber Cove Rd.
Ft. Ross State Historic Park
Stewarts Pt.-Skaggs Springs Rd.
Tin Barn Rd.
Annapolis Rd.
SAN ANDREAS FAULT ZONE
Gualala River
S.Fork
Horseshoe Cove
Ocean Cove
Black Point
Fish Rock Rd.
Old Stage Rd.
Iversen Rd.
Ten Mile Rd.
Eureka Hill Rd.
Garcia R.
Mtn. View Rd.
Brush Cr.
Alder Creek
Point Arena
Greenwood Rd.
Philo-Greenwood Rd.
NAVARRO RIVER
ANDERSON VALLEY
Flynn Cr. Rd.
Comptche Ukiah Rd.
S. Fork
Big River
DH32
DH22
DH24
DH27
DH29
DH10
TE-A
TE-B
TE-C
TE-D
TE-E
TE-F
TE-G
TE-H
I
(II)

DH29 Jenner – Albion (Mendocino)

Highway 1

Distance:	76.0 mi / 122.3 km	Traffic:	Moderate

At a Glance

Google has maintained that (unlike Microsoft?) they would "do no evil" and "make the world a better place" while making "all the world's information universally accessible and useful." So goo guys, what's with the 43,756 pages of irrelevant goozak when you just want a little road info? Not to worry, riders. TIRES only comes up with relevant results. And, in this case, you can cast your online vote for CalTrans, which not only keeps the Pavement up to snuff on this romantic coastal route, but also throws in extra Engineering help when necessary. There's lots of archetypal California beach and offshore islet Scenery as you cruise the bluffs and benches just inland from the Pacific. That is, if the cold California Current isn't shrouding everything in a heavy, wet blanket of fog. It can be quite cool here even when it's sunny. And when it actually precipitates, you can freeze *and* drown if not properly attired. Towns are generally small and don't sprawl much but the popularity of the Mendocino coast for holiday home development does impact Remoteness, although many places seem rarely used. Twistiness is good with the southern half scanning better than the north. Certainly, this long, Character-filled DH should make your world a better place. But don't take our word for it – given our history of crashing, we could be part of Gates' Evil Empire. So go on and google DH29. That is, as long as you're not behind the Great Firewall of China.

TIRES	
Twistiness	24.0/ 30
Pavement	17.0/ 20
Engineering	5.5/ 10
Remoteness	4.0/ 10
Scenery	11.0/ 15
Character	11.1/ 15
Total	**72.6**

Access

From Jenner

On Hwy 1

Head north out of town and you'll be on the road.

From Mendocino

Via Hwy 1

Albion is a few miles south of Mendocino and north of the junction of Hwy 1 with Hwy 128 (**TE-G**). Take Hwy 1 south from this junction and you're on the road.

J's Camp Outback
707.869.3102
16209 First St
877.644.9001
Forestville Club
River Bend CG
707.887.7662
Mirabel CG
707.887.2383
Foresthill Market
Rotten Robbie
Russian River Pub
707.887.7932
Hilton Park Family CG
707.887.9206
River Bend RV CG
707.887.7662
Ridenhour Inn B&B
707.887.1033
Faerie Ring CG
707.869.2746
CazSonoma Inn
707.632.5255
Pink Elephant
Santa Rosa BMW
800 American
707.838.9100
Raford House B&B Inn
800.887.9503
Underwood Bar & Bistro
707.823.7023
Mexico Lindo
707.823.4154
Willow Wood Mkt
Cape Fear Café
707.865.9246
Blue Heron
707.865.9135
Cassini Ranch CG
707.865.2255
Santa Nella House B&B
800.440.9031
Topolos Vineyards
707.887.1562
Occidental Mkt
Farmhouse Inn B&B
800.464.6642
Wildflower Bakery
Green Apple Inn B&B
707.874.2526
Freestone Store
265 S Main
707.823.3032
Sizzling Tandoor
707.865.2984
Rivers End
707.865.2484
Jenner Inn B&B
800.732.2377
10439 Hwy 1
707.865.9757
For detail see DH37
NON-FEATURED DH SERVICES NOT SHOWN
DH10
DH10 TE-B
DH10 TE-A
DH53 TE-B
DH37 TE-H
DH29
DH37
TE-A
TE-B
TE-B ALT
TE-C
I
II
To Cloverdale & DH27
To Calistoga & DH53 Pg. 73
To mid-DH29
To Santa Rosa To DH34 Pg. 61 To DH53 Pg. 73
To San Fransisco
To Petaluma
To Tamalpais Valley
To San Francisco
Jimtown
Healdsburg
Windsor
Cazadero
Guerneville
Hacienda
Forestville
Monte Rio
Jenner
Duncans Mills
Graton
Occidental
Sebastopol
Freestone
Bodega Bay
Bodega Harbor
Valley Ford
Dillon Beach
Tomales
LAGUNA WILDLIFE AREA
RUSSIAN RIVER
PACIFIC OCEAN
GABES ROCK
IRISH HILL
Alexander Vly. Rd.
SodaRock Ln.
W. Dry Ck. Rd.
Dry Creek Rd.
Lambert Bridge Rd.
Dry Creek
Mill St.
Dry Creek Rd.
Westside Rd.
Arata Rd.
Conde Ln.
Shiloh Rd.
Eastside Rd.
Russian River Valley
Wohler Rd.
Sweetwater Springs Rd.
Armstrong Woods Rd.
Odd Fellows Rd.
Fort Ross Rd.
Cazadero Hwy.
Austin Creek
Mark West Creek
River Rd.
Trenton Healdsburg Rd.
Laguna Rd.
Vine Hill Rd.
Guerneville Rd.
Forestville Hwy.
Green Valley
Green Valley Rd.
Bohemian Hwy.
Graton Rd
Laguna de Santa Rosa
Occidental Rd.
Coleman Valley Rd.
Salmon Creek
Bodega Hwy.
Valley Ford-Freestone Rd.
Valley Ford Estero Rd.
Marsh Rd.
Petaluma - Valley Ford Rd.
Valley Ford - Franklin School Rd.
Middle Rd.
Fallon - Two Rock Rd.
Dillon Beach Rd
101
128
116
12
1
2 km
2 miles
N
SONOMA
MARIN
38°40'
38°30'
38°20'
123°00'
122°50'

On The Road

Fine pavement twists along grass-topped, ocean side cliffs as soon as you boot out of Jenner. Pointed rocks form small islands just offshore. A loop in the road provides a view at 1.3 mi (2.1 km) back toward the beach stretching north of town. Then you're on bench land cutting straight through treeless fields.

The route turns inland on the eastern slope of a gorge. The pavement kinks and crosses the ravine. As you begin to climb up its western side, a hairpin flips you back southward. There's more climbing before a second flops you back northward. Looking down to the right, the asphalt you just rode loop-de-loops down the slope, while farther back you can see the ocean and beach at the mouth of the canyon. Caution: riding under the influence of this Hwy 1 oceanscape can impair your ability to operate a motorcycle.

The road levels off, bumps you over a badly laid cattleguard and passes Meyers Grade Rd (**TE-D**), right at 4.3 mi (6.9 km). The gray-blue ocean stretches all the way to Japan. You're so high now you can almost make it out.

The winding pavement continues across a grassy slope and heads slowly back down to the Pacific as coastal views toward the north open up and close again. On one corner there's another cattleguard you wouldn't want to hit in wet conditions at speed. Uh, CalTrans, how about not putting it *right* in the middle of a curve?

At 7.3 mi (11.7 km), the road enters a patch of forest and cranks in its curve radii. You're quickly back out in the open, although still descending slightly. Judging by the enormous but placid bull at the road edge this side of the fence, those cattleguards aren't just for show. Nor are the helpful little pieces of shoulder that CalTrans has been nice enough to plop down. They're even more helpful when the pylons use them to pull over and let you get by.

After a brief straight, you're soon curving sweetly again, more or less at the same level as the water but slightly inland. After you pass the turnoff left for the Fort Ross State Historic Park, the road straightens again, this time considerably, before re-twisting above a beach. The townlet of Fort Ross is reached at 12.3 mi (19.8 km).

TOUR NOTE: Fort Ross was the most southerly fur-trading post the Russians established during their presence on the West Coast. Several buildings from their period of occupation (1815-1841) have been reconstructed at the State Historic Park.

The road is straight again and there's a fair bit of development until you pass Timber Cove Rd (**TE-D**), right at 13.2 mi (21.2 km). While the signs of humanity don't disappear for some time after that, at least curves slowly reappear. In a reasonable number and variety at that.

The DH climbs away from Ocean Cove at 16.0 mi (25.7 km) on a particularly nice set of tight, linked curves through shade-creating forest that soon evolves into the Salt Point State Park. Gradually, the forest thins, shrinks and then disappears on the left to reveal a rocky shoreline, your first view of the ocean in awhile. The twisties are tight enough that if you have the misfortune of getting caught behind any pylons, it's quite hard to get by them. That straight through more forest at 20.0 mi (32.2 km) should help.

It's not long before you're back among friendly curves. The uniform pavement's pretty gregarious too, ranging from good to excellent. Leaving the state park, the forest shortly disappears on the left. Where the road straightens at 22.5 mi (36.2 km), you can glance back to get a look at the promontory on the south side of Horseshoe Cove. Time to take in those ocean vistas. Or just use the dotted yellow to dispense with some pylons.

ROUTING OPTION: At 25.6 mi (41.2 km), Stewarts Point-Skaggs Springs Rd provides back-door access to the superlative ***DH10 Skaggs Springs Rd - Dry Creek Rd****. This bumpy track is a rather painful way to get to it, though.*

Straights broken up by high-speed sweepers are the order of the day as you continue to streak north just inland from the Pacific. The only disconcerting sign is the one at 27.3 mi (43.9 km) advising you of deer for the next 8 mi (13 km). Unless, of course, you look at the map and notice that the San Andreas Fault is paralleling your path.

What will make you happy is the return of curves, cutting through the forest. They dissipate gradually though, and by 31.0 mi (49.9 km), you're straight-shotting it past strewn-about vacation developments and closing in on the town of Gualala, which you enter at 36.6 mi (58.9 km).

Guanolala continues to splatter development along the coast before spitting you out onto a long straight. A sign demands that slow traffic pull over, a sure sign of pylonic irregularity. Relief comes in the form of gentle curves tugging the road this way and that, before you reach Anchor Bay at 40.5 mi (65.2 km).

The curves are considerably tighter and more in the trees once you exit this microtown, though quite a few buildings linger roadside. Gradually, the excellent pavement re-straightens and, at 46.2 mi (74.3 km), the trees and buildings clear to open up more views of the ocean. The road then pulls away from the coast to proffer a few curves in a canyon before entering Point Arena at 51.1 mi (82.2 km).

Hwy 1 hooks hard left in the middle of town. Once completely out of this burb, your course provides a view inland of green Adams Ridge. Past Rollerville Junction, a 25-mph (40-kmh) corner turns the road east whereupon it curves sweetly down to the edge of some farmland before crossing it. Once over the Garcia River, you pass a sentinel line of tall roadside trees on the east shoulder. Then you pass Mountain View Rd (**TE-E**), right at 55.5 mi (89.3 km) before entering Manchester at 56.7 mi (91.2 km).

Leaving Red Devil town, you ride straight between open fields, sidling back toward the water. Cliff Ridge angles in from the right, inspiring a few more undulations in the geography. Not many curves though, at least until a linked, sweeperish three-set ess cuts through the terrain at 60.2 mi (96.9 km). The road straightens again the past an ocean view. The perfect place for... a bunch of buildings.

Cliff Ridge gets closer and at 62.6 mi (100.7 km), a sharp, blind, downhill, 25-mph (40-kmh) right-hander loops the road east. It then straightens abruptly among more fields in the shadow of the looming ridge. A slightly higher advisory introduces a couple more curves before the road straightens yet again.

Two linked, wide-shouldered, 20-mph (30-kmh) corners start off a tight, winding descent – complete with several hairpins – through some jumbled terrain covered in scrubby brush. More sweet curves on the other side of the hollow take you up onto another flat. A few more cliff-side curves and then the road drops down to Greenwood Creek. It climbs once more to junction with Philo-Greenwood Rd (**TE-F**) at 69.4 mi (111.7 km). Welcome to the charming little town of Elk, perched high on a cliff.

The road has one final flourish after leaving Elk. Fine cliff top pavement above the Pacific combines with a flurry of spaced and tighter, linked curves. The DH drops down through a forest, crosses the Navarro River and junctions with Hwy 128 (**TE-G**) at 76.0 mi (122.3 km).

Twisted Edges

TE-A Forestville – Guerneville (Hwy 116)
Not exactly a TE to pop open a bottle of California bubbly over but the tight corners through forest and past a couple of vineyards may provide enough effervescence for you. Though, because it's hard to pass here, it doesn't take much traffic to leave you feeling flat.

TE-B Monte Rio – Freestone (10.0 mi / 16.1 km) *Bohemian Hwy*
This rhapsody of variably paved, but consistently twisty, asphalt fandangos through farmland, the town of Occidental and some forest.

TE-B ALT Occidental – Graton (5.5 mi / 8.9 km) *Graton Rd*
This alternative in or out of Occdot bears a fair bit of resemblance to the main TE, particularly its more smoothly paved southern end. It does tend to be more trafficky though, as it provides major access to Santa Rosa.

TE-C Jenner – Monte Rio (Hwy 116) (7.6 mi / 12.2 km)
This designated scenic highway lives up to its billing with smooth gray pavement, wide shoulders and fast, banked sweepers. The scenery isn't bad either, varying from farmland framed by thickly wooded ridges west of Duncans Mills to a rock-walled and forested setting along the Russian River near Monte Rio.

TE-D Meyers Grade Rd - Ft Ross Rd - Seaview Rd - Timber Cove Rd (10.8 mi / 17.4 km)
Pretty, rolling countryside on the mostly open Meyers Grade - Ft Ross climb is followed by the twistier, more forested Seaview - Timber Cove section. Yahoo!

TE-E Manchester – Boonville (24.7 mi / 39.7 km) *Mountain View Rd*
Starts off well enough from Manchester with pretty good pavement ripping through some lovely farmed terrain before venturing into the woods. But then it gets bumpy and narrows into frequent one-lane sections. Those are easy to forget, however, once you get on the great M6 pavement that takes you down the final 21 per cent grade into Boonieville.

TE-F Elk – Philo (17.8 mi / 28.6 km) *Philo-Greenwood Rd*
Cold, thick fog socking in the DH? Or are you just hankering for a little vino? Whatever your reason for getting off the coast, this option has interesting layers and is certainly not flaky. Except for maybe the shake-and-bake pavement. Remote with little traffic, the TE climbs up from Elk and runs along forested Greenwood Ridge past a couple of orchards. Then a curvier descent heads down through denser forest before a steeper, tighter descent deposits you in the middle of Anderson Valley vineyards. Rouge *ou* Blanc?

TE-G Albion – Navarro (Hwy 128) (14.3 mi / 23.0 km)
Most of this curvy scoot along the Navarro River valley lies in the Navarro River Redwoods State Park, so you spend a lot of time in a cool, dark tunnel of trees, marveling at how this forest managed to be spared. Actually, it wasn't; what you see here is all second growth, which leaves you wondering what the old growth would have looked like. Probably as magnificent as this asphalt.

TE-H Mendocino – Navarro (23.1 mi / 37.2 km)
Comptche-Ukiah Rd - Flynn Creek Rd
While Flynn Creek Rd cannot compare to the near-perfection of **TE-F**, it's nonetheless impressive to see good pavement in such a remote location. And it's way better than the initial segment of Ukiah–Mendocino Rd east of Comptche that has great engineering but is horribly bumpy. But once that's over you're in like Flynn as newer pavement takes over at the top of the ridge and whips you all the way down into Mendocino.

RIDER'S LOG: **DATE RIDDEN:** **YOUR RATING: /10**

Map Tip: Services on non-featured DHs and TEs are generally shown as bare icon only and sometimes as no icon. For the full detail, just turn to the featured map.

To Leggett
DH5
OCEAN
Hollow Tree Ck.
To Leggett
Rattlesnake Creek
Laytonville
CAHTO PEAK
BLACK ROCK
Laytonville Dos Rios Rd.
To Covelo
EEL RIVER
Eel River Rd.
N
Branscomb Rd.
Branscomb
S. Fk. Eel River
DH5 TE-B
FARLEY PEAK
Westport
Wages Creek
Redwood Hwy.
Leisure Time RV CG
707.964.5994
332 N Main
707.961.6300
2 km
2 miles
DH15
BRUSH MTN.
STRONG MTN.
North Fork
Ten Mile River
Longvale Jct
Sleepy Hollow RV CG
707.459.0613
Middle Fork
Mackerricher State Park
S. Fork
Hidden Valley BCG
Sherwood Rd.
Outlet Cr.
Quail Meadows RV CG
707.459.6006
Cleone
Pine Beach Inn
888.987.8838
Playa
707.964.4074
North Fork
Hearst-Willits Rd.
Fort Bragg
Annie's Jughandle Beach B&B
707.964.1415
LITTLE LAKE VALLEY
BIG DARBY PEAK
239 S Main
707.459.7910
Noyo
Noyo River
THREE CHOP RIDGE
Willits
JACKSON STATE FOREST
Camp One BCG
CHAMBERLAIN CREEK CONSERVATION CAMP
KOA CG
707.459.6179
Caspar
Camp 20 BCG
DH32
IRENE PEAK
North Fork
Big River
WILLIAMS PEAK
IMPASSABLE ROCKS
Ridgewood Summit (1953ft/ 595 m)
LOUGHLIN RANGE
Mendocino
735 Main
707.937.5397
DH29 TE-H
Comptche Ukiah Rd.
Comptche
To Ukiah & DH22
Little River
Little River Airport Rd.
Comptche Ukiah Rd.
S. Fork
Big River
Albion
Orr Springs Rd.
Flynn Creek Rd.
DH22 TE-A
To Ukiah & DH22
Cameron Rd.
DH29 TE-G
Navarro
Elk
Greenwood
NAVARRO RIVER
DH29 TE-F
Philo Greenwood Rd.
PINE RIDGE
Robinson Creek
DH29
Creek
Philo
ANDERSON VALLEY
Mtn. View Rd.
Ukiah Boonville Rd.
Boonville
To Ukiah
DH22
To Jenner
To mid-DH29
DH29 TE-E
DH27
To Cloverdale

DH32 FT BRAGG – WILLITS

Highway 20

DISTANCE:	31.0 mi / 49.9 km	TRAFFIC:	Heavy

AT A GLANCE

Ever wondered why DH5 Cleone (Ft Bragg) – Leggett is devoid of traffic? Because it's all here on DH32. Yes, this beautifully paved, steadily twisting artery through the heavily forested mountains has lots of pullouts and even signs to encourage their use. But there's always some pylon pilot who has an issue with the fact that while he's just trying to get there, you're trying to enjoy the ride. It's double yellow all the way, so if the flashing high beams don't work, you may be left with few choices. So why is it the same passing restrictions apply to a Yamaha R1 as a Toyota Echo? Just wondering.

TIRES	
Twistiness	30.0/30
Pavement	18.0/20
Engineering	5.5/10
Remoteness	4.6/10
Scenery	8.2/15
Character	6.0/15
TOTAL	**72.3**

ACCESS

From Ft Bragg

Coming in on DH5 Leggett – Cleone (Ft Bragg)

Hwy 20 turns east off Hwy 1 at the southern end of Ft Bragg. Take it. When you pass the 55-mph sign, you're on the road.

From Willits

Head west on Hwy 20. When you clear town, you're on the road.

ON THE ROAD

There's a bit of straight at first as you track through the half-developed houses, private sale used cars and other suburban detritus outside Ft Bragg. But that's hardly typical of what to expect on this DH. The "Slower Vehicles Must Pull Over To Permit Passing" sign at 1.7 mi (2.7 km) is much more of an indicator of what's coming up. At first it's just a sweeper and a couple of linked curves. But by 2.2 mi (3.5 km), you're on an eight-curve S series through tall roadside woods.

Houses linger in clearings among the trees and you're pretty much stuck with them – and their attendant access roads – until 4.1 mi (6.6 km) when you weave into the redwoods of the Jackson Demonstration State Forest. If you'd like to demonstrate how effectively you can slide your pucks, there's another fine series of climbing esses and close-knit curves coming right up.

The steady, gradual climb tops out at 7.2 mi (11.6 km) and you begin a not-quite-as-gradual descent. Some rockfaces peeking out of the trees along with a 25-mph (40-kmh) corner speak to the rougher terrain. Not that sharp curves are a problem – on this pavement, the sharper the better.

You're in the trees most of the time on this road, but there are some occasional views, such as the long one of Three Chop Ridge to the northeast at 10.0 mi (16.1 km) and the grassy valley of the Big River's north fork at 10.9 mi (17.5 km). An out-of-place bit of farmland in the valley's short flat bottom offers more variety. But at 12.1 mi (19.5 km), the redwoods are back.

A straightish section follows, running by the Chamberlain Creek Conservation Camp at 15.0 mi (24.1 km). There's a nice picnic area across the road from it in case you you're waiting to visit any friends or relatives who got caught passing on the double yellow here. Don't expect to find any drivers of RVs and other pylons doing hard time for refusing to use the pullouts. They get off without even a slap on the wrist.

The trees get taller and the curves become tighter at 16.5 mi (26.6 km). Inevitably, the traffic gets gummed up by some heavy truck or other slow pylon. And when it finally pulls over, no one else does. Seems everyone who was following him suddenly thinks they're Jimmie Johnson. Which would be fine, except that you're Nicky Hayden.

If you're fortunate enough to get a clear shot at this road, you're entering its best section. If you're stuck behind a convoy, you'll be weeping at the waste. Near-perfect pavement oscillates back and forth and up and down along the edge of a treed canyon while a wall of forest climbs to your right and openings in the trees to your left offer more views of Three Chop Ridge. Likely the only things you want to chop right now are a few axles.

But at the right time, on the right day, it can be simply amazing through here. Sweet pavement, tight, semi-shouldered, well-contoured corners, reasonably good sightlines, no driveways, and even a vista or two, such as the high one at 25.0 mi (40.2 km). From here, you look south over to Williams Peak, Irene Peak, and something called the Impassable Rocks. Seems someone else had a little trouble passing around here, too.

A nine-per-cent grade drops you down off the crest for the journey's final leg. It's not as tight and twisty now, a change made apparent by the section of dotted yellow line at 27.0 mi (43.4 km). Riding this DH, you wouldn't think they made this kind of paint anymore, but there it is. Unfortunately, it's too little too late for the really great stuff. But there's still lots to enjoy as you linger on the long, sweeping corners that guide you rhythmically down an open slope into a widening valley and hence to Willits' 30-mph (50-kmh) zone, where the road ends at 31.0 mi (49.9 km).

Rider's Log: **Date Ridden:** **Your Rating:** /10

Just what is an "STC" or "maxburner" anyway?
Check out these and other Twisted Terms in the Glossary at p.??

To Garberville & DH66 Pg. 145
Leggett Mkt SM
Angelo's Pizza Parlor 707.925.6200
Janice's Redwood Diner 707.925.6442
Patriot
Lost Coast Inn B&B 707.964.5584
Westport Community Store
To Shelter Cove & DH66TE-A Pg. 147 via 20 mi (32km) gravel
Leggett
TE-A
271
EEL RIVER
SHELL ROCK
River's Run Lodge 707.984.6321
Stonegate Villas 707.925.6226
Shoreline Hwy.
Hollow Tree Creek
BRUSH MTN.
Budget Inn 707.984.8492
Express Inn 707.984.8456
Boomers Bar & Grill 707.984.6534
Laytonville Inn 707.984.8213
Geiger's Groceries SM
Chevron
Rattlesnake Summit (1769ft/547m)
101
N
Rattlesnake Creek
2 km
2 miles
BLACK ROCK
DH5
Redwood Mercantile SM
Wages Creek Beach CG 707.964.2964
Westport Beach BCG 707.937.5804
Pacific 707.964.1155
CAHTO PEAK
Laytonville
Laytonville Dos Rios Rd.
TE-B
ADMIRAL WILLIAM STANDLEY SRA
S. Fk.
Branscomb Rd.
Branscomb
Branscomb GS
FARLEY PEAK
OCEAN
Wages Creek
Westport
Chadbourne Gulch
Leisure Time RV CG 707.964.5994
332 N Main 707.961.6300
Eel River
Redd Fox Casino 707.984.6800
Redwood Hwy.
Coast Motel 707.964.2852
Shoreline Cottages 707.964.2977
Hidden Pines CG 707.961.5451
US
Mackerricher SP CG 707.964.9112
North Fork
BRUSH MTN.
STRONG MTN.
Ten Mile River
Longvale Junction
To Covelo
Woodside RV CG 707.964.3684
Middle Fork
Cleone Gardens Inn 800.400.2189
Cleone Grocery
Cleone CG 707.964.4589
Purple Rose 707.964.6507
DH15
To Willits & DH32
Sherwood Rd.
Mackerricher State Park
S. Fork
Pomo CG 707.964.3373
Inglenook
Cleone
Pine Beach Inn 888.987.8838
Playa 707.964.4074
PACIFIC
North Fork
Fort Bragg
Annie's Jughandle Beach B&B 707.964.1415
Noyo
Noyo River
THREE CHOP RIDGE
20
Caspar Inn 707.964.5565
To Willits
JACKSON STATE FOREST
Caspar
Caspar Beach RV Park CG 707.964.3306
DH32
North Fork
To Mendocino & DH29
Russian Gulch SP CG 707.964.3306
Big River
123°50'
123°40'
123°30'
39°50'
39°40'
39°30'
39°20'

DH5 Cleone (Ft Bragg) – Leggett

Shoreline Highway (Hwy 1)

Distance:	39.8 mi / 64.1 km	Traffic:	Moderate

At a Glance

TIRES	
Twistiness	30.0/ 30
Pavement	19.0/ 20
Engineering	4.9/ 10
Remoteness	6.7/ 10
Scenery	10.2/ 15
Character	11.7/ 15
Total	82.5

Ironically, the best section of the Shoreline Hwy isn't along the shoreline at all. Sure, when you think of riding Hwy 1, you think of essing precariously atop steep cliffs, peering over the crashing surf below. And in fact, once you stop dipping and climbing off the beaches and waterside towns north of Cleone, you do get a bit of that on this DH. But the superb part actually comes when the road moves off the coast and a sign announces "Narrow Winding Road Next 22 Miles." This remote collection of endless S-curves beneath the tall redwoods not only has good camber and decent sightlines, it's been recently repaved as well. And when you factor in that more than one million Californians hold a Class M license, there's an odds-on chance that at least one of those colorful guys on the screaming Gixxers is an off-duty speed tax collector. And isn't that the greatest irony of all.

Access

From Ft. Bragg

Coming in on DH32 Willits – Ft Bragg (Hwy 20)

Turn north on Hwy 1 and suffer through Ft Bragg. When you finally leave Cleone, you're on the road.

From Leggett

On Hwy 101

Take the well-marked Hwy 1 turnoff and go south. You're on the road.

On The Road

"End 35" reads the sign coming out of Cleone, the present end of the suburban sprawl creeping up from Ft Bragg. Not that it's particularly remote in the early miles north of Cleone. Houses and cottages still linger along the meandering, impeccably paved route. It is scenic, though. At 0.8 mi (1.3 km), you break out of the trees and get a look at the dunes of MacKerricher Beach. With the inevitable fog bank beyond.

The sea view comes and goes as you dip and climb, passing through groves of redwoods and the small, but spread out town of Inglenook.

After Nookytown, you get closer to the dunes as you angle north toward the coast. And there's a great view of the ocean breakers from the bridge over Ten Mile River at 4.2 mi (6.8 km). Then an S-curve sweeps you right down to the windswept beach at 5.0 mi (8.1 km).

The coastal landscape is a strange marriage of lush rainforest and hardy, wind- and salt-resistant shrubs. You continue to rise and fall with the terrain, though at 5.5 mi (8.9 km), some serious side-to-side is introduced as well with a chain of esses that twists up to more misty views of the coastline. At 6.0 mi (9.7 km), a long straight crosses a large tract of oceanside grassland. Great passing opportunity. But for the mystifying double yellow.

There's a vista point just off the road at 8.5 mi (13.7 km) and it's a stop to consider given that the constant bobbing up and down of this road does impact the views you get from the saddle. If not, there are still a couple of okay viewing points that you don't have to brake for at 8.9 mi (14.3 km) and 9.2 mi (14.8 km). Of course, you may want to engage your right finger a little for some of the tight corners that come when the road dodges inland, winds through Chadbourne Gulch, then climbs and twists back out to the coast. You'll have to, anyway, if there's some trailer-towing pylon in front of you.

Assuming you're lucky and have the road to yourself, the scene does feel remote as you come out of the shrub-blanketed gulch and wind steadily along a low bank above the sea. At least for a minute. At 11.4 mi (18.3 km), you arrive at the speed zone of Westport. It's followed by some sweet corners along and above the beach. For grumpy Sullivan-seekers who prefer bumpy, one-and-one-half lane pavement and poor engineering, Branscomb Rd (**TE-B**) turns off for Laytonville at 13.4 mi (21.6 km). (Unfortunately for them, this TE turns into a beautifully paved and engineered road in the middle.)

The road is straight past the **TE-B** junction, but the sign that says "Narrow Winding Road Next 22 Miles" at 16.0 mi (25.7 km) is bound to cheer you up. It's a little premature, since the big, open, well-engineered sweepers that drift elegantly between the crashing ocean and layered, calcified cliff could hardly be described as "narrow" or "winding." But they can be described as "fantastic."

At 17.8 mi (28.6 km), however, you move off the ocean and the DH begins to take on some of its advertised features. Winding more tightly and steadily on an upward cant through a thickening redwood forest, it's the kind of road that gets the most out of a lacquer of new pavement. And what do you know, there it is.

The essing curves continue when the descent comes at 19.2 mi (30.9 km). You get a break – whether you want it or not – at 21.8 mi (35.1 km) where the road rolls out onto a flat. Here, the corners are unlinked and far more modest as they pass through some rare patches of grassland amid all the trees. At 25.4 mi (40.9 km), however, you climb again.

Tilt, tilt, tilt through the redwood canopy on a long, sinuous and unyielding ascent. Northern California has some special pieces of pavement and this is one of them. This section is like an extended, director's cut of **DH39 Boulder Creek – Saratoga**. And without the lineups.

You catch your breath on a brief, straighter section beginning at 30.2 mi (48.6 km). A few buildings in the towering trees interrupt the hitherto uninterrupted feeling of remoteness. The fact they belong to a wood products company gives cause for concern. Especially since they've yet to hire a logging truck driver who knows how to use a pullout.

You've gained elevation, as evidenced by the forest-veiled views of the Sinkyone Wilderness off to the left at 30.9 mi (49.7 km). The openness allows some light in on the often dark, shaded pavement. Which makes the intense S-curves look even better as they slither along the top of this ridge and then snake down its southern side.

Considering the tightness of the curves, the sightlines really aren't too bad. That's the nice thing about redwoods – not a lot of low branches. It's nice to see all the way around the corners, especially at 35.4 mi (57.0 km) when the descending grade steepens to seven per cent.

Despite the grade, it's hard not to go heavy on the throttle as you flit down through the unrelenting S-curves. The smoothness of the pavement just keeps calling for more. Like some siren from Homer's Odyssey, it draws you closer and closer to the edge. Just don't pass the point of no return.

The DH twists and turns to its rather abrupt end. Your only warning is a house in the trees at 39.0 mi (62.8 km) just before you cross the south fork of the Eel River. You emerge from the woods and arrive at the stop sign right beside the north end of Leggett, at 39.8 mi (64.1 km).

ROUTING OPTION: The non-freeway section of Hwy 101 just north of Leggett is a great piece of winding, well-paved road if you can catch it without traffic – which is probably later in the day. The section of the 101 south of ***TE-A*** *over the Rattlesnake Summit ain't bad either.*

Twisted Edges

TE-A Highway 271 (7.4 mi / 11.9 km)
This renumbered piece of the old Hwy 101 is smooth, well-engineered and quite twisty with views of the Eel River valley and the new Hwy 101, which it crisscrosses. Best of all, it has absolutely no traffic. A truly excellent TE.

TOUR NOTE: The local drive-thru tree down the gravel access road just south of Leggett has a picnic area, visitor information and, of course, a gift shop.

TE-B Laytonville – Westport (25.0 mi / 40.2 km) *Branscomb Rd*
Another of those Cinderella stories you find between Hwy 101 and Hwy 1. The eastern half is a smooth, wide, fairy tale of well-engineered pavement that sweeps gracefully through the wild grasslands and open forests of the Admiral William Standley State Recreation Area. Then, after the clock

strikes 15.4 mi (24.8 km), it pumpkins into a tight, paintless, poorly engineered, one-and-one-half laner that rolls steeply off a ridge through thick trees down to the coast.

Rider's Log: **Date Ridden:** **Your Rating: /10**

DH37 DH29 DH32 DH5 DH15 DH22 DH27 DH24 DH10

How does this book work again? RTFM. "What is Destination Highways Northern California?" and "How to Use Our Maps" appear at the front of the book.

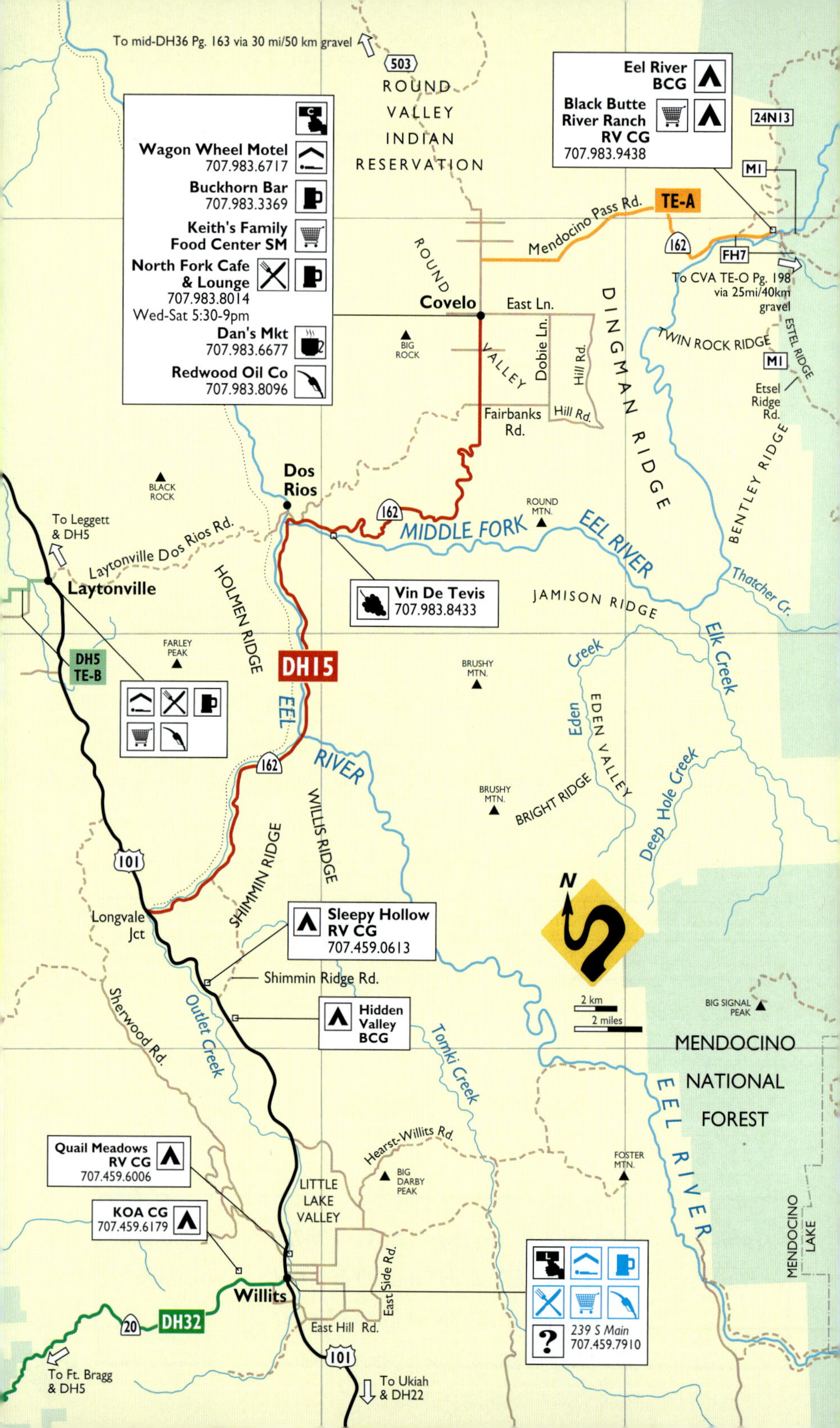

To mid-DH36 Pg. 163 via 30 mi/50 km gravel
503
ROUND VALLEY INDIAN RESERVATION
Wagon Wheel Motel
707.983.6717
Buckhorn Bar
707.983.3369
Keith's Family Food Center SM
North Fork Cafe & Lounge
707.983.8014
Wed-Sat 5:30-9pm
Dan's Mkt
707.983.6677
Redwood Oil Co
707.983.8096
Eel River BCG
Black Butte River Ranch RV CG
707.983.9438
24N13
M1
TE-A
Mendocino Pass Rd.
162
FH7
To CVA TE-O Pg. 198 via 25mi/40km gravel
ROUND VALLEY
Covelo
East Ln.
Dobie Ln.
Hill Rd.
Hill Rd.
Fairbanks Rd.
DINGMAN RIDGE
TWIN ROCK RIDGE
ESTEL RIDGE
M1
Etsel Ridge Rd.
BENTLEY RIDGE
BIG ROCK
BLACK ROCK
Dos Rios
ROUND MTN.
MIDDLE FORK EEL RIVER
To Leggett & DH5
Laytonville Dos Rios Rd.
Laytonville
HOLMEN RIDGE
Vin De Tevis
707.983.8433
JAMISON RIDGE
Thatcher Cr.
Elk Creek
FARLEY PEAK
DH5 TE-B
DH15
BRUSHY MTN.
Eden Creek
EDEN VALLEY
EEL RIVER
162
BRUSHY MTN.
BRIGHT RIDGE
Deep Hole Creek
WILLIS RIDGE
SHIMMIN RIDGE
101
N
Longvale Jct
Sleepy Hollow RV CG
707.459.0613
Shimmin Ridge Rd.
Hidden Valley BCG
2 km
2 miles
BIG SIGNAL PEAK
Sherwood Rd.
Outlet Creek
Tomki Creek
MENDOCINO NATIONAL FOREST
EEL RIVER
Hearst-Willits Rd.
Quail Meadows RV CG
707.459.6006
BIG DARBY PEAK
FOSTER MTN.
LITTLE LAKE VALLEY
KOA CG
707.459.6179
East Side Rd.
MENDOCINO LAKE
Willits
239 S Main
707.459.7910
20
DH32
East Hill Rd.
101
To Ft. Bragg & DH5
To Ukiah & DH22

DH15 Longvale Jct – Covelo

Highway 162

Distance:	28.9 mi / 46.5 km	Traffic:	Light

At a Glance

The roads that time forgot. You know the ones. They run from places like Longago Junction to a place like Nocovelo, a small, fading town in Nobody's Around Valley tucked away in a backwater corner of Mendontcomeno County. These historical curiosities are often deadenders with only gravel providing an alternate escape. But this helps keep traffic down and Remoteness up. Twistiness comes alive when these forgotten roads climb up and down over ridges and track waterway valleys – which can make for varied and stimulating hill and vale Scenery. Trouble is, the attractive qualities of such ancient byways are often tempered by asphalt that feels like it hasn't been updated since the 50s – and often hasn't been. Not so here. For some reason – probably relating to Pavement-barrel politics – the road's surface is rarely less than adequate and is often superior. And with the asphalt being this good, you don't mind some challenging Engineering; in fact, you often prefer it. If you're lucky, you'll find a few highways like this in your time, classics that suit a timeless mount – a Crocker say or perhaps a Brough Superior. But even a modern-era Ducati won't beat you up too badly on this one. Because, while it may be one of those roads that time forgot, CalTrans certainly hasn't.

TIRES	
Twistiness	29.5/ 30
Pavement	15.9/ 20
Engineering	5.7/ 10
Remoteness	7.5/ 10
Scenery	10.0/ 15
Character	10.1/ 15
Total	**78.7**

Access

From Longvale Jct

On Hwy 101

Whether coming from north or south, head east on Hwy 162 from its junction with 101 and you'll be on the road.

From Covelo

As soon as you leave town south on 162, you are on the road.

On The Road

You're outta here – the present, that is, although this will only become evident later. What you do notice right away, however, as you turn off 101, are the surprisingly well-paved curves alongside Outlet Creek. And the surprisingly rough and badly angled wooden railway crossing (whump) just before the bridge.

The creek's valley is quite narrow, though the hills on either side are low and mostly treed. What's impressive, however, is the sense of remoteness you feel. At least after you pass the gravel dump/pit that appears left at 2.1 mi (3.4 km). The curves are continuous but mild. The mix of deciduous and conifer trees are loosely scattered and rarely press in on the road, though sightlines are sometimes obscured by the steep grass or rock slopes shimmying down from Shimmin Ridge.

The 25-mi (40-kmh) corner at 4.8 mi (7.7 km) precedes a short, more wide-open stretch nicely interrupted by a quintuple S-curve. As the terrain opens up, the hillsides lose trees. At 6.6 mi (10.6 km), you're in the middle of a straighter stretch where some buildings set up beside the road.

The sign at the foot of Willis Ridge warns of rock falls ahead for 7 mi (11 km). Encouraging. And indeed, there's an electric set of twisties before you cross the bridge over the Eel River at 8.2 mi (13.2 km). The Eel runs along to your left while the steep eastern side of its valley hatches some curves and sweepers. They're pretty harmless, except when they're obscured by vegetation.

A little climb has you a little above the right side of the river by 11.7 mi (18.8 km). More low-speed advisories interspersed with higher-speed stretches provide an entertaining, ever-changing potpourri. A widening in the shoulder at 12.4 mi (20.0 km) provides access to the wide gravel bars flanking the river's shores. That's the old railway line running along the other side of the river.

At 15.1 mi (24.1 km), you hit the Dos Rios bridge crossing. It takes you sharply east away from the Eel and over the Middle Fork Eel River. Almost immediately, you start to climb up from the Middle Fork into the larger hills on the river's north side. The slightly uphill curves tighten and multiply. More low-speed advisories offer their counsel. As always, they're a little conservative.

A sharp left-hander at 16.9 mi (27.2 km) takes the road up a subsidiary canyon where the curves constrict even more on what is the DH's most memorable stretch. That little bit of a shoulder is a nice touch. Especially when some of the corners decrease-radius on you.

The tops of Dingman, Bentley and Etsel Ridges stretch away to the east as the route turns back northward while continuing to curve upward. The vegetation gradually thins and by 20.9 mi (33.6 km), the hillside is grassy and mostly bare of trees. A big sweeper north soon puts you back among trees, though. And by 22.6 mi (36.4 km), they're often thick enough to block your views of the surrounding landscape. Not to mention some of your views around the corners.

There are no blocked views, however, where a widening in the gravel shoulder at 23.9 mi (38.5 km) reveals a panorama over Round Valley and its surrounding ridges. The curves don't diminish as the vista unfolds but you have stopped climbing. By the time you get to the two near-hairpins – one right, then a little further on, one left – the road is clearly descending.

Then it's basically over. You exit the trees and curves at 26.4 mi (42.5 km) and level out on Round Valley's floor. It's a straight shot through fields and past the occasional building to semi-deserted Covelo where the DH ends at 28.9 mi (46.5 km). If you stop and remove your helmet, you may hear the faint strains of "Dueling Banjos" echoing over the valley from some far-off porch. Even if it's only in your head.

Twisted Edges

TE-A Mendocino Pass Rd (Hwy 162/FH 7) (8.4 mi / 13.5 km)
Looking for a place to hang out before heading back to Hwy 101? This remote, variably paved extension that cuts through golden fields, winds along shaded creeks and finally emerges onto the benchlands above the Middle Fork Eel River is worth the few extra miles. If only because the Black Butte Ranch is as cool a destination as anything Covelo has to offer.

ROUTING OPTION: If you continue beyond the pavement, you'll be traveling the gravel for approximately 26.5 mi (42.5 km) before the pavement resumes at Eel River as ***CVA TE-O Alder Springs Rd (FH 7/Hwy 162)****.*

Rider's Log: **Date Ridden:** **Your Rating:** /10

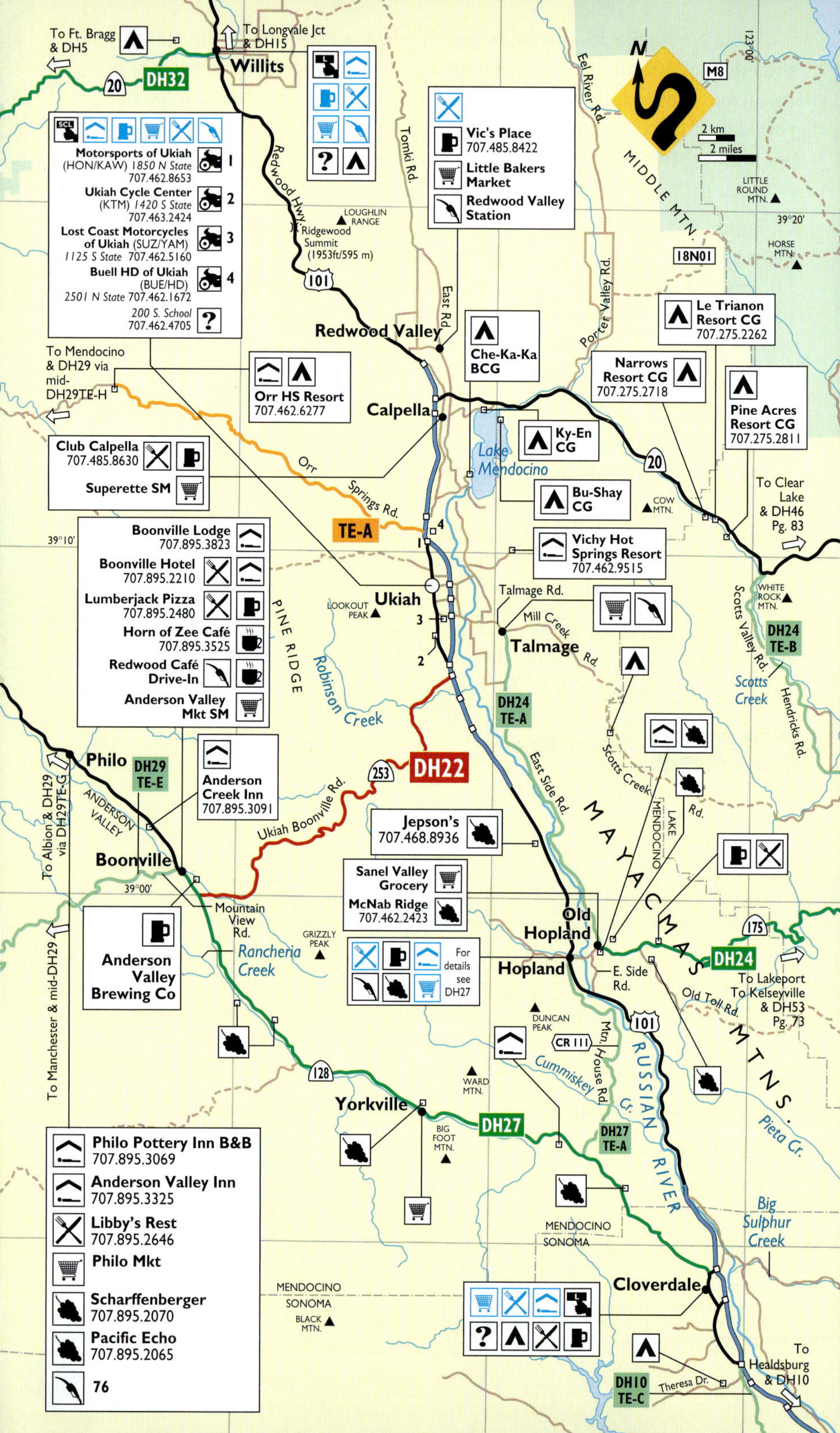

To Ft. Bragg & DH5
To Longvale Jct & DH15
Willits
20
DH32
Motorsports of Ukiah (HON/KAW) 1850 N State 707.462.8653 1
Ukiah Cycle Center (KTM) 1420 S State 707.463.2424 2
Lost Coast Motorcycles of Ukiah (SUZ/YAM) 1125 S State 707.462.5160 3
Buell HD of Ukiah (BUE/HD) 2501 N State 707.462.1672 4
200 S. School 707.462.4705
Redwood Hwy.
Ridgewood Summit (1953ft/595 m)
LOUGHLIN RANGE
Tomki Rd.
Vic's Place 707.485.8422
Little Bakers Market
Redwood Valley Station
Eel River Rd.
N
M8
2 km
2 miles
123°00'
MIDDLE MTN.
LITTLE ROUND MTN.
39°20'
HORSE MTN.
18N01
101
Redwood Valley
East Rd.
Che-Ka-Ka BCG
Porter Valley Rd.
Le Trianon Resort CG 707.275.2262
Narrows Resort CG 707.275.2718
Pine Acres Resort CG 707.275.2811
To Mendocino & DH29 via mid-DH29TE-H
Orr HS Resort 707.462.6277
Calpella
Ky-En CG
Lake Mendocino
20
Club Calpella 707.485.8630
Superette SM
Orr Springs Rd.
Bu-Shay CG
COW MTN.
To Clear Lake & DH46 Pg. 83
TE-A
4
1
39°10'
Boonville Lodge 707.895.3823
Boonville Hotel 707.895.2210
Lumberjack Pizza 707.895.2480
Horn of Zee Café 707.895.3525
Redwood Café Drive-In
Anderson Valley Mkt SM
Vichy Hot Springs Resort 707.462.9515
Talmage Rd.
WHITE ROCK MTN.
Scotts Valley Rd.
PINE RIDGE
LOOKOUT PEAK
Ukiah
3
Mill Creek Rd.
Talmage
2
DH24 TE-B
Robinson Creek
DH24 TE-A
Scotts Creek
Hendricks Rd.
Philo
DH29 TE-E
Anderson Creek Inn 707.895.3091
DH22
253
East Side Rd.
Scotts Creek Rd.
To Albion & DH29 via DH29TE-G
ANDERSON VALLEY
Ukiah Boonville Rd.
Jepson's 707.468.8936
MAYACMAS MTNS.
LAKE MENDOCINO
Boonville
Sanel Valley Grocery
McNab Ridge 707.462.2423
39°00'
Mountain View Rd.
Old Hopland
175
Anderson Valley Brewing Co
GRIZZLY PEAK
Rancheria Creek
For details see DH27
Hopland
DH24
E. Side Rd.
To Lakeport To Kelseyville & DH53 Pg. 73
Old Toll Rd.
To Manchester & mid-DH29
DUNCAN PEAK
CR 111
101
Mtn. House Rd.
128
WARD MTN.
Cummiskey Cr.
RUSSIAN RIVER
Yorkville
DH27
BIG FOOT MTN.
DH27 TE-A
Pieta Cr.
Philo Pottery Inn B&B 707.895.3069
Anderson Valley Inn 707.895.3325
Libby's Rest 707.895.2646
Philo Mkt
Scharffenberger 707.895.2070
Pacific Echo 707.895.2065
76
MENDOCINO SONOMA
Big Sulphur Creek
MENDOCINO SONOMA
BLACK MTN.
Cloverdale
DH10 TE-C
Theresa Dr.
To Healdsburg & DH10

DH22 Ukiah – Boonville

Highway 253

Distance:	17.1 mi / 27.5 km	Traffic:	Moderate

At a Glance

This road is impossible to resist. Silky smooth Pavement, sweet Engineering, gaga Scenery and an unforgettable body of curves. The only rub on Hwy 253 is that when it comes to Character, it's a little "length challenged," shall we say. But, after all, it's not what you got it's how you use it. After teasing you through the pretty vineyards south of Ukiah, this beauty wiggles its overachieving asphalt up and over Pine Ridge, writhing in a passionate series of desperate, almost unceasing esses. As if that's not stimulating enough, it caresses your eyeballs at the same time with remote mountain and valley views. And being a relatively minor highway, chances are you'll get to enjoy its pleasures without a drove of geeky pylons trying to cut in on your action. So go ahead and hook up. C'mon, you've always got time for a quickie.

TIRES	
Twistiness	30/30
Pavement	16.1/20
Engineering	5.7/10
Remoteness	5.1/10
Scenery	11.6/15
Character	7.9/15
Total	**76.4**

Access

From Ukiah

On State St

State St is the main drag through Ukiah. Follow it south almost to Hwy 101. Hwy 253 goes west from here. Take it. You're on the road.

From Hwy 101

Take the Hwy 253 exit at the south end of Ukiah and follow the signs. They'll put you on the road.

From Boonville

Coming in on DH27 Cloverdale – Boonville (Hwy 128)

Turn right where Hwy 253 junctions with Hwy 128. You're on the road.

On The Road

It's scenic from the start as this DH shoots off Hwy 101 at the south end of Ukiah. Vineyards stretch out from a road cloistered by overhanging oaks. The newer blacktop doesn't look too bad either. Nor does the "Twisties Next 15 Miles" sign at 1.0 mi (1.6 km).

The bucolic scene continues as the road starts to climb ever so subtly into the layered hills ahead. At 2.7 mi (4.3 km), it follows a 25-mph (40-kmh) curve around the rock and grass cliff that's erupted to the right, essing back then forth. A sign foretells twisties for the next two miles. Uh, CalTrans, thought you said it was 15. Get it together, will ya?

Actually, what CT probably means is that the next part of the DH is *especially* twisty. Because that turns out to be the case. All development ends as tight, well-contoured turns climb a steep, grass and tree-covered embankment. Gorgeous views continue with rock formations so thickly treed, they look like emerald-colored clouds.

Back on the ground, the pavement quality drops a touch at 3.8 mi (5.4 km) as a turnout gives any conscientious pylons the opportunity to do the right thing. Actually, the right thing would be to pull over on the shoulder well before now.

The sinuous road keeps on climbing. And twisting. Then, at 4.2 mi (6.8 km) the terrain levels enough to make room for a vineyard. You keep on curving through the grapes, just not quite as steeply and intensely as before.

Oops, spoke too soon. The flurry of S-curves starting at 5.5 mi (8.8 km) is pretty tight. But it's just a flurry. Then the curves ease enough to let you cast your eyes left over the rugged, tree-filled expanse of the Feliz Creek Valley. Fitting somehow, as right now you're one *feliz motocylista.*

Twisties continue along the bank, sometimes coming at you as long sweepers. The road's nice and wide, giving you a reasonable sense of confidence despite the lack of any guardrail on the opposite, drop-off side. At 6.9 mi (11.1 km), you come over a crest and… wow! A tremendous view opens up over the valley toward the blue outlines of Grizzly Peak as well as Sanel, Snow and Ward Mtns.

The view lingers, expanding from the right side of the road at 7.6 mi (12.2 km). What's so striking is the relief and detail in the landscape. The valleys have sub-valleys, which, in turn, roll with smaller dips and mounds. Shaved brown hills covered with lush oaks roll out to every horizon. It's beautiful.

The right side of the road banks up again at 7.9 mi (12.7 km) and the road responds with a quintuple S-sweeper. More esses follow as the road eases down a nine- per-cent grade in a continuing chain of corners. Despite losing some height, the view is still great. And so is everything else.

Another pair of sweepers, extra large this time, switchback at 10.4 mi (16.7 km). Now the panoramic views are gone and the road enters a straight across a level section of land. Take a breath while you can.

At 12.9 mi (20.8 km), you pass a lone house, enter a fold in the terrain and the big corners come back. After effortlessly twisting on the fine pavement through this vale of sweepers, you drop down another nine per cent grade, starting at 14.3 mi (23.0 km). At least you don't have to worry if you're low on gas – it's steep enough to coast into town.

There's more great scenery as the road comes down an embankment high above Soda Creek. The slope angles steeply down to your right, opening up a chasm filled with an elaborate detail of grass, rock and trees. A ridge and mountainside in the distance provide a further backdrop for the DH's remaining curves. The DH ends just east of Boonville at the T-junction with Hwy 128 and **DH27 Boonville – Cloverdale** at 17.1 mi (27.5 km).

Twisted Edges

TE-A Ukiah – Orr Hot Springs (11.9 mi / 19.2 km) *Orr Springs Rd*
After gliding through a short sheet of grass, this road zigs and zags up a rocky slope as a pair of fantastic blond and green valleys open up below. Pavement could use a Zamboni but the engineering's good enough that you can win the battles in the tight corners, at least until the road narrows for the 10 per cent drop toward the end. It's a shame this TE has to hang up its skates at Montgomery Woods. But at least you can stop and soak your aching knees – or wrist – in the hot springs.

NAVIGATION: From Ukiah, go north on N State Street. As soon as it takes you under the freeway, look for the Orr Springs Rd sign.

ROUTING OPTION: The bumpy, one-lane stuff at the end of the TE continues another 16.9 mi (27.2 km) to Comptche and the mid point of ***DH29TE-H Navarro – Mendocino****.*

Rider's Log: **Date Ridden:** **Your Rating:** **/10**

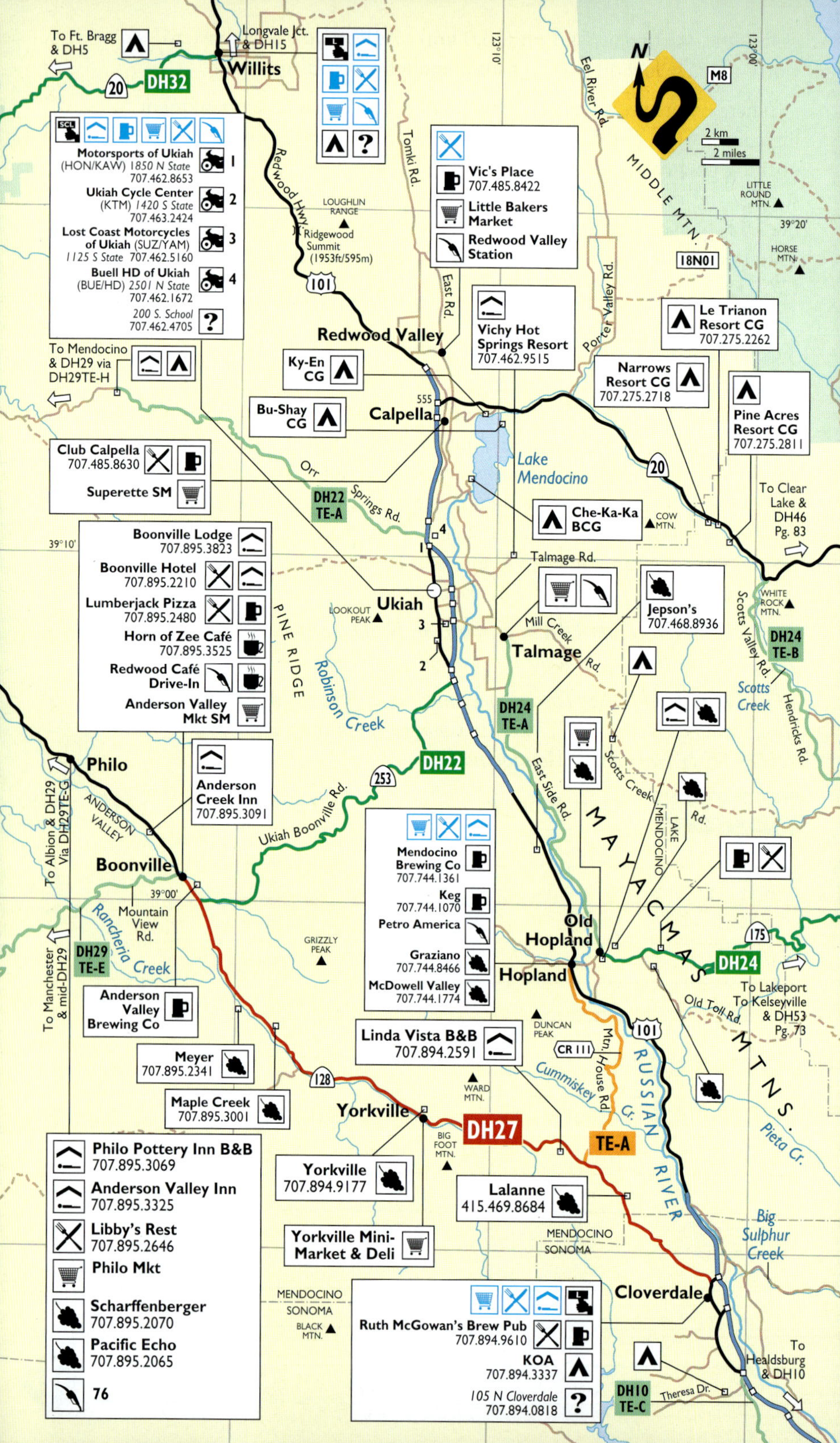

To Ft. Bragg & DH5
Longvale Jct. & DH15
Willits
DH32
Motorsports of Ukiah (HON/KAW) 1850 N State 707.462.8653 1
Ukiah Cycle Center (KTM) 1420 S State 707.463.2424 2
Lost Coast Motorcycles of Ukiah (SUZ/YAM) 1125 S State 707.462.5160 3
Buell HD of Ukiah (BUE/HD) 2501 N State 707.462.1672 4
200 S. School 707.462.4705
Redwood Hwy.
LOUGHLIN RANGE
Ridgewood Summit (1953ft/595m)
Tomki Rd.
Vic's Place 707.485.8422
Little Bakers Market
Redwood Valley Station
Eel River Rd.
MIDDLE MTN.
M8
2 km
2 miles
LITTLE ROUND MTN.
39°20'
HORSE MTN.
18N01
East Rd.
Redwood Valley
Vichy Hot Springs Resort 707.462.9515
Porter Valley Rd.
Le Trianon Resort CG 707.275.2262
To Mendocino & DH29 via DH29TE-H
Ky-En CG
Narrows Resort CG 707.275.2718
Pine Acres Resort CG 707.275.2811
Bu-Shay CG
Calpella
555
Lake Mendocino
Club Calpella 707.485.8630
Superette SM
Orr Springs Rd.
DH22 TE-A
To Clear Lake & DH46 Pg. 83
Che-Ka-Ka BCG
COW MTN.
39°10'
Boonville Lodge 707.895.3823
Boonville Hotel 707.895.2210
Lumberjack Pizza 707.895.2480
Horn of Zee Café 707.895.3525
Redwood Café Drive-In
Anderson Valley Mkt SM
Talmage Rd.
Jepson's 707.468.8936
WHITE ROCK MTN.
LOOKOUT PEAK
Ukiah
PINE RIDGE
Robinson Creek
Mill Creek Rd.
Talmage
Scotts Valley Rd.
DH24 TE-B
Scotts Creek
Hendricks Rd.
DH24 TE-A
Philo
Anderson Creek Inn 707.895.3091
DH22
253
Ukiah Boonville Rd.
East Side Rd.
Scotts Creek Rd.
MAYACMAS MTNS.
LAKE MENDOCINO
ANDERSON VALLEY
To Albion & DH29 Via DH29TE-G
Boonville
Mendocino Brewing Co 707.744.1361
Keg 707.744.1070
Petro America
Graziano 707.744.8466
McDowell Valley 707.744.1774
39°00'
Mountain View Rd.
Rancheria Creek
GRIZZLY PEAK
Old Hopland
Hopland
175
DH24
To Lakeport To Kelseyville & DH53 Pg. 73
To Manchester & mid-DH29
DH29 TE-E
Anderson Valley Brewing Co
Linda Vista B&B 707.894.2591
DUNCAN PEAK
Old Toll Rd.
Mtn. House Rd.
CR 111
101
Meyer 707.895.2341
Cummiskey Cr.
RUSSIAN RIVER
128
WARD MTN.
Maple Creek 707.895.3001
Yorkville
DH27
TE-A
BIG FOOT MTN.
Pieta Cr.
Philo Pottery Inn B&B 707.895.3069
Anderson Valley Inn 707.895.3325
Libby's Rest 707.895.2646
Philo Mkt
Scharffenberger 707.895.2070
Pacific Echo 707.895.2065
76
Yorkville 707.894.9177
Lalanne 415.469.8684
Yorkville Mini-Market & Deli
MENDOCINO SONOMA
Big Sulphur Creek
Cloverdale
MENDOCINO SONOMA
BLACK MTN.
Ruth McGowan's Brew Pub 707.894.9610
KOA 707.894.3337
105 N Cloverdale 707.894.0818
To Healdsburg & DH10
DH10 TE-C
Theresa Dr.
123°10'
123°00'

DH27 Cloverdale – Boonville

Highway 128

Distance:	26.0 mi / 41.8 km	Traffic:	Light

At a Glance

Back in the early 1900s, Boonville residents invented their own language to baffle outsiders. With its originators gradually dying off, the old dialect is *pikin' to the dusties* as they say. Fortunately, this twisty, smoothly paved and generally well-engineered ride that esses through the woods up and down from the scenic Yorkville Highlands vineyards and then sweeps across a farming flat is a *deep moshe with much bahlness* (a great ride) in any language. Traffic's never too bad on this DH, even on summer weekends when bright-lightners come up from the Bay Area *deekin' on frattey nooks* (looking for wine tasting rooms). Back in the day, got so Boontling was used so often, local folks forgot how to speak English altogether. Just imagine – a whole town full of motorcycle mechanics.

TIRES	
Twistiness	29.2/ 30
Pavement	16.3/ 20
Engineering	5.9/ 10
Remoteness	3.7/ 10
Scenery	9.7/ 15
Character	9.0/ 15
Total	**73.8**

Access

From Cloverdale

On Hwy 101

Turn off onto Hwy 128 and follow the signs to Ft Bragg and Boonville. When N Cloverdale Blvd splits off south, you're on the road.

Via Cloverdale Blvd

Take N Cloverdale Blvd north from the city center. Turn left onto Hwy 128. You're on the road.

From Boonville

Coming in on DH22 Ukiah – Boonville (Hwy 253)

Turn left onto Hwy 128. You're on the road.

On The Road

Leaving Cloverdale, the DH treks westward through the shallow, brown hills of the Oat Valley. It's not particularly remote at first, with houses and vineyards about but it's still pretty, especially when large oaks create a canopy over the road at 1.3 mi (2.1 km). The valley is short and narrows quickly. At 2.3 mi (3.7 km), you feel your own oats as the nicely paved road starts essing and climbing into the hills.

It's getting tighter. That was a 15-mph (25-kmh) curve there. It triggers a steeper S-curving climb up the tree-lined ridge. While your views are largely restricted by the multitude of roadside oaks, it's feeling much more remote up here. Only the occasional mailbox reminds you to keep an eye out for intermittent driveways.

At 4.7 mi (7.6 km), the terrain flattens out and the road enters Mendocino County. It's level enough in this high valley to create room for some vineyards. Yorkville Highlands Appellation, it turns out. It seems they grow deer as well as grapes around here – a sign warns you to look out for them for the next 35 miles (55 km).

But the next sign's a better one, advising of twisties for the next six miles. Not that they've ever really stopped. It's just that at 5.3 mi (8.5 km), they ess and tighten up again coming down off the highlands along a slope covered by small trees. "Slower Vehicles Must Pull Over," proclaims a third sign. Yes, Mr. and Mrs. Pylon, that means you.

The road rises again briefly at 6.4 mi (10.3 km) and enters another high plain. No worries, there are far more esses to come. So you might want to think twice before bailing out to Hopland via Mountain House Rd (**TE-A**) at 7.1 mi (11.4 km). Unless you're hankering for a barley sandwich.

The DH undulates as it descends. Going down, it's an unusual scene. The terrain rolls like a green coverlet knotted with clumps of trees. The road nestles into its folds. It all makes you want to snuggle up with the S-curves.

The valley opens up, exposing grassy sections on both sides of the road at 9.9 mi (16.0 km). Dry Creek is visible, running to the right alongside the treed slope. With the easing of the terrain comes the inevitable loosening of the curves. They tighten up at little more at 10.7 mi (17.2 km), but only briefly. At 11.1 mi (17.9 km), the road itself widens, smoothes and straightens. There's some minor shifting in direction going on but nothing that requires shifting gears.

Even with the straightness, the road still holds your interest. The scenery is compelling enough at first, particularly with the creek in view. But it's not long before the increasing number of houses and farms, not to mention lack of curves starts to get a little old. Almost as old as the shacks in the one-store town of Yorkville at 14.2 mi (22.8 km).

TOUR NOTE: Might be a good time to stop for a tasting at the Yorkville Cellars at 15.1 mi (24.3 km). Best bets are the Semillon or the Malbec.

The road climbs beyond Yorkville and starts to drift from side to side. Then it drops again, narrowing at the same time. You cross and run briefly beside a creek at 16.4 mi (26.4 km) – all telltale signs that curves are on the way. However, at 17.3 mi (27.8 km)… you come across a scrap heap, a vineyard and a flat field full of cows.

Don't despair. The terrain slopes a little and you climb again. There's a curve at 17.9 mi (28.8 km) and an actual S-curve at 18.5 mi (29.8 km). More follow. Not lots, mind you. But as a thirsty traveler in a desert, you'll gulp down anything that comes your way.

At 20.5 mi (33.0), you're high enough again to get some wider views of the surrounding rolling hills. You pass through another vineyard valley that brings a resumption in straightness. But then, at 22.8 mi (36.7 km) the left side drops off and opens a view over Rancheria Creek. The steeper side slope delivers some curves and at 23.7 mi (38.1 km), you descend down an eight-per cent grade. Steep grades and tight corners drop through a grassy brown landscape clustered with oaks. Just like old times.

At 25.0 mi (40.2 km), the good times end as the pavement smoothes and straightens again, this time onto a broad plain. The DH ends at the junction with **DH22 Boonville – Ukiah** at 26.0 mi (41.8 km).

Twisted Edges

TE-A Mountain House Rd (C 111) (9.1 mi / 4.7 km)
Not as well paved as the DH, this remote side trip to Hopland passes through a variable landscape of oak forests, open fields and rolling hills. Lots of challenging curves on the southern part. Not so many to the north. The only pylon was a killer UPS truck.

Rider's Log: **Date Ridden:** **Your Rating:** /10

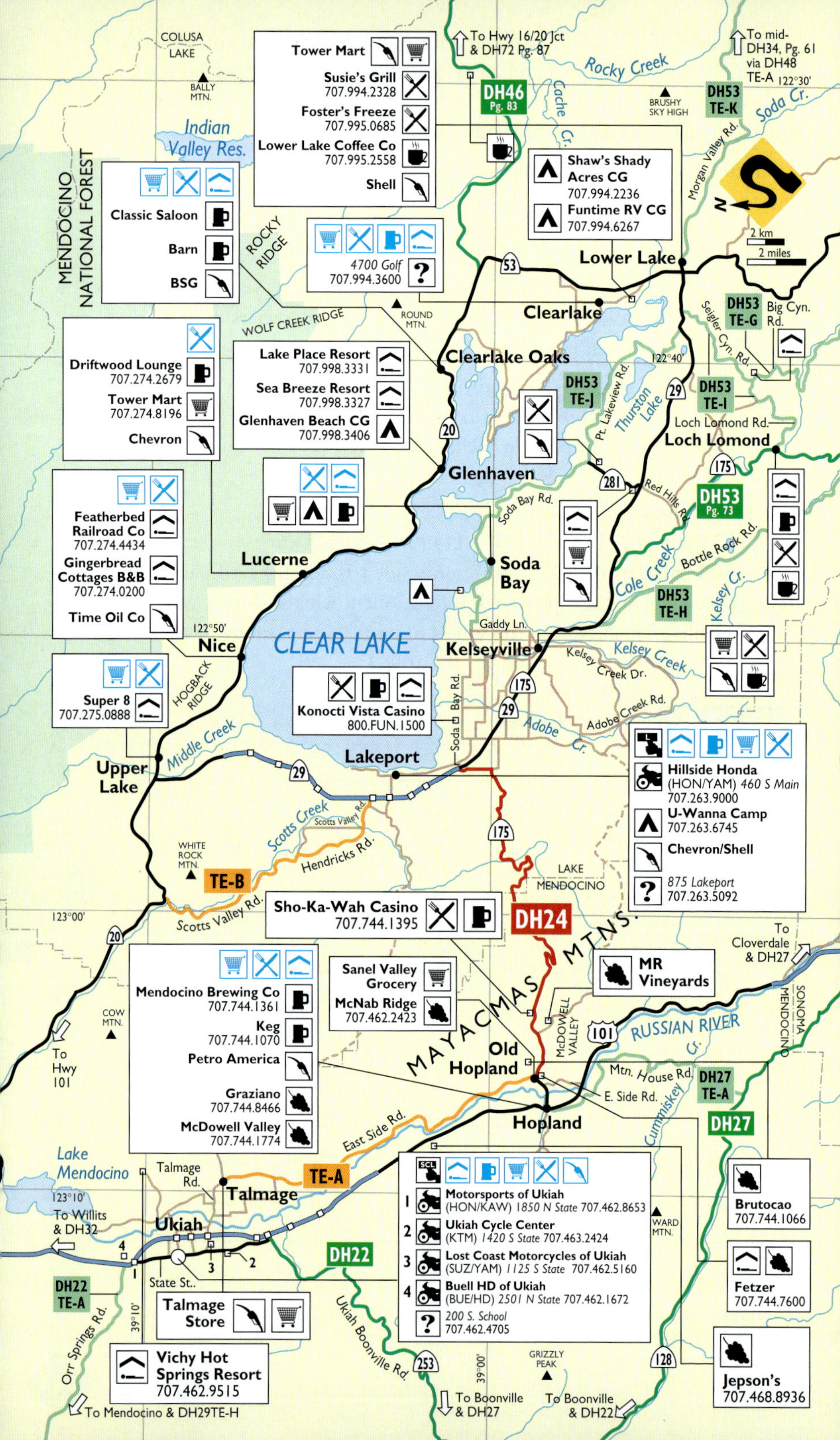

COLUSA LAKE
BALLY MTN.
Indian Valley Res.
MENDOCINO NATIONAL FOREST
Tower Mart
Susie's Grill 707.994.2328
Foster's Freeze 707.995.0685
Lower Lake Coffee Co 707.995.2558
Shell
To Hwy 16/20 Jct & DH72 Pg. 87
DH46 Pg. 83
Rocky Creek
Cache Cr.
BRUSHY SKY HIGH
DH53 TE-K
To mid-DH34, Pg. 61 via DH48 TE-A
122°30'
Soda Cr.
Morgan Valley Rd.
Shaw's Shady Acres CG 707.994.2236
Funtime RV CG 707.994.6267
2 km
2 miles
N
Classic Saloon
Barn
BSG
ROCKY RIDGE
4700 Golf 707.994.3600
53
Lower Lake
Clearlake
ROUND MTN.
WOLF CREEK RIDGE
DH53 TE-G
Big Cyn. Rd.
Seigler Cyn. Rd.
Driftwood Lounge 707.274.2679
Tower Mart 707.274.8196
Chevron
Lake Place Resort 707.998.3331
Sea Breeze Resort 707.998.3327
Glenhaven Beach CG 707.998.3406
Clearlake Oaks
DH53 TE-J
Pt. Lakeview Rd.
Thurston Lake
122°40'
29
DH53 TE-I
Loch Lomond Rd.
Loch Lomond
20
Glenhaven
281
175
Red Hills Rd.
DH53 Pg. 73
Soda Bay Rd.
Featherbed Railroad Co 707.274.4434
Gingerbread Cottages B&B 707.274.0200
Time Oil Co
Lucerne
Soda Bay
Cole Creek
Bottle Rock Rd.
DH53 TE-H
Kelsey Cr.
122°50'
Nice
CLEAR LAKE
Gaddy Ln.
Kelseyville
Kelsey Creek Dr.
Kelsey Creek
HOGBACK RIDGE
Super 8 707.275.0888
Konocti Vista Casino 800.FUN.1500
Soda Bay Rd.
175
29
Adobe Creek Rd.
Adobe Cr.
Middle Creek
Upper Lake
29
Lakeport
Hillside Honda (HON/YAM) 460 S Main 707.263.9000
U-Wanna Camp 707.263.6745
Chevron/Shell
875 Lakeport 707.263.5092
Scotts Creek
Scotts Valley Rd.
175
Hendricks Rd.
WHITE ROCK MTN.
TE-B
LAKE MENDOCINO
Scotts Valley Rd.
Sho-Ka-Wah Casino 707.744.1395
DH24
123°00'
20
MAYACMAS MTNS.
To Cloverdale & DH27
Mendocino Brewing Co 707.744.1361
Keg 707.744.1070
Petro America
Graziano 707.744.8466
McDowell Valley 707.744.1774
Sanel Valley Grocery
McNab Ridge 707.462.2423
MR Vineyards
SONOMA
MENDOCINO
COW MTN.
To Hwy 101
McDOWELL VALLEY
101
RUSSIAN RIVER
Old Hopland
Mtn. House Rd.
DH27 TE-A
E. Side Rd.
Cummiskey Cr.
Hopland
DH27
East Side Rd.
Lake Mendocino
Talmage Rd.
TE-A
Talmage
123°10'
To Willits & DH32
Ukiah
Motorsports of Ukiah (HON/KAW) 1850 N State 707.462.8653
Ukiah Cycle Center (KTM) 1420 S State 707.463.2424
Lost Coast Motorcycles of Ukiah (SUZ/YAM) 1125 S State 707.462.5160
Buell HD of Ukiah (BUE/HD) 2501 N State 707.462.1672
200 S. School 707.462.4705
WARD MTN.
Brutocao 707.744.1066
Fetzer 707.744.7600
DH22
State St.
DH22 TE-A
Talmage Store
39°10'
Orr Springs Rd.
Vichy Hot Springs Resort 707.462.9515
Ukiah Boonville Rd.
253
39°00'
GRIZZLY PEAK
128
Jepson's 707.468.8936
To Mendocino & DH29TE-H
To Boonville & DH27
To Boonville & DH22

DH24 Old Hopland – Lakeport

Highway 175

Distance:	16.5 mi / 26.6 km	Traffic:	Light

At a Glance

So, what's on tap out of ol' Hopland? Sure, the Mendocino Brewing Company can offer you specialties like Red Tail, Blue Heron, or Eye of the Hawk. But no microbrewery could produce the kind of crisp, clean, full-bodied flavor you'll find on this refreshing section of Hwy 175. This balanced mixture of yeasty Twistiness, hopped-up Scenery and often unfiltered Remoteness, this DH starts curving almost from the start, shifting past some vineyards in the Sanel Valley and climbing into the lush Mayacmas Mtns, where almost the entirety of the ride takes place. The newer asphalt, fine sightlines and cambered corners give this ride a smoothly paved and engineered finish, despite the steepness of the grade and tightness of the turns. And as long as you make them all, you won't be left with any bad aftertaste. Try a sip of this fine brew. You'll want to drink the whole pitcher.

TIRES	
Twistiness	30.0/30
Pavement	15.9/20
Engineering	4.8/10
Remoteness	6.2/10
Scenery	10.9/15
Character	8.2/15
Total	**76.0**

Access

From Hopland

Via Hwy 175

Hopland is on Hwy 101. Old Hopland is situated 1.1 mi (1.8 km) west on Hwy 175. When you reach the east end of Old Hopland's 35-mph zone, you're on the road.

From Lakeport

Via Hwy 29

Ride south of town until Hwy 175 turns off west. Take it. You're on the road.

On The Road

Gee, a vineyard on the left. No real surprise since you're in a wide valley and you just crossed the Russian River. But what is surprising is how little time it takes this DH to traverse a couple of straights eastward across the valley floor and slip into the nearest cut in the Mayacmas Mtns. Just like that, at 1.6 mi (2.6 km), you're climbing among forest and low cliffs. And on curves.

The flurry ends at 2.5 mi (4.0 km) as you enter the McDowell Valley. A line of oaks to the right guides you straight across another piece of flatland. At 3.0 mi (4.8 km), trees line the left as well and the road narrows a touch to squeeze between them. As they do, the road begins to curve between the shortening straights. The valley ends at 4.1 mi (6.6 km) and you're once more in thick forest.

Warmed up yet? Because you don't want to blow the ascending 15-mph (25-kmh) curve at 4.4 mi (7.1 km). And that's just the beginning. You're climbing sharply and tightly now, with oaks spreading their branches across the road from the vertical bank on your left and the gully to your right. Both curves and terrain open up a little at 5.1 mi (8.2 km) when you come around a ridge, the right roadside rises and the left drops off into a wide, lush vale of trees.

Rhythmic esses repeat along the edge of the steep slope. Sightlines aren't bad at all, considering all the right-hand corners are going around red rock cliffs. Though with very few guardrails on the left, you're inclined to keep careful note of the advisories. Like that 20-mph (30-kmh) one at 6.3 mi (10.1 km). Whoa….

The views get better the higher you climb into the heart of these rugged mountains. Too bad the pavement seems to be getting gradually worse. But that changes at 7.7 mi (12.4 km) when it mysteriously improves a grade. Though it still sports those irritating troughs CalTrans digs out to install cat's eyes.

At 8.5 mi (13.7 km), you reach the top of the climb and enter Lake County. Coming over the cusp, you begin a descent down a six-per cent grade and get a tremendous, panoramic view over the Clear Lake basin to the north-south running High Valley, Wolf Creek and Rocky Ridges. But nothing looks better than the new, silky smooth blacktop that commences at 10.2 mi (16.4 km).

Not so fast. The pavement's very nice but this scenery really is something else. It's not just the breadth of the view that's attention-grabbing. The lee side of the mountains is totally covered in a sea of sage that resembles a thick film of algae. It's as if you're looking at the bottom of the ocean. And maybe that's what it once was. Though that would have been thousands of years ago. Like before fuel injection.

It's steep downhill; it's tight and it's twisty. But the superb pavement and surprisingly good engineering make it all work. The esses continue all the way down until the slope levels out and you cross the narrow bridge over Scotts Creek at 11.5 mi (18.5 km). The tightness of the corners eases, but only momentarily. Then a sharp curve around a right-side rockface at 11.9 mi (19.1 km) spirals the road upward through a rough and tumble landscape of bare and shrub-covered gullies, mounds and crevices.

More tight stuff, enhanced by a short-lived narrowing of the road at 12.9 mi (20.8 km). Pressed against the side of a cliff, the DH continues to ess relentlessly, though now the terrain has leveled out significantly. Of course, after that six-per cent grade, this should be a snap.

Oaks dripping with dried moss now line the winding road. A bit of marshland fed by Manning Creek adds a dash of bright green to the silver and sage-colored vegetation. Then, at 14.2 mi (22.8 km), you wind into a tiny canyon and cross the creek, now visible on your right. This little cut through some rock on the left and treed slope rising up to the right lasts but a moment before the terrain flattens and the creek gets slurped up by a vineyard at 14.7 mi (23.7 km).

This is one solid ride. Even when the farms and vineyards take over completely at 15.6 mi (25.1 km), it delivers its share of corners. And when the north and south horizons stretch out and you think a long straight is inevitable, the DH suddenly ends at the traffic light at the junction of Hwy 29, just south of Lakeport at 16.5 mi (26.5 km).

Another round?

Twisted Edges

TE-A Talmage (Ukiah) – Old Hopland (13.0 mi / 20.9 km) *East Side Rd*
This bumpy but tolerably paved trip through the quiet vineyards of Mendocino's Hopland Wine Region features long, sweeping 35-mph (55-kmh) turns. And pylon traffic is so light, chances are you'll have them all to yourself. Except, of course, for the other two-wheeled curve tasters.

NAVIGATION: To get to Talmage, turn off Hwy 101 onto Talmage Rd at the Talmage Exit and head east. Or, from Ukiah, turn of S. State St onto Talmage Rd (Hwy 222) and head east. Turn right at the Ten Thousand Buddhas Monastery (at least in this life).

ROUTING OPTION: After a short jog west on Hwy 175 at the TE's south end, East Side Rd continues another 1.4 mi (2.3 km) to connect with Hwy 101.

TE-B Scotts Valley Rd Part 1 - Hendricks Rd - Scotts Valley Rd Part 2 (10.2 mi / 16.4 km)
The smooth-flavored grain of SV Part 1's straight pavement is hopped up nicely by the yeastier cornering on Hendricks and more especially on the SV Part 2 section where it winds along the crystal-clear Myacmas Mountain water of Scotts Creek. Urp.

NAVIGATION: The Scotts Valley Rd exit off Hwy 29 in Lakeport is clearly marked. No matter which way you drink this one in, make sure you turn off Scotts Valley Rd and onto Hendricks Rd. It's easy to blow right by Hendricks and stay on the flat, flavorless middle part of Scotts Valley.

Rider's Log: **Date Ridden:** **Your Rating:** **/10**

To Boonville & DH22
To Hopland & DH24
DH27
KOA Cloverdale CG 707.894.3337
Dutcher Creek Village CG 230 Theresa Dr 707.894.4829
Fritz 707.894.3389
Lake Sonoma 707.473.2987
Pedroncelli 800.836.3894
Liberty Glen CG
David Caffaro 707.433.9715
Chateau Souverain 707.433.8281
Cloverdale
Geysers Rd.
Big Sulphur Creek
Ruth McGowan's Brew Pub 707.894.9610
KOA 707.894.3337
105 N Cloverdale 707.894.0818
LAKE SONOMA WILDLIFE AREA
River Rd.
Theresa Dr.
TE-C
TE-D
Dutcher Creek Rd.
RUSSIAN RIVER
Geyser Peak 707.857.9400
Big John's Mkt SM
Little Sulphur Creek
Geysers Rd.
Lake Sonoma
Rockpile Rd.
LAKE SONOMA REC. AREA
Geyserville
Canyon Rd.
Red Winery Rd.
Pine Flat Rd.
To Calistoga & DH53 Pg. 73
Las Lomas
Skaggs Springs Rd.
DH10
To mid-DH29
Pena Creek
Dry Creek
W. Dry Ck. Rd.
Alexander Valley CG 707.431.1453
Clos du Bois 707.857.1651
ALEXANDER VALLEY
Jimtown
Alexander Vly.
Alderbrook 800.405.5987 1
Mill Creek 707.431.2121 2
Armida 707.433.2222 3
De La Montanya 707.433.3711 4
Roshambo 888.525.9463 5
Rabbit Ridge 707.431.7128 6
Belvedere 800.433.8296 7
Rochioli 707.433.2305 8
Hop Kiln 707.433.6491 8
WALBRIDGE RIDGE
Teldeschi 707.433.6626
Passalacqua 877.825.5547
Seghesio 707.433.3579
Lambert Bridge Rd.
W. Dry Creek Rd.
LAGUNA WILDLIFE AREA
Jimtown Store
SodaRock Ln.
Healdsburg
TE-B
217 Healdsburg 707.433.6935
Mill St.
Davis Bynum 800.826.1073
Mill Creek Rd.
RED OAK RIDGE
Madrona Manor 800.258.4003
Westside Rd.
TE-A
Raford House B&B 800.887.9503
Farmhouse Inn B&B 800.464.6642
Santa Rosa BMW 800 American 707.838.9100
Armstrong Woods Rd.
Sweetwater Springs Rd.
Arata Rd.
Windsor
To Santa Rosa
Fort Ross Rd.
Cazadero
Ridenhour Inn B&B 707.887.1033
Porter Creek 707.433.6321
Eastside Rd.
Conde Ln.
Shiloh Rd.
Austin Creek
Cazadero Hwy.
Berry's Mkt
Hacienda
Wohler Rd.
RUSSIAN RIVER VALLEY
Trenton Healdsburg Rd.
GABES ROCK
Guerneville
Odd Fellows Rd.
RUSSIAN RIVER
River Rd.
Mark West Creek
2 km
2 miles
DH29 TE-C
Guerneville Rd.
Forestville
116
DH29 TE-A
Monte Rio
GREEN VALLEY
Vine Hill Rd.
Laguna Rd.
To Santa Rosa
To Mendocino
DH29
Jenner
Duncan Mills
DH29 TE-B
Bohemian Rd.
Green Valley Rd.
PEAKED HILL
Russian River Pub 707.887.7932
Hilton Park Family CG 707.887.9206
River Bend RV CG 707.887.7662
Graton Rd.
Graton
PACIFIC OCEAN
Occidental
DH29 TE-B ALT
Occidental Rd.
Sebastopol
12
To Santa Rosa
Coleman Valley Rd.
NON-FEATURED DH SERVICES NOT SHOWN
Santa Nella House B&B 800.440.9031
Freestone
Bodega Hwy.
To San Francisco
IRISH HILL
Salmon Creek
265 S Main 707.823.3032
To Tomales & DH37

DH10 Dry Creek Rd - Skaggs Springs Rd

Distance:	22.4 mi / 36.1 km	Traffic:	Moderate

At a Glance

TIRES	
Twistiness	26.9/ 30
Pavement	19.0/ 20
Engineering	8.6/ 10
Remoteness	5.6/ 10
Scenery	10.9/ 15
Character	9.3/ 15
Total	**80.3**

Skaggs Springs Rd, also known as Skaggs Springs International Raceway. And why is that? It sure ain't the 30-mph (50-kmh) – yes that's *30-mph!* – speed zone that yellow flags the best part. No, the nickname is the reason *why* there's a 30-mph speed zone. It's well blogged that this road is a Mecca for speed lovers and those who hunt them by land and air. But c'mon. How cynical can CalTrans get? In a sane world, this wide, seamlessly paved, perfectly banked and contoured invitation to rip would be posted at 55 mph (90 kmh). This would at least give you a fighting chance with the speed tax collectors. But no. It's only when the DH peters out and the road transforms into a horrendously bumpy and brutally engineered one-and-narrow-two-lane trail to the coast that the restrictive speed zone ends and you can legally crank it up. Sure, sure, the Lake Sonoma Rec Area's lush landscape of rolling treed mountains and valleys is nice to look at, but let's face it – that's not why you're here. So, given there's a good chance Officer Marien is waiting, there's really only one question: Who wants to go first?

Access

From Healdsburg

On March Ave/Dry Creek Rd

March Ave becomes Dry Creek Rd when it crosses Headsburg Ave. Head west on Dry Creek under Hwy 101 (at Exit 505), then north out of town. When you hit the 50-mph zone, you're on the road.

From mid-DH29 Jenner – Albion (Mendocino) (Hwy 1)

Turn onto Annapolis Rd, just north of the Sea Ranch Resort. Ride 30.8 mi (49.6 km) of rough, often-one-lane pavement and then you're on the DH. Nothing ever felt so good.

On The Road

So what's the big deal, anyway? All you see at first are a few easy wide-shouldered, smoothly paved sweepers on an otherwise straight road drifting through the Dry Creek Valley vineyards outside Healdsburg. And perhaps some pretty views of Pritchett Peaks to the north as you approach the stop-signed junction for Lambert Bridge Rd (**TE-B**) at 6.0 mi (9.7 km). Just be patient. Carry on past Dutcher Creek Rd (**TE-C**) at 7.3 mi (11.7 km) and cross the creek at 8.8 mi (14.2 km).

The first long, perfectly paved and engineered sweeper comes at 9.4 mi (15.1 km). It's followed immediately by a 35-mph (55-kmh) speed sign and a steady climb through a broad V-cut. Watch for the painted turn left lane at 10.8 mi (17.4 km) for Skaggs Springs Rd. Definitely **go left**.

Great, now the speed limit's posted at 30 mph (50 kmh). Like, can your bike even go that slow? At least the marina turnoff at 11.4 mi (18.3 km) is the last side road you'll see for a while. In fact, all you're going to see are amazing curves and fantastic overlooks as the road continues to climb through mountainous terrain, along the northwest side of a ridge. Lake Sonoma's shoreline is visible far below.

You don't get more than glimpses of the lake, though at times you're witness to a literal sea of trees. But who cares? There are better things to look at here than scenery. Like flawless pavement and predictable lines. Roads like this are why sportbikes are made. But just when you may be hoping that speed limit sign you saw was the local Vintage Motorcycle Club's idea of a joke, there's another one at 12.0 mi (19.3 km). Painted on the road and easily visible from an altitude of 3000 feet.

You've probably never seen so many ridiculous speed signs. It's so absurd they've got to keep reminding you so you don't think you're hallucinating. Just for fun, try telling the STC you missed them. Maybe he'll laugh.

The road has the feel of one of those long climbs that's going to continue indefinitely. So it's a bit of a surprise at 13.1 mi (21.1 km) when you dive suddenly and steeply below the face of Walbridge Ridge. There's a vista off to the right over the Lake Sonoma Recreation and Wildlife Areas at 13.6 mi (21.9 km). Not a bad place to stop on the return trip. Assuming you're doing the sane thing and doubling back once the DH turns to crap further on.

The up and down along here creates magnificent views over the valley to your right. And the back and forth creates magnificent S-curves at the same time. You move onto the far side of a ridge and a couple of deep sweepers dip you southward, then back north again. But even with the long, tight curves, the engineering is incredible.

At 16.8 mi (27.0 km), you ess onto the top of a ridge and enter the shortest of straights. There are amazing panoramas either side as vibrant oaks cluster on the undulating, park-like landscape. At 18.7 mi (30.1 km), you drop back down onto the north side of the ridge and wind downward along a 45-degree bank. At 19.7 mi (31.7 km) the speed limit leaps to a blazing 40 mph (60 kmh). What, is it turning into a four-lane divided highway or something?

Actually, it means the great corners have become merely good. But with the continuing great pavement and engineering, the lack of tightness is simply a matter of making some basic throttle adjustments. Like… that.

A steep descent at 21.2 mi (34.1 km) takes you down and over a high bridge. Off the crossing and rising up, there's a rare stretch when you're actually on the center of your tire. No worries – it lasts but a moment and you're back on your rims. But hold on. Seems it's time to worry after all. That's because, like a prince turning into a toad, the road suddenly narrows, the center paint disappears and the pavement starts to upchuck. The DH ends as the speed limit is lifted, at 22.4 mi (36.1 km).

ROUTING OPTION: Yes, you can carry on and ride Stewarts Point-Skaggs Springs Rd all the way to the coast. It's a pretty bumpy, grueling ride for 17.1 mi (27.5 km) until you turn right over the one-lane bridge and take the better-paved and engineered, two-lane Annapolis Rd the rest of the way. Total distance from the DH: 53.2 mi (85.6 km).

Twisted Edges

TE-A Hacienda – Healdsburg (12.4 mi / 20.0 km) *Westside Rd*
Most maps show this TE to be equivalent to River Rd, from which it splits. But unlike that busy, straight piece of pavement, this minor route curves tightly and quietly just into the trees above the Russian River before turning north, straightening out and wandering among more wineries and vineyards.

NAVIGATION: There is direct access from Hwy 101 only if you are coming from the north. If you're on 101 from the south, take the previous exit (502), head into Healdsburg and turn west on Mill St under 101 where Mill is renamed Westside.

TE-B West Dry Creek Rd - Lambert Bridge Rd (5.6 mi / 9.0 km)
Mostly straight but lots of grapes. Almost exactly the same as the northern part of **TE-A**. Another option to help you mix and match this area's riding.

TE-C Dutcher Creek Rd (4.1 mi / 6.6 km)
It's straightish with excellent pavement, much like the Dry Creek Rd part of the DH. Done together, both roads make a good Hwy 101 avoidance route.

NAVIGATION: The TE starts south of Cloverdale at the Hwy 101 exit for Theresa Dr/Dry Creek Rd. A non-TE part of Dry Creek also extends south along 101 from downtown Cloverdale's main drag (South Cloverdale Blvd).

TE-D Red Winery Rd - Geysers Rd (15.4 mi / 24.8 km)
Prepare yourself. The gush of smooth, though poorly maintained pavement and engineering that explodes off Red Winery Rd turns into a one-lane dribble when the TE ends at the geothermal plant. But, up to that point, this panoramic climb out of the Alexander Valley is the best traffic-free motorcycling escape around.

Rider's Log: **Date Ridden:** **Your Rating:** /10

Find more information about camping in Northern California, including how to make a reservation, in the "Touring Northern California – What You Should Know" section at the front of the book.

WILD RIVER
Pg. 183
REDWOODS
RUSSIAN COAST
Pg. 91
WINE COUNTRY
PACIFIC OCEAN
INTER-MOUNTAIN
CVA I
CVA II
CVA III
Crescent City
Klamath
Orick
McKinleyville
Arcata
Eureka
Ferndale
Fortuna
Carlotta
Rio Dell
Bridgeville
Weott
Phillipsville
Redway
Garberville
Shelter Cove
Leggett
Covelo
Laytonville
Longvale Jct
Cleone
Fort Bragg
Willits
Mendocino
Albion
Navarro
Elk
Ukiah
Happy Camp
Somes Bar
Willow Creek
Weaverville
Douglas City
Hyampom
Hayfork
Mad River
Triangle Junction
Yreka
Weed
Shasta
Redding
Anderson
Red Bluff
Corning
Orland
Willows
DH20
DH50
DH23
DH12
DH2
DH18
DH31
DH13
DH33
DH44
DH6
DH36
DH66
DH64
DH11
DH15
DH5
DH32
1C01
A16
A9
10 km
10 miles
(D-SUZ)
(D-BUE/HD)
(D-HON/YAM)
(D-KAW/KTM/SUZ)
(D-HD)
(D-HON/KAW/VIC)
(D-KTM/SUZ)
(D-YAM)
(D-KAW/SUZ)
(D-BUE/HD)
(D-HON/KAW)
(D-KTM)
(D-SUZ/YAM)
(D-HON/YAM)

Redwoods

RANK DH#/74	TIRES Total/100	DESTINATION HIGHWAY	PAGE
DH66	60.6	Avenue of the Giants 31.6 mi / 50.9 km	145
DH64	61.2	Lost Coast 66.6 mi / 107.2 km	151
DH6	82.2	Carlotta (Fortuna) – Triangle Jct 65.3 mi / 105.1 km	157
DH36	70.8	Mad River Loop 44.3 mi / 71.3 km	163
DH11	79.6	Triangle Jct – Red Bluff 65.3 mi / 105.1 km	169
DH33	71.7	Shasta (Redding) – Douglas City (Weaverville) 31.9 mi / 51.3 km	175
DH44	67.5	Triangle Jct – Douglas City (Weaverville) 35.3 mi / 56.8 km	179

To Eureka, Arcata & DH31 Pg. 201
To Ferndale & DH64
Grizzly Bluff Rd.
Hydesville
Carlotta
Murrish's Mkt
For detail see DH64
Van Dusen River
Brentville
DH64 TE-A
Blueside Rd.
Rio Dell
Scotia
Stafford RV CG 707.764.3416
Scotia Inn 707.764.5683
Hoby's Deli Mkt
MT. PIERCE
CHALK MTN.
DH6
Bridgeville
To Triangle Jct. & DH11/44
McCLELLAN MTN.
LARABEE BUTTES
Pepperwood
Immortal Tree
Avenue of the Giants
Redcrest
Redcrest Resort Cabins/CG 707.722.4208
Eternal Tree Café 707.722.4247
Redcrest Grocery 707.722.4291
3 km
3 miles
Eel River
BEAR RIVER RIDGE
Dyerville Loop Rd.
Miranda Gardens Cottages 707.943.3011
Redwood Palace 707.943.3037
Miranda Café 707.943.9945
Miranda Mkt SM
Alderpoint Rd.
THE PEAKS
To Garberville To mid-DH36
HUMBOLDT REDWOODS STATE PARK
40°20'
Mattole Rd.
DH64
Burlington SP CG
Weott
Founder's Grove Nature Trail
707.946.2409
Avenue of the Giants
Mama Sue's Store
Living Chimney Tree Café 707.923.2265
CATHEYS PEAK
Williams Grove
Elk Crk. Rd.
MATTOLE RIVER
Honeydew
To Ferndale
Trading Post Saloon
Myers Flat Mkt SM
Giant Redwoods RV CG 707.943.3198
DH66
Myers Flat
Salmon Creek
Miranda
Dean Creek Resort/CG 707.923.2555
Phillipsville
101
Wilder Ridge Rd.
Madrona Motor Court 707.943.1708
Riverwood Inn 707.943.1766
Deerhorn Mkt
40°10'
Brass Rail Steakhouse 707.923.3188
Shopmart SM
Shell
Dazey's MS (YAM) 591 Briceland 707.923.4332
Redway Inn Motel 707.923.2660
KING NATIONAL CONSERVATION AREA
Horse Mtn. Rd.
Horse Mtn BCG
Tolkan BCG
Sentry Mkt SM
784 Redwood 707.923.2613
Briceland Thorn Rd.
Redway
Redwood Dr.
Alderpoint Rd.
Briceland Rd.
Garberville
To mid-DH6 To mid-DH36
TE-A
Shelter Cove Rd.
Benbow
Benbow Inn 800.355.3301 Recommended
Benbow Rd.
Benbow Lake SRA CG 707.923.3238
Shelter Cove
Chemise Mtn. Rd.
124°10'
40°00'
Mario's Marina 707.986.7595
Lighthouse Inn 707.465.4778
Beachcomber Inn 707.986.7551
Shelter Cove GS
Chartroom 707.986.9696
Shelter Park RV CG 707.986.7474
Richardson Grove SP CG
French's Camp
123°50'
431
435
Richardson Grove RV CG 707.247.3380
Redwood Family Camp CG 707.247.3380
76
124°00'
To mid-DH5 Pg. 115 via 20 mi (32km) gravel
To Leggett & DH5 Pg. 115
36
101
40°30'

DH66 Avenue of the Giants

Distance:	31.6 mi / 50.9 km	Traffic:	Moderate

At a Glance

TIRES	
Twistiness	19.7/30
Pavement	16.0/20
Engineering	5.6/10
Remoteness	3.7/10
Scenery	10.5/15
Character	5.1/15
Total	**60.6**

Forget about Willie McCovey, Willie Mays or Barry Bonds. The Tall, Giant and Founders Trees are just some of the MVPs you'll see on this steadily winding, Hwy 101 crisscross through Humboldt Redwoods State Park. Unfortunately, these evergreens on steroids attract so many tourists, concessions and souvenir stands, it can sometimes feel like you're on the concourse at Pacific Bell Park. Though the Pavement is major league pretty much all the way, Engineering only bats about .500 on this road, its average brought down by some of the tighter turns and lack of shoulders in the taller-treed sections. Of course, if you've just come off DH64 Lost Coast, the P & E here will feel so great, you might start thinking the Giants can't be beat. Then again, that's what everyone thought back in '02.

Access

NOTE: There are several access points from Hwy 101 along this DH. The DH stretches between the northern and southernmost of them.

From Hwy 101 (North Access)

Take the Pepperwood Exit. You're on the road.

From Hwy 101 (South Access)

Leave the freeway two exits north of Garberville. You're on the road.

From DH64 Lost Coast

The southern end of **DH64** junctions with the middle of **DH66** at the Honeydew Exit of Hwy 101.

On The Road

You enter Humboldt Redwoods State Park as soon as you leave Hwy 101 at the Avenue's northern end and are subsumed beneath a canopy of redwoods. Traffic's at its lightest here on the DH's least busy segment. Unfortunately, curves are at their lightest too, as brief straightaways jut east, then south, to incorporate the mapdot of Pepperwood.

At 2.0 mi (3.4 km), you pass the first of many spurs back to the freeway. Unfortunately, as you continue south, these access points will add more traffic than they'll take away. But for now, it should still be relatively peaceful as you cross Bear Creek and get a view eastward through a gap in the ever-taller trees to the mountains across the Eel River.

It seems the taller the trees, the better the curves on this DH. Perhaps that's because even in America, you're not going to chop down a 2000-year-old redwood to make way for a road that's being put in for the purpose of viewing those same redwoods. As a result, the pavement curves around the trees. The way nature intended.

And it doesn't hurt that these sexy little sections, such as the one beginning at 4.3 mi (6.9 km), tend to coincide with newer pavement. This burst of corners leads to something called the Immortal Tree, so named for its tendency to survive fire, lightning and flood. You pass its obligatory gift shop at 5.0 mi (8.0 km) and a straight section gives you a chance to admire any kitsch you've just attached to your instrument display before a few short S-curves guide you to the settlement of Redcrest, site of something called the Eternal Tree – a stump with 3500 rings – at 6.6 mi (10.6 km).

You continue south past another 101 access point, enduring the rather incongruous sight of a sawmill by the road before you commune again with the trees at 7.1 mi (11.4 km). Here, you're treated to a chain of sweeping and essing curves followed by a section of monster trees. This in turn is followed by another short essy section at 9.3 mi (15.0 km) before the road opens up again along the broad Eel. Then it's a straight shot to the first Hwy 101 access point and the southern junction with **DH64 Lost Coast**.

*TOUR NOTE: Even if you're intimidated by the thought of riding **DH64**, you can see one of the best, accessible, remaining stands of old redwoods by taking a short detour west on the first part of it. The narrow, 5.3 mi (8.5 km) trail through part of Founders Grove is pure magic. If you're prepared to actually get off your bike, you can turn east onto Dyerville Loop Rd and check out the Founders Grove Nature Trail.*

Continuing south, you bridge the Eel River and pass through another tall treed section that abuts either side of a Hwy 101 crossing. Not a lot of curves to check your speed, but you're too busy gawking to be cracking it too hard through here anyway.

At 12.9 mi (20.8 km), the forest parts to offer a view over the river before you re-enter the now-not-so tall redwoods. Weott, another small settlement with Hwy 101 access, interrupts the flow at 13.2 mi (22.2 km). South of that, a solid curvy section above the river takes you as far as the large Burlington campground.

More big trees at 15.3 mi (24.6 km). That's becoming a mantra on this road. But they rarely coincide with any curves. One exception is the section beginning at 16.2 mi (26.1 km) when giants and twisties come together for a shining moment. Not atypically, the promising leans quickly deteriorate into what can best be described as "minor wavering." It is pretty in here, though. Your passenger will like it.

At 18.1 mi (29.1 km), you pass Williams Grove trails/day use area, another of the Avenue's destinations. Or maybe you'd prefer the drive-thru tree in the berglet of Myers at 18.8 mi (30.3 km). The latter is partnered with the inevitable gift emporium. But at least the Trading Post Saloon is right next door.

At the far end of Myers, you pass under a Hwy 101 exchange and switch to the other side of the highway. There are a few curves through some medium-height woods but the road straightens when the view opens up along the river. Then, at 21.8 mi (35.1 km), with the fine pavement still lingering, the esses come. This combination of S-curves and asphalt are still present at 23.5 mi (37.8 km) when the big fellahs return. The road drops low down toward the river in here, creating a feeling of pure biking synchronicity.

You reach yet another settlement at 24.9 mi (40.1 km). In Miranda, you have the right to stop at a couple of restaurants, a market, a gas station and some cottages. If you can't afford to stop, some long curves over the river south of town will be appointed for you.

There's another freeway access point across from the glassblowing joint at 26.8 mi (43.1 km). No big trees south of here but there are some wide sweepers, some of which actually ess together. There's also less traffic on this leg to Phillipsville, the DH's final town, where you arrive at 28.9 mi (46.5 km).

The long, open sweepers continue along the river south of Phillipsville. Not many tourist attractions here, with the possible exception of the hollow "Living Chimney Tree". You pass the tree and attendant coffee shop at 30.9 mi (49.7 km), just before the DH ends at the exit ramp from Hwy 101, at 31.6 mi (50.9 km).

ROUTING OPTION: If you're heading to or from Garberville, little Benbow Rd south of Benbow offers a tiny postcard version of the DH. Short but fun with just a touch of gravel where the road slid away into the water. Easy river access for you, too.

Twisted Edges

TE-A Redway – Shelter Bay (19.4 mi / 31.2 km) *Briceland Thorn Rd - Shelter Cove Rd*

Shelter Bay posts a phone number to call in case of RV crashes. And you can see why. After starting nicely through some tall redwoods and then essing in a long series of moderate curves and sweepers through mixed woods along Redwood Creek, this TE gets bumpy and narrow as it contorts steeply, though scenically, down to Shelter Bay.

RIDER'S LOG: **DATE RIDDEN:** **YOUR RATING:** /10

Remember, you'll find video clips of all of Northern California's DHs at destination highways.com.

Samoa Boat Launch SP CG
Eureka
Humboldt Bay
To Arcata & DH31 Pg. 201
Old Arcata Rd.
Jacoby Creek
Fickle Hill Rd.
FICKLE HILL
MAD RIVER
MapleCreek Rd.
Eureka Motorsports (KAW/KTM/SUZ) 1601 Broadway 707.445.3093
Redwood Buell (BUE/HD) 21 West 4th St. 707.444.0111
Richard Miller Motorcycles (HON/YAM) 1725 Tomlinson 707.443.8031
2112 Broadway 707.442.3738
LCS
Victorian Inn 707.786.4949
Palace Saloon 707.786.4165
Curley's Bar & Grill 707.786.9696
Valley Grocery SM
Restaurant Matias 707.786.4648
Tipple Motors
Humboldt Gables Motel 707.764.5609
Mingo's Sports Bar
Corner Market SM
Pizza Factory 707.764.2233
DJ's Burger Bar 707.764.2924
Ruby's Coffee Shop
Shell
124°00'
40°40'
101
N
3 km
3 miles
Fortuna
Eel River
Centerville Rd.
Ferndale
TE-A
Grizzly Bluff Rd.
BEAR
Price Creek
RIVER
Oil Creek
Murrish's Mkt
L/S
735 14th St 707.725.3959
Hydesville
Carlotta
Van Dusen River
Brentville
DH6
36
Blueslide Rd.
Rio Dell
Scotia
40°30'
PACIFIC OCEAN
Rd.
Mattole
Bear River
Cape Mendocino
CAPE
Scotia Inn 707.764.5683
Hoby's Deli Mkt
101
RIDGE
To Triangle Jct & DH11/44
DH66
Pepperwood
Avenue of the Giants
CHALK MTN.
Stafford RV CG 707.764.3416
MT. PIERCE
Redcrest
BEAR RIVER RIDGE
Eel River
DH64
RIDGE
TAYLOR PEAK
RAINBOW RIDGE
THOMAS HILL
BIG HILL
HUMBOLDT
Albee Creek
REDWOODS
GRASSHOPPER MTN.
STATE PARK
40°20'
BUCKEYE MTN.
Petrolia
Mattole Rd.
Weott
101
To Garberville
Mattole BCG
MOORE HILL
Lighthouse Rd.
Honeydew Store 707.629.3310
A.W. Way CP CG
CATHEYS PEAK
Albee Creek SP CG
MATTOLE RIVER
Honeydew
Myers Flat
COOSKI RIDGE
Salmon Creek
Wilder Ridge Rd.
OAT HILL
Mattole River Organic Farms Country Cabins/CG 707.629.3445
Honeydew Creek BCG
40°10'
KING
KING PEAK
To Garberville (Hwy 101)
Lost Coast Lodge 707.629.3355
The Lost Inn 707.629.3394
Petrolia Store 707.629.3455
Horse Mtn BCG
Horse Mtn. Rd.
PARADISE RIDGE
S. Fork Bear Ck.
RANGE
Briceland Thorn Rd.
Briceland Rd.
DH66 TE-A
Tolkan BCG
Shelter Cove Rd.
GIBSON RIDGE
Shelter Cove
435
Abalone Point
Chemise Mtn. Rd.
124°20'
124°10'
124°00'
To mid-DH5 Pg. 115 via 20 mi (32km) gravel

DH64 Lost Coast
Mattole Road

Distance:	66.6 mi / 107.2 km	Traffic:	Light

At a Glance

TIRES	
Twistiness	28.8/ 30
Pavement	6.2/ 20
Engineering	2.6/ 10
Remoteness	7.1/ 10
Scenery	11.1/ 15
Character	5.4/ 15
Total	**61.2**

California classic? Or a poorly paved bumpfest not worth the trouble? Admittedly, this one could go either way. But if you're a buff for coastal remoteness and don't mind when things get a little rough, this is a DH not to be missed. Coming from the south, the first five one-lane miles of this county loop provide one of the best old-growth redwood experiences you'll find anywhere. Then the road widens into a steep, tight, switchbacking section of deteriorated asphalt that travels up and over a treed ridge and down into the one-store stop of Honeydew. Engineering improves and Pavement is marginally better when the road runs through the part forest, part field and part tumbledown shack environs of the Mattole River Valley to the next lonely gas stop of Petrolia. The next segment is the most memorable despite the fact the surface quality dips again. This is where the road tumbles down to a breathtaking piece of wild, Northern California coastline. Scenically, it's most intense on the straight section that runs between the dunes and the pounding surf, but you continue to get fantastic ocean views when you rise steeply up to the barren, windswept highlands above the water. From there, you twist through a high, partly treed valley, before clambering over a last ridge and plunging steeply through thick forest down into the Victorian village of Ferndale.

Access

From Hwy 101 (Honeydew Exit)

Exit Hwy 101 and follow the sign to Honeydew. You're on the road.

From mid-DH66 Avenue of the Giants

Turn west and cross under Hwy 101 where you see the sign for Honeydew, 20.8 mi (33.5 km) from the Avenue's south end and 10.8 mi (17.4 km) from the north end. You're on the road.

From Ferndale

From downtown, head west along Ocean Ave. Look for a large, elaborate ironworked sign showing the way to Capetown and Petrolia. Turn left here. You're on the road.

On The Road

The adventure begins from the Honeydew exit of Hwy 101 where you find yourself on a dark, narrow, paved trail along Albee Creek through the enormous redwoods of Founders Grove. Though the road is not that curvy, not that well paved, horribly engineered and sports a 25-mph (35-kmh) speed limit, the chance to commune with these ancient giants – without being badgered by trinket shops – makes this section of the DH magic nonetheless. It's actually a disappointment when you see the dotted yellow line at 5.3 mi (8.5 km) and the path turns into a road.

The giants disappear, replaced by smaller redwoods dispersed across an open plain. The average-at-best pavement curves gently over the flat towards the modest mound of Grasshopper Mtn. At 7.3 mi (11.8 km), a climb commences along with some tight curves through a thicker, overhanging section of trees. The forest extends to cover the surrounding topography of Thomas Hill, Big Hill and Rainbow Ridge. Your immediate destination? Cathey's Peak.

The remote climb continues, sometimes cloistered by trees, sometimes open to views of the surrounding terrain. The switchbacks are tight and not particularly well cambered. The pavement doesn't help, going from bad to worse as you ascend. Your only relief is the patches of new asphalt the county has mercifully put down in some of the rougher spots. Why don't they just put a whole new layer of fresh hot mix down, you ask? Well, as the local sheriff at the Honeydew Store so succinctly put it, "Humboldt County doesn't have a pot to piss in."

You arrive at the top of the winding climb at 14.3 mi (23.0 km) and begin a descent. Despite the gentleness of the grade, at first it's quite essy coming off the top. At 15.1 mi (24.3 km), the thick forest opens up to reveal that you're on a grassy ridge overlooking the Mattole River Valley. The road flips over to the other side of the ridge at 19.0 mi (30.6 km). Then, you're in and out of the thick, overhanging trees, gingerly picking your way down the slope through yet more dismally paved and poorly engineered curves and switchbacks. Oh, well, at least it's curvy and there's no traffic. And the remote mountain, ridge and river valley views, more enduring the farther down you go, are marvelous.

You finally reach bottom at 22.2 mi (35.7 km) and wind toward the river, crossing it on a slatted three-quarter lane wooden trestle bridge. Assuming you dodge the errant two-by-fours that could use another nail or two, you pull into the one-store stop of Honeydew at 22.5 mi (36.2 km). "Ferndale 45" says the sign. It may feel like you've journeyed far but you're still only one third of the way there.

ROUTING OPTION: If you've had enough, you can always head south out of Honeydew on the 19.3 mi (31.0 km) Wilder Ridge Rd, which intersects with ***DH66TE-A Redway – Shelter Cove*** *just east of the nifty seaside berg of Shelter Cove. It may only have one lane but – except for the brief gravel section near Honeydew – has better pavement.*

The road is straighter as you head out through the flat fields northwest of Melon-town. The terrain roughens quickly again, though. At 23.6 mi (38.0 km), you re-enter forest and rise above the Mattole River, streaming below to your left. While the pavement is only marginally better than the descent into Honeydew, and there's the unwelcome introduction of cattle-guards, the engineering is much improved. But that's as much a testament to the lack of pitch and tight corners as to any special attention by the county to camber or shoulder width. Still, it's nice to be cruising easily along the leafy riverside at the foot of Buckeye Mtn without slamming against your tank.

The forest thins at 25.3 mi (40.7 km). Then, just beyond the small graveyard of broken-down cars, the landscape opens up to reveal a broad, burnt grass plain ringed by brown hillsides in turn dabbed with small, dark green splotches of trees. A rare, long sweeper careens the road westward through the broad valley toward the low line of Prosper Ridge.

It becomes quite scenic when the DH returns to the hills at 27.2 mi (43.8 km). The grassy shrub and low-tree-covered terrain is open enough to provide good sightlines but rugged enough to resurrect some tighter corners. You climb up into a number of thicker treed sections, but by and large, broad valley views remain. It's not as remote as it was, with the smattering of houses and ranches abutting the road. Some look lived in, some look abandoned and some, well, it's not entirely clear.

You drop down through the trees, cross some fields and arrive back at the river, crossing it via a one-lane bridge at 30.4 mi (48.9 km). On the far side, you pass the turnoff to the Mattole Camp and Retreat Center. Must be a destination for Presbyterian riders who like their pavement bumpy.

No retreat for you, however, as you press on. The trees and hills back away opening another flat section of narrow, bush-lined, toast-colored fields. At 32.8 mi (52.8 km), you pop up into another set of low, mottled hills. It's nice going up, but the section where you start coming down is another of those tightly wound, pitifully paved and engineered sections for which this DH is infamous. Fortunately, it lasts but a few curves before the corners, pavement and overall grade mellow out again.

TOUR NOTE: For a remote, oceanside camping experience, or just to check out a piece of lonely beach, take the turnoff at 36.2 mi (58.3 km) down Lighthouse Rd to the Mattole BCG. If you're not a maxburner however, be warned: more than half of the 5.0 mi (8.1 km) is gravel.

At 37.2 mi (59.9 km), you pass through the sleepy little gas stop of Petrolia, historic site of California's first commercial oil well. Seems things have gone dry, judging from the boarded up businesses. But the rolling fields are still open and some dandy sweepers steer you on a gradual rise through tawny grass. Stands of eucalyptus add a touch of green to the roadside. At 38.9 mi (62.6 km), the fields flatten out, the road straightens and the pavement even improves, if only slightly.

At 40.9 mi (78.8 km), the road starts to curve again; long, easy serpentine corners slither above a steepening gorge. It's about here you'll feel a change as the cool coastal air creeps up the hillside and into your vents. You'll see your first glimpse of the breakers foaming in along the remote stretch of coast 41.7 mi (67.1 km). Enjoy the view. It's what you came for.

You drop down toward the coast, experiencing a drop in pavement quality at 42.7 mi (68.7 km), but who cares? By now, you're immune. But there's no inoculation against the euphoria that comes with seeing a misty, wind-blown stretch of wild, untamed, rock-strewn coastline. "Drifting Sand" warns the sign as you turn north right along the low dunes. No problem. After all that crappy pavement, what's a little sand on the road?

You cross an iron bridge at 47.3 mi (76.1 km) and start to angle away from the coastline and the big, black bicuspid that marks Cape Mendocino. You cross a creek and at 48.4 mi (77.9 km), begin a steep climb inland and away from the water. The narrow two-lane asphalt is more depressing than ever as it traces a rough, zig-zag pattern along the brown, grass edge of a deep gorge to your right. If you were going the other way, you'd get a fantastic ocean panorama but even on the upward climb, the steep valley to your right makes for great viewing. Still, what's going through your mind is, I did all this bumping and grinding for that? Yes, and you might even come back.

You continue to climb the exposed ridge through the hardy shrubs and small trees that manage to grow despite the wind and salt air. The road gradually straightens and, at 50.6 mi (81.4 km), reaches the top of the ridge. From there, you descend into the Bear River Valley. The vegetation is more familiar now as redwoods start to reappear. The grade of the descent sharpens. So do some of the corners.

The terrain plateaus briefly when you cross the river at 52.2 mi (84.0 km) and straighten past a handful of farms. Then, at 52.5 mi (84.5 km), you're over a cattleguard and twisting and climbing again, U-ing back up onto another largely barren, windswept ridge that offers a last view of the sea before you flip over the top and come steeply down the other side.

Though pitched, the short descent through the equally barren, grass landscape is not as twisty as the climb up was, giving you some chances to glance over Bear River Ridge, the collection of countless peaks and crests that paw the sky to the southeast. Then, climbing yet again, at 57.0 mi (91.7 km) you enter another clump of redwoods and the tight curves resume. More high, striking views – now to west as you break back out into what feels like the Scottish Highlands at 58.4 mi (94.0 km). Where's John Loudon MacAdam when you need him?

At 58.7 mi (94.5 km), you begin the final descent into the forest. It's a gentle grade at first and a cool ocean mist lingers in the trees as you negotiate the moderate corners. Patches of decent pavement tease you, giving a false sense of security. But then the woods darken, the grade steepens and at 61.9 mi (99.6 km), the road narrows along a precarious cliff. Typical. On this road, you don't get to relax for even a minute.

ROUTING OPTION: At 60.4 mi (97.2 km), you pass a turnoff to a signed, one-lane paved road right. This part-pavement/part-gravel route crosses the Bear River Ridge and connects with Rio Dell on Hwy 101 at the south end of ***TE-A****.*

The turns get a little tighter and the slope remains steep as you continue the long drop. Great views continue through frequent breaks in the forest. Though at this point, the only break you're thinking of is the long one you're going to take in the charming town of Ferndale, where you finally arrive at 66.6 mi (107.2 km).

Twisted Edges

TE-A Ferndale – Rio Dell (11.3 mi / 18.2 km) *Grizzly Bluff Rd - Blueside Rd*

This shoulderless TE is bumpy, mostly straight and generally uninspiring as it travels east across the farming flat out of Ferndale. However, when it turns south along the leafy bluffs of the Eel River, the twistiness, pavement and scenery all improve dramatically.

NAVIGATION: From Ferndale, head west on Ocean Ave. It turns into Grizzly Bluff Rd.

From Rio Dell, head to the north end of town. Belleview Ave turns west across from the freeway on ramp and turns into Blueside Rd.

Rider's Log: **Date Ridden:** **Your Rating:** **/10**

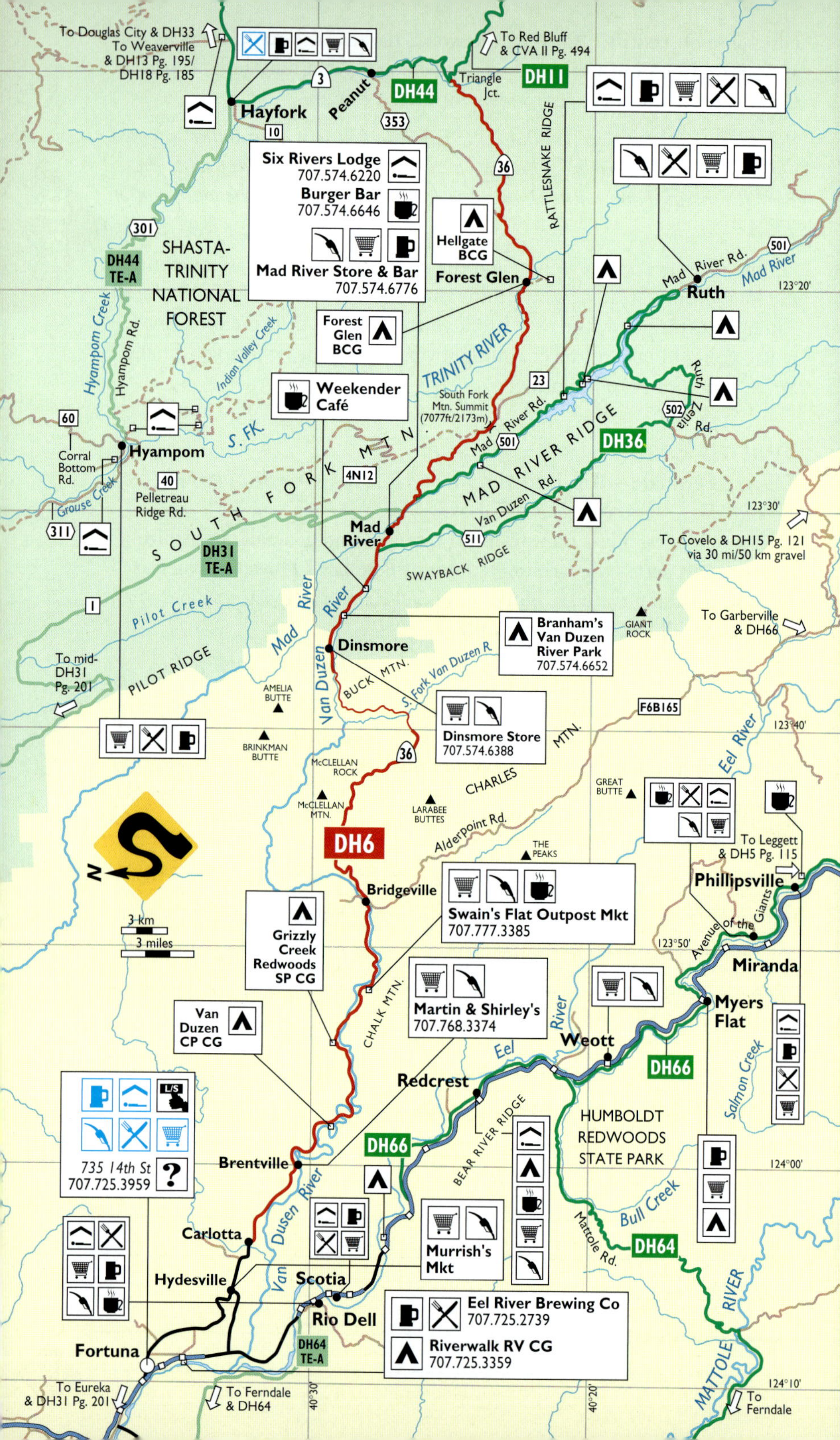

To Douglas City & DH33
To Weaverville
& DH13 Pg. 195/
DH18 Pg. 185
To Red Bluff
& CVA II Pg. 494
Hayfork
Peanut
DH44
Triangle Jct.
DH11
RATTLESNAKE RIDGE
Six Rivers Lodge
707.574.6220
Burger Bar
707.574.6646
Mad River Store & Bar
707.574.6776
Hellgate BCG
Forest Glen
SHASTA-TRINITY NATIONAL FOREST
DH44 TE-A
Hyampom Creek
Hyampom Rd.
Indian Valley Creek
Forest Glen BCG
Mad River Rd.
Mad River
Ruth
Weekender Café
TRINITY RIVER
South Fork Mtn. Summit (7077ft/2173m)
Ruth Zenia Rd.
DH36
Corral Bottom Rd.
Hyampom
S. FK.
SOUTH FORK MTN
4N12
MAD RIVER RIDGE
Pelletreau Ridge Rd.
Grouse Creek
Van Duzen Rd.
Mad River
DH31 TE-A
SWAYBACK RIDGE
To Covelo & DH15 Pg. 121 via 30 mi/50 km gravel
Pilot Creek
Mad River
Dinsmore
Branham's Van Duzen River Park
707.574.6652
GIANT ROCK
To Garberville & DH66
To mid-DH31 Pg. 201
PILOT RIDGE
AMELIA BUTTE
BUCK MTN.
S. Fork Van Duzen R
Van Duzen
Dinsmore Store
707.574.6388
F6B165
BRINKMAN BUTTE
McCLELLAN ROCK
McCLELLAN MTN.
LARABEE BUTTES
CHARLES MTN.
Eel River
GREAT BUTTE
DH6
Alderpoint Rd.
THE PEAKS
To Leggett & DH5 Pg. 115
Phillipsville
N
3 km
3 miles
Bridgeville
Swain's Flat Outpost Mkt
707.777.3385
Grizzly Creek Redwoods SP CG
Avenue of the Giants
Miranda
Martin & Shirley's
707.768.3374
CHALK MTN.
Myers Flat
Van Duzen CP CG
Weott
Eel River
DH66
Redcrest
Salmon Creek
HUMBOLDT REDWOODS STATE PARK
BEAR RIVER RIDGE
DH66
735 14th St
707.725.3959
Brentville
Van Dusen River
Bull Creek
Mattole Rd.
Murrish's Mkt
Carlotta
DH64
Hydesville
Van
Scotia
Eel River Brewing Co
707.725.2739
Rio Dell
MATTOLE RIVER
Riverwalk RV CG
707.725.3359
Fortuna
DH64 TE-A
To Eureka & DH31 Pg. 201
To Ferndale & DH64
To Ferndale
123°20'
123°30'
123°40'
123°50'
124°00'
124°10'
40°30'
40°20'

DH6 Carlotta (Fortuna) – Triangle Jct

Highway 36

Distance:	65.3 mi / 105.1 km	Traffic:	Light

At a Glance

The British TV series "The Office", which has spawned an American version, was a hit from Liverpool to Livermore because people could relate to a dilbertian workplace where the boss is a complete wanker and most co-workers are a bunch of dull-normal wallys. Well, when the grind gets you down, why not hop on your Triumph for a little out-of-the-office roadwork? And legendary DH6 is a fave spot for that, in spite of its one inferior single-lane section. From Carlotta, the road darts in and out of impressive redwood forest to take meetings with the Van Duzen River before winding inland for follow-up committees composed of more sedate forest and fields. The big presentation, however, occurs on the eastern third past DH36 Mad River Loop. From here on, Twistiness, Pavement, Engineering and Remoteness all rocket higher than employee self-evaluation scores, coming together as a team to create what is unquestionably one of NorCal's most profitable riding experiences. By its end, this ride can leave you as knackered as a hard day at work. But as David Brent might quip, "Even a bad day on a DH is better than a good day at the orifice, yeh?"

TIRES	
Twistiness	30/30
Pavement	15.9/20
Engineering	6.4/10
Remoteness	6.4/10
Scenery	9.7/15
Character	13.8/15
Total	**82.2**

Access

From Fortuna

Whether you take Rohnerville Rd from Fortuna or the Hwy 36 exit a few miles south of F-town off Hwy 101, both options junction at Hydesville. From there, take Hwy 36 east. Several miles later, you motor through Carlotta and are on the road.

From Triangle Jct

Coming in on DH11 Red Bluff – Triangle Jct (Hwy 36)
Coming in on DH44 Douglas City (Weaverville) – Triangle Jct (Hwy 3)
From this three-DH junction, head west on Hwy 36 and you're on the road.

On The Road

As you leave Carlotta, you may notice a simple white wooden cross tacked to a roadside tree, presumably commemorating someone's untimely death.

Strangely, as is so often the case with these markers, this one is posted on a straight stretch. Still, when you're on a bike, it's never a bad idea to be reminded of one's mortality and the tenuous hold we all have on life. That is before you crack the throttle and lunge into a deep, dark forest.

The curves commence immediately and, though they're not extreme, they are quite close to intimidating tree trunks (any of which provides a suitable mounting spot for a memorial.) Good thing the pavement is smooth; it won't be the reason you'll have any problems. At 1.6 mi (2.6 km), the forest backs away as the Van Duzen River appears over to your right. Some development also appears – the store/gas station and fire hall that make up the mapdot of Brentville.

Soon you're back among trees. Now, they crowd right up to the road edge, causing the asphalt to narrow in response. Why not just chop a few down? Seems you're in an official grove of redwoods, that's why. The most impressive of them don't last long before you're back in the open alongside the river. The soaring big fellahs come back before you reach the Van Duzen County Park "Swimmers Delight" at 4.7 mi (7.6 km).

Thanks, but you'll probably stay with this "Bikers Delight." After a brief straight, a bridge escorts you across the waterway. Not long after, a second crossing puts the river back on your right. The pavement's quality picks up just in time for some mellow curves and sweepers along the water. Then you're back on a straight out in the open, away from the river.

At 7.1 mi (11.4 km), the road re-enters the redwoods and curves once more along the Van Duzen. Once a 30-mph (50-kmh) corner turns the road south, you'll see that the river gorge has narrowed considerably. In fact, you're now in a rockslide area. With tight, fun corners to match.

You enter the Grizzly Creek Redwoods State Park and by 8.9 mi (14.3 km) are in the middle of another marked grove. The continuous curves have unclenched for the most part. That's probably a good thing, given how close some monstrous trunks are to the asphalt's edge. And, accordingly, how close you are to them.

Guess you must have left the state park. That is if the miscellaneous buildings and shrunken forest after the third crossing of the Van Duzen are any guide. The curves gentle even more as the terrain widens and flattens into a valley surrounded by mountain ridges that slant in from either side. At 11.9 mi (19.1 km), you enter a place called Swains Flat. But it doesn't flatten the curve index for long. A fourth crossing of the waterway marks the return of tighter topography and better corners when river and road both turn northeast.

A vista of bare-rock ridge running south from Black Butte opens up from a curve at 13.8 mi (22.2 km). Development's gone missing, at least for the moment. Unfortunately, so has the great pavement once the river flips back to the right side of the road.

Superlative asphalt returns after your final crossing of the Van Duzen at the townlet of Bridgeville at 16.3 mi (26.2 km). It's drier now; for the first time the surrounding hills are less than completely forested. It's also warmer as you head further inland, away from the cooler, coastal air.

Three signs arrive in quick succession: a low-speed advisory, a 10 per cent uphill grade and a twisty yellow. Sure enough, a tight left-hander puts you in a climb. The curves are okay but don't seem as tight as promised, at least at first. The pavement also drops a level but it's only momentary. A sharp right-hander with wide shoulders marks the return of the good black stuff at 19.3 mi (31.1 km).

By now, the road has climbed quite high onto the top of a ridge where you get a glimpse of more hilltops on the far, north side of the now distant and unseen Van Duzen River. A short passing lane gets you by any pylons on the continuing climb. At 20.4 mi (32.8 km), the incline decreases and the road straightens across the middle of a grassy slope. The ridge of Charles Mtn is in the middle distance over to your right. There is the odd building, mailbox and driveway hereabouts, but at least the scattered development doesn't spawn much traffic.

You're soon off the top of the slope and back in the trees. But you still see the massive, black hulk of McClellan Rock looming above what looks like the right side of the road at 23.0 mi (35.4 km). Then a taut right-hander makes it clear that this monolithic chunk of igneous is actually on the left. The curves stay chilled as the landscape alternates between open grassy and partially forested.

A short downhill grade begins a mile later, where you skirt the end of a big swath of rolling grassland that stretches out to the left. After a few curves through the forest, you'll find yourself on a dotted-yellow straight shooting across the largely open area that appears at 25.1 mi (40.4 km). More straights follow.

The crossing of Buck Creek marks the return of forest and decent curves while the curving bridge across the South Fork Van Duzen River at 27.9 mi (44.9 km) indicates the start of your next climb. At first, the ascent is fairly straight and the pavement is pretty good. There's even a bit of the shoulder. The "road narrows" sign doesn't imply anything unusual; after all you've seen a few of them before now. So unless you've read this, you may be unprepared when the center line disappears and the road narrows into a single lane at 28.6 mi (46.0 km).

TOUR NOTE: We first rode this piece at night and it's not much fun to do in the dark. It's strange enough to find a primitive section like this in the middle of a two-digit highway, though that certainly isn't unheard of in the Golden State. But, stranger still, we caught up to a colorfully painted circus convoy winding its laborious way slowly uphill and the night scene took on a kind of surreal, Felliniesque tone in the glare of our headlights. Memorable, indeed.

Daylight can turn to darkness here when you're surrounded by the dense forest pressing up against the edges of this narrow stretch of road. Many corners are tight in here and dirt slopes beside the road impinge on the sight lines. Not interesting enough? Okay, let's throw in the possibility of deer.

Truth be told, the pavement's not that terrible and there are a few short teaser stretches where you even get a bit of mid-yellow back. Moreover, there is more open terrain and the single lane straightens the further uphill you go. At 32.9 mi (52.9 km), you're finally back on normal pavement for yet another bridging of the prodigal Van Duzen River. That's better. Actually, it's excellent.

Now you can really enjoy the curves. But where did they go? The road mostly straightens out just prior to Dinsmore at 34.2 mi (55.0 km). After D-town, you're in a little valley with fields, buildings and a gravel runway. The curves peter out completely by the time you enter the Six Rivers National Forest at 35.5 mi (57.1 km). How can you tell you're in a national forest? You pass the cone of an inactive acorn burner followed by a conclave of immobile vehicles around a mostly nonfunctioning café. As far as the road goes, it's a little disappointing here as well, showing nothing but a few mellow sweepers. Relax and take advantage of this breather; things will soon change.

A rather large, industrial gravel operation sits off to the right just past the Humboldt/Trinity County line. After that, the valley you have been following east turns to the south, taking the Van Duzen River with it. Mad River Ridge stretches north-south at right angles to your direction. Industrious riders will take the turnoff for the Van Duzen Rd arm of **DH36 Mad River Loop** south at 38.9 mi (62.6 km). Everyone else, **stay straight**.

Continuing onward, you immediately begin a climb up Mad River Ridge. It's crested quickly and soon you're descending down its eastern side. Across the east side of the Mad River valley, you can see the extended length of South Fork Mtn, running parallel to the ridge you're on.

The decline down the eastern slope of Mad River Ridge and into the valley is an easy one. You're in and quickly curving out of what constitutes metropolitan Mad River. A few corners later a bridge crosses the actual river and the DH junctions with FSR 1 (**DH31TE-A**), left at 41.2 mi (66.3 km).

The climb up the western slope of South Fork Mtn begins where you pass the junction for the Mad River Rd leg of **DH36**, which turns south at 41.6 mi (66.9 km). Whether or not **DH36** is in your plans, you don't want to miss this next piece of Highway 36.

The excellently paved and still climbing curves tighten, multiply in number and link up. The pavement stays great and after one last building, all signs of development disappear. The twisties-for-the-next-three-miles sign seems somewhat belated. At a few points, there are good views back over the Mad River valley to your right. The best view? The roadscape ahead.

You're now on one of those pieces of road so well laid out that you can pretty much go as fast as your skills, your bike and the weather conditions will allow. After digging deep and confidently onto a set of particularly sweet sweepers, the DH summits and you enter the Shasta-Trinity National Forest at 47.7 mi (76.8 km). Initially, there is no obvious descent. And no obvious reason to ease up on the throttle.

The forest thickens on the rain shadow side of the slope but it causes no sight line impairment. Which is good considering that the continuing, predictable, consistent curves and sweepers keep on coming as the road slides obliquely down the western pitch of South Fork Mtn.

Okay, it's not perfect. At 52.5 mi (84.5 km), an imposing, white rock face drops down to the right-hand roadside to obscure your view around the corners, which is a bit of an issue given the tight S-curve section that begins here. And what's with the pock-marks in the road? That's what happens when CalTrans buys its anti-erosion coating at Wal-Mart.

This rockface gives way to less intimidating, tawny rock slopes. They don't contort the road quite as much and the path straightens to cross a bridge at 54.7 mi (88.0 km). You ford the South Fork Trinity River and pass the few buildings that make up Forest Glen.

Can it get better? Well, in some ways. The pavement you're on is currently the best of the whole DH. It usually even has a shoulder outside the white edge line that you like to see. But there's a break in the long string of twisties as the road straightens across the bottom of the valley. But it's not a wide passage, so before long, the marvelous gray stuff is throwing curves at you again while it heads gradually uphill through the narrowing gorge at the base of Rattlesnake Ridge. Just don't get too close to the threatening black rock that rears up on the right at 57.4 mi (92.4 km).

High-speed cornering opportunities abound as you cross two more bridges and climb through rock cuts on the north side of the gentling gorge. Increased forest cover beginning at 59.3 mi (95.4 km) tempers the terrain's rockiness. The curves lighten up in intensity as well and the occasional straight shows up between what are now relaxed sweepers. Your cool-down ends with one last, tighter flurry of corners before you reach Triangle Jct and the end of the DH at 65.3 mi (105.1 km). Not to mention the start of **DH11 Triangle Jct – Red Bluff** and **DH44 Triangle Jct – Douglas City.**

TOUR NOTE: This is the best three-way junction in Northern California. Someone should drop a couch in the middle of this special spot so enthusiasts can pause and comfortably contemplate what they just experienced. And are about to experience.

RIDER'S LOG: **DATE RIDDEN:** **YOUR RATING: /10**

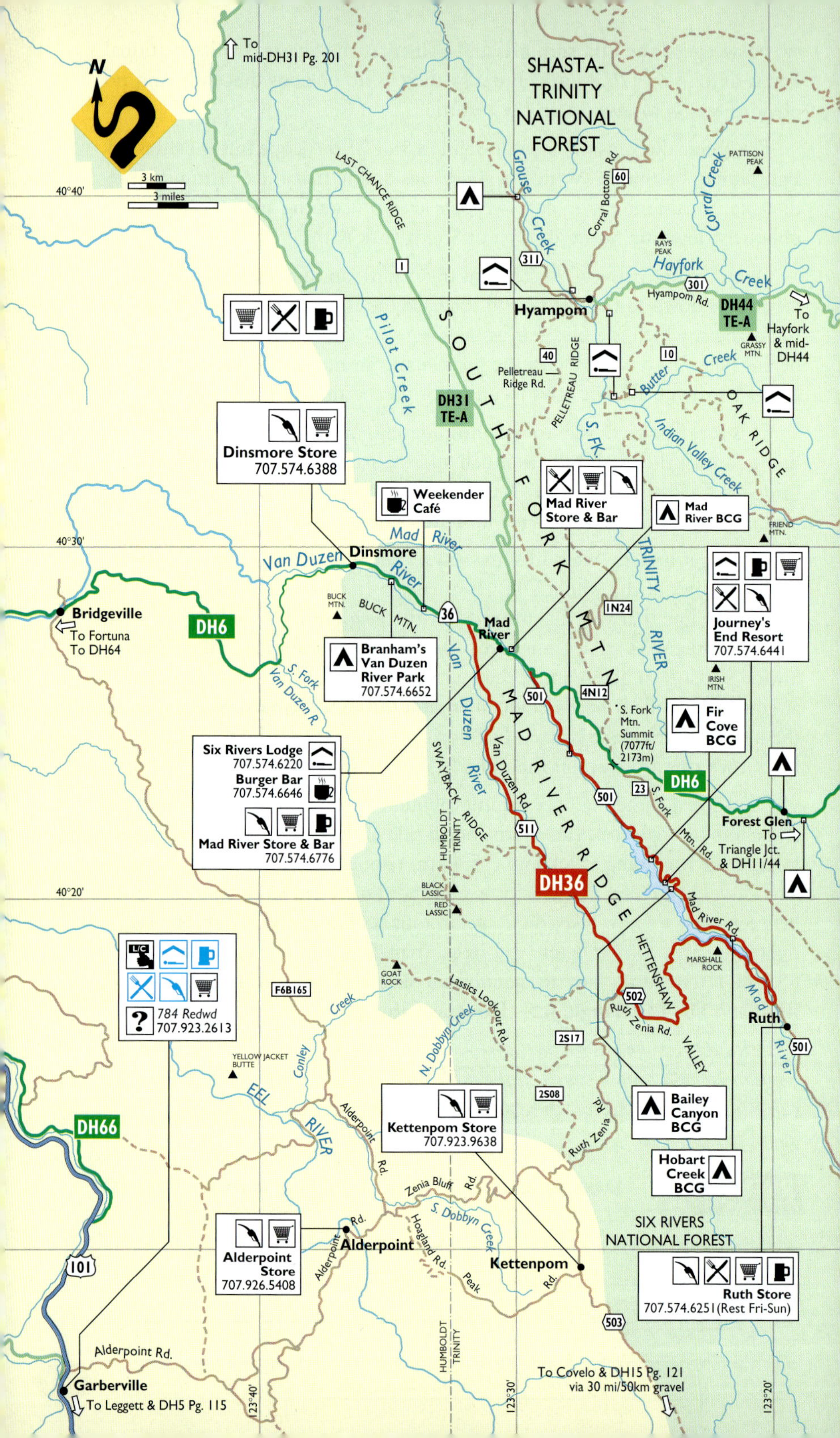

To mid-DH31 Pg. 201
SHASTA-TRINITY NATIONAL FOREST
3 km
3 miles
40°40'
LAST CHANCE RIDGE
Grouse Creek
Corral Bottom Rd.
60
Corral Creek
PATTISON PEAK
RAYS PEAK
311
Hayfork Creek
301
Hyampom Rd.
Hyampom
DH44 TE-A
To Hayfork & mid-DH44
GRASSY MTN.
Pilot Creek
SOUTH FORK MTN
DH31 TE-A
40
Pelletreau Ridge Rd.
PELLETREAU RIDGE
10
Butter Creek
OAK RIDGE
S. FK.
Indian Valley Creek
Dinsmore Store
707.574.6388
Weekender Café
Mad River Store & Bar
Mad River BCG
FRIEND MTN.
40°30'
Mad River
Van Duzen River
Dinsmore
Journey's End Resort
707.574.6441
TRINITY RIVER
BUCK MTN.
BUCK MTN.
36
1N24
Bridgeville
DH6
To Fortuna
To DH64
Mad River
Branham's Van Duzen River Park
707.574.6652
S. Fork Van Duzen R.
Van Duzen
IRISH MTN.
501
4N12
MAD RIVER RIDGE
S. Fork Mtn. Summit (7077ft/2173m)
Fir Cove BCG
Six Rivers Lodge
707.574.6220
Burger Bar
707.574.6646
Mad River Store & Bar
707.574.6776
SWAYBACK RIDGE
Van Duzen Rd.
River
501
23
DH6
S. Fork Mtn. Rd.
Forest Glen
To Triangle Jct. & DH11/44
HUMBOLDT TRINITY
511
DH36
40°20'
BLACK LASSIC
RED LASSIC
Mad River Rd.
HETTENSHAW
MARSHALL ROCK
784 Redwd
707.923.2613
F6B165
GOAT ROCK
Creek
Lassics Lookout Rd.
N. Dobbyn Creek
502
Ruth Zenia Rd.
VALLEY
Ruth
Mad River
501
2S17
YELLOW JACKET BUTTE
Conley
EEL RIVER
2S08
Alderpoint Rd.
Ruth Zenia Rd.
Kettenpom Store
707.923.9638
Bailey Canyon BCG
Hobart Creek BCG
DH66
Zenia Bluff Rd.
S. Dobbyn Creek
SIX RIVERS NATIONAL FOREST
Alderpoint Store
707.926.5408
Rd.
Alderpoint
Alderpoint
Hoagland Rd.
Kettenpom
Peak Rd.
Ruth Store
707.574.6251(Rest Fri-Sun)
101
503
Alderpoint Rd.
HUMBOLDT TRINITY
Garberville
To Leggett & DH5 Pg. 115
123°40'
123°30'
To Covelo & DH15 Pg. 121
via 30 mi/50km gravel
123°20'

DH36 MAD RIVER LOOP

Mad River Rd / Ruth Zenia Rd / Van Duzen Rd

DISTANCE:	44.3 mi / 71.3 km	TRAFFIC:	Light

AT A GLANCE

TIRES	
Twistiness	26.3/ 30
Pavement	16.6/ 20
Engineering	5.2/ 10
Remoteness	6.6/ 10
Scenery	9.1/ 15
Character	7.0/ 15
TOTAL	**70.8**

For years, motorcyclists had been railing about the maddening quality of the asphalt on this southern loop route off DH6. And the outrageous thing is that when the county finally stepped in, it broke the first rule of Destination Highway maintenance: "Don't straighten it, just repave it, stupid." So many curves were ripped up while refurbishing the Pavement on the Mad River Rd piece that Twistiness no longer maxes out. Nice work, guys. And don't give us any drivel about better sightlines – they only enable the pylons to drive off the road faster. You want to improve Engineering? How about lane and shoulder width? Sigh. Still, you won't be irritated by the Scenery; the green forests in the Mad River and Van Duzen River valleys, the panorama from the top of Mad River Ridge and the views along Ruth Lake are still intact. Nor does the Remoteness in this sparsely developed area give any cause for resentment. So stop fulminating and get out and enjoy this road. 'Cause we all know that when the new stuff starts to heave and crack, it'll be years before anything's done about it. So there'll be plenty of time to get pissed all over again.

ACCESS

From mid-DH6 Carlotta (Fortuna) - Triangle Jct (Hwy 36)

Mad River and Van Duzen Rds junction with Hwy 36 only 2.5 mi (4.0 km) apart. Take either one and you are on the road.

ON THE ROAD

The flat, open rangeland of the Van Duzen River valley floor stretches out to the right as you turn off **DH6** and onto Van Duzen Rd. Smooth pavement winds through a non-town consisting of a school and some straggly looking, mostly mobile buildings. It's enough of a place to have a 25 mph (40 km) speed limit, though. After the lots-of-canines-please-drive-slow sign at 2.3 mi (3.7 km), you curve past what seems like the hamlet's last building and head into scattered forest.

Looks like it's not the last edifice after all. Seems you're barely in the trees before you pop out into an open area with a few more bland structures strewn casually about. From the clearing, you can see the low hills either side of the valley but they're soon blocked from sight by more trees. At 3.1 mi (5.0 km), the initial speed limit ends. Since there is no new limit posted, you might assume the authorities are leaving the rate of progress up to your own good judgment rather than the usual determinant: the speed at which a '57 Chevy in poor mechanical condition can be safely driven by a drunk.

So you might feel free to exercise your own considered opinion as to what speed is appropriate on the continuous curves at the base of the slope forming the valley's east side. They've been mellow so far but out to your right, it appears the flat valley bottom is narrowing. And there it is – the sign advising curvier stuff for the next 8 mi (13 km).

Initially, there doesn't seem to be much improvement. Then at 5.1 mi (8.2 km), a 15-mph (25-kmh) curve introduces a tighter stretch through increasingly dense forest. Thankfully, this greenery stays far enough back from the road that it doesn't impair your views much around the delectably paved corners.

There's a slight climb with another low-speed corner before the pavement quality decreases a bit at 6.9 mi (11.1 km). Those two forested mounds over to your right are the peaks of Black Lassic and Red Lassic. Funny, both are green.

The pavement grade drops even more after the one-lane bridge across the Van Duzen River. The asphalt is pretty new so obviously the problem is that not enough time and money was spent preparing the base. Perhaps because they wasted all the money straightening out the other arm of this DH. Not to exaggerate too much, though. The asphalt's still not bad and at least the curves are still good.

A second one-lane bridge has you back across the Van Duzen at 7.7 mi (12.4 km). The road tracks slightly uphill as it continues to wind through uniform forest. The landscape slopes slightly down to your left showing Mad River Ridge rising in the near distance. To your right, the landscape tilts upward, producing a sharp left-hander at 9.5 mi (15.3 km).

The pavement improves in texture and width on a brief straight (of course) beginning at 10.0 mi (16.1 km). A third one-lane bridge at 10.5 mi (16.9 km) crosses a tributary of the Van Duzen River as the water slants away to the southwest. The traffic-free curves come back in force, some of them even tighter than before.

At 12.1 mi (19.5 km), a dotted yellow line heralds the beginning of another straight but, this time, on a less-smooth part of the road. The better pavement returns at 14.4 mi (23.2 km) where the terrain opens up considerably. Fields stretch out to your left, but don't let the long straight entice you into increasing your speed. You should actually be slowing down so you don't blow by the junction with Ruth Zenia Rd at 15.0 mi (24.1 km). To stay on the DH, **turn left**.

ROUTING OPTION: Ruth Zenia Rd also continues straight ahead. Staying on this rough piece of it will eventually get you (via gravel) to ***DH15 Covelo – Longvale Jct.*** *Alternately, it will also give you the option of paved Alderpoint Rd either out to Garberville on Hwy 101 or back up to* ***DH6 Carlotta – Triangle Jct*** *at Bridgeville.*

The DH runs through the trees and skirts the edge of the open fields as it heads east. There are a fair number of curves and a middling number of buildings before you straighten across the open Hettenshaw Valley and aim directly toward Mad River Ridge. There's the odd sweeper lying about this flat stretch.

A twisties sign at 17.5 mi (28.2 km) marks the start of a climb off the valley floor and back into the trees. And this sign is as good as its word. Better actually, if you like those hairpins you're experiencing. Too bad about the pavement quality, which degrades slightly as you climb up the partly treeless ridge and angle north. Scenery's okay, if you look left back over the valley.

A few more hairpins are featured on the climb up to the crest of the bare ridge at 19.0 mi (30.2 km) where you get one more view of Hettenshaw Valley to your left. Out to your right, you can see the southern tip of Ruth Lake and the low mountains beyond to the east. Then, in a flash, you're descending through forest. And while there is no mid-road yellow on the tight and continuous corners, at least the pavement 's better. Despite the fact that the white paint is only on the one, downhill edge of the asphalt, the road isn't that narrow. Still, lots of fun to be had; perhaps even more if you ride it uphill in the other direction.

The road has occasional bumpy stretches along with another hairpin or two on the descent. In truth, it probably won't be too long before the quality of the pavement on this slope degrades significantly. Again, you get the feeling that they didn't spend a lot of time preparing the roadbed but simply laid down a layer of black stuff. Perhaps that's because all the money was wasted… but we repeat ourselves.

At 22.0 mi (35.4 km), standard mid-yellow/edge-white paint returns along with better pavement. There's a terrific sweeper with a short-lived shoulder. You should be able to nail it too, as long as you don't T-bone one of the local deer bolting across the road after stopping for a drink at the creek coming off Ruth Lake.

The DH runs along the south side of the arm of Ruth Lake and, at 22.8 mi (36.7 km), there is a view straight north down the middle of the lake. As the route swings south, the road continues to flow with the water. This is a particularly sweet stretch: a beautiful triptych of scenery, curves and asphalt.

The terrain flattens, the curves gentle and Ruth Lake, never very wide to begin with, narrows into Ruth River. A left-hander puts you across a bridge over the river where you Y-junction with Mad River Rd at 27.3 mi (43.9 km). To remain on the DH, **bear left**.

The surface quality drops briefly and the road is a little more linear as you gently wind your way through the thickening forest. Soon, you can see the river-about-to-become-a-lake-again glinting through the trees on the left. The curves gradually begin to dance again. And so do you.

Tsk, tsk, what's this? Unsightly tar strips begin to mar the surface of the road. Fortunately, they are mostly parallel to your path rather than across it, so they don't present too much of a problem, especially because the underlying pavement is still pretty smooth.

At 32.7 mi (52.6 km), the view left over the lake confirms that the road has actually gained some altitude above the east shore. It sometimes pulls away from the lake but always returns. At 34.4 mi (55.4 km), there's another nice lakeside vista. You may experience more traffic now but the road's relaxed demeanor and dotted yellow help you dispense with it effectively.

A sweeping, uphill right-hander affords an excellent view of Mad River Ridge on the western side of the lake. You pass the dam that created Ruth Lake and leave the lake behind for good at 37.3 mi (60.0 km). You don't see Mad River that now takes its place. What you do see is the excellent pavement beneath your spinning rubber.

There are definitely fewer curves than there were along the lake. And why would that be? It's not just because you're running along a narrow, straight and nondescript valley. The raw roadside shows that the road crews took advantage of the recent opportunity presented by repaving this stretch to take some of its curves away. And the reason for that? Well, someone obviously has a problem with this DH scoring 30/30 for Twistiness. What else could it be?

Of course with such great pavement, what curves are left are terrific. Though your enjoyment might be restrained somewhat by the killjoy 35-mph (55-kmh) sign. Especially if there are party-poopers around, if you know what we mean. Hopefully, your soiree will continue uninterrupted until the junction with mid-**DH6** at 44.3 mi (71.3 km).

RIDER'S LOG: **DATE RIDDEN:** **YOUR RATING: /10**

DH66

DH64

DH6

DH36

DH11

DH33

DH44

Map Tip: To see the next good motorcycle road, look for the white navigation arrows at the edge of the Local maps.

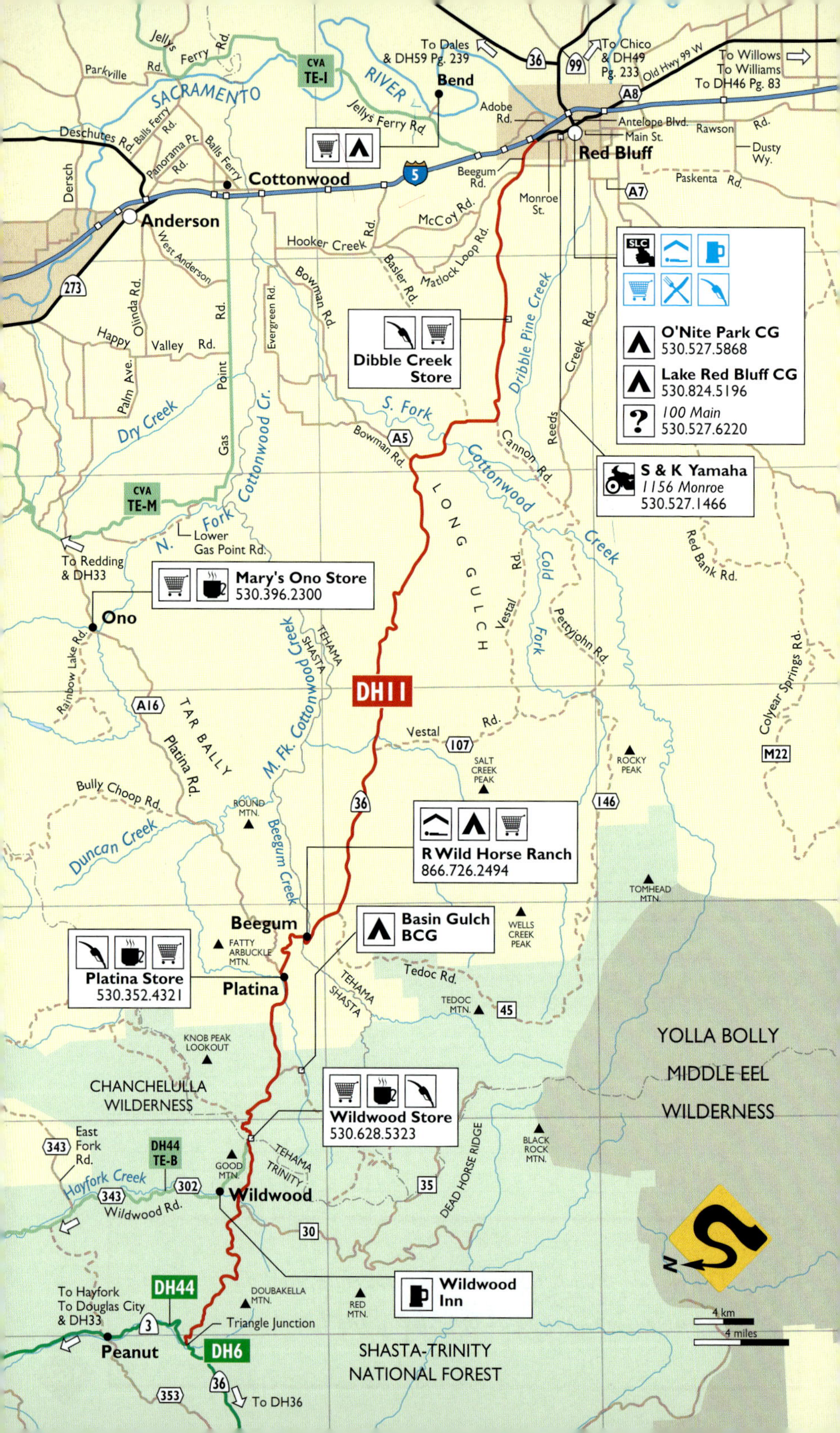
DH11
Red Bluff
Cottonwood
Anderson
Bend
Ono
Beegum
Platina
Wildwood
Peanut
Triangle Junction
O'Nite Park CG
530.527.5868
Lake Red Bluff CG
530.824.5196
100 Main
530.527.6220
S & K Yamaha
1156 Monroe
530.527.1466
Dibble Creek Store
Mary's Ono Store
530.396.2300
R Wild Horse Ranch
866.726.2494
Basin Gulch BCG
Platina Store
530.352.4321
Wildwood Store
530.628.5323
Wildwood Inn
To Dales & DH59 Pg. 239
To Chico & DH49 Pg. 233
To Willows
To Williams
To DH46 Pg. 83
To Redding & DH33
To Hayfork
To Douglas City & DH33
To DH36
SACRAMENTO RIVER
CHANCHELULLA WILDERNESS
YOLLA BOLLY MIDDLE EEL WILDERNESS
SHASTA-TRINITY NATIONAL FOREST
LONG GULCH
TAR BALLY
DH44
DH6
4 km
4 miles

DH11 Triangle Jct – Red Bluff
Highway 36

Distance:	65.3 mi / 105.1 km	Traffic:	Light

At a Glance

TIRES	
Twistiness	28.1/ 30
Pavement	17.9/ 20
Engineering	5.7/ 10
Remoteness	7.6/ 10
Scenery	8.9/ 15
Character	11.4/ 15
Total	**79.6**

Ho-hum, just another day of drudgery at the Hwy 36 office. And this continuation of the renowned NorCal east-wester starts out from the three-DH junction possibly as an even better ride than the superlative DH6 from Carlotta, as hard as that is to believe. It's exceedingly rare to find the intense, lengthy barrage of Twistiness that's thrown at you right off the top, especially when it's combined with excellent Pavement. Though the road-hugging forest and rugged close-to-the-road terrain initially impair Engineering, both T&E mellow out the nearer you get to Red Bluff in the Central Valley. But Remoteness stays consistently – and surprisingly – good; there's as yet little development even close to Blufftown. As for Scenery, thickly forested mountains eventually give way to more moderately treed and sage-covered foothills before a combination of open flat and partly treed, rollicking n' rolling countryside takes you home. The magnificence of the upper reaches and the wide variety of experience throughout helps keep Character within striking distance of its Hwy 36 colleague. It's just too bad these particular workdays aren't pensionable time.

Access

From Triangle Jct

Coming in on DH6 Carlotta (Fortuna) – Triangle Jct (Hwy 36)
Coming in on DH44 Douglas City – Triangle Jct (Hyw 36)

After an appropriate amount of contemplation at the three-DH jct, head east and you're on the road.

From Red Bluff

West of I-5 and north of Antelope Blvd, Main St/I-5BR is also Hwy 36. Stick with 36 (aka Beegum Rd) when it heads west off Main/I-5BR. You're on the road.

From I-5

Head west from the Adobe St Exit 649. Turn right on triple identified Main/I-5BR/Hwy 36. Stick with 36 (Beegum Rd) when it heads west off Main. You're on the road.

NAVIGATION: If you are coming from the north on I-5, you can take the exit north of Adobe onto Main St. Turn right on Hwy 36/Beegum and you'll be on the road.

On The Road

Are you ready for some riding? Hope so, since the curving and sweeping begin immediately off the junction. Engineering could be better as gravelly side slopes and dense forest crowd the road to the point you might even drop under the 55 mph (90 kmh) speed limit at times. Like that ever happens.

Traffic is light with the lack of development up here; the only impediments you'll likely have to watch out for are deer. At 3.4 mi (5.5 km), you begin to get brief views out to the left of not only the forest below you but of Stone Ridge and other mountains in the distance. When the road curves to the south on the north slant of Dubakella Mtn, you can see the DH snake up ahead on another incline. Moments later you're on it, slithering north. Ssss...

The forest is beginning to thin a little among all the continuing curves. At 6.0 mi (9.7 km), the rocky gradient to your right changes its complexion from tawny brown gravel to gray-white rock and the tight corners tighten even more. As forested ridge after forested ridge stretches north and east to the horizon it's hard to imagine being in a better place or on a better road. Or having a better time.

Suddenly at 8.3 mi (13.4 km), you find yourself on the first curveless section you've seen since the DH began. Rockfaces rise from both sides of the road as you head downhill toward a crossing of Hayfork Creek. The junction left for Wildwood Rd (**DH44TE-B**) is at 12.2 mi (19.6 km). You'd never suspect it, but you're also at a 3805 ft (1168 m) summit. The six-per-cent grade sign hints at this. Let's see if the twisties come back on the way down.

They do. A twisties sign marks the return of curves on rock gradients. Then the topography gentles and low, scrubby bush encroaches on terrain previously covered entirely by trees. You pass a ranger station at 16.9 mi (27.2 km) and the road begins to stretch out; longer straights link its still frequent, but more gradual corners. The road exits the Shasta-Trinity National Forest at 19.7 mi (31.7 km) and runs you down the middle of a shallow valley bottom that contains some light, scattered development and light, scattered sweepers. They escort you through Platina at 21.3 mi (34.3 km).

ROUTING OPTION: If you really need to get to Redding (God knows why you'd want to, other than for a bike shop), you can take bumpy Platina Rd (A 15) left at 21.5 mi (34.6 km). Be warned though: it's one rough son of a bitch.

The terrain flattens out ahead, though entirely brush-covered hillsides still surround you. Whatever that plant stuff is, it'll fill your nostrils with a pungent, tobacco-like aroma, at least if it's rained recently. You smoke down the terrific, large-sweeper descent into the valley of Beegum Creek. The bridge crossing the creek at 24.7 mi (39.7 km) also marks the boundary between Shasta and Tehama Counties.

The road straightens as it climbs up more scrub-covered hills and into another little valley. The few buildings at its west end constitute the map-dot of Beegum. The surrounding hills decrease rapidly in size while more open areas appear among the trees. Straights begin to predominate and there's not much reason to restrain your throttle hand through the few graceful curves that do appear. Despite the drop in twistiness there's still something about this slightly rolling, foothill terrain that makes for very attractive riding. The excellent pavement and still-strong sense of remoteness undoubtedly has something to do with that.

A road narrows sign at 36.2 mi (58.3 km) is followed quickly by a 30-mph (50-km) left-hander that introduces a curvier but undulating section. You're riding along the south side of a creek bed but it's likely dry. Which might explain why there are lots of cattle warning signs but no cattle. So, despite the low-speed advisories, you can safely ride this entertaining, consistent piece of road without much fear of cow splatter.

The creek slants left as the road angles right and finally leaves the shallow valley floor, straightening at 41.3 mi (66.5 km) through flatter but still largely treed topography. But it's not long before more corners – similar to the last batch, but even more undulating – appear. Though some are nicely banked, it's a little more challenging here because the trees have multiplied enough to obscure sightlines around the increased numbers of curves. The increasingly up-and-down terrain doesn't help. But you're up for all this, right?

ROUTING OPTION: Still gotta get to Redding? You've obviously never been there. Piece-of-cake Bowman Rd (A 5) left at 47.7 mi (76.8 km) short cuts you over to I-5. Look for the sign indicating Cottonwood.

There are a few tighter curves at 49.1 mi (79.0 km) before the road relaxes once more. After some high-speed sweepers, the asphalt curves tighter again too. This catchy rhythm is repeated several times through what is now scattered forest. The curves nod up and down harder as the terrain rock 'n' rolls to a heavier beat.

By 53.0 mi (85.3 km), the road is on the top of a ridge and displaying some pretty wild and surreal S-curves. The ground normalizes at 54.4 mi (87.5 km) and the road straightens out big-time on the flat. More development appears. Man, it seems like ages since you and Dali left the coast this morning....

Zzzz... mnft, what? You awaken in the townlet of Dibble Creek at 60.8 mi (97.8 km). Seems like somebody didn't wake up, judging by the service truck rolled over on its side with the telephone pole it had taken dibs on resting on its bottom. Once again, we meditate on the fragility of life. And the sentience of pyloneers that wipe out on straight sections.

The road stays straight until Baker Rd, past which there are a few final cool-down curves. You cross the railway tracks and junction with Main St/I-5BR, where the DH ends just north of – and outside – Red Bluff at 65.3 mi (105.1 km).

Rider's Log: **Date Ridden:** **Your Rating:** **/10**

Don't forget to print the DH Rider Discount list of service providers from destinationhighways.com *and take it with you. Then, just show 'em your book and ask for the discount.*

Bear Mtn. Resort CG
530.275.4728
To DH38 Pg. 245
Millville Plains Rd.
Old 44
SACRAMENTO RIVER
Deschutes Rd.
Dry Creek Rd.
Bear Mountain
WHISKEYTOWN SHASTA-TRINITY NATIONAL REC. AREA
CVA TE-K
Stillwater Wy.
Panorama Pt. Rd.
Balls Ferry
Dersch
Airport
Anderson
To Red Bluff & DH11
Old Oregon Trail
Twin View Blvd.
Hilltop Dr.
Alta Mesa Dr.
Larkspur Ln.
Churn Cr. Rd.
West Anderson
Shasta Lake
Ashby Rd.
Oasis Rd.
Lake Blvd.
Cypress Ave.
Redding
Olinda Rd.
Happy Valley Rd.
Bransletter Ln.
Creek Rd.
China Gulch Dr.
Hawthorne Ave.
Palm Ave.
Point Rd.
Gas
Keswick Dam Rd.
CVA TE-L
Lower Springs Rd.
Placer Rd.
Texas Spgs. Rd.
Clear
Dry Creek
SHASTA LAKE
Iron Mtn. Rd.
Swasey Rd.
Shasta
Centerville
Cloverdale Rd.
122°30'
SUGARLOAF MTN.
J's Market
CVA TE-M ALT
CVA TE-M
Whiskeytown Lake
Muletown
Clear Creek
Gas Point Rd.
Cottonwood Cr.
Igo
Lower Gas Point Rd.
JF Kennedy Mem. Dr.
KANAKA PEAK
TE-A
MONARCH MTN.
MAD MULE MTN.
Brandy Creek Day Use Area
S. Shore Dr.
Ono GS
Ono
Yamaha of Redding
3119 Twin View
530.275.7300
Redding Harley-Davidson
1268 Twin View
530.241.7117
Lee's Honda Kawasaki
(HON/KAW/VIC)
2230 Larkspur 530.221.6788
Fator's MS (KTM/SUZ)
682 Grove 530.221.6612
747 Auditorium
530.225.4433
Clear Creek
WHISKEYTOWN SHASTA-TRINITY NRA
Trinity Mountain Rd.
122°40'
Rainbow Lake Rd.
North Fork
2 km
2 miles
TAR BALLY
DH33
East County Line Rd.
Blackhorn Summit 3213ft/979m
Grass Valley Creek
PARADISE PEAK
Platina Rd.
Bully Choop Rd.
DH18 TE-A
BULLY CHOOP MTN.
LOOKOUT PEAK
JOES PEAK
Trinity Dam Blvd.
Duncan Creek
MIKES PEAK
Lewiston
Lewiston Rd.
Creek
Indian Creek Lodge
530.623.6294
Middle Fork Cottonwood Creek
122°50'
DH18 TE-B
TRINITY RIVER
SHASTA TRINITY
Steel Bridge Rd.
Indian
Indian Cr. Rd.
Timber Lodge Motel
530.623.6624
Douglas City GS
ARBUCKLE MTN.
BROWNS MTN.
Browns Mtn. Rd.
31N02
Reading Cr. Rd.
CHANCHELULLA WILDERNESS
Browns Creek
Douglas City
Deer Lick Springs Rd.
To Weaverville & DH13 Pg. 195/ DH18 Pg. 185
123°00'
Douglas City NRA CG
KNOB PEAK LOOKOUT
DH11
DH44
40°40'
To Triangle Jct. & DH6/11
40°30'
STONE RIDGE
To Triangle Jct. & DH6/44

DH33 Shasta (Redding) – Douglas City (Weaverville)

Highway 299

Distance:	31.9 mi / 51.3 km	Traffic:	Heavy

At a Glance

Pour yourself a smooth blend of Pavement, Engineering and Remoteness. The only rough edges to this DH's Character are the heavy traffic that bog it down and extra-wide passing lanes that straighten it out as it noses through the pure forest and rock landscape. The longest straight shot out of Shasta is particularly hard to swallow, even though it provides a long, scenic view over Whiskeytown Lake. The western third shows reasonable complexity as it sweeps steadily through refined, but watered-down curves off the Buckhorn Summit. Yet connoisseurs will find it's the middle section that will make or break this offering. If you catch it when the pylons are bumper to bumper sticker, it can be more frustrating than a bartender putting ice in your Balvenie. But if you can savor the tight, peaty, well-banked esses on the climb up the summit without being cut off, it's a ride that matches up with the finest single malts. Now, if only you could bottle and sell it.

TIRES	
Twistiness	25.3/ 30
Pavement	17.2/ 20
Engineering	8.6/ 10
Remoteness	5.5/ 10
Scenery	9.9/ 15
Character	5.2/ 15
Total	**71.7**

Access

From Redding

Via Hwy 299

Follow Hwy 299 out of Redding. When you pass through Shasta, about 6.0 mi (9.7 km) west, you're on the road.

From Douglas City

Coming in on DH44 Triangle Jct – Douglas City (Weaverville) (Hwy 3)

Turn right on Hwy 299. You're on the road.

From Weaverville

Coming in on DH18 Callahan – Weaverville (Hwy 3)

Coming in on DH13 Willow Creek – Weaverville (Hwy 299)

Head south of Weaverville on Hwy 3/299. When you turn west out of Douglas City, you're on the road.

On the Road

Shasta, once the Queen City of California's northern mining towns, is now reduced to a row of roofless brick buildings along Hwy 299. It's in stark contrast to the asphalt breezeway that flows straight and wide through the middle of the former boom town. Sad to report that the straight and wide continues well past Shasta on the gradual climb up to Whiskeytown Lake and the turnoff to JFK Memorial Dr (**TE-A**) at 1.4 mi (2.3 km).

But, wow, what a view you're presented with past the TE. The grand, blue lake spreads out below you, beyond the dam to the distant mountains. The road remains straight, though as it bridges a couple of inlets and ventures through some colorful rock cuts. Red, brown, ochre, tawny, grey. There's green in the scene too, consisting of low trees and sun-withered shrubs. But whither curves?

Powerhouse Rd turns off at 8.1 mi (13.0 km), marking the end of the lake. You climb now, crossing Clear Creek and passing the Crystal Creek Rd access to the Juvenile Detention Facility at 9.7 mi (15.6 km). With so many kids on 600s crossing the double yellow lines to overtake pylons, guess it made some sense to build this nearby.

ROUTING OPTION: Trinity Mtn Rd, turning off at 9.3 mi (15.0 km), is paved for several miles before gravelling out. It offers a maxburning opportunity through the Trinity Mtns all the way north of Trinity Lake that connects with ***DH18 Weaverville – Callahan*** *just south of Coffee Creek as E Side Rd.*

What was that at 10.2 mi (16.4 km)? A curve? And another? Finally. And a pickup in the pavement quality to boot. The best section of the DH comes suddenly as you enter a winding pass up to Buckhorn Summit. The right side of the road angles up sharply, the left drops off into an oak and pine-filled gulch that deepens on the steepening climb. The curves are moderate at first, but the 20-mph (30-kmh) advisory at 12.8 mi (20.6 km) indicates compressed radii are ahead. From here, it's a pitched, tightly curving and sweeping ascent on a road so wide, smoothly paved and sweetly banked, that it's a piece of NorCal perfection. There are even a few winding passing lanes. And because this is California, chances are you're going to need them.

You reach the Buckhorn Summit (3213 ft /979 m) at 17.8 mi (28.6 km) and cross the Shasta/Trinity County line. It's decidedly less interesting over the top. A long, wide-shouldered, downhill straight gives you lots of time to shake out your right wrist. The heavily treed and granite landscape, while still rugged, levels significantly at 19.8 mi (31.9 km) when you lose the right upslope that so effectively created the S-curves on the ascent. The long, easy, sweeping curves that come as you approach the marked turnoff to Trinity Dam Blvd (**DH18TE-A**) at 22.7 mi (36.5 km) are pleasant enough, but nothing in comparison to what you just experienced.

ROUTING OPTION: ***DH18TE-A*** *is a prudent bypass if you're planning to ride* ***DH18 Weaverville – Callahan*** *and want to avoid the boring slog between Douglas City and Weaverville. You can also use it to get to* ***DH13 Weaverville – Willow Creek.*** *It's a longer way to go, but curvier and far less trafficked.*

*TOUR NOTE: Even if you don't want to ride **DH18TE-A** all the way north, another feature of the Trinity Dam Blvd turnoff is its access to the nifty little ghost town of Lewiston . It's a great little stop, featuring a riverside B&B, restaurant, antique shops and a laid-back ambience. You can avoid backtracking by looping back to the DH via Lewiston Rd.*

Staying on the DH, you sweep around a corner past the junction and see the ridge-shaped outline of Browns Mtn ahead in the distance. At 23.8 mi (38.3 km), you enter a minor canyon. Rockfaces rise up to the right as the road bridges a creek. The canyon lasts but a few corners, ending after the sweeper at 24.5 mi (39.4 km). There are still some curves and sweepers after that. As long as you're riding fast enough.

At 26.6 mi (42.8 km), you pass the turnoff to Lewiston Rd, the back route into Lewiston (see *TOUR NOTE* above). This is followed by a couple of long, easy curves and a passing lane up to a mini-summit. There's a nice close-in view of Browns Mtn as you reach the apex and ride along the crest past Poker Bar Rd at 27.6 mi (44.4 km). By this point, however, the curves have pretty much folded.

You enter a rock slide area at 29.3 mi (47.1 km). The left roadside steepens upward and squeezes the road against the Trinity River. You'd think with all this sliding, squeezing and steepening, the DH might eke out a few corners. Have another think.

You see the first development in a while at 29.9 mi (48.1 km). Seems some dude named "Dave" offers everything from marine products to taxidermy. At this point the DH may as well be dead and stuffed for all the excitement it's delivering. If it's excitement you're looking for, turn south at 31.9 mi (51.3 km) when this DH ends at the junction with **DH44 Douglas City (Weaverville) – Triangle Jct**.

Twisted Edges

TE-A JFK Memorial Dr (5.1 mi / 8.2 km)
Easy-sipping pavement with a few curves through the woods provides dead-end access to the swimming and campgrounds of Whiskeytown Lake. It ends at the marina about a half mile past the Brandy Creek Day Use Area. It's not clear if you have to pay to hang out at the marina like you do at Brandy Creek.

Rider's Log: **Date Ridden:** **Your Rating: /10**

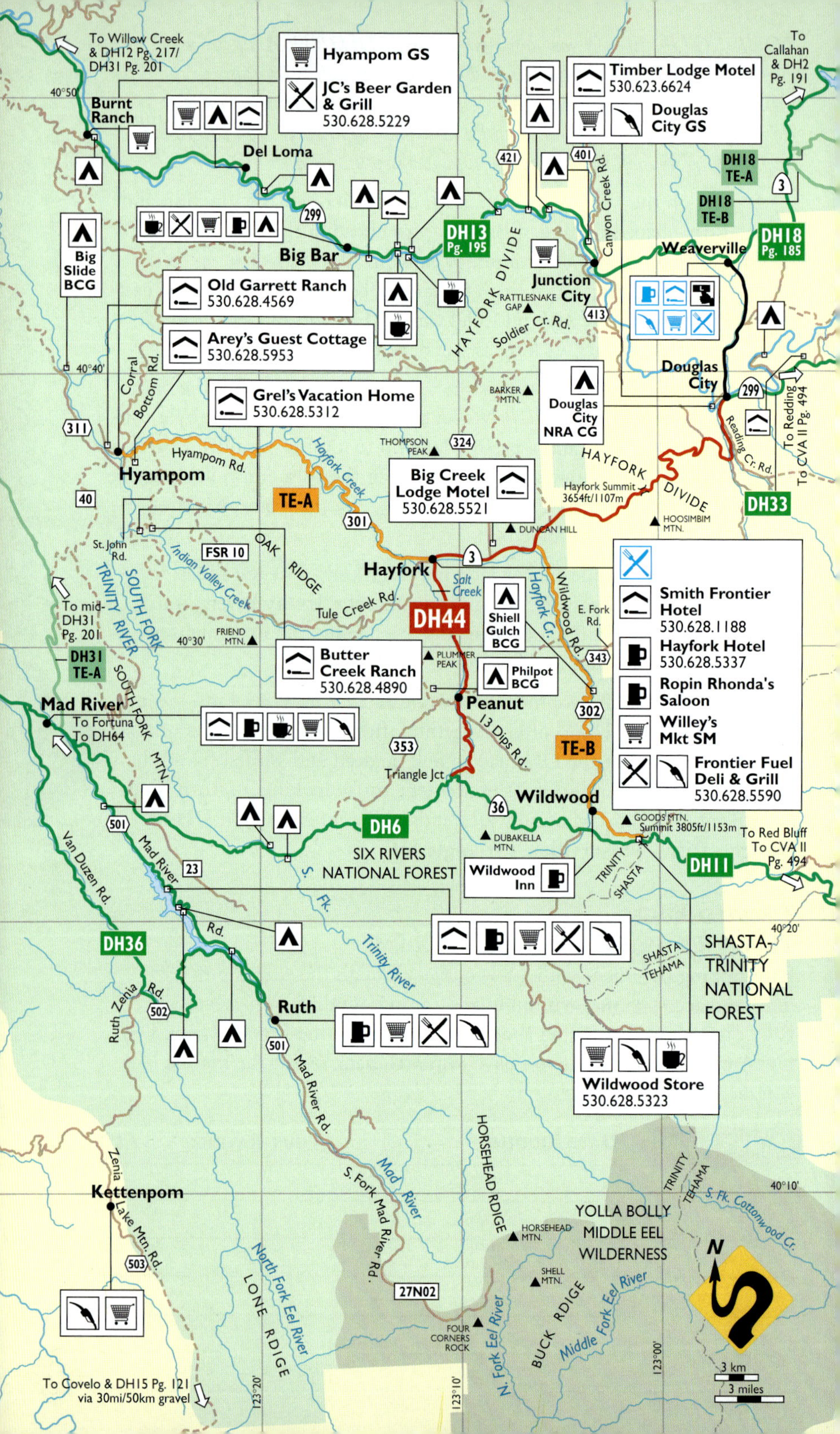

To Willow Creek & DH12 Pg. 217/ DH31 Pg. 201
Hyampom GS
JC's Beer Garden & Grill
530.628.5229
Timber Lodge Motel
530.623.6624
Douglas City GS
To Callahan & DH2 Pg. 191
40°50'
Burnt Ranch
Del Loma
299
421
401
Canyon Creek Rd.
DH18 TE-A
DH18 TE-B
3
DH13 Pg. 195
DH18 Pg. 185
Big Bar
Weaverville
Big Slide BCG
Old Garrett Ranch
530.628.4569
HAYFORK DIVIDE
Junction City
RATTLESNAKE GAP
413
Soldier Cr. Rd.
Arey's Guest Cottage
530.628.5953
40°40'
Corral Bottom Rd.
Douglas City
Grel's Vacation Home
530.628.5312
BARKER MTN.
Douglas City NRA CG
299
To Redding To CVA II Pg. 494
311
THOMPSON PEAK
324
Reading Cr. Rd.
Hyampom Rd.
Hyampom
Hayfork Creek
HAYFORK DIVIDE
Big Creek Lodge Motel
530.628.5521
40
TE-A
Hayfork Summit 3654ft/1107m
DH33
301
HOOSIMBIM MTN.
DUNCAN HILL
St. John Rd.
FSR 10
OAK RIDGE
Hayfork
3
Indian Valley Creek
Salt Creek
Smith Frontier Hotel
530.628.1188
TRINITY RIVER
SOUTH FORK
To mid-DH31 Pg. 201
Tule Creek Rd.
Hayfork Cr.
Wildwood Rd.
E. Fork Rd.
Hayfork Hotel
530.628.5337
DH44
Shiell Gulch BCG
FRIEND MTN.
40°30'
DH31 TE-A
Butter Creek Ranch
530.628.4890
PLUMMER PEAK
343
Ropin Rhonda's Saloon
Philpot BCG
SOUTH FORK
Mad River
Peanut
302
To Fortuna To DH64
Willey's Mkt SM
13 Dips Rd.
353
TE-B
MTN.
Frontier Fuel Deli & Grill
530.628.5590
Triangle Jct
Wildwood
36
501
GOODS MTN.
Summit 3805ft/1153m
To Red Bluff To CVA II Pg. 494
DH6
DUBAKELLA MTN.
Van Duzen Rd.
Mad River
SIX RIVERS NATIONAL FOREST
Wildwood Inn
DH11
23
TRINITY SHASTA
S. Fk.
40°20'
Rd.
Trinity River
DH36
SHASTA TEHAMA
SHASTA-TRINITY NATIONAL FOREST
Ruth Zenia Rd.
Ruth
502
501
Wildwood Store
530.628.5323
Mad River Rd.
HORSEHEAD RDIGE
S. Fork Mad River Rd.
Mad River
TRINITY TEHAMA
40°10'
Kettenpom
Zenia Lake Mtn. Rd.
YOLLA BOLLY MIDDLE EEL WILDERNESS
S. Fk. Cottonwood Cr.
HORSEHEAD MTN.
North Fork Eel River
N
503
SHELL MTN.
LONE RDIGE
27N02
Middle Fork Eel River
BUCK RDIGE
FOUR CORNERS ROCK
N. Fork Eel River
To Covelo & DH15 Pg. 121 via 30mi/50km gravel
123°20'
123°10'
123°00'
3 km
3 miles

DH44 Triangle Jct – Douglas City (Weaverville)

Highway 3

Distance:	35.3 mi / 56.8 km	Traffic:	Moderate

At a Glance

Put it almost anywhere else and this DH would be a superstar. But with so many celebrated routes to the north and south, this lightly trafficked bit of road candy gets about as many casting calls as Brent Chapman. But it's sure not for lack of talent. This respectably well paved and engineered road gives a shining performance in the early and late frames, curling down exquisitely off the popular Triangle Jct and essing admirably up and down the lush, forested slopes either side of the Hayfork Summit. Too bad its Remoteness and Character get assassinated by the excruciatingly long straights when the DH mails it in through the stretched out farming community of Hayfork. But if you can deal with a few boring scenes, there are moments on this route that rival the region's best. So is this B-road ready for a leading role? Well, as Mr. Chapman would say, "What have Tom Cruise and Russell Crowe got that I don't?"

TIRES	
Twistiness	26.7/ 30
Pavement	14.9/ 20
Engineering	5.9/ 10
Remoteness	5.3/ 10
Scenery	9.0/ 15
Character	5.7/ 15
Total	**67.5**

Access

From Triangle Jct

Coming in on DH6 Carlotta (Fortuna) – Triangle Jct (Hwy 36)
Coming in on DH11 Red Bluff – Triangle Jct (Hwy 36)
Go north on Hwy 3. You're on the road.

From Douglas City

Coming in on DH33 Shasta – Douglas City (Weaverville) (Hwy 299)
Turn south on Hwy 3 just before Douglas City. When you do, you're on the road.

From Weaverville

Coming in on DH13 Willow Creek – Weaverville (Hwy 299)
Coming in on DH18 Callahan – Weaverville (Hwy 3)
Head south of Weaverville on Hwy 3/299. Turn west out of Douglas City and then immediately south on Hwy 3. You're on the road.

On The Road

Wow, what a gorgeous section off the top of the ridge where this DH heads north from its junction with **DH6** and **DH11**. Long, tight, beautifully paved curves ess through a pine forest along dirt and rock banks. Views open up to the west toward Chanchelulla Peak and the Chanchelulla Wilderness. Although there are some nice sections to come, nothing will quite compare to these first few miles.

The great pavement drops a grade at 4.0 mi (6.4 km) as the road levels out on the bottom of the Salt Creek valley. Farmhouses, shacks and a few too many mobile homes appear in the dry terrain and the road bends alongside them. The curves aren't bad; they just don't compare with what you just rode coming down. But don't relax too much. After all, you've got to keep a lookout for the "Deer Next 6 Miles".

The landscape gets progressively drier as you continue due north toward Hayfork. Sage appears, but the oaks still thrive. As, it seems, does Hayfork; its 45-mph (70-kmh) speed zone appears at 10.4 mi (16.7 km). The limit drops to 35 mph (55 kmh) at 11.1 mi (17.9 km) where you reach the junction with Hyampom Rd (**TE-A**) and the road shifts east.

Hayfork could probably be crammed into about 10 per cent of the space it occupies. But it's largely irrelevant since the road is dead straight after the turn. At 13.1 mi (21.1 km), you're out of town into the hayfields and scrub. Apart from the green, forested walls of Wells and Hoosimbim Mtns looming ahead, it's hardly scenic. Maybe you'd feel more charitable if the curves weren't keeping you waiting.

The scenery does improve, albeit briefly. At 15.1 mi (24.3 km), the wide, rock-strewn bed of Hayfork Creek scars the land to the left. Its presence creates a few curves as the road veers north and passes Wildwood Rd (**TE-B**), which follows the creek. You continue, straight again, through a scene of pines and golden hay backed by treed mountains. It would be pretty but for the collection of broken down cars rusting quietly by the side of the road.

At 18.6 mi (29.9 km), the magic resumes. You're back in peaceful woods riding through a little canyon and enjoying the first S-curves you've seen in a while. The pavement improves; it's not perfect, but is certainly better. The easy esses rapidly evolve into tight, snaking corners as the pitch steepens and the climb up to Hayfork Summit begins in earnest. There's not a lot of traffic up here, but one always appreciates a passing lane like the one at 20.3 mi (32.7 km). Sometimes these improvements in engineering mean a loss of twistiness. Not this time, though. You're tilting as much as ever.

The extra lane ends at 20.8 mi (33.5 km). As you continue to climb and curve, the pavement starts to suffer the effects of the higher altitude. The scenery doesn't though. The views over the dense, steep forests of the Hayfork Divide are tremendous.

You get the benefit of another brief passing lane at 22.0 mi (35.4 km). Forest is thick on the left above the red dirt cliffs that define that side of the road. The sweeping views off to the right remain as you cross the 3654 ft (1107 m) Hayfork Summit at 23.0 mi (37.0 km).

The corners are even tighter essing down off the summit. Or maybe they just feel that way. Looking up, you catch panoramic vistas over the divide of Mike's Peak, Joe's Peak and Bully Choop Mtn. Looking down… well, given you're on the edge of a chasm, maybe that's not a great idea.

You lose the long views in a wall of trees as you slither downward on improving pavement. Although the picture of a road looping back upon itself from 26.2 mi (42.2 km) is as beautiful a sight as any peak or ridge. Or the deep gorge you enter at 27.6 mi (44.4 km).

How long can this road keep it up? S after S after S twists through the gorge. But hang on, maybe shouldn't have asked. The grade begins to ease and the straight at 29.8 mi (48.0 km) is the first you've seen in miles.

The curves resume at 30.9 mi (49.7 km), but they're not quite as tight. They are still great though, sweeping along a chalk white rockface that contrasts with the usual red rock and dirt bank. Though the setting is still rugged, natural and green when the sweepers take over, you can't help but feel the end is near.

And so it is. At 33.5 mi (53.9 km), you finally reach the end of the long descent and settle down into the flat, forested bottom. A roadside wrecking yard brings you back to earth. And the junction with **DH33 Shasta – Douglas City** brings you to the end of the DH, just east of Douglas City, at 35.3 mi (56.8 km).

Twisted Edges

TE-A Hayfork – Hyampom (29.8 mi / 48.0 km) *Hyampom Rd*
Pavement and engineering are below average on this twisty TE. But it's remote and very scenic as you climb from the depths of the spectacular canyon outside of Hayfork to the panoramic heights above Hayfork Creek. But the tremendous views of the wilderness peaks and valleys have a price: the middle of this road goes to one lane for at least four harrowing miles (6.4 harrowing km) before widening for the long, steady descent into Hyampom.

TE-B Wildwood Rd (17.7 mi / 28.5 km)
Rougher pavement than the DH but there are lots of curves through the forest along this Hayfork Creek valley/gorge tracker. The northern third is pretty good but the middle third is single lane. (Take the corners like there's a big truck coming the other way because there sometimes is.) The southern third has some development and just enough population to support a bar.

Rider's Log: **Date Ridden:** **Your Rating:** /10

OREGON
CALIFORNIA
WILD RIVER
INTER-MOUNTAI
Pg. 231
CVA I
CVA II
CVA III
REDWOODS
Pg. 143
RUSSIAN COAST Pg. 91
PACIFIC OCEAN
O'Brien
Crescent City
Klamath
Orick
McKinleyville
Arcata
Blue Lake
Eureka
Happy Camp
Somes Bar
Willow Creek
Cecilville
Weaverville
Yreka
Fort Jones
Gazelle
Weed
Callahan
Mount Shasta
Fortuna
Carlotta
Rio Dell
Bridgeville
Hyampom
Mad River
Triangle Junction
Douglas City
Shasta
Redding
Anderson
Weott
Phillipsville
Redway
Garberville
Shelter Cove
Red Bluff
Corning
Leggett
Covelo
DH20
DH50
DH23
DH12
DH2
DH31
DH13
DH18
DH33
DH44
DH6
DH64
DH36
DH66
DH11
DH5
(D-SUZ)
(D-BUE/HD)
(D-HON/YAM)
(D-KAW/KTM/SUZ)
(D-HD)
(D-HON/KAW/VIC)
(D-KTM/SUZ)
(D-YAM)
10 km
10 miles

Wild River

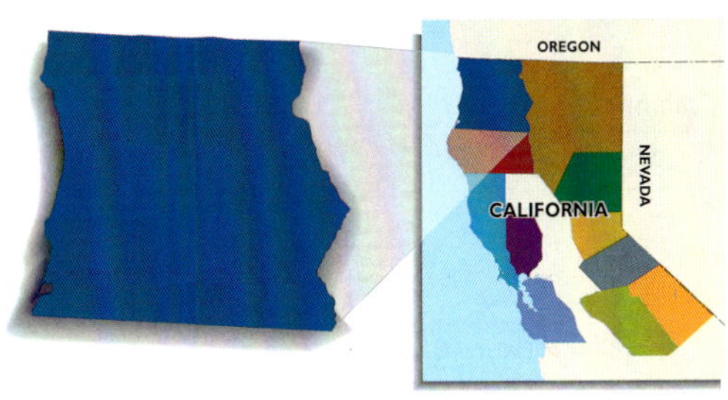

RUSSIAN WILDERNESS
To Ft. Jones
To Yreka & DH23
E. Callahan Rd.
TE-C
DH2 TE-A
Gazelle-Callahan Rd.
LOVERS LEAP
Masterson Rd.
Callahan
Callahan Emporium
RUSSIAN PEAK
GRIZZLY PEAK
SUGAR HILL
SISKIYOU
TRINITY
Scott Mountain BCG
Scott Mtn. Summit
MTNS.
SCOTT
Summit (6100 ft/1848m)
DH2
To Cecilville
Edson-Foulke Guest Ranch B&B 530.435.2627
Blue Creek
Trinity River
Forest Café 530.266.3575
Coffee Creek CG 530.266.3534
Coffee Creek Country Store
Carrville Inn B&B 530.266.3511
DH18
Eagle Creek BCG
Enright Gulch Cabins & Motel 530.266.3600
Trinity River BCG
Coffee Creek
E. Side Rd.
Wyntoon Resort/CG 800.715.3337
Mini Kat Burgers NL 530.266.3851
Coffee Cr.
Carville Loop
Sasquatch 530.266.3250
Yellow Jacket 530.266.3866
Jaktri Mkt SM
SHASTA-TRINITY NATIONAL FOREST
Preacher Meadow BCG
N. Fk
Swift Cr.
Cedar Stock Resort 530.286.2225
Timbers Rest & Lounge 530.286.2225 (Wed-Sat only)
Minersville NRA CG
Estrellita Marina/RV CG 530.286.2215
Trinity Lake
Trinity Center
TRINITY ALPS
Alpine View FS CG
Pinewood Cove Resort/CG 800.988.5253
Hayward Flat NRA CG
Rush Creek BCG
Stoney Point NRA CG
Mary Smith NF CG
Tannery Gulch CG SM
Sidney Gulch RV CG 530.623.6621
215 Main 530.623.6101
Trinity Alps Marina
Trinity Lake
Ackerman NRA CG
Trinity Dam Blvd.
TE-A
Tunnel Rock BCG
East Weaver BCG
204
Rush Creek Rd.
TE-B
Pine Cove Marina
To Willow Creek & DH12/31
DH13
MUSSER HILL
Weaverville
Lakeview Terrace Resort 530.778.3803
Dam Blvd.
Lewiston
Cooper Gulch BCG
Weaver Creek
TRINITY RIVER
Trinity
Trinity Mtn. Rd.
Douglas City
DH44 Pg. 179
To Triangle Jct & DH6 Pg. 157/DH11 Pg. 169
DH33 Pg. 175
To Redding
To CVA II Pg. 494
Old Lewiston Hotel B&B 800.286.4441
Trinity River Lodge/RV CG 800.761.2769
Lakeview Terrace Resort 530.778.3803
Lewiston Valley Motel 530.778.3942
River Oaks Resort CG 530.778.0220
Old Lewiston Bridge RV CG 800.922.1924
Mama's Mountain Valley Grill 530.778.3177
76
CVA TE-C
5
Old 99 Hwy.
Old Westside Rd.
W. Louie Rd.
Gazelle
Scarface Rd.
BONNER ROCK
Willow Creek
MALLETHEAD ROCK
TE-C
Gazelle Summit (4921ft/1491m)
GAZELLE MTN.
Gazelle-Callahan Rd.
Rail Cr. Rd.
Noyes Valley Creek
LOVERS LEAP
Masterson Rd.
Callahan
3 km
3 miles

DH18 Weaverville – Callahan

Highway 3

DH18

Distance:	61.7 mi / 99.3 km	Traffic:	Light

At a Glance

"If it wasna for the weavers, what wod ye do?" goes the old Irish ditty. And love 'em or hate 'em, you'd have to say the same for the dreamweavers down at CalTrans. California's asphalt artisans have taken time out of their busy schedule of straightening perfectly good motorcycle roads to thread a smooth, wide-shouldered seam of well-engineered tarmac through the glorious tapestry of the Shasta Trinity National Forest. Needling north from Weaverville, perfectly paved S-turns weave up and down past an appliqué of snowy peaks en route to the bright blue shoreline of Trinity Lake. North of the campground-dotted reservoir, it's more remote but much straighter too, at least until the DH scissors off the trickling Trinity River. Then, the shoulders narrow and the road sews tightly through some blind corners up to the Scott Mtn Summit. The north side of the summit is cut from a different cloth as straights and wide open sweepers shear a path down to the Scott Valley and the tiny outpost of Callahan. Now, if it wasna for the speed tax collectors…

TIRES	
Twistiness	26.3/ 30
Pavement	18.2/ 20
Engineering	6.6/ 10
Remoteness	8.1/ 10
Scenery	10.2/ 15
Character	8.8/ 15
Total	**78.2**

DH2 DH13 DH31 DH20 DH50 DH12 DH23

Access

From Weaverville

Coming in on DH13 Willow Creek – Weaverville (Hwy 299)

Go north at the well-marked turn onto Hwy 3 north. You're on the road.

From Douglas City

Coming in on DH33 Shasta (Redding) – Douglas City (Weaverville) (Hwy 299)

Coming in on DH44 Triangle Jct – Douglas City (Weaverville) (Hwy 3)

Go north on Hwy 3 to Weaverville. Follow Hwy 3 north out of town. You're on the road.

From Callahan

On Hwy 3

Coming in on DH2 Cecilville – Callahan

Go south on Hwy 3. You're on the road.

On The Road

Heading north from Weaverville, the outline of the Trinity Alps shapes the northwest horizon as you pass the 50-mph sign and come up over a rise. The road bends east and starts curving through the houses and small ranches that populate the pine forest near town. With fine pavement and esses right away, the future bodes well.

The minor development dwindles quickly and airy woods now define the surroundings on the straightish section that follows the early flurry of corners. A small slope rises on the right producing a sweeper, but that's about it. At 3.7 mi (6.0 km), you enter the Shasta-Trinity National Forest. Great name. So what happened to the great curves?

They resume at 6.1 mi (9.8 km) on a descent that follows a lengthy, climbing straight. A fetching little series takes you down through a short ravine to the junction with Rush Creek Rd (**TE-B**) at 6.6 mi (10.6 km). The road drops and sweeps some more to the junction with Trinity Dam Blvd (**TE-A**) at 7.5 mi (12.1 km).

ROUTING OPTION: Either one of these options is an excellent short cut if you're traveling to or from ***DH33 Shasta – Douglas City****. More to the point, they're great ways of bypassing the busy, boring stretch of Hwy 299 between Douglas City and Weaverville.*

The up and down continues. You climb again north of the twin TEs on a relatively remote, steadily winding ascent along a treed and sometimes terraced red dirt roadside to a modest summit. At 9.0 mi (14.5 km), you begin to descend and a fabulous, glacier view of the Alps hits you square in the face. It disappears as you plummet sharply back into the forest. The grade is as pitched as it was on the ride up and it has the tight sweepers to prove it, seemingly that much tighter since you're going downhill. This terrific section ends with a long straightaway at 10.6 mi (17.1 km).

The aquamarine of Trinity Lake comes into view at 11.6 mi (18.7 km), followed by a rapid succession of lakeside campgrounds, picnic and swim areas. Blue water and soaring mountains. It's a sublime scene while it lasts. And while it's a pity the water views are blocked by thick forest when the road climbs high above the shoreline, the tight, perfectly paved sweepers more than make up for it.

You top the ascent at 15.3 mi (24.6 km) and head down on some spaced, open sweepers, slowed down by the turn offs for the string of picnic areas and campgrounds. Of course, if you barely make it around the huge, 25-mph (40-km) advised sweeper at 16.7 mi (26.9 km), the fact you checked your speed may not be such a bad thing.

There are lots more tight curves on the steep decline and more excellent asphalt as you leave the lake area. Apart from a glimpse of the occasional alp such as the one at 21.3 mi (34.3 km), however, there's not much in the way of scenery since the forest is thick and closes you in most of the time. Despite the woodsy setting, the well-manicured corners remain predictable and well sighted. Your speed? Predictable as well.

The road straightens at 22.4 mi (36.0 km). And when this DH straightens, it doesn't fool around. Minor changes in direction are all you get through the long, flat stretch of thinning forest. This relatively dull state of affairs prevails all the way past the turnoff for Trinity Center at 28.7 mi (46.2 km).

In fact, you don't see another curve until 30.3 mi (48.8 km) when the road comes back against the shoreline of Trinity Lake. Once again, the presence of the lake inspires the DH to curve. Gotta love balanced TIRES: the steady stream of corners are not as tight as they were in the last lakeside stretch, but this one has far more enduring water vistas.

At 33.3 mi (53.6 km), you emerge from the forest and straighten across the wide, dry estuary of the Trinity River. The watercourse has narrowed beyond the north end of the lake and a scape of grass and gravel mounds spreads out flat over a once-flooded plain. If you want to explore it further, Eastside Rd, a paved/gravel route that that goes along the east side of the lake through the Trinity Mtns and down to intersect with mid-**DH33**, turns off right at 34.1 mi (54.9 km).

More great scenes. At 35.8 mi (57.6 km), you round a lazy corner and face Billy's Peak, fronting the Scott Mtns to the north. Beside you, the Trinity River percolates through the open trees. At 36.6 mi (58.9 km), you cross the river and reach the turnoff to the one-store berg of Coffee Creek, hidden in the trees just down Coffee Creek Rd.

Coffee Creek feels like the end of the line. Heading north from there into the foothills of the Scott Mtns, a sense of high remoteness sets in. Supple curves track the Trinity River through a setting that's sometimes thick forest and sometimes low brush. California's water levels have been low so long, hardy, drought-resistant trees have sprouted in the river's coarse islands.

ROUTING OPTION: The 29.0 (46.7 km) gravel route across to Castella on the I-5 is right at 42.0 mi (67.6 km).

You cross the river at 42.8 mi (68.9 km) and the terrain roughens. A treed bank rises on the left across from the creek that runs on your right for a brief spell. You traverse the creek at 44.6 mi (71.8 km) but whichever side it's on, the broad swath of riverbed creates a sense of breadth and openness to the scene. It's a softer landscape as you head north; the rock and moraine are often covered by a layer of green and gold grass that sprouts between the trees and along the roadside.

If you're objecting to the lack of tight curves, your objection's about to be sustained. You cross the river one last time at 46.8 mi (75.3 km) and see a yellow sign warning "Narrow Winding Road". No, that's not referring to the rough and narrow Parks Creek Rd that turns off east to the I-5 at 48.0 mi (77.2 km). It's referring to the DH.

Which transforms suddenly. The shoulders on the wide swath of highway narrow to almost nothing as the road turns northeast and skirts Blue

Creek before mounting a twisting assault on the Scott Mtn summit. The esses are back and they're tighter than ever as the still smoothly paved road cuts sharply – and sometimes awkwardly – up a steep incline through the trees and along pitched rockfaces. You get extra points if you ride this section proficiently.

The gain in altitude is quick before the grade lessens at 51.2 mi (82.4 km). You're high enough that views of the Scott Mtns are visible to the southwest. And with the curves lengthening, you might even be able to look up and catch a glimpse of them without riding off a cliff.

You continue to climb, tightly but evenly through an increasingly subalpine setting of rock, shrinking trees, small meadows and colorful shrubs, reaching the 5401 ft (1646 m) Scott Mtn Summit at 53.6 mi (86.2 km). Don't expect more of the same on the way down. Your first hint? The 55-mph sign that begins the descent.

It's hard to imagine a greater contrast than that between the north and south sides of the summit. Where the south had nothing but tight curves, the descent off the north side begins with a long, leisurely straight toward a distant line of snow-patched mountains. In fact, there are but a handful of curves and sweepers on the fast ride down. Not too fast, though – the DH's last long sweeper at 57.8 mi (93.0 km) can be a little tricky.

The distant mountains dip below the nearer, brown mound of Smith Mtn as you come through that last big corner and pass through a striking gray and brown rock canyon. The steep descent continues down to the stop sign and junction with the Gazelle-Callahan Rd (**TE-C**) at 60.0 mi (96.5 km). To stay on the DH to Callahan, **turn left**.

You're down in the Scott Valley now. And it's quite pretty as you negotiate the final flat and curveless miles. The DH ends in the one-bar town of Callahan at 61.7 mi (99.3 km).

Twisted Edges

TE-A Trinity Dam Blvd (25.1 mi/ 40.4 km)
The long way round offers views through the pines over Lewiston and Trinity Lakes before jutting west through a less interesting forested section over to Hwy 3. Well paved, wide and sweepy for the southern half; shoulderless, not so well paved and a little tighter curved in the north. But quiet, quiet, quiet throughout.

TE-B Rush Creek Rd (9.1 mi / 14.6 km)
For riders in a hurry, this easy, wide, smoothly paved bypass of the Weaverville strip features the sort of long, easy, well-engineered curves that won't slow you down.

NAVIGATION: From the south, this TE turns left off Trinity Dam Blvd north of Lewiston. If you go through town, you can pick up the TE off the Lewiston Turnpike Rd.

TOUR NOTE: Lewiston's an inviting little place with funky antique stores and a quiet, old-fashioned riverside ambience. The old gas pumps in town seem frozen in time. Too bad the gas prices aren't.

TE-C Gazelle-Callahan Rd (25.3 mi / 40.7 km)
The tumbledown hotel in Callahan was a stop on the Oregon Trail between 1852 and 1887. Maybe you'll sense the ghosts of those who rode the prairie schooners when you do this decently paved, remote though straight-ish, high-speed dash through forest and farmland up to the tight corners either side of Gazelle Summit and then down to the Shasta Valley. Last time we were in Gazelle, the gas station there had regular posted for 63 cents and super on for 69. Too bad it's been closed for thirty years.

RIDER'S LOG: **DATE RIDDEN:** **YOUR RATING:** **/10**

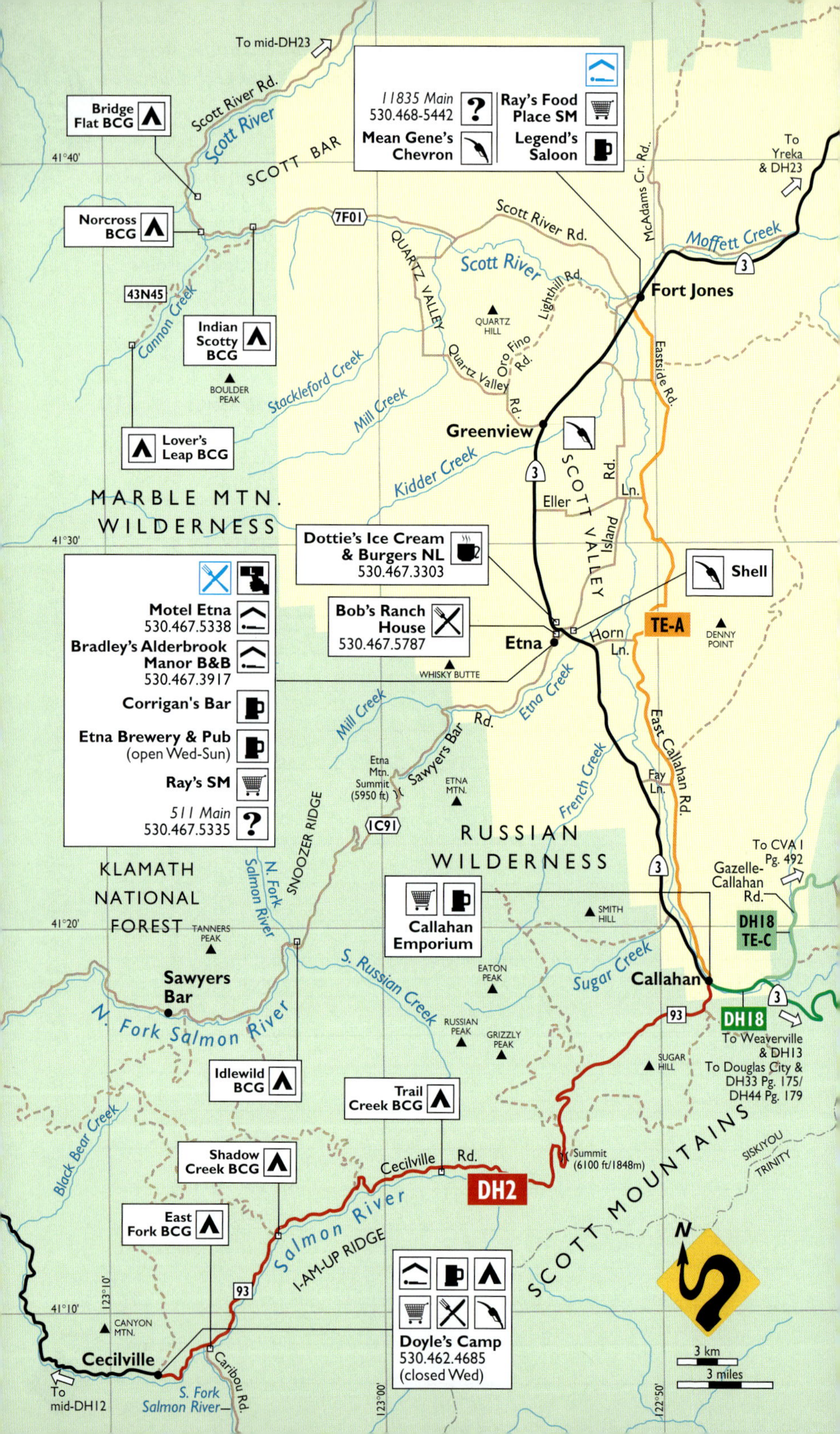

To mid-DH23
Bridge Flat BCG
Scott River Rd.
Scott River
SCOTT BAR
11835 Main
530.468-5442
Ray's Food Place SM
Mean Gene's Chevron
Legend's Saloon
To Yreka & DH23
McAdams Cr. Rd.
Norcross BCG
7F01
Scott River Rd.
Moffett Creek
Scott River
Lighthill Rd.
Fort Jones
QUARTZ VALLEY
QUARTZ HILL
43N45
Cannon Creek
Indian Scotty BCG
Eastside Rd.
Oro Fino Rd.
Quartz Valley Rd.
BOULDER PEAK
Stackleford Creek
Mill Creek
Greenview
Lover's Leap BCG
Kidder Creek
SCOTT VALLEY
Rd.
Ln.
Eller
Island
MARBLE MTN. WILDERNESS
Dottie's Ice Cream & Burgers NL
530.467.3303
Shell
Motel Etna
530.467.5338
Bradley's Alderbrook Manor B&B
530.467.3917
Corrigan's Bar
Etna Brewery & Pub
(open Wed-Sun)
Ray's SM
511 Main
530.467.5335
Bob's Ranch House
530.467.5787
Etna
Horn Ln.
TE-A
DENNY POINT
WHISKY BUTTE
Mill Creek
Etna Creek
Rd.
East Callahan Rd.
Etna Mtn. Summit (5950 ft)
Sawyers Bar
ETNA MTN.
French Creek
Fay Ln.
1C91
SNOOZER RIDGE
RUSSIAN WILDERNESS
To CVA I Pg. 492
Gazelle-Callahan Rd.
KLAMATH NATIONAL FOREST
N. Fork Salmon River
Callahan Emporium
SMITH HILL
DH18 TE-C
TANNERS PEAK
Sawyers Bar
S. Russian Creek
EATON PEAK
Sugar Creek
Callahan
N. Fork Salmon River
RUSSIAN PEAK
GRIZZLY PEAK
93
DH18
To Weaverville & DH13
To Douglas City & DH33 Pg. 175/ DH44 Pg. 179
SUGAR HILL
Idlewild BCG
Trail Creek BCG
SCOTT MOUNTAINS
Black Bear Creek
Shadow Creek BCG
Summit (6100 ft/1848m)
SISKIYOU
TRINITY
Cecilville Rd.
DH2
East Fork BCG
Salmon River
I-AM-UP RIDGE
N
93
CANYON MTN.
Doyle's Camp
530.462.4685
(closed Wed)
Cecilville
Caribou Rd.
To mid-DH12
S. Fork Salmon River
3 km
3 miles
41°40'
41°30'
41°20'
41°10'
123°10'
123°00'
122°50'

DH2 CALLAHAN – CECILVILLE
Cecilville Road

DISTANCE:	29.8 mi / 48.0 km	TRAFFIC:	Very Light

AT A GLANCE

“It is Unlawful to Ski or Toboggan on a County Road,” says the sign just out of Callahan. With nothing in Cecilville but a tiny all-purpose bar and a further 30 miles of goat path between it and the next piece of decent asphalt, the pylon quotient can obviously get pretty low around here. Of course, since they’ve laid a blanket of fresh blacktop, it soon won’t be just bobsledders and biathletes wanting to take advantage of this lonely mountain road. Motorcyclists will be tempted to go for a run up and down the steep ridge out of Callahan. After taking in the glorious alpine views off the summit, you’ll schuss down through steep straights and tight sweepers, then slam through a long, steady slalom course of S-curves that follows the Salmon River almost all the way to C-ville. With all the riders coming to check out this black diamond, the county may well need a new sign. How about: “It is Unlawful to Operate a Pylon on this County Road?”

TIRES	
Twistiness	30/30
Pavement	19.4/20
Engineering	5.8/10
Remoteness	9.0/10
Scenery	9.7/15
Character	11.1/15
TOTAL	**85.0**

ACCESS

From Callahan

Coming in on DH18 Weaverville – Callahan (Hwy 3)

The turnoff to Cecilville is just north of Callahan on Hwy 3. Take it. You’re on the road.

From Cecilville

Go east. You’re on the road.

ON THE ROAD

It’s sweet pavement from the start as you turn off Hwy 3 and roll west of Callahan on a short bit of straight along the south fork of the Scott River. The first series of climbing S-curves and sweepers at 2.1 mi (3.4 km) are pretty sweet, too, as you twist along the steepening gorge that separates the road from the slopes of Sugar Hill.

Treed slopes roll south and west like swells in a forested sea. But from close up you can see they’re darkened by patches of shiny black obsidian.

The drier slope that's visible at 6.2 mi (10.0 km) when the climb steepens through the narrowing canyon only serves to accentuate the green.

Not too tight; not too gentle. The curves so far have been predictable and well-cambered. Now they tighten and lose some of that perfect banking at 6.6 mi (10.6 km) where long sweepers switchback up the steepening ridge. Sightlines suffer on these long turns, particularly on the right-handers around the sharp bluffs. And you don't want to find yourself coming off an apex in the oncoming lane. That'll be just about the time you'll see your first car. Or last UPS truck.

The radius and length of the curves settle back down at 8.3 mi (13.4 km). Or do they? Just when you're back charging into the corners, a long, sweeping hairpin at 9.3 mi (15.0 km) sends a jolt of electricity through you. As may the patches of gravel.

That long corner has shifted you to the north side of the ridge and the slope now rises to your left and falls to the right. Views through the trees reveal the southern end of Scott Valley and the upward reaches of Russian Peak. No more widowmakers for a while, as the terrain flattens and the road shifts you back to a south-facing slope.

The Scott Mtns, spreading to the south, have gotten progressively closer as you've ridden west. And when you come back to the south side of the ridge, they're more up front than ever. Alpine meadows, bold tusks of rock and brilliant mini-glaciers create a stunning scene. You reach the DH's 6100 ft (1859 m) summit at 11.7 mi (18.9 km).

Unfortunately, the fabulous scenery disappears behind the trees as you begin to descend. The curves disappear, too, but don't be kicking it into high gear just yet. There's a sharp left-hander at 12.5 mi (20.1 km) and more steep straights tagged by tight sweepers after that.

The corners gentle down but resume their steady rhythm at 15.1 mi (24.3 km). They get tighter again at 17.5 mi (28.2 km) after the road joins the Salmon River and follows its course. You're still descending, at times steeply, as you negotiate the long strings of lower-speed S-curves and sweepers that snake along the dirt and rock slopes through the ever-thickening forest. I-Am-Up Ridge soars high above the treetops. Enjoying the DH's best section without a pylon in sight, You-Are-Up, too.

The endless S-curves don't let up at 19.9 mi (32.0 km) when the grade of the descent eases to just a few degrees. The slightly downward pitch is perfect if you like to stay in a middle gear and carry some speed into the next curve. Come to think of it, it's perfect even if you don't.

A few short straights appear and the corners aren't quite as tight once you curve over the bridge at 23.0 mi (37.0 km). There are some winding fits and starts in this section but only one comes anywhere close to your recent curve-after-curve-after-curve experience. Entering a linear section at 25.0 mi (40.2 km), you see a farm to the right – the first sign of civilization you've seen since the bar in Callahan.

But not to worry. This is Siskiyou County. Civilization is a relative term here. At 26.4 mi (39.6 km), you and the DH are back in a groove as you enter a final canyon stretch of S-curves. The grade of the descent continues to be so slight it's barely noticeable, but for a few extra scrapings off your pegs from the speed boost that gravity gives you in the corners.

The esses end at 28.7 mi (46.2 km), right about the time the sign for the Cecilville Hose Company tells you you're almost there. But you won't feel you've been hosed as a straightaway takes you past some cleared land to Cecilville's 25-mph zone, and end of the DH, at 29.8 mi (48.0 km).

*ROUTING OPTION: What's it like if you carry on from Cecilville and connect with mid-**DH12 Happy Camp – Willow Creek**? Well, it's nothing like the DH, that's for sure. If you continue on, you'll find 27.6 mi (44.4 km) of narrow, crumbling and sometimes very narrow one-lane road. But this crap does make the beautiful final 7.0 mi (11.3 km) from Butler Flat (**DH12TE-A**) feel even better.*

Twisted Edges

TE-A Callahan – Fort Jones (22.6 mi / 36.4 km) *E Callahan Rd - Eastside Rd*

You'd always take this option over parallel Hwy 3, which has slightly better pavement but no other redeeming features. The quiet, rural flavor of the scenery contrasts sharply with all the light commercial zoning along the main highway. Running along the base of the hills at the eastern edge of Scott Valley causes a fair number of turns and the engineering is pretty good too, except at the very south end of Eastside Rd where the asphalt gets a little narrow.

Rider's Log: **Date Ridden:** **Your Rating: /10**

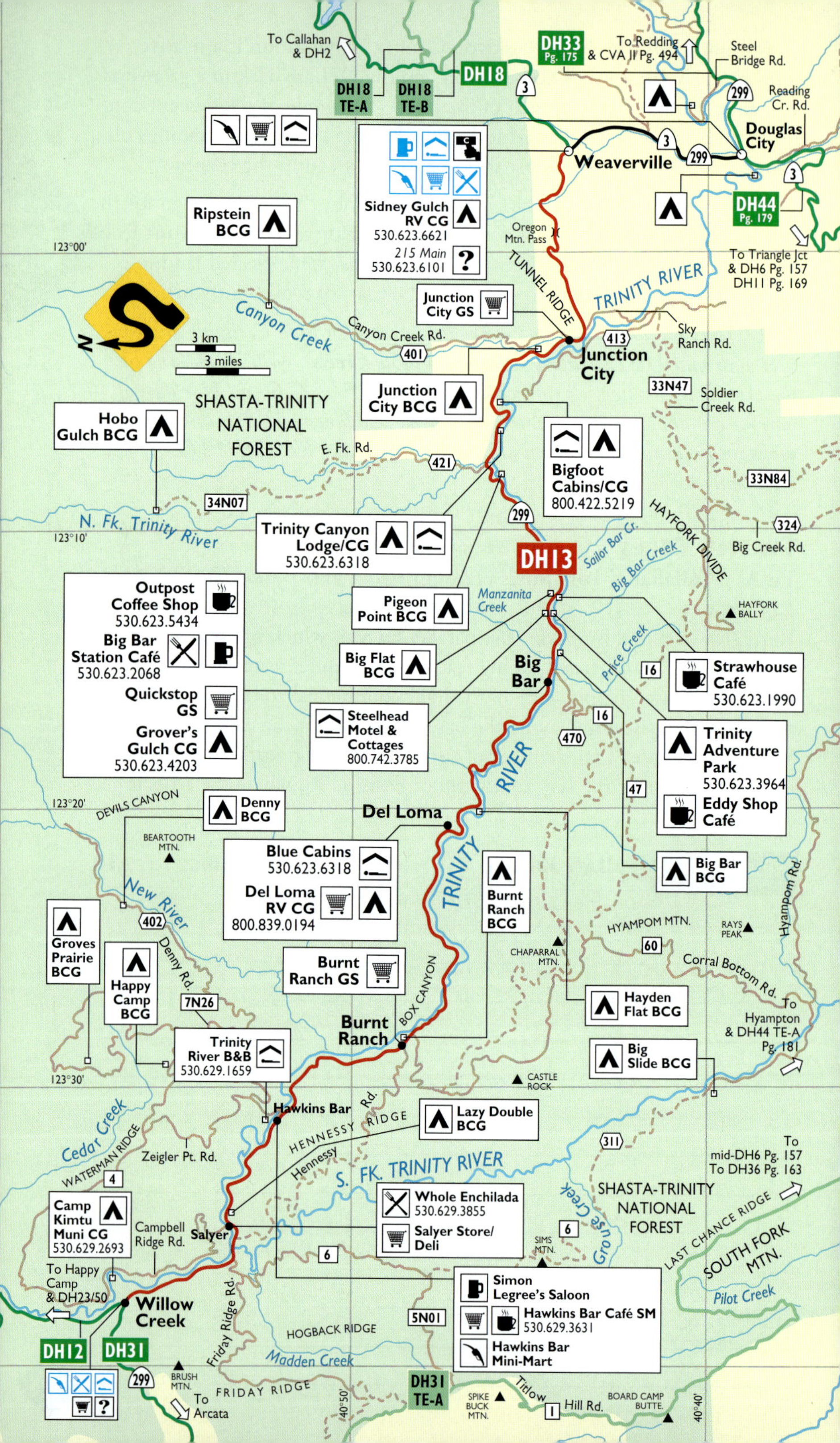

To Callahan & DH2
DH18
DH18 TE-A
DH18 TE-B
DH33 Pg. 175
To Redding & CVA II Pg. 494
Steel Bridge Rd.
Reading Cr. Rd.
Douglas City
Weaverville
Sidney Gulch RV CG 530.623.6621
215 Main 530.623.6101
Ripstein BCG
DH44 Pg. 179
To Triangle Jct & DH6 Pg. 157 DH11 Pg. 169
Oregon Mtn. Pass
123°00'
TUNNEL RIDGE
TRINITY RIVER
Junction City GS
Canyon Creek
Canyon Creek Rd.
3 km
3 miles
Sky Ranch Rd.
Junction City
Junction City BCG
33N47
Soldier Creek Rd.
SHASTA-TRINITY NATIONAL FOREST
Hobo Gulch BCG
E. Fk. Rd.
Bigfoot Cabins/CG 800.422.5219
33N84
34N07
N. Fk. Trinity River
123°10'
HAYFORK DIVIDE
Trinity Canyon Lodge/CG 530.623.6318
Big Creek Rd.
DH13
Sailor Bar Cr.
Big Bar Creek
Outpost Coffee Shop 530.623.5434
Big Bar Station Café 530.623.2068
Quickstop GS
Grover's Gulch CG 530.623.4203
Pigeon Point BCG
Manzanita Creek
HAYFORK BALLY
Big Flat BCG
Big Bar
Price Creek
Strawhouse Café 530.623.1990
Steelhead Motel & Cottages 800.742.3785
RIVER
Trinity Adventure Park 530.623.3964
Eddy Shop Café
123°20'
DEVILS CANYON
Denny BCG
Del Loma
BEARTOOTH MTN.
Blue Cabins 530.623.6318
Del Loma RV CG 800.839.0194
TRINITY
Burnt Ranch BCG
Big Bar BCG
Hyampom Rd.
New River
Groves Prairie BCG
Denny Rd.
HYAMPOM MTN.
RAYS PEAK
CHAPARRAL MTN.
Corral Bottom Rd.
Happy Camp BCG
Burnt Ranch GS
BOX CANYON
7N26
Burnt Ranch
Hayden Flat BCG
To Hyampton & DH44 TE-A Pg. 181
Trinity River B&B 530.629.1659
Big Slide BCG
123°30'
CASTLE ROCK
Hawkins Bar
Rd.
HENNESSY RIDGE
Lazy Double BCG
Cedar Creek
WATERMAN RIDGE
Zeigler Pt. Rd.
Hennessy
S. FK. TRINITY RIVER
To mid-DH6 Pg. 157 To DH36 Pg. 163
Camp Kimtu Muni CG 530.629.2693
Whole Enchilada 530.629.3855
Salyer Store/ Deli
Grouse Creek
SHASTA-TRINITY NATIONAL FOREST
Campbell Ridge Rd.
Salyer
LAST CHANCE RIDGE
SOUTH FORK MTN.
SIMS MTN.
To Happy Camp & DH23/50
Simon Legree's Saloon
Hawkins Bar Café SM 530.629.3631
Hawkins Bar Mini-Mart
Pilot Creek
Willow Creek
Friday Ridge Rd.
5N01
HOGBACK RIDGE
DH12
DH31
Madden Creek
BRUSH MTN.
To Arcata
FRIDAY RIDGE
DH31 TE-A
SPIKE BUCK MTN.
Titlow Hill Rd.
BOARD CAMP BUTTE
40°50'
40°40'

DH13 WEAVERVILLE – WILLOW CREEK

Highway 299

DISTANCE:	54.9 mi / 88.3 km	TRAFFIC:	Moderate

TIRES	
Twistiness	26.8/ 30
Pavement	17.5 20
Engineering	6.8/ 10
Remoteness	5.3/ 10
Scenery	10.2/ 15
Character	12.6/ 15
TOTAL	**79.2**

AT A GLANCE

Shangri-la – a beautiful natural environment of snow-capped mountains, steep canyons and winding rivers where man lives in harmony with nature. James Hilton, who conceived this idyllic Tibetan paradise for his novel, *Lost Horizons*, actually described the landscape east of Weaverville as the closest place on earth to match that definition. And you can see his point once you transcend the strip malls of modern Weaverville and embark on your journey toward the coast through the Shasta and Six Rivers National Forests. Enlightened Engineering is apparent throughout, as is the rapturous Pavement that sweeps you upward on a winding passing lane to the Oregon Mtn Pass and then down to commune at length with the peaceful Trinity River in moderate, predictable corners that rarely drop below a 40-mph (60-kmh) advisory. Often remote and always scenic, Hilton's mountains, canyons and rivers are all around you. The question is: Can motorcyclists live in harmony with speed tax collectors? Maybe in Tibet.

ACCESS

From Weaverville

On Hwy 299
Head west and follow the signs to Eureka. You're on the road when you leave town.

Coming in on DH18 Callahan – Weaverville (Hwy 3)
Turn right on Hwy 299. Once out of town, you're on the road.

From Willow Creek

Coming in on DH12 Happy Camp – Willow Creek (Hwy 96)
Coming in on DH31 Blue Lake (Arcata) – Willow Creek (Hwy 299)
Head west on Hwy 299. Clear Willow Creek and you're on the road.

ON THE ROAD

The charred evidence of Year 2000's wildfires covers the hill to the left as you leave Weaverville. It contrasts starkly with the unsullied slopes of

Tunnel Ridge dead ahead. But your attention is refocused at 1.4 mi (2.3 km) on the passing lane that tracks a huge, ascending series of S-sweepers all the way up to the Oregon Mtn Pass (2888 ft / 880 m). It's a long one, and combined with the steepening grade, provides a sure remedy to any pylon angst you may have suffered in the early miles.

Ah, the joy of effortlessly flicking your wrist and blurring past some decelerating motorist with his gas pedal plastered to the floor. Especially if you can squeak past that very last, lingering Accord and get the road ahead to yourself at 2.8 mi (4.5 km) when you reach the top of the pass and the passing lane shifts across the highway. The views are wide as the road straightens and you settle into a valley characterized by forest to the left and a sparsely treed, burnt-brown, grassy slope to the left. In the background, the blue peaks of the Hayfork Divide pitch skyward.

All that's missing are a couple of 30-mph (50-kmh) curves. No problem. You'll find them at 3.7 mi (6.0 km) when you sweep into a dramatic, steep-walled canyon, dotted by rock and trees. The terrain is rough and the descent is steep, but the engineering is excellent on this gorge descent. Essy, higher-speed curves resume and the canyon ends as suddenly as it began, giving way to grass, forest and a long straight into Junction City. Arrival: 7.5 mi (12.1 km).

There's not much going on in J-City, no doubt related to the fact it's barely more than a mapdot with a 45-mph (70-kmh) speed trap. After you cross Canyon Creek, the standard 55-mph (90-kmh) shackle resumes along a fresh rockface over the Trinity River. This major waterway treks up from the south to bond with the DH for the remainder of the journey. Pavement's less impressive here, with tar strips and rectangular patches the rule rather than the exception. Still smooth, though. Which is a good thing considering the speed you need to get a lot of lean out of the gentle corners.

Rivers and rockfaces. This usually means great curves. But not here in the land of uberengineering. Some easy sweepers are all you get. CalTrans' efforts at straightening are aided by the fact the slope regularly recedes, flattening out the landscape so much that there's even room for a small house or two. These anomalies fade at 11.5 mi (18.5 km) as a series of respectable mirror-tilters guide you through a narrow section of the Trinity Canyon.

At 14.3 mi (23.0 km), you bridge the north fork of the Trinity River and enter the Shasta National Forest. As you do, you pass the turnoff to the ghost town of Helena, a main street of boarded-up buildings that belies its wild heyday in the mid-1850s when the same building served as a school by day and a brothel by night. Makes as much sense as a bike shop doubling as a police station.

The entrance to Shasta is striking, consisting of a gateway of high, glinting rockfaces. It's almost as striking as the curves that arc gracefully along the river through a remote landscape of precarious cliffs and forested hills. This scenic, high-speed, sweeping section of road is best ridden without a stream of traffic in front. Then again, what road isn't?

But there can be traffic on this DH, especially in high summer when motorcyclists have to share the road not only with fishermen, but with narrow-tired cyclists and Subaru-driving rafters who hang out in places like the Trinity Adventure Park at 20.4 mi (32.8 km). The presence of organic visitors from Marin County no doubt explains an organic coffee house in what's supposed to be the middle of nowhere.

The next few miles are a bit of a letdown. The road struggles to wiggle, the endless patch jobs make the pavement look tired and the formerly cinematic scenery has about as much drama as a later episode of ER. "Nurse CalTrans, this patient needs an infusion of tight curves and new pavement. Stat!"

Sorry, Doc. Seems the state's on Medicaid these days, so you'll just have to suffer, at least until you're beyond Big Bar, where there's a campsite and a couple of cafés at 23.5 mi (37.8 km). A series of 40-mph (60-kmh) curves begins at 25.4 mi (40.9 km), followed by some big, rounding sweepers. And check out the like-new, face-lifted pavement.

The small service dot of Del Loma comes and goes at 29.5 mi (47.5 km), giving way to more high-grade scenery – skyrocketing cliffs, deep green, thickly treed hillsides and the Trinity River drifting off into the distance. Not to mention a solid grey ribbon of pavement crinkled into corners and wrapping around the red rock.

Although you're riding consistently along the river, perspectives change depending upon the nature of the curve and where you are in one. Sometimes you're turning square to the river; other times, you're sweeping in tandem through a mélange of forest and rock. More scenic variety comes at 36.9 mi (59.4 km) when you cross the river and begin the twisting climb up the 75-degree sides of Box Canyon.

You reach the top o' the climb at 39.7 mi (63.9 km) and straighten out onto Burnt Flat. But the curves aren't over yet. Scenically enhanced by high views to the granite face across the river, a series of essing sweepers snakes you into the green sea of the Six Rivers National Forest. A passing lane begins at 44.2 mi (71.1 km) and the sweepers separate but continue through the bitty berg of Hawkins Bar.

You're off the river past Hawkins Bar for a brief spell at 47.1 mi (75.8 km). Then the river dips back in under a couple of high bridges inspiring a four-curve ess. With this flurry of curves, however, comes a flurry of development as a bench along the river is suddenly filled with cottages among the thinned trees. This bit of blight is interrupted at 49.1 mi (79.0 km) when the bottom drops out of the terrain and the road curves along a steep-angled cliff. But it seems your experience of winding along a river through thick, uninterrupted forest is about over. At 49.4 mi (79.5 km), a line of lazy pines guides you past another campground and into the 45-mph (70-kmh) zone of Salyer.

At 50.7 mi (81.6 km), the 55-mph (90-kmh) resumes. Just as you accelerate, the DH throws a disarmingly tight ess at you. But that's about it for remaining thrills. The South Fork Trinity River spills in from the south, marking the boundary between Trinity and Humboldt Counties. As the South Fork joins with the main flow, the DH straightens, with just enough subtle bending left through the oaks, pines and fir to keep your attention till your arrival in Willow Creek, at 54.9 mi (88.3 km).

RIDER'S LOG: **DATE RIDDEN:** **YOUR RATING: /10**

What are the Top Ten Rides based on Twistiness, Pavement, Engineering, Remoteness, Scenery and Character? You'll find the answers in the TIRES Charts at the back of the book. The complete list of DHs by TIRES components is at destinationhighways.com.

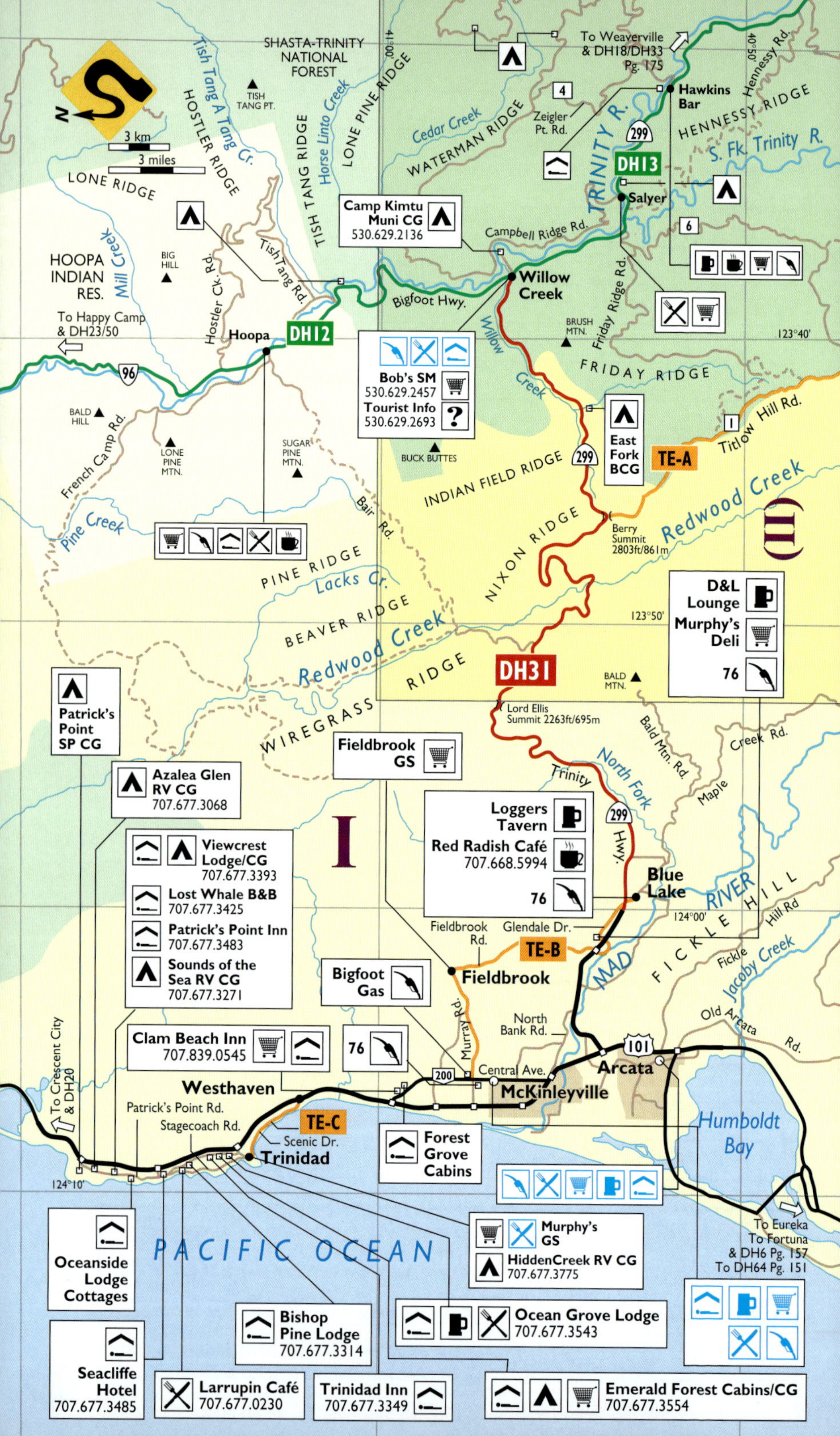
SHASTA-TRINITY NATIONAL FOREST
To Weaverville & DH18/DH33 Pg. 175
Hawkins Bar
HENNESSY RIDGE
Hennessy Rd.
S. Fk. Trinity R.
TRINITY R.
DH13
Salyer
Zeigler Pt. Rd.
WATERMAN RIDGE
Cedar Creek
LONE PINE RIDGE
Horse Linto Creek
TISH TANG RIDGE
Tish Tang A Tang Cr.
HOSTLER RIDGE
TISH TANG PT.
3 km
3 miles
LONE RIDGE
HOOPA INDIAN RES.
Mill Creek
BIG HILL
Hostler Ck. Rd.
TishTang Rd.
Camp Kimtu Muni CG 530.629.2136
Campbell Ridge Rd.
Willow Creek
Bigfoot Hwy.
Friday Ridge Rd.
BRUSH MTN.
FRIDAY RIDGE
To Happy Camp & DH23/50
Hoopa
DH12
Bob's SM 530.629.2457
Tourist Info 530.629.2693
BALD HILL
LONE PINE MTN.
SUGAR PINE MTN.
BUCK BUTTES
French Camp Rd.
Pine Creek
Bair Rd.
Willow Creek
East Fork BCG
TE-A
Titlow Hill Rd.
INDIAN FIELD RIDGE
NIXON RIDGE
Berry Summit 2803ft/861m
Redwood Creek
II
PINE RIDGE
Lacks Cr.
BEAVER RIDGE
Redwood Creek
RIDGE
WIREGRASS
DH31
D&L Lounge
Murphy's Deli
76
BALD MTN.
Lord Ellis Summit 2263ft/695m
Patrick's Point SP CG
Azalea Glen RV CG 707.677.3068
Fieldbrook GS
Trinity
North Fork
Bald Mtn. Rd.
Creek Rd.
Maple
Viewcrest Lodge/CG 707.677.3393
Lost Whale B&B 707.677.3425
Patrick's Point Inn 707.677.3483
Sounds of the Sea RV CG 707.677.3271
I
Loggers Tavern
Red Radish Café 707.668.5994
76
Hwy.
Blue Lake
MAD RIVER
FICKLE HILL
Fickle Hill Rd
Jacoby Creek
Fieldbrook Rd.
Glendale Dr.
TE-B
Bigfoot Gas
Fieldbrook
Murray Rd.
North Bank Rd.
Old Arcata Rd.
Clam Beach Inn 707.839.0545
76
To Crescent City & DH20
Westhaven
Central Ave.
McKinleyville
Arcata
Humboldt Bay
Patrick's Point Rd.
Stagecoach Rd.
TE-C
Scenic Dr.
Trinidad
Forest Grove Cabins
To Eureka To Fortuna & DH6 Pg. 157 To DH64 Pg. 151
PACIFIC OCEAN
Murphy's GS
HiddenCreek RV CG 707.677.3775
Oceanside Lodge Cottages
Bishop Pine Lodge 707.677.3314
Ocean Grove Lodge 707.677.3543
Seacliffe Hotel 707.677.3485
Larrupin Café 707.677.0230
Trinidad Inn 707.677.3349
Emerald Forest Cabins/CG 707.677.3554

DH31 Willow Creek – Blue Lake (Arcata)

Highway 299

Distance:	32.3 mi / 52.0 km	Traffic:	Moderate

At a Glance

Sometimes you just want to take it easy. You're not into tight, blind, decreasing radius hairpins. You don't want to deal with patched and bumpy asphalt. All you want to do is pour it on through smooth, carefree, perfectly engineered sweepers. If that's your mood, this is your DH. Wide and pristinely paved, this gently sweeping lark effortlessly wings its way over two summits before dropping to the Pacific. The Willow Creek end is the best, with a high concentration of moderate, often-linked sweepers and lots of passing lanes climbing up to the Berry Summit. The wide, natural scenes over the Six Rivers National Forest culminate in a spectacular vista as you come over the top. The much straighter and solid-yellow-limited descent isn't as enthralling. But you soon get another curving, passing-laned climb up to the Lord-Ellis Summit. The final descent is a high-speed, straight and long-sweeper coast to the coast. Now that was easy, wasn't it?

TIRES	
Twistiness	24.0/ 30
Pavement	17.9/ 20
Engineering	9.3/ 10
Remoteness	5.8/ 10
Scenery	10.2/ 15
Character	5.2/ 15
Total	**72.4**

Access

From Willow Creek

Coming in on DH12 Happy Camp – Willow Creek (Hwy 96)
Coming in on DH13 Weaverville – Willow Creek (Hwy 299)
Go west on Hwy 299. You're on the road

From Arcata

Via Hwy 299
Turn off Hwy 101 onto Hwy 299. The DH begins east of Blue Lake when the freeway ends.

On The Road

You leave Willow Creek on a passing lane, power-sweeping your way on near-perfect pavement high along the bank of Willow Creek toward the beckoning, rounded green outline of Indian Field Ridge. The climbing, passing lane ends at 0.9 mi (1.4 km) only to resume at 1.2 mi (1.9 km). Pylons? What pylons?

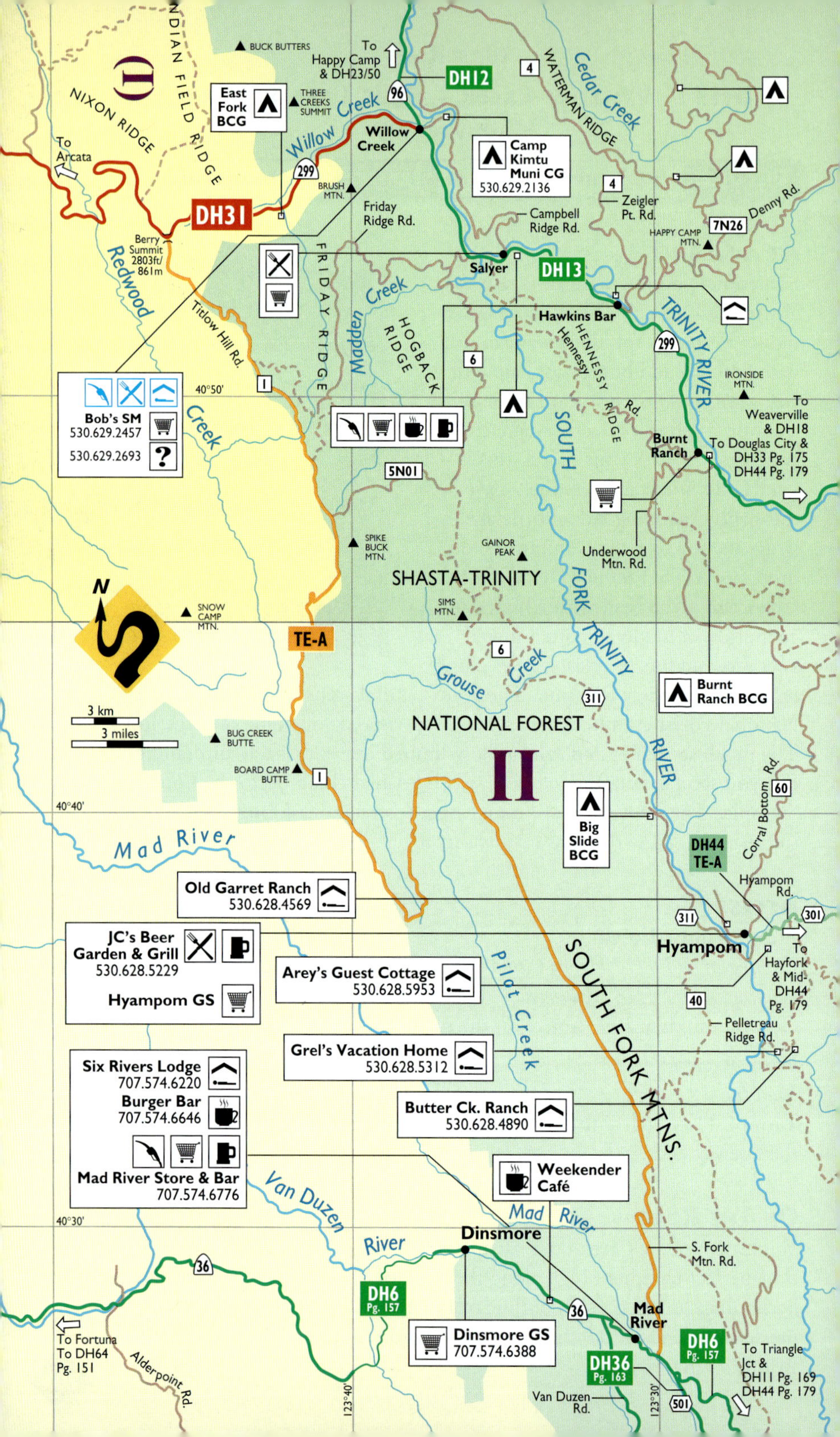

I
II
BUCK BUTTERS
To Happy Camp & DH23/50
96
DH12
4
WATERMAN RIDGE
Cedar Creek
NIXON RIDGE
INDIAN FIELD RIDGE
East Fork BCG
THREE CREEKS SUMMIT
Willow Creek
Willow Creek
To Arcata
299
Camp Kimtu Muni CG
530.629.2136
BRUSH MTN.
DH31
4
Zeigler Pt. Rd.
Denny Rd.
Friday Ridge Rd.
Campbell Ridge Rd.
7N26
HAPPY CAMP MTN.
Berry Summit 2803ft/ 861m
Redwood
FRIDAY RIDGE
Salyer
DH13
Madden Creek
HOGBACK RIDGE
Hawkins Bar
Hennessy
HENNESSY RIDGE
Rd.
TRINITY RIVER
Titlow Hill Rd.
6
299
IRONSIDE MTN.
Bob's SM
530.629.2457
530.629.2693
40°50'
1
Creek
SOUTH
To Weaverville & DH18
To Douglas City & DH33 Pg. 175
DH44 Pg. 179
Burnt Ranch
5N01
Underwood Mtn. Rd.
SPIKE BUCK MTN.
GAINOR PEAK
SHASTA-TRINITY
FORK
SNOW CAMP MTN.
N
SIMS MTN.
TRINITY
TE-A
6
Grouse Creek
Burnt Ranch BCG
311
3 km
3 miles
NATIONAL FOREST
RIVER
BUG CREEK BUTTE
BOARD CAMP BUTTE
1
Corral Bottom Rd.
60
40°40'
Big Slide BCG
Mad River
DH44 TE-A
Hyampom Rd.
Old Garret Ranch
530.628.4569
311
301
JC's Beer Garden & Grill
530.628.5229
Hyampom
To Hayfork & Mid-DH44 Pg. 179
Arey's Guest Cottage
530.628.5953
Pilot Creek
SOUTH FORK MTNS.
Hyampom GS
40
Pelletreau Ridge Rd.
Grel's Vacation Home
530.628.5312
Six Rivers Lodge
707.574.6220
Burger Bar
707.574.6646
Butter Ck. Ranch
530.628.4890
Mad River Store & Bar
707.574.6776
Weekender Café
Van Duzen
Mad River
40°30'
Dinsmore
River
S. Fork Mtn. Rd.
36
DH6 Pg. 157
36
Mad River
To Fortuna
To DH64 Pg. 151
Dinsmore GS
707.574.6388
DH6 Pg. 157
DH36 Pg. 163
To Triangle Jct & DH11 Pg. 169
DH44 Pg. 179
Alderpoint Rd.
123°40'
Van Duzen Rd.
123°30'
501

The passing lane ends at 2.5 mi (4.0 km). Though you're zipping through a large tract of undeveloped forest, you're anything but closed in. The chasm over the creek bed, the gentle sloping of the landscape and the width of the road itself create a rare sense of openness. They do wonders for the sightlines, too.

You move off the creek but the steady S-curves continue, wending their way into a broad, forested bowl. The right side of the road angles upward, usually treed but sometimes sharpening into a rockface. At 4.1 mi (6.6 km), the terrain shifts again as the road ducks behind a large chunk of rock on the left. But what you really notice is that huge, pullout-width swath of shoulder to the right. Too bad no one else does.

No problem. Another passing lane starts at 4.6 mi (7.4 km). And despite the fact you're keeping a close eye on the red line, it's always interesting to check out the profiles of the pullout-averse drivers as you blast by them. Despite some variation in features, the look of general obliviousness is common to all.

The sweepers aren't quite as tight on this swatch of passing lane. But there's enough there that you can get some definite lean out of them. Especially if you want to wind it all the way up to the speed limit. And what was it again?

The passing lane ends at 5.4 mi (8.7 km). You cross another bridge and leave the Six Rivers Forest. No highrises quite yet, just a fantastic set of sweeping esses through what may as well still be national forest. Another passing lane comes at 7.2 mi (11.6 km). And another at 8.7 mi (14.0 km). Just in time to get you by the logging trucks. Unless you don't want to miss the turnoff left to the challenging, but remote and scenic Titlow Hill Rd (**TE-A**).

At 9.6 mi (15.4 km), you reach the top of the world. Or at least it feels like it. At a mere 2803 ft (854 m), the Berry Summit looks modest on paper. But with its big drop and deep, broad view, it has a sense of drama that others twice its height don't have. Makes you want to stop and hang out. And you might want to think about doing just that – it gets very cold dropping down into the bank of marine fog that often settles on the coast.

And away we go. Or do we? As is common on a long descent, any passing lane settles in on the other side of the road. With the gawking views, it's easy to get stuck in a pylon caravan here. But keep your eyes peeled for brief bits of dotted yellow doling out leftovers from the lanes o' plenty.

Unfortunately, the road loses a bit of its curvitude on the downward slope. Indeed, it's starting to get downright straight by the time you hit the fat 40-mph (60-kmh) sweeper at 12.9 mi (20.8 km). It's a long one, lasting all the way to 13.4 mi (21.6 km).

The panoramic view that smacked you full in the face when you came over the top has dissipated as well. There are still some terrific scenes, especially when you can see the road bending ahead and below. But as the pitch of the overall terrain levels, the large switchbacks move you into stands of trees. And when they do, the scenery can seem rather commonplace.

Likewise the corners. The curves on the climb up weren't exactly sharp, but they had a definite, well-defined arc to them. And where they didn't, it was nothing a little shot of throttle couldn't fix. Coming down off Berry, the road curves and even esses on occasion, but without much commitment. And the combination of traffic, single-wide lane and double yellow line on this stretch can remove the power of change from your hand. At least for now.

At 16.3 mi (26.2 km), you cross the long, high bridge over Redwood Creek and begin the climb up to the Lord-Ellis Summit. There's a big, presidential view to the left over Redwood Creek's valley to Wiregrass, Beaver and Nixon Ridges before the curving road straightens through the densest swath of forest so far. The best news? A long-awaited series of passing lanes provides a handful of opportunities to impeach any stubborn semis.

You reach the 2263 ft (690 m) Lord-Ellis Summit at 20.8 mi (33.5 km). Closed in by forest, it's far less interesting than its predecessor. With a twist of the wrist, however, the long, gentle sweepers on the descent might generate some level of interest as the DH makes a couple of bows north and brings Tip Top Ridge into view ahead and to the left. And some wrist twisting may just be possible since you've just passed all that traffic on the ascent and still have occasional permission to use one of the two lanes coming the other way.

At 25.4 mi (40.9 km), you swing back south for the last time and at 26.6 mi (42.8 km), cross the north fork of the Mad River. A passing lane comes and the mad river of pylons rushes to the left to pass whatever even slower camper is holding up the parade. Fortunately, it's a long stretch of double lane and there's lots of room for them to do their thing. And for you to do yours.

The timing's not bad either. The final flurry of gentle, reliable corners starts in the passing stretch and carries on after the road narrows back to one lane at 27.8 mi (44.7 km). Fittingly, they end with a view of Fickle Hill to the left at 29.7 mi (47.8 km).

The last few miles are uneventful. There's nothing quite like the weigh scale at 30.4 mi (48.9 km) to scuttle your sense of remoteness. Or how about the "Begin Freeway 1/2 Mile" sign at 31.8 mi (51.2 km). You're outta here. The DH ends as the freeway begins at the Blue Lake/Glendale Dr exit where your clock reads 32.3 mi (52.0 km).

Twisted Edges

TE-A Titlow Hill Rd - South Fork Mountain Rd (54.3 mi / 87.4 km)
This connection down to mid-**DH6 Carlotta – Triangle Jct** is not for everyone. But don't let the tight, bumpy, poorly engineered northern end of this one-lane road turn you off. The pavement and curves soon mellow

out so you can enjoy the perfect remoteness and incredible high views northeast to the Marble Mtns and west all the way to the Pacific. It's so quiet up here chances are you may not see a single car. Bikes on the other hand…

ROUTING OPTION: Pelletreau Ridge Rd (FSR 40) offers a steep, washboarded connection down to Hyampom, ***DH44TE-A Hyampom Rd*** *and ultimately* ***DH44 Triangle Jct – Douglas City****. Not for the faint of tread.*

TE-B Blue Lake – McKinleyville (9.9 mi / 15.9 km) *Glendale Dr - Fieldbrook Rd - Murray Rd*

A reasonably well paved, semi-rural ride that bypasses two dull, divided stretches of Hwys 299 and 101. Winds a fair bit south of Fieldbrook but is more or less straight on the birch-lined connector out to Central Ave (Hwy 200).

NAVIGATION: If you're coming off Hwy 299 from the east into Blue Lake, just keep on going right onto Glendale Dr. If you're coming from the town of Blue Lake, just follow Blue Lake Blvd out of town and under the freeway. In either case, when you reach the next freeway access point at 1.7 mi (2.7 km), go left under the freeway, then take the next right onto Fieldbrook Rd. This takes you back north, nipping under the freeway again.

TOUR NOTE: Women on Wheels beware: Some smartass has scratched out the R, I, O and E on the sign for Primose Lane off the TE near the southern end.

TE-C Scenic Dr (2.8 mi / 4.5 km)

This narrow bypass is bumpy but beautiful as it guides you slowly along a rocky coastline filled with foaming breakers and sharp, protruding rocks. You only want to ride this one for the scenery.

NAVIGATION: From the south, take the Westhaven Rd exit off Hwy 101, cross under the freeway and turn right at the T-junction. (Left takes you down to Moonstone Beach.)

ROUTING OPTION: If you enjoyed this TE, and don't mind another 2.8 mi (4.5 km) of narrow pavement, go through Trinidad toward the ocean and turn right on Stagecoach Rd. After a straight first half through a few houses, it winds up through some dripping, sweet-smelling woods to its junction with the straightish, mostly well paved Patrick's Point Rd.

RIDER'S LOG: **DATE RIDDEN:** **YOUR RATING: /10**

To Washington
To I-5 & Washington
DH50
O'Brien
To Happy Camp & DH12/DH23
SISKIYOU NATIONAL FOREST
Nielsen's Almost Heaven Resort 541.596.2952
1001 Front 707.464.3174
1111 2nd St 707.464.6101
Hiouchi Café & Motel 888.881.0819
Houchi Hamlet RV CG 800.722.9468
Hiouchi Hamlet Mkt
OREGON
CALIFORNIA
CURRY
DEL NOTRE
Oregon Mtn. Rd.
TE-A
Hazel View Summit (2100ft/ 1636m)
Elk Creek
HIGH DOME
N. FORK SMITH RIVER BOTANICAL AREA
Rowdy Cr.
Rowdy Creek Rd.
Smith River
Sandy Cr.
She-She's Drive In 707.457.3434
Gasquet GS
Patrick Creek Lodge 707.457.3323
Monkey Creek
MONKEY CREEK RIDGE
Mid. Fk. Smith River
BROKEN RIB MTN.
Crescent City Redwoods KOA 707.464.5744
Sarina Rd.
Smith R.
Moseley Rd.
Morehead Rd.
Fort Dick
North Bank Dr.
Hardscrabble Creek
N. Fork Smith River
Old Gasquet Toll Rd.
Patrick Creek
Gasquet
Myrtle Creek
Patrick Creek NRA CG
French Hill Rd.
DH20
Lake Earl Dr.
King Valley Rd.
Parkway Mkt
Madrone Motel 541.596.2498
McGrew's 541.596.2202
O'Brien Country Store
Hiouchi
CRAIGS CREEK MTN.
Hurdygurdy Rd.
Creek
Elk Valley Rd.
S. Fork Rd.
S. Fk. Smith River
Coon Creek
Grassy Flat BCG
Crescent City
Jedediah Smith Redwoods SP CG 707.464.6101
Redwood Hwy
Mill Creek
Hurdygurdy
FOX RIDGE
Jones Creek
SIX RIVERS NATIONAL FOREST
Village Camper Inn 800.283.7183
Panther Flat NRA CG
LITTLE RATTLESNAKE MTN.
42°00'
41°50'
41°40'
SMITH RIVER NATIONAL RECREATION AREA
Gasquet-Orleans Rd.
Goose Creek
TE-B
Motel Trees 800.848-2982
Forest Café 707.482.5585
RATTLESNAKE MTN.
De Martin BCG
Woodland Villa 888.866.2466
Camp Marigold CG 707.482.3585
Mystic Forest RV CG 707.482.4901
Don's
Requa Inn B&B 866.800.8777
Trees of Mystery
Redwood Nat'l Park Ranger Station
MYNOT RIDGE
Tuna Creek
Rainy season closure due to Port-Orford Cedar Disease
14N01
Ravenswood Motel 866.520.9875
The Country Club
Klamath Mkt
Sweet Street Café 707.482.3125
Alder Camp Rd.
Klamath
RED MTN.
Goose Cr.
Crivelli's 707.482.3713
Klamath Glen
Coastal Dr.
Rhodes' End B&B 707.482.1654
NICKOWITZ PEAK
41°30'
Kamp Klamath CG 866.552.6284
Blue Creek
Slide Creek
Gold Bluffs SP/NP CG
Summit (1485ft/456m)
Newton B. Drury Scenic Pkwy.
KLAMATH RIVER
N
BLUE CREEK MTN.
DEL NOTRE
HUMBOLDT
Green Valley Motel 707.488.2341
Elkhorn Saloon
Lumberjack Tavern
Shoreline Mkt
Orick Mkt
76
TE-C
Elk Prairie SP/NP CG
3 km
3 miles
REDWOOD NATIONAL PARK
Davidson Rd.
Rolf's Park Rest & Motel 707.488.3841
41°20'
124°10'
124°00'
123°50'
Orick
To Arcata & DH31
To Eureka

DH20 Crescent City – O'Brien, OR

Highway 199

Distance:	41.4 mi / 66.6 km	Traffic:	Moderate

At a Glance

TIRES	
Twistiness	24.7/ 30
Pavement	20.0/ 20
Engineering	8.1/ 10
Remoteness	5.5/ 10
Scenery	9.6/ 15
Character	9.1/ 15
Total	**77.0**

Legendary Jedediah Strong Smith was certainly not your typical frontiersman, given that he didn't drink, smoke or use profanity, never boasted and exhibited the open faith of an NFL wide receiver. Seems JS wouldn't match the profile of today's average rider either. But with his sense of adventure and predilection for leather, you can see him Riding for the Son on this route along the middle branch of the last wild river system in California. Jed'd particularly like the early tight stuff among the majestic redwood Scenery but he'd also enjoy slicing through the less impressive, but still dense, forest all the way to O'Brien in Oregon. The road does have some straight four-lane stretches, yet when the Twistiness strikes, it hits as hard as a grizzly. Combine these curves with the buckskin-smooth Pavement and excellent Engineering and even Jedediah might show some uncharacteristic exuberance. Certainly, as an early seeker of Remoteness, he would be displeased with the ungodly traffic that can clog what's become a major trail to and from the I-5 at Grants Pass, OR. He just wouldn't be cussin' at it. Yet, despite his probity, Smith was still well respected by his more ribald colleagues. He was always invited to the annual Mountain Man Rendezvous – a kind of Wild West precursor to show-and-shines. In fact, his 1832 eulogy could easily apply to this DH: "One whom none could approach without respect, and whom none could know without esteem."

Access

From Crescent City

On Hwy 101

A few miles north of Crescent City, Hwy 199 junctions east. Take it. Once you leave the short freeway bit, you're on the road.

From O'Brien, OR

Coming in on DH50 Happy Camp - O'Brien, OR

When you junction with 199, turn south. Exit O'Brien and you are on the road.

On The Road

Deep, dark redwood forest presses in tightly once you leave Hwy 101 and begin a shallow climb on very good pavement. A twisties sign emerges from the mist and the curves start batting you from side to side. The 25-mph (40-kmh) advisory seems a little bearish and is probably unnecessary since the imposing trees just off your kneecap tend to encourage prudence. And since there's no trail of dotted yellow through this forest, you'll probably be going slower anyway because of the traffic. No cussin', now.

What's this? Well, if it ain't a gol-danged passing lane! It don't last long, so use it or lose it. It's unclear why it disappears, since the road stays pretty straight until you cross the Smith River bridge and junction with Hwy 197 (an alternate route back to Hwy 101) at 3.6 mi (5.8 km). Beyond the turnoff, you're quickly winding again through the dense forest of the Jed Smith Redwoods State Park. Just as quickly, you bust out of the brooding giants and coochy coo into the tiny hamlet of Hiouchi at 4.8 mi (7.7 km).

Past the townsite flat, a left-hander puts you north along a rockface, back in the forest – albeit sans the big redwoods – and above the river. Once you pass the turnoff right for the South Fork Rd (CR 427) river access at 6.5 mi (10.5 km), you'll be right beside the Middle Fork Smith River.

The big trees may be gone but the curves are back in a big way, along with more conservative, low-speed advisories. Because of the excellent pavement and good engineering, you may be inclined to ride as fast as the 55-mph (90-kmh) limit allows.

You should feel it getting warmer now, unless some huge coastal weather front has penetrated this far inland. You might also be getting warmer under the collar if the pylons in front of you refuse to use the pullouts provided. C'mon Durango, even pulling over two feet will do.

If you've ridden much in NorCal, what you see at 9.7 mi (15.6 km) will seem familiar – river to one side of you, rockfaces to the other and trees carpeting both sides of the gorge you are in all the way to the top. And, of course, continuing curves. What you don't always find, however, is pavement this smooth. In other words, Hardscrabble Creek, crossed at 10.4 mi (16.7 km), wasn't named for the asphalt.

You bridge the Middle Fork Smith and find yourself in suburban Gasquet, entering the town proper at 12.3 mi (19.8 km). Once you blow this tiny but strangely sprawling town, you're on four lanes of straightness. Up to your left in the now-widened valley are the variegated bumps of Elk Camp Ridge. The road crosses the Middle Fork once more at 16.5 mi (26.6 km) and offers up a few gentle high-speed sweepers. It drops back to two lanes at 18.9 mi (30.4 km) when the gorge re-tightens its grip.

The 30-mph (50-kmh) curve confirms you're back in the good stuff. Rockfaces? Check. River? Roger. Narrow, tree-covered gorge? Ten four. Curves? Oh, yeah. And a twisties sign that promises them for another eight miles….

The gorge steepens and the road contorts even better past the old stage-coach stop of Patrick Creek at 21.5 mi (34.6 km), crossing the river a couple of more times as each fight for primacy. A great stretch? Well, that will depend entirely on the number of pylons in front of you. It's not easy to get by 'em so make sure to take advantage of the brief passing lanes.

The curves challenge you even more as you enter a world of 20/25-mph (30/40-kmh) advisories. This is sometimes not a great world to be in, depending on what's going on with pavement and engineering. But here, the asphalt maintains its impeccable, well-cambered composure and CalTrans even gives you those nice, little extra bits of widened shoulder to help your lines. If tight curves have any meaning in your life, this is a place you definitely want to be. At least if the traffic holds off. The intensity abates at the CalTrans works yard, left at 27.5 mi (44.3 km). Touch hand to helmet in homage, please.

ROUTING OPTION: There is a sign at the yard informing you it's only 295 mi (475 km) to Portland, OR and the start of contiguous Destination Highways coverage of Washington and British Columbia. Thanks, guys.

The road widens to four lanes once more and the curves devolve into gentle changes in direction while you continue gradually uphill. Winking blue and red lights behind the pylon on the shoulder opposite serve as a reminder that speed taxing can affect you anytime, anywhere on this road. Ah well, better them than you.

You're back to a solo lane in each direction at 29.2 mi (47.0 km). And back to twistin' and turnin' with sweet pavement and engineering. Oregon Mountain Rd (**TE-A**) junctions left at 30.8 mi (49.6 km) before a straighter stretch with a passing lane in your direction interrupts your reverie. When the extra lane ends and you enter the Collier Tunnel under Hazel View Summit at 32.8 mi (52.8 km), you're heading downhill.

You emerge from the perfectly straight tunnel a little under a mile later. There's a passing lane on the slight, straightish descent. Unfortunately, it's coming in the other direction. The other end of Oregon Mountain Rd (**TE-A**) is right at 34.6 mi (55.7 km). You cross into Oregon itself at 36.0 mi (57.9 km).

Judging from the quality of the pavement, the state of Oregon thinks as highly of this road as California does. But if the Beaver State really wanted to respect this DH, it wouldn't have allowed the development past the Dwight Creek crossing. Just as the road begins to curve again, a profusion of fences, driveways and buildings rear their ugly heads. Four lanes appear at 39.7 mi (63.9 km) then almost immediately disappear. Not that it matters much. You enter O'Brien and reach the end of the DH at 41.4 mi

(66.6 km), where an old highway patrol car sits in front of the grocery store/gas station.

ROUTING OPTION: You are now only 280 mi (450 km) from Portland, OR and the start of Destination Highways coverage of the great riding in both Washington and British Columbia.

Twisted Edges

TE-A Oregon Mountain Rd (CR 324) (4.3 mi / 6.9 km)

The Collier Tunnel eliminated the need for travelers to go over the old summit road's 128 curves and hairpin switchbacks. That doesn't mean you can't experience some of them on what's left of it, though. As you'd expect, the pavement is narrow and old but you can bet the scenic views from up here are a lot better than those you get driving through the mountain.

TE-B Trees of Mystery – Crescent City (Hwy 101) (14.0 mi / 22.5 km)
Redwood Hwy

Sometimes it seems this place would be better called the RVs of Mystery. A sweepy stretch of misty coast north of the T of M gives way to some winding sections amid the tall, thick, tight-to-the-roadside trees of Del Norte Coast Redwood State Park. Smooth pavement all the way.

TE-C Newton B Drury Scenic Pkwy (7.6 mi / 12.2 km)

Newton's Fourth Law stipulates that a bypass TE to a major highway should be twistier than the main road. Apparently, speed tax laws aren't the only ones meant to be broken. Whether you're on the open prairie at the south end or deep in the majestic redwoods, the high-quality asphalt here has only a paltry 10 curves. And they're all huddled together for protection on the brief climb toward the northern end just before you swing back to rejoin 101.

Rider's Log: **Date Ridden:** **Your Rating:** **/10**

How do YOU rate Northern California's 74 Destination Highways? Go to destinationhighways.com, *and let other riders know.*

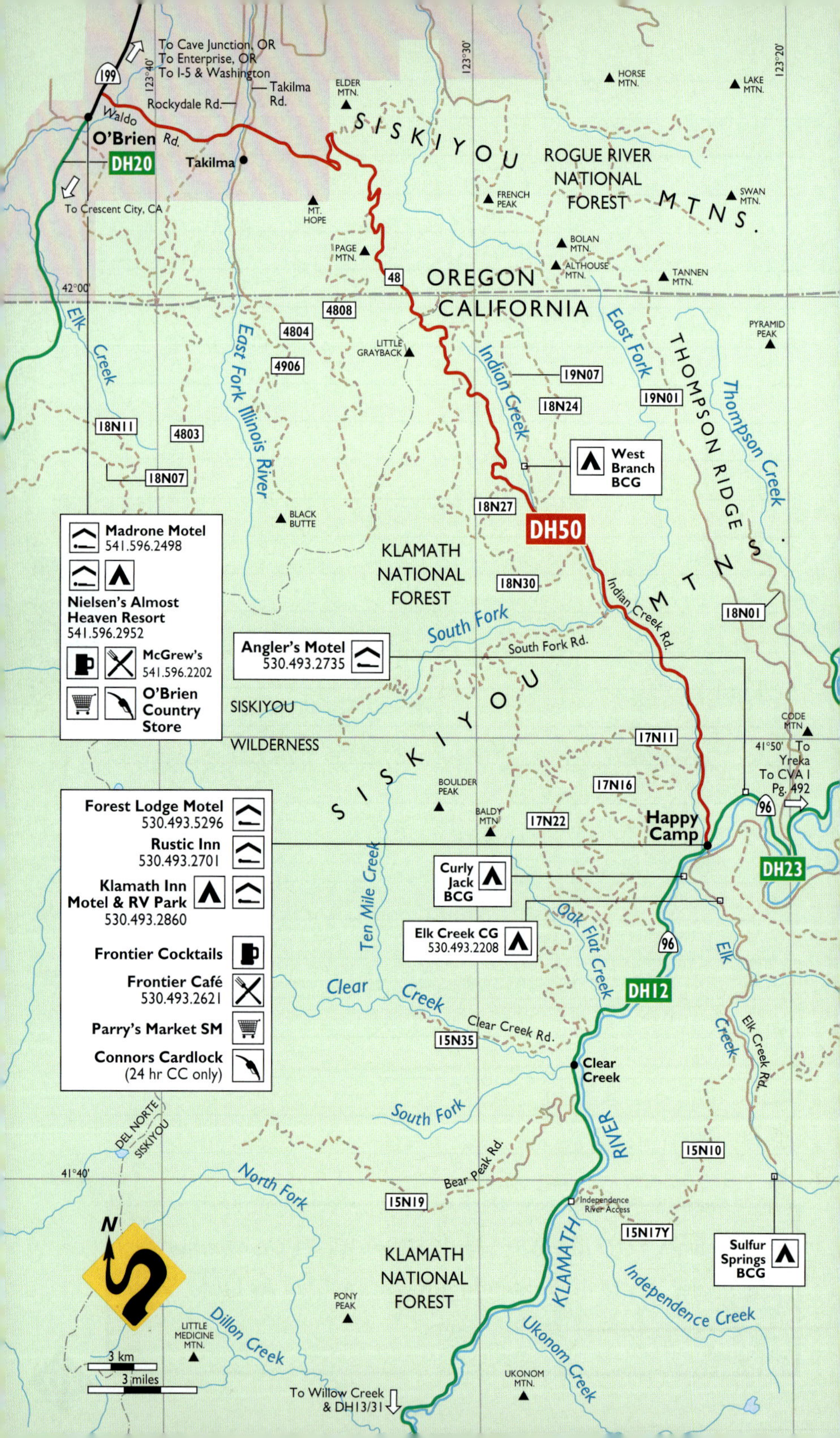

To Cave Junction, OR
To Enterprise, OR
To I-5 & Washington
199
Takilma Rd.
Rockydale Rd.
Waldo Rd.
O'Brien
DH20
Takilma
To Crescent City, CA
ELDER MTN.
SISKIYOU MTNS.
ROGUE RIVER NATIONAL FOREST
HORSE MTN.
LAKE MTN.
FRENCH PEAK
SWAN MTN.
MT. HOPE
PAGE MTN.
BOLAN MTN.
ALTHOUSE MTN.
TANNEN MTN.
48
OREGON
CALIFORNIA
42°00'
123°40'
123°30'
123°20'
4808
4804
4906
LITTLE GRAYBACK
PYRAMID PEAK
Elk Creek
East Fork Illinois River
Indian Creek
East Fork
THOMPSON RIDGE
Thompson Creek
19N07
18N24
19N01
18N11
4803
18N07
West Branch BCG
18N27
BLACK BUTTE
DH50
KLAMATH NATIONAL FOREST
18N30
Indian Creek Rd.
SISKIYOU MTNS.
18N01
Madrone Motel
541.596.2498
Nielsen's Almost Heaven Resort
541.596.2952
McGrew's
541.596.2202
O'Brien Country Store
Angler's Motel
530.493.2735
South Fork
South Fork Rd.
SISKIYOU WILDERNESS
CODE MTN
41°50'
To Yreka
To CVA I Pg. 492
17N11
17N16
BOULDER PEAK
BALDY MTN
17N22
Happy Camp
96
DH23
Forest Lodge Motel
530.493.5296
Rustic Inn
530.493.2701
Klamath Inn Motel & RV Park
530.493.2860
Frontier Cocktails
Frontier Café
530.493.2621
Parry's Market SM
Connors Cardlock
(24 hr CC only)
Curly Jack BCG
Elk Creek CG
530.493.2208
Ten Mile Creek
Oak Flat Creek
Elk Creek
DH12
Clear Creek
Clear Creek Rd.
15N35
Clear Creek
Elk Creek Rd.
South Fork
KLAMATH RIVER
DEL NORTE
SISKIYOU
41°40'
North Fork
Bear Peak Rd.
15N10
15N19
Independence River Access
15N17Y
KLAMATH NATIONAL FOREST
Sulfur Springs BCG
Independence Creek
N
PONY PEAK
LITTLE MEDICINE MTN.
Dillon Creek
Ukonom Creek
UKONOM MTN.
3 km
3 miles
To Willow Creek & DH13/31

DH50 O'BRIEN, OR – HAPPY CAMP

Waldo Rd / Indian Creek Rd

DISTANCE:	37.3 mi / 60.0 km	TRAFFIC:	Very Light

TIRES

Twistiness	30/30
Pavement	9.0/20
Engineering	4.9/10
Remoteness	7.8/10
Scenery	9.0/15
Character	4.9/15

TOTAL 65.6

AT A GLANCE

Twisted Edge Publishing's controversial decision to publish *Destination Highways Northern California* before coming out with *DH Oregon* has residents of the Webfoot State fuming. So here's another little bone to at least whet their appetites. Yes folks, this not-so-well-paved DH actually begins in Oregon, heads south from O'Brien and winds up in California. And winds is the operative word here. Despite some asphalt issues, this road is overflowing with nicely engineered twisties amid the Siskiyou National Forest's wild landscape of remote mountains, canyons and ridges. Oregonians point to the fact it's the straight, moderately developed southern end leading into Happy Camp, CA, that drags this DH's TIRES numbers down. Perhaps that's why they keep asking, "Is your Oregon book out yet?" Yes, well, sort of. We've got DHWA18 Asotin – Enterprise, OR, DHNCA20 Crescent City – O'Brien, OR and now, DHNCA50 O'Brien, OR – Happy Camp.

ACCESS

From O'Briens, OR

Coming in on DH20 Crescent City – O'Brien, OR (Hwy 199)

Go south on the well-marked turnoff to Happy Camp. You're on the road.

From Happy Camp

Coming in on DH12 Willow Creek – Happy Camp (Hwy 96)

Coming in on DH23 Yreka – Happy Camp (Hwy 96)

Go north on Indian Creek Rd. You're on the road.

ON THE ROAD

Not too much going on curvewise in the first few miles south of O'Brien. Just a regiment of trees standing guard along the roadside. The landscape opens up at 2.7 (4.3 km), where pine trees with large, exploded fronds pose against the sky and layered hills. At 3.2 mi (5.1 km), a few curves come as a soft descent begins. Redwoods, arbutus and occasional oak mix with the pines. Rockydale Rd asphalts off left at 4.0 mi (6.4 km).

At 4.5 mi (7.2 km), you cross the East Fork of the Illinois River, just before you approach the stop sign at the 4.8 mi (7.7 km) junction of Takilma Rd. This is your last paved chance to turn left and backtrack to Cave Junction and the Oregon Caves National Monument. Is the ride out the caves worth it? Sorry, have to check out *Destination Highways Oregon* for that.

"Happy Camp 38 Miles" reads the sign as you head into the snow zone. Snowplows, salt and sand. Guess that explains the scraped and inconsistent pavement. But there's nothing inconsistent about the corners that finally start at 5.3 mi (8.5 km) when the road begins its gradual assault through the open range up the slopes of Page Mtn.

Sweepers and curves repeat along a crumbling slope. The bank angles up to your right. The green thickness of the Siskiyou National Forest spreads out to the left. You officially enter the nat forest at 7.2 mi (11.6 km), riding north then south high above the steep-sided Althouse Creek Canyon.

The curves on this winding trip along the canyon's edge are even and predictable. Can't say the same for the sometimes slippy-slidey surface. This is especially noticeable when a lingering sweeper carries you overtop the ridge at 9.1 mi (14.6 km). On a positive note, the traffic count's so low that if you do enter into a rear wheel slide, your chances of meeting a semi head on across the line are extremely slim.

The angle of the terrain has shifted, now going up left and down right. Views of the rough, surrounding landscape are eye-catching, but they're often shielded and sometimes completely cloaked by a canopy of pines and oaks. You're descending now, but the grade isn't steep – a perfect match for the parade of moderately arced S-curves.

Altitude decreases and redwoods join the storybook scene of trees overhanging a winding trail. You're now twisting more tightly between solid walls of forest, slowing – or not – for a 10-mph (15-kmh) hairpin at 11.8 mi (19.0 km). With it comes a shift in the angle of the terrain back to a left side dropoff as well as glimpses of the misty climes of Althouse Mtn.

The constant curves ease up a little at 14.8 mi (23.8 km) and a mini-straightaway extends pretty much to the Page Mtn Snowpark at 15.5 mi (24.9 km). Nothing much here but a couple of outhouses. Of course, that can be enough, depending on the circumstances.

When you gotta go, you gotta go. After all, the chain of S-curves that links up again past the potty park is waiting. The road curls down into the bowl below and crosses the unmarked state boundary in the longest and most satisfying series of esses on the DH. A great, and fitting, introduction to the Golden State.

A small retaining wall at 17.5 mi (28.2 km) adds a rare manmade element to the unbroken landscape. What is broken is the string of S-curves, which terminates at 18.1 mi (29.1 km). But to compensate, the straight that follows offers a striking southeast view of green and buttermilk-blue layers of Thompson Ridge. It's so nice someone thought to install a viewpoint and picnic area at 18.9 mi (30.4 km). The spectacular view from this spot is worth at least a slow-down, even if it is in the middle of a curve.

Here we go again. Not quite as essy as before, but the curves are great and there are lots of them. Add in the scenery, the wider road and a bump up in overall pavement quality at 23.8 mi (38.3 km), and this road's got something going on. And so do you.

The curves start to dwindle at 24.7 mi (39.7 km) along with your hopes of better pavement. In fact, the stretch of asphalt starting at 26.9 mi (43.3 km) is the worst so far. You cross Indian Creek, traverse a brief flat, enter a shallow valley and wind through a last hurrah of curves above the creek. They slowly devolve from moderate…to gentle…to mere wisps of directional change.

Trees rise tall atop the red cliffs to your left as you cruise more or less straight along the banks of the unseen creek. The domes and billowed ridges enclose you in a deep, flat-bottomed valley. You feel far away, so it's strange to see a pedestrian walking on the road or a pick-up emerging from a… driveway? What be this place?

California, friend. You really think flat land beside a creek is going to stay unoccupied? Even if it is in the middle of absolutely frickin' nowhere? Not a chance. Could be worse, though – at least the homesteads coincide with the straightest and bumpiest part of the road.

Not that there aren't a few easy curves through here. And if you were going fast enough, you might even be able to get some lean out of them. But despite these bends and the roadside oaks and attractive treed ridges surrounding the brown fields that spread out to your right beginning at 30.8 mi (49.6 km), you have the definite sense it's almost over and you're just putting in time. And you're right.

The most you have to look forward to is the little stretch starting at 34.0 mi (54.7 km) when you're right along the creek and you can clearly see the shining granite that defines its western bank. This scenic moment is a prelude to a wide, sweeping ess that gets your mirrors tilting one last time. But the Indian Creek Trailer Park at 34.4 mi (55.3 km) puts to rest any hopes of a comeback for this DH.

There are a few final curves starting at 35.7 mi (57.4 km) as the road rises off the creek and out of its now-shallow valley. You arrive in the town of Happy Camp and junction with **DH12 Happy Camp – Willow Creek** and **DH23 Happy Camp – Yreka** at 37.3 mi (60.0 km).

RIDER'S LOG: **DATE RIDDEN:** **YOUR RATING:** **/10**

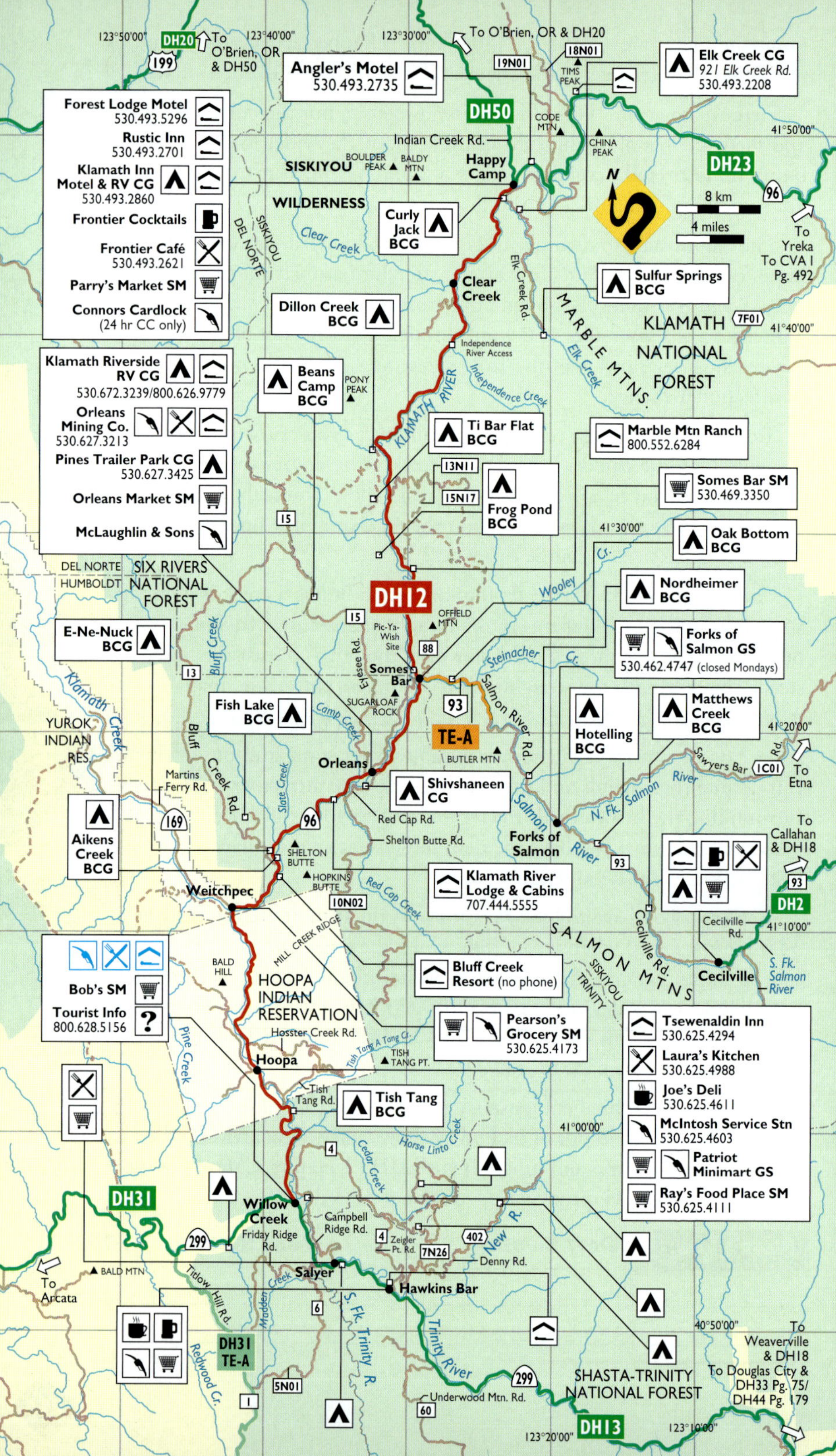

Angler's Motel 530.493.2735
Elk Creek CG 921 Elk Creek Rd. 530.493.2208
Forest Lodge Motel 530.493.5296
Rustic Inn 530.493.2701
Klamath Inn Motel & RV CG 530.493.2860
Frontier Cocktails
Frontier Café 530.493.2621
Parry's Market SM
Connors Cardlock (24 hr CC only)
Curly Jack BCG
Sulfur Springs BCG
Dillon Creek BCG
Klamath Riverside RV CG 530.672.3239/800.626.9779
Orleans Mining Co. 530.627.3213
Pines Trailer Park CG 530.627.3425
Orleans Market SM
McLaughlin & Sons
Beans Camp BCG
Ti Bar Flat BCG
Frog Pond BCG
Marble Mtn Ranch 800.552.6284
Somes Bar SM 530.469.3350
Oak Bottom BCG
Nordheimer BCG
Forks of Salmon GS 530.462.4747 (closed Mondays)
Hotelling BCG
Matthews Creek BCG
E-Ne-Nuck BCG
Fish Lake BCG
Aikens Creek BCG
Shivshaneen CG
Klamath River Lodge & Cabins 707.444.5555
Bluff Creek Resort (no phone)
Bob's SM
Tourist Info 800.628.5156
Pearson's Grocery SM 530.625.4173
Tsewenaldin Inn 530.625.4294
Laura's Kitchen 530.625.4988
Joe's Deli 530.625.4611
McIntosh Service Stn 530.625.4603
Patriot Minimart GS
Ray's Food Place SM 530.625.4111
Tish Tang BCG
DH12
DH20
DH50
DH23
DH2
DH31
DH13
TE-A
DH31 TE-A
To O'Brien, OR & DH50
To O'Brien, OR & DH20
To Yreka To CVA I Pg. 492
To Etna
To Callahan & DH18
To Arcata
To Weaverville & DH18 To Douglas City & DH33 Pg. 75/ DH44 Pg. 179
8 km
4 miles
Happy Camp
Clear Creek
Somes Bar
Orleans
Forks of Salmon
Weitchpec
Hoopa
Willow Creek
Salyer
Hawkins Bar
Cecilville
SISKIYOU WILDERNESS
KLAMATH NATIONAL FOREST
SIX RIVERS NATIONAL FOREST
SHASTA-TRINITY NATIONAL FOREST
MARBLE MTNS.
SALMON MTNS
HOOPA INDIAN RESERVATION
YUROK INDIAN RES.
DEL NORTE
HUMBOLDT
Klamath River
Salmon River
Trinity River
S. Fk. Trinity R.
Indian Creek Rd.
Elk Creek Rd.
Salmon River Rd.
Red Cap Rd.
Shelton Butte Rd.
Martins Ferry Rd.
Bluff Creek Rd.
Hosster Creek Rd.
Tish Tang Rd.
Campbell Ridge Rd.
Friday Ridge Rd.
Zeigler Pt. Rd.
Denny Rd.
Tidlow Hill Rd.
Underwood Mtn. Rd.
Cecilville Rd.
Sawyers Bar Rd.
Eyesee Rd.
Independence River Access
Pic-Ya-Wish Site

DH12 HAPPY CAMP – WILLOW CREEK
Highway 96

DISTANCE:	82.0 mi / 132.0 km	TRAFFIC:	Light

AT A GLANCE

Mirror, mirror on the wall. Who's the fairest road of all? Well actually, DH1 dwells in a different region. But not to worry. Though its Character's not perfectly snow-white, even Grumpy would love this long, remote and pretty-darn-fair ride along the rugged cliffs of the Klamath and Trinity Rivers down from Happy Camp. The Engineering of its steady, Sleepy curves along the Klamath and tight esses along the Trinity either side of Hoopa is certainly nothing to get Sneezy at. And while its Pavement shows signs of age here and there, all it needs is a little attention from the Docs at CalTrans. With so little traffic on the empty, undeveloped northern eighty-per cent of this ride, you've got a sporting chance to slow down a bit before Dopey flicks on the radar. So c'mon, don't be Bashful. *Hi Ho, Hi Ho, it's off to bike we go.*

TIRES	
Twistiness	28.9/ 30
Pavement	13.6/ 20
Engineering	6.7/ 10
Remoteness	7.0/ 10
Scenery	10.3/ 15
Character	12.8/ 15
TOTAL	**79.3**

ACCESS

From Happy Camp

Coming in on DH50 O'Brien, OR – Happy Camp
Turn right on Hwy 96. You're on the road.

Coming in on DH23 Yreka – Happy Camp (Hwy 96)
Keep going straight on Hwy 96. When you leave Happy Camp, you're on the road.

From Willow Creek

Coming in on DH31 Blue Lake (Arcata) – Willow Creek (Hwy 299)
Coming in on DH13 Weaverville – Willow Creek (Hwy 299)
Go north on Hwy 96. You're on the road.

ON THE ROAD

TOUR NOTE: There are many marked river access spots along the Klamath River. They can be a little hazardous to access on a bike though, unless you're particularly skilled at turning around a fully loaded tourer in deep gravel. As a result, you may want to suss it out on foot before riding down. Or leave your bike at the top.

You're on a narrow bit of benchland for the first couple miles out of Happy Camp, one that provides enough space for some cottages, campers and a small field before the steepening slope puts an end to all that. At 2.0 mi (3.2 km), the highway starts to look like a motorcycle road, sweeping against a bare rock cliff looking across a wild river at an unspoiled background of thickly-treed mountains.

The road continues to curve as it rises and falls along the riverbank. A few horizontal tar strips patch the winter cracks on this pretty ride along the river. The left roadside either shoots up sharply as granite cliffs or angles up gently as brown and silver-green grassland clustered with yew, black oak, Ponderosa Pine and juniper. It's an easy ride, too, with good visibility around most of the big sweepers.

There's a surprise house perched on a rare bit of flat as you cross the Clear Creek Bridge at 8.1 mi (13.0 km). Despite his screwing around with this DH's remoteness, you can understand why this suburban pioneer would decide to plant his footings above this visually striking stretch of river.

Fortunately, Clear Creek won't be turning into another Weaverville very soon. The pitched right hand slope quickly re-establishes its presence, though it's overshadowed by the lichen-tinged bluff that bulges forcefully out into the river from the other side. A tunnel of foliage temporarily blocks the view, but soon the dominant theme re-emerges: a lonely road curling steadily along the river with layers of mountains in the distance fading from green to blue.

Just when you think you're finally moving into the Siskiyou Wilderness, there'll be a couple of mailboxes like the ones by the Independence River access at 11.5 mi (18.5 km) to spoil the sensation. Not that there aren't plenty of other sensations to focus on. Like that feeling of suspending your weight over blurred pavement, surrendering to the forces of speed and gravity.

The fast sweepers continue, twisting off into the distance. And in the distance, they get even better. Esses link up, starting at 15.4 mi (24.8 km), carrying you along two sections of chalky cliffs. Looking down at the river from the high vantage point at 16.1 mi (25.9 km), the river appears as still as mirrored glass. If only H-D would hurry up and produce an amphibious motorcycle. Hey, after the V-Rod, anything's possible.

"Bicycles Next 20 Miles" reads the sign at 17.5 mi (28.2 km). Sigh. It seems that wherever you have a quiet, scenic, well-paved road, you can always trust Mr. and Mrs. Spandex to try and get into the act. Given the sweeping nature of most of the curves on this road, maybe you can let them have the paved shoulder all to themselves this time. All six inches of it.

There's a bit of straightening now as the terrain plateaus into a bench spun with trees and gold grass. But it's brief. At 18.9 mi (30.4 km) a pair of sweepers signal the commencement of another lean-lady-lean set of twisties. The road contorts as it dives downward into a steep gorge, passing the Dillon Creek BCG at 21.3 mi (34.3 km).

You cross the river for the first time at 22.1 mi (35.6 km). The bank is not as steep on this side but the road's still nice and sweepy. Since the road never wavers from its course along the river, this gives you the variety of the opposite bank's perspective on the river and surrounding mountains. The terrain's gentler, though, and this takes its toll when you enter a short section of straight at 24.4 mi (39.3 km). No cause for alarm as there are many more curves to come.

Indeed, the road starts to gently curve again as soon as 25.8 mi (41.5 km) – right about the point the pavement takes a downturn. You don't see much of the river here, just the slope off to the right angling down through mixed, interleafed forest. The trees covering the contoured mountains, ridges and vales create a soft, fairytale scene.

The river reappears at 28.2 mi (45.4 km) and with the slight eastward shift, you can make out the blue, bear-market shape of Offield Mtn. You lose the scenery as the DH rallies with a run of shallow curves. But then at 29.9 mi (48.1 km), you get it all – a long, steep, sweeper steers you around a steep rockface to a wide view over and across the river.

There are a few impressive curves as you negotiate downwards at 31.9 mi (51.3 km) toward the river crossing. But the dramatic span of the H. Lyle Davis Memorial Bridge itself is far more impressive. As is the fact that CalTrans had the class to name it after the heavy equipment operator whose number came up while building it.

At 35.9 mi (57.8 km), Sugarloaf Rock, a big piece of mossy rock reminiscent of a chia pet gets thrown into the scenic mix. It overlooks Somes Bar, the confluence of the Salmon and Klamath Rivers and locale of the Pic-Ya-Wish Ceremonial Site at 36.6 mi (58.9 km). So *that's* what's going on here. You've been wishing upon a star for a remote, winding, well-engineered road with no traffic and nary an speed tax collector. And your wish is finally being granted.

Salmon River Rd (**TE-A**) turns off left at 37.9 mi (60.1 km). Then a bridge takes you across the deep gorge of Salmon River and into Humboldt County. The jurisdictional change makes no difference to the scenery, however. At 38.9 mi (62.6 km), you glimpse the road ahead twist atop an enormous face that verticals straight down to the river. Think it looks great? It feels even better. The 39.4 mi (56.2 km) mark puts you into the first S-curves you've seen in a while.

By 40.7 mi (65.5), the road has resumed its familiar, gently winding form. The scene changes a little as you gradually descend. The white foam of the riffling river bubbles beneath black and brown cliffs across the way. At 96 degrees in the shade, chances are you'll be in that water before this ride is out. Even if it does require a trip down a third world road to one of the gravel river access bars to get to it.

The curves undergo some minor tightening at 42.2 mi (67.9 km). But just as things were starting to feel like they might get interesting again, a sign welcomes you to Orleans at 43.8 mi (70.5 km) and you cross the river into town. Orleans is a bit of a disappointment, too. Its French Quarter offers a choice of the Bigfoot Country Store and the Orleans Market Pizza & BBQ. Oh, well. *C'est la vie.*

The speed zone's back up to 55 mph (90 kmh) at 45.3 mi (72.9 km). You cross Camp Creek and begin a long, steady, increasingly-curvy descent along the west side of the river. The pavement roughs up a bit at 48.4 mi (77.9 km), probably a result of the crumbly slopes and rockfaces that get in your face as you ess gently along the slope. At 51.1 mi (82.2 km), the pavement resumes its fine form. And so do you.

Despite its high rating for scenery, this DH has few real mind blowing scenic events. Its attractiveness lies in the consistent reel of low treed mountains, rock faces and river perspectives that unfold before you in different ways as you travel southeast through the rugged Siskiyou, Marble and Salmon Ranges. The scene at 52.2 mi (84.0 km) offers a classic example. From the Slate Creek crossing, the road ahead banks upward off the river, climbing the glinting, slate slopes that lie bald beneath a tousled combover of trees .

The river curves off to the left while the road turns to the right at 53.4 mi (85.9 km). You cross the steep-sided Bluff Creek, then the highway nips behind a huge rocky knoll that marks the creek's confluence with the Klamath River. Now the steepness is on your left in the form of a bare, dominating curtain of rock that hides the river on the other side.

The road continues to sweep respectably through the rock and treed landscape, toward the distinctive outline of Mill Creek Ridge. The buildings on the left at 54.8 mi (88.2 km) are part of the low-key Bluff Creek Resort. You're back along the river at 57.3 mi (92.2 km) where you cross the Yurock Reservation Boundary. And you do indeed rock, all the way through the steady curves that carry you across the Klamath to Weitchpec, the townlet where the Trinity and Klamath Rivers meet at 59.2 mi (95.3 km).

You were riding downriver on the Klamath. Now you're riding upriver along the Trinity. Though you wouldn't know it at first as you move into a deeply treed section. The mega-foliage is short lived and you emerge along a slope to your first clear view of the Trinity River at 60.7 mi (97.7 km). There's nothing short-lived about the mega-curves, though. They continue and get tighter to boot, a trend exemplified by the particularly sphincter-clenching sweeper at 61.3 mi (98.6 km).

Your whole tire is in play as the sweetest piece of this road so far flits in an out of the trees, winding and weeping along cliffs above the river. At 63.2 mi (101.7 km), the DH narrows, with the expected twisty consequences. Despite the tightness of the corners, visibility is outstanding around most of them. And with the pavement holding its own, there's no reason not to be adding that little extra wear to the outer edges of your rubber. Unless it's that rather-too-cliff-like slope that pitches off to the right.

The tight stuff climaxes with a long chain of S-curves hanging precariously over the river, clinging to a sharp, extruding rockface. Then, more moderate esses take over, winding you down to the Indian town of Hoopa at 66.7 mi (107.3 km). What's the Hoopa all about? It sure ain't the straightaway that bisects the long and wide Hoopa Valley.

This broad valley seems particularly vast compared to the narrow, steep sides of the Klamath. That may be interesting enough that you're not immediately thrown by the sudden development, lack of curves and inevitable speed zone. But by the time you hit Hoopa's uneven block of services at 69.3 mi (111.5 km), the novelty has long worn off.

Doo de doo de doo de.... Hey, what happened? After the drab straightness along the river, the DH surprises you with a curve. But Hoopa's not a memory yet. After all, if the land's flat, you've gotta put buildings on it. Or at least some junked out cars. You're not officially out of this tidbit of scenic misery until the river bends at 73.6 mi (118.4 km). And takes the road with it.

This was worth the wait. Smooth, brilliantly engineered pavement lashes up a steep granite slope. There's a commanding view of the Trinity River before the blacktop contorts into the thick trees. Despite the mostly forested setting, sightlines are great. As is the feeling you get honing your cornering technique on this virtually faultless piece of road.

You know it's over when you notice an RV Park on your left at 79.1 mi (127.27 km). Nothing against alternative lifestyles, but why here? Not that it matters; the land has flattened out again, leaving few if any curves for these burly pylons to negotiate on the final miles to Hwy 299 and the not-so princely town of Willow Creek, at 82.0 mi (132.0 km).

Twisted Edges

TE-A Somes Bar – Butler Flat (7.0 mi / 11.3 km) *Salmon River Rd*

Why is the first 7.0 mi (11.3 km) of Salmon River Rd paved and engineered like a fantasy when the rest of route to Cecilville hasn't been upgraded since about the year Grimm's Fairy Tales were written? Maybe when we're older, we'll understand. Meanwhile, just enjoy the reverie of this enchanted, traffic-free stretch of road through the riverside woods.

TOUR NOTE: Butler Flat, right down beside the river, provides a natural spot to stop before turning around and heading back. For braver souls, the road continues as a paved, but mostly one-lane goat path for another 27.6 mi (44.4 km) to Cecilville. There are some extremely precarious sections where this sullivan is crumbling away atop a straight drop down to the Salmon River and is so narrow, you'd be lucky to get a trike through by itself, let alone edge past a pylon coming the other way. Your reward for taking your life in your hands? Direct access to the fabulous ***DH2 Cecilville - Callahan.***

RIDER'S LOG: **DATE RIDDEN:** **YOUR RATING: /10**

Map Tip: Services on non-featured DHs and TEs are generally shown as bare icon only and sometimes no icon. For the full detail, just turn to the featured map.

To Oregon
5
River
Phillipe Ln.
Oberlin Rd.
Foothill
3
263
Shasta
Hawkinsville
Yreka
Ash Creek River Access
Ash Creek
COTTONWOOD PEAK
LITTLE COTTONWOOD PEAK
RIVERVIEW
BADGER MTN.
Humbug Rd.
Westside Rd.
To Weed
To Mt. Shasta
To McDoel & DH62
Pg. 261
CVA TE-C
Yreka Motorsports
(SUZ) 1409 S Main
530.841.0861
Waiiaka Trailer Haven CG
530.842.4500
117 W Miner
530.842.1649
Tree of Heaven BCG
7J02
Humbug Creek
Humbug Creek Rd.
Ridge Rd.
Greenhorn Creek Rd.
Cayuse River Access
Skeahan River Access
CRAGGY MTN.
CHINA PEAK
RIVER
96
Gottville River Access
45N30
KLAMATH
Yreka-Walker Rd.
Eliza Gulch Rd.
McKINLEY MTN.
Forest Mtn. Summit
4097 ft/1258 m
3 km
3 miles
N
Ray's Food Place SM
Legend's Saloon
Mean Gene's/ Chevron
11835 Main
530.468.5442
3
Oak Bar Lodge
530.465.2340
Rainbow Resort
530.496.3242
Sportsmans Lodge
530.465.2366
McAdams Cr. Rd.
Eastside Rd.
Fort Jones
Klamath River
7J01
DH2 TE-A
Scott River Rd.
Greenview
Quigley RV CG
530.465.2224
SCOTT
BAR
RUSSELL PEAK
Scott River
QUARTZ HILL
Quartz Valley Rd.
To Callahan & DH2/18
MONUMENT PEAK
FOREST
Mill Creek
Mill Creek Rd.
Brown Bear River Access
Buckhorn Creek
LITTLE BALDY
DH23
Steelhead Lodge
530.496.3256
QUARTZ VALLEY
Horse Creek
NATIONAL
MTN.
Scott Bar
Scott River Rd.
Indian Scotty BCG
Sarah Totten BCG
Horse Cr. Rd.
Horse Creek
96
KLAMATH
Hamburg
7F01
Scott River Lodge
530.496.3167
TOM MARIN PEAK
JOHNNY O'NEIL RIDGE
RIVER
Mid River RV CG
530.496.3400
Seiad Valley GS
Seiad Café NL
530.496.3340
Wildwood
530.496.3195
Seiad Card Lock
Scott River
Bridge Flat BCG
Seiad Creek
Seiad Creek Rd.
KLAMATH
SLINKARD PEAK
Kelsey Creek
O'Neill Creek BCG
Grider Creek Rd.
Seiad Valley
Sluice Box River Access
Grider Creek
Forest Lodge Motel
530.493.5296
Rustic Inn
530.493.2701
Klamath Inn Motel & RV Park
110 Nugget St. 530.493.2860
Frontier Cocktails
Frontier Café
530.493.2621
Parry's Market SM
Connors Cardlock
(24 hr CC only)
46N03
Fort Goff BCG
HUCKLEBERRY MTN.
BUCKHORN MTN.
Savage Rapids River Access
CHINA PEAK
China Grade Rd.
Thompson Creek Lodge
530.496.3505
TIMS PEAK
Seattle Cr. River Access
CODE MTN.
MTNS.
MARBLE
Angler's Motel
530.493.2735
Elk Creek Rd.
Elk Creek
Indian Creek Rd.
Happy Camp
To O'Brien, OR & DH20
DH50
Curly Jack BCG
96
DH12
To Willow Creek & DH13/31
Elk Creek CG
921 Elk Creek Rd.
530.493.2208
Sulfur Springs BCG
41°40'
41°50'
122°40'
122°50'
123°00'
123°10'
123°20'

DH23 Happy Camp – Yreka

Hwy 96 / Hwy 263

Distance:	70.5 mi / 113.5 km	Traffic:	Light

At a Glance

TIRES	
Twistiness	23.7/30
Pavement	18.1/20
Engineering	6.5/10
Remoteness	4.5/10
Scenery	10.0/15
Character	13.4/15
Total	**76.2**

"Yreka!"– ancient Greek for "I got it!"– was famously exclaimed by the great Syracusean thinker Archimedes when the solution to a thorny problem suddenly hit him while getting into his bath. Being a mathematician, he'd certainly appreciate the TIRES algebra that you get to immerse yourself in on this, the Klamath River basin's second most famous DH. The western fraction of this road is between the sedate Siskiyou and Marble Mountains, so the Scenery doesn't equal the alternate Klamath ride. But it does divide nicely, gradually becoming drier as you click on the miles heading east towards the Shasta Valley. This road is not as twisty as its derivative cousin but it does have superior Pavement that integrates just fine with its invariable Engineering. Tragically, the recurring buildings do subtract from Remoteness, though Character still adds up nicely and is remarkably similar to that of DH12. And because it is a state highway, you can probably count on speed tax professors checking your speedo numbers. If you manage to get a passing grade from them, it's mathematically certain that you'll "get it" too. And like Arch, end up a happy camper.

Access

From Happy Camp

Coming in on DH12 Willow Creek - Happy Camp (Hwy 96)
When you hit Happy Camp, stay straight on Hwy 96. When you leave town, you're on the road.

Coming in on DH50 O'Brien, OR - Happy Camp
When you junction with Hwy 96, turn left. When you exit Happy Camp, you are on the road.

From Yreka

At the north end of town, take Hwy 263. When you leave town, you're on the road.

From I-5

Take the north (Hwy 3) Yreka exit west. When you hit N Main St, turn right. It becomes Hwy 263 and, when you leave town, you're on the road.

On The Road

You're out of Happy Camp quickly, with an open, grassy area to your right and a beautiful smooth sheet of asphalt underpeg. It's not long before the Klamath River replaces the open area on your right. It'll be your friend for most of the trip.

The valley bottom is fairly wide here, so initially there's not a lot in the way of curves. Which means you might have even more of a tendency to wick it up along here... ah, shit... nailed by Dopey.

TOUR NOTE: Where'd he come from? Oh, followed us out of town. Fortunately, this local sheriff rides, as a fair number of STCs here in California do. After a polite chat, during which we discuss the number of bugs that can hover above the road, we fork over a leaflet and, thankfully, receive no paper in exchange. Yesss!

Back on the road, you're into curves mixed with some sweepers. These start at about 3.0 mi (4.8 km) where the trees and terrain close in, impeding your sightlines. That, and maybe a lingering sense of dopeyness, restrains you from going full bore on the great, well-banked pavement.

You get a quick view down the valley ahead though a screen of trees before a river access road slants right at 5.6 mi (9.0 km). After a 25-mph (40-kmh) advised left-hander standing on its own, you're on a straight and heading downhill, edging closer to the Klamath as the trees retreat from the roadside.

Gradually, the curves come back and there's a quick flurry of mellow, linked turns before the trees return and you reach another river access point at 9.3 mi (15.0 km). A loose collection of buildings, not quite enough to coalesce into a mapdot, loiter about the bridge across Thompson Creek. At this spot, you are 383 mi (616 km) by highway from San Francisco, 397 mi (639 km) from Portland, 569 mi (916 km) from Seattle and 712 mi (1146 km) from Los Angeles. A little farther of course, by *Destination* Highway.

You're back in the open and sweeping along the river at 13.4 mi (21.6 km). Gently to be sure, but sweeping nonetheless. If you've done much river road riding in Northern California, you're starting to feel quite at home.

You blow through another collection of buildings on a flat. Quickly, you're up above the river; a rockface sliding past on your left spawns a couple more high-speed corners. Repeat. And enjoy.

The green bump rearing none too majestically ahead is Slinkard Peak. The Klamath seems drawn toward it, slanting off east as the road slants north. You're on another flat and entering tinytown Seiad Valley at 18.7 mi (30.1 km) but you exit it almost immediately. A few more buildings come and go. The Klamath is back, now on your left. The curves... well, they're just gone.

A single changing-radius sweeper follows the terrain and the river southward but it's not until 23.8 mi (38.3 km) that you get any real corners back. With the excellent pavement continuing as it has from the start, they are easily dealt with. As if to mirror your ride, the Klamath, close left, has gone placid and glassy. At 27.1 mi (43.6 km), you enter Hamburg.

The long and not too winding road continues as you exit the burg. As does the excellent pavement and engineering. But suddenly, more curves appear along the Klamath. You bridge the Scott River at 29.8 mi (48.0 km), disinclined to take the Scott River Rd turnoff right. You want to see whether these curves continue. And they do.

They even get a little tighter just as the trees move back in to briefly shadow the road, although you're probably beginning to wonder what's with the speed advisory signs. For example, this one's only 30 mph (50 kmh). Sure, the side slope blocks your sight lines around the corners a little bit but you'd have to be riding an incredibly poorly set up motorcycle incredibly poorly to take these signs at anywhere near face value.

Loping back and forth, the road starts to descend slightly at 31.9 mi (51.3 km). If you're observant, you will notice the trees thinning on the hillsides to the left, becoming interstitially separated by patches of dry, open ground. It's fairly subtle but the terrain is also starting to change, becoming less green. Something else to note: the first deer-advisory sign.

A couple of miles later, you'd have to be a dead ungulate to miss the drying and de-greening of the landscape. A bit of open farmland pops up on the left, complete with a weathered farm building. At 34.7 mi (55.8 km), you're in Horse Creek. And after a sparse collection of buildings, you're leaving it.

That mostly brown mass of Monument Pt over to the right is the last big lump of rock you'll see this close to the road. As the terrain continues to open up, the temperature gets much warmer. By the time you flash by the Brown Bear river access point, you're getting increasingly tempted by the Klamath, now shuffling away on your right.

The curves gentle into shallow sweepers and decrease in number. If watching for potential deer wasn't enough, you're now informed that bicyclists may be a menace for the next 20 mi (32 km). You'd like to be able to share the road but there's no real shoulder here to offer your spandex-clad brethren. Sorry.

A few more curves later and beyond some buildings, the ridge of Craggy Mtn appears in the distance at right angles to your path. Conifers have by now completely given away to deciduous trees, mostly large, rounded oaks. You pass the optimistic sign announcing the town of Klamath River but it's not until sometime later, and a half-dozen more usable curves, that you hit any sign of civilization at 43.5 mi (70.0 km).

But you're not quite in Metro Klamath yet. A proto-rockface crowds the left-hand side of the road against the river, causing curves under wheel. As you round one, you may spot Mom and two Bambis hidden under the cooling shade of the trees on the right shoulder. As you slow, they skitter across the road right in front of you. Ah yes, deer. The only animals that make cattle look smart.

More houses, immobile homes and assorted flotsam appear before you enter Klamath River's downtown core at 46.5 mi (74.8 km). Blowing out of the city center, more riverside corners appear as do more buildings and fields. The easy bends continue but it's not until a few miles have passed that the last of the buildings are gone. Once they leave, there's a nice piece where the terrain tightens up alongside the Klamath.

Scattered buildings return at 51.7 mi (83.2 km). At the same time, a sign indicates cows for the next 15 mi (24 km). Curves are still around but they have devolved into a more sweeper-like species. The hills have fewer and fewer trees, though there are still a fair number down here in the Klamath River Valley bottom and some occasionally move in to the road's edge. If the increasing heat is getting to you, there's another river access point at 54.5 mi (87.7) and one more about a mile after.

The high, almost completely treeless hillside angles down toward the left of the road from Little Cottonwood Peak. Farther to the right lie the hulks of Riverview and Badger Mtns. Look right. You can see you've edged up high above the Klamath. The corners carry on, though they rarely challenge. The only exception: the 25-mph (40-kmh) one at the turnoff for the Tree of Heaven BCG. Hopefully you've been good enough to get in if you mishandle this curve and nail the tree.

It's getting drier and the trees on the rocky hillsides are overcome by sagebrush as you descend once more to the river. The waterway's gorge has tightenened when you leave the Klamath National Forest at 60.7 mi (97.9 km). Some black, crumbly, volcanic-looking extrusions stick off the shoulder of Riverview Mtn just before you reach the junction with the north end of Hwy 263 at 62.5 mi (100.6 km). To stay on the DH, **turn right** on 263.

The pavement remains smooth and the engineering good even as the rougher terrain manhandles the road. Here, you get what might just be the best stretch of the DH – especially if you like high-speed sweepers. Just hope it's a pylon-free experience 'cause there's not much passing room here.

You round a tight bluff at 63.3 mi (101.9 km) and cross a short high span over the Shasta River. Once across, you climb the right-hand side of the gorge. Intermittent rockfaces press very close to your right-hand side, resulting in one 35-mph (55-kmh) advisory. Glimpses of I-5 can be seen on the other side of the gorge. It replaced Hwy 263 and is the reason traffic should be light where you are. Gotta love the interstates.

A right-hander through a cut at 64.6 mi (104.0 km) puts you on the high, long Pioneer Bridge crossing of the Shasta River, still far below you. Past the bridge, you're on the left side of the dry, steeply sided gorge. Round another tight, left side rock bluff, and, on the clear day, magnificent Mt Shasta shimmers white – albeit briefly – over the road.

You are still climbing, but strangely enough, the gorge to your right is getting shallower. A couple more rock cuts and corners and you leave the gorge behind, emerging between fields on the Shasta Valley plateau. After one long sweeper, there's nothing left to do but cruise the straight shot to Yreka, where the DH ends at 70.5 mi (113.5 km). Get it?

RIDER'S LOG: **DATE RIDDEN:** **YOUR RATING:** **/10**

Just what is an "STC" or "maxburner" anyway?

Check out these and other Twisted Terms in the Glossary at p.??

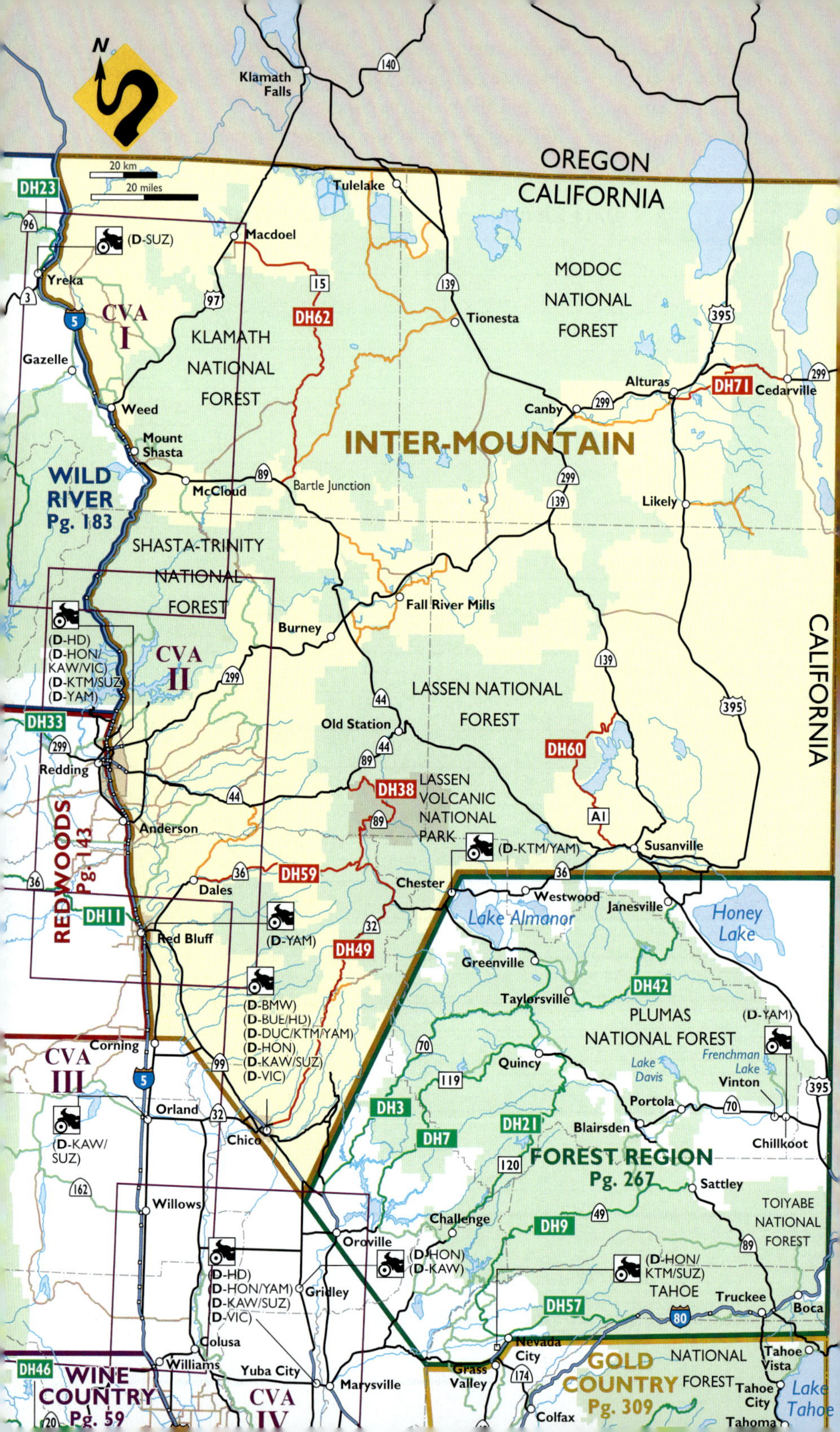

OREGON
CALIFORNIA
Klamath Falls
Tulelake
Macdoel
Yreka
Gazelle
Weed
Mount Shasta
McCloud
Bartle Junction
Tionesta
Alturas
Cedarville
Canby
Likely
KLAMATH NATIONAL FOREST
MODOC NATIONAL FOREST
INTER-MOUNTAIN
WILD RIVER Pg. 183
SHASTA-TRINITY NATIONAL FOREST
CVA I
CVA II
CVA III
CVA IV
Fall River Mills
Burney
LASSEN NATIONAL FOREST
Old Station
LASSEN VOLCANIC NATIONAL PARK
Redding
Anderson
Dales
Red Bluff
Susanville
Chester
Westwood
Janesville
Lake Almanor
Honey Lake
Greenville
Taylorsville
PLUMAS NATIONAL FOREST
Quincy
Lake Davis
Frenchman Lake
Vinton
Portola
Blairsden
Chillkoot
FOREST REGION Pg. 267
Sattley
TOIYABE NATIONAL FOREST
Challenge
Oroville
Gridley
Corning
Orland
Chico
Willows
Colusa
Williams
Yuba City
Marysville
Nevada City
Grass Valley
Colfax
TAHOE NATIONAL FOREST
Truckee
Boca
Tahoe Vista
Tahoe City
Tahoma
Lake Tahoe
GOLD COUNTRY Pg. 309
WINE COUNTRY Pg. 59
REDWOODS Pg. 143
CALIFORNIA
20 km
20 miles
DH23 DH62 DH71 DH33 DH38 DH60 DH59 DH11 DH49 DH42 DH3 DH7 DH21 DH9 DH57 DH46
(D-SUZ)
(D-HD) (D-HON/KAW/VIC) (D-KTM/SUZ) (D-YAM)
(D-KTM/YAM)
(D-YAM)
(D-BMW) (D-BUE/HD) (D-DUC/KTM/YAM) (D-HON) (D-KAW/SUZ) (D-VIC)
(D-KAW/SUZ)
(D-HD) (D-HON/YAM) (D-KAW/SUZ) (D-VIC)
(D-HON) (D-KAW)
(D-HON/KTM/SUZ)
(D-YAM)

INTER-MOUNTAIN

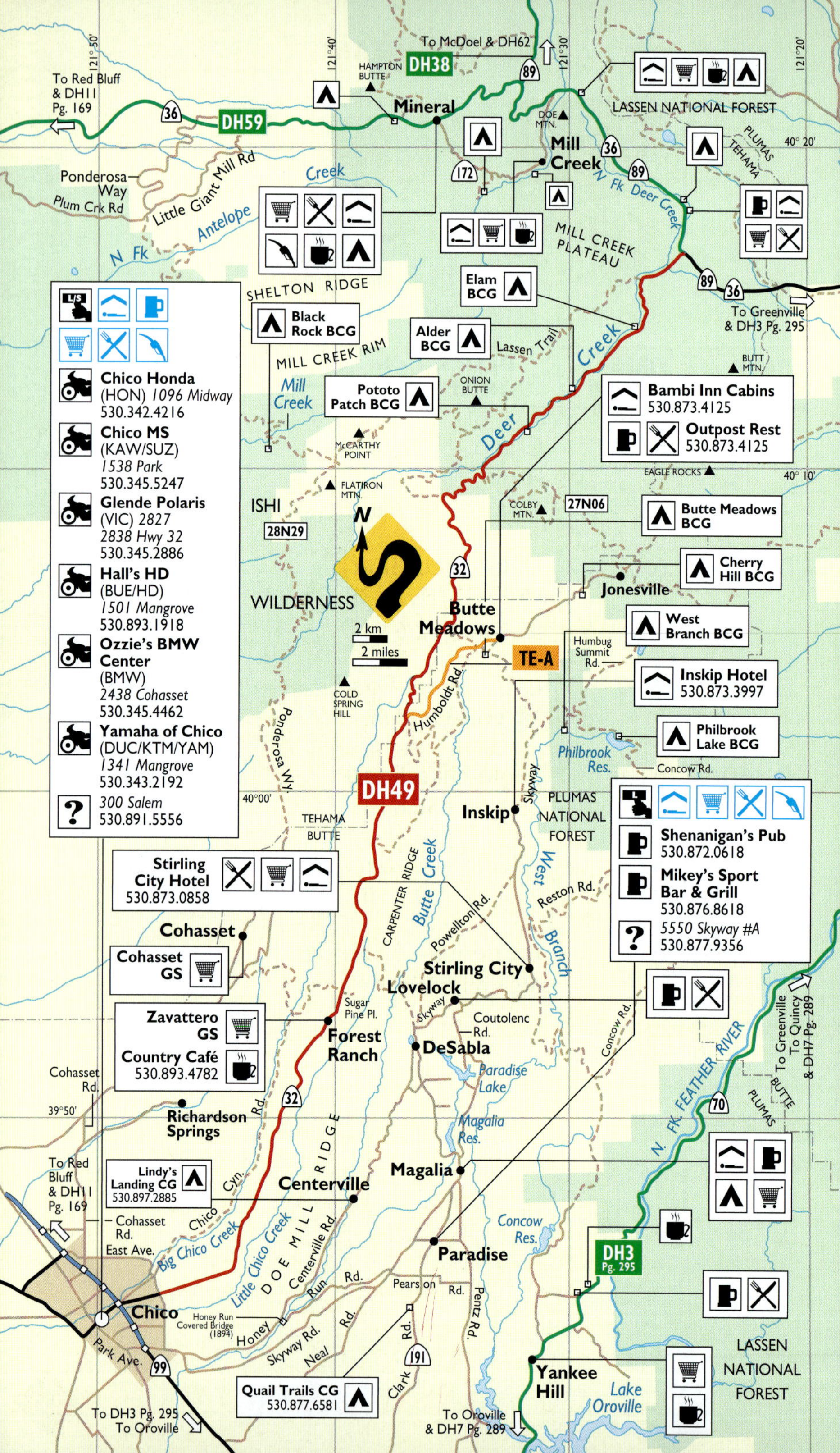

To McDoel & DH62
DH38
HAMPTON BUTTE
Mineral
To Red Bluff & DH11 Pg. 169
DH59
LASSEN NATIONAL FOREST
DOE MTN.
Mill Creek
PLUMAS
TEHAMA
Ponderosa Way
Plum Crk Rd
Little Giant Mill Rd
Creek
Antelope
N Fk
N Fk Deer Creek
MILL CREEK PLATEAU
To Greenville & DH3 Pg. 295
SHELTON RIDGE
Elam BCG
Black Rock BCG
Alder BCG
Lassen Trail
MILL CREEK RIM
Mill Creek
Pototo Patch BCG
ONION BUTTE
BUTT MTN.
Bambi Inn Cabins 530.873.4125
Outpost Rest 530.873.4125
McCARTHY POINT
Deer
EAGLE ROCKS
FLATIRON MTN.
COLBY MTN.
27N06
Butte Meadows BCG
ISHI
28N29
Cherry Hill BCG
Jonesville
WILDERNESS
Butte Meadows
2 km
2 miles
West Branch BCG
Humbug Summit Rd.
TE-A
Inskip Hotel 530.873.3997
COLD SPRING HILL
Humboldt Rd
Ponderosa Wy.
Philbrook Lake BCG
Philbrook Res.
Concow Rd.
Chico Honda (HON) 1096 Midway 530.342.4216
Chico MS (KAW/SUZ) 1538 Park 530.345.5247
Glende Polaris (VIC) 2827 2838 Hwy 32 530.345.2886
Hall's HD (BUE/HD) 1501 Mangrove 530.893.1918
Ozzie's BMW Center (BMW) 2438 Cohasset 530.345.4462
Yamaha of Chico (DUC/KTM/YAM) 1341 Mangrove 530.343.2192
300 Salem 530.891.5556
40°00'
DH49
Inskip
Skyway
PLUMAS NATIONAL FOREST
TEHAMA BUTTE
Shenanigan's Pub 530.872.0618
Mikey's Sport Bar & Grill 530.876.8618
5550 Skyway #A 530.877.9356
Stirling City Hotel 530.873.0858
CARPENTER RIDGE
Butte Creek
West Branch
Reston Rd.
Powellton Rd.
Cohasset
Cohasset GS
Stirling City
Lovelock
Sugar Pine Pl.
Zavattero GS
Country Café 530.893.4782
Forest Ranch
Coutolenc Rd.
DeSabla
Paradise Lake
Cohasset Rd.
39°50'
Richardson Springs
Magalia Res.
N. FK. FEATHER RIVER
To Greenville To Quincy & DH7 Pg. 289
BUTTE
PLUMAS
To Red Bluff & DH11 Pg. 169
Lindy's Landing CG 530.897.2885
Centerville
DOE MILL RIDGE
Magalia
Cohasset Rd.
East Ave.
Big Chico Creek
Little Chico Creek
Centerville Rd.
Concow Res.
Paradise
DH3 Pg. 295
Chico
Honey Run Covered Bridge (1894)
Honey Run Rd.
Skyway Rd.
Neal Rd.
Pearson Rd.
Pentz Rd.
Clark Rd.
Park Ave.
Yankee Hill
Lake Oroville
LASSEN NATIONAL FOREST
Quail Trails CG 530.877.6581
To DH3 Pg. 295 To Oroville
To Oroville & DH7 Pg. 289

DH49 Chico – Hwy 32/Hwy36/89 Jct

Highway 32

Distance:	51.4 mi / 82.7 km	Traffic:	Moderate

At a Glance

Tires	
Twistiness	23.5/ 30
Pavement	13.6/ 20
Engineering	7.2/ 10
Remoteness	7.0/ 10
Scenery	8.8/ 15
Character	6.1/ 15
Total	**66.2**

Chico was a character in the mid-70s sit-com that took place in a garage. He was played by Freddy Prinze whose untimely suici... make that "accident, while playing with a loaded gun" was probably due to the fact that he never got out of that garage and away from working on pylons. If only Pie had become addicted to motorcycle roads instead of quaaludes, maybe he wouldn't have been so accident-prone. Granted, this ride can be a bit sedated during the first third, but once you get into the terrain conched between the north end of the Sierra Nevada and Mt Lassen, you'll find enough uplifting Twistiness to naturally elevate your mood. Because it's not as high as this nearby topography, the Scenery is over the counter, up-country forest but it's still good enough to prevent psychosis. It's true that Chico's size affects the Remoteness, but only at the start, so there's no reason to get depressed. And sure, the Pavement might not be quite as good as other nearby DHs but both it and Engineering manage to hold it together for the show. And, speaking of performers, who da Man? Well, on this DH, you get to play that role. Loo-king good!

Access

From Chico

On Hwy 32

Hwy 32 cuts east-west through Chico. Get on it and head east. Once you cross Bruce Rd, you're on the road.

Via Hwy 99

Whether you're coming from the north or south, look for the Hwy 32 exit east. Take it and once you cross Bruce Rd, you're on the road.

From Hwy 36/89

Coming in on DH59 Dales (Red Bluff) – Hwy 32/Hwy 36/89 Jct

At the end of the DH, turn right on Hwy 32. You're on the road.

On The Road

Damn, it's hot down here in the Central Valley. Fastest way to escape Chico's heat is to go east. And you can do that quickly on the straight shot that heads toward Dole Mill Ridge. The number of trees in the foreground increases to the point where the ridge is barely noticeable. At 3.0 mi (4.8 km), the road inclines slightly and a long, gradual sweeper swings you north.

At 4.7 mi (7.6 km), the ground to the right drops down to unseen Little Chico Creek. The heights behind make up Doe Mill Ridge. There's lots of time to check out the scenery since all the road's giving up is the odd, lazy sweeper. Over to your left at 6.3 mi (10.1 km), an even larger chasm down to the Big Chico Creek canyon makes it clear you're on top of a ridge of your own. While yours is treed, Musty Buck Ridge across the gorge is mostly rock.

The curveless asphalt gets a bit tar-strippy here but the snakes mostly run in the same direction as your tires and cause little insecurity. What might, however, is the sheriff's car going in the other direction. Curiously, it only has amber lights on top. Phew… apparently he's not interested in collecting speed tax. Yellow, your new favorite color.

You're climbing now, the trees are multiplying and, at 8.3 mi (13.4 km), you get one of those short, slow-traffic-move-to-the-right, widening-of-the-shoulder passing lanes that most pylons refuse to believe are meant for them. Right after that, a deer warning sign indicates a fresh meat zone for the next 4 mi (6 km). A few curves – mostly sweepers – add some extra challenge to the hunt.

The road descends and you flash through Forest Ranch at 12.7 mi (20.4 km) commencing a long, straight forested stretch. You can't see any terrain above the trees so you deduce that it's relatively flat around here. At least there's nice pavement, good shoulder and lots of dotted yellow.

It is getting more remote and pleasingly cooler, too. In fact, it's one of those pieces of road where your mind, focused but at the same time free, can wander off to some of those special places it sometimes needs to go. Everyone needs a little bikeotherapy.

At 18.7 mi (30.1 km), the topography gets shaken up a little as cuts through the landscape create sweepy curves broken up by straights. Some quick views out to the right across Butte Creek toward Carpenter Ridge precede another sign warning of a venison stretch, this time for 9 mi (15 km). Man, where have all the hunters gone? Wish they'd get out here with their assault weapons and do some serious deer damage.

Humboldt Rd (**TE-A**) turns off right for Butte Meadows at 26.0 mi (41.8 km). If you don't go down it, the next thing you'll see is the twisty sign promising 25 mi (40 km) of heaven. The forest moves to the edge of the road, the engineering tightens up and the curving begins.

A vista on the left side affords a view of tree-covered Cold Spring Hill just before you get your butt out of Butte County and enter Tehama at 26.8 mi (43.1 km). Not that you're likely to notice, what with the increased cornering opportunities. Unless you're stuck behind a pylon, of course. And they're not easy to pass in here, no matter how slow they're going. Dum-de-dum-de-dum...

The curves slacken and you pounce on the dotted-yellow opportunity at 28.9 mi (46.5 km). It only lasts half way along that straight, so don't waste it, since you'll soon be back winding tightly through the trees. The asphalt roughs up temporarily but quickly reverts to its perfectly adequate, if not exceptional, nature.

Bogged down in traffic as usual? A legitimate, one-mile passing lane at 32.0 mi (51.5 km) is there to help you out. There are some big sweepers on it but frankly, they're kind of tough to enjoy at the posted 55 mph (90 kph). Fortunately, you get one mile of tight stuff prior to another, shorter passing lane. After this, you're back in sweet and steady twisties through the trees.

The giant, tight sweeper at the end of a short straight heralds a brief opening in the terrain. On your left the forest disappears to reveal McCarthy Point and environs. No point getting your speed up, though. You're quickly reined in by a series of tight, blind and essed-together, 30-mph (50-kph) turns slicing through rock cuts. They're great if you get 'em swept clean of traffic.

You enter the Lassen National Forest at 37.6 mi (60.5 km). And the road tightens up even more. It doesn't get any more remote, though. That's because it doesn't need to. You haven't seen so much as a forest road turnoff in eons.

You didn't know it, but the road's actually been following Deer Creek for quite some time. A bridge takes you across to its western side at 39.8 mi (64.0 km). Sadly, the pavement across the creek is a little more beaten up. And it's less twisty for a while too, though encroaching trees still keep a lot of these lesser corners blind. Looking away to the left, you could savor Onion Butte but you'd have to peel some layers of forest away to do it.

The warmth that comes the deeper you plunge into the interior is set off by the coolness of the mountains. The increase in temperature is all the more noticeable if a crawling pylon has you jacked up on this tough-to-pass section.

Another two bridges criss and cross the creek, returning you to the western side at 44.4 mi (71.4 km). The trees get bigger and the slope either side of the road steepens as you climb above the waterway. The reliable curves continue – just hope you get to enjoy them. Because it's not until a short straight arrives with yet another crossing of the Deer that you get any chance to pass.

Once clear, you can whack your throttle and enjoy the turning once again. It's more or less continuous until the slope on the right pulls away, you cross the creek for the last time and the first little meadow appears right side. From here, it's a simple matter of looking good for the mellow victory stretch across an open valley and into a few more trees before the DH ends at 51.4 mi (82.7 km).

Twisted Edges

TE-A Humboldt Rd (5.2 mi / 8.4 km)

The Bambi Inn is biker friendly. The road you take to get to it is pretty receptive as well. Despite being bumpy and poorly cambered at times, the road curves easily upward through tall, airy forest. There are some agreeable views at the end toward Cold Spring Hill to the west.

Rider's Log: **Date Ridden:** **Your Rating:** **/10**

How does this book work again? RTFM. "What is Destination Highways Northern California?" and "How to Use Our Maps" appear at the front of the book.

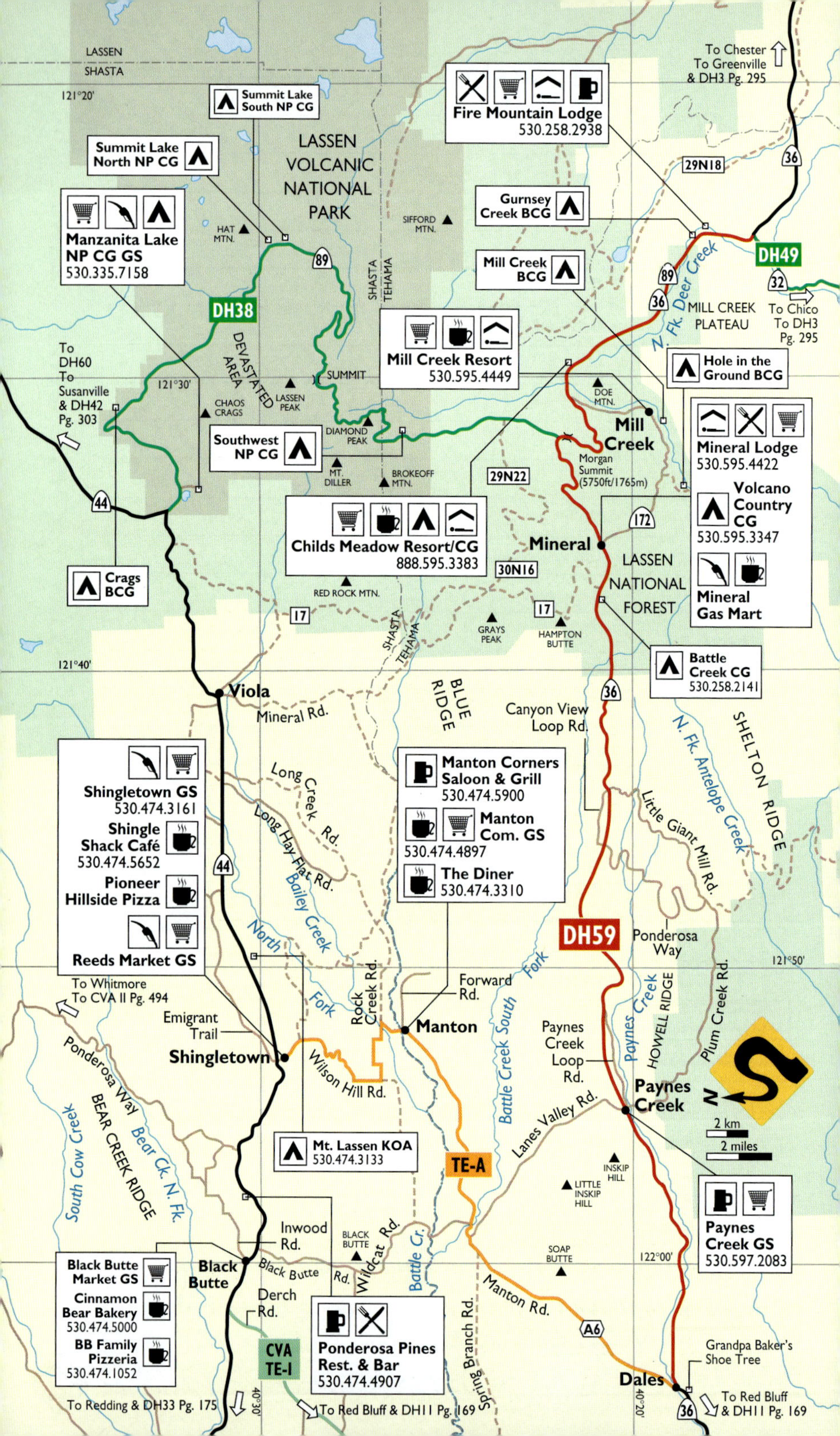

LASSEN
SHASTA
LASSEN VOLCANIC NATIONAL PARK
Summit Lake South NP CG
Summit Lake North NP CG
Manzanita Lake NP CG GS
530.335.7158
Fire Mountain Lodge
530.258.2938
To Chester
To Greenville
& DH3 Pg. 295
Gurnsey Creek BCG
Mill Creek BCG
Mill Creek Resort
530.595.4449
Hole in the Ground BCG
Mineral Lodge
530.595.4422
Volcano Country CG
530.595.3347
Mineral Gas Mart
Southwest NP CG
Childs Meadow Resort/CG
888.595.3383
Crags BCG
Battle Creek CG
530.258.2141
To DH60
To Susanville
& DH42
Pg. 303
To Chico
To DH3
Pg. 295
MILL CREEK PLATEAU
N. Fk. Deer Creek
DEVASTATED AREA
LASSEN PEAK
CHAOS CRAGS
HAT MTN.
SIFFORD MTN.
SUMMIT
DIAMOND PEAK
MT. DILLER
BROKEOFF MTN.
DOE MTN.
Mill Creek
Morgan Summit
(5750ft/1765m)
Mineral
LASSEN NATIONAL FOREST
RED ROCK MTN.
GRAYS PEAK
HAMPTON BUTTE
SHASTA
TEHAMA
DH38
DH49
DH59
TE-A
CVA TE-I
29N18
29N22
30N16
Viola
Mineral Rd.
BLUE RIDGE
Canyon View Loop Rd.
SHELTON RIDGE
N. Fk. Antelope Creek
Little Giant Mill Rd.
Shingletown GS
530.474.3161
Shingle Shack Café
530.474.5652
Pioneer Hillside Pizza
Reeds Market GS
Manton Corners Saloon & Grill
530.474.5900
Manton Com. GS
530.474.4897
The Diner
530.474.3310
Long Creek Rd.
Long Hay Flat Rd.
Bailey Creek
North Fork
Ponderosa Way
HOWELL RIDGE
Plum Creek Rd.
Paynes Creek
To Whitmore
To CVA II Pg. 494
Emigrant Trail
Shingletown
Rock Creek Rd.
Forward Rd.
Manton
Battle Creek South Fork
Paynes Creek Loop Rd.
Wilson Hill Rd.
Lanes Valley Rd.
Paynes Creek
2 km
2 miles
Mt. Lassen KOA
530.474.3133
South Cow Creek
BEAR CREEK RIDGE
Bear Ck. N. Fk.
INSKIP HILL
LITTLE INSKIP HILL
Paynes Creek GS
530.597.2083
Inwood Rd.
BLACK BUTTE
Wildcat Rd.
Battle Cr.
SOAP BUTTE
Black Butte Market GS
Cinnamon Bear Bakery
530.474.5000
BB Family Pizzeria
530.474.1052
Black Butte
Black Butte Rd.
Derch Rd.
Ponderosa Pines Rest. & Bar
530.474.4907
Spring Branch Rd.
Manton Rd.
Dales
Grandpa Baker's Shoe Tree
To Redding & DH33 Pg. 175
To Red Bluff & DH11 Pg. 169
To Red Bluff & DH11 Pg. 169
121°20'
121°30'
121°40'
121°50'
122°00'
40°30'
40°20'

DH59 Dales (Red Bluff) – Hwy 32/Hwy 36/89 Jct

Hwy 32 / Hwy 36/89

Distance:	45.1 mi / 72.6 km	Traffic:	Moderate

DH49 DH59 DH38 DH60 DH71 DH62

At a Glance

TIRES	
Twistiness	14.6/ 30
Pavement	19.9/ 20
Engineering	8.4/ 10
Remoteness	6.0/ 10
Scenery	9.7/ 15
Character	3.6/ 15
Total	62.2

After Disney comedy duo Chip 'n' Dale broke up, Dale – the party animal with the larger, redder nose – ended up running a self-named bar/café here in Middle of Nowhere, CA. And while this business is now just as often out of business, you can always rely on the DH east of Dales to provide some madcap merriment. There's a well-drawn background of Pavement and Engineering throughout, though the plot of curves is a little slow to build as the show moves east. The open plateau at the beginning is renowned for its vibrant explosion of wildflower color in March/April but the Scenery becomes less animated as you leave the heat of the Central Valley behind and move into the cooler, forested ridges on the approach to Lassen Volcanic National Park. The entertainment on this ride is light, so you don't expect to find a huge amount of Character. But with the great Twistiness in the higher country on the other side of the spinoff, DH38 Lassen Park Road, you may find yourself smiling, even chuckling at times before the story ends. Oh, and what happened to CHiP, you ask? He's the cartoon character behind you in glorious black and white.

Access

From Red Bluff (and I-5)

Via Hwy 36

Hwy 99 starts in Red Bluff off I-5. Follow Hwy 36 east when it splits off from Hwy 99. Take it for about 13 mi (21 km). Don't blink or you may miss Dales and not realize you've left town and are on the road.

From Hwy 32/Hwy 36/89 Jct

Coming in on DH49 Chico – Hwy 32/Hwy 36/89 Jct

At the end of Hwy 32, turn left. You're on the road.

On The Road

As you scamper out of Dales, excellent quality pavement strikes east along the edge of a plateau. To your right, the shallow valley of Paynes Creek descends from the high land surrounding it. At 2.0 mi (3.2 km), you can see Inskip Hill ahead to the left of the road as the trees begin to increase in number.

There are a few curves around an open field, followed by one long sweeper and then several more past some buildings at 5.1 mi (8.2 km). All preface a shallow climb up the northern side of the creek's valley, which you may notice, has suddenly become a lot deeper.

Reaching cruising speed, you soon level off among taller trees. Far ahead and above the road, you can see some of the higher, beige terrain around Lassen Peak. The turnoff for Paynes Creek is at 8.8 mi (14.2 km).

ROUTING OPTION: Those not attracted by narrow, poor pavement with few curves through boring terrain will pass on the remote Plum Creek Rd-Little Giant Mill Rd bypass to the straightest stretch of the DH. The rest of you, hang a right at Paynes Creek.

Now, the DH begins another climb, though it re-levels for awhile at 2000 ft (614 m). You're on the southern edge of a broad, open plateau stretching out to Battle Creek South Fork while the higher country around Lassen lies blue in the distance. Down to your right, fields of bright green on the bottom of Paynes Creek valley contrast with the darker green of the trees covering the nearby slopes. No curves here, but at least the surfeit of dotted yellow helps you get by any leisurely pylons heading to the National Park.

After a lon-n-n-ng sweeper, a passing lane at 13.0 mi (20.9 km) provides more ease of passage. Paynes Creek valley continues to offer scenic variation with its collection of foothills folding away to your right. If it's a clear day, you might be able to catch a glimpse of the top of Mount Shasta far to the north just before you hit 3000 ft (921 m) at 15.9 mi (25.6 km). Strangely enough, you can't see Lassen Peak at this point, even though it's much closer than Shasta.

You're now on top of a long ridge riding parallel to Shelton Ridge right and Blue Ridge left. Just prior to the junction with Canyon View Loop and Little Giant Mill Rd at 20.1 mi (32.3 km), you lose the passing lane and the speed limit drops to 55 mph (90 kmh). Both good signs. You don't even mind giving up a bit of engineering in favor of the curves that contort the still-smooth asphalt here. The trees in the thickening forest suddenly seem taller and more majestic. But that may just be psychological.

Near as you can tell among all the increased flora, you're still on a ridge, though you no longer seem to be on its spine. This becomes more evident when you see the large chasm gaping off to your left. Hopefully, there's no traffic blocking your enjoyment of this nice stretch. Because, all too quickly, the road straightens at 20.3 mi (32.7 km). Well, at least if you were stuck behind pylons you're probably… not now.

You enter Lassen National Forest at 25.7 mi (41.4 km). Its dense green completely cloaks the surrounding valley walls and presses thickly against the roadside. At least it does for a mile or so, then the terrain opens up into a mix of fields and--uh, sewage lagoons, how nice--to the south. Some scattered buildings on the outskirts of Mineral preface the downtown that comes at 28.1 mi (45.2 km).

TOUR NOTE: Mineral is at nearly 5000 ft (1535m). If you are wrung out by the California heat, you'll be happy to know it cools down quite nicely here in the evening. Or just drop a couple of Mineral's waters and move on.

You'll see a few buildings as you leave town, but you're soon back in the deep forest. Initially, there's not much in the way of cornering opportunities through the trees. But, gradually, things pick up. A few sweepers – one even has a 40-mph (65-kph) advisory – begin at 29.3 mi (47.1 km), where the road cuts into the hillside on the left. You reach the turnoff left for **DH38 Lassen Park Road** at 32.6 mi (52.5 km).

More bikes may join the cast as you carry on from the junction and clear Morgan Summit (5750 ft / 1765 m) at 32.9 mi (52.9 km). As you start down, the excitement builds. A rockface appears to your right and a co-slope slants down to your left, conspiring to create a bunch of linked curves. They vary in intensity, though true to this DH, they're never extreme.

At 36.3 mi (58.4 km), you stop descending and the flurry is over. Past the junction right with Hwy 172, you emerge from the forest onto a flat valley floor. Quickly, you're across it and briefly back among trees before zipping out onto sprawling Child's Meadow. The pavement toddles across it before re-entering the forest.

At 39.4 mi (63.4 km), some fields open up below the heights of Mill Creek Plateau to the west and then you're back among the trees. And that's pretty much it until the DH ends at the junction with Hwy 32 at 45.1 mi (72.6 km). Turn right and you're on **DH49 Hwy 32/Hwy 36/89 Jct – Chico**.

Twisted Edges

TE-A Dales – Shingletown (A 6) (23.8 mi / 38.3 km) *Manton Rd - Rock Creek Rd - Wilson Hill Rd*

The first part of this little-traveled TE goes straight across the wide-open, wildflower-covered-in-springtime plateau that presents some long-distance views of Mts Lassen and Shasta. After a few curves on the way down to and back up from Battle Creek, it straightens again through scattered trees all the way to Manton where A 6 ends. The second part, the climb up to Shingletown, has curves, although the mostly okay pavement does narrow to almost one lane for most of Wilson Hill Rd. Oh yes, there can be ambulatory venison on Wilson.

TOUR NOTE: Heat getting to you? A good spot to cool down is in Battle Creek South Fork at the little bridge just before the junction of Manton Rd and Wildcat Rd.

Rider's Log: **Date Ridden:** **Your Rating:** /10

Find more information about camping in Northern California, including how to make a reservation, in the "Touring Northern California – What You Should Know" section at the front of the book.

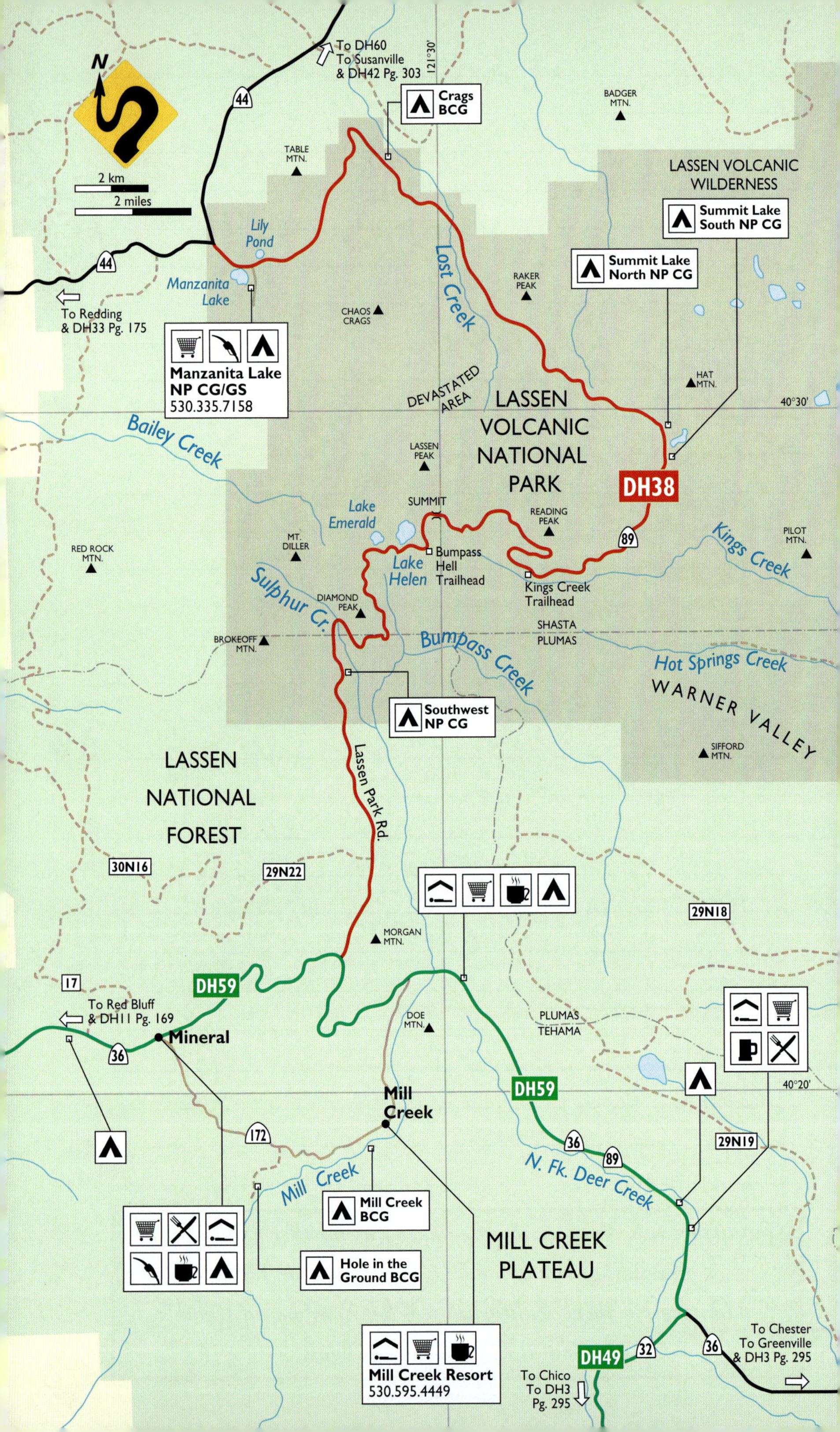

N
2 km
2 miles
To DH60
To Susanville
& DH42 Pg. 303
121°30'
44
Crags BCG
BADGER MTN.
TABLE MTN.
LASSEN VOLCANIC WILDERNESS
Summit Lake South NP CG
Summit Lake North NP CG
Lily Pond
Manzanita Lake
44
To Redding
& DH33 Pg. 175
Lost Creek
RAKER PEAK
CHAOS CRAGS
Manzanita Lake NP CG/GS
530.335.7158
HAT MTN.
DEVASTATED AREA
LASSEN VOLCANIC NATIONAL PARK
40°30'
Bailey Creek
LASSEN PEAK
DH38
SUMMIT
Lake Emerald
READING PEAK
89
PILOT MTN.
Kings Creek
MT. DILLER
RED ROCK MTN.
Lake Helen
Bumpass Hell Trailhead
Kings Creek Trailhead
Sulphur Cr.
DIAMOND PEAK
SHASTA
PLUMAS
BROKEOFF MTN.
Bumpass Creek
Hot Springs Creek
WARNER VALLEY
Southwest NP CG
SIFFORD MTN.
Lassen Park Rd.
LASSEN NATIONAL FOREST
30N16
29N22
29N18
MORGAN MTN.
17
DH59
To Red Bluff
& DH11 Pg. 169
DOE MTN.
PLUMAS
TEHAMA
Mineral
36
DH59
40°20'
Mill Creek
172
36
89
29N19
N. Fk. Deer Creek
Mill Creek
Mill Creek BCG
MILL CREEK PLATEAU
Hole in the Ground BCG
To Chester
To Greenville
& DH3 Pg. 295
DH49
32
36
Mill Creek Resort
530.595.4449
To Chico
To DH3
Pg. 295

DH38 Lassen Park Road

Highway 89

Distance:	34.3 mi / 55.2 km	Traffic:	Moderate

At a Glance

TIRES	
Twistiness	26.0/30
Pavement	15.1/20
Engineering	5.2/10
Remoteness	6.1/10
Scenery	12.7/15
Character	5.6/15
Total	**70.7**

You'd think with these kinds of TIRES numbers, you'd find a lot of sportbikes converging on this twisty, question-mark-shaped route through California's least visited national park. But while cruisers love this smoothly paved ride through the snowy, volcanic peaks, rugged, red-rock slopes, alpine forests and floral meadows, something keeps their knee puck-dragging brothers away. It's sure not the lack of Twistiness or Scenery. The Forest Service Pavement is good to great and Engineering is more than adequate. You might think it had something to do with the 35-mph (55-kmh) zone that covers the twistier southern half. Or the tourist traffic that can descend like a blanket of ash on summer weekends. But the real reason? The same guys who will spend two grand on a set of Akrapovic racing pipes and four hundred bucks on the latest radar detector can't bring themselves to part with a measly $5 toll, no matter how great a road is.

Access

From Mid-DH59 Dales – Hwy 32/Hwy 36/89Jct (Hwy 36)

Turn north on Hwy 89, 12.4 mi (20.0 km) west of the Hwy 32/Hwy 36/89 Jct. You're on the road.

From Hwy 44

Look for the well-marked turnoff south onto Hwy 89, approximately 40 mi (60 km) east of Redding. Once on 89, you're on the road.

On The Road

Lassen National Park's volcanic past is obvious as you turn off **DH59 Dales – Hwy 32/Hwy 36/89 Jct** and head north on Hwy 89 through a light pine forest. Red dirt banks, numerous peaks and tumbling waterfalls of rock like the one off to the left at 3.6 mi (5.8 km). Wow. And you're not even officially in the park until 3.9 mi (6.3 km).

The Forest Service assumes responsibility for the pavement once you cross the park boundary. While engineering isn't their forte, they like to keep their blacktop fresh and new, at least in national parks. And those high standards are apparent here. Their scenic standards aren't bad either, as snowy cones and saddles fill the eastern sky.

At 5.3 mi (8.5 km), it's time to stop the bike, drop the stand, peel off the gloves, zip open the jacket, fish out the wallet, find five bucks, pass it to the smiling summer student, stick a flimsy piece of paper to your windscreen, reverse the process and try to get some cool air moving through the vents again. Cool? Well, when you're sweating like you've just been clocked at 100 mph (160 kmh), any air will do.

It's Sub-Alpine City, Arizona, as you pass the Chalet. Stands of dwarfed pines and rock-strewn meadows stuffed with manzanita and gooseberry roll beneath a panoply of gleaming glaciers. Forget 100 mph (160 kmh). The speed limit here is 35-mph (55-kmh). And if that weren't sufficiently ridiculous, at 6.3 mi (10.1 km), you cross West Sulphur Creek and the limit drops to a glacial 15 mph (25 kmh). This ensures you get a good strong whiff of the sulphur that wafts up from the water by the trail access parking lot.

Back up to a sizzling 35-mph (55-kmh), you curl around east to parallel the creek, bringing the higher, longer views across the Warner Valley to Pilot Mtn and the Crystal Cliffs beyond. Climbing up a series of switchbacks, the curves on the narrow road thicken as the air thins. With distance opening up between parking lots, there's even some sense of remoteness.

At 7.5 mi (12.1 km), the road's right side drops off, opening a big, soft and hazy view over the green and blue peaks to the south. Then you turn north again along a huge rockface. Its brown and white chalk surface is all the more striking backed as it is by the glacier-laden heights of Lassen Peak. Try taking all this in while keeping an eye on the crumbling rock above the road to the left and the lack of guardrail to the right. It could be you holding up the pylons for a change.

The right side dropoff eases a little, the curves elongate and the sightlines improve. One big sweeper at 8.6 mi (13.8 km) esses into another. A chunk of rock, like a giant, black bicuspid juts up from the ridgeline. Turning back toward Lassen Peak, the road levels. It seems you're near the top. But not quite yet.

It's extremely tight through the pass. Curves and sweepers crunch together to create a tight, continuously essing section. Snow by the road is common through here, even in high summer. And you can feel the cool of the mini-glaciers as you lean by. The tightness eases at 10.5 mi (16.9 km) where you spurt east and get another striking southward view before curving past Lakes Emerald and Helen. Feel like instantly dropping your core body temperature 50 degrees? Jump right in.

TOUR NOTE: Across from Lake Helen is the Bumpass Hell Basin trailhead. If you wish to take in some of the steaming pools, mudpots and vents of this volcanically active area but don't feel like going on a major hike, this easy, level trail is the best place in the park to do it. "Bike-hikes" not permitted.

You push onward to the top, rubble sliding down the glaciated slopes as you clear the treeline. The red-orange color of the roadside rock formations belies their volcanic origins. Looking up at the peak ahead, a distinctive rock resembles an eye glaring down from above. It watches you erupt through the sweepers that climb through the barren, snow-spotted terrain on the final summit approach.

You reach the 8512 ft (2594 m) summit at 12.5 mi (20.1 km) and the road straightens into another world. Rock, gnarly bristlecone pines, lots of snow patches and, if you're lucky, one lonely rider – you. The road takes on a different rhythm as you begin the sharp descent. Long sweepers separated by short straights switchback down the slope on Lassen's north side. It's a fast road with a fast drop. Not too much traffic either, with most of the pylons hunting for parking back on the south side of the peak. So where's the sign bumping the speed limit on this quiet stretch up to at least 55 mph (90 kmh)? Must have missed it.

The barren slopes disappear and the trees thicken and grow taller as you rapidly lose altitude. The slope's steep, so you don't lose the views straight ahead to the east of the bright white peaks of the Lassen Volcanic Wilderness. The terrain ultimately levels out at 16.5 mi (26.6 km) where you enter a short, dry zone. The pines recede and a large tract of rocky moonscape unfurls from either side of the road. Hardy, sage-like shrubs give the surface a hint of silver-green. Then, a verdant meadow, fed by King's Creek, fills the left roadside at 17.1 mi (27.5 km), contrasting starkly with the parched right side. Speaking of parched, how about some curves?

Funny you should ask. At 17.5 mi (28.2 km), just beyond the concentration of pylons at the Kings Creek trailhead, a concentration of corners juices along the red base of Reading Peak. The right roadside drops off and the trees return in number. Not thick enough to block the views over the Warner Valley, though.

At 19.7 mi (31.7 km), you drop below 7000 ft (2133 m) and enter a flowing series of partially linked corners. The ponderosas crowd and shadow the road as you pass the Summit Lake campground and picnic area entrances. But then the road straightens. Not just for a short spell between a couple curves but for a long and drawn out stretch. Troubling. The great view of the east side of Lassen Peak to the left is not enough to quell your concern.

At 22.5 mi (36.2 km), the streaked slopes of Raker Peak burst out of the forest to the right. Does this close-in slope mean a return to sweepiness? Well, not quite. You do ess big past the trailhead at 23.8 mi (38.3 km) but then straighten again onto a sparselytreed flat. And, what's this? At 24.5 mi (39.4 km), a 45-mph (70-kmh) sign confirms the speed limit. Right – um, you knew that.

It seems you're turning back to thick forest and sloped terrain as you round the solid corner at 25.1 mi (40.4 km) – but not yet. The flat, dusty, volcano-devastated area – not to mention the general straightness - continues to Lost Creek at 26.7 mi (43.0 km). There are some good curves to be found here among the encroaching pines. And some even better ones that loop the road southward at 29.2 mi (47.0 km).

But that's it. At 31.1 mi (50.0 km), it's pretty much over. The road is all too orderly as you emerge from the woods back into the devastated area and take in the eroding slopes of Chaos Crags. Short trees somehow find a way to poke through the thick layer of rubble that fans out over the level landscape. A couple of curves lead to the Manzanita Lake turnoff at 32.7 mi (52.6 km), which is notable as the start of a major jump in the pavement grade. It's a teaser though, since the road is utterly straight as it runs briefly along the shore of Lily Pond to the right, then Lake Manzanita to the left before the stop sign appears at the park's north entrance. From here, it's a little skip to the junction of Hwy 44, and end of road, at 34.3 mi (55.2 km).

RIDER'S LOG: **DATE RIDDEN:** **YOUR RATING: /10**

Remember, you'll find video clips of all of Northern California's DHs at **destination highways.com.**

To Alturas & DH71
139
North Eagle Lake BCG
Mariners Resort/CG
530.825.3333
N
3 km
3 miles
LASSEN NATIONAL FOREST
Stones Landing
LOWER SIGNAL BUTTE
A1
ICE CAVE RIDGE
Eagle Lake Rd.
EAGLE LAKE
Eagle Lake RV Park/ Cabins/CG
530.825.3133
Lakeview Inn
530.825.3555
Spalding GS
Spalding
Horse Lake
40°40'
WHALEBACK MTN.
DH60
BROCKMAN FLAT LAVA BEDS
21
Gallatin Marina
BLACK MTN.
HORSE LAKE MTN.
FOX MTN.
GALLATIN PEAK
MAHOGANY PEAK
Merrillville Rd.
Willow Creek
MERRILL MTN.
Aspen Grove CG
139
TUNNISON MTN.
GREENS PEAK
Round Valley Res.
40°30'
Merrill CG
Eagle Lake Summit (6340ft/1946m)
Eagle CG
Christie CG
SUSANVILLE PEAK
Antelope Summit (5472ft/1680m)
ROOP MTN.
To Mt. Lassen & DH38
ANTELOPE MTN.
Rice Cyn. Rd.
40
GOAT MTN.
Susanville
Susan River
204
Johnstonville Center Rd.
Leavitt
A27
FEDONYER BUTTE
Leavitt Ln.
Gold Run Creek
Richmond Rd.
Leavitt Lake
Lake Leavitt
395
36
Gold Run Rd.
To DH49
To Greenville & DH3 Pg. 295
Willard Creek
Wingfield Rd.
Beyers Pass Rd.
40°20'
HAMILTON MTN.
LASSEN
PLUMAS
84 N Lassen
530.257.4323
222
East
Baxter Creek
A3
29N46
Janesville
COYOTE PEAK
Main St.
Buntingville
Janesville Grade
29N43
01
DH42 Pg. 303
To Reno, NV
To DH9TE-I Pg. 276
28N08
213
PLUMAS NATIONAL FOREST
28N02
To Greenville & DH3 Pg. 295
120°50'
120°40'
120°30'

DH60 Eagle Lake Road

County Road A 1

Distance:	35.2 mi / 56.6 km	Traffic:	Light

At a Glance

Let the Eagle soar
Like she's never soared before
From rocky coast to golden shore
Let the mighty Eagle soar

TIRES	
Twistiness	20.8/ 30
Pavement	11.2/ 20
Engineering	5.8/ 10
Remoteness	7.6/ 10
Scenery	9.8/ 15
Character	6.4/ 15
Total	**61.6**

Former Attorney General John Ashcroft will forever be remembered for his stirring paean to NorCal's DH60. This quiet flight through the varied, if unspectacular dry-country Scenery that surrounds the state's second largest natural lake won't be hurt by a little eulogizing though. That's because it's located in one of the least populated counties in California. The initial hop through loose, pine forest north of Susanville prefaces a soaring climb up the flanks of Roop Mtn. On the subsequent descent, the road hunts through the Brockman Flat lava beds on the golden, western shore of the lake before thermalling up, down and back up the gentler topography that faces the lake's rockier eastern coast. The first third has concentrated Twistiness, while the remainder sweeps more gently and is more suitable to flying at higher speeds. The older variety of Pavement causes few problems, though you probably wouldn't mind if it was a little wider on that first piece. And there's so little roadside development that even a large convocation of riders won't impair its remote feeling. Yes, the Eagle soars all right but – no offense, John – we still prefer the sound of pipe music.

Access

From Susanville

Via Hwy 36

The turnoff for Eagle Lake Rd is a couple of miles west of Susanville, almost exactly halfway to 36's junction with Hwy 44. Turn north at the boat shop and you're on the road.

From Hwy 139

At the north end of Eagle Lake, turn west on Eagle Lake Rd. You're on the road.

On The Road

The speed limit from the south end starts out at a leisurely 45 mph (70 kmh). And don't be looking for it to get any higher. Which is rather surprising since the numerous curves through the forest are pretty leisurely as well. The speed limit does go lower, however. The few houses set back in the trees foreshadow a drop to 35 mph (55 kmh).

You pass an even larger collection of abodes at 2.2 mi (3.5 km) when the road tightens up and starts to climb the eastern flank of Roop Mtn. When the 25-mph (40-kmh) advisory comes at 4.1 mi (6.6 km) – of course, just *after* an off-camber corner – you'll know you're getting into the gamiest curves of this gradual ascent.

By 5.8 mi (9.3 km), the road has climbed high enough that, with a little help from logging and fire, sage has largely replaced the trees. The lack of a woody screen to the right allows for a clear view between Greens and Susanville Peaks of shallow Round Valley and east of that, Horse Lake Mtn and Tunnison Mtn. More importantly, it allows for clear sightlines around the tightish, demanding, sometimes off-camber corners.

It's kind of hard to tell when you clear the unmarked Eagle Lake Summit (6340 ft / 1946 m). You know you've passed it by 7.9 mi (12.7 km), since you're back in the forest and descending. A glimpse of Eagle Lake flashes over the road far in the distance just before four tight corners refocus you. And stop you whining about the trees blocking the view.

Don't be complaining about the pavement, either. Although it's the roughest looking stuff you've seen so far, it doesn't feel that bad. And it's about to get smoother (and wider) anyway. Not only that, but when the descent gentles to almost nothing at 11.6 mi (18.7 km), the speed limit soars back to a lordly 45 mph (70 kmh).

The curves lengthen out to stretched sweepers down on the flat as you enter the Lassen National Forest Eagle Lake Recreation Area at 12.8 mi (20.6 km). Gallatin Rd – to the right at 13.5 mi (21.7 km) – provides your first access to the lake. The DH continues almost perfectly straight as it parallels the southwestern edge of the water. You just might be able to spot it through the trees to your right.

You get a better look at the lake at 15.8 mi (25.4 km) when the road comes closer and fewer trees stand in the way. This first close-up look at the water is also your last for a while. As you pass by the turnoff for Christie NF CG, the road heads north away from the lake, more or less paralleling the low north-south ridge between Fox and Whaleback Mtns.

The trees thin in number, matching the lack of curves through the openness of the unspectacular Brockman Flat lava beds. After a short while, the trees come back, complete with scrubby underbrush. This increased vegetation doesn't bring a lot of corners with them, though. Let's see: no curves, no traffic and no development. So why's the speed limit staying at 45 mph (70 kmh)? The remnants of a dead deer at the edge of the road provide one answer.

The flat on the left turns to a gradual slope as the road slides closer to the base of Whaleback Mtn. But at 23.1 mi (37.2 km), a right-hand sweeper turns your bearing east. Soon you're back in the middle of another wide flat dominated by brush. You breach Pine Creek and cross the barely perceptible southern end of Ice Cave Ridge, reaching the turnoff to Spalding at 26.4 mi (42.5 km).

Just past the turn, the trees on the right disappear, leaving a broad, sage-filled plain that stretches all the way to the lake. The terrain gets even drier as you formally exit the Lassen National Forest – which is appropriate, given the absence of trees. There are not many curves either.

At 28.7 mi (46.2 km), you cross a cattle guard, curve to the north and start a steep climb up the side of a ridge and away from the lake. Lower Signal Butte is that bump across the chasm over to your left. An easterly sweeper cuts a short gorge through the ridge and takes you back down to the lake.

The road stops descending at 30.9 mi (49.7 km), hangs a left and heads through the middle of Bucks Bay's ratty collection of summer places and trailers. It then sweeps up and away from the lake in a repeat of the previous pattern. One curve later and you turn back to parallel the shoreline again, though this time it's closer. Another curve and the turnoff right for Stones Landing appears at 34.0 mi (55.4 km). Past Stones, it's a short, straight scream to Hwy 139, and the end of the DH, at 35.2 mi (56.6 km).

RIDER'S LOG: **DATE RIDDEN:** **YOUR RATING: /10**

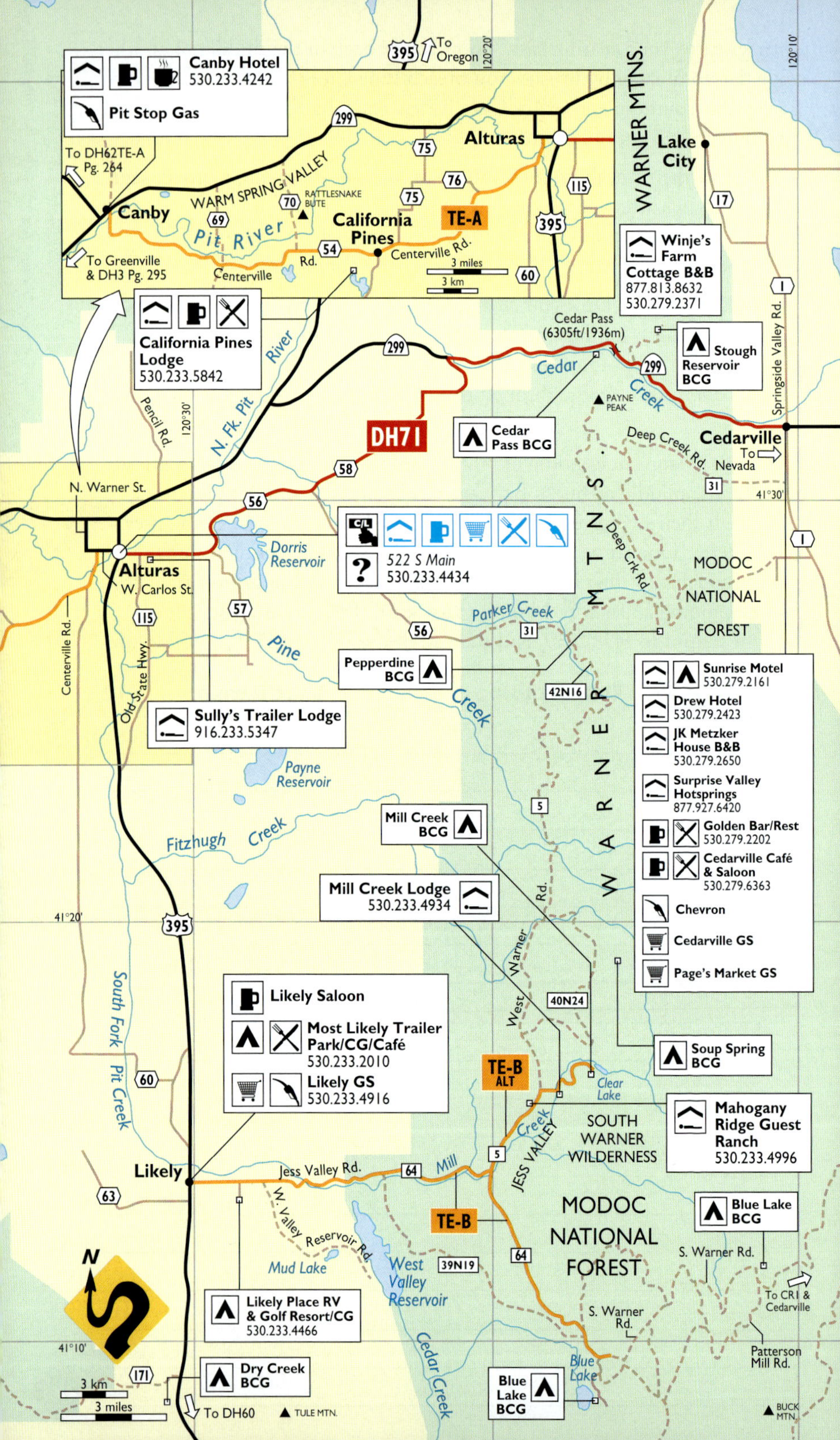

Canby Hotel
530.233.4242
Pit Stop Gas
To DH62TE-A
Pg. 264
To Greenville
& DH3 Pg. 295
Canby
WARM SPRING VALLEY
RATTLESNAKE BUTE
Pit River
Centerville Rd.
California Pines
Centerville Rd.
TE-A
Alturas
3 miles
3 km
To Oregon
California Pines Lodge
530.233.5842
WARNER MTNS.
Lake City
Winje's Farm Cottage B&B
877.813.8632
530.279.2371
Cedar Pass
(6305ft/1936m)
Stough Reservoir BCG
Cedar Creek
PAYNE PEAK
Cedar Pass BCG
DH71
N. Fk. Pit River
Pencil Rd.
Cedarville
To Nevada
Deep Creek Rd.
Springside Valley Rd.
N. Warner St.
Alturas
W. Carlos St.
Dorris Reservoir
522 S Main
530.233.4434
Deep Crk Rd.
MODOC NATIONAL FOREST
Parker Creek
Pine Creek
Pepperdine BCG
Centerville Rd.
Old State Hwy.
Sully's Trailer Lodge
916.233.5347
Sunrise Motel
530.279.2161
Drew Hotel
530.279.2423
JK Metzker House B&B
530.279.2650
Surprise Valley Hotsprings
877.927.6420
Golden Bar/Rest
530.279.2202
Cedarville Café & Saloon
530.279.6363
Chevron
Cedarville GS
Page's Market GS
WARNER MTNS.
Payne Reservoir
Fitzhugh Creek
Mill Creek BCG
Mill Creek Lodge
530.233.4934
West Warner Rd.
South Fork Pit Creek
Likely Saloon
Most Likely Trailer Park/CG/Café
530.233.2010
Likely GS
530.233.4916
TE-B ALT
Soup Spring BCG
Clear Lake
Mahogany Ridge Guest Ranch
530.233.4996
SOUTH WARNER WILDERNESS
JESS VALLEY
Likely
Jess Valley Rd.
Mill Creek
TE-B
W. Valley Reservoir Rd.
MODOC NATIONAL FOREST
Blue Lake BCG
S. Warner Rd.
To CR1 & Cedarville
Mud Lake
West Valley Reservoir
S. Warner Rd.
Likely Place RV & Golf Resort/CG
530.233.4466
Cedar Creek
Blue Lake
Patterson Mill Rd.
Dry Creek BCG
Blue Lake BCG
To DH60
TULE MTN.
BUCK MTN.
3 km
3 miles
N

DH71 Alturas – Cedarville

CR 56 / CR 58 / Hwy 299

Distance:	24.4 mi / 39.3 km	Traffic:	Light

DH49 DH59 DH38 DH60 DH71 DH62

At a Glance

Citius. Alturas. Fortius. The Olympic motto could well apply to this little *Via Destinatum* that takes you fast and high into the paralympic Warner Mountains and then finishes strong with a sweeping descent down to the quiet, quaint village of Cedarville in the Surprise Valley, close by the Nevada border. It may be a couple of miles short of a marathon but it will still appeal to some competitors. Modern bi-wheeled athletes will find it a little narrower, rougher and not too curvy when they cross-country the portions where CR 56 skirts the edge of the Modoc National Wildlife Refuge and CR 58 bisects a sloped foothill plain. But the Hwy 299 sprint track has moderate, sweeping *Twistius* and better *Pavementus* that allows you to ride faster, higher and stronger while striving for a personal best. Just remember: this is a state sanctioned venue, so you do have to watch for those pesky *Accelero Tributum Exactors* eager to javelin a ticket into you. If they do, take heart from your own motto: *Illegitimus non carborundum.*

TIRES	
Twistiness	12.2/ 30
Pavement	14.8/ 20
Engineering	6.8/ 10
Remoteness	6.1/ 10
Scenery	11.4/ 15
Character	5.9/ 15
Total	**57.2**

Access

From Alturas

On Hwy 395

At the southern outskirts of town, watch for CR 56 heading east. Take it and when you leave the development, you're *ilico via.*

From Cedarville

On Hwy 395

Head west. When you leave town, you're on the road.

On The Road

TOUR NOTE: Just west of Hwy 395 lies a cool green park on your left, shaded by tall oak trees. It's a great spot for a nap before the big event.

ROUTING OPTION: CR 115 (Old State Hwy) comes up on your right at 0.6 mi (1.0 km). If you're coming off the DH from Cedarville and heading south, it provides a bypass to the first few miles of Hwy 395 south of Alturas.

Trees border both sides of the road on your way out of Alturas. Once out of town, the road splits two scrubby fields – one bare, one brush covered – while it arrows toward the pocket Warner Mountains on the horizon. Irrigation quickly turns both fields green. The odd farm building, usually surrounded by trees, completes the scene.

CR 57 – catchy name – junctions right at 2.8 mi (4.5 km), smack in the middle of a shallow sweeper that turns the DH north and around the western shore of the Dorris Reservoir.

Tree-scattered, gently rolling terrain is what you'll find once you curve round the northern side of the res. You'll also discover that apart from a few gentle curves, most of the road's motion is up and down. Just after the blind-hill corner, the road goes right at 6.6 mi (10.6 km). But you **turn north** here, off CR 56 (which continues straight) and onto CR 58.

ROUTING OPTION: CR 56 eventually connects to the gravel FSR 5. This runs parallel to the western slope of the Warners and eventually junctions with the end of ***TE-B ALT****.*

Most of the middle-of-the-road paint disappears after the turn. So does most of the decent asphalt as the road here is narrower and a tad rougher. On the upside, at least there are a few more corners and even an occasional curve advisory sign as you plough deeper into the rolling ranch and farm countryside, continuing to angle toward the Warners. Traffic is almost nonexistent. The same can't be said for the yapping, bike-chasing dogs that protect collections of vehicles parked at the occasional roadside farm. At 13.6 mi (21.9 km), CR 58 junctions with Hwy 299. **Turn right.**

Craving curves, you roll on the throttle and head straight for the mountains. As the terrain becomes more rugged, paint reappears in the middle of the road and on the shoulders. Pavement and engineering quality upgrades just in time for the sweepers that appear after a mile or so. At 17.0 mi (27.4 km), the trees increase markedly in size, confirming that you've entered the Modoc National Forest. If you feel high, there's a reason – you're at nearly 6000 ft (1842 m).

There's an upslope on your left and a downslope to a creek bed on your right. With Payne Peak to the south and Cedar Mtn to the north, the Warners, which are actually a short spur of the Cascades, get up close and personal. Their knobbly, ancient looking rock is mostly either black basalt lava flow or light-colored rhyolitic volcanic ash. Okaaay. Apparently many people stop to collect samples of the unique obsidian deposits found here. You, presumably, are not one of them.

One assumes you're far more interested in sampling the sweepers that appear just before you enter the cut of Cedar Pass (6305 ft / 1936 m) at 18.7 mi (30.1 km) and start descending a 5-mi (8-km) grade down Cedar Creek's canyon. Around the next sweeper, Nevada's Hays Canyon Range appears in the distance beyond the last of the Warners. The latter decrease in height and grandeur and the forest thickens as you round the corner by the ski hill turnoff.

Middle Alkali Lake washes a light-colored swath over the road ahead, though it's actually down on the floor of Surprise Valley. By 23.0 mi (37.0 km), you're back down to an elevation of 5000 feet (1535 m) and the gorge rapidly widens out onto the valley's bottom. You're at the end of the DH when you hit the Cedarville speed limit at 24.4 mi (39.3 km). *Via brevisque dulcis est.*

TOUR NOTE: The Surprise Valley Hot Springs are 6.0 mi (9.7 km) straight ahead from the stop sign in Cedarville. They offer Fly 'n' Soak packages for pilots, if that sounds like you. Open 8am – 8pm for day trippers. Overnighters can escape to their own private patio hot tub and choose from a library of more than 500 complimentary movies. Maybe something in Latin with English subtitles.

Twisted Edges

TE-A Alturas – Canby (CR 54) (20.4 mi / 32.8 km) *Centerville Rd*
Alturas ad Canbius est straightius, especially through the open countryside west of A-town. Although there are a few gentle curves on the second half once the road hurdles along Portuguese Ridge closer to the Pit River. Because of the absence of pylons and STCs, it beats the purgatorium on Hwy 299 if you're going this way (or the reverse).

NAVIGATION: In Alturas, you get to this TE either via W Carlos St off Hwy 395 or via N Warner St off Hwy 299. Centerville Rd is not marked at the beginning. The sign to Cal Pines/California Pines Lodge is your clue that you are at the right junction.

TE-B Jess Valley Rd (FSR 64) (16.1 mi / 25.9 km)
Jonathan Swift couldn't write satire this good. Tiny-town Likely ended up with its moniker after the townsfolk kept getting their name choices rejected by the houyhnhnms asses at the post office. Exasperated, the tiny-townsfolk submitted the "most Likely name to be accepted." You'll have no trouble accepting this excellently paved road winding through the juniper and sagebrush-filled Mill Creek canyon and out into the verdant, picturesque little Jess Valley at the foot of the blefuscudian Warner range. At 9.4 mi (15.1 km), it Y(ahoo)s south from **TE-B ALT** with narrower, tar-strippier pavement that continues around the edge of the valley and twists up through forest before ending at the turnoff for the beautiful, natural and appropriately lilliputian Blue Lake.

ROUTING OPTION: Brobdingnagian maxburners won't be afraid to continue on the 18 mi (29 km) or so of good gravel across the South Warner Wilderness to the Surprise Valley Rd so they can do the DH east to west.

TE-B ALT West Warner Rd (FSR 5) (4.7 mi / 7.6 km)
This arm meanders north around the Jess Valley and up into the forest of the Warner foothills before terminating at the Clear Lake CG. Clear Lake is also natural, although not as big or as cute as Blue Lake.

ROUTING OPTION: Another maxburning option is to continue on the gravel part of West Warner (FSR 5). You can stay on this side of the Warners and do the approximately 20 mi (32 km) to where the DH turns off CR 56. Or you can take FSR 31 across the Warners to just south of Cedarville.

RIDER'S LOG: **DATE RIDDEN:** **YOUR RATING: /10**

Map Tip: *To see the next good motorcycle road, look for the white navigation arrows at the edge of the Local maps.*

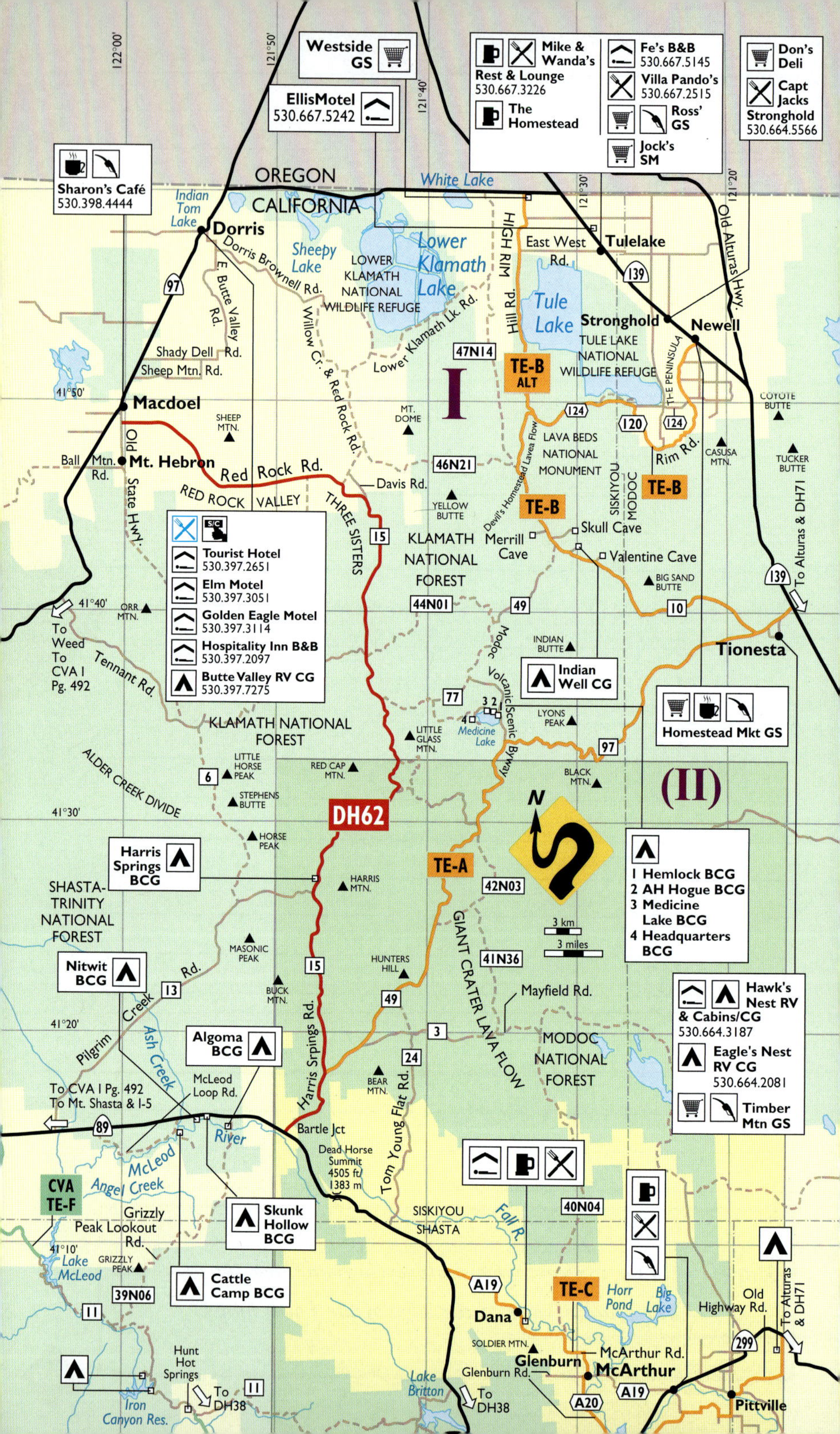
Westside GS
EllisMotel 530.667.5242
Mike & Wanda's Rest & Lounge 530.667.3226
The Homestead
Fe's B&B 530.667.5145
Villa Pando's 530.667.2515
Ross' GS
Jock's SM
Don's Deli
Capt Jacks Stronghold 530.664.5566
Sharon's Café 530.398.4444
OREGON
CALIFORNIA
White Lake
Indian Tom Lake
Dorris
Sheepy Lake
Lower Klamath Lake
LOWER KLAMATH NATIONAL WILDLIFE REFUGE
Dorris Brownell Rd.
E. Butte Valley Rd.
Willow Cr. & Red Rock Rd.
Lower Klamath Lk. Rd.
HIGH RIM
Hill Rd.
East West Rd.
Tulelake
Tule Lake
Stronghold
Newell
TULE LAKE NATIONAL WILDLIFE REFUGE
TI-E PENINSULA
Old Alturas Hwy.
Shady Dell Rd.
Sheep Mtn. Rd.
47N14
TE-B ALT
I
Macdoel
SHEEP MTN.
MT. DOME
COYOTE BUTTE
Ball Mtn. Rd.
Mt. Hebron
Old State Hwy.
Red Rock Rd.
RED ROCK VALLEY
THREE SISTERS
Davis Rd.
46N21
LAVA BEDS NATIONAL MONUMENT
Devil's Homestead Lava Flow
SISKIYOU
MODOC
Rim Rd.
CASUSA MTN.
TUCKER BUTTE
TE-B
YELLOW BUTTE
Skull Cave
Merrill Cave
Valentine Cave
KLAMATH NATIONAL FOREST
BIG SAND BUTTE
To Alturas & DH71
Tourist Hotel 530.397.2651
Elm Motel 530.397.3051
Golden Eagle Motel 530.397.3114
Hospitality Inn B&B 530.397.2097
Butte Valley RV CG 530.397.7275
ORR MTN.
To Weed
To CVA I Pg. 492
Tennant Rd.
44N01
Modoc Volcanic Scenic Byway
INDIAN BUTTE
Indian Well CG
Tionesta
Homestead Mkt GS
KLAMATH NATIONAL FOREST
LITTLE HORSE PEAK
LITTLE GLASS MTN.
Medicine Lake
LYONS PEAK
BLACK MTN.
RED CAP MTN.
ALDER CREEK DIVIDE
STEPHENS BUTTE
DH62
(II)
HORSE PEAK
Harris Springs BCG
HARRIS MTN.
TE-A
42N03
1 Hemlock BCG
2 AH Hogue BCG
3 Medicine Lake BCG
4 Headquarters BCG
SHASTA-TRINITY NATIONAL FOREST
MASONIC PEAK
GIANT CRATER LAVA FLOW
3 km
3 miles
41N36
Nitwit BCG
Creek Rd.
Pilgrim
HUNTERS HILL
BUCK MTN.
Mayfield Rd.
Hawk's Nest RV & Cabins/CG 530.664.3187
Eagle's Nest RV CG 530.664.2081
Timber Mtn GS
Algoma BCG
Ash Creek
Harris Srpings Rd.
MODOC NATIONAL FOREST
BEAR MTN.
Tom Young Flat Rd.
To CVA I Pg. 492
To Mt. Shasta & I-5
McLeod Loop Rd.
River
Bartle Jct
Dead Horse Summit 4505 ft/1383 m
McLeod
Angel Creek
CVA TE-F
Grizzly Peak Lookout Rd.
Skunk Hollow BCG
SISKIYOU
SHASTA
Fall R.
40N04
Lake McLeod
GRIZZLY PEAK
39N06
Cattle Camp BCG
TE-C
Horr Pond
Big Lake
Old Highway Rd.
To Alturas & DH71
Dana
SOLDIER MTN.
Glenburn
McArthur Rd.
McArthur
Glenburn Rd.
Hunt Hot Springs
To DH38
Lake Britton
To DH38
Iron Canyon Res.
Pittville
122°00'
121°50'
121°40'
121°30'
121°20'
41°50'
41°40'
41°30'
41°20'
41°10'
97
139
124
120
15
49
10
77
6
13
3
24
89
A19
A20
299
11

DH62 Bartle Jct – Macdoel

Harris Springs Rd / Davis Rd / Red Rock Rd (FSR 15)

Distance:	59.1 mi / 95.1 km	Traffic:	Very Light

At a Glance

Perennially snowcapped Mt Shasta dominates the landscape hereabouts. Unfortunately, the main effect of the volcano's effluvial efforts has been to smother this road's surrounding terrain in a thick, pacifying layer of lava. But it has extruded some pretty fiery TIRES numbers as well. While not exactly the twistiest DH in the state, the curves that do exist are more than adequately served by the quality of the Pavement and Engineering. Remoteness is excellent too; the only man-made things you're likely to see are hell-bent-for-your-leather logging trucks. And although the Scenery consists largely of evergreen trees of various species and sizes, there are some views of the breathtaking volcano toward the ride's north end in the wide-open, curveless Red Rock Valley. There's no question that until Shasta rumbles back into action and changes the landscape, this hasta be the best riding in the area.

TIRES	
Twistiness	14.0/ 30
Pavement	13.8/ 20
Engineering	7.0/ 10
Remoteness	8.0/ 10
Scenery	10.0/ 15
Character	8.6/ 15
Total	**61.4**

Access

From Bartle Jct

On Hwy 89

The long-forgotten train stop of Bartle is approximately 18 mi (29 km) east of McCloud. Turn north here and you're on the road.

From Macdoel

On Hwy 97

Turn south on Old State Hwy. Red Rock Rd junctions to the east 1.0 mi (1.6 km) later. Take it and you're on the road.

On The Road

Crossing the train tracks, you leave the first and last sign of Bartle – one house – behind. The road runs straight through a forest of indeterminate age. By 2.0 mi (3.2 km), you're into your first few curves and climbing slightly. Soon you get a brief glimpse of magnificent Shasta – a massive, glowing white cone dominating the horizon to the west – at least until the trees screen it from view. You stop climbing and FSR 49 (**TE-A**) junctions to the right at 4.7 mi (7.6 km).

DH49 DH59 DH38 DH60 DH71 DH62

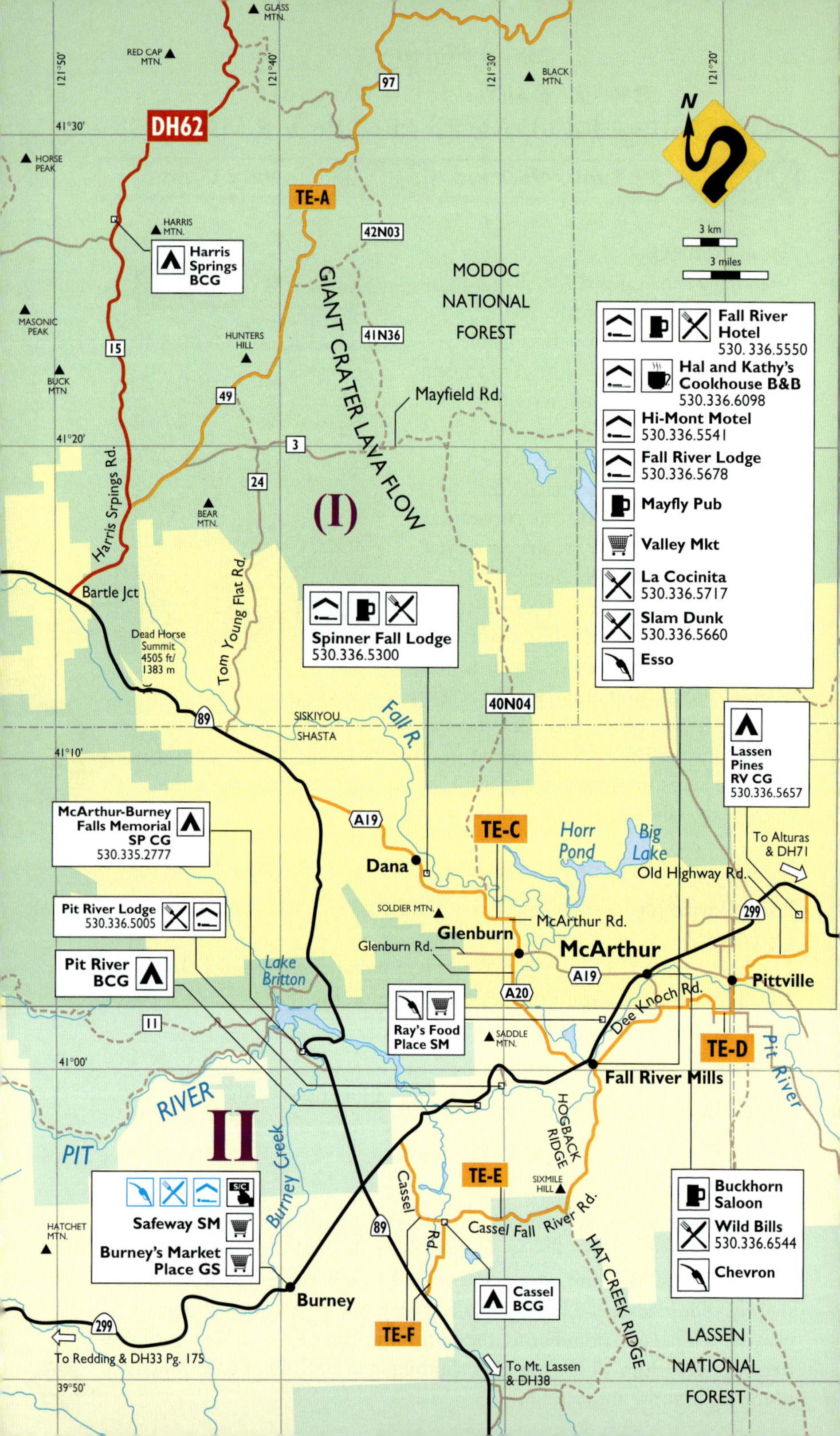

DH62
Harris Springs BCG
Harris Srpings Rd.
Bartle Jct
Dead Horse Summit 4505 ft/ 1383 m
Tom Young Flat Rd.
GIANT CRATER LAVA FLOW
MODOC NATIONAL FOREST
Mayfield Rd.
(I)
TE-A
Fall River Hotel 530.336.5550
Hal and Kathy's Cookhouse B&B 530.336.6098
Hi-Mont Motel 530.336.5541
Fall River Lodge 530.336.5678
Mayfly Pub
Valley Mkt
La Cocinita 530.336.5717
Slam Dunk 530.336.5660
Esso
Spinner Fall Lodge 530.336.5300
Lassen Pines RV CG 530.336.5657
To Alturas & DH71
3 km
3 miles
SISKIYOU
SHASTA
Fall R.
McArthur-Burney Falls Memorial SP CG 530.335.2777
Pit River Lodge 530.336.5005
Pit River BCG
TE-C
Horr Pond
Big Lake
Old Highway Rd.
Dana
Glenburn
McArthur
McArthur Rd.
Glenburn Rd.
Pittville
Dee Knoch Rd.
Lake Britton
Ray's Food Place SM
TE-D
Fall River Mills
Pit River
HOGBACK RIDGE
RIVER
PIT
II
Burney Creek
Safeway SM
Burney's Market Place GS
TE-E
Cassel Rd.
Cassel Fall River Rd.
HAT CREEK RIDGE
Buckhorn Saloon
Wild Bills 530.336.6544
Chevron
Cassel BCG
Burney
TE-F
To Redding & DH33 Pg. 175
To Mt. Lassen & DH38
LASSEN NATIONAL FOREST

Past the turnoff, the pavement quality increases and a few more corners appear, disappearing just as quickly when the terrain turns as flat as a frying pan. At 8.3 mi (13.4 km), there's a slight upshift in the land and, with it, another flurry of curves. There's an upshift in the forest as well as the trees get larger and somewhat more impressive.

Alas, the curves don't last, leaving you little to do but blow out some carbon until 12.0 mi (19.3 km) when you're awakened by some sweepers. They tighten up at 15.5 mi (24.9 km) and at the same time the good pavement gets even better. A combination squiggly/35-mph (55-kmh) advisory sign appears. Some of the corners even ess together, although, at the prescribed velocity, they're still pretty mellow.

A sudden rough patch of pavement at 18.4 mi (29.6 km) rattles your back teeth. It takes you by surprise since there are no visual clues to explain why it should feel that bumpy. You shrug as the curving asphalt immediately smoothes out again and starts another slight climb.

Jumbled, black mounds of lava show up among the scattered trees at 23.9 mi (38.5 km). It's the first time since that one view of Shasta that the scenery is anything other than forest. Bald, round Red Cap Mtn appears over the road as you round one corner at 25.3 mi (40.7 km). Too bad about the return of the rough pavement and the skittery patches of sand.

You continue to climb and the trees become stunted. Black-slag Little Glass Mtn on the right glints in the sunshine like it was made of… well, broken glass. It's obsidian actually. Which, according to Webster, is pretty much the same thing.

But curves have many definitions and the ones you're now on are the tightest and most concentrated of the DH. By 28.5 mi (45.9 km), the road is in a descent and the trees get taller again. The asphalt, however, gets rougher. You may even spot the odd pothole among the cracks. Or (ouch) you may not.

All the shaking got your bladder calling? Rumor has it some local wusses are petitioning to have the restrooms at the 4 Corners Winter Recreation Area at 33.0 mi (53.1 km) open in the summer as well as the winter. They obviously can't get used to the old iron butt relief tube.

ROUTING OPTION: In a hurry to enjoy the delights of Weed? You could turn left here on Tennant Lava Beds Rd (FSR 77) for a shortcut to Hwy 97. It bypasses the straightest portion of the DH, though about 10 mi (16 km) of it is gravel.

The pavement smoothes out as you continue on the DH, weaving in a short series of shallow curves through more forest. The "Range Cattle" sign might suppress the temptation to increase your speed when the curves thin out and the road straightens. The arboreal cover thins as well, replaced by scrub and sage. To the left, Sharp Mtn pokes up behind what trees are left.

When a 35-mph (55-kmh) zone shows up at 38.0 mi (60 km), the road is plumb straight. A completely unkinked road, wide-open terrain and a speed zone–if this is someone's lame attempt at humor, no one's laughing.

The round, volcanic-looking mound dead ahead is Mt Dome. It's appropriately named, as are the Three Sisters, whose protruberances are visible to the south through a brief screen of trees when a big sweeper reorients the road from north to west at 40.9 mi (65.8 km). Shortly, another sweeper turns your attention away from them and back to the north. This north/west pattern repeats itself until 42.4 mi (68.2 km), where the DH leaves Davis Rd (which slants off to the right) and continues its sojourn on Red Rock Rd. You exit the Klamath National Forest and soon the trees retreat once more, leaving a southern vista toward Shasta and a bunch of smaller acolytes.

The curves dissipate completely at 42.5 mi (68.4 km). Naturally, this is when the pavement gets better. Manicured green fields backed by low forest-covered mountains lying on the western side of Hwy 97 replace the scrubby open areas. By 50.0 mi (80.0 km), you've definitely seen the last of any cornering possibilities. So it's really up to you how quickly you finish off this last, straight stretch in the Red Rock Valley. The DH ends when Red Rock Rd does, at the junction with Old State Highway on the outskirts of Macdoel at 59.1 mi (95.1 km).

Twisted Edges

TE-A Tionesta – Bartle Jct (48.8 mi / 78.5 km) *FSR 97 - FSR 49*
This epic, very remote TE is boringly straight for the first 10 mi (16 km) out of Tionesta (though the rough railway crossing near its beginning might wake you up). And it's pretty dull for most of the 20 mi (32 km) out of Bartle too. But once you get into the volcanic high country, there are some good curves and pavement on 97. You pay for it though, on straight, sometimes one-lane 49 where at times you'll feel like you're hardtailing it directly on the Giant Crater Lava Flow itself.

TE-B Tionesta – Newall (29.2 mi / 47.0 km) *FSR 10 - CR 124 - CR 120*
Prefer lava beds and wildlife to Lavalife and wild beds? Then, you'll want to check out this bypass to Hwy 139. Very rough at the beginning, it runs through the Lava Beds National Monument, skirts the southern edge of the Tule Lake National Wildlife Refuge and edges along the base of that piece of geology named The Peninsula. Technically speaking, you are supposed to pay to go through the LBNM but when we said we were just riding straight through, they just waved us on. Maybe they just liked our profile.

TE-B ALT Hill Rd (12.9 mi / 20.8 km)
After your rough treatment at the hands of **TE-A** and **TE-B**, it's a pleasant surprise how smooth the pavement is on this one, especially once you're along the base of High Rim. It's pretty straight until you reach Tule Lake, where the lake and the rim pinch out a few, lazy sweepers. North of East-West Rd, the asphalt is not as good.

TOUR NOTE: Hwy 161 at the TE's north end serves as the border between California and Oregon.

TE-C McArthur Rd (A 19) - Glenburn Rd (A 20) (17.7 mi / 28.5 km)
From its north end at Hwy 89, this TE descends from the forest (and traffic) down into the quiet pastureland of the Fall River valley. It's mostly straight through the peaceful farmland, especially before and after Glenburn. Toward its south end, where the TE gets squeezed between the base of Saddle Mtn and Fall River, you do get a few curves, though they come with a little Fall River Mills development. If you want something less tame, you'll have to check out the wild rice this area is famous for. Or **TE-E**.

TE-D Old Hwy Rd (CR 407) - Pittville Rd - Dee Knoch Rd (14.4 mi / 23.2 km)
The old main road is now just another quiet road through valley bottom farmland. The only curves are farmland 90s, outside of a few real ones at the Fall River Mills end. But it does provide a welcome bypass to Hwy 299 getting to or from FRM. Tacking on remoter, twistier **TE-E** to this one will allow you to avoid twice as much of the main highway.

TE-E Cassel-Fall River Rd (11.7 mi / 18.8)
Consistent, mellow curves and remoteness are the main attractions of this part of the Hwy 299 bypass. It runs from downtown Fall River Mills mostly through forest and then sneaks between Highback Ridge and Hat Creek Ridge. Next it buzzes around Sawmill Hill before finally heading west to junction with mid-**TE-F** at no-town Cassel, just off Hwy 89. The pavement's not fabulous, but you'll get by.

TE-F Cassel Rd (7.1 mi / 11.4 km)
This one's back in the farmland. Great pavement here but you've got more chance of catching the famous local trout than any curves. Okay, there are a *few* small ones to land north of Cassel but don't expect 'em to put up much of a fight.

RIDER'S LOG: **DATE RIDDEN:** **YOUR RATING: /10**

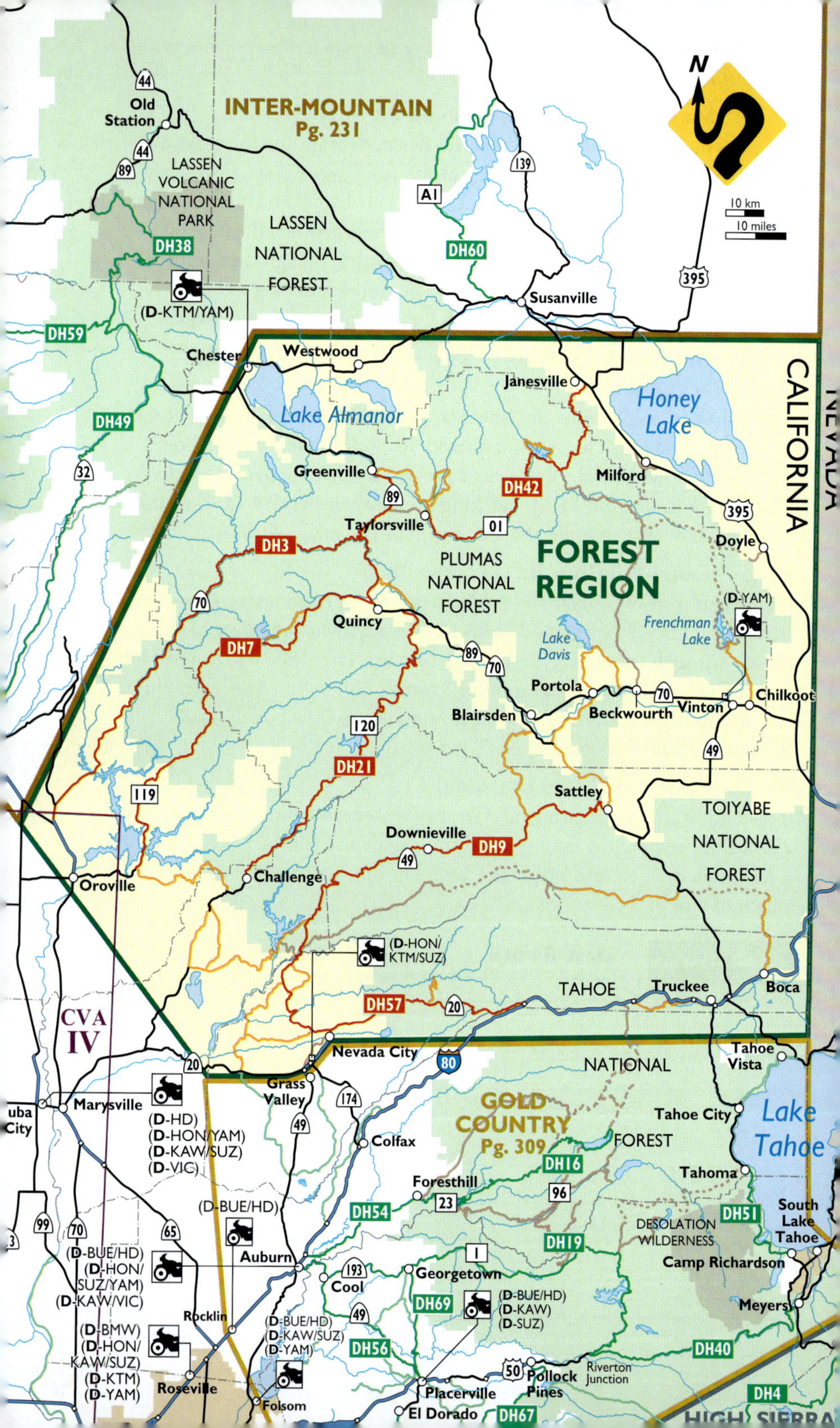

INTER-MOUNTAIN
Pg. 231
N
10 km
10 miles
Old Station
LASSEN VOLCANIC NATIONAL PARK
LASSEN NATIONAL FOREST
DH38
DH59
DH49
DH60
A1
(D-KTM/YAM)
Susanville
Chester
Westwood
Janesville
Lake Almanor
Honey Lake
CALIFORNIA
NEVADA
Greenville
Milford
DH42
Taylorsville
01
Doyle
DH3
PLUMAS NATIONAL FOREST
FOREST REGION
(D-YAM)
Frenchman Lake
Lake Davis
Quincy
DH7
Portola
Beckwourth
Vinton
Chilkoot
Blairsden
120
DH21
119
Sattley
TOIYABE NATIONAL FOREST
Downieville
DH9
Oroville
Challenge
(D-HON/KTM/SUZ)
TAHOE
Truckee
Boca
DH57
CVA IV
Nevada City
NATIONAL
Tahoe Vista
Grass Valley
Marysville
uba City
(D-HD)
(D-HON/YAM)
(D-KAW/SUZ)
(D-VIC)
GOLD COUNTRY
Pg. 309
Tahoe City
Lake Tahoe
Colfax
FOREST
DH16
Tahoma
Foresthill
DH54
DH51
South Lake Tahoe
(D-BUE/HD)
DESOLATION WILDERNESS
DH19
(D-BUE/HD)
(D-HON/SUZ/YAM)
(D-KAW/VIC)
Auburn
Camp Richardson
Georgetown
Cool
(D-BUE/HD)
(D-KAW)
(D-SUZ)
DH69
Meyers
Rocklin
(D-BMW)
(D-HON/KAW/SUZ)
(D-KTM)
(D-YAM)
(D-BUE/HD)
(D-KAW/SUZ)
(D-YAM)
DH56
DH40
Riverton Junction
Pollock Pines
Roseville
Folsom
Placerville
El Dorado
DH67
DH4
HIGH SIERRA

Forest Region

RANK DH#/74	TIRES Total/100	DESTINATION HIGHWAY	PAGE
DH9	81.0	Nevada City – Sattley 72.6 mi / 116.8 km	269
DH57	62.5	Nevada City – Hwy 20/I-80 Jct 26.6 mi / 42.8 km	279
DH21	76.5	Challenge – East Quincy (Quincy) 51.8 mi / 83.4 km	283
DH7	81.9	Quincy – Oroville 58.5 mi / 94.1 km	289
DH3	83.4	Oroville – Greenville/Quincy 71.2 mi / 114.6 km 67.6 mi / 108.8 km	295
DH42	69.5	Taylorsville – Janesville (Susanville) 41.0 mi / 66.0 km	303

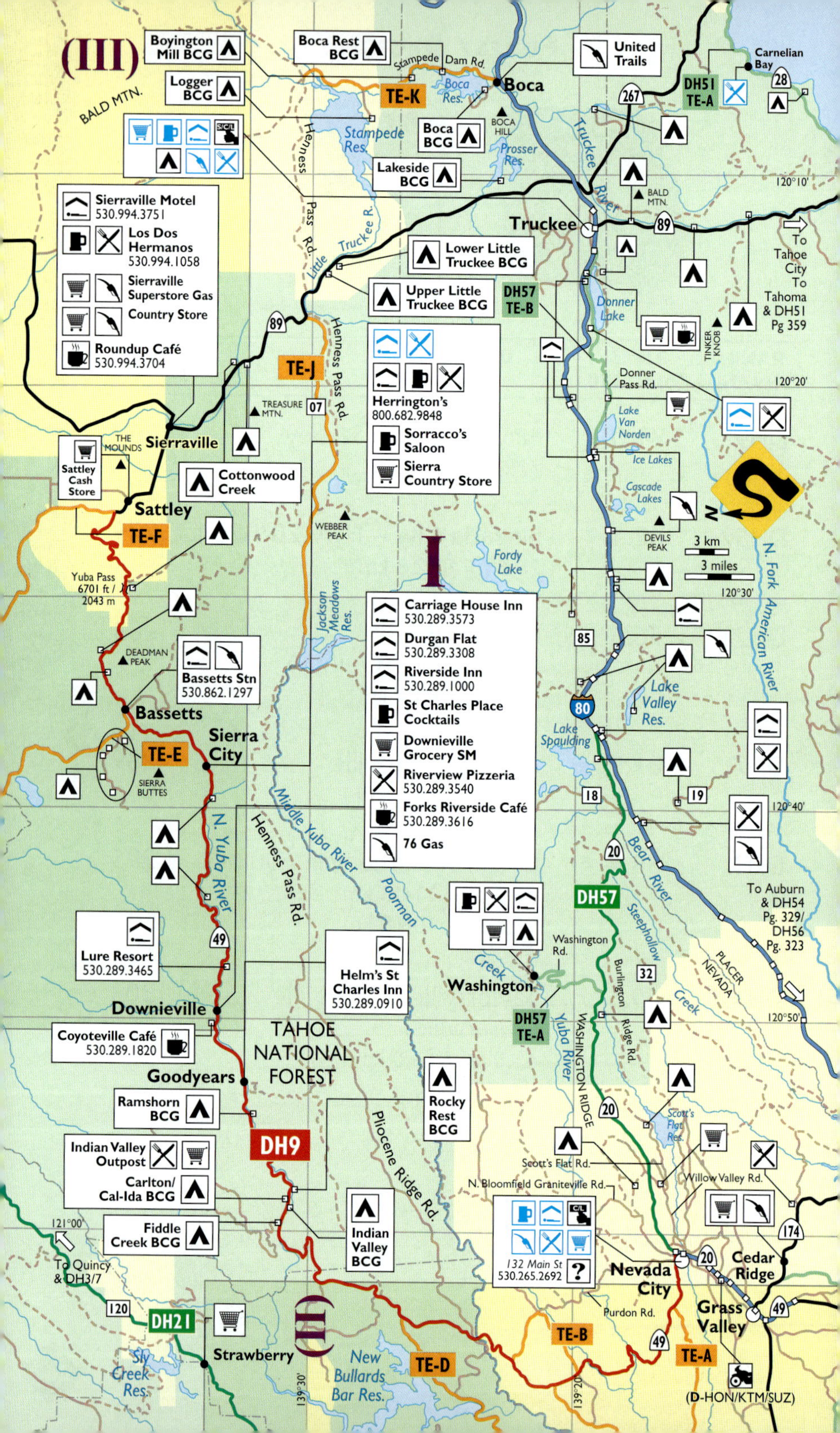
(III)
Boyington Mill BCG
Logger BCG
Boca Rest BCG
Stampede Dam Rd.
TE-K
Boca
Boca Res.
United Trails
Carnelian Bay
28
DH51 TE-A
267
BALD MTN.
Stampede Res.
Boca BCG
BOCA HILL
Prosser Res.
Lakeside BCG
Truckee River
Henness Pass Rd.
BALD MTN.
120°10'
Sierraville Motel
530.994.3751
Los Dos Hermanos
530.994.1058
Sierraville Superstore Gas
Country Store
Roundup Café
530.994.3704
Little Truckee R.
Lower Little Truckee BCG
Truckee
89
To Tahoe City
To Tahoma & DH51 Pg 359
Upper Little Truckee BCG
DH57 TE-B
Donner Lake
TINKER KNOB
89
Henness Pass Rd.
TE-J
Herrington's
800.682.9848
Sorracco's Saloon
Sierra Country Store
Donner Pass Rd.
120°20'
TREASURE MTN.
07
Lake Van Norden
THE MOUNDS
Sierraville
Satley Cash Store
Cottonwood Creek
Ice Lakes
Cascade Lakes
Sattley
TE-F
WEBBER PEAK
DEVILS PEAK
3 km
3 miles
N
Fordy Lake
I
Yuba Pass
6701 ft / 2043 m
120°30'
N. Fork American River
Carriage House Inn
530.289.3573
Durgan Flat
530.289.3308
Riverside Inn
530.289.1000
St Charles Place Cocktails
Downieville Grocery SM
Riverview Pizzeria
530.289.3540
Forks Riverside Café
530.289.3616
76 Gas
Jackson Meadows Res.
DEADMAN PEAK
Bassetts Stn
530.862.1297
85
Bassetts
80
Lake Valley Res.
Lake Spaulding
Sierra City
TE-E
SIERRA BUTTES
18
19
120°40'
Middle Yuba River
Henness Pass Rd.
N. Yuba River
20
Bear River
DH57
Poorman
To Auburn & DH54 Pg. 329/ DH56 Pg. 323
Steephollow
Washington Rd.
PLACER
NEVADA
Lure Resort
530.289.3465
49
Helm's St Charles Inn
530.289.0910
Creek
Washington
32
Burlington Ridge Rd.
Creek
Downieville
DH57 TE-A
Yuba River
WASHINGTON RIDGE
120°50'
Coyoteville Café
530.289.1820
TAHOE NATIONAL FOREST
Goodyears
Ramshorn BCG
Rocky Rest BCG
Pliocene Ridge Rd.
20
Scott's Flat Res.
DH9
Indian Valley Outpost
Carlton/ Cal-Ida BCG
Scott's Flat Rd.
N. Bloomfield Graniteville Rd.
Willow Valley Rd.
Indian Valley BCG
Fiddle Creek BCG
121°00'
To Quincy & DH3/7
132 Main St
530.265.2692
174
20
Cedar Ridge
Nevada City
Grass Valley
Purdon Rd.
49
120
DH21
Strawberry
II
Sly Creek Res.
New Bullards Bar Res.
TE-D
TE-B
49
TE-A
(D-HON/KTM/SUZ)
139°30'
139°20'

DH9 Nevada City – Sattley

Highway 49

Distance:	72.6 mi / 116.8 km	Traffic:	Moderate

At a Glance

Master, why do we ride this DH? Ah, close your eyes and look inside your mind, Grasshopper. Can you not sense the movement of wheels on smooth, contoured pavement as you leave the mundane, Sacramento-induced bustle of Nevada City and wind sharply down to and back up from the South Yuba River? With training and self-discipline – or by taking one of the bypass TEs – you can overcome your impatience with the straightaway through the long suburb of North San Juan. Whatever path you take, your mind will quiet once you enter the stillness of the Tahoe National Forest. Mile after mile of sublime rivers, trees, mountains and corners prepare you for the road's "Dead Man's Curves" – a steep, tightly essing culmination that drops steeply off the Yuba Pass and down to a simple farming community in the Sierra Valley. Finished meditating? Snatch this chain lube from my hand; it will be time for you to go.

TIRES	
Twistiness	30/30
Pavement	15.6/20
Engineering	5.8/10
Remoteness	6.2/10
Scenery	9.0/15
Character	14.4/15
Total	**81.0**

Access

From Nevada City

On Hwy 49

The DH begins at the Broad Street turnoff, just before the 55-mph sign.

From Sattley

Via Hwy 89

Head north and go left on Hwy 49 just north of Sattley. You're on the road.

On The Road

The terrific pavement is the first thing you notice as you strike out from Nevada City. The fantastic curves are the second. At 2.1 mi (3.4 km), just beyond Newtown Rd (**TE-A**), the descending road esses through the forest, slightly at first and then with greater intensity. There are some straight sections but they soon dwindle, leaving behind corners, trees, and some southward views over Kentucky Ridge. And a few too many driveways to the houses that are hidden in the woods.

Some tight sweepers at 4.6 mi (7.4 km) introduce a new sharpness to the waves of corners. The landscape comes into sharp focus as well. The road-

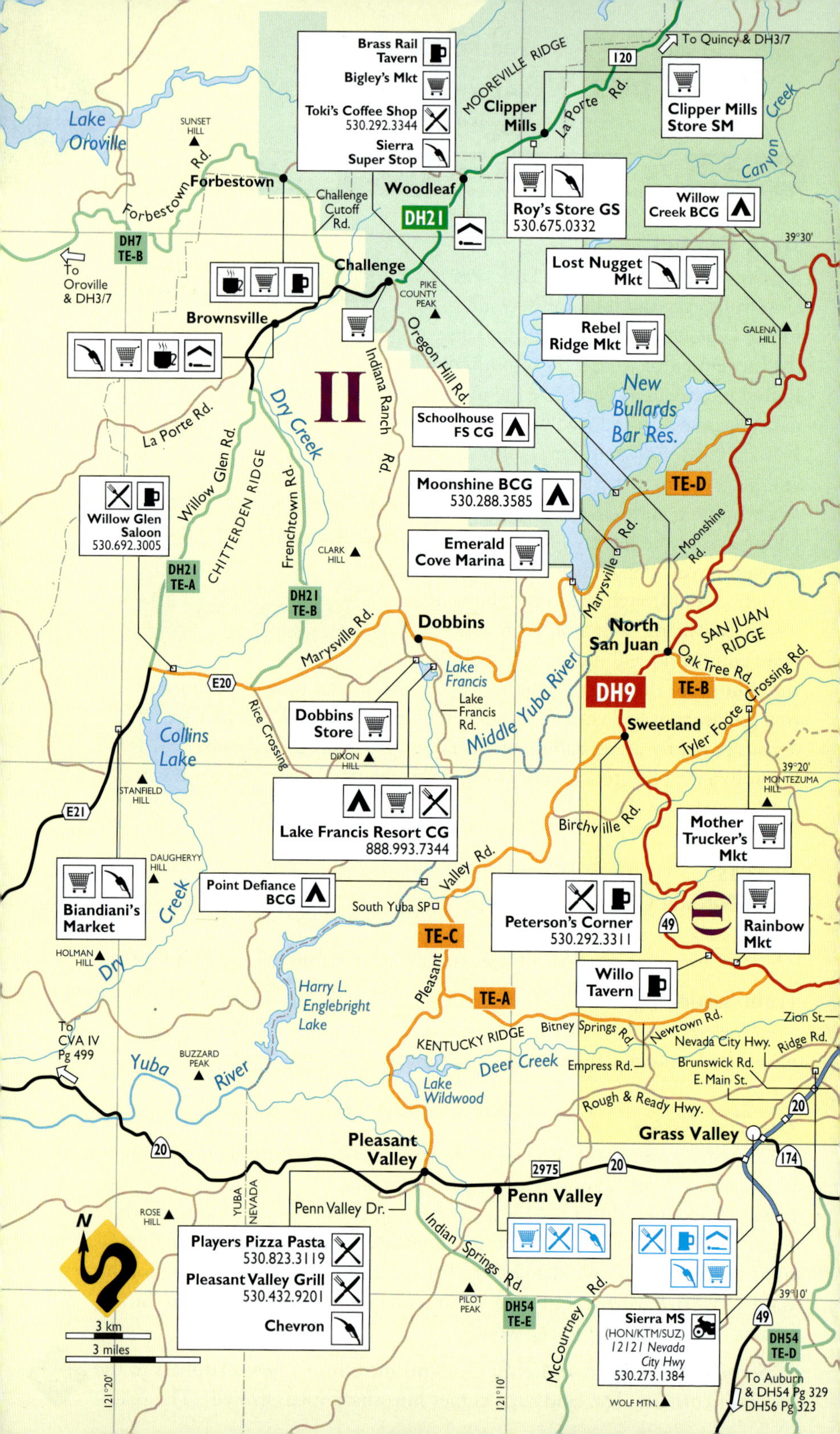

Brass Rail Tavern
Bigley's Mkt
Toki's Coffee Shop 530.292.3344
Sierra Super Stop
MOOREVILLE RIDGE
Clipper Mills
La Porte Rd.
120
To Quincy & DH3/7
Clipper Mills Store SM
Creek
Canyon
Lake Oroville
SUNSET HILL
Forbestown Rd.
Forbestown
Challenge Cutoff Rd.
Woodleaf
DH21
Roy's Store GS 530.675.0332
Willow Creek BCG
39°30'
Lost Nugget Mkt
DH7 TE-B
To Oroville & DH3/7
Challenge
PIKE COUNTY PEAK
Brownsville
Rebel Ridge Mkt
GALENA HILL
Oregon Hill Rd.
Indiana Ranch Rd.
II
Dry Creek
New Bullards Bar Res.
La Porte Rd.
Schoolhouse FS CG
Willow Glen Rd.
CHITTERDEN RIDGE
Frenchtown Rd.
Moonshine BCG 530.288.3585
TE-D
Willow Glen Saloon 530.692.3005
Emerald Cove Marina
Moonshine Rd.
Marysville Rd.
CLARK HILL
DH21 TE-A
DH21 TE-B
Dobbins
Marysville Rd.
North San Juan
SAN JUAN RIDGE
Oak Tree Rd.
Lake Francis
Lake Francis Rd.
E20
Middle Yuba River
DH9
TE-B
Tyler Foote Crossing Rd.
Rice Crossing
Dobbins Store
Sweetland
Collins Lake
DIXON HILL
39°20'
MONTEZUMA HILL
STANFIELD HILL
Lake Francis Resort CG 888.993.7344
E21
Birchville Rd.
Mother Trucker's Mkt
DAUGHERYY HILL
Valley Rd.
Biandiani's Market
Point Defiance BCG
South Yuba SP
Peterson's Corner 530.292.3311
Rainbow Mkt
Creek
49
HOLMAN HILL
Dry
TE-C
Pleasant
Willo Tavern
Harry L. Englebright Lake
TE-A
To CVA IV Pg 499
Yuba
BUZZARD PEAK
River
KENTUCKY RIDGE
Bitney Springs Rd.
Newtown Rd.
Zion St.
Nevada City Hwy.
Ridge Rd.
Deer Creek
Lake Wildwood
Empress Rd.
Brunswick Rd.
E. Main St.
Rough & Ready Hwy.
20
Grass Valley
Pleasant Valley
2975
174
YUBA NEVADA
Penn Valley
Penn Valley Dr.
ROSE HILL
N
Players Pizza Pasta 530.823.3119
Pleasant Valley Grill 530.432.9201
Chevron
Indian Springs Rd.
PILOT PEAK
DH54 TE-E
McCourtney Rd.
Sierra MS (HON/KTM/SUZ) 12121 Nevada City Hwy 530.273.1384
39°10'
49
DH54 TE-D
3 km
3 miles
121°20'
121°10'
WOLF MTN.
To Auburn & DH54 Pg 329 DH56 Pg 323

side foliage is lush. The slopes just beyond, rising above the South Yuba, are chock-a-block with oaks. The driveways disappear as you continue your winding descent to the river, crossing it via a big, sweeping bridge at 6.0 mi (9.7 km). And then it's back up the other side on a long chain of more tightly linked curves.

At 7.3 mi (11.8 km), the road straightens and a brief passing lane shoots you further up the slope through a sandstone cut and onto a flat, up-and-down section characterized by long straights, the return of driveways, and long, 50-mph (80-kmh) curves. Two TEs intersect the DH in this straightaway. Tyler Foote Crossing Rd (**TE-B**), right at 9.8 mi (15.8 km) and Pleasant Valley Rd (**TE-C**), which goes south from Peterson's Corner at 10.9 mi (17.5 km).

Overall, this is a pretty remote DH. But riding this section, you don't feel it. Houses and driveways multiply as you get nearer North San Juan, which you reach at 13.1 mi (21.1 km). The DH's sprawliest settlement is also the northern end of **TE-B**, the little bypass that comes in from the east as Oak Tree Rd.

Fortunately, the development ends with the town. At 13.8 mi (22.2 km), you enter the Tahoe National Forest and drop sharply downhill, sweeping past the hunks of sharp shale and mossy granite that line the road along with thick trees. A feeling of remoteness settles once you cross the Middle Yuba River and enter Yuba County at 16.1 mi (25.9 km). You ride the steady, climbing curves above the unseen watercourse, skirting a rock-face on your left. Doesn't matter how much of a maxburner you are, forget about the turnoff at 17.1 mi (27.5 km) marked "To Pike and Allegheny." The road ahead is too good to miss even for you.

A short, dotted-lined straight gets you by any traffic you've caught up to and at 18.6 mi (29.9 km), you're curving again on those, easy, free-flowing S-curves that are the hallmark of this road. There are more of them to be found on the excellent northern section of E 20, (**TE-D**), the county road that intersects with the DH from the west at 19.7 mi (31.7 km).

TOUR NOTE: If you're looking for a place to stop for refreshment, you don't have to wait till Downieville. The terrific section of ***TE-D Marysville Rd*** (E 20) *down to Dobbins is a rewarding detour.*

You spend most of this DH in the trees. But there are occasional views when the DH gets high on a ridge. At 20.2 mi (32.5 km), for example, a panorama of the northern end of heavily forested San Juan Ridge unfolds over the river's valley. But the experience is brief. Within moments, you're back in heavy woods, peering around the base of volcanic rock that juts sharply off the roadside.

The easy, spaced, predictable curves continue, letting you husband your strength for the tighter, more intense stuff to come. At 25.5 mi (41.0 km), you cross from Yuba to Sierra County and a road sign pronounces this a "scenic route." Sure, trees are scenic, to a point. But you'd think it would require something more.

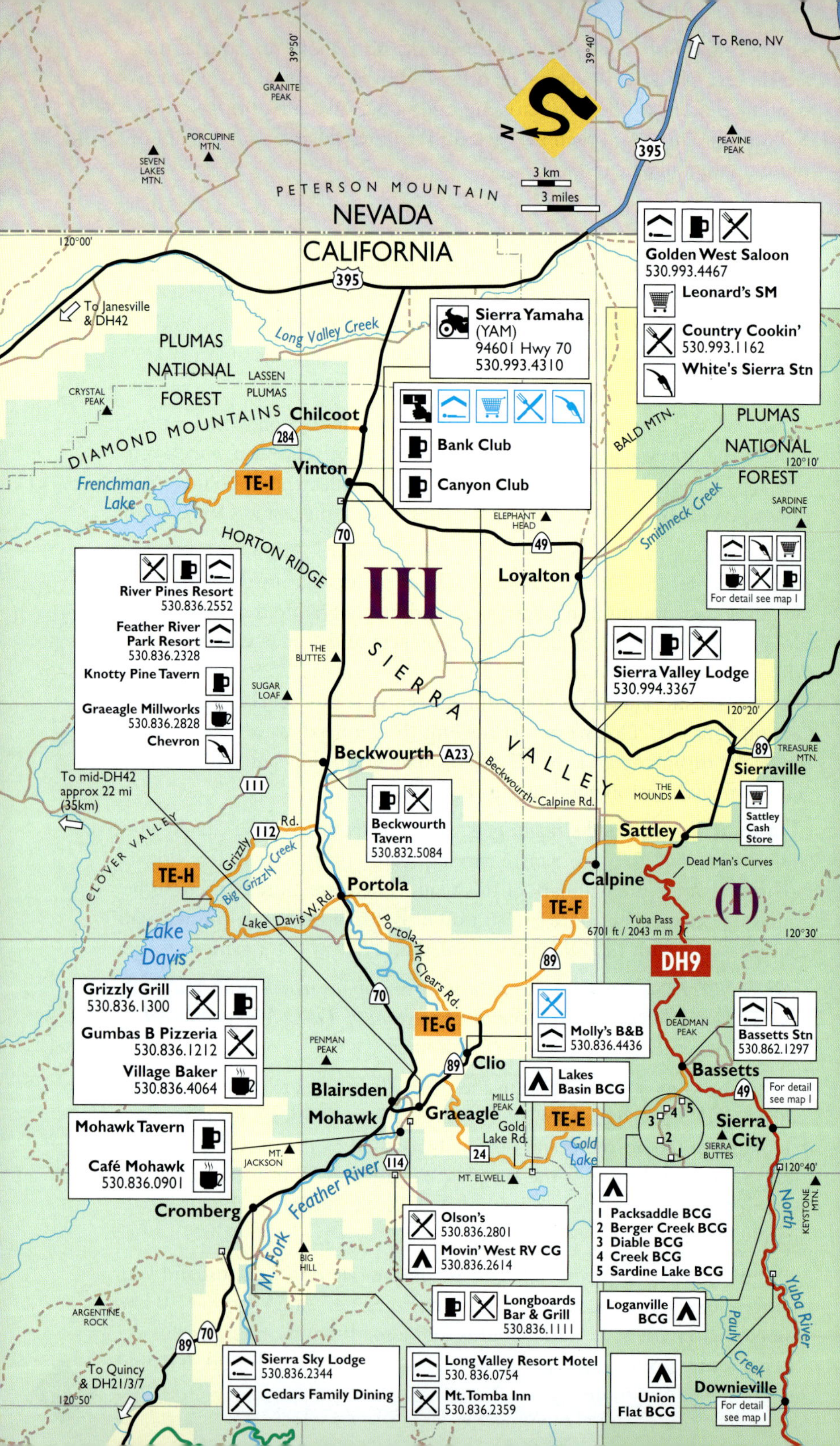

NEVADA
CALIFORNIA
PETERSON MOUNTAIN
To Reno, NV
To Janesville & DH42
PLUMAS NATIONAL FOREST
DIAMOND MOUNTAINS
Long Valley Creek
Chilcoot
Vinton
TE-I
Frenchman Lake
HORTON RIDGE
Sierra Yamaha (YAM)
94601 Hwy 70
530.993.4310
Bank Club
Canyon Club
Golden West Saloon
530.993.4467
Leonard's SM
Country Cookin'
530.993.1162
White's Sierra Stn
Loyalton
III
SIERRA VALLEY
Smithneck Creek
For detail see map I
Sierra Valley Lodge
530.994.3367
River Pines Resort
530.836.2552
Feather River Park Resort
530.836.2328
Knotty Pine Tavern
Graeagle Millworks
530.836.2828
Chevron
Beckwourth
Beckwourth Tavern
530.832.5084
Beckwourth-Calpine Rd.
Sierraville
Sattley Cash Store
Sattley
Calpine
Dead Man's Curves
To mid-DH42 approx 22 mi (35km)
CLOVER VALLEY
TE-H
Grizzly Rd.
Big Grizzly Creek
Lake Davis
Lake Davis W. Rd.
Portola
Portola-McClears Rd.
TE-F
Yuba Pass
6701 ft / 2043 m
DH9
(I)
TE-G
Grizzly Grill
530.836.1300
Gumbas B Pizzeria
530.836.1212
Village Baker
530.836.4064
Molly's B&B
530.836.4436
Bassetts Stn
530.862.1297
Clio
Lakes Basin BCG
Bassetts
For detail see map I
Blairsden
Mohawk
Graeagle
Gold Lake Rd.
TE-E
Gold Lake
Sierra City
Mohawk Tavern
Café Mohawk
530.836.0901
Feather River
Cromberg
M. Fork
Olson's
530.836.2801
Movin' West RV CG
530.836.2614
1 Packsaddle BCG
2 Berger Creek BCG
3 Diable BCG
4 Creek BCG
5 Sardine Lake BCG
North Yuba River
Longboards Bar & Grill
530.836.1111
Loganville BCG
Pauly Creek
To Quincy & DH21/3/7
Sierra Sky Lodge
530.836.2344
Cedars Family Dining
Long Valley Resort Motel
530. 836.0754
Mt. Tomba Inn
530.836.2359
Union Flat BCG
Downieville
For detail see map I
3 km
3 miles

And the DH delivers. Coming down beside a moss-dripping cliff, you cross the 3000 ft (914 m) elevation line at 26.5 mi (42.6 km), and the left-side forest opens, revealing a vista to the west over Canyon Creek to Mooreville Ridge beyond. Your Victor Foxtrot Roger continues down into a gorge, radioing especially tight, beautifully paved, award-winning twisties all the way. Wow.

Too bad this great segment has to end. At 29.2 mi (47.0 km), you cross the North Yuba River and enter the flat Indian Valley Recreation Area. The road then stretches out past a few campgrounds and even a restaurant. As advertised, it's pretty scenic riding the gentle bends along the quietly riffling river. Even if your rear views don't move much for a while.

The river valley narrows and the road starts winding again at 32.1 mi (51.7 km). Bisecting the North Yuba and the corrugated red rock that rises above it, the smooth road sweeps effortlessly through the lush gorge. It is truly gorgeous in here. One could even see hanging out at the Comdick Flat Day Use Area at 32.3 mi (52.0 km). Except that would involve stopping.

And it's hard to think about stopping when you're in a groove. It doesn't matter what you're riding, the irresistible flow of this section keeps beckoning you on, drawing you around the next bend, and the one after that. The call of the road, maybe? The quest for the perfect turn? Something to contemplate when you pull into Downieville, softly nestled in the mountains at 41.7 mi (67.1 km). It's a natural place to stop.

Leaving Downieville, you're back on the road beside the river, fording upstream through some big sweepers, including a particularly long one at 44.1 mi (70.1 km). There are a couple of riverside resorts along here. The wooden buildings fit so well into the natural setting that you'd hardly notice they were there. If it weren't for the bright, artificial green shuffleboard court that blends into the woods about as well as a Bimota Delirio at Sturgis.

Although it stays true to the river's course, the road doesn't remain constantly at water level. Instead it rises and falls along the steep rock wall to the left, providing different perspectives on the frequent rapids as well as fleeting glimpses of Keystone Mtn, Bald Ridge and the Sierra Buttes. Your thoughts segue and you wonder if some balding Keystone cop isn't just waiting somewhere nearby to get *your* butt.

At 50.3 mi (80.9 km), a small ranch occupies a rare piece of flat land to the left of the river. The road keeps curving though, reaching 4000 feet (1219 m) before entering the burgeoning metropolis of Sierra City at 53.9 mi (86.3 km).

TOUR NOTE: If you're here on a Friday night in July or early August, the Kentucky Mine Museum Amphitheater offers "foot stompin' fun" at their folk/bluegrass Summer Concert Series. As long as you can handle the banjoes.

Despite the name, Sierra City is no more a city than a Vespa is a motorcycle. That said, it's got more services than any other place on this remote road. Not quite as much charm as Downieville, but nice just the same. It's also a lot closer to the upcoming best part of the DH, not to mention fantastic **TE-E Gold Lake Rd**. The TE goes off left after a rapidly climbing straight from the old stage stop of Bassetts at 59.8 mi (96.2 km). Just past the turnoff, the North Yuba River, which has traced the DH for so many miles, disappears into its headwaters. You're on your own.

"Bikers Beware. Dead Man's Curves Next 15 Miles." Yes, the sign really says that. Now that's your kind of invitation. You've gained a fair bit of altitude and are now riding through the Yuba Pass, a section of meadow and airy lodgepole pines that has a definite sub-alpine feel. The road, however, has yet to recover its tightly curving feel. It's straight and mildly sweepy at best. While the pair of 35-mph (55-kmh) curves at 61.2 mi (98.5 km) are nice, they're hardly to die for.

But the ones coming up are. The corners get deeper as you keep climbing up to the 6701 ft (2042 m) summit, their advisories tightening to 20 and 25 mph (30 and 40 kmh). Think it's hairy now? Next you get to try it coming downhill. However you'll find solace and support in the excellent asphalt that kicks in just over the top at 67.0 mi (107.8 km). If you're going to kill yourself, it's nice to do it on good pavement.

The last miles are a dream. They'd be more of a dream riding up, but they are marvelous just the same. Smoothly paved. Remote. Good sightlines. Some nice vistas over the Sierra Valley. And enough little straights so you can really get your speed up for those 15- and 20-mph (25- and 30 kmh) hairpins. You leave the Tahoe National Forest at 69.3 mi (111.5 km). "Land of many uses," indeed.

The elevation markers count down and you gradually flatten out into the Sierra Valley, reaching the end of the DH at the junction with Hwy 89 at 72.6 mi (116.8 km). From there, you can head north on Hwy 89 to Clio (**TE-F**) or ride south through the warm, straw-colored, pine-peppered grass and farmland to pat the dog on the porch of the Sattley Cash Store.

Twisted Edges

TE-A Newtown Rd - Empress Rd - Bitney Springs Rd

(8.5 mi / 13.7 km)

As Bitney herself might sing, "The mostly great pavement, remoteness and seductive curvaceousness of this TE make you come. They make you complete. They make you completely happy." Guess she's not that innocent after all.

NAVIGATION: If you are coming from the DH, make sure you 90 degree right off Newton and onto Empress at 3.4 mi (5.5 km). When you hit Bitney at 3.9 mi (6.3 km), turn right. Bitney left will take you to Rough and Ready. Just hope her kid's in its car seat.

If you are coming from the ***TE-C*** *end, slide off Bitney and onto Empress at 5.1 mi (8.2 km).*

TE-B Oak Tree Rd - Tyler Foote Crossing Rd (5.9 mi / 9.5 km)
Who cares if **DH9 Nevada City – Sattley** is the second longest DH in Northern California? There's always some joker who wants those few extra quiet, well-paved miles and those few extra sections of curves. **TE-B** obliges.

NAVIGATION: Going south, turn right at the stop sign at Mother Truckers Market.

Going north, turn left at Mother Truckers at 3.3 mi (5.3 km)

TE-C Pleasant Valley Rd (14.5 mi / 23.3 km)
After starting out at its northern end as a quiet, gently turning, sometimes bumpy country road, this TE transforms first into a steep, curling, one-lane drop through the wondrous green gorge of S Yuba State Park. Then it evolves into a well-paved, winding trip through some rolling oak and ranchland before broadening into a wide-shouldered, over-engineered suburban feeder road around Lake Wildwood to the busy junction with Hwy 20.

TOUR NOTE: There's a popular swimming spot at the south end of the bridge over the S Yuba River.

TE-D Marysville Rd (E 20) (19.1 mi / 30.7 km)
Despite its smooth pavement, this merry TE's quite contrarily straight out on the barren flat west of Dobbins. But east of town, pretty sweepers all in a row climb through a garden of solid pines, then descend to cross the southern tip of the New Bullards Bar Reservoir. Once you goose it back up along a winding cliff above the water, the road straightens out again toward the DH.

TE-E Gold Lake Rd (15.3 mi / 24.6 km)
There's no apparent reason for this well paved and engineered route winding high up into the pass between the snow caps of Mount Elwell and Mills Peak and offering terrific in-your-face views of the Sierra Buttes. With nothing but a couple of campgrounds and a lonely lodge, you gotta wonder what gives. No complaints, though.

TE-F Sattley – Clio (Hwy 89) (12.4 mi / 20.0 km)
Surprisingly scenic, curvy, remote and traffic free, this high, smooth section of Hwy 89 through Plumas National Forest winds up to the top of a summit. Then, after a brief straight, it descends on a curving run through the pines to the junction of **TE-G Clio-Portola** south of Clio.

TE-G Clio – Portola (7.7 mi / 12.4 km) *Portola-McClears Rd (A 15)*
A quieter route than Hwy 70 on the other side of the Middle Fork Feather River, at least until the large "planned community" around the golf course at Gold Mountain is finished. Some nice curves between GM and Hwy 89. Decent pavement throughout.

NAVIGATION: In Portola, take Gulling St south over the river to the old town. Take the first street to your right (Commercial St) and follow the signs south for A 15. You'll end up on Main St. Turn right from Main onto 3rd Ave, which becomes Portola-McClears Rd.

TE-H Lake Davis Loop (13.2 mi / 21.2 km) *West St – Lake Davis Rd W – Grizzly Rd*

Good pavement but you could use more curves, especially on the west arm of this gradual climb into Plumas National Forest's Lake Davis Rec Area and back down to Hwy 70. Apparently, the deer like to come out and play with you here.

NAVIGATION: On Hwy 70 in Portola look for the brown Davis Lake sign at West St. And is that four-way stop really necessary?

ROUTING OPTIONS: Maxburners may want to circumnavigate the lake. Intrepid maxburners who've seen a little fire and rain may wish to continue on the gravel past the north end of the lake for about 27 mi (43 km) to get to Genesee on ***DH42 Taylorsville – Janesville.*** *Or they can do about the same distance on paved Genesee-Beckwourth Rd north from Beckwourth, which becomes gravel FSRs 177/111 and ride along the Clover Valley to the same DH arriving five or so miles east of Genesee.*

Less fearless bump-and-grind explorers can take the slightly longer but almost entirely paved (there's 4.4 mi (7.1 km) of pebbles) route north from Beckwourth. It changes FSR designations several times (177/11/70/03/01) then lands you on ***DH42****, just south of Antelope Lake after 35.2 mi (56.6 km). It's remote going this way but because there are few useful curves, it's a little boring for twistiness mavens. Oh, and you may find logging trucks attempting to kill you. Which at least makes a change from Brown.*

TE-I Chilcoot – Frenchman Lake (Hwy 284) (8.3 mi / 14.1 km)

Eh cheri, dis lil' gem get you straight cross da hopen plain at da begin. Wonce you in da Plumas Nashnul' Fores' Homme de Francais Area de Recreation, da 'igher, treed cuntree 'tween da Diamon' Mountuns an' 'Orton Ridge make for da good twisties, no? An' da narrow, jumble black ignus rock canyon in da en time heven better dan dat. Tabernac!

ROUTING OPTION: Maxburners who'd rather see a lonely day that they thought would never end rather than backtrack can gravel it cross country some 30 mi (50 km) to ***DH42 Taylorsville – Janesville*** *by taking either of the two roads north around Frenchman Lake. Then FSR 101 will lead you to the Plinco Mine Rd-Milford Grade Rd route down to Milford on Hwy 395. If you make it, head north to Janesville and turn left at the Chevron about 10 mi (15 km) later.*

TE-J Jackson Meadows Rd - Henness Pass Rd (FSR 7) (14.9 mi / 24.0 km)

Mellow. That's the word that best describes this remote, traffic-free and sometimes tar-strippy TE that wanders through pine forest and past soothing meadows on its way out to the campgrounds on the Jackson Meadows Reservoir.

TE-K Stampede Dam Rd (10.6 mi / 17.1 km)

Except when a stampede of boat-towing pylons is rushing through the extremely well-paved, steady curves up to the Stampede Reservoir, this is a quiet ride along water, through piney sage and beside some rockfaces.

TOUR NOTE: You reach the turnoff to the Stampede Reservoir at 8.5 mi (13.7 km). If you turn left here, you'll cross over the dam and wend the 0.8 mi (1.3 km) through a couple campgrounds down to the boat launch.

ROUTING OPTION: The gravel road that T-junctions at the top of the TE is the old Henness Pass Rd. Left will take maxburners to Hwy 89 (12.0 mi / 19.3 km), right to I-80 (8.0 mi / 12.9 km)

RIDER'S LOG: **DATE RIDDEN:** **YOUR RATING:** **/10**

Don't forget to print the DH Rider Discount list of service providers from* destinationhighways.com *and take it with you. Then, just show 'em your book and ask for the discount.

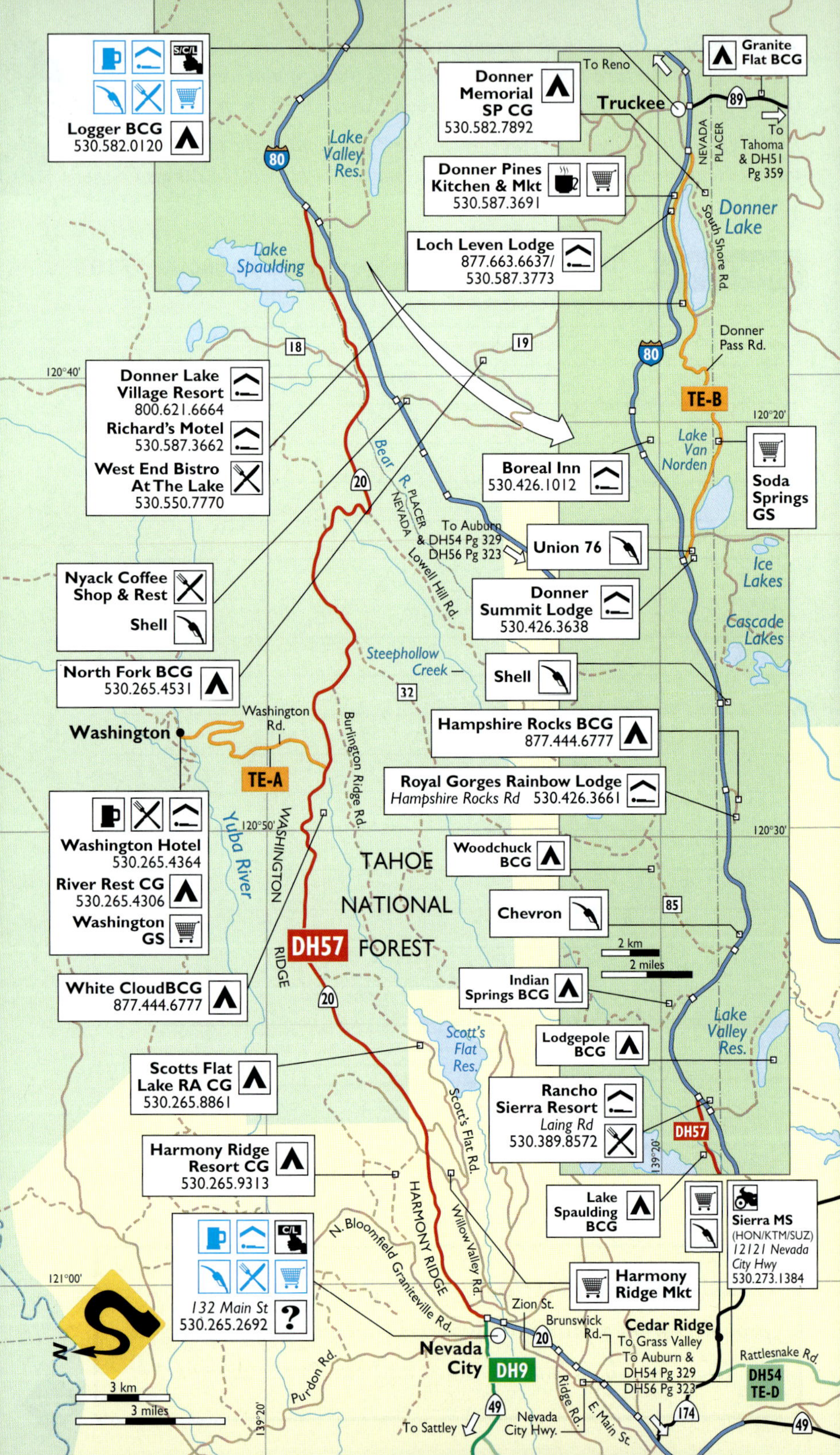

S/C/L
Logger BCG
530.582.0120
Donner Memorial SP CG
530.582.7892
To Reno
Granite Flat BCG
Truckee
89
To Tahoma & DH51 Pg 359
Donner Pines Kitchen & Mkt
530.587.3691
NEVADA
PLACER
Donner Lake
South Shore Rd.
Loch Leven Lodge
877.663.6637/
530.587.3773
Lake Valley Res.
80
Lake Spaulding
18
19
Donner Pass Rd.
TE-B
120°40'
120°20'
Donner Lake Village Resort
800.621.6664
Richard's Motel
530.587.3662
West End Bistro At The Lake
530.550.7770
Lake Van Norden
Soda Springs GS
Boreal Inn
530.426.1012
20
Bear R.
PLACER
NEVADA
To Auburn & DH54 Pg 329
DH56 Pg 323
Union 76
Lowell Hill Rd.
Ice Lakes
Nyack Coffee Shop & Rest
Shell
Donner Summit Lodge
530.426.3638
Cascade Lakes
Steephollow Creek
Shell
North Fork BCG
530.265.4531
32
Washington Rd.
Washington
Hampshire Rocks BCG
877.444.6777
TE-A
Burlington Ridge Rd.
Royal Gorges Rainbow Lodge
Hampshire Rocks Rd 530.426.3661
120°50'
120°30'
Yuba River
WASHINGTON
Washington Hotel
530.265.4364
River Rest CG
530.265.4306
Washington GS
TAHOE
NATIONAL
FOREST
Woodchuck BCG
85
Chevron
2 km
2 miles
DH57
RIDGE
White CloudBCG
877.444.6777
Indian Springs BCG
Lake Valley Res.
Scott's Flat Res.
Lodgepole BCG
Scotts Flat Lake RA CG
530.265.8861
Rancho Sierra Resort
Laing Rd
530.389.8572
Scott's Flat Rd.
DH57
139°20'
Harmony Ridge Resort CG
530.265.9313
Lake Spaulding BCG
Sierra MS
(HON/KTM/SUZ)
12121 Nevada City Hwy
530.273.1384
C/L
HARMONY RIDGE
Willow Valley Rd.
N. Bloomfield Graniteville Rd.
121°00'
Harmony Ridge Mkt
132 Main St
530.265.2692
Zion St.
Brunswick Rd.
Cedar Ridge
To Grass Valley
To Auburn & DH54 Pg 329
DH56 Pg 323
Rattlesnake Rd.
Nevada City
DH9
DH54
TE-D
Purdon Rd.
Ridge Rd.
E. Main St.
174
49
3 km
3 miles
139°20'
To Sattley
Nevada City Hwy.
N

DH57 Nevada City – Hwy 20/I-80 Jct

Highway 20

Distance:	26.6 mi / 42.8 km	Traffic:	Heavy

DH9 DH57 DH21 DH7 DH3 DH42

At a Glance

Bigger is better. At least on this DH. Folks riding heavy, powerful 1300cc sport-tourers, 1800cc cruisers or six-cylinder luxo-tourers are going to drool over this ride. The expertly paved and engineered, moderately long-leaning sweepers featured on this secondary route are just the ticket for those who've got what it takes and know how to use it. Sweeping up out of Nevada City, the DH climbs along the south-facing slopes of Harmony and Washington Ridges. That's followed by a long, gently climbing straight through an airy forest of tall, cabin-filled pines. Where the road and your throttle really start cracking is on the remote, stretched out descent to the eastern junction. There are some views at the west end over the Deer Creek Valley, a vista point by the TE-A turnoff and some distant mountain sightings coming down toward the interstate, but most of this ride is in the tall trees of the Tahoe National Forest. They don't affect the sightlines, however. So you and your big baby are free to delight in the endless, roll-on sweepers that ess down the easy slope. Sure, bring your Rocket III.

TIRES	
Twistiness	16.7/ 30
Pavement	20.0/ 20
Engineering	7.3/ 10
Remoteness	5.4/ 10
Scenery	8.8/ 15
Character	4.3/ 15
Total	**62.5**

Access

From Nevada City

Coming in on DH9 Sattley – Nevada City (Hwy 49)

Follow Hwy 49 to its junction with Hwy 20. Turn left. You're on the road.

From I-80

Take the well-marked exit to Hwy 20. Go west – the only way you can. You're on the road.

On The Road

There's a bit of development by the wide-shouldered roadside as the DH leaves Nevada City. It dwindles, however, at 1.2 mi (1.9 km), as gentle corners serenade you into a brief passing lane above the Deer Creek Valley. Climbing Harmony Ridge, you'll find more melodic curves and sweepers begin at 1.7 mi (2.7 km) and carry on to 3.1 mi (5.0 km). Music to your tires.

"Driveways Next 2 Miles" reads the sign. Despite the news, it is nice to be forewarned for a change. Guess that explains why there's no dotted line on the long straight that cuts geometrically through the tall, striking pines hugging the roadside. You enter the Tahoe National Forest at 4.2 mi (6.8 km) bringing an end to most of the cabins, driveways and side roads. But it doesn't bring an end to what's becoming a ridiculously long straightaway.

Another sign warns of populated area ahead. Thought we were in a national park here? But the cabins and driveways return in force at 6.0 mi (9.7 km). Ah, land of many useless things. How about a sign warning of twisties? You know, those curvy things.

At 10.8 mi (17.4 km), you cross a crest and begin a descent. The drop triggers a series of long, high-powered sweepers through the forest. Great pavement and fine engineering whip you past a splendorous vista at 12.1 mi (19.5 km) over the Washington River Valley to Grouse Ridge, Fall Creek Mtn, the Black Buttes and other peaks of the Sierra Nevada.

You enter another straight – don't worry it's brief – but this time, you have an option. Washington Rd (**TE-A**) carries on down to the river and offers a tight and twisty contrast to the sweepiness of the DH. It's conveniently located to your left at 12.7 mi (20.4 km).

The lines of tall, shadowy pines are something to look at. Especially when they curl in front of you at 13.9 mi (22.4 km) and mark the beginning of the excellent second half of this DH.

It's a fast ride on the big essing sweepers forced on the road by Washington Ridge. Even here, however, the DH does not curl consistently. There are still some straight sections, like the one that runs between 16.1 mi (25.9 km) and 17.1 mi (27.5 km). But when you pick that line through the big honkin' sweepers and hold… hold… hold it, accelerating all the way, it's a powerful feeling that stays with you through a straight or two. Did someone say power? You can use all you got here.

But it's not all just open 'er up and go. Take, for example, the 35-mph (55-kmh) advised sweeper at 19.2 mi (30.9 km). Or, more to the point, that unadvised one that immediately follows it. But hey, motorcycling is more fun if you have to lean a little more than you planned once in a while, right?

More big curves bank into smaller ones. Zion Hill rises in the distance, breaching the scenic protocol of solid trees. Of greater concern is the breach of your cornering agenda that occurs with the straight at 20.8 mi (33.5 km).

But at 21.6 mi (34.8 km), you're curving again – albeit not like before – through what's becoming a more level landscape. A wide, grassy powerline cut marks the line between Nevada and Placer counties at 21.9 mi (35.2 km).

You are back in the forest at 22.4 mi (36.0 km), although it's set well back from the wide shoulder. The trees soon creep back closer to the roadside, but the road doesn't capture the perfect balance between forest atmosphere and sightlines that existed back in Nevada County. Not that it matters much, since there are only a few more curves on which you can stake a claim before the DH ends, at the junction with I-80, at 26.6 mi (42.8 km).

Twisted Edges

TE-A Washington Rd (5.4 mi / 8.7 km)

This TE offers a little Yin to the DH's Yang. Where the DH is big, sweepy and well-engineered, this deadender is unceasingly tight and twisty. Where the DH eases up and down over a low summit through a forest of mature, spaced pines, this road winds steeply down a scenic cliff onto a deeply forested valley bottom. Where the DH has flawless pavement, this road has a few minor bumpy spots. So why should you ride this road? Because you own a 600. Or maybe just want to stop at the Washington Hotel for a Babeweiser by the river.

TE-B Donner Pass Rd (10.6 mi / 17.1 km) *Old Hwy 40*

Ever been at a dinner party gone horribly wrong? You know, not enough food or cranky guests that end up at each other's throats? The infamous Donner Dinner Party lasted eight months through the winter of 1846-47 and was so awful that history abbreviated the name simply to the Donner Party. But you won't starve on this little soiree up to Donner Pass. Though the appetizer that runs along the north side of Donner Lake is a little straight and developed, it's followed by a twisty climb through raw and rocky terrain that's a real feast for the tires. And you can gorge on the view from the top over Donner Lake and the landscape on the east side of the Sierra Nevada. Dessert is a piece-of-cake ride back to I-80. Weather can sock in quickly up here though, so if you ride late in the season, you may want to pack some food along. Or at least a "dinner companion" on the back. For as Carlos Santana reminds us, "Those who forget history are doomed to re-eat it."

NAVIGATION/TOUR NOTE: To get to the TE from the Truckee end, take the I-80 exit for the Donner Memorial State Park, where the Emigrant Trail Museum has a large section dedicated to the story of the Donner Party.

Rider's Log: **Date Ridden:** **Your Rating:** **/10**

To Greensville
To Taylorsville & DH42
DH3
DH3 TE-A
DH3 ALT
Chandler Rd.
East Quincy
Quincy
Sweet Lorraine
530.283.5300 (Recommended)
EUREKA RIDGE
BACHS CREEK RIDGE
SIERRA NEVADA MTNS.
Twain
Bucks Lake Rd.
Meadow Valley
Running Deer FS CG
Red Feather FS CG
Little Beaver FS CG
Wyandotte BCG
Peninsula FS CG
Black Rock BCG
ONION VALLEY
PILOT'S PEAK
Little Grass Valley Res.
Johnsville Rd.
Gold Country Resort/B&B
530.675.2322
LaPort Cabin Rentals
530.675.0850
The Union Hotel
530.675.2860
Union Hotel Dining Room and Saloon
530.675.2830
Riley's Saloon & Café
La Porte Deli GS
Rabbit Creek Deli
NON-FEATURED DH SERVICES NOT SHOWN
DH7 TE-A
Bucks Lake
Bucks Creek
Grizzly Creek
Grizzly Summit
MT. ARARAT
La Porte
LA PORTE BALD MTN.
DH21
La Porte Rd.
PLUMAS NATIONAL FOREST
2 km
2 miles
Strawberry GS
Mtn. Rose Motel
530.675.2480
Gold Eagle Market Shell
530.675.2681
Bonny Lou's Café
530.675.1824
Shell
Clipper Mills Store SM
Roy's Store
530.675.0332
N. FK. FEATHER RIVER
MIDDLE FK. FEATHER RIVER
S. FK. FEATHER RIVER
Sly Creek Res.
Strawberry
Clipper Mills
Woodleaf
DH9
DH7
DH3
Oroville-Quincy Hwy.
FIELDS RIDGE
Forbestown Rd.
Forbestown
Challenge
Challenge GS
Challenge Cutoff Rd.
DH7 TE-B
New Buffalo Bar Res.
Concow Res.
Yankee Hill
Pentz Rd.
To Paradise
Bald Rock Rd.
Lake Oroville
Brownsville
TE-B
Frenchtown Rd.
Marysville Rd.
Willow Glen Rd.
DH9 TE-D
Willow Glen Saloon
530.692.3005
Forbestown Rd.
NORTH TABLE MTN.
Cherokee Rd.
Oregon Gulch Rd.
Clark Rd.
SOUTH TABLE MTN.
Miners Ranch Rd.
Oroville Bangor Rd.
MILLER HILL
SUGARLOAF
Rice Crossing Rd.
Oroville
Wyandotte Rd.
Dunstone Rd.
Verjeles Rd.
TE-A
DAUGHERTY HILL
HOLMAN HILL
To Chico & DH49 Pg. 233
To Orland
To CVA III Pg. 498
To Marysville
To CVA IV Pg 499
Biandiani's Market
To Hwy. 20
To Sattley & DH9
Lee Summit
LAVA PEAK
ARGENTINE ROCK
GRIZZLY DOME
PLUMAS
BUTTE
YUBA

DH21 Challenge – East Quincy (Quincy)
La Porte Road (FSR 120)

Distance:	51.8 mi / 83.4 km	Traffic:	Light

DH9 DH57 DH21 DH7 DH3 DH42

At a Glance

Roll that throttle. Push on those bars. Drop those knees. Sure, the punishing pavement and agonizing, drawn-out speed zones through the townlets south of La Porte hurt. But you gotta ride through the pain to get in the zone – the smooth-toned Pavement, buff Engineering and tight, muscular twisties that wind north of La Porte into the remote alpine Scenery of the unspoiled Onion Valley. Feel that tire burn off as you shift your weight through those low-pylon corners. All right, now take a breath. Don't strain yourself on the narrow hairpin turns that crunch down the steep, forested cliff to the Feather River's wild Middle Fork. Save something for the last winding blast through the woods between the gentle curves of the Willow Creek valley and the high-speed, cool-down sweepers through the hayfields at the end. That's it! Way to go! Looking great! One more time!

TIRES	
Twistiness	30/30
Pavement	13.6/20
Engineering	4.7/10
Remoteness	6.9/10
Scenery	8.6/15
Character	12.7/15
Total	**76.5**

Access

From Challenge

On E 21

Head north from this one horse town. You're on the road.

From Quincy

Coming in on DH7 Oroville – Quincy (Oroville-Quincy Hwy)

Coming in on DH3 Oroville – Quincy (Hwy 70)

Approximately 3.0 mi (4.8 km) east of Quincy on Hwy 70/89, and just past East Quincy, you'll see the turnoff for La Porte. Take it. You're on the road.

On The Road

At first, this ride seems quite remote. Challenge's 25-mph (40-kmh) speed zone ends and the DH begins with gentle curves and easy engineering through tall, dense, shadowy woods. After a little straight, the cracked, bumpy pavement tightens up into a series of esses at 1.7 mi (2.7 km).

The early sense of awayness continues until 3.1 mi (5.0 mi) when you reach Woodleaf, the first of a series of 35-mph (55-kmh) building zones that litter the southern section of this DH. All you can say about Woodleaf is that the pavement improves for its duration. When it ends at 3.6 mi (5.8 km), the surface returns to not-great.

The remoteness doesn't have a chance to recover before you're in another 35-mph (55-kmh) speed zone – this time for the town of Clipper Mills – at 4.5 mi (7.2 km). Ironic, really, given that the town derives its name from the speedy clipper ships that whipped across the bounding main in the 1800s. Today, not only does the sluggish zone persist past the houses, farms, stores and long-closed lodge at 6.6 mi (10.6 km), but there isn't even any improvement in the pavement.

The speed zone ends but the development lingers. A couple of dilatory industrial complexes scar the left roadside at 7.5 mi (12.0 km) before the green curtain of forest is finally drawn again. And even then, it lasts only until 8.9 mi (14.3 km), when you straightaway past another closed lodge. Strawberry Valley, at 9.4 mi (15.1 km), brings the last in this string of speed zones. It's the site of a wedding chapel and a closed general store. Could the honeymoon be far off?

Despite the fact that Strawberry Valley is the least sprawling of this trilogy of towns there's never a sign saying "End 35-mph Speed Zone". Though there is a yellow advisory warning of 35-mph (55-kmh) twisties at 10.6 mi (17.1 km). Now that's the best kind of speed zone – one you can usually ignore.

The experience of curving through largely unblemished forest is back. And this time, it's not ending in such a hurry. At 12.7 mi (20.4 km), a stand of enormous pines rockets up from the side of the road. Trees step back from the widened surface, the pavement improves and the road starts to sweep, sweep, sweep.

And it gets better. Engineering remains good as your mirrors tilt deeper and deeper through alternating sections of sweepers and tight turns. Towering trees, good, predictable pavement, well-sightlined corners and no one else around. There's even a brief passing lane at 20.0 mi (32.2 km). Like you really need it on this traffic-sparse road.

It's a steep, straight climb up the three lanes of pavement. Coming over the crest at 20.4 mi (32.8 km), the lanes converge toward a view of La Porte Bald Mtn. Its odd name suggests a compromise of some kind. You have to compromise as well – apart from a couple of gentle sweepers, the road is straight right to the town of La Porte at 22.3 mi (35.9 km).

Great, another town. But at least this one follows some decent riding, has a bar that's actually open and doesn't sprawl more than it has to. It would be considerate of them to mark the end of the 25-mph (40-kmh) zone, though. But maybe the town believes in leaving that to the rider's discretion. In any case, at 24.7 mi (39.7 km), you reach a junction. Left will take you down to the Little Grass Valley Reservoir and its campgrounds. To stay on the DH, **turn right**.

Well, well, what have we here? This pavement seems almost new. And there's even a bit of paved shoulder. But can the DH coax a few curves out of this terrain? You bet your patootie it can. Some pretty nice ones, too. An S-curve here, another there. In a couple of spots, the Forest Service has elected to put up a sign saying "Rough Road" rather than fix a gopher lump in the pavement, but other than those anomalies, this is one smooooth stretch of road. And it seems even smoother after what you've ridden to get here.

The Pilot Lake Baptist Camp is down the Johnsville Rd to the right at 29.5 mi (47.5 km). Given what's coming up, you'd have to be pretty self-sacrificing to make that turn. Because it's here that the DH really starts to find its divine purpose. Chains of S-curves and the occasional sweeper link together on a steep, weaving climb. You ascend so quickly you can feel the temperature dropping. Coming around a half-hairpin at 31.4 mi (50.5 km), you're suddenly in the sub-alpine, with narrowed trees, high views, high-country meadows and maybe even a little lingering snow.

The top of Pilot's Peak appears at twelve o'clock as you easily navigate the mountain curves. Then, at 32.7 mi (52.6 km), the road drops below the ridgeline, signaling the start of a descent. The corners continue, more gently now, with the exception of the get-down sweeper across the South Fork Feather River at 33.7 mi (54.2 km). If you really enjoyed this section, you can always loop back left at 33.9 mi (54.6 km) on the unpaved road back to the Little Grass Valley Reservoir and ride it all over again. Just imagine how good this pavement will feel after a little gravel. Or, if you're a maxburner, how good the gravel will feel after that great pavement.

Past the intersection, a vast view westward over the Middle Fork Feather River's canyon lingers below as you edge tightly back upward along a drop-off mountainside. At 35.2 mi (56.6 km), the terrain flattens through the high Onion Valley. But then the pungent climb continues through an alpine landscape layered with glaciated rock, bright green meadows and more touches of snow.

At 35.9 mi (57.8 km), there's another big view, this one east to Eureka Ridge. It's momentary though, as you rapidly descend back into sub-alpine forest. A large clearing amid the narrow trees abounds with low shrubbery and banks of bright yellow flowers. The steep decline allows peek-a-boo views of the blue-green layers of ridges and mountains to the north and east.

Gentler curves characterize the descent. Good thing, since the soaring view and steep sideslope down to the right starting at 37.2 mi (59.9 km) is enough to give a Flying Wallenda vertigo. Nothing but a few piddling white stakes lie between you and the other kind of motorcycling heaven. Well, at least you know there'd be no speed tax collectors there.

There's lots of time for such metaphysical contemplation as you continue to drop into more and more temperate forest. It's obvious from the long, tree-gap view off the opposite side at 37.8 mi (60.8 km) that you're still on top of a ridge. The road glides down its west side, composes a view of

Bach's Ridge, then flips to the eastern slope, its tighter turns exaggerated by the steepening grade. The green, brown and slate-colored bluffs of Eureka Ridge offset by dabs of snow are impressive. But better keep your eyes on the road. It's a pretty long drop beyond that two-inch shoulder. "Winding Road" reads the sign at 39.9 mi (64.2 km). The Forest Service – masters of the obvious.

Well, maybe it wasn't so obvious. The road completely changes here. It narrows, steepens even more and starts to hairpin all at the same time. Oh yes, and the pavement quality drops a level. All of which make it much more challenging to ride this road like Mat Mladin. Truth be told, this tough descent is more like a trials course. Moving slow. Heavy concentration. Death or injury a slip away. This is one section you might wish you were riding the other way.

The engineering improves at 42.4 mi (68.2 km) and you pick up speed accordingly. Curves are not as tight and the visibility around them is markedly better but it's still plenty twisty along the side of the cliff as you ride down into the forest-filled valley. At 44.5 mi (71.6 km), you cross the wild Middle Fork Feather River and the path widens a little.

Willow Creek runs unseen in a ravine to your right. Following its course, you wind gently through rugged but now much lower terrain. After the ordeal of the long cliffside descent, the grassy strips and meadows by the road look like a welcome mat. And indeed they are. At 45.9 mi (73.9 km), you're welcomed to a small settlement whose only name seems to be "25 mph."

The reason for the speed zone is not entirely clear since there are a couple of houses on the left and a broad, wind-ruffled meadow on your right. Once again, no one bothers to tell you when you can wind it out again. At 46.6 mi (75.0 km), a 25 mph marker for the other direction appears in your left rear-view. That's good enough. Back up to speed.

Pavement dives a bit as you re-enter the forest. Just in time for an out-of-the-blue hairpin at 48.0 mi (77.2 km). From here, the road narrows and winds sharply along a steep slope through a section of dark, storybook woods. The story ends when 49.7 mi (80.0 km) brings the first straightaway in a long time. Perturbed by the prospect of motorcyclists getting out of third gear, the Forest Service has posted a 45-mph (70-kmh) speed sign at 49.9 mi (80.3 km).

When is this DH going to end? Well, the appearance of mailboxes should give you a clue. The straight ends in a series of light, smoothly paved sweepers that guide you past the hayfields and couple of barns to the junction with Hwy 70 where the DH concludes at 51.8 mi (83.4 km).

Twisted Edges

TE-A E 20/E 21 Jct – Brownsville (E 21) *Willow Glen Rd* (7.0 mi / 11.3 km)

Forest, a couple of clearings and steady, gentle to moderate curves winding beneath Chitterden Ridge. Yes, it's very peaceful here in Willow Glen. That is until your tire slips on a one of the thousands of tar strips.

TE-B Frenchtown Rd (7.6 mi / 12.2 km)

While this quiet TE does its best to appease riders with some conciliatory twisties and scenery that varies from forest at the north end to ranchland at the south, the pavement's still *comme çi, comme ça*. Perhaps that's why there are still those who would see the name changed to "Freedomtown Rd."

Rider's Log: **Date Ridden:** **Your Rating:** **/10**

What are the Top Ten Rides based on Twistiness, Pavement, Engineering, Remoteness, Scenery and Character? You'll find the answers in the TIRES Charts at the back of the book. The complete list of DHs by TIRES components is at destinationhighways.com.

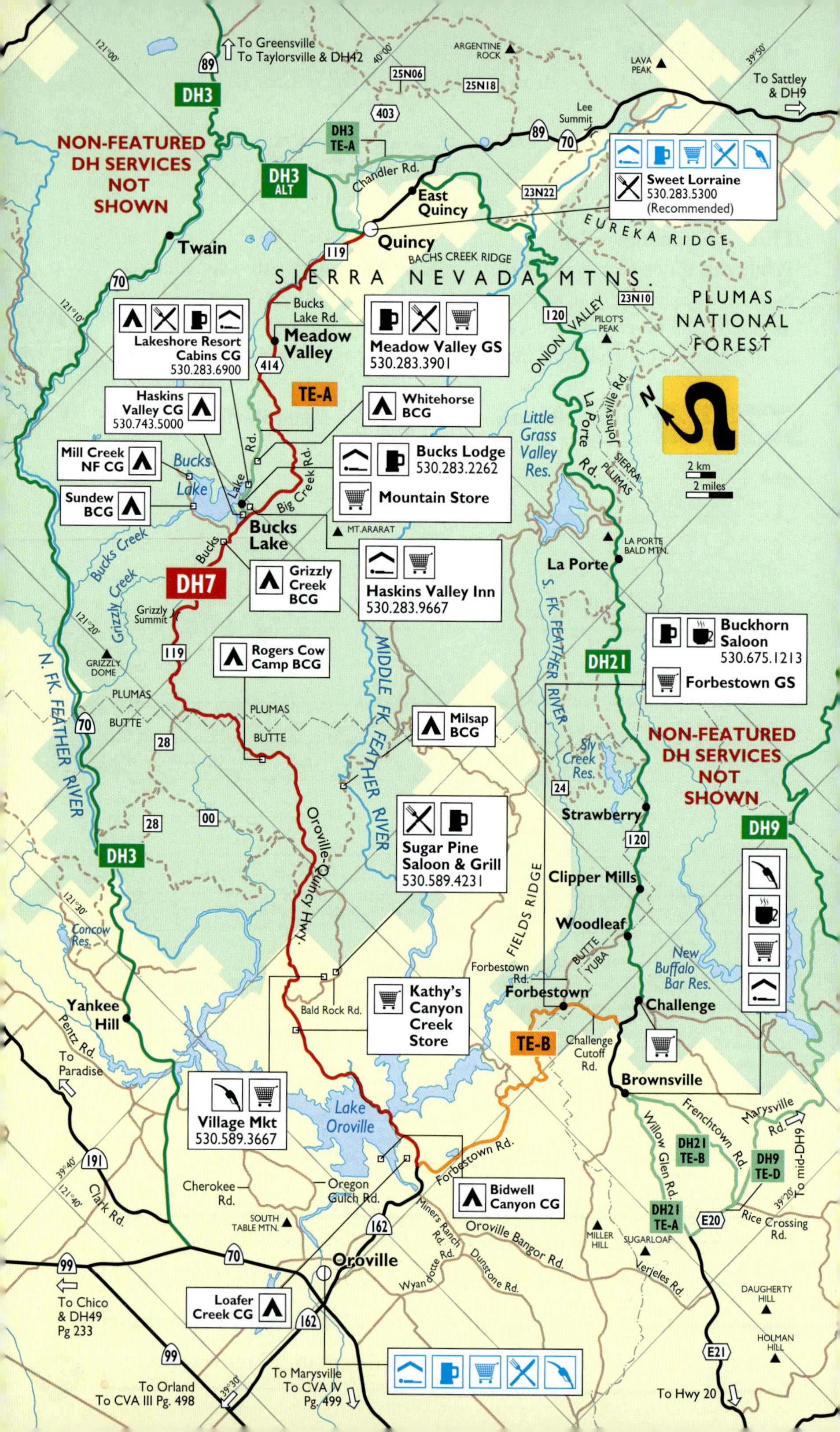

To Greensville
To Taylorsville & DH42
ARGENTINE ROCK
LAVA PEAK
To Sattley & DH9
NON-FEATURED DH SERVICES NOT SHOWN
DH3
DH3 TE-A
DH3 ALT
Chandler Rd.
Lee Summit
East Quincy
Sweet Lorraine
530.283.5300
(Recommended)
EUREKA RIDGE
Twain
Quincy
BACHS CREEK RIDGE
SIERRA NEVADA MTNS.
PLUMAS NATIONAL FOREST
Bucks Lake Rd.
Meadow Valley
Lakeshore Resort Cabins CG
530.283.6900
Meadow Valley GS
530.283.3901
ONION VALLEY
PILOT'S PEAK
TE-A
Haskins Valley CG
530.743.5000
Whitehorse BCG
Mill Creek NF CG
Bucks Lake
Big Creek Rd.
Bucks Lodge
530.283.2262
Mountain Store
Little Grass Valley Res.
La Porte Rd.
Johnsville Rd.
SIERRA PLUMAS
2 km
2 miles
Sundew BCG
Bucks Lake
MT. ARARAT
LA PORTE BALD MTN.
Bucks Creek
Grizzly Creek
DH7
Grizzly Creek BCG
Haskins Valley Inn
530.283.9667
La Porte
Grizzly Summit
GRIZZLY DOME
Rogers Cow Camp BCG
MIDDLE FK. FEATHER RIVER
S. FK. FEATHER RIVER
DH21
Buckhorn Saloon
530.675.1213
Forbestown GS
PLUMAS
BUTTE
N. FK. FEATHER RIVER
Milsap BCG
Sly Creek Res.
NON-FEATURED DH SERVICES NOT SHOWN
Oroville-Quincy Hwy.
Strawberry
DH9
Sugar Pine Saloon & Grill
530.589.4231
DH3
Clipper Mills
FIELDS RIDGE
Concow Res.
Woodleaf
BUTTE YUBA
New Buffalo Bar Res.
Forbestown Rd.
Forbestown
Challenge
Yankee Hill
Kathy's Canyon Creek Store
Bald Rock Rd.
Pentz Rd.
TE-B
Challenge Cutoff Rd.
To Paradise
Brownsville
Village Mkt
530.589.3667
Lake Oroville
Frenchtown Rd.
Marysville Rd.
Willow Glen Rd.
DH21 TE-B
DH9 TE-D
To mid-DH9
Forbestown Rd.
Cherokee Rd.
Oregon Gulch Rd.
Bidwell Canyon CG
Miners Ranch Rd.
Clark Rd.
SOUTH TABLE MTN.
Oroville Bangor Rd.
MILLER HILL
SUGARLOAF
DH21 TE-A
Rice Crossing Rd.
Oroville
Wyandotte Rd.
Dunstone Rd.
Verjeles Rd.
To Chico & DH49 Pg 233
Loafer Creek CG
DAUGHERTY HILL
HOLMAN HILL
To Orland
To CVA III Pg. 498
To Marysville
To CVA IV Pg. 499
To Hwy 20

DH7 Quincy – Oroville

Bucks Lake Rd / Big Creek Rd / Oroville-Quincy Hwy

Distance:	58.5 mi / 94.1 km	Traffic:	Light

DH9 DH57 DH21 DH7 DH3 DH42

At a Glance

TIRES	
Twistiness	30/30
Pavement	17.4/20
Engineering	6.3/10
Remoteness	6.4/10
Scenery	8.6/15
Character	13.2/15
Total	**81.9**

When the Impressionist painters spoke about light and dark, they meant the imagery of shape and emotion as interpreted by the texture and translucent color of their paint. Frankly, while their stuff may be hanging in the Musée d'Orsay in Paris, it doesn't compare to this Post-Impressionist work of art painted against the background of the Plumas National Forest. And as fine a composition as this is on the steadily winding climb from Quincy up to Grizzly Peak, it's south of the summit that the road artist has really created a masterpiece. Here, the dark Pavement has been colored with a light Engineering touch that has allowed this tour de force to retain an almost transcendent Twistiness. The landscape's scenic motif throughout is largely varied forest, though the contrasting juxtaposition of Lake Oroville in the lower part of the picture does intrigue. The piece's Character is enhanced by the variety of valley, high country and lakeside climatic themes. There's a balanced symmetry in the inherent Remoteness: it's heightened the higher up you are and it's lower down low. No doubt you'll appreciate all three state-of-the-art DHs curated south of Quincy, even if normally you just mean toast when you speak about light and dark. Yes, to be exposed to sublime asphart like this makes one weep for what can be. After all, while you may not know much about art, you know what you like.

Access

From Oroville

On Hwy 162

Take 162 east all the way through town. Once you pass Forbestown Rd (**TE-B**), you are on the road.

Coming in on DH3 Greenville/Quincy – Oroville (Hwy 70)

Continue south on Hwy 70 until you get to the Hwy 162 jct at Oroville. Follow the instructions above.

From Quincy

Coming in on DH3 Oroville – Quincy (Hwy 70)

As you enter downtown Quincy, watch for the Buck's Lake Rd junction on your right. Take it. When you pass the "End 30 mph (50 kmh)" zone, you'll be on the road.

Coming in on DH21 Challenge – East Quincy (Quincy)
Head west to and then through Quincy on one-way Lawrence St. At the end of Lawrence, turn left on Crescent St and then right on Buck's Lake Rd. Once the 30-mph (50-kmh) zone ends, you're on the road.

On The Road

The road starts out in the Spanish Creek valley. It's fairly straight at first as it runs alongside open fields, gradually leaving the straggly bits of Quincy behind. At 2.0 mi (3.2 km), the valley narrows to a forested gorge. The excellently paved but blasé curves tighten into enthusiastic, high-speed sweepers.

The route rests briefly along the creek before a short incline takes it up across a rockface. This is followed by a descent that puts you back on the bottom of the now-widened gorge. An easing straight is interrupted by a turnoff for Shake Lake at 4.0 mi (6.4 km). The sharp right-hander at the end of the straightaway marks the retightening of the gorge, the return of corners and the disappearance of the bit of intermittent shoulder. Too bad the curves disappear as well when you enter the outskirts of the small but sprawling community of Meadow Valley at 5.2 mi (8.4 km).

The "End 35 mph" sign presages the last bit of Meadow Valley at 7.5 mi (12.1 km). Immediately, the road begins to wind and climb along a right side rockface. At 8.3 mi (13.4 km), you reach a Y junction. Bucks Lake Rd (**TE-A**) continues straight on. To stay on the DH (now Big Creek Rd), **bear left**.

The pavement's a little coarser but the tight, essing curves are now plentiful as the road tracks a side slope in the narrowed, heavily forested gorge. In fact, some of them are so tight, they're a little blind. Despite that, the heightened sense of remoteness entices you confidently into them. At least, when the crumbling shoulder inclines haven't shed gravel all over the road.

At 14.6 mi (23.5 km), the pavement picks up a grade but alas, straightens out at the same time. This trend continues as you rejoin Buck's Lake Rd at 16.9 mi (27.2 km). The south end of **TE-A** is right. The DH, taking up its old moniker, continues **straight ahead**.

Bucklin Rd comes in right at 18.9 mi (30.4 km), providing access to the west side of Bucks Lake. Despite the fact that you begin curving again after this junction, a chill soon passes over you. That's because the next sign you see is for something called "The Bucks Lake Meadow Subdivision". Brrr….

But soon you're back in the forest warming your tires through a consistent collection of curves interrupted by only the occasional straight. The terrain changes and the air cools as you climb gradually but steadily. The valley of Grizzly Creek opens to your right. The trees assume a shrunken, alpine character as they crowd in closer to the road. Tiny, pink wildflowers try to restrain the erosion on the bare, shallow left-side slope at 22.4 mi (36.1 km). Whether you notice any of this will depend to a large extent on whether you're riding an SV 800 or a ZX-10R.

The road finally levels off at 26.5 mi (42.6 km). Somewhere before the early downhill grade sign is the unmarked Grizzly Summit (5840 ft / 1793 m). After a brief straight through the thinned-out forest, the twisting recommences on the downward slope along with the same even pavement and consistent engineering. You'd be forgiven for thinking that it can't get much better. But you'd be mistaken.

At 29.1 mi (46.8 km), the asphalt smoothes out brilliantly. Dark gray perfection right down to the bit of extra paved comfort you like to have outside the white edge markers. Don't let that little bit of a straight bother you. The 25-mph (40-kmh) advisory/twisties ahead sign at 30.7 mi (49.4 km) is your cue to snick down a couple gears, bring your engine to a boil and tuck in.

At first, you think it's just another overcautious advisory. But the three bikes whooshing by on the opposite shoulder suggest that this may not be the case. The right-hander is definitely tight. If you're not quite ready for it, the extra three feet outside the white line should help.

Take a breather. Some mellower curves and one more brief straight bracket a second warning sign indicating the 13 per cent downhill grade. Another low-speed advisory marks the return of curving prior to yet a *third* grade sign saying the same thing. They're sure worried someone's not paying attention.

You ease gently into the multiple and often-essed curves that begin at 32.7 mi (52.6 km). And whenever they're extra tight or have degraded sightlines due to their radius or encroaching shrubbery, the road artist has lovingly laid down as wide a piece of pavement as he could outside the white sidelines. As you dive from one apex to another, the S-curves feel virtually continuous. You're on one of those beautiful works that invites you to fully explore your bike's – and your own – abilities. If anyone asks why you ride, send 'em here.

A few buildings make up Mountain House either side of the road at 39.3 mi (63.2 km). It's straighter past the mapdot and you quickly reach the north turnoff for Bald Rock Rd and the end of the Plumas National Forest, at 41.1 mi (66.1 km).

TOUR NOTE: If you need to stop for precious fluids, access to the bar and/or gas on rough Bald Rock is less painful from its smoother southern access just ahead.

Past the first Bald Rock turnoff, you're raving once again in a mosh pit of curves that's interrupted by a straight through some scattered development. The turns return to escort you around the end of the western arm of tiny Lake Madrone at 46.8 mi (75.3 km). Then the pavement quality drops slightly, the road straightens and the terrain opens up before you reach the south turnoff for Bald Rock Rd at 47.9 mi (77.1 km).

A set of esses past the southern turnoff gradually gives way to straights along with another loose collection of buildings. Its 45-mph (70-kmh) speed zone ends just after you get your first distant glimpse of Lake Oroville. You are now on the west side of the widening Canyon Creek valley. There's the odd curve but it's pretty straight along here. Then, at 51.8 mi (83.4 km), you see your first Hwy 162 sign. The roadside terrain steepens abruptly and you're into another sweet section.

Suddenly, at 52.7 mi (84.8 km), the rockface on the right shoulder disappears and you're on a bridge crossing an arm of Lake Oroville. A right-hander after the bridge has you winding south along a rocky incline on the eastern side of one of the large lake's lesser arms. And, yes, this terrain does make for lots more corners, many of them essed together. Another great stretch. The downside is that it can be tough to get by any traffic but, hey, if that's the case, check out how huge Lake Oroville is.

At 55.7 mi (89.6 km), you start across a mini-Golden Gate bridge. That huge arm of water it crosses eventually becomes the Mid Fork Feather River far away somewhere to your left. On the south side of the bridge, there are only a few more curves as the terrain flattens out and the road moves off the lake. At 58.5 mi (94.1 km), you reach Forbestown Rd (**TE-B**) and the end of the DH. Sure is nice and warm down here.

Twisted Edges

TE-A Bucks Lake Rd (7.4 mi / 11.9 km)
Bypass TEs aren't generally short cuts, but this particular one is. It offers better views, less traffic and less scattered gravel than on the better-engineered parallel section of the DH. Pavement's variable and not quite up to the DH's standards, but the twisties are tighter on the climb through the trees from the north end. Then it straightens to let you enjoy some high, east-facing views before dropping down to the lakeside bars and resorts at its south end. Even in its twistiest sections, the road's dotted center line ensures constant passing opportunities for the bold and powerful. Good for when you do get behind a pylon trailer-queening his boat out to the lake.

TE-B Forbestown Rd - Challenge Cutoff Rd (16.6 mi / 26.7 km)
Despite the good blacktop and the "Twisty Next 8 Miles" indicators coming out of Oroville, the market for curves is pretty flat for the first two quarters. And when the twistiness index goes up on the forested climb west of Forbestown, the pavement index goes down, making it hard to get a decent return on your investment until after the asphalt corrects, east of town. Expect little traffic but modest remoteness and scenery dividends. Though you do get some sporadic dead cat bounce views of Lake Oroville.

RIDER'S LOG: **DATE RIDDEN:** **YOUR RATING: /10**

How do you rate Northern California's 74 Destination Highways?
Go to destinationhighways.com *and let other riders know.*

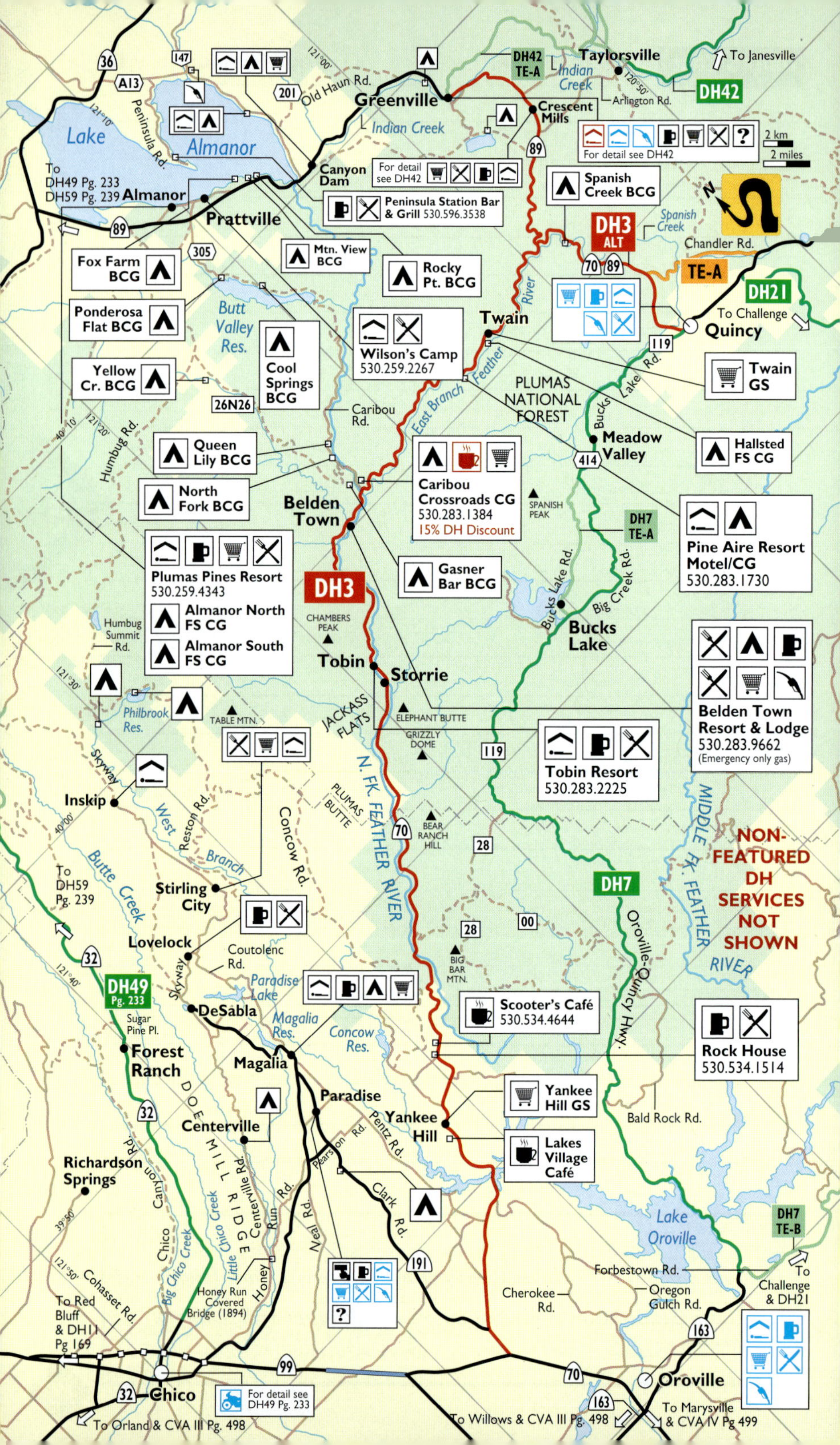
Taylorsville
To Janesville
DH42
DH42 TE-A
Indian Creek
Arlington Rd.
Greenville
Old Haun Rd.
Crescent Mills
Indian Creek
For detail see DH42
2 km
2 miles
Lake Almanor
Peninsula Rd.
Canyon Dam
For detail see DH42
To DH49 Pg. 233
DH59 Pg. 239
Almanor
Prattville
Peninsula Station Bar & Grill 530.596.3538
Spanish Creek BCG
DH3 ALT
Spanish Creek
Chandler Rd.
TE-A
DH21
To Challenge
Quincy
Fox Farm BCG
Mtn. View BCG
Rocky Pt. BCG
Ponderosa Flat BCG
Butt Valley Res.
Cool Springs BCG
Wilson's Camp 530.259.2267
Twain
Twain GS
Yellow Cr. BCG
Caribou Rd.
East Branch
Feather River
PLUMAS NATIONAL FOREST
Bucks Lake Rd.
Meadow Valley
Hallsted FS CG
Queen Lily BCG
North Fork BCG
Caribou Crossroads CG 530.283.1384
15% DH Discount
Humbug Rd.
Belden Town
SPANISH PEAK
DH7 TE-A
Pine Aire Resort Motel/CG 530.283.1730
Plumas Pines Resort 530.259.4343
Almanor North FS CG
Almanor South FS CG
DH3
Gasner Bar BCG
Bucks Lake Rd.
Big Creek Rd.
Bucks Lake
Humbug Summit Rd.
CHAMBERS PEAK
Tobin
Storrie
Belden Town Resort & Lodge 530.283.9662
(Emergency only gas)
Philbrook Res.
TABLE MTN.
JACKASS FLATS
ELEPHANT BUTTE
GRIZZLY DOME
Tobin Resort 530.283.2225
Skyway
Inskip
West Branch
Reston Rd.
Concow Rd.
PLUMAS BUTTE
N. FK. FEATHER RIVER
BEAR RANCH HILL
MIDDLE FK. FEATHER RIVER
NON-FEATURED DH SERVICES NOT SHOWN
To DH59 Pg. 239
Butte Creek
Stirling City
DH7
Oroville-Quincy Hwy.
Lovelock
Coutolenc Rd.
BIG BAR MTN.
DH49 Pg. 233
Paradise Lake
Sugar Pine Pl.
DeSabla
Magalia Res.
Concow Res.
Scooter's Café 530.534.4644
Rock House 530.534.1514
Forest Ranch
Magalia
DOE MILL RIDGE
Paradise
Yankee Hill GS
Yankee Hill
Bald Rock Rd.
Centerville
Pentz Rd.
Pearson Rd.
Lakes Village Café
Richardson Springs
Canyon Rd.
Centerville Rd.
Run Rd.
Clark Rd.
Lake Oroville
DH7 TE-B
Chico Creek
Neal Rd.
Big Chico Creek
Little Chico Creek
Honey Run Rd.
Honey Run Covered Bridge (1894)
Forbestown Rd.
To Challenge & DH21
Cherokee Rd.
Oregon Gulch Rd.
Cohasset Rd.
To Red Bluff & DH11 Pg 169
Chico
For detail see DH49 Pg. 233
Oroville
To Orland & CVA III Pg. 498
To Willows & CVA III Pg. 498
To Marysville & CVA IV Pg 499

DH3 Oroville – Greenville/Quincy

Hwy 70 / Hwy 89

Distance:	71.2 mi / 114.6 km 67.6 mi / 108.8 km	Traffic:	Can Be Heavy

At a Glance

Whether you're an aging boomer taking your Harley out on the open road for the first time or an experienced belly-shover about to flip the dial on his trusty ZX9R, there are a lot of reasons to point your wheels toward the Feather River Canyon. With its true surface, consistent camber and fine sightlines, this riverside DH has none of those nasty surprises that can cause a novice to piss their chaps. And yet there's enough bite to the frequent S-curves and sweepers to keep the interest of those who like riding a little closer to the edge. Engineering is not only great on the side to side, it's refined on the up and down as well. Apart from one sharp, doodle-dandy climb up Yankee Hill after the straight wheatfield flat and foothills north of Oroville, the grades along the river are never steep. Rather, the road moves gradually from high, essing cliffside sections to low, sweepier, waterside segments. Frequent changes in elevation and numerous bridge crossings provide changing perspectives on scenes that range from barren rock to thick forest to dramatic granitescapes around Grizzly Dome and Elephant Butte Tunnels. Unless you ride it on a busy summer weekend, this road's Remoteness scores high as well with little development and no speed-zoned towns to interrupt the flow. Now if only those crotchrockets would get a move on.

TIRES	
Twistiness	26.8/ 30
Pavement	17.8/ 20
Engineering	7.0/ 10
Remoteness	6.1/ 10
Scenery	11.5/ 15
Character	14.2/ 15
Total	**83.4**

Access

From Oroville

Coming in on DH7 Quincy – Oroville (Oroville-Quincy Hwy)

Follow Hwy 162 through Oroville. When you reach Hwy 70, head north. The divided highway ends at the junction with Hwy 149 (the spur to Hwy 99). Veer right to keep going on Hwy 70. You're on the road.

From Greenville

On Hwy 89

Go south. You're on the road

From Quincy (ALT)

Coming in on DH7 Quincy – Oroville (Oroville-Quincy Hwy)

Turn left on Hwy 70. When you clear town, you're on the road.

Coming in on DH21 Challenge – East Quincy (Quincy)
Go left on Hwy 70. Pass through Quincy. When you clear town, you're on the road.

On The Road

It's a boring start to this DH from the busy Hwy 70/149 intersection north of Oroville. In fact, there's not a curve to be seen on the yellow-dotted straightaway that blasts east through the brushcut wheatfields. Necklaces of green oak drape over the blonde landscape in the foothills ahead. But even when you reach the hills the road doesn't waver, despite the many dips, depressions, hollows and grass-covered cuts in the rising landscape.

The first actual curve comes at 6.8 mi (10.9 km). It's not much but it is enough to result in the dotted line being replaced by a double one. Then a long, slow sweeper crests atop the steep, grassy embankment that rolls down to a tiny finger of Lake Oroville. The road switches to four lanes at 7.7 mi (12.4 km) just in time to cross a broad, northern arm of the lake. Red-Tailed Hawks fly overhead. Honda Hawks fly below them.

The bridge ends and the steep but excellently engineered, gently sweeping climb up Yankee Hill begins. There are broad overlooks to the left and right, made broader since the confederacy of oaks is defeated and reduced to shrubbery on the drying ascent. If you want a better view, there's a vista point to your left at 11.4 mi (18.3 km). But who wants to break up the steady rhythm of a good Acura Grand Slalom?

You're back into a forested setting at 11.1 mi (17.9 km). Pines settle on the striking, red-hued rock. Four lanes resolve into two at 12.4 mi (20.0 km) and once past the dot of Yankee Hill, the DH starts to feel more like a typical NorCal Destination Highway. Especially when the curves begin at 13.9 mi (22.4 km).

You sense you're in the right place when you pass the motorcycle-themed Scooters Café on the left at 15.1 mi (24.3 km). Your instincts are confirmed as a short series of esses sweeps you toward the blue skyline defined by low domes, mountains and ridges of the northern Sierra Nevada.

At 16.1 mi (25.9 km), you pass a closed café, the last structure you'll see for a while, and snuggle up against the high bank of the Feather River Canyon. It's a beautiful scene looking right over the chasm to Big Bar Mtn. And there's an even more beautiful view ahead: your first twisties sign.

And so begins the absolutely stellar section that snakes along the canyon's edge before entering Plumas National Forest at 17.5 mi (28.2 km). Pavement and engineering continue to be outstanding across the line, matched by the captivating scenery over the gorge. If you find it too captivating to keep your eyes on the road, there's a wide pullout/viewpoint where you can stop and take it all in.

More sets of twisties follow more twisties signs as you nose past 2000 ft

(606 m) in elevation. The curves get progressively tighter as the road battles the terrain, hugging the steep, granite cliff that rises above the river's dramatic gorge, lined here by retained walls. The riding drama intensifies on the approach to a high, steel girder bridge that crosses the river at 20.8 mi (33.5 km).

Once on the south side of the water, you're back into a bit of woods. The pavement's improved but the curves are much gentler since the roadside's not as steep as it was on the previous side. It's still very charming though as the corners ess together on a steady descent that takes you down closer to the river. The sight of the road winding ahead against the treed and mountained backdrop is so pretty, you might want to take a longer look. Which you can do at the riverside rest stop at 26.6 mi (42.8 km).

At 27.0 mi (43.4 km), you pass through a short tunnel and emerge to find big slabs of solid granite slanting down to the river. Huge boulders fill the watercourse forcing the river to roil around them. Linear stains on the vertical granite that define the west side of the bubbling river give the appearance of endlessly dripping water. It's a magnificent scene, its centerpiece a massive, purple monolith towering above the road, dwarfing the tiny tunnel at its bottom. From a distance, the entrance looks so small, you might think you'd need to have a pocket bike to get through.

This is Grizzly Dome Tunnel, constructed 1936. You're quickly in and out of its blackness, emerging at 28.8 mi (46.3 km), but almost immediately you're spelunking again through the much longer Elephant Butte Tunnel. There's a bit of an opening in the middle of this bore to add some light to the otherwise pitch darkness. Which is helpful, considering you probably haven't bothered to remove your Serengetis.

And if it's summertime, you definitely need them as you shimmy along shining water at the bottom of a gleaming rockface. What you don't need on this stretch, however, is a whole lot of side tread since the road straightens at 27.9 mi (44.9 km) and continues this way with but a handful of curves once you cross the river again at 31.0 mi (49.9 km). The ensuing section west of the river, site of a hydro-electric substation and a popular roadside swimming spot is known as Jackass Flats. Oddly, the speed tax collectors rarely seem to lie in wait here.

You pass what's left of historic Storrie and cross back to the east side of the river at 33.7 mi (54.2 km) for just enough time to pass what's left of historic Tobin. There may be some history here but there's not much in the way of geography. All that's left of the canyon's elegant granite-filled setting is a few smooth boulders in the river. The surrounding terrain has returned to more commonplace California pine forest. These bridges are getting mighty commonplace, too. You're quickly over another one and across the river at 35.0 mi (56.3 km).

The valley is wider now or at least seems that way since the upward slope on either side of the river is not as steep as it was before. Or maybe it's the widened road with the short passing lane at 37.2 mi (59.9 km) that gives that impression. Curves return, mostly in the form of gentle, consistent sweepers. These become tighter and more concentrated through some rough, steeper-sided spots beyond 38.1 mi (61.3 km). Tiny Rock Creek Dam at 40.4 mi (65.0 km) creates a small pool in the river. Or swimming hole, depending on how hot it is. If you'd rather have a cold beverage, the optional bridge crossing to the funky little settlement of Belden Town is at 42.8 mi (68.9 km).

Things continue sweet past the Belden turn. Sweep, sweep, sweep, then cross the river again at 44.6 mi (71.8 km). The North Fork Feather River heads toward Lake Almanor while you continue east above what is now the East Branch North Fork Feather. The A-1 pavement gives up more sweepers and that first one's even a bit tricky – a little longer and tighter than it seems at first. And if you feather your brake a little as you apex, well, no one has to know.

ROUTING OPTION: Caribou Rd starts as pavement but gravel makes up roughly 50 per cent of the route along the river and the Butt Valley Reservoir up toward Hwy 89 on the south shore of Lake Almanor.

You're high above the East Branch, but immediately start descending a variably graded slope of sharp, jutting rock. Its grey and black shading gives way to bright red hues at 48.6 mi (78.2 km) as you venture into the river's oven-like canyon. It's not so dry that you're surprised to see pine trees dot the patches of topsoil that layer the rock on the higher levels above the road. But it is strange to see a few water-loving cedars amid the pines.

It's not strange, however, to see sweeper-loving motorcyclists on this stretch of asphalt. The curves are tight enough to get you leaned over but well-engineered enough that you can keep your speed up entering into the next one. Perfect.

The sweepers are interrupted at 52.2 mi (84.0 km) by a short four lane straight. It shoots you into a thickly treed section that comes as a cool relief after all the heat-reflecting rock. An old, closed gas station at 53.2 mi (85.6 km) bears a sign that says "Crisis Coming." Whatever crisis they're referring to, it's hard to understand why that justifies shutting down a perfectly good gas station. Especially if you're on reserve.

A longer straightaway ensues at 54.5 mi (87.7 km). It takes you past the Twain Store and lasts to 55.6 mi (89.5 km) where a couple of curves provide minor relief. But then the road unkinks again to 57.1 mi (91.9 km). It's not only straight here, it's not particularly scenic. Though you're again edging along the river, your view of it is blocked by a thick pine and oak forest sprinkled with out-of-place cedar.

"Slower Traffic Please Use Turnouts to Allow Passing" announces the sign at 57.7 mi (92.8 km). Why add "to allow passing"? Obviously the duller pylons need further admonishment.

The pattern of moderate sweepers separated by straights continues, though the curves gradually tighten to 30-35 mph (50-55- kmh) corners.

The ever-thickening forest is interrupted only by a barren, uprising grey cliff. At 61.1 mi (98.3 km), you reach the junction with Hwy 89. Here the East Branch divides into Indian Creek going north and Spanish Creek heading south. The DH splits, too, with the primary route turning left on Hwy 89 to Greenville and the alternative continuing on Hwy 70 to Quincy*.

Hwy 70/Hwy 89 Jct – Greenville (Hwy 89)

A beautiful water vista awaits after you turn left at the junction and sweep low along the quiet shoreline of Indian Creek. You gain a little elevation at 62.8 mi (101.0 km) giving you a nice vantage point over to the distinctively shaped boulders across the water. With their white sheen, the stalactite-like droopings remind you of icicles. Which, in turn, remind you of how unbelievably hot you are.

Long, lingering curves propel you up along a cliff of red and white rock in and out of the forest. More remarkable rock forms abutting the creek take on the likeness of totems or statues. The road drops back to creek level at 65.2 mi (104.9 km) and straightens a little. Then it rises back up at 65.9 mi (106.0 km) and delivers a few more sweepers before dropping down again into Indian Valley. You reach Arlington Rd, an access route to **DH42 Taylorsville – Janesville**, right at 67.1 mi (108.0 km).

The little berg of Crescent Mills lies just beyond the turnoff at 67.9 mi (109.3 km). Not a bad stop if you plan on doing **DH42** rather than continuing to Greenville. After a short stretch through some wheatfields, the road re-enters the forest at the northern edge of the valley where it climbs and drops down a six-per-cent grade in a sinewy section of winding sweepers, aided by a passing lane. The speed zone for the charming town of Greenville comes at 71.2 mi (114.6 km).

**DH ALT Hwy 70/Hwy 89 Jct – Quincy (Hwy 70/89)*

There may be an increase in traffic as you bridge Indian Creek and edge along the canyon wall above what is now Spanish Creek. And that would be a shame since the section of the *ALT* immediately south of the intersection is its best part. If you're in luck, a conscientious pylon or two will use the mid-climb pullout at 62.7 mi (100.9 km).

You gain height above the river from the steep canyon wall that rises above the creek. The easy, graceful sweepiness continues up to the high bridge across Spanish Creek at 63.6 mi (102.3 km). Over the crossing, with the cliff now dropping to your left, the sweepers clench up a little. The road moves off this watercourse at 65.9 mi (106.0 km) and onto Little Blackhawk Creek. It then delivers a final flurry of corners before straightening out at 66.3 mi (106.7 km) for the straight run into Quincy. This is where the speed tax collectors like to park on the shoulder. The DH ends in the tall pines when it junctions with Chandler Rd (**TE-A**), at 67.6 mi (108.8 km).

NAVIGATION: ***TE-A*** *can be easy to miss. It goes off left about a quarter mile north of the Mt Hough Ranger Station. If you see the ranger station you've passed the TE.*

Twisted Edges

TE-A Chandler Rd (6.0 mi / 9.6 km)

This mellow, mostly straight bypass up the American Valley avoids the bright lights of Quincy/East Quincy. You'll still find development, children and dogs at the western end, and sometimes the local sheriff. But at least you get away from the State Stormtroopers for a spell.

TOUR NOTE: At 2.3 mi (3.7 km) from the western end, there is a swimming hole where the road crosses Spanish Creek. At the eastern end of the TE, there's another one a quarter mile back toward Quincy on the main road.

Rider's Log: **Date Ridden:** **Your Rating: /10**

Map Tip: Services on non-featured DHs and TEs are generally shown as bare icon only. For the full detail, just turn to the featured map.

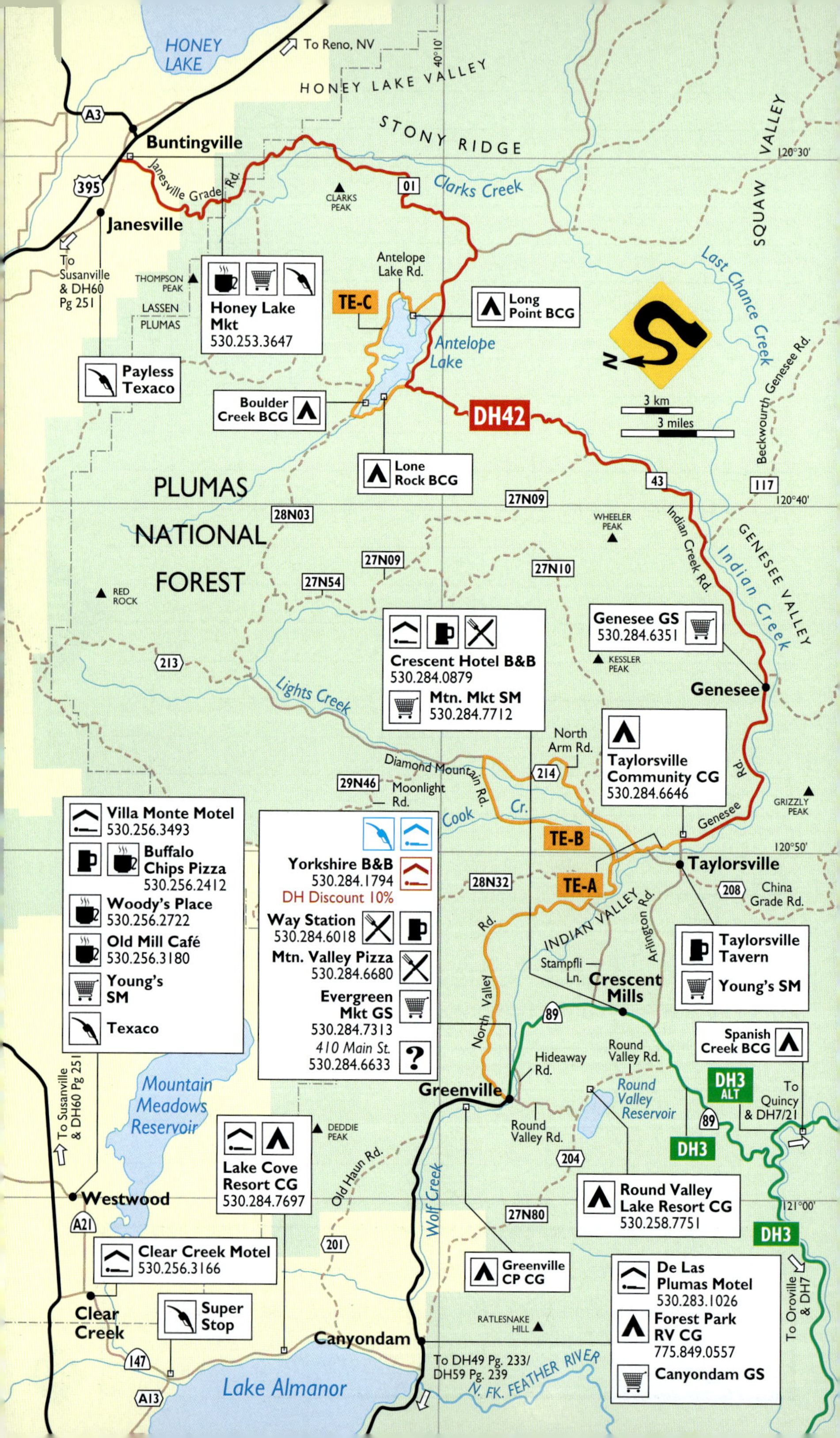

HONEY LAKE
To Reno, NV
HONEY LAKE VALLEY
STONY RIDGE
40°10'
A3
Buntingville
395
Janesville Grade Rd.
Janesville
To Susanville & DH60 Pg 251
01
Clarks Creek
CLARKS PEAK
THOMPSON PEAK
LASSEN
PLUMAS
Honey Lake Mkt 530.253.3647
Antelope Lake Rd.
TE-C
Long Point BCG
Antelope Lake
Payless Texaco
Boulder Creek BCG
DH42
Lone Rock BCG
SQUAW VALLEY
120°30'
Last Chance Creek
Beckwourth Genesee Rd.
3 km
3 miles
43
117
120°40'
PLUMAS NATIONAL FOREST
28N03
27N09
WHEELER PEAK
Indian Creek Rd.
GENESEE VALLEY
Indian Creek
27N09
27N54
27N10
RED ROCK
Genesee GS 530.284.6351
KESSLER PEAK
213
Crescent Hotel B&B 530.284.0879
Mtn. Mkt SM 530.284.7712
Genesee
Lights Creek
North Arm Rd.
Taylorsville Community CG 530.284.6646
Diamond Mountain Rd.
214
29N46
Moonlight Rd.
Cook Cr.
Genesee Rd.
GRIZZLY PEAK
TE-B
120°50'
Taylorsville
TE-A
28N32
208
China Grade Rd.
Villa Monte Motel 530.256.3493
Buffalo Chips Pizza 530.256.2412
Woody's Place 530.256.2722
Old Mill Café 530.256.3180
Young's SM
Texaco
Yorkshire B&B 530.284.1794
DH Discount 10%
Way Station 530.284.6018
Mtn. Valley Pizza 530.284.6680
Evergreen Mkt GS 530.284.7313
410 Main St. 530.284.6633
INDIAN VALLEY
Arlington Rd.
Stampfli Ln.
Crescent Mills
Taylorsville Tavern
Young's SM
North Valley Rd.
89
Spanish Creek BCG
Hideaway Rd.
Round Valley Rd.
DH3 ALT
To Quincy & DH7/21
Mountain Meadows Reservoir
To Susanville & DH60 Pg 251
Greenville
Round Valley Reservoir
Round Valley Rd.
89
DH3
DEDDIE PEAK
Lake Cove Resort CG 530.284.7697
204
Old Haun Rd.
Wolf Creek
Round Valley Lake Resort CG 530.258.7751
Westwood
A21
27N80
121°00'
201
DH3
Clear Creek Motel 530.256.3166
Greenville CP CG
De Las Plumas Motel 530.283.1026
Forest Park RV CG 775.849.0557
Canyondam GS
To Oroville & DH7
Clear Creek
Super Stop
RATLESNAKE HILL
Canyondam
147
To DH49 Pg. 233/ DH59 Pg. 239
N. FK. FEATHER RIVER
Lake Almanor
A13

DH42 Taylorsville – Janesville (Susanville)

Genesee Rd / Indian Creek Rd / Janesville Grade Rd (FSR 43/01)

Distance:	41.0 mi / 66.0 km	Traffic:	Light

At a Glance

Some roads are like an old friend – comfortable to be with, welcoming and dependable. This remote, crustily paved curmudgeon, however, is not one of them. Oh, it starts off pleasantly enough, sweeping south of Taylorsville along Indian Creek, where it graciously offers you some easygoing curves on the embankment. And there's nothing objectionable about the mostly straight, scenic ride through the mountain-backed ranches and hayfields on the flat Genesee Valley floor, either. That's why you're so taken aback by the temperamental Pavement, fickle, off-camber Engineering and all the sand in the corners on the canyon climb out of the valley. Even when the camber improves, the asphalt smoothes and the sand settles down around Antelope Lake, the high-maintenance S-curves can be very demanding. You can live with the fact there are very few curve advisories, but you'd think a center line that wasn't faded to invisibility would be a basic courtesy. You miss its guidance, especially when the road widens on the tightly sweeping FSR 01 section. The yellow finally brightens up – albeit as a solid double – on the steep, scenic final descent into Janesville. Thing is, at the same time the views over the Honey Lake Valley are attracting your attention, the steep switchbacks are bumpy enough to betray you if you don't keep an eye on them. As with most difficult and complex personalities, it may take a few encounters to really bond with this DH. But once you do, you'll be riding buddies for life.

TIRES	
Twistiness	30/30
Pavement	11.9/20
Engineering	4.3/10
Remoteness	7.2/10
Scenery	9.4/15
Character	6.7/15
Total	**69.5**

Access

From Taylorsville

Head east through town to the junction at the campground. Turn right. You're on the road.

Coming in on TE-A North Valley Rd

Arlington Rd, the junction for Taylorsville, is at the south end of the TE. When you pass it, you're on the road.

From Susanville

Via Hwy 395

Look for the Chevron Station/Honey Lake Market. Janesville Grade Rd turns off Hwy 395 here. Take it. You're on the road.

On The Road

If you want to bed down at the west end of this road, the Community CG is Taylorville's best and only option. It's not a bad one though, especially as the DH starts right outside its entrance and heads south through unusually tall, airy pines on Genesee Rd. Grizzly Peak rises up in the distance above the road while Indian Creek is visible on the right. All in all, pleasantly scenic. Now if could just become pleasantly curvy.

And it does. Easy curves guide you along some rock cliffs that lift up the road starting at 1.4 mi (2.3 km). The corners tighten as you gain height. The terrain roughens too, especially once you pass the ranch on the right at 2.4 mi (3.9 km). Nice spot to raise horses. Particularly iron ones.

The curves get faster and sweepier as the ride bends east through the forest. Glimpses of the mountains through the pines are more frequent since the taller trees have few low branches. This improves the sightlines as well and it all adds up to a good rhythm section of long S-curves. At 5.3 mi (8.5 km), the forest recedes and you emerge into the broad Genesee Valley. Yellow hayfields and black cows. And the one-store town of Genesee at 6.0 mi (9.7 km).

It's quaint here in the Genesee Valley. And it's even more charming when you realize that you may not have to sacrifice too much curvitude. A sharp, 25-mph (40-kmh) curve kicks off a winding series that takes you back up the valley's side and into some loose stands of trees. When you subsequently come back down onto its floor, you enter a bucolic scene of chestnut horses grazing in the pastures of the Walking Ranch and Children's Summer Camp. "Slow Children at Play" says the sign. Not a word about dodging the somewhat faster wild turkeys.

Unless you count some very minor wig-wagging, you're now on a straightaway riding beside the fields through some archways of pines. There are houses and trailers scattered about. Some appear lived in, some don't. There's a kind of randomness to the whole scene. So you're not too surprised to see the locals veering their pickups across the centerline as you approach. Could be they're just off-duty UPS drivers.

Somehow you don't really mind the curveless break in the action. And if you do, you haven't much time to stew since the sweeper at 10.0 mi (16.1 km) marks the end of the only real straight section of the DH. Back in the trees, you climb and are met by a crude, homemade "Rocks on Road" sign at 11.1 mi (17.9 km). At least someone thought to mention it.

The change in the road's character is fast. A moment ago, you were drifting on a mellow plain and now you're essing tightly against a sandstone wall with a steep slope dropping off to the right. Too bad the off-camber corners are covered with dust, sand and tar snakes. Sure is remote, though. And scenic too, as gently sloped ridges dappled with rock and trees overlook the canyon where Last Chance Creek dribbles into Indian Creek. The view's even better if you're riding this section the other way.

The curves lengthen when you start a gradual descent. But this still doesn't prepare you for what happens at 13.3 mi (21.4 km). Here, all by itself in the middle of nowhere is an honest-to-God passing lane. Rub your visor – no, you haven't inadvertently gotten onto Hwy 395. This aberration lasts, oh, until 13.6 mi (21.9 km). It's so short and there's so little traffic that your chances of needing it are about the same as seeing a speed tax collector.

Curve, STC and scenery-wise, it's a nice section, but it's too bad about the dust-on-the-road thing. True, the blackness of the asphalt shows it off well but you really don't trust the integrity of the surface around the next corner until you're all the way down beside Indian Creek at 17.6 mi (28.3 km). It's no coincidence that this is when the camber improves and the road stretches out enough that you can see around the curves.

As nice as this scenery's been, you're ready for a change. The hardened shapes of sandstone on the left and in the creek at 20.1 (32.3 km) are interesting, but they're by in a flash. As you approach Antelope Lake, the landscape flattens and opens, revealing huge swaths of forest blackened by fire. At 21.6 mi (34.8 km), you reach Antelope Lake and the junction with **TE-C**. To stay on the DH, **turn right**.

The lake is pretty but you don't see that much of it once you cross the small causeway and wind tightly up away from the water through a forest of matchsticks. The burnt area is striking in its contrast to the road's otherwise woodsy feel. But at least it's good for the sightlines.

At 23.3 mi (37.5 km), you're back in un-charcoaled forest, descending in extremely twisty fashion through dense pines. Although there are still a few grains here and there, sand's no longer really a factor. Camber's okay in here too. This is also where you'll find some of the road's better pavement. At 24.9 mi (40.1 km) you reach an intersection signed "Janesville 16 Miles." Straight ahead is the other end of the **TE-C** loop. To stay on the DH, **follow the sign right**.

The pavement turns to grey after you make the turn. It's not quite as smooth but that's not the only difference. The curves aren't anywhere near as tight either. And the occasional off-camber corners are back. The road widens at 26.4 mi (42.5 km) as a sign warns of an upcoming stop sign. Good thing, since the stop sign itself is skillfully hidden behind a tree. This is the T-junction with FSR 01. **Turn left**.

ROUTING OPTION: Turning right will put you on a mostly paved 35.2 (56.7 km) route via FSRs 01, 03, 70, 111 and 177 down to Beckwourth on Hwy 70. (See ***DH9TE-H*** *for more information on this route.)*

Pavement's back to black on FSR 01, curving evenly through a flat scape of mixed pines and shrubs. The narrow, stunted trees, the sub-alpine-like openness and the terrain you can see below to the right give the feeling of high elevation. And if you don't get that sense yet, you soon will.

This section of the DH is much wider than it was before Antelope Lake. Camber's much better, too. Which is good, since a steep descent starts here and you can use all the road they give you to make it through the hairpinning S-curves. The juvenile Ponderosas by the roadside tend to stick their long, soft fronds right out over the pavement. As a result, they caress your helmet as you stay tight to the right before choosing your line through the next corner. Where's a fire when you need it?

The dome of Clark's Peak rises ahead and shows you the way. There's a clear view of it across the golden clearing at 31.6 mi (50.8 km). Despite the fact that most of the corners are blind, you're swooping downhill with speed through the tall, spaced, red-barked pines.

At 36.2 mi (58.2 km) a double yellow centerline appears, signaling the start of the Janesville Grade. Yellow markings on a road – what a concept. Big, tight switchbacks follow where the yellow is a definite plus. Not to nitpick, but a *single* dotted line would have been sufficient.

There are sweeping panoramas over the guardrails as you come down. The slope is steep enough that you get views over the trees to the dry Honey Lake Valley and the brown, wrinkled Amedee and Skedaddle Mtns beyond. At 37.1 mi (59.7 km), you skedaddle out of Plumas National Forest. Strange that past this point you get some of the road's best scenery. Don't get too caught up in it, though. That long, tight, bumpy-in-the-middle sweeper at 37.7 mi (60.7 km) can sneak up on you.

Corners continue sharp, lingering and bumpy the rest of the way down. At 38.9 mi (62.6 km), there's a 35-mph (55-kmh) sign and the terrain flattens. There's not too much development outside of Janesville apart from a few houses and couple of hobby ranches. There's one last overlook of the valley before you reach Hwy 395, and the end of the road at 41.0 mi (66.0 km).

Twisted Edges

TE-A Taylorsville – Greenville (11.3 mi / 18.2 km) *North Valley Rd*
There is a bit of development on this skirt around the edge of Native American Valley but you'll also find good pavement and some curves.

TE-B North Arm Rd - Diamond Mtn Rd (13.1 mi / 21.1 km)
This one rounds the edge of the farms, fields and forest of the Indian Valley offshoot. Similar to **TE-A**, the pavement is good and so are the curves.

*NAVIGATION/ROUTING OPTION: At the junction of North Arm and Diamond Mtn, make sure you don't take the non-TE part of the latter (unless you're a maxburner of course). It tracks Light Creek and leads to a gravel FSR road that connects with **TE-C** at the western end of Antelope Lake.*

TE-C Antelope Lake Rd (7.8 mi / 12.6 km)

Locals like to ride part way up the DH, loop around Antelope Lake and head back. The equally paved longer route around the north side of the lake is not as tight and twisty as the south. It stays much flatter but has more scenic lake views, particularly on the west end. Some pylon potential since this TE provides access to fishing spots, a picnic area and a couple campgrounds.

ROUTING NOTE: Maxburners might seek out the gravel turnoff left (straight if you're riding west) option 1.9 mi (3.1 km) from the west end of this TE. This half-gravel, half-paved road loops all the way back to ***TE-B****.*

RIDER'S LOG: **DATE RIDDEN:** **YOUR RATING: /10**

Just what is an "STC" or "maxburner" anyway?

Check out these and other Twisted Terms in the Glossary at p.??

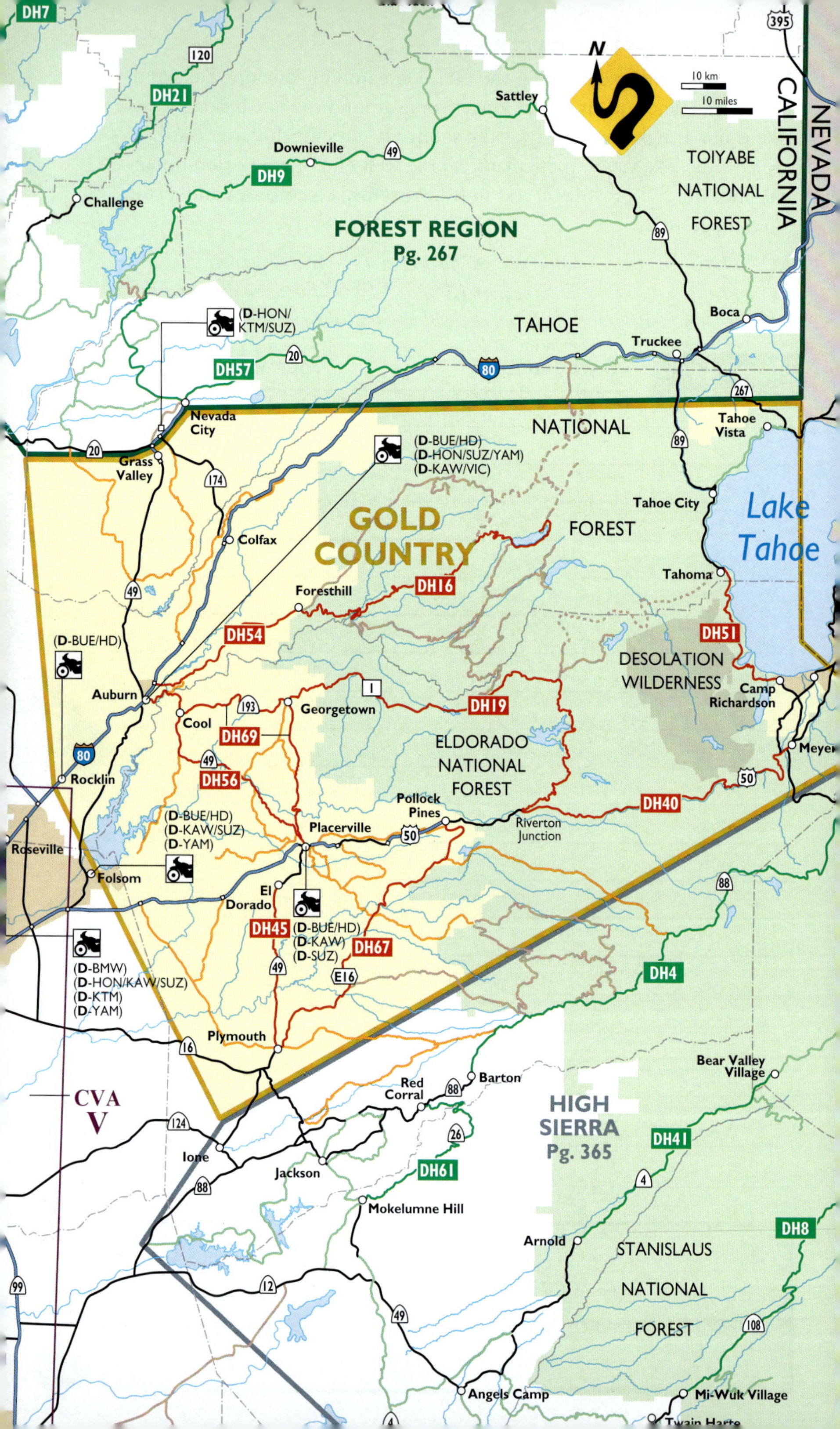

FOREST REGION
Pg. 267
GOLD COUNTRY
HIGH SIERRA
Pg. 365
TOIYABE NATIONAL FOREST
TAHOE NATIONAL FOREST
ELDORADO NATIONAL FOREST
STANISLAUS NATIONAL FOREST
DESOLATION WILDERNESS
Lake Tahoe
CALIFORNIA
NEVADA
10 km
10 miles
N
CVA
V
DH7
DH21
DH9
DH57
DH16
DH54
DH51
DH19
DH69
DH56
DH40
DH45
DH67
DH4
DH41
DH61
DH8
(D-HON/KTM/SUZ)
(D-BUE/HD)
(D-HON/SUZ/YAM)
(D-KAW/VIC)
(D-BUE/HD)
(D-BUE/HD)
(D-KAW/SUZ)
(D-YAM)
(D-BUE/HD)
(D-KAW)
(D-SUZ)
(D-BMW)
(D-HON/KAW/SUZ)
(D-KTM)
(D-YAM)
Sattley
Downieville
Challenge
Boca
Truckee
Nevada City
Grass Valley
Tahoe Vista
Tahoe City
Colfax
Foresthill
Tahoma
Auburn
Cool
Georgetown
Camp Richardson
Meyers
Rocklin
Roseville
Folsom
Pollock Pines
Placerville
Riverton Junction
El Dorado
Plymouth
Barton
Red Corral
Bear Valley Village
Ione
Jackson
Mokelumne Hill
Arnold
Angels Camp
Mi-Wuk Village
Twain Harte

Gold Country

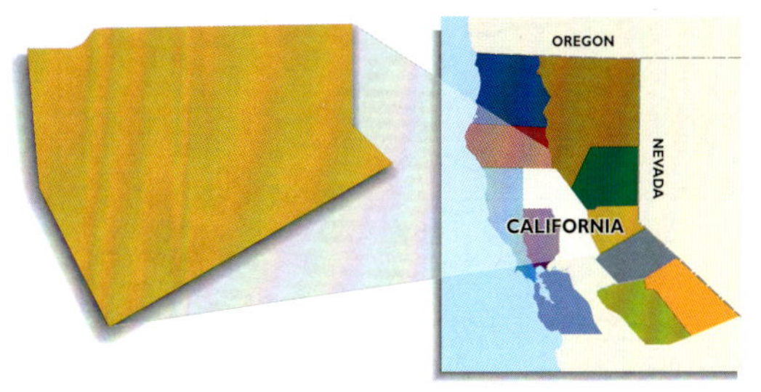

N
2 km
2 miles
To Cool & DH69
To Auburn & DH54
Pilot Hill
38°50'
121°00'
DH69
TE-A
Marshall Rd.
Black Oak Mine Rd.
To Georgetown & DH19
193
121°50'
NON-FEATURED DH SERVICES NOT SHOWN
RPS MS
(SUZ)
4516 Missouri Flat
530.295.8286
DH69
SLC
Lotus
Coloma
DH56
S. FORK AMERICAN RIVER
Hangtown HD
(BUE/HD)
629 Main
530.344.0401
High Country
530.642.1034
DH56
TE-C
FLAGSTAFF HILL
Folsom Lake
Cold Springs Rd.
Coloma Rd.
49
DH67
TE-A
To Pollock Pines & DH67
Placerville KOA CG
4655 Rock Barn Rd
530.676.2267
Salmon Falls Cutoff
Gold Hill Rd.
Weber Creek
Lotus Rd.
DH56
TE-B
Commelback Rd.
Middletown Rd.
PJ's Roadhouse
Aloha Gas
Placerville Dr.
Rd.
Placerville
Green Valley Rd.
Rescue
Green Valley Rd.
DH56
TE-A
Missouri Flat Rd.
Big Cut Rd.
DH67
TE-C
Silva Valley Pkwy.
Cameron Park
Exxon
50
Missouri Flat Rd.
Diamond Springs
DH67
TE-C
ALT
El Dorado Hills Blvd.
Serano Pkwy.
Rd.
Bass Lake
Greenstone Rd.
Lode Dr.
El Dorado
Mother Lode Dr.
38°40'
Shingle Springs
50
49
Irish Pub
530.622.2045
Chevron
Exxon
Mike's Cycle
(KAW)
291 Placerville
530.622.0209
To Sacramento
To CVA V
Pg. 500
TE-B
Golden Chain Hwy.
Union Mine Rd.
Toscana Winery & Bistro
209.245.3800
EL DORADO
SACRAMENTO
South Shingle Rd.
BEN BOLT RIDGE
El Dorado Grocery & Deli SM
Poor Red's BBQ
530.622.2901
El Dorado Gallery Café
530.622.3593
Sand Ridge Rd.
Plymouth Hotel
209.245.4544
Pokerville Mkt SM
Marlene & Glen's Diner
209.245.5578
Café in the Park
Incahoots
209.245.5544
Sierra Trading Post
Latrobe Rd.
SUGARLOAF
Nashville Cantina & Grill
530.620.5585
Shenandoah Inn
209.245.4491
Colina De Oro Mexican Rest
209.245.3278
Gold Country Café
209.245.6218
Texaco
Gold Beach Park CG
TE-A
Big Indian Creek
Bell Rd.
To Pollock Pines
DH67
EL DORADO
AMADOR
Cosumnes River
Shenandoah Rd.
To mid-DH4 Pg. 379
DH45
38°30'
Old Sacramento Rd.
TE-A
E16
Fiddletown Rd.
DH67
TE-F
To CVA V Pg 500
To Sacramento
Ione Rd.
SACRAMENTO
AMADOR
Plymouth
S. Fork Dry Creek
16
Carbondale Rd.
Imperial Hotel
209.267.9172
Mine House Inn B&B
209.267.5900
DH Discount 10%
Aquatic Cow
209.267.0605
Buffalo Emporium
209.267.0570
Drytown
Old Well Motel & Grill
209.245.6467
Irish Hill Rd.
Drytown Cellars
Willow Cr. Rd.
124
49
Amador City
DH67
TE-G
To Mokelumne Hill & DH61 Pg 385
Tonzi Rd.
To Stockton

DH45 PLYMOUTH – EL DORADO (PLACERVILLE)

Golden Chain Highway (Hwy 49)

DISTANCE:	14.3 mi / 23.0 km	TRAFFIC:	Moderate

DH45
DH67 DH56 DH54 DH16 DH69 DH19 DH40 DH51

AT A GLANCE

TIRES	
Twistiness	25.1/ 30
Pavement	15.6/ 20
Engineering	5.7/ 10
Remoteness	4.5/ 10
Scenery	9.4/ 15
Character	7.1/ 15
TOTAL	**67.4**

Erudite riders know that the mythical *Road to El Dorado* refers to Voltaire's novel, *Candide*. For everyone else, it's the title of a mediocre Disney film. But for all motorcyclists, the phrase is an evocative reminder that it's in the journey that the true riches lie. This surprisingly lightly trafficked stretch of the otherwise busy Hwy 49 isn't long, but it is memorable. Elysian Pavement and idyllic Engineering make for a whimsical and easy cornering ride through the quiet fields and cloistered groves north of Plymouth. There's a hint of suspense in the couple of tight turns into and out of a gorge in the middle but nothing you can't handle. Despite suffering great hardship on their travels, Candide's ever-optimistic companion, Dr. Pangloss, always insisted that life couldn't be better. Riding this road to El Dorado in the cooler, later part of the day and watching the sun set behind the curtain of oaks, you'll agree that Pangloss was right: even though we share it with speed tax collectors, this is indeed the "best of all possible worlds."

ACCESS

From Plymouth

On Hwy 49

Coming in on DH67 Pollock Pines – Plymouth (E 16)

Go north on Hwy 49. Leave Plymouth and you're on the road.

From Placerville

On Hwy 49 or Hwy 50

Coming in on DH56 Auburn – Placerville (Hwy 49)

Coming in on DH69 Cool – Placerville (Hwy 193)

Follow Hwy 49 as it climbs south out of Placerville. The DH starts south of El Dorado.

ON THE ROAD

The road begins as a straight cut through a wide but shallow bowl of brown ranchland. Big Indian Creek flows in along the right, unnoticed but for the silver-green band of oak, ash and eucalyptus that charts its course. The road bends gently, then the sides of the bowl steepen and the thickening trees guide your Chief through some more pronounced turns. With the only signs of life a few fences and a little shack at 2.3 mi (3.7 km), it almost feels like 1948 again.

The curves ease up at 3.4 mi (5.5 km) when the terrain flattens and the trees back away behind the fields. But when you pass the 35-mph (55-kmh) advisory at 3.9 mi (6.3 km), they come back, encompassing that sharp, but quick corner as well as the milder, sweepier ones that bridge the Cosumnes River at 4.8 mi (7.7 km). No drop in pavement quality here as you enter El Dorado County. If anything, it's even better.

There is a little more development north of the county line, though. Some houses perch above and below the road, providing local trade for the Nashville Cantina & Grill, the DH's only refreshment option at 6.8 mi (10.9 km). 'Course, mebbe y'all are jest too busy pickin' and grinnin' your way through the well-tuned turns to be stoppin' right now, anyhoo.

A sense of remoteness returns at 7.9 mi (12.7 km), right about the point you pass the one-lane Union Mine Rd. And if that pickup in front of you would take that turn off, it would be timely. The twisty section that dips down into a gorge, curves tight right and then esses up a lightly treed bank is one of the more memorable tidbits on this road. If you get to ride it unimpeded, that is.

The scenery's been pretty so far but it's more or less a study in what nature can do with an oak tree – in other words, speckle them across tawny grasscapes or concentrate them into canopied groves. So it's a refreshing change of pace after you accelerate out of the big sweeper at 8.8 mi (14.2 km) and catch the view to the right over to Logtown Ridge.

The view is short-lived as a hillock rises to block it. The terrain tilts westward for the first time, turning the bleached grass toward the hot sun. The sporadically curving climb through the wide vale is a capped by a final dash through a chute of trees. You emerge onto a broad plateau at 11.0 mi (17.7 km).

Although there are some houses and other structures on the broad swaths of ranchland that expand on either side of the road, the DH still manages to retain its charm, largely due to the receiving line of oaks that silhouette either side of the route. The road meanders through this landscape and the occasional sprouting shoots of suburban sprawl. At 14.3 mi (23.0 km), the road ends on the outskirts of El Dorado.

Twisted Edges

TE-A Latrobe Rd - Old Sacramento Rd (21.3 mi / 34.3 km)
Once you get past the traffic lights and the burgeoning business parks near Hwy 50, this TE has some pleasant surprises. Unfortunately the pavement, which ranges from sort of okay to barely acceptable, is not one

of them. Nonetheless, what you lose in surface quality, you gain in remoteness. With virtually no further development and no traffic, you and the evening riders out of Sacramento are free to shoot down the frequent straights, weave through the rolling brown grasslands and navigate the twisty, oak-filled hollows with nothing to worry about but the local sheriff.

TE-B South Shingle Rd (8.1 mi / 13.0 km)
Yeah, well, the pavement being what it is, at times it feels like you're riding over shingles on this well-engineered but only subtly curving road. Bumpier, less twisty and more developed than **TE-A** with small ranches and country houses most of the way. Not a lot of traffic, though.

RIDER'S LOG: **DATE RIDDEN:** **YOUR RATING: /10**

How does this book work again? RTFM. "What is Destination Highways Northern California?" and "How to Use Our Maps" appear at the front of the book.

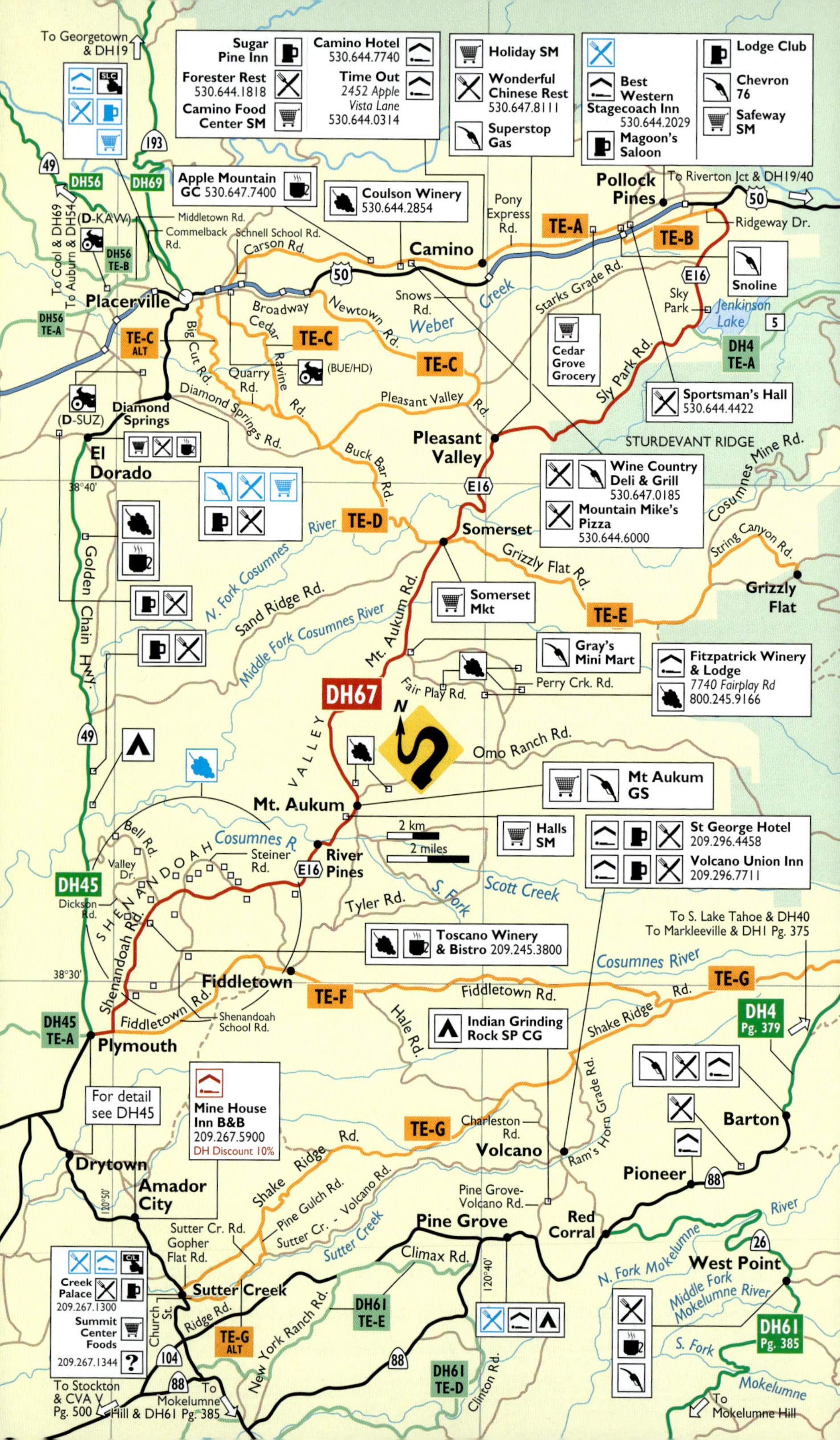

To Georgetown & DH19
Sugar Pine Inn
Forester Rest 530.644.1818
Camino Food Center SM
Camino Hotel 530.644.7740
Time Out 2452 Apple Vista Lane 530.644.0314
Holiday SM
Wonderful Chinese Rest 530.647.8111
Superstop Gas
Best Western Stagecoach Inn 530.644.2029
Magoon's Saloon
Lodge Club
Chevron 76
Safeway SM
Apple Mountain GC 530.647.7400
Coulson Winery 530.644.2854
Pollock Pines
To Riverton Jct & DH19/40
Ridgeway Dr.
Pony Express Rd.
TE-A
TE-B
Camino
Middletown Rd.
Commelback Rd.
Schnell School Rd.
Carson Rd.
(D-KAW)
DH56
DH69
DH56 TE-B
DH56 TE-A
To Cool & DH69
To Auburn & DH54
Placerville
Snows Rd.
Weber Creek
Starks Grade Rd.
Snoline
Sky Park
Jenkinson Lake
DH4 TE-A
Broadway
Newtown Rd.
Cedar Ravine Rd.
Big Cut Rd.
Quarry Rd.
(BUE/HD)
TE-C ALT
TE-C
Cedar Grove Grocery
Sly Park Rd.
Sportsman's Hall 530.644.4422
Diamond Springs
Diamond Springs Rd.
(D-SUZ)
Pleasant Valley Rd.
Pleasant Valley
STURDEVANT RIDGE
El Dorado
Buck Bar Rd.
Wine Country Deli & Grill 530.647.0185
Mountain Mike's Pizza 530.644.6000
Cosumnes Mine Rd.
38°40'
River
TE-D
Somerset
Grizzly Flat Rd.
String Canyon Rd.
Grizzly Flat
N. Fork Cosumnes
Golden Chain Hwy.
Sand Ridge Rd.
Somerset Mkt
TE-E
Middle Fork Cosumnes River
Mt. Aukum Rd.
Gray's Mini Mart
Fitzpatrick Winery & Lodge 7740 Fairplay Rd 800.245.9166
Perry Crk. Rd.
Fair Play Rd.
DH67
VALLEY
N
Omo Ranch Rd.
Mt Aukum GS
Mt. Aukum
2 km
2 miles
Halls SM
St George Hotel 209.296.4458
Volcano Union Inn 209.296.7711
Bell Rd.
Valley Dr.
SHENANDOAH
Cosumnes R.
Steiner Rd.
River Pines
DH45
Dickson Rd.
S. Fork
Scott Creek
Tyler Rd.
Toscano Winery & Bistro 209.245.3800
To S. Lake Tahoe & DH40
To Markleeville & DH1 Pg. 375
Cosumnes River
38°30'
Shenandoah Rd.
Fiddletown
TE-F
Fiddletown Rd.
TE-G
Hale Rd.
Shenandoah School Rd.
DH45 TE-A
Plymouth
Indian Grinding Rock SP CG
Shake Ridge Rd.
DH4 Pg. 379
For detail see DH45
Mine House Inn B&B 209.267.5900 DH Discount 10%
Charleston Rd.
Volcano
Ram's Horn Grade Rd.
Barton
Drytown
Amador City
120°50'
Pioneer
Pine Gulch Rd.
Sutter Cr. - Volcano Rd.
Pine Grove-Volcano Rd.
Sutter Cr. Rd.
Gopher Flat Rd.
Sutter Creek
Pine Grove
Red Corral
Climax Rd.
River
West Point
N. Fork Mokelumne
Middle Fork Mokelumne River
120°40'
Creek Palace 209.267.1300
Summit Center Foods 209.267.1344
Church St.
Ridge Rd.
TE-G ALT
DH61 TE-E
New York Ranch Rd.
DH61 TE-D
Clinton Rd.
DH61 Pg. 385
S. Fork
Mokelumne
To Mokelumne Hill
To Stockton & CVA V Pg. 500
To Mokelumne Hill & DH61 Pg. 385

DH67 Pollock Pines – Plymouth

Sly Park Rd / Mt Aukum Rd / Shenandoah Rd (E 16)

Distance:	32.9 mi / 52.9 km	Traffic:	Moderate

At a Glance

Shenandoah. Traditionally, the title of the famous folk song brings to mind the Appalachians, the Missouri River and the story of an Indian chief with a beautiful daughter. But here in Northern California, the word evokes something entirely different. The Shenandoah Valley is synonymous with rolling vineyards, cozy tasting rooms, and, most notably, a catchy little Destination Highway. DH67 strums down from the shady groves south of Pollock Pines, picks along Sturdevant Ridge and slides into the valley's grassy shoals. And as long as crowds of pylons aren't flooding out of the small, sold-out houses that populate this tour, you'll be humming along through the tight corners between Pleasant Valley and Somerset and the wider, sweepier, better engineered chorus of sweepers down toward Plymouth. The legendary Pete Seeger once asked, "Why should this favorite sea shanty concern an Indian chief, and a midwestern river? And why does everyone love it so and refuse to change it?" Well, Pete, we couldn't agree more. Here's our version: *Oh Shenandoah, I long to ride you…*

TIRES	
Twistiness	25.2/ 30
Pavement	12.6/ 20
Engineering	6.2/ 10
Remoteness	3.8/ 10
Scenery	7.1/ 15
Character	5.3/ 15
Total	**60.2**

Access

From Pollock Pines

Via TE-B Ridgeway Dr

Head south under the highway overpass and follow Ridgeway Dr to the junction with E16. Turn right. You're on the road.

From Hwy 50

E 16 is a well-marked exit off of Hwy 50. Take it and head south on E16. You're on the road.

From Plymouth

On Hwy 49

Coming in on DH45 El Dorado (Placerville) – Plymouth (Hwy 49)

Turn east on the well-marked Shenandoah Rd (E16). When you clear the speed zone, you're on the road.

On The Road

Those tall Pollock Pines that line the early miles south of Hwy 50 sure are impressive. So much so that you don't tend to notice the panoply of houses dwarfed beneath them. You can't help but notice the traffic that tends to collect on the DH's northern end, though. Especially if you're trying to take a run at the nice esses that wend through the trees.

TOUR NOTE: If it's getting a little sweaty under those leathers, Sly Park, on the shore of Jenkinson Lake, offers an easy-access swimming opportunity.

At 4.6 mi (7.4 km), you pass the junction with Mormon Emigrant Trail (**DH4TE-A**). A grassy field on the right hints at a change in the landscape. But the landscape doesn't take the hint, reverting to pine forest, albeit one mixed with aspen, dense undergrowth and driveways from the all-too-frequent houses. Curves are nice, though, twisting respectably on pavement that ranges from good to very good.

You've probably noticed the double yellow dividing the road from the beginning. This legal restriction is compounded by a practical one at 8.2 mi (13.2 km) when the road enters its tightest and twistiest section – the piece along the slope of Sturdevant Ridge. It's particularly frustrating to be stuck behind a heavily laden Subaru Justy when the pavement jumps a grade at 8.6 mi (13.8 km).

But what a great piece of road. If you get it without traffic and keep an eye on the driveways, you can really get down in these S-curves. The climb continues steadily, even as the left-side bank flattens out at 9.7 mi (15.6 km) and oak-shaded grassland takes over. You keep waiting for the development to dwindle. But if anything, the presence of houses and hobby ranches is getting worse. And what's this at 11.4 mi (18.3 km)? A supermarket parking lot? Let's get out of here. Turn left onto Mt Aukum Rd.

*ROUTING OPTION: Turning right will put you on the spur of Pleasant Valley Rd that connects to **TE-C**.*

If you're riding a Rune, you'll be pleased to know there's relief from the tight twisties after the turn. Long, smooth curves and sweepers drift across a plateau, then down a seven-per cent grade. But it's not until 13.1 mi (21.1 km) that you get any relief from the houses still sprouting out of the long grass and light forest.

A four sweeper S-series whips you along a curving ridge high over the confluence of Camp Creek and the North Fork Cosumnes River. The terrain changes to sun-blanched rock and dark green flora. This nice segment ends once you cross the bridge over the river at 14.1 mi (22.7 km) where the road straightens and the landscape devolves into a hodgepodge of eclectic shrubs and inconsistent forest. The stop sign at 15.0 mi (24.1 km) marks the intersection with Bucks Bar Rd (**TE-D**) and Grizzly Flat Rd (**TE-E**). To stay on the DH, **go straight**.

The shoulders are wide and the pavement is good south of the junction. Scenery's above average, too, due to the hunks of granite and thickly forested hillsides that slope down to the Middle Fork Cosumnes River on the left. But the only curve to speak of is a milquetoast sweeper that bridges the river at 16.6 mi (26.7 km). Okay, granted. If you really pour it on, you can just just detect it bending back into a discernable ess at the end.

The junction with Fairplay Rd at 17.5 mi (28.2 km) marks the commencement of the Shenandoah Valley wine region. The change to flatland is sudden; the terrain is mainly ranchland but colored by vineyards and some forested sections. There are houses along with the barns and buildings but it still feels mainly rural, despite the chichi airs that gentrifying wine areas like to put on.

The ride is pretty easy from here on in. The most challenging aspect is keeping the speed in the non-felony range and resisting the temptation to flick past the pylons on the stubborn double yellow. The previously hard shoulders soften to gravel but the curves are long, sweepy and predictable. Just hope you can predict precisely when a tractor will pull out of a side road.

You see your first DH-side vineyard at 18.9 mi (30.4 km). Though there are more to come, this is no Napa – yet. There's still a lot of rolling ranchland waiting to be converted to grapes by yuppies returning to the land.

But for now, it's just great. Curves are fast, concentrated and well-sight-lined in the bit between Fairplay Rd and the Mt. Aukum mapdot, despite the fact the terrain undulates slightly. The pavement is neutral enough and not a factor either way. Perhaps what's best is that this is not only one of the twistier sections of the DH, but also the quietest and least developed.

At 22.5 mi (36.2 km), you pass Omo Ranch Rd and the shoulders widen. It's not clear why that junction would give rise to such an improvement in engineering, given that Omo Ranch Rd itself is such a piece of crap. If you don't believe this, try negotiating your way over its lunar-like surface to mid-**DH4 Hwy 88/Hwy 89 Jct – Barton**.

Assuming you've taken our word for it and remain on the DH, the route continues southward, curling into the woodsy section at 24.0 mi (38.6 km) and the not entirely uncharming little mapdot of River Pines. Then it sweeps back out into the grassland, where a tapestry of billowing, golden grass, splotches of oak, and tailored vineyards unfolds. The road is narrow and soft-shouldered but the curves are moderate enough that it makes little difference. After the tight and twisty section earlier, it's a nice contrast to be able to roll the throttle on and off without constantly shifting gears. Just how high a gear is up to you.

TOUR NOTE: You're in the heart of serious wine country now. Steiner and Shenandoah Schoolhouse Rds are two winery loops that form a large S bisected by the DH. Steiner turns off at 27.3 mi (43.9 km), circles back to the DH at 28.3 mi (45.5 km) to connect with Shenandoah Schoolhouse, which in turn links back to the DH at 31.5 mi (50.7 km). Be prepared to see pylons stumbling out of the side roads anywhere along here.

There are just a couple minor curves and a big sweeper past the Fiddletown Rd (**TE-F**) junction at 32.7 mi (52.6 km) left before a sign welcomes you to Old Pokerville, Plymouth's former, less refined self. You reach Plymouth/Pokerville's 25-mph (40-kmh) zone at 32.9 mi (52.9 km).

Twisted Edges

TE-A Placerville – Pollock Pines *Carson Rd - Pony Express Trail*
There's lots of development along this wandering, smoothly paved, semi-rural bypass. But there are lots of trees and, more importantly, it's not the freeway.

NAVIGATION: From Placerville, Carson Rd turns off Broadway right beside the freeway at the east end of town. Cross the freeway and turn right.

*This TE hooks up nicely with **TE-B** at the east end. Just turn right at the Snoline Gas Station, cross under the freeway and veer left onto Ridgeway.*

TE-B Ridgeway Dr (2.7 mi / 4.3 km)
A short but convenient detour between two Hwy 50 exits. Mostly through pine forest with a few houses. Considering its tight sweepers and smooth, not-too-tar-strippy pavement, there's really no reason not to take it.

TE-C Cedar Ravine Rd - Pleasant Valley Rd - Newtown Rd (16.3 mi / 26.2 km)
A nice loop out of Placerville. Cedar Ravine boasts the best marriage of pavement and curves as well as some great open views of the surrounding ridges. There are lots of houses and driveways though, and a single pylon can ruin the fun in some of the tight sections. The busy Pleasant Valley section is pleasant enough with good pavement, pretty oak canopies and modest sweepers ranging across flat, open countryside. What you lose in pavement turning on to Newtown, you get back in remoteness as this quiet road twists narrowly, but predictably along a creek until it stretches out through fields and back to Hwy 50 and Placerville.

NAVIGATION: Cedar Ravine Rd connects off Placerville's Main Street right by the Harley shop.

If you want to go in the other direction from Placerville, get to Broadway and Main and just follow Broadway east as it parallels the freeway and turns into Newtown.

If you're riding from the east on Hwy 50, take the exit for the Placerville Airport. Pass under the highway and turn left.

TE-C ALT Big Cut Rd - Quarry Rd (4.7 mi / 7.6 km)
Big Cut is very tight and twisty when you climb out of suburban Placerville, with more trees and fewer houses the farther you go. It's scenically varied, with some valley views off the crest before you drop into a grassy, oak hollow and onto the more refined Quarry Rd. Overall, it's not nearly as well paved as **TE-C**, but your chances of getting stuck behind a Volvo are way lower.

NAVIGATION: From Hwy 49 in Placerville (Sacramento St), turn onto Pacific St, go a very short block and turn right on Benham. Benham turns into Big Cut Rd. At 3.1 mi (5.0 km), turn left on Quarry Rd.

TE-D Bucks Bar Rd (5.0 mi / 8.1 km)
The sealed pavement isn't as appealing as the smooth asphalt of **TE-C**. The surprising level of traffic isn't so appealing, either. It's twisty enough though, with nice curves drifting through pine and oak forest. And the relative lack of houses gives it a boost. Scenic highlight: the sandstone formations beside the one-lane bridge over Squaw Hollow Creek.

TE-E Grizzly Flat Rd - String Canyon Rd (11.6 mi / 18.7 km)
Nicely engineered S-turns climb up onto Grizzly Flat and great pavement sweeps you out into vineyards, forests and hobby ranchland. Too bad this gorgeous little run turns into a bear trail at the serviceless settlement of Grizzly Flat.

NAVIGATION: Heading east, there's a poorly signed fork at 8.2 mi (13.2 km). Go left.

*ROUTING OPTION: Fans of paved, one-lane backcountry trails will find all kinds of options beyond Grizzly Flat. Drift north to hook up with **DH4TE-A Mormon Emigrant Rd** or south to connect with **DH4 Hwy 88/89 Jct – Barton**. Note the nicely paved two lane stretch of FSR 6.*

TE-F Fiddletown Rd (15.9 mi / 25.6 km)
This lightly trafficked, well-paved ol' time TE bows gently through the rolling hills on the climb out of the Shenandoah Valley. The asphalt could use a little more rosin, though, after the quick burn through Fiddletown. Especially since it's here the road's easy rhythm changes to a quickstep of curves. Largely a tree-cloistered ditty, except for some high, lonesome stretches toward the end as you approach the junction with **TE-G**.

TE-G Shake Ridge Rd - Gopher Flat Rd (15.4 mi / 24.8 km)
Starts (or ends) right in Sutter Creek. Reasonably consistent curves, great pavement and barely noticeable development that thins out even more as you head east. The speed limit tops out at 45 mph (70 kmh) though you might not mind much since it's a bit cloistered by trees and deer warning signs anyway. Not to mention its own engineering on the Shake Ridge Rd part. Beats busy Hwy 88 as a way to get on or off **DH4 Hwy 88/89 Jct – Barton** to or from Hwy 49.

*NAVIGATION: If you are coming from the east, make sure you bear right at 8.9 mi (14.3 km) and stay on Shake Ridge. Your tendency will be to stay straight on Ram's Horn Grade because it seems like the main road. Oh well, there is beer in Volcano. But the pavement on Sutter Creek Rd west of Volcano can get pretty rough. At 13.2 mi (21.2 km), once again bear right to start Gopher Flat Rd and stay on the TE. If you stay straight, you'll be on **TE-G ALT**. No compensating beer down here. Well, at least not until you get to Sutter Creek.*

TE-G ALT Pine Gulch Rd - Sutter Creek Rd - Church St

(3.1 mi / 5.0 km)

This starts right in Sutter Creek as well and might be a little cooler as it flows alongside the burbling waters of Sutter Creek. Pavement is almost as good as the main TE but it's a little less curvy.

ROUTING OPTION: You might be tempted to stay straight on Sutter Creek (to Volcano). If you do, be prepared for rougher pavement.

RIDER'S LOG: **DATE RIDDEN:** **YOUR RATING: /10**

Find more information about camping in Northern California, including how to make a reservation, in the "Touring Northern California – What You Should Know" section at the front of the book.

Auburn KOA CG
530.885.0990
To DH57 Pg 279
To Colfax
Auburn HD/Buell (BUE/HD)
12075 Locksley Lane 530.885.7161
13411 Lincoln
530.887.2111
Foresthill
To French Meadows
DH16
DH54 TE-B
Placer Hills Rd.
Meadow Vista
Sugar Pine Mtn.
Arthur Rd.
80
N. FORK AMERICAN RIVER
DH54
MIDDLE FORK AMERICAN RIVER
Buckeye Point
American River Inn
530.333.4499
Recommended
DH Discount 15%
For detail, see DH16
To Nevada City & DH9 Pg. 269 & DH57 Pg. 279
Lake
Clipper Gap
Bowman Rd.
Placer
El Dorado
Hindquarter House
530.878.1906
Pilot House Mkt
Sierra Super Stop
To Riverton Jct & DH40
Luther Rd.
Lincoln Wy.
Foresthill Rd.
DH19
Wentworth Springs Rd.
49
DH54 TE-A
For detail see DH 69
Georgetown Rd.
Lower Main St.
Georgetown
Old Auburn-Forest Hill Rd.
Auburn
To Sacramento & CVA V Pg 500
Cool
DH69
193
ELDORADO NATIONAL FOREST
Coloma Club Café & Saloon
530.626.6390
Marco's Café
530.642.2025
Texaco
DH69 TE-A ALT
Greenwood Rd.
Marshall Rd.
Garden Valley
Auburn SRA BCG
GARDEN VALLEY
Black Oak Mine Rd.
Georgetown Rd.
Venezio
530.885.9463
Auburn Power Sports (KAW/VIC)
1460 Canal
530.823.5768
Pilot Hill
38°50'
DH56
DH69 TE-A
Marshall Rd.
Mt. Murphy Rd.
Garden Valley Rd.
Coloma Country Inn B&B
345 High St
530.622.6919
Coloma Resort CG
Sutter Center Mkt SM
American River CG
6019 New River Rd
530.622.6700
Apex (HON/SUZ/YAM)
446 Hwy 49
530.885.7105
Sierra Nevada House
530.626.8096
Coloma
Kelsey
Rock Creek Rd.
TE-C
Lotus
S. FORK AMERICAN R.
Adam Lohry's Red Brick Rest
530.622.4562
Camp Lotus
5461 Bassi Rd
530.622.8672
Flagstaff Hill
Folsom Lake
Cold Springs Rd.
Coloma Rd.
Lotus Rd.
Gold Hill Rd.
Gold Hill Vineyard & Brewery
530.626.6522
Salmon Falls Cutoff Rd.
TE-B
Sleepy Hollow Rd.
Middletown Rd.
Commelback Rd.
DH67 TE-A
To Pollock Pines & DH67
Deer Valley Rd.
Gold Hill Olive Oil Co.
530.621.7073
Flyers Gas
Starbuck Rd.
Pine Hill
Placerville
Placerville Dr.
TE-A
Green Valley Rd.
Rescue
Cameron Park
Green Valley Rd.
N. Shingle Rd.
Missouri Flat Rd.
Cedar Creek
Weber
Diamond Springs
Silva
Rescue Jct
Ponderosa Rd.
50
Cameron Park Dr.
DH67 TE-C ALT
DH67 TE-C
Big Cut Rd.
Ravine Rd.
El Dorado Hills Blvd.
Valley Pkwy.
Serano Pkwy.
Bass Lake Rd.
38°40'
Greenstone Rd.
El Dorado
Mother Lode Dr.
Pleasant Valley Rd.
Hangtown HD (BUE/HD)
629 Main
530.344.0401
Shingle Springs
Golden Chain Hwy.
To Sacramento To CVA V Pg. 500
Latrobe Rd.
N
South Shingle Rd.
Mike's Cycle (KAW)
291 Placerville
530.622.0209
2 km
2 miles
RPS MS (SUZ)
4516 Missouri Flat
530.295.8286
French Creek Rd.
DH45
DH45 TE-A
DH45 TE-B
121°00'
120°50'
To Plymouth & DH67

DH56 Placerville – Auburn

Highway 49

Distance:	23.6 mi / 38.0 km	Traffic:	Brutal

At a Glance

TIRES	
Twistiness	26.6/30
Pavement	16.4/20
Engineering	5.8/10
Remoteness	2.3/10
Scenery	8.2/15
Character	3.9/15
Total	**63.2**

Dry Diggins was the original name of *both* gold rush towns at either end of this DH back in the day when they attracted legions of '49ers. So one settlement changed its name to Auburn while the other became known as Old Hangtown, due to the tendency of the short-fused gold diggers to mete out rough, rope-based justice to local miscreants. Tempers cooled and the latter's name was eventually changed to the more benign-sounding Placerville. These days, there's so much traffic on this connector between I-80 and Hwy 50, especially north of Cool, that you'll probably want to string up a few ne'er-do-wells yourself on the nearest oak tree. But, with patience, you can still sluice out some glittering Pavement and Twistiness from this claim. Scenery on the ride down to along and back up from the South Fork American River is a mother lode mix of golden open and forested countryside. And there's more gilded viewscapes on the descent to the seam where the other two other American River forks join up, as well as on the final climb up to Auburn. Engineering assays out as better than average but, unfortunately, Remoteness has been played out by an amalgam of pylons and development, leaving only the smallest nugget of Character. Today's fortune seekers are continuing to develop the whole area around here at such a rapid pace that the state capital is effectively merging with the two communities into one big Sacramauburnville. So if you want to strike it rich, you'll have to dig up a time to avoid all the pylon riff-raff. Otherwise, there's a good chance these particular DH diggings will come up dry.

Access

From Placerville

On Hwy 49 or Hwy 50

Stay on 49 north through Placerville or take it from the 49/50 Jct. When you run outta town, you're on the road.

Coming in on DH69 Cool – Placerville (Hwy 193)

This DH junctions with Hwy 49 on the northern outskirts of P-ville. Turn right on 49 and you're on the road.

Coming in on DH45 Plymouth – El Dorado (Placerville) (Hwy 49)
Continue north on 49 into Old Hangtown. Once you pass through, you're on the road.

From Cool

Coming in on DH69 Placerville – Cool (Hwy 193)
The north end of Hwy 193 junctions with the DH 6.7 mi (10.8 km) south of Auburn and 16.9 mi (27.2 km) north of Placerville.

From Auburn

On I-80 or Hwy 49
Take Hwy 49 south from the 49/80 Jct in Auburn. You'll quickly drop out of town and be on the road.

Coming in on DH54 Foresthill – Auburn
Turn left on I-80 and follow the signs for Hwy 49. When you abruptly dive out of Auburn, you are on the road. Better yet, use **DH54TE-A Old Auburn-Foresthill Rd** as a short cut.

On The Road

The DH starts at the edge of Placerville where **DH69 Placerville – Cool** slants off right and begins its plunge down to the South Fork American River. Although there are lots of houses tucked away in among the trees at first, they peter out after about a mile or so. Too bad you can't say the same about the pylons.

The land to your left slopes gently up to the ridge that forms the south side of the South Fork American River valley. The somewhat worn but still-smooth pavement curves mildly through a pleasing mix of open terrain and statuesque oaks. Unfortunately with the slow rate of the traffic and the lack of passing lanes, you could be feeling pretty statuesque yourself.

At 1.3 mi (2.1 km), the corners tighten up and the trees coalesce into thick brush, obscuring the sightlines. One notable – and sharp – righthander has a 15-mph (25-kph). When you pass the Gold Hill Rd turn off left at 2.6 mi (4.2 km), both geography and road open up again. But then a steep-grade-ahead advisory suggests more tight cornering may be on the way. And indeed it is.

A high-bank lefthander at 4.2 mi (6.8 km) offers a quick glance out to the right where you see the heights on the north side of the South Fork American River. As you descend, the road gets increasingly S-curvy. Caltrans helps out for a change by widening the lanes as much as it can. At 6.2 mi (10.0 km), you enter Coloma under a cooling canopy of shade trees. Left, Cold Springs Rd (**TE-B**) heads south.

TOUR NOTE: Tiny Coloma, a semi-ghost town, was where gold was first discovered in 1848, setting off the 49er Gold Rush. It was found at Johan Sutter's Mill by Sutter's partner, James Marshall. The Marshall Gold Discovery State Historical Park marks the actual location. Neither Sutter nor

Marshall benefited from the find – Sutter's business was ruined by it and Marshall died penniless – but at least you did.

After leaving Coloma, you cross the South Fork American River at 7.3 mi (11.7 km). Down here in the drier and more open valley bottom, the road straightens. The upside? You've finally got some dotted yellow working in your favor. As you wick it up past the pylons, you might miss the fact that in some strange microclimatic twist, the hills to your left appear mostly treed while the ones to your right are mostly bare.

The crossing of Greenwood Creek at 10.2 mi (16.4 km) marks the start of a shallow climb. Curves? Except for the rare and very lazy sweeper, there are none. The terrain's getting pretty relaxed around here. So much so that a vineyard appears on the right.

Finally, by 11.0 mi (17.7 km), you've climbed high enough to put you back in thick forest. The cornering opportunities aren't exactly thick but at least there are some. Even if they are relatively gentle and separated by straights. Seems this is often the price of great pavement and engineering.

You climb further into the forest and the number of curves increases. But then the geography plateaus and the twistiness struggles yet again. The gas station/dinner house at 14.4 mi (23.2 km) marks Pilot Hill, the turn off for Salmon Falls Cutoff Rd (**TE-C**). If you have to bail and get back to Sacramento in time for dinner, this twisty TE's a great way to get there.

Or forget the time and press ahead on the newer pavement through the rolling, open countryside. Maybe chill out in Cool, the northern terminus of **DH69 Cool – Placerville** at 16.9 mi (27.2 km). Or not, since north of Hiptown, the DH immediately takes a turn for the better when it starts its descent to the North Fork American River. Shrubbery and curves thicken quickly. Unfortunately, north of the junction of the two state highways, so to do the pylons.

The road is now too tight to have much in the way of passing opportunities. Even if it did, the volume of traffic coming in the other direction would tend to dissuade you. Might as well enjoy the view over the mining operation, to the right at 19.3 mi (31.1 km).

It really is too bad about the lack of passing lanes. As this section continues downward, it's as good as the great winding descent coming into Coloma. Actually, if it had no traffic, it would be even better. Right. And if a pylon had two wheels, it would be a motorcycle. Or cut in half.

At least the view over the river valley to your right is pretty. And that soaring bridge across the North Fork American River high above you ahead is downright spectacular. All the more so since it's part of **DH54 Auburn – Foresthill**. But down where you are, the midpoint of a less-imposing bridge at 21.4 mi (34.4 km) marks the end of El Dorado and the beginning of Placer County at the junction of the Middle and North Forks of the American River. To hightail it to high-bridge **DH54**, turn right at the end of the low bridge onto Old Auburn-Foresthill Rd (**DH54TE-A**).

The DH turns 90 degrees left at the **DH54TE-A** junction and starts an immediate climb up the steep, west-side slope of the Middle Fork. The asphalt is fairly new, twists wonderfully and is probably completely unusable. Where's a lynch mob when you need one?

The road cuts west into a side gully away from the river at 22.4 mi (36.0 km) where a short pullover lane appears. Nice try but it's a little too late. A few more wonderful, useless curves and the DH ends at 23.6 mi (38.0 km) in Auburn.

Twisted Edges

TE-A Green Valley Rd (10.7 mi / 17.2 km)

How green was my valley? Depends what time of the year you're riding here. But at least there's more remoteness than you'd expect from this reasonably paved, suburban TE. Not a lot of great curves but the forested hollows, hobby ranches, strawberry fields and lots of oaks make it a pleasant, meandering cruise. To borrow from Llewellyn: "There is no fence nor hedge around rides that are done. You can go back and have what you like of it, if you can remember."

*NAVIGATION: There's a junction with Missouri Flat Rd at 1.8 mi (2.9 km). Turn right. At 6.4 mi (10.3 km), Lotus Rd comes in from the right. Stay left. At 6.9 mi (11.1 km), when N. Shingle Rd comes in from the south, stay right. (Turning south on N Shingle Rd will put you on **DH45TE-B S Shingle Rd.**)*

*Coming the other way, stay left when N Shingle comes from the south at 3.8 mi (6.1 km), right when Lotus Rd comes in from the north at 4.3 mi (6.9 km) and left at the junction with Missouri Flat Rd at 8.9 mi (14.3 km). (Going south on Missouri Flat Rd is a good short cut if you're headed for **DH45 El Dorado – Plymouth.**)*

ROUTING OPTIONS:

(1) You can extend this ride by tacking on Deer Valley Rd. Be prepared for some poor pavement, though.

*(2) If you're using **TE-A** as a Hwy 50 bypass, Bass Lake Rd – 0.3 mi (0.5 km) west of Cameron Park Dr, and the western end of the TE – is the least worst connection to Hwy 50.*

TE-B Coloma – Placerville (8.4 mi / 13.5 km) *Cold Springs Rd - Middletown Rd - Commelback Rd*

Cold Springs Mobile Manor is a pretty pretentious name for a mobile home park. But somehow fitting on a TE where nouveau pavement and bourgeois engineering make the rich curves stand out. The treed residential lots of the great unwashed are steadily encroaching from the south, threatening the ranch and forested remoteness at the northern end. But still a fine ride – sniff – for a TE.

NAVIGATION: Coming from the north, there's a stop sign for Pierroz Rd, then another where arrows split the road right and left. Go left onto Middletown, which turns into Commelback.

Coming from the south, Commelback turns into Middletown, which merges into Cold Springs. Easy.

TE-C Salmon Falls Cutoff Rd (11.8 mi / 19.0 km)

The best TE close to Sacramento, fins down. Excellent pavement. A little fatty and farmed at the south as it swims through the fields and ritzy housing developments on the east side of Folsom Lake. But north of Falcon Crest, this fish is 100% wild, twisting down to cross the south fork of the American River, then fishladdering up tightly through the drop-off rock cuts of Pilot Hill.

RIDER'S LOG: **DATE RIDDEN:** **YOUR RATING: /10**

***Remember, you'll find video clips of all of Northern California's DHs at* destination highways.com.**

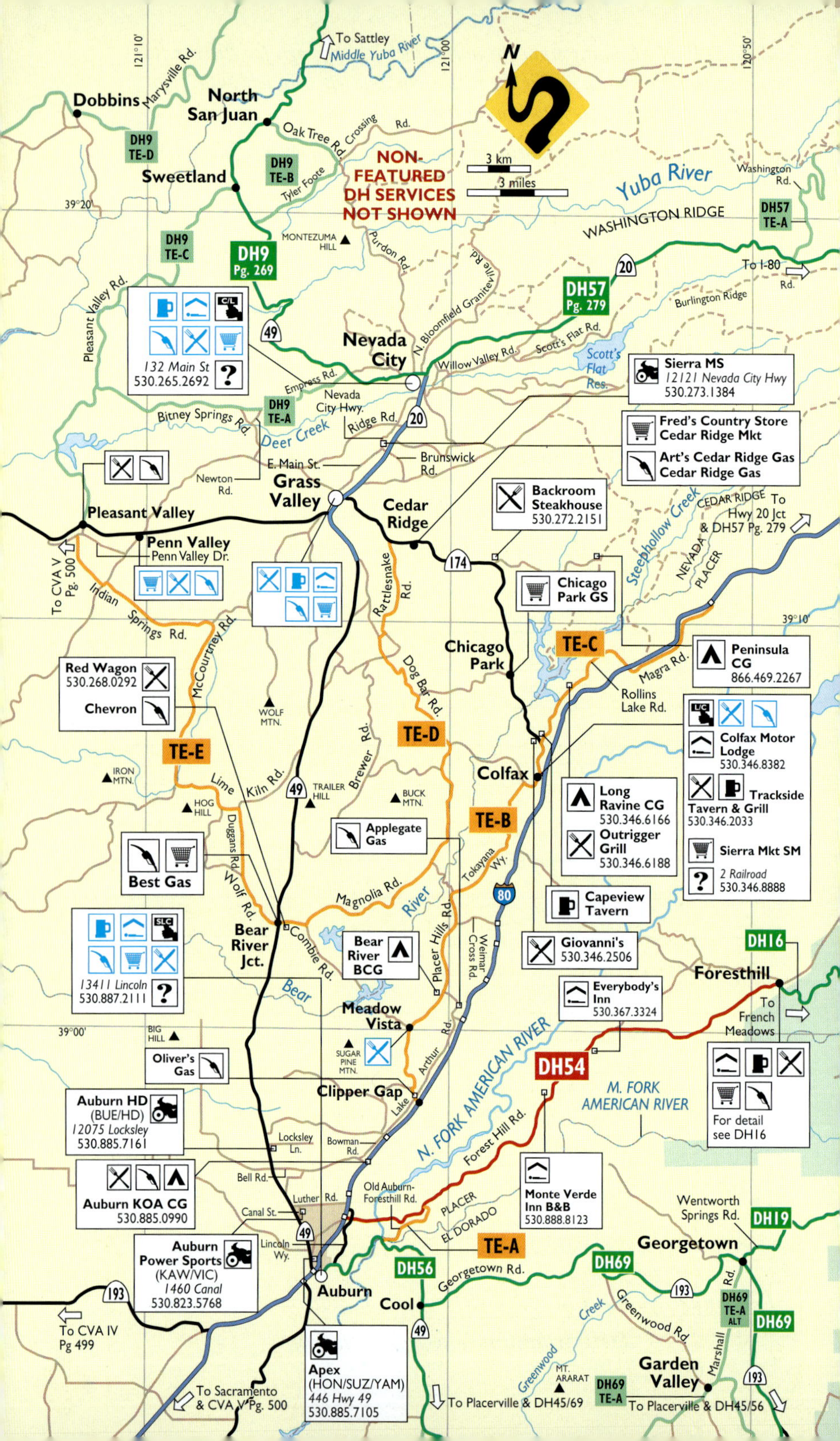

NON-FEATURED DH SERVICES NOT SHOWN
3 km
3 miles
N
Dobbins
North San Juan
Sweetland
Nevada City
Grass Valley
Cedar Ridge
Pleasant Valley
Penn Valley
Chicago Park
Colfax
Bear River Jct.
Meadow Vista
Clipper Gap
Auburn
Cool
Foresthill
Georgetown
Garden Valley
To Sattley
Middle Yuba River
Yuba River
WASHINGTON RIDGE
Washington Rd.
To I-80 Rd.
Burlington Ridge
Scott's Flat Res.
Deer Creek
Steephollow Creek
CEDAR RIDGE
NEVADA
PLACER
EL DORADO
N. FORK AMERICAN RIVER
M. FORK AMERICAN RIVER
Bear River
DH9 TE-D
DH9 TE-B
DH9 TE-C
DH9 TE-A
DH9 Pg. 269
DH57 Pg. 279
DH57 TE-A
DH16
DH54
DH56
DH69
DH19
DH69 TE-A ALT
DH69 TE-A
TE-A
TE-B
TE-C
TE-D
TE-E
132 Main St 530.265.2692
Sierra MS 12121 Nevada City Hwy 530.273.1384
Fred's Country Store Cedar Ridge Mkt
Art's Cedar Ridge Gas Cedar Ridge Gas
Backroom Steakhouse 530.272.2151
Chicago Park GS
Peninsula CG 866.469.2267
Colfax Motor Lodge 530.346.8382
Trackside Tavern & Grill 530.346.2033
Sierra Mkt SM
2 Railroad 530.346.8888
Long Ravine CG 530.346.6166
Outrigger Grill 530.346.6188
Capeview Tavern
Giovanni's 530.346.2506
Everybody's Inn 530.367.3324
For detail see DH16
Monte Verde Inn B&B 530.888.8123
Red Wagon 530.268.0292
Chevron
Applegate Gas
Best Gas
Bear River BCG
13411 Lincoln 530.887.2111
Oliver's Gas
Auburn HD (BUE/HD) 12075 Locksley 530.885.7161
Auburn KOA CG 530.885.0990
Auburn Power Sports (KAW/VIC) 1460 Canal 530.823.5768
Apex (HON/SUZ/YAM) 446 Hwy 49 530.885.7105
To CVA IV Pg 499
To Sacramento & CVA V Pg. 500
To CVA V Pg. 500
To Placerville & DH45/69
To Placerville & DH45/56
To Hwy 20 Jct & DH57 Pg. 279
To French Meadows
Marysville Rd.
Oak Tree Rd.
Crossing Rd.
Tyler Foote
Purdon Rd.
Graniteville Rd.
N. Bloomfield
Willow Valley Rd.
Scott's Flat Rd.
Empress Rd.
Nevada City Hwy.
Ridge Rd.
Bitney Springs Rd.
Brunswick Rd.
E. Main St.
Newton Rd.
Penn Valley Dr.
Pleasant Valley Rd.
Indian Springs Rd.
McCourtney Rd.
Rattlesnake Rd.
Dog Bar Rd.
Magra Rd.
Rollins Lake Rd.
Lime Kiln Rd.
Brewer Rd.
Duggans Rd.
Wolf Rd.
Combie Rd.
Magnolia Rd.
Placer Hills Rd.
Tokayana Wy.
Weimar Cross Rd.
Arthur Rd.
Lake
Locksley Ln.
Bowman Rd.
Bell Rd.
Canal St.
Luther Rd.
Lincoln Wy.
Old Auburn-Foresthill Rd.
Forest Hill Rd.
Georgetown Rd.
Greenwood Rd.
Greenwood Creek
Wentworth Springs Rd.
Marshall Rd.
MONTEZUMA HILL
WOLF MTN.
IRON MTN.
HOG HILL
TRAILER HILL
BUCK MTN.
BIG HILL
SUGAR PINE MTN.
MT. ARARAT
39°20'
39°10'
39°00'
121°10'
121°00'
120°50'
20
49
174
80
193

DH54 Auburn – Foresthill
Foresthill Road

Distance:	17.0 mi / 27.4 km	Traffic:	Heavy

At a Glance

Is this fast trip along the mountainous Foresthill Divide any kind of warm-up for DH16? C'mon, get real. On what planet can long, pour-it-on sweepers and top-tier Pavement prepare anyone for a contorted twistfest like Mosquito Ridge? It would sure make matters easier if you had to deal with a few steep, blind curves or the occasional heart-stopping cliff. *Something* to get you out of fifth gear. But noooooo. Instead, every time you flick your eyes back to the road from checking out the canyon view of the Middle Fork of the American River or the remote acres of empty meadows and lush trees off past the wide shoulders, this Engineering exhibitionist is switching to three and four lanes. Which does have its advantages for the massive new development that'll make Foresthill look more like a bedroom community than the "community of rugged individualists and creative people" it proclaims itself to be. But whatever the justification, the fact remains: by the time you finish acing the essing supersweepers and zipping effortlessly by the standstill pylons to turn down the precarious DH16, you're feeling too cool for words. Hopefully not too cool for what's to come.

TIRES	
Twistiness	22.5/ 30
Pavement	18.5/ 20
Engineering	9.7/ 10
Remoteness	3.1/ 10
Scenery	7.9/ 15
Character	2.7/ 15
Total	**64.4**

Access

From Auburn

Via I-80

Via Lincoln Way/East Lincoln Way

Foresthill Rd is a marked exit off I-80, just north of Auburn. You can also get to that exit from Auburn by riding north on Lincoln Way. Either way, head east to Foresthill and you're on the road.

Coming in on DH56 Placerville – Auburn (Hwy 49)

Turn right on Lincoln Way. When Lincoln Way (now East Lincoln Way) intersects with Foresthill Rd, turn right. You're on the road.

Via TE-A Old Auburn-Foresthill Rd

If you've no reason to plow through Auburn, just shoot up this TE and pick up the DH 3.1 mi (5.0 km) in. You're on the road.

From Foresthill
Coming in on DH16 Mosquito Ridge Road
Turn left on Foresthill Rd. Once you leave Foresthill, you're on the road.

On The Road

Blasting off the light at the intersection with Lincoln Way, you head down a splendidly paved road. The world of the Foresthill Divide opens up with mountains rising far off, soft-looking, tree-coated hills in the middle distance and 45-degree rockfaces either side of the road. The sense of remoteness feels sudden after the heavy urbanity of Auburn.

At 0.6 mi (1.0 km), you cross the North Fork American River on an unusual, concrete-sided divided bridge. Apparently, this distinctive span (the highest in America) was designed to cross a dam that – hard to believe in California – was never built. Out of context, it resembles a Roman aqueduct. In fact, put yourself on a Ducati 999 Testastretta and you could feel as if you're in Lazio.

You flow straight over the bridge and into the first of the many passing lanes that CalTrans has pasted down every time there's a hint of a climb. The passing lane ends at 1.7 mi (2.7 km) but the road continues to ascend through deep V-cuts, emerging now and then onto a high bluff overlooking the breadth of the Middle Fork American River valley. At 3.1 mi (5.0 km), you arrive at the junction of the Old Auburn-Foresthill Rd (**TE-A**).

If you've come by way of **TE-A** and just turned right on this DH, don't worry, you haven't missed much. The heart of this DH doesn't really start beating until 3.6 mi (5.8 km) when a series of long and steady sweepers and curves gets your blood pumping. Stuck behind a little rush hour traffic on this artery? No need to perform unauthorized surgery on the double yellow lines. Brief passing lanes at 5.0 (8.1 km) and again at 6.0 mi (9.7 km) help you easily bypass clots of pylons.

There's some flattening of the terrain at 6.4 mi (10.3 km) as the steep climbing ends and the land spreads out. Gentle fields of brown and olive-green grass line the way along with Ponderosa Pines and oaks. The gentling of the topography doesn't last long. Chains of long, smooth S-curves soon forge their way along a revitalized cliff face and through a thickly forested section of the DH. It becomes obvious you're riding along the top of a divide when the terrain tilts northward at 7.4 mi (11.9 km) and faces the North Fork American River. It's a quick shift though – at 7.9 mi (12.7 km), an extra large sweeper sucks you back onto a southward slant.

A passing lane at 8.3 mi (13.4 km) sees you climbing again on a steep but perfectly engineered climb along a dynamited rockface. With forever sightlines and a ton of blacktop to work with, you can laugh at the gaping valley below to your right. Laugh away, friend. **DH16 Mosquito Ridge Road** will have the last one.

The extra lane ends at 9.4 mi (15.1 km) and the road straightens. The sweepers resume just as the next passing lane does at 10.9 mi (17.5 km) on the DH's swan song – an essing ascent through a setback forest of Black Oak, Douglas Fir, Incense Cedar, Ponderosa Pines and huge, red-barked laurelwoods. At 12.4 mi (20.0 km), however, the road turns into an ugly duckling, straightening through a gauntlet of signs advertising one-acre home sites. From here, it's a curveless and uneventful ride through a thickly treed canopy to the sprawling town of Foresthill, where you arrive at 17.0 mi (27.4 km).

Twisted Edges

TE-A Old Auburn-Foresthill Rd (3.2 mi / 5.2 km)

A much twistier way to start the DH, if you don't mind average pavement and engineering. You start low, bridge the American River's North Fork, then rapidly gain altitude as you ess neatly up a steep, red-rocky slope above the Middle Fork to the Foresthill Rd junction.

*TOUR NOTE: If it's so hot you don't need a fork to see if you're done, there's an easy, albeit popular, river access at the west end of the TE just east of the junction with **DH56 Auburn – Placerville**. Mammoth Bar River Access, at the TE's halfway point is more remote, but you need to negotiate a steep gravel road to get down to it.*

TE-B Clipper Gap – Colfax (11.4 mi / 18.3 km) *Placer Hills Rd - Tokayana Way*

Great engineering on the southern beginning gives way to a tighter, twistier jaunt through pleasing, hilly countryside north of Meadow Vista. Tokayana's even tighter. Excellent pavement all the way. Yes, there's still a little gold in these here Placer Hills.

NAVIGATION: At the Colfax end, look for either Grass Valley St or W Church St west off Main Street downtown. Both get you to Rising Sun St, which connects to Tokayana.

TE-C Rollins Lake Rd - Magra Rd (8.3 mi / 13.4 km)

For those of you who want to avoid as much of I-80 as you can, this TE north from Colfax ties in nicely with the TE running south from Colfax, though the ride here pales a little in comparison.

TE-D Bear River Jct – Grass Valley (17.2 mi / 27.7 km)

Combie Rd - Magnolia Rd - Dog Bar Rd - Rattlesnake Rd

The well-engineered, sweet-smelling asphalt on Magnolia continues through a partly treed, rangeland setting to the remote hollows of Dog Bar's northern end where both pavement and engineering, well, go to the dogs for a spell. P & E scale up again in the residential woods of Rattlesnake Rd. Great, tight curve combos throughout.

NAVIGATION: From the south, go left at the stop sign at 5.7 mi (9.2 km) onto Dog Bar Rd, then right onto Rattlesnake at 13.0 mi (20.9 km).

From Grass Valley, head down Hwy 174 to Rattlesnake Rd. Go right onto Rattlesnake, then left when you reach the Dog Bar Rd T-junction. When you reach Magnolia (11.5 mi (18.5 km) from the Rattlesnake Rd/Hwy 174 Jct), veer right.

TE-E Pleasant Valley – Bear River Jct (17.6 mi / 28.3 km) *Indian Springs Rd - McCourtney Rd - Lime Kiln Rd - Duggans Rd - Wolf Rd*
This road's only semi-curvy, which kind of goes with its semi-rural, semi-suburban environs. Too bad, since the undulating, gently bending pavement is more than semi-sweet.

NAVIGATION: From the north, if you're at the junction of ***DH9TE-C Pleasant Valley Rd*** *and Hwy 20, Penn Valley Dr runs parallel to Hwy 20 immediately south of it. Going just west on Penn Valley Rd will take you to the northern end of Indian Springs Rd. Heading south on Indian Springs Rd, there's a stop sign at 2.1 mi (3.4 km). Jog left and right to continue south on Indian Springs. There's another stop sign at 5.8 mi (9.3 km) where you turn right onto McCourtney Rd. At 10.8 mi (17.4 km), McCourtney Rd drifts off right. You continue straight on what is now Lime Kiln Rd and then right at 13.3 mi (21.4 km) onto Duggans Rd. Finally, turn left at 15.2 mi (16.6 km) onto Wolf Rd.*

From the south, turn right off Wolf Rd onto Duggans Rd at 2.4 mi (3.9 km), then left at the stop sign onto Lime Kiln Rd at 4.3 mi (6.9 km). Stay right at 6.8 mi (10.9 km) when Lime Kiln merges into McCourtney. At 11.8 mi (19.0 km), jog left onto Indian Springs Rd.

RIDER'S LOG: **DATE RIDDEN:** **YOUR RATING: /10**

Map Tip: To see the next good motorcycle road, look for the white navigation arrows at the edge of the Local maps.

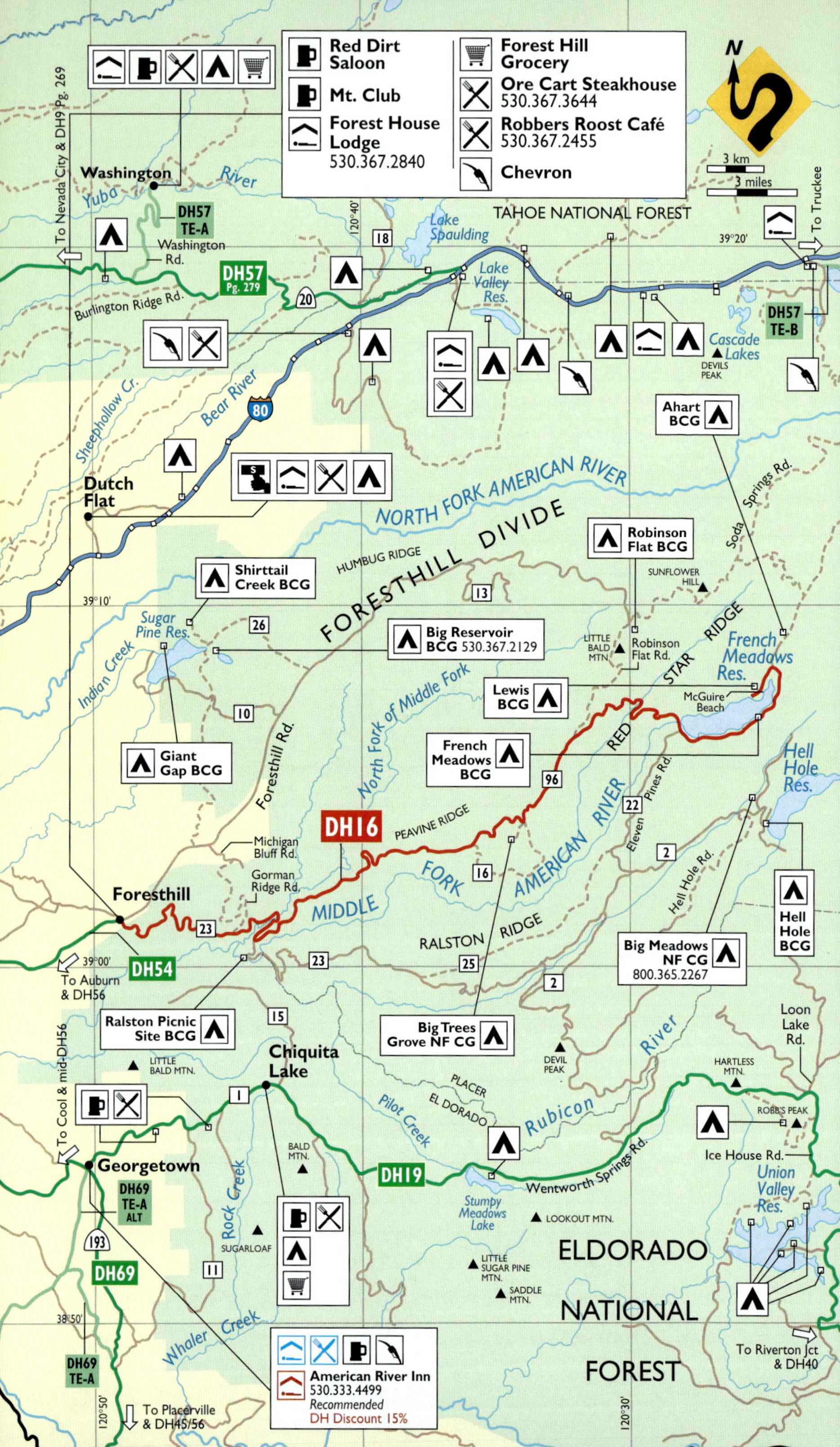
Red Dirt Saloon
Mt. Club
Forest House Lodge 530.367.2840
Forest Hill Grocery
Ore Cart Steakhouse 530.367.3644
Robbers Roost Café 530.367.2455
Chevron
3 km
3 miles
To Truckee
To Nevada City & DH9 Pg. 269
Washington
Yuba River
DH57 TE-A
Washington Rd.
Burlington Ridge Rd.
DH57 Pg. 279
TAHOE NATIONAL FOREST
Lake Spaulding
Lake Valley Res.
Cascade Lakes
DEVILS PEAK
DH57 TE-B
Sheephollow Cr.
Bear River
Dutch Flat
Ahart BCG
Soda Springs Rd.
NORTH FORK AMERICAN RIVER
FORESTHILL DIVIDE
HUMBUG RIDGE
Robinson Flat BCG
SUNFLOWER HILL
Shirttail Creek BCG
Sugar Pine Res.
Indian Creek
Big Reservoir BCG 530.367.2129
LITTLE BALD MTN
Robinson Flat Rd.
RED STAR RIDGE
French Meadows Res.
McGuire Beach
Lewis BCG
French Meadows BCG
North Fork of Middle Fork
Giant Gap BCG
Foresthill Rd.
Hell Hole Res.
Eleven Pines Rd.
DH16
PEAVINE RIDGE
Michigan Bluff Rd.
Gorman Ridge Rd.
MIDDLE FORK AMERICAN RIVER
Hell Hole Rd.
Hell Hole BCG
Foresthill
RALSTON RIDGE
Big Meadows NF CG 800.365.2267
To Auburn & DH56
DH54
Ralston Picnic Site BCG
Big Trees Grove NF CG
Loon Lake Rd.
DEVIL PEAK
River
To Cool & mid-DH56
LITTLE BALD MTN.
Chiquita Lake
PLACER
EL DORADO
Pilot Creek
Rubicon
HARTLESS MTN.
ROBB'S PEAK
Ice House Rd.
Georgetown
DH69 TE-A ALT
BALD MTN.
DH19
Wentworth Springs Rd.
Stumpy Meadows Lake
LOOKOUT MTN.
Union Valley Res.
Rock Creek
SUGARLOAF
DH69
LITTLE SUGAR PINE MTN.
SADDLE MTN.
ELDORADO NATIONAL FOREST
Whaler Creek
DH69 TE-A
American River Inn 530.333.4499 Recommended DH Discount 15%
To Riverton Jct & DH40
To Placerville & DH45/56

DH16 Mosquito Ridge Road

FSR 23 / FSR 96

Distance:	41.3 mi / 66.5 km	Traffic:	Light

At a Glance

Mosquitoes have been a growing concern lately. But you'd never think Northern California's most remote motorcycle road could be a breeding ground for an outbreak of the West Nile Speed Tax Virus. But despite its high Remoteness, a silent killer lurks among the endless S-curves that buzz up and down the rocky ridges and swarm through the thickly treed canyons of Tahoe National Forest. Even though the Pavement and Engineering are well above average for a Forest Service Road, so many squids have left their sneakered and t-shirted carcasses on this famous DH that during prime feeding periods, the CHP has air-assisted speed tax collectors hiding in the fetid swamps, hungry to suck the blood out of any motorcyclist daring to exceed the 40-mph (60-kmh) speed limit. So you might want to wave down a fellow rider (or in a pinch, a pyloneer) returning on this amazing dead-ender to see if anyone's been stung recently. If so, you'll just have to turn on the radar repellent and hope *Culex errati taxus* is too busy sucking on a big, tasty SUV to off you.

TIRES	
Twistiness	30.0/ 30
Pavement	12.2/ 20
Engineering	4.1/ 10
Remoteness	9.8/ 10
Scenery	10.0/ 15
Character	12.5/ 15
Total	**78.6**

Access

From Foresthill

Coming in on DH54 Auburn – Foresthill

Keep going through Foresthill until you get to the Chevron Station. Turn right. You're on the road.

On The Road

You're immediately out of town right away as you turn down FSR 23 and skirt a wall of tall, heavy pines. Your first curve esses into another, and another. At 0.6 mi (1.0 km) and 1.2 mi (1.9 km), you get your first killer views over to the steep, ripple-sided canyon wall on the far side of the North Fork of Middle Fork American River, not to mention the stately spires of Buckeye and Cock Robin Points. Who'll ride the road? I, said the motorcyclist.

You may be surprised by the 40-mph (60-kmh) sign at 1.5 mi (2.4 km), partly because it seems rather low for a middle-of-nowhere road and partly because it suggests the limit's been something less than that up till now. Oops. At any rate, as you begin your steep, edging, tightly winding descent along a steep rockface down to the river, you'll realize that nature and not some Forest Service bureaucrat sets the real limit on this road.

The view over the steep gorge is magnificent, just one more thing to divert your attention from the shoulderless, sometimes-bumpy and often-blind corners. You enter the Tahoe National Forest at 2.3 mi (3.7 km). Rips in this blanket of trees reveal mounds of rich, iron-red earth and black-streaked hunks of white granite. The rock angles immediately up from the left edge of the road and briefly on the right as well, creating a natural gateway to the NF. There's not a hint of development in sight. Not a hint of straightaway either as the unabated S-curves continue.

"Road Narrows" announces the sign at 6.7 mi (10.8 km). This can be a little disconcerting, given there's a solid rock wall on your left and a free fall on your right. We recommend you squeeze by any logging trucks carefully (these harrowing events are par for this moto-course). Like here at 8.1 mi (13.0 km) and again at 8.6 mi (13.8 km). At least the road never drops below two lanes.

The long descent ends as you cross the bridge over the river at 9.3 mi (15.0 km) and reverse direction up the other side. The narrowing of the canyon creates a dramatic bottleneck of steep, slate-colored shale. But enough scenery. Get yourself off the brakes, out of second and onto the throttle. You were dying to do some digging in these corners but had to take it easy coming down the precarious slope. As the first real climb of this ride begins, it's time to start shoveling.

Ah, curves can feel so much nicer going up than down. And unlike those steep ascents where the slope is in your face and all you see are trees, this one doesn't ask for a scenic sacrifice. The reversing climb up the other side of the gorge presents a broad and striking view of the west side of the canyon's steep, furry green slopes. At 10.8 mi (17.4 km), you reach a fork where the DH continues as FSR 96. Unless you've got a special thing for goat paths, there's no reason for any self-respecting sport-rider to stick right down FSR 23 except to check out the waterside Ralston Picnic area 2.0 mi (3.2 km) on. To remain where the real biking is, **stay left**.

The road switches back again, completing a zee. After a brief flit through the trees, you edge along the sharply detailed rock that forms Mosquito Ridge, looking across at the serrated green top of Peavine Ridge. Not a bad time for the road to widen and the pavement to jump a notch in quality. The curves moderate and lengthen. There's even a sweeper or two. Don't get too comfortable, though. It's a loooong way down. Straight down.

You enter the trees and resume climbing at 13.7 mi (22.0 km). You're in and out of them all along this ridge as the road curls steadily upward. The DH mounts the very top of the ridge at 17.1 mi (27.5 km), as evidenced by the fact that when you emerge from the forest at this point, the drop is suddenly on your right and you're overlooking a different fork of the American River. The forks may change, but the curves remain the same.

The pattern is much the same on the south slope of Mosquito Ridge as on the north, ascending in and out of the trees on a combination of predictable S-curves and sweepers. At 20.1 mi (32.3 km), you move deep into the forest where the shoulderless but wide road cuts a rare, straight swath through some unexpectedly tall pines.

As if to apologize for this uncharacteristic moment of straightness, a road sign announcing "Twisties Next 1 Mile" appears at 21.8 mi (35.1 km). Seems rather redundant given the 230 curves thus far, but you're not objecting. Particularly when it's followed by a sexy series of big, tight sweeping S-turns. If too many turns are making your eyes go funny, you can pull into the Big Trees Grove and Picnic Site at 24.4 mi (39.3 km). There a couple short walking loops through the northernmost grove of the few remaining virgin old-growth Giant Sequoia still in existence. In other words, the perfect place for a smoke break.

After a decent run, the pavement drops back to average grade at 24.8 mi (39.9 km). It's surprising that it's not better, considering the road is little used and covered by snow much of the year. It must get particularly deep here, where the dropping temperature and stunted trees serve as a reminder of how high you've climbed.

There are a couple of impressive, arcing sweepers at 25.0 (40.2) and 25.2 mi (40.6 km). They are so impressive, in fact, that the Forest Service has marked the second with a warning sign. Assuming you make the turn, there's a definite thinning of the corners past it to go with the thinning trees. The terrain flattens and you enter the straightest section of the DH so far. In fact, there's not another curve until you reach 27.4 mi (44.1 km). Outrageous!

Okay, calm down. This road's not done yet. At 27.9 mi (44.9 km), just past the gravel turnoff to Robinson Flat Rd and the sign saying "French Meadows 7 Miles", the pavement improves and the road resumes its essing ways through a series of narrow, tight, blind corners. The green, flat-topped mountains of Red Star Ridge across Duncan Canyon flash through spaces in the trees.

The veneer of trees opens up briefly on the right at 30.1 mi (48.4 km) marking the end of this corkscrewy section. Even though there are now some sweepers interspersed with the curves and the corners are more spaced, they're still pretty tight. In fact, the road throws a few hairpins at you starting at 30.9 mi (49.7 km). Add to this a steep, downward pitch through a darkening forest of pine, fir and cedar and you're happy to slow for the narrow bridge over Duncan Canyon Creek at 31.7 mi (51.0 km) after which you begin climbing again.

There's a bit of relief from the corners on the climb out of the canyon. Well at least until 32.4 mi (52.1 km), when the road curves from southwest to east. From your vantage point atop Red Star Ridge, the view is now to the left, back across the creek to the other bank.

At 33.5 mi (53.9 km), you clear the ridge and get your first look at the French Meadows Reservoir below, a view entirely unobstructed by trees. That's because any semblance of forest has been completely blighted, burned or chopped. There's obviously a lot of re-creation to be done here in the French Meadows Recreation Area. You descend through the few matchsticks left on a combination of steep, tight corners, leveling out at the dam crossing at 34.7 mi (55.8 km). Cross the dam and **turn left**.

*ROUTING OPTION: Turning right onto Eleven Pines Rd will take you the approximately 32 horribly paved miles (51.5 horribly paved kilometers) to mid-**DH19 Georgetown – Riverton Jct**. If that's not enough for you, you can add some distance to the trip by taking the turnoff right another mile on and going via Hell Hole Rd. Yeah, exactly.*

The veto on trees ends at the dam. Once on the other side, you're back into them and tall ones at that. The forest seems particularly beautiful compared to the carnage you witnessed coming down off the ridge. And you can relax and enjoy it since the curves that run along the flat lakeside meander easily through the firs. At 38.5 mi (62.0 km), the pavement smoothes and the sightlines improve, the latter a direct result of the shrinking and thinning of the trees. You cross the rivulet at the eastern tip of the reservoir and reach a junction at 40.4 mi (65.0 km). **Turn left here**. Another mile straight down this narrow paved road will take you to the McGuire Beach entrance and end of the DH at 41.3 mi (66.5 km).

*ROUTING OPTIONS: Rather than turning left to the McGuire Beach entrance, a maxburning option is to continue straight on gravel. Two miles (3.2 km) on, you'll reach a junction. Turn left to stay on Mosquito Ridge Rd. After a twisting climb, you'll reach the junction with Foresthill Rd (left) and Soda Springs Rd (right). Going left takes you 35 mostly paved but narrow miles (55 km) back to Foresthill and the start of the DH. The latter takes you approximately 18 gravel miles (29 km) up to I-80 and **DH57TE-B Donner Pass Rd** just west of Truckee.*

RIDER'S LOG: **DATE RIDDEN:** **YOUR RATING: /10**

Don't forget to print the DH Rider Discount list of service providers from destinationhighways.com *and take it with you. Then, just show 'em your book and ask for the discount.*

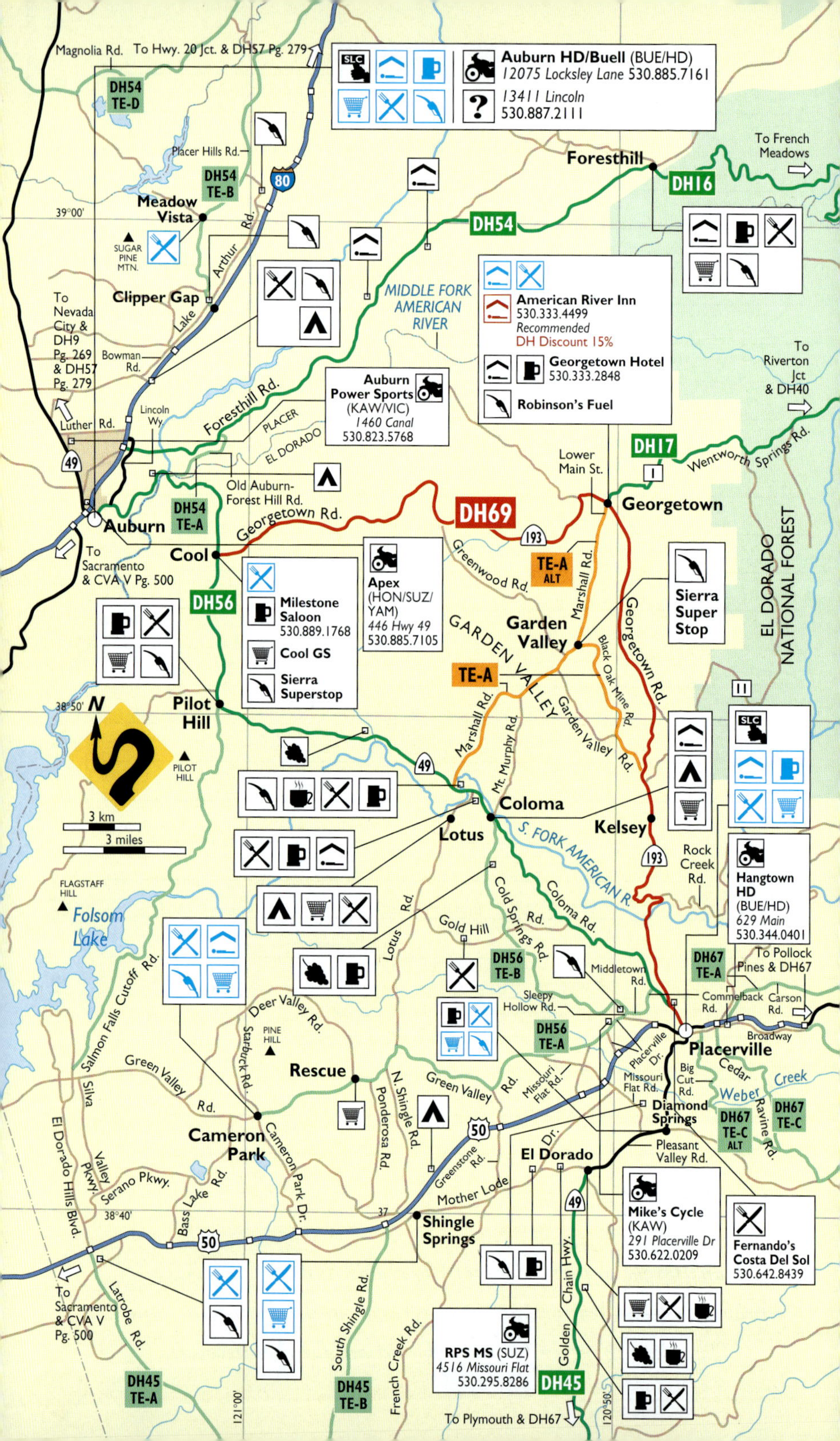

Auburn HD/Buell (BUE/HD)
12075 Locksley Lane 530.885.7161
13411 Lincoln
530.887.2111
Magnolia Rd.
To Hwy. 20 Jct. & DH57 Pg. 279
DH54 TE-D
Placer Hills Rd.
DH54 TE-B
Meadow Vista
Foresthill
To French Meadows
DH16
DH54
SUGAR PINE MTN.
Arthur Rd.
Clipper Gap
Lake
To Nevada City & DH9 Pg. 269 & DH57 Pg. 279
Bowman Rd.
MIDDLE FORK AMERICAN RIVER
American River Inn
530.333.4499
Recommended
DH Discount 15%
Georgetown Hotel
530.333.2848
Robinson's Fuel
To Riverton Jct & DH40
Auburn Power Sports
(KAW/VIC)
1460 Canal
530.823.5768
Foresthill Rd.
PLACER
EL DORADO
Lincoln Wy.
Luther Rd.
DH17
Wentworth Springs Rd.
Lower Main St.
Old Auburn-Forest Hill Rd.
DH54 TE-A
Auburn
Georgetown Rd.
DH69
Georgetown
To Sacramento & CVA V Pg. 500
Cool
Greenwood Rd.
TE-A ALT
Marshall Rd.
Sierra Super Stop
EL DORADO NATIONAL FOREST
DH56
Milestone Saloon
530.889.1768
Cool GS
Sierra Superstop
Apex
(HON/SUZ/YAM)
446 Hwy 49
530.885.7105
GARDEN VALLEY
Garden Valley
Black Oak Mine Rd.
Georgetown Rd.
TE-A
Pilot Hill
Marshall Rd.
Mt. Murphy Rd.
Garden Valley Rd.
PILOT HILL
3 km
3 miles
Coloma
Lotus
Kelsey
S. FORK AMERICAN R.
Rock Creek Rd.
Hangtown HD
(BUE/HD)
629 Main
530.344.0401
FLAGSTAFF HILL
Folsom Lake
Lotus Rd.
Gold Hill
Cold Springs Rd.
Coloma Rd.
Salmon Falls Cutoff Rd.
DH56 TE-B
Middletown Rd.
DH67 TE-A
To Pollock Pines & DH67
Sleepy Hollow Rd.
Commelback Rd.
Carson Rd.
Deer Valley Rd.
PINE HILL
Starbuck Rd.
DH56 TE-A
Placerville Dr.
Broadway
Placerville
Cedar
Green Valley Rd.
Rescue
N. Shingle Rd.
Green Valley Rd.
Missouri Flat Rd.
Missouri Flat Rd.
Big Cut Rd.
Weber Creek
Silva Valley Pkwy.
Cameron Park
Ponderosa Rd.
Diamond Springs
DH67 TE-C ALT
DH67 TE-C
Ravine Rd.
El Dorado Hills Blvd.
Cameron Park Dr.
Greenstone Rd.
El Dorado
Pleasant Valley Rd.
Serano Pkwy.
Bass Lake Rd.
Mother Lode Dr.
Mike's Cycle
(KAW)
291 Placerville Dr
530.622.0209
Fernando's Costa Del Sol
530.642.8439
Shingle Springs
To Sacramento & CVA V Pg. 500
Latrobe Rd.
South Shingle Rd.
French Creek Rd.
RPS MS (SUZ)
4516 Missouri Flat
530.295.8286
Golden Chain Hwy.
DH45 TE-A
DH45 TE-B
DH45
To Plymouth & DH67

DH69 Cool – Placerville

Georgetown Road (Hwy 193)

Distance:	26.8 mi / 43.1 km	Traffic:	Moderate

At a Glance

TIRES	
Twistiness	25.0/ 30
Pavement	12.7/ 20
Engineering	4.4/ 10
Remoteness	3.8/ 10
Scenery	7.8/ 15
Character	5.3/ 15
Total	**59.0**

The name is 69. DH69. Frankly, you don't have to be James Bond to look cool at the northern end of this route where the Engineering is wide and charismatic, the Pavement is smooth not shaken and tight corners are as rare as a natural nine. Not to mention that when it shoots as straight as a bullet from a 7.65 Walther PPK between Georgetown and the junction with TE-A. But be forewarned. This DH is going to test your mettle when the action starts south of Black Oak Rd. Here, the forces of Twistiness mercilessly crunch the road in the rocky jaws of the South Fork American River canyon, bending the asphalt thousands of feet down to the river and back up the closely treed west side. The climax is not only steep and tight, it's narrow. So please ensure you don't get stuck behind an Aston-Martin for the best part. And one more thing: do try and remember that this is a state highway. SPECTRE (SPecial Executive for Collection, Ticketing, Revenue and Extortion) patrols it. So you might want to pick up a radar detector from Q Division on your way out. After all, you do want to keep your license to ride.

Access

From Cool (mid-DH56 Placerville - Auburn)

Turn east from Hwy 49 at the well-marked turnoff for Hwy 193. You're on the road.

From Placerville

On Hwy 49 or Hwy 50

Follow Hwy 49 north out of Placerville. Turn right at the well-marked turnoff out to Hwy 193 and you're on the road.

Coming in on DH56 Auburn – Placerville (Hwy 49)

Turn left onto the well-signed Hwy 193 on the outskirts of P-ville. You're on the road.

Coming in on DH45 Plymouth – El Dorado (Placerville) (Hwy 49)

Continue north on Hwy 49 as it passes through Placerville. After you cross Hwy 50, look for the turnoff onto Hwy 193. Take it. You're on the road.

On The Road

Hwy 49 is pretty straight around Cool. So you'll feel right at home as you turn off 49 and head straight east through burnt fields, some scrubby trees, a vineyard and one too many houses. But apart from the three curves at 1.4 mi (2.3 km), it's hard to see what's so cool about this DH in the early frames.

More curves, albeit gentle ones, start at 3.8 mi (6.1 km). With the landscape getting progressively hillier and woodsier, the scenery and remoteness improve as well. The pavement? Smooth sailing so far.

The road widens at 5.7 mi (9.2 km), just in time for a fast, easy sweeper that turns the road south. The woods recede, leaving room for some scattered roadside development. While the scene is still dominated by light-to-heavy forest, the trend is nonetheless disturbing. As is the lack of any well-developed curves.

At 8.4 mi (13.5 km), the structures disappear and you actually enter a corner that you can't see the end of until you're in it. It's followed by others as the shoulder narrows again and sucks the forest against the road. We're not talking Mosquito Ridge here, but these are unquestionably S-curves and those things bobbing up and down are unquestionably your mirrors. **DH16** eat your heart out.

Better eat fast. The road widens for a turnoff at 10.1 mi (16.3 km) and the gentle, drifting bends return. With them comes a trickle of development, building to a stream and then a river at 11.9 mi (19.2 km) when you enter Georgetown, once known as Growlersburg. Won't be doing much growling through here, though – the speed limit's only 30 mph (50 kmh).

The DH's longest straight begins south of Georgetown, interrupted only by a couple of barely detectable shifts at 13.1 mi (21.1 km) and 14.1 mi (22.7 km) through the flat landscape of culled pines. Never known for their forbearance, impatient Placervillians squeezing in an after-work ride are inclined to use Black Oak Mine Rd (**TE-A**) at 15.6 mi (25.1 km) to cut off the northern half of this DH and make a loop using the southern half of **DH56 Auburn – Placerville**.

The pavement improves but it still adds scenic insult to twistiness injury when dull fields and ranchland replace much of the forest on the flat south of the TE. But the 17.6 mi (28.3 km) mark introduces a trio of curves. A tickler, but not enough to prepare you for the tight sweeper that brings you rudely out of your reverie at 18.1 mi (29.1 km). You've been cruising along, drifting in and out of biking consciousness and then suddenly it's all you can do to stay in your lane.

Yes, things have definitely changed. Whoa, there's a 25-mph (40-kmh) advisory preceding the next corner. Sure, now they tell you. But there's no time to complain since, out of the blue, the curves are coming fast and tight, and on a descent to boot. Low foliage interspersed with pines creeps along the road's edge to create a completely new feel in the suddenly remote and rolling terrain.

This steep twisting precursor to what lies ahead ends at 18.7 mi (30.1 km) as the terrain flattens, the ranch houses return, and the curves ease and lengthen. Take a breath as you weave through light trees and structural debris spread around the non-town of Kelsey, because you may not have a chance later.

The last bit of straightness starts at 20.2 mi (32.5 km) and ends at 21.5 mi (34.6 km), where you enter a "Rock Slide Area." Usually a good sign, as long as the rock isn't actually sliding. And this area's better than most, though, as is common, you pay for it with a drop in the quality of the asphalt. But these twisties are certainly worth the pavement price as you begin to pick your way through the first of the many long chains of tight esses that curve high above the canyon of the South Fork American River.

Check out that speedo. This section may not represent a lot of miles, but with one 20 to 30-mph (30 to 50-kmh) curve following the other on a sharp descent it takes some time to ride it, especially if you want to take in the spectacular view while avoiding becoming part of it. And if you were beginning to wonder where all those Twistiness points came from, you're not now.

The pavement's not so pockmarked come 22.5 mi (36.2 km). This, and the widened, guard-railed shoulders at the apex of the corners, give cause for a little extra juice. Not too much, though – the narrower, zitty asphalt is back at 23.0 mi (37.0 km).

It's dry here in the canyon, not to mention hot, as you descend into its bowels. Green becomes scarcer and brown more common as the vegetation shrinks, exposing rock and hardy grass. For hardier souls, the one-lane Rock Creek Rd turns off left at 23.6 mi (38.0 km) just before the DH hairpins to put the cliff on your right.

ROUTING OPTION: If you're a maxburner, Rock Creek Rd back to Placerville is a twisting, dipping, paved one laner that gives you many of the benefits of a crappy gravel road without actually being gravel.

The corkscrew continues as you pick your way down the steep slope. The tar strips that splatter across the asphalt make you think Jackson Pollock was alive and well and working for CalTrans. Of course, given the post-modern corners, abstract downslope and cubist engineering, you better be more skilled at riding your bike than Jackson was at driving his Caddy. Or at least more sober.

You reach the bottom of the gorge and cross the South Fork American River at 24.5 mi (39.4 km). The broad, smooth bridge is but a brief respite. Once you're across it, the twisting resumes as tightly as ever through a tunnel of trees. At least you're climbing now and there's even the occasional pullout that the occasional pylon deigns to use.

This is a nice, flowing section of S-curves. Not just because of the better pavement, though that always helps. It's more the improved sightlines, rising slope and lack of hairy hairpins that make it a piece of road you can shake and stir on, whether you're riding a Ninja 250 or a VTX 1800. The mission ends as you come over a rise to meet the junction of Hwy 49 and the southern HQ of **DH56 Placerville – Auburn** at 26.8 mi (43.1 km). Time for a dry martini?

Twisted Edges

TE-A Marshall Rd Part 1 - Black Oak Mine Rd - Garden Valley Rd (6.5 mi / 10.5 km)

Whether you're gunning it through the huge sweepers on the climb up Marshall Rd to a piney plateau or enjoying the spectacular views of the South Fork American River on the way down, the patches of slick pavement that shine through the gritty but smooth surface are easy to overlook. As is the short section of bumpy stuff that coincides with Garden Valley's 35-mph (55-mph) zone. And if you can't overlook them, well, you're back up to smooth when you pitch down the hill on Black Oak Mine.

TE-A ALT Garden Valley – Georgetown (3.5 mi / 5.6 km)

Marshall Rd Part 2

Despite the below-average pavement, this narrow, but decently cambered zig-zag along Empire Creek is just the ticket if you just can't get enough of those silly curves.

NAVIGATION: From Georgetown, go down Lower Main St and turn right down Marshall Rd.

Rider's Log: **Date Ridden:** **Your Rating: /10**

DH45 DH67 DH56 DH54 DH16 DH69 DH19 DH40 DH51

What are the Top Ten Rides based on Twistiness, Pavement, Engineering, Remoteness, Scenery and Character? You'll find the answers in the TIRES Charts at the back of the book. The complete list of DHs by TIRES components is at destinationhighways.com.

Yellowjacket BCG
Fashoda Beach BCG
Wolf Creek BCG
38°50'
To S. Lake Tahoe & DH51
Strawberry Point BCG
To mid-DH4 Pg. 379
120°20'
Northwind BCG
Ice House Res.
Cheese Camp Creek
Ice House Rd.
50
Silver Creek BCG
3
Loon Lake Rd.
36
30
To Tahoma & DH51 via about 25m/40km 4WD gravel
ROBB'S PEAK
DH40
5
Ice House Resort/CG
530.293.3321
Union Valley Res.
EL DORADO NATIONAL FOREST
BIG HILL
Big Silver C.
Robb's Hut BCG
HARTLESS MTN.
3
DH4 TE-A
Riverton Jct.
31
St Pauli Inn
530.293.3384
SILVER HILL
Silver Creek
Camino Cove BCG
Sunset BCG
11N60
11N65
IRON MTN. RIDGE
Mormon Emigrant Tr.
Camp Creek
North-South Rd.
Uncle Tom's Cabin
120°30'
2
DESOLATION WILDERNESS
Pilot Creek
ELDORADO NATIONAL FOREST
Jones Fork BCG
DH19
Stumpy Meadows BCG
S. FORK AMERICAN RIVER
Jenkinson Lake
N
2 km
2 miles
LOOKOUT MTN.
Chiquita Lodge
530.333.1147
Camp Chiquita
530.333.4673
Worton's SM
E16
Stumpy Meadows Lake
Pollock Pines
Sly Park Rd.
Rubicon River
DH67
To Plymouth & DH45
50
Starks Grade Rd.
Pilot Creek
Wentworth Springs Rd.
PLACER
EL DORADO
SAND MTN.
American River Inn
530.333.4499
Recommended
DH Discount 15%
Creek
Pleasant Valley
13
Camino
120°40'
Whaler Creek
Weber
DH67 TE-A
Newtown Rd.
DH67 TE-C
Quintette
Georgetown Hotel
530.333.2848
Hangtown HD
(BUE/HD)
629 Main
530.344.0401
Bucks Bar Rd.
BALD MTN.
Pleasant Valley Rd.
15
Robinson's Fuel
DH67 TE-D
Volcanoville Rd.
Chiquita Lake
SUGARLOAF
Rock Creek
DH67 TE-C
1
Camp Virner Rest
530.333.4674
Mike's Cycle
(KAW)
291 Placerville Dr
530.622.0209
Carson Rd.
Broadway
Cedar Ravine Rd.
11
DH67 TE-C
Quarry Rd.
Springs Rd.
DH67 TE-C ALT
Buckeye Rest
530.333.2600
Placerville
Commelback Rd.
Big Cut Rd.
Diamond
Diamond Springs
LITTLE BALD MTN.
Rock Creek Rd.
193
Missouri Flat Rd.
DH45
DH69
Georgetown Rd.
Pleasant Valley Rd.
120°50'
Black Oak Mine Rd.
Rd.
NON-FEATURED DH SERVICES NOT SHOWN
Georgetown
Marshall Rd.
Garden Valley Rd.
Middletown Rd.
El Dorado
Lower Main St.
Garden Valley
Coloma Rd.
To Plymouth & DH67
DH69 TE-A ALT
Greenwood Rd.
GARDEN VALLEY
Marshall Rd.
DH69 TE-A
Cold Springs Rd.
Green Valley Rd.
Coloma
DH56 TE-A
MIDDLE FORK AMERICAN RIVER
Lotus
DH56 TE-B
Gold Hill Rd.
To Sacramento & CVA V Pg. 500
Lotus Rd.
193
49
N. Shingle Rd.
RPS MS
(SUZ)
4516 Missouri Flat
530.295.8286
Ponderosa Rd.
DH69
DH56
Rescue
Deer Valley Rd.
To Cool & mid-DH56
To Cool & DH69

DH19 Georgetown – Riverton Jct

Wentworth Springs Rd / Ice House Rd

Distance:	54.0 mi / 86.9 km	Traffic:	Light

At a Glance

TIRES	
Twistiness	27.2/ 30
Pavement	16.0/ 20
Engineering	6.1/ 10
Remoteness	7.5/ 10
Scenery	8.1/ 15
Character	12.9/ 15
Total	**77.8**

During his brief tenure as governor, Gray Davis took on the maxburning confederacy and proclaimed the abolition of gravel on Wentworth Springs Rd. Thanks to California's modern-day Abraham Lincoln, this mountain pass would no longer be the sole domain of the dual sport elite. The entirety of this route to motorcycling freedom astride the Desolation Wilderness is now beautifully paved for all to enjoy, regardless of tread, clearance or displacement. Predictably, carpetbaggers were quick to move in and shackle the inconsistently curved western end of this DH with side roads and driveways. But east of the historic outpost of Uncle Tom's Cabin, you're free at last. Development is officially abrogated where beautiful black asphalt esses along a perfectly sightlined ridge. And though the dream of equal Pavement the rest of the way is compromised once you turn south on Ice House Rd, at least the Remoteness keeps you out from under the lash of the speed tax collectors. This twisting exodus through quiet woods ends with a tight, steep descent down to the South Fork of the American River. Of course, some rebel maxburners will remain unreconstructed, but, in time, most will come to accept the notion of liberty for all. And Davis will live on in motorcycling history not as a silent, gray fellow shot down in the prime of his political life, but as The Great Emancipator.

Access

From Georgetown (mid-DH69 Cool – Placerville (Hwy 193))

Follow Georgetown's Main St northeast from Hwy 193. When you reach the 45-mph sign at the edge of town, you're on the road.

From Riverton Jct

Coming on DH40 Meyers (South Lake Tahoe) – Riverton Jct (Hwy 50)

Ice House Rd is a signed turnoff 30.8 mi (49.6 km) west of the Hwy 50/89 Jct in Meyers. Turn north. You're on the road.

On The Road

Houses linger as you leave Georgetown. You figure you've cleared them when the 45-mph (70-kmh) speed limit ends and a sweeper guides you up a north-facing slope. Especially with the natural view you see of Little Bald Mtn as you curve and sweep steadily along the treed sideslope. But when the terrain plateaus at 2.0 mi (3.2 km), houses again settle on the forested flat.

Despite the fact the landscape is flat, you don't stop curving. And the corners tighten at 3.8 mi (6.1 km) when the terrain roughens. Both left and right roadsides angle up intermittently, inhibiting the construction tendencies of the local population. The pavement quality drops from good to not so good, but then rebounds at 6.4 mi (10.3 km).

Another mini-hamlet appears, this time squeezed between the road and tiny, hidden Chiquita Lake. The curves are gentle until you pass the paved turnoff to the old ghost town of Volcanoville at 7.7 mi (12.4 km). Then they erupt into a climbing series of hot, flowing sweepers.

The DH continues to improve. Great pavement gets the most out of the long, leaning curves. It's remote, though you can't see much since you're hemmed in by thick forest. Of course, if you want to interrupt the action for a bird's eye view, you can take the marked turnoff for short but steep gravel run up Bald Mtn at 10.2 mi (16.4 km).

ROUTING OPTION: Maxburners looking for a hair-brained connection down to Placerville can continue south beyond Bald Mtn on this mostly gravel road.

Houses again – just a few in the trees as you traverse a short straight through the once-town of Quintette. The great pavement drops to merely good as the straight ends and you sweep back beside a tall wall of solid green. You're still climbing steeply as you nip through this cut. Openness in the right-side trees ahead hints at a view. And there it is, a fleeting glimpse over the Whaler Creek Valley.

You continue to ascend above Whaler Creek, harpooning the separated curves and sweepers. The trees separate and shrink as the increase in altitude starts to have its effect. It's hardly sub-alpine wilderness – the fences and gravel driveways preclude any such illusion – but the lingering, snowy view of Lookout Mtn at 13.1 mi (21.1 km) is something. Too bad you have to endure a descending straightaway to get it.

The straightaway flattens at 14.3 mi (23.0 km), a sign you're entering Stumpy Meadows. Junior pines emerge from the indeed stumpy landscape. Compared to the terrain, the sight of Stumpy Meadows Lake at 15.9 mi (25.6 km) seems spectacular. The boat launch just beside the road seems like a nice place to stop. But that road beyond the twisties sign across the dam seems like a nicer place to… go.

Or so it seems. A few S-curves bunch together on the blacktop, but then separate. There's a sense of remoteness among these sweepers in the pine forest. But then, 19.0 mi (30.6 km) brings a long straightaway that traverses the thinning trees as well as some recently razed and reforested sections. Don't even think of bailing by turning at the paved turnoff at 22.3 mi (35.9 km). Unless you're really a dyed-in-the-wool maxburner.

ROUTING OPTION: Technically, this is a paved 32-mile (51.5-km) connection to ***DH16 Mosquito Ridge Road****. Practically, the asphalt's so crummy it may as well be gravel.*

The magic starts when you pass the turnoff to Uncle Tom's Cabin at 23.5 mi (37.8 km). Beautiful sweepers arc along the ridge between the Rubicon River valley to the north and Pilot Creek down to the south. Excellent engineering propels you through a series of endless esses along the granite and red rock cliffs overlooking the Desolation Wilderness. Perfect pavement, wide shoulders, great sightlines. Even guardrails – just in case.

Motorcycling may not get better than this. At 28.0 mi (45.1 km), the long, steady climb ends and a descent begins. It's just pitched enough to open up a view of the Sierra Nevada's sparkling blue, snow-topped Crystal Range, crossing the horizon ahead. But not so pitched that you can't accelerate effortlessly through the curves. The vastness of the mountain landscape suits this wide, sweeping road perfectly. The scene is full of motorcycling portraits, like the framed memory of the road curving downward through the tall, airy, cone-shaped pines at 29.4 mi (47.3 km).

S-curve after s-curve after s-curve. It feels like it's going to go on forever. But, of course, it doesn't. Wentworth Springs Rd ends at 30.8 mi (49.6 km), at the stop-signed T-junction with Ice House Rd. Not much you can do about it but **turn right**.

TOUR NOTE: Turning left will put you on Loon Lake Rd and the Rubicon route to the north end of ***DH51 Camp Richardson – Tahoma****. You'll get about eight miles (13 km) of pavement before you cross your own rubicon and the road turns into a rough, 4WD route. For serious maxburners only.*

It's got a tough act to follow, but Ice House Rd holds its own. The flawless pavement drops a grade after the turn although it's still very good. There are still respectable curves as you venture south as well, back amid thicker forest. If you're really having trouble adjusting, you can turn back and do that last section of Wentworth Springs again.

At 33.8 mi (54.4 km), the landscape opens up a little and you catch some glimpses to the south of the tops of Big Hill Mtn and the distant Iron Mtn Ridge. The mostly gravel Union Valley Rd down to the campgrounds on the north side of the Union Valley Reservoir is right at 34.4 mi (55.4 km). Too bad there's only a token glimpse of the water itself.

TOUR NOTE: There's a good swimming beach at the Fashoda Beach CG. Hot coin-op showers, too.

Interesting granite formations appear on the right, both before and after you bridge Cheese Camp Creek at 35.1 mi (56.5 km). But the terrain is getting less rugged, leveling out beside a processed flat of pines on the left. Though it is level on the right as well, there's just enough slope to provide one more glimpse of the reservoir at 36.7 mi (59.1 km). You then turn away from the water and veer east, U-ing over Big Silver Creek at 37.3 mi (60.0 km).

Apart from the big hairpins, there's been a definite straightening trend. It continues as you turn south again to parallel the eastern end of the lake's southern arm. There are several more turnoffs to waterside campgrounds along here. If an overloaded RV lumbers out of one of them, the dotted line sections will undoubtedly come in handy.

It's not much of a straight and it ends soon, transforming back into a serious sweepfest through the trees and meadows of stumps starting at 39.2 mi (63.1 km). Don't be too concerned about the cattleguards starting at 39.6 mi (63.7 km). They're mostly restricted to the short straights between the long, tight turns.

The forest thickens as you lose altitude. At 43.2 mi (69.5 km), there's an uncharacteristic section of bumpy pavement. It's short, though, and the surface is quickly back up to snuff. The altitude drop doesn't last long, either. At 45.2 mi (72.7 km), you're climbing again and out onto a wide, clearcut ridge, sweeping tightly through the recently planted trees.

The terrain, while razed, is striking nonetheless. It's a rocky landscape dabbed with thousands of tiny green trees. The land pitches and rolls down to the right, adding texture to the scene. As does the green and brown-tinged ridge just ahead and the hazy line of blue mountains beyond that.

At 46.5 mi (74.8 km), you begin the final descent. You're heading down a straightaway toward a big looping S-turn at 46.9 mi (75.5 km). Then the pitch steepens and, for the first time in a long while, the road is sloping down sharply to your left, rather than right. More ridges gnaw at the sky to the south. The pitch is definitely a factor now. All those miles of gunning it unconcerned out of the corners are over.

The DH presents a different face as it descends into the empty basin. Gone is the lush forest and feeling of sub-alpine wilderness. Now sage mixes with stunted trees that barely puncture the rocky red earth. It adds character, especially since the rapidly descending road is as twisty as ever. But what's that suspicious-looking development down there below? Something called "Mountain Acres"? Please, say it ain't so.

Down, down, down. At 51.3 mi (82.5 km), there are a few taller pines lining the switchbacks that guide the road through the steep terrain. The trees multiply just in time to obscure the side road that arrives mid-corner to interrupt your focus at 53.0 mi (85.3 km). So much for that line. Just a few more turns through the trees and Hwy 50 appears, in all its arterial glory, marking 54.0 mi (86.9 km) and the end of this DH.

Rider's Log: **Date Ridden:** **Your Rating:** /10

How do YOU rate Northern California's 74 Destination Highways? Go to destinationhighways.com*, and let other riders know.*

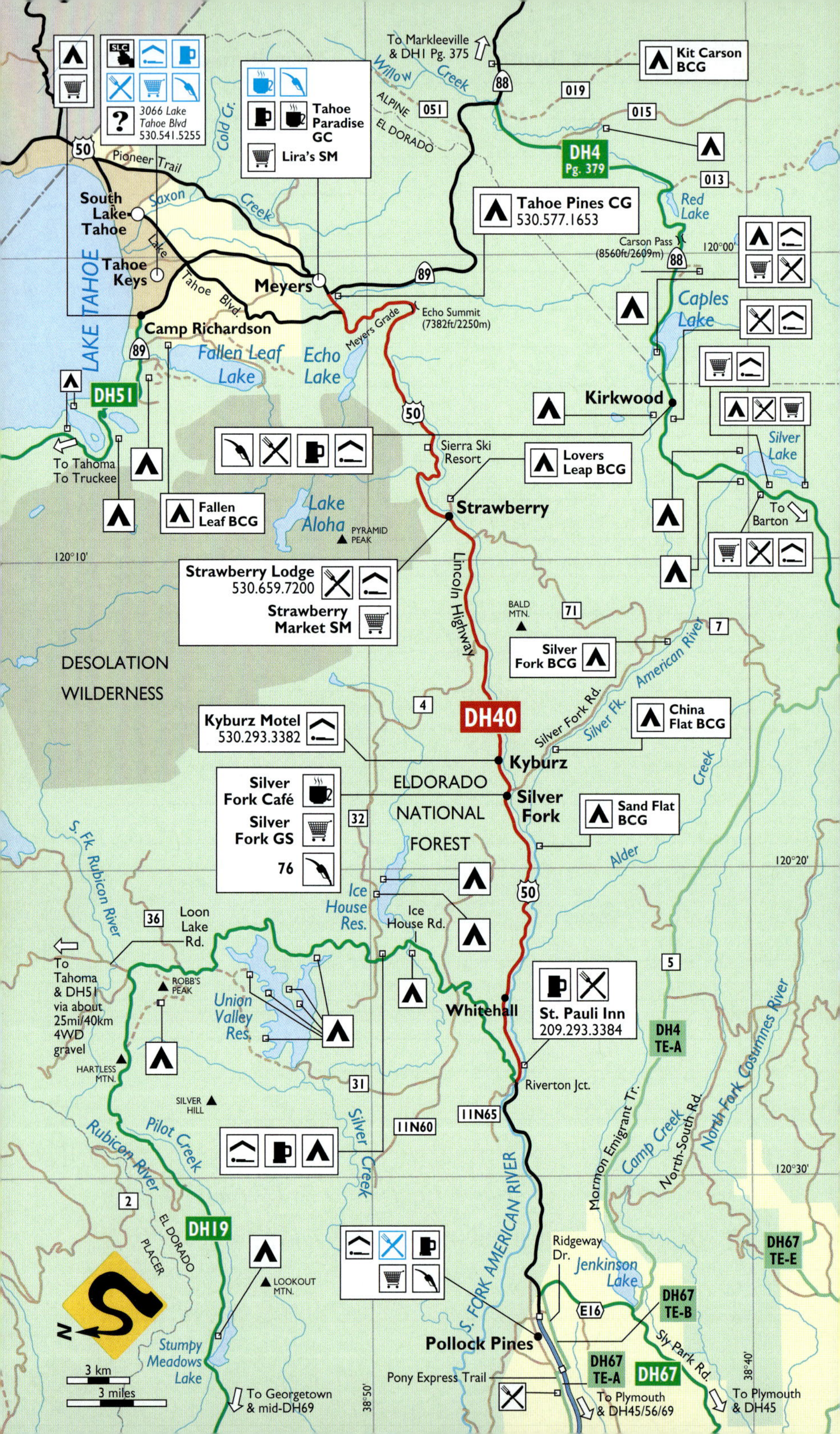

3066 Lake Tahoe Blvd 530.541.5255
Tahoe Paradise GC
Lira's SM
To Markleeville & DH1 Pg. 375
Kit Carson BCG
DH4 Pg. 379
Tahoe Pines CG 530.577.1653
South Lake Tahoe
Tahoe Keys
Meyers
Camp Richardson
LAKE TAHOE
Fallen Leaf Lake
Echo Lake
Echo Summit (7382ft/2250m)
Meyers Grade
Pioneer Trail
Carson Pass (8560ft/2609m)
Red Lake
Caples Lake
Kirkwood
DH51
To Tahoma
To Truckee
Fallen Leaf BCG
Sierra Ski Resort
Lovers Leap BCG
Strawberry
Silver Lake
To Barton
Lake Aloha
PYRAMID PEAK
Strawberry Lodge 530.659.7200
Strawberry Market SM
Lincoln Highway
BALD MTN.
Silver Fork BCG
DESOLATION WILDERNESS
DH40
China Flat BCG
Kyburz Motel 530.293.3382
Kyburz
Silver Fork Rd.
Silver Fk. American River
ELDORADO NATIONAL FOREST
Silver Fork Café
Silver Fork GS
76
Silver Fork
Sand Flat BCG
Alder Creek
Ice House Res.
Ice House Rd.
S. Fk. Rubicon River
Loon Lake Rd.
To Tahoma & DH51 via about 25mi/40km 4WD gravel
ROBB'S PEAK
Union Valley Res.
Whitehall
St. Pauli Inn 209.293.3384
DH4 TE-A
HARTLESS MTN.
SILVER HILL
Riverton Jct.
11N65
11N60
Pilot Creek
Rubicon River
Silver Creek
Mormon Emigrant Tr.
Camp Creek
North-South Rd.
North Fork Cosumnes River
DH19
ELDORADO
PLACER
S. FORK AMERICAN RIVER
Ridgeway Dr.
Jenkinson Lake
DH67 TE-E
LOOKOUT MTN.
DH67 TE-B
E16
Sly Park Rd.
Pollock Pines
Stumpy Meadows Lake
Pony Express Trail
DH67 TE-A
DH67
3 km
3 miles
To Georgetown & mid-DH69
To Plymouth & DH45/56/69
To Plymouth & DH45

DH40 Riverton Jct – Meyers (South Lake Tahoe)

Lincoln Highway (Hwy 50)

Distance:	30.8 mi / 49.6 km	Traffic:	Brutal

At a Glance

TIRES	
Twistiness	24.0/ 30
Pavement	18.6/ 20
Engineering	7.8/ 10
Remoteness	4.1/ 10
Scenery	10.3/ 15
Character	5.0/ 15
Total	**69.8**

The Lincoln Highway, completed in 1913, was America's first true intercontinental highway. "The Loneliest Road in America" is lonely no more, however, especially on this section that traces the original southern route through the Sierras to South Lake Tahoe. Scores of gamblers now roll along the bank of the glittering South Fork of the American River, trying their luck through the fast, low-risk curves. Yet despite the traffic, lots of throttle-cracking passing lanes go far to reduce the pylon vigorish on the long, steep climb through the sugar pines. Scenery's glamorous throughout, changing from green to granite as the road crosses into the sub-alpine to summit at the Sierra Ski Resort. And while the DH parlays its esses into a Twistiness jackpot on the narrow strand of asphalt that edges down Meyers Grade, the panoramic view over Lake Tahoe and the surrounding peaks is of historic proportions. This road proved so popular way back in the teens and twenties that the Lincoln Highway Association published a best selling tour book. This guide rated the road, described its best parts and pointed out the places where motorists could stop along the way to sleep, eat or gas up… Hey, wait a second!

Access

From Riverton Jct

Coming in on DH19 Georgetown – Riverton Jct

Turn left. You're on the road.

From South Lake Tahoe

Coming in on DH51 Tahoma – Camp Richardson (South Lake Tahoe) (Hwy 89)

Continue south on Hwy 89. It will merge with Hwy 50 south of South Lake Tahoe. At Meyers, when Hwy 89 splits off south to Markleeville, keep going straight on Hwy 50. You're on the road.

On The Road

"Twisties Next 30 Miles." Now, there's a sign. Heading east from Riverton Jct, it's hard to believe that Hwy 50 was a freeway not too many miles back. The smooth blacktop that winds along the sparkling South Fork American River is enveloped by rugged terrain of emerald pine, dark green shrubs, brown grass and gray rock. Now if only that pylon in front of you would only take advantage of the pullouts at 2.0 and 2.3 mi (3.2 and 3.7 km).

There's definitely an intimacy to this scene, due largely to the fact that when this road was constructed a century ago, it wasn't built very high off the river. In fact, at 2.6 mi (4.2 km), you drop right down along its bank to the frequently flooded settlement of Whitehall. Not much to see here. Despite the important-sounding name, it's nothing but a couple blocks of waterlogged cabins connected by wooden bridges across the river.

The DH stays low to the river as its valley widens. The landscape opens up and you pick up speed as the curves stretch out. You pick up more velocity at 4.1 mi (6.6 km) when the first sweeping passing lane veers upward and across Alder Creek. The extra width ends at 4.7 mi (7.6 km), and you're back down beside bubbling rapids.

The constant twisting and turning, dashing over rocks and splitting to go around little islands creates lots of whitewater on this wild little river. Its spirited flow somehow makes the linked curves and sweepers that ebb and flow along the low bank seem even more abundant. Not that that's really necessary in these beginning miles.

Well, maybe it is necessary. At 6.0 mi (9.7 km), you climb up the sharply rising left bank and lose the great river views. Then, at 6.9 mi (11.1 km), another passing lane also introduces an element of straightness. And it settles in, lingering even after the passing lane ends at 7.7 mi (12.4 km) and you run Silver Fork's small gauntlet of cabins.

The setting is heavily treed now, elegant sugar pines glazing not only the roadside but the slopes and summits of Bald Mtn and Pyramid Peak. At 8.6 mi (13.8 km), you cross the 4000 ft (1220 m) barrier and pass through the little burglet of Kyburz.

The twisties that resume out of Kyburz are neither tight nor concentrated. But you're never too far from a tilting moment. Even the passing lane at 11.6 mi (18.7 km) has a little lilt in it. At 12.5 mi (20.1 km), you're at 5000 feet (1524 m). You see the elevation too, as the break in the trees to the right reveals how high the road has clambered above the river.

Up, up and away. The views off to the right are so compelling, the RVs are actually using the pullouts, albeit for parking. The trees shrink and the colorful Sierra granite dominates the landscape. You're already feeling high as another passing lane rockets upward.

It seems you've reached the summit at 14.9 mi (24.0 km). You tilt downward, tempted to pass that last remaining pylon in defiance of the whiny "Do Not Pass" sign and get a clear glimpse of the stony mountains of the Desolation Wilderness. There's still a steep drop on the right but the width of the road and paucity of curves make the injunction irrelevant.

The terrain flattens as the gentle descent continues. And with the exception of a decent sweeper at 17.2 mi (27.7 km), what curves there are get gentler, too. Even though there was the sense of having gone through a pass, when you find the river flowing by again on your right at 17.8 mi (28.6 km), it's clear you're still gaining altitude. Unless, of course, water flows uphill. Which is unlikely, despite the current governor's election promises.

There's a nice meadow view on the right, spoiled only by a 45-mph (70-kmh) sign. The two-service town of Strawberry ripens beneath a looming cliff named Lover's Leap. Despairing lovers in ancient Greece would plunge from the original Leap into the Ionian Sea hoping to cure themselves of their passions. Fortunately, your passion for motorcycling needs less dramatic treatment.

The cabins lining the road are dwarfed by a stand of enormous pines as you exit Strawberry's small residential area. The lushness of the trees, grass and shrubs beneath them stand out against the granite faces looming above. At 19.0 mi (30.6 km) in the midst of another four-lane stretch, you're at 6000 feet (1829 m). Rock takes over from forest again. And that alpine feeling resumes.

The passing lane ends at 20.0 mi (32.2 km), at the turnoff to the small mountain community of Twin Bridges. A big, wide, well-sightlined sweeper is incongruously cautioned at 35 mph (55 mph). Make up your own mind.

More big sweepers bring big views. All you can see of the river far below is the top of its gorge opening up on your right. Granite monoliths, huge molars stained with trees, protrude out of the void. On the left, the black and white kaleidoscope formed by the chalk and shadows of the rough cut rock blur as you flash through the perfectly engineered esses.

At 20.7 mi (33.3 km), a passing lane begins again – a blessing if you've been stuck behind anything for those recent turns. You may have the extra lane, but the corner is still tight and your right mirror lingers low as you blast by any underpowered obstacles that interfere with your wrist-twisting enjoyment. You'll want your speed up to enjoy the more moderate curves that lie just ahead.

At 23.7 mi (38.1 km), you reach the Sierra Ski Resort. Can it be that it's just a basic November to May ski area? No golf course, tennis courts or rollerblading paths? None of that "four-season" crap attracting summer traffic and damaging otherwise great motorcycle roads? Finally, a responsible corporate citizen. Supporter of Greypeace, too, no doubt.

The curves fall off as you continue on the wide pavement through the cabins and trees, and don't resume until you pass Echo Summit (7382 ft / 2250 m) at 26.7 mi (43.0 km) and curl north. Signs warning of steep downgrades and tight turns don't prepare you for the eye-bugging views over Lake Tahoe to the 10,000 foot (3050 m) plus peaks. The mountain peaks are eye-catching, but then so are the curves that eke out a narrow line between the rock going straight up on the left and straight down on the right.

A nifty little series of S-curves later, the terrain flattens enough to permit a brief passing lane – too bad it's for bikes coming the other way – at 28.0 mi (45.1 km). When the road narrows to two lanes again, it maintains a bit of shoulder for the equally nifty series of S-sweepers that follow. The layer of green that has been thickening as you descend is interrupted by a large, blackened granite face to the left at 29.0 mi (46.7 km).

At 29.6 mi (47.6 km), the road sweeps west, away from the mountainside, leaving the curves behind. The super-broad shoulders are back as the DH eases down onto the wide valley floor, arriving at the junction with Hwy 89, on the outskirts of Meyers, at 30.8 mi (49.6 km).

RIDER'S LOG: **DATE RIDDEN:** **YOUR RATING: /10**

Map Tip: Services on non-featured DHs and TEs are generally shown as bare icon only. For the full detail, just turn to the featured map.

To Truckee
To DH57
Pg. 279
To I-80
Granite Flat BCG
To I-80
Martis Creek Lake BCG
Safeway SM
To Reno
431
Sandy Beach CG
267
LOOKOUT MTN.
Goose Meadows BCG
Incline Village
Tahoe Vista
Kings Beach
28
89
MT. PLUTO
Crystal Bay
Crystal Bay
Silver Creek BCG
Carnelian Bay
Carnelian Bay
MT. WATSON
Sunnyside Resort
530.583.7200
Cottage Inn B&B
530.581.4073
SIERRA
28
TE-A
Lake Forest BCG
Sunnyside Market
Tahoe Park GS
Tahoe City
Fire Sign Café
530.583.0871
39°10'
SCOTT PEAK
Waro Creek Blvd.
Sunnyside
William Kent CG
Black Bear Tavern
530.583.8626
28
Tahoe State BCG
Kaspian BCG
LAKE
Barker Pass Rd.
3
Tahoe Pines
Fluer de Lac
530.525.5261
50
To Reno
89
Glenbrook
Obexer's GS
Homewood
Glenbrook Bay
Wentworth Springs Rd.
TAHOE
Sugar Pine Point SP BCG
Tahoma
NEVADA
50
Chamber's Landing
530.525.7262
Lakeridge
4WD
PLACER
EL DORADO
To mid-DH19 via about 25mi/40km 4WD gravel
Meeks Bay
Rubicon Bay
Skyland
Tut Rite GS
ELDORADO NATIONAL FOREST
LOST CORNER MTN.
DH51
Zephyr Cove
Tahoma Market GS
39°00'
Round Hill Village
RUBICON PEAK
Meeks Bay BCG
Meeks Bay Resort
877.326.3357/
530.525.6946
Tahoe Village
207
SLC
Emerald Bay
Stateline
Meeks Bay GS
NEVADA
CALIFORNIA
DL Bliss SP CG
Cascade Lake
South Lake Tahoe
380 North Lake Blvd
530.581.6900
Tahoe Keys
Emerald Pt BCG
Fallen Leaf Lake
Camp Richardson
Lake Tahoe Blvd.
Pioneer Trail
DESOLATION WILDERNESS
MT. TALLAC
SLC
Eagle Point CG
89
TWIN PEAKS
N
3066 Lake Tahoe Blvd
530.541.5255
Lake Aloha
Echo Lake
Meyers
FREEL PEAK
Bayview BCG
3 km
3 miles
89
To DH4 Pg. 379
38°50'
To Riverton Jct & DH19
DH40
50
120°10'
120°00'
EL DORADO
ALPINE

DH51 Camp Richardson (South Lake Tahoe) – Tahoma

Highway 89

Distance:	15.0 mi / 24.1 km	Traffic:	Almost Always Brutal

At a Glance

TIRES	
Twistiness	26.7/ 30
Pavement	17.8/ 20
Engineering	5.7/ 10
Remoteness	2.0/ 10
Scenery	10.7/ 15
Character	2.4/ 15
Total	65.3

Lake Tahoe, the "Jewel of the Sierra" as Mark Twain called it, is a brilliant, cornflower blue sapphire set between the Sierra Nevada's Desolation Wilderness and the Carson Range. At 6,229 ft (1912 m), it's the highest lake of its size in the US, the third deepest lake in North America and the tenth deepest lake in the entire world. This short but scintillating necklace of tight curves running up the often busy, southwest shoreline of Tahoe also rates a high evaluation, especially for its Twistiness and Pavement facets. The Scenery is particularly lustrous around the glittering pendant of Emerald Bay but it does have a few development blemishes at the northern end. Flaws in Remoteness, in the intensity and distribution of traffic and length all take away from its Caratcter. This minor gem may not be perfect but if you appraise it in less-busy times of the year, you'll be glad you added it to your collection of precious rides.

Access

From South Lake Tahoe

On Hwy 89

Camp Richardson is 2.2 mi (3.5 km) to the west of where joint Hwy 50/89 splits into its constituent parts in South Lake Tahoe. Stay on Hwy 89. Once through Camptown, you're on the road. Doo-dah, doo-dah.

Coming in on DH40 Riverton Jct – Meyers (South Lake Tahoe) Hwy 50

Continue north on Hwy 50/89 past Meyers. When the duo highway splits in South Lake Tahoe, take 89 to Camp Richardson. Once through it, you're on the road.

From Tahoe City

On Hwy 89

Tahoma is on the southwestern shore of Lake Tahoe about halfway between Tahoe City and South Lake Tahoe. Keep south on Hwy 89 past town and you are on the road.

On The Road

Traffic is likely bad as you leave Camp Richardson. Better get used to it, since it might be there the whole way. Why not admire the great pavement? Or turn your attention to the loose forest crowding the edge of the road? Enjoy the mountains you can make out between the white trunks of the birch trees. Or read the sign indicating the National Forest Baldwin Lake turnoff at 0.4 mi (0.6 km).

Whoa, check out the curves. Double yellow's a bummer, though. Better get used to it, too. See the straight? Any pylons coming? Probably. Sometimes it's better to keep your throttle closed and let people think you are a fool than open it and remove all doubt.

Wow, at 1.8 mi (2.9 km) there is actually a passing lane. In both directions, no less. That's because the road straightens out as it starts to climb. Going north, you quickly lose the dotted yellow but a nice view over the lake at 2.0 mi (3.2 km) provides at least some compensation.

A fence barely restrains big, round, white rocks on the left side from tumbling onto the road. Then, a small viewpoint and a 15-mph (25-kmh) corner appear. This curve abruptly turns the road from northeast to southwest before you're down into the flat, glacier-debris field to the north of Cascade Lake.

More curves come through the thinning trees and the increasingly prevalent, jumbled, white moraine rock. Not much soil left here from the heavy glaciation. Not even the pavement's been spared; check out those deep gouges in the asphalt on the 10-mph (15-kmh) curve at 2.8 mi (4.5 km) that swings the road back north. Or are those from Gold Wing trailer hitches?

You're again heading north, slanting upward. As before, there's a view over Lake Tahoe to the Nevada shore. Then another wide but sharp corner returns the road to a southwest heading. The turnoff for Eagle Point is at 3.3 mi (5.3 km) prior to another 10-mph (15-kmh) curve that points you north again. Déjà vu. Right down to the gouges in the asphalt.

This time though, a fourth sharp corner quickly returns the road to a southwest tack. And you discover that somehow, through all this, you've climbed up onto a lateral moraine ridge, the remnant of a retreating glacier. From up here, you can see Cascade Lake in its bowl down to your left and Emerald Bay below through the trees to the right. Both bodies of water are backed by the Desolation Wilderness peaks of the Sierra Nevada, including Mt Tallac on the far side of Cascade Lake.

The road is having a rare straight section so there's lots of time to look at the view before Cascade Lake sinks out of sight. Past the turnoff left for one of the Tahoe Rim Trail (TRT) trailheads at 4.1 mi (6.6 km), you start to head down around the end of Emerald Bay.

TOUR NOTE: If you're feeling like a bit of exercise, the TRT is a 170-mi (274-km) long hike that completely encircles Lake Tahoe. (Sorry maxburners, motorcycles are verboten.)

The mountains up behind the bay are incredibly white at the top. Which is odd, considering there is no snow on them. Below them, and over the guard rail to your right, tiny, perfect Fannette Island – the only island in Lake Tahoe – is nestled in its green water setting at this end of the bay. The left upslope off the road mirrors the light hue of the mountains with white sandstone, mudstone, and limestone weathered into a variety of interesting shapes.

A bit of a shoulder is now added to the excellent, sweeping pavement that takes you past the turnoff at 5.3 mi (8.5 km) for Vikingsholm – a medieval-style, Scandihoovian house built in the late 1920s. Maybe it's a Norwegian thing but for some reason, the asphalt surface of the road changes briefly to concrete. It's still smooth and sweet though, as are the continuing views over the bay. It'd just be nice if there were a few more serious curves. But no, you have to settle for more of that bright, white-rock road edge, now on both sides of the road at 7.2 mi (11.6 km).

North of the Emerald Point State Park CG, the road turns into the trees. You're back along the main shore of Lake Tahoe here, although you can't actually see the water again until 7.8 mi (12.6 km) when the terrain slopes down to the right. More importantly, you're into a nice set of loosely linked sweepers and curves, but one that comes with a drop in pavement quality. Oh well, there's a good chance pylons are impeding your progress anyway.

A sign welcomes you to Rubicon Bay at 9.9 mi (15.9 km). Gradually, development appears, along with more (and slower) traffic. The former doesn't last long but, by the time it's gone, so have most of the curves. The latter is likely to stay.

By 11.7 mi. (18.8 km), you've descended almost down to lake level and at 12.5 mi (20.1 km), you enter and exit the townlet of Meeks Bay. What's left? Not much. A little more cornering through the forest and then you follow a pylon into Tahoma where this little bauble stops glinting at 15.0 mi (24.1 km).

Twisted Edges

TE-A Tahoe City – Kings Beach (Hwy 28) (13.6 mi / 21.9 km)
If you liked that stretch of the DH between Meeks Bay and Tahoma, this TE has more of the same. A few more regal curves and more majestic pavement skirt the northwest Tahoe lakeshore. Past Carnelian Bay though, the development gets increasingly extravagant, culminating in the palatial Nevada casinos in Crystal Bay.

ROUTING OPTIONS: There are a few good roads nearby in Nevada you may want to do:

(1) Smooth, twisty, well-paved and wide-shouldered, Hwy 431 from Incline Village up to the Mt Rose Summit (8900 ft / 2732 m) and then down to Hwy 395 just south of Reno can have you riding above the snowline in June.

Nice views over Nevada and Lake Tahoe too. Pylons can easily bog you down, though, and there are few legal passing opportunities in the twistiest spots either side of the Summit. It's 17.6 mi (28.3 km) from Incline Village to where the good stuff peters out alongside grotesquely large houses and another 6.0 mi (9.6 km) to the jct with 395, where you are just a short interstate hop south to Reno.

(2) Hwy 28 along the north eastern shore of the Lake Tahoe is also a good scoot, in large part because no development seems to be allowed on a lot of this stretch. How enlightened of somebody.

(3) A little farther east, Hwy 341 either side of Virginia City between Hwy 395 and Hwy 50 provides some mild amusement. Makes a nice addition to the Rose Summit Rd (possibly with break for a little Reno action in the middle).

RIDER'S LOG: **DATE RIDDEN:** **YOUR RATING: /10**

Just what is an "STC" or "maxburner" anyway?
Check out these and other Twisted Terms in the Glossary at p.??

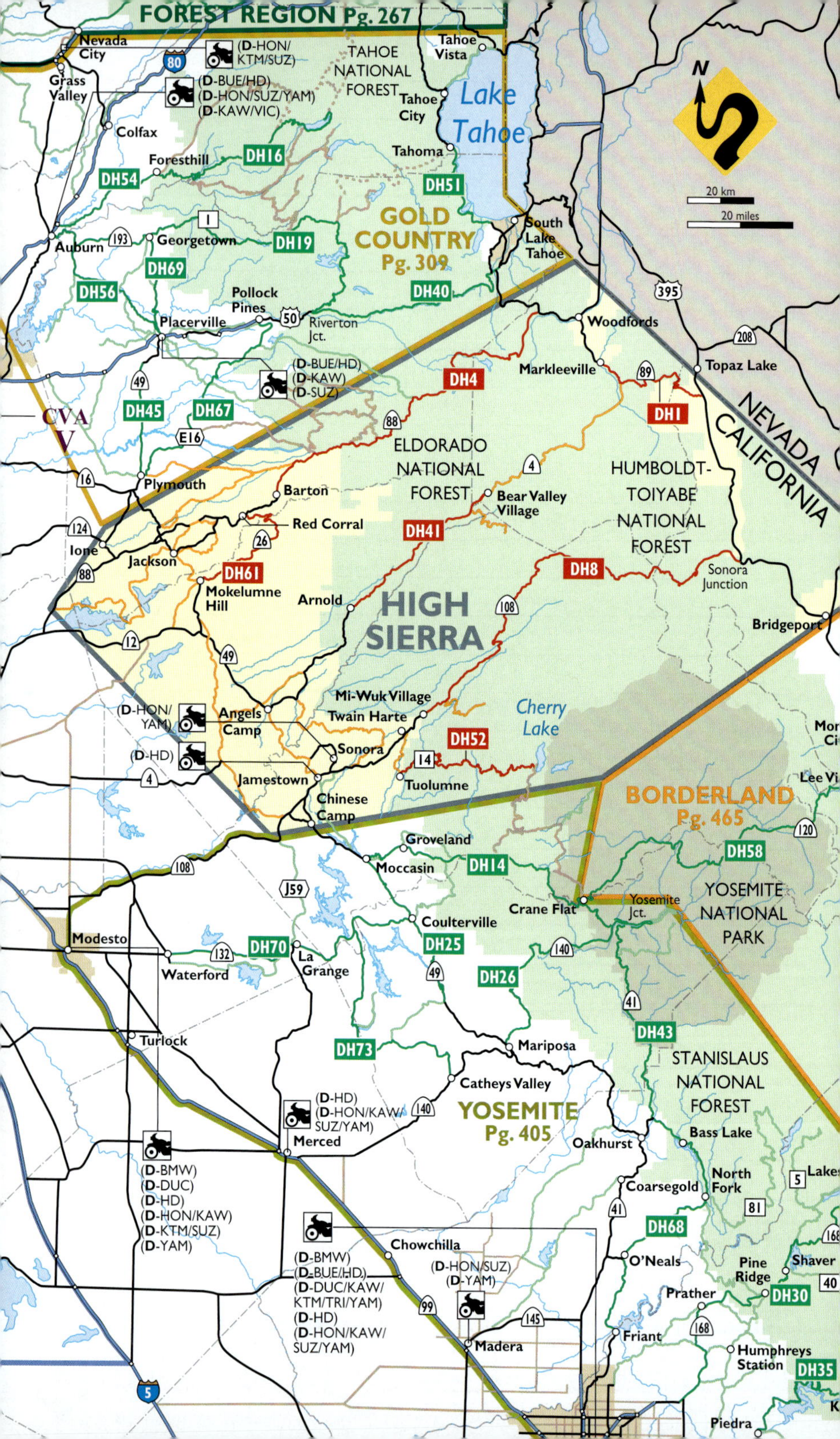

FOREST REGION Pg. 267
GOLD COUNTRY Pg. 309
HIGH SIERRA
BORDERLAND Pg. 465
YOSEMITE Pg. 405
CVA
NEVADA
CALIFORNIA
TAHOE NATIONAL FOREST
ELDORADO NATIONAL FOREST
HUMBOLDT-TOIYABE NATIONAL FOREST
STANISLAUS NATIONAL FOREST
YOSEMITE NATIONAL PARK
Lake Tahoe
Cherry Lake
20 km
20 miles
N
Nevada City
Grass Valley
Colfax
Foresthill
Auburn
Georgetown
Pollock Pines
Placerville
Riverton Jct.
Tahoe Vista
Tahoe City
Tahoma
South Lake Tahoe
Woodfords
Markleeville
Topaz Lake
Plymouth
Barton
Red Corral
Ione
Jackson
Mokelumne Hill
Arnold
Bear Valley Village
Sonora Junction
Bridgeport
Mi-Wuk Village
Twain Harte
Angels Camp
Sonora
Jamestown
Tuolumne
Chinese Camp
Groveland
Moccasin
Crane Flat
Yosemite Jct.
Coulterville
Modesto
Waterford
La Grange
Turlock
Mariposa
Catheys Valley
Merced
Oakhurst
Bass Lake
Coarsegold
North Fork
Chowchilla
O'Neals
Pine Ridge
Shaver
Prather
Friant
Madera
Humphreys Station
Piedra
Lee Vi
Mor Ci
Lakes
DH1
DH4
DH8
DH14
DH16
DH19
DH25
DH26
DH30
DH35
DH40
DH41
DH43
DH45
DH51
DH52
DH54
DH56
DH58
DH61
DH67
DH68
DH69
DH70
DH73
80
1
193
50
395
208
89
49
88
E16
16
4
124
26
108
12
14
120
J59
132
140
41
5
81
168
40
99
145
(D-HON/KTM/SUZ)
(D-BUE/HD)
(D-HON/SUZ/YAM)
(D-KAW/VIC)
(D-BUE/HD)
(D-KAW)
(D-SUZ)
(D-HON/YAM)
(D-HD)
(D-HD)
(D-HON/KAW/SUZ/YAM)
(D-BMW)
(D-DUC)
(D-HD)
(D-HON/KAW)
(D-KTM/SUZ)
(D-YAM)
(D-BMW)
(D-BUE/HD)
(D-DUC/KAW/KTM/TRI/YAM)
(D-HD)
(D-HON/KAW/SUZ/YAM)
(D-HON/SUZ)
(D-YAM)

High Sierra

NON-FEATURED DH SERVICES NOT SHOWN
To Hwy 88/89 Jct
Cosumnes River
Middle Fork
Ham's Station
Cook's Station
DH4
9N17
PEDDLER HILL
Lower Bear River Res.
Bear River Res.
ELDORADO NATIONAL FOREST
To Barton
To Red Corral & DH61
38°30'
120°20'
120°10'
DOAKS RIDGE
N. Fork Mokelumne River
AMADOR
CALAVERAS
DEVILS NOSE
Silver Valley NF CG
Pine Marten NF CG
Lake Alpine Lodge 209.753.6358
Alpine NF CG
MOKELUMNE PEAK
MT. REBA
Silver Tip NF CG
Salt Springs Res.
CALAVERAS DOME
Base Camp 209.753.6556
Bear Valley Lodge 209.753.2327
Bear Valley Pizza
Bear Valley GS SM
Headwaters Coffee House 209.753.2708
Bear Valley Adventure Co
Big Meadow BCG
Bear Valley Village
Lake Alpine
TE-C
Tamarack
Union Res.
Spicer Res. Rd.
ALPINE
TUOLUMNE
7N01
Spicer Res.
TE-A
DH41
BAILEY RIDGE
Middle Fork Mokelumne River
Dorrington Hotel & Rest 209.795.5800
Dorrington Inn 888.874.2164
Dorrington GS 209.795.2027
Chevron
North Fork Stanislaus River
LIBERTY HILL
Tamarack Lodge B&B 209.753.2830
Tamarack Pines Inn B&B 209.753.2895
Stanislaus River BCG
38°20'
S. Fork Mokelumne
SUMMIT LEVEL RIDGE
Golden Pines RV Resort CG 209.795.2820
Camp Connell
Dorrington
Wa Ka Luu Hep Yoo NF CG
Spicer Reservoir BCG
Calveras Big Trees SP
Boards Crossing BCG
MCKEE HILL
To Sonora Jct (Hwy 395)
San Antonio Cr.
SLC
Arnold
STANISLAUS NATIONAL FOREST
Griswold Creek
Golden Pines RV CG 209.795.2820
Beardsley Lake
Strawberry
CALAVERAS
TUOLUMNE
Oak Hollow SP CG
M. Fk. Stanislaus River
Cold Springs
Pinecrest
38°10'
DARBY KNOB
North Grove SP CG
DH8
Murphys
TABLE MTN.
Knight Creek
SCL
Goldrush (HON/YAM) 358 W Stockton 209.532.2371
RIDGE
Rose Creek
STAR RIDGE
Long Barn
Vallecito
S. Fk Stanislaus River
Tuolumne River
DODGE
DH8 TE-A
Sugar Pine
Mi-Wuk Village
N
Stanislaus
Yankee Hill Rd.
Big Hill Rd.
Columbia
DH8 TE-B
Twain Harte
Confidence
MARBLE MTN.
Clavey
Reed Creek
3 km
2 miles
Phoenix Lake Rd.
Tuolumne Rd.
38°00'
Sonora
DH52 TE-A
THOMPSON PEAK
DH52
To Cherry Lake
Soulsbyville
E17
TE-E
E5
To Moccasin & DH14 Pg. 421 & DH25 Pg. 417
Tuolumne
DUCKWALL MTN.
Jamestown
DH14 TE-A
DH14 TE-A ALT
Jamestown HD 18275 Hwy 108 209.984.4888

DH41 Arnold – Bear Valley Village

Highway 4

Distance:	25.0 mi / 40.2 km	Traffic:	Moderate

At a Glance

Listen and understand. The Speed Tax Collector is out there. It can't be bargained with. It can't be reasoned with. It doesn't feel pity, or remorse, or fear. And it absolutely will not stop, ever, until you are dead broke.

TIRES	
Twistiness	23.4/ 30
Pavement	16.5/ 20
Engineering	8.2/ 10
Remoteness	6.2/ 10
Scenery	9.5/ 15
Character	6.0/ 15
Total	69.8

Well, at least that's how Kyle Reese would have described the Terminator if he were a motorcyclist. Fortunately, whether you see STCs as terminators, predators or just bungling kindergarten cops, this piece of road offers some measure of sanctuary, despite being a state highway. That's because there's far better pillage before the DH begins amid the barbaric traffic west of Arnold. The route starts out easy as you pump your iron horse through tight but basic reps of S-curves in the thick forest of Calveras Big Trees State Park. But past Dorrington, it takes all your muscle to ride strong and fast through the long, linked, perfectly paved and sculpted sweepers that make this DH a contender for Mr. Pavement and Engineering Universe. Scenery accents are increasingly alpine and European as you climb. In fact, by the time you reach the road's more remote higher points, the sparsely treed, granite mountains and ridges look like something naturalized from Austria. All you need are clothes, boots and a motorcycle. *Hasta la vista, baby.*

Access

From Arnold

On Hwy 4

Continue east on Hwy 4. You're on the road.

From Bear Valley

On Hwy 4

Ride west. You're on the road.

On The Road

There's a "Scenic Route" sign on the eastern edge of Arnold, a sure indication that you are finally out of the busy, curveless, suburban sprawl that constitutes Hwy 4 between Hwy 49 and Ahnuld. And if the proposition

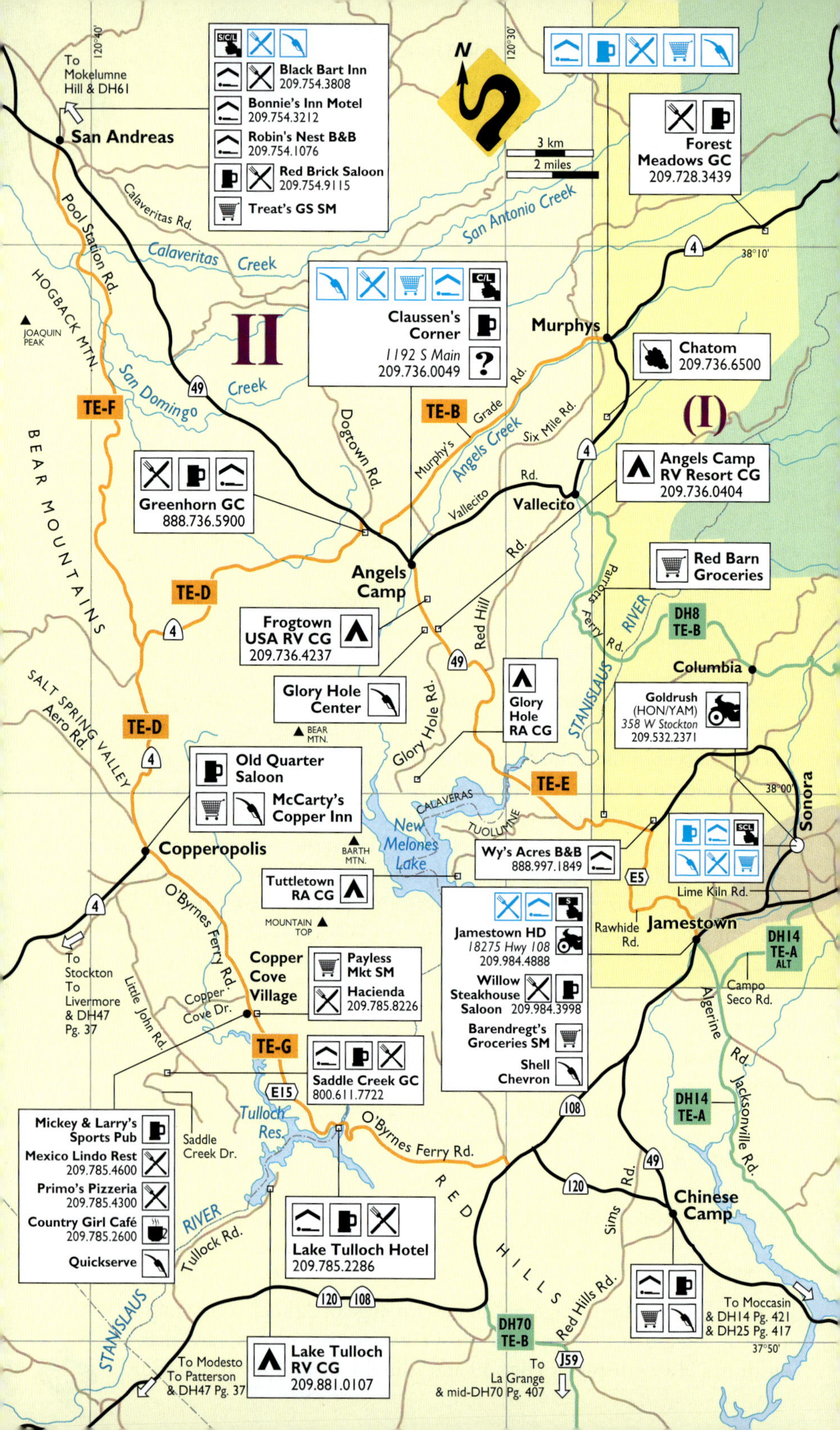

To Mokelumne Hill & DH61
San Andreas
Black Bart Inn 209.754.3808
Bonnie's Inn Motel 209.754.3212
Robin's Nest B&B 209.754.1076
Red Brick Saloon 209.754.9115
Treat's GS SM
3 km
2 miles
Forest Meadows GC 209.728.3439
San Antonio Creek
Calaveritas Rd.
Calaveritas Creek
Pool Station Rd.
HOGBACK MTN.
JOAQUIN PEAK
Claussen's Corner
1192 S Main
209.736.0049
II
Murphys
Chatom 209.736.6500
(I)
San Domingo Creek
TE-F
TE-B
Dogtown Rd.
Murphy's Grade Rd.
Angels Creek
Six Mile Rd.
BEAR MOUNTAINS
Greenhorn GC 888.736.5900
Angels Camp RV Resort CG 209.736.0404
Vallecito Rd.
Vallecito
Angels Camp
TE-D
Red Barn Groceries
Frogtown USA RV CG 209.736.4237
Red Hill Rd.
Parrotts Ferry Rd.
RIVER
DH8 TE-B
Columbia
Glory Hole Center
Glory Hole RA CG
STANISLAUS
Goldrush (HON/YAM) 358 W Stockton 209.532.2371
SALT SPRING VALLEY
Aero Rd.
BEAR MTN.
Glory Hole Rd.
Old Quarter Saloon
McCarty's Copper Inn
CALAVERAS
TUOLUMNE
TE-E
Sonora
Copperopolis
BARTH MTN.
New Melones Lake
Wy's Acres B&B 888.997.1849
E5
Lime Kiln Rd.
Tuttletown RA CG
MOUNTAIN TOP
Jamestown HD 18275 Hwy 108 209.984.4888
Rawhide Rd.
Jamestown
DH14 TE-A ALT
To Stockton To Livermore & DH47 Pg. 37
O'Byrnes Ferry Rd.
Copper Cove Village
Payless Mkt SM
Hacienda 209.785.8226
Willow Steakhouse Saloon 209.984.3998
Campo Seco Rd.
Little John Rd.
Copper Cove Dr.
Barendregt's Groceries SM
Algerine Rd.
TE-G
Saddle Creek GC 800.611.7722
Shell Chevron
Jacksonville Rd.
E15
DH14 TE-A
Mickey & Larry's Sports Pub
Saddle Creek Dr.
Tulloch Res.
O'Byrnes Ferry Rd.
Mexico Lindo Rest 209.785.4600
RED HILLS
Primo's Pizzeria 209.785.4300
Chinese Camp
Sims Rd.
Country Girl Café 209.785.2600
RIVER
Quickserve
Tullock Rd.
Lake Tulloch Hotel 209.785.2286
Red Hills Rd.
To Moccasin & DH14 Pg. 421 & DH25 Pg. 417
STANISLAUS
DH70 TE-B
To Modesto To Patterson & DH47 Pg. 37
Lake Tulloch RV CG 209.881.0107
To La Grange & mid-DH70 Pg. 407
J59

passes to move the state capital to this burgeoning town, the traffic will only get worse.

But that shouldn't trouble you as you make your escape. If there are any nagging pylons beyond Swartzenville, a passing lane that lasts to 0.7 mi (1.1 km) should be enough to dispense with them. Hope it does, because at 1.1 mi (1.8 km), the road narrows into some tight S-turns through a rock slide area and the tall pines of Calveras Big Trees State Park. If there is still anyone jamming you up in the esses, you'll hopefully lose them to the park's turnoff at 2.8 mi (4.5 km).

Traces of red volcanic dust color parts of the forest floor. Granite has hardened close to the roadside in some places, while tall trees continue to choke the shoulder in others. It's still great pavement, though. At 3.6 mi (5.8 km), you're at 5000 ft (1524 m) but the asphalt shows no signs of winter stress. If anything, it's improving the higher you go. The only stress comes from the lack of curves on this bipolar road that's suddenly gone straight.

It's not just twistiness that suffers from the infusion of beelines. The change confirms the fact well known to motorcyclists that scenery looks considerably better when the road through it is curving. As opposed to mindlessly droning straight like some victim of pavement electroshock therapy. If that was your trip, you'd be a resident of the Golden Pines RV Park, on the left at 4.7 mi (7.6 km).

You're not completely into the woods yet. At 5.3 mi (8.5 km), you pass through the short-lived town of Dorrington. You see some houses in the trees beyond and a few side roads heading off into a hidden residential area. However, compared to Arnold, this town feels like pristine wilderness.

The increased remoteness is fine, of course, but you're still waiting for the curves to return. It's hardly encouraging as a widened shoulder and long straightaway provide a lengthy legal passing opportunity. But your spirits are lifted by the deep set of sweepers and curves that shape the perfect pavement starting at 10.4 mi (16.7 km).

You pass a closed ski area and reach the 6000 ft (1829 m) elevation mark at 11.9 mi (19.1 km). Big, sweet, constant curves. Generously wide, silky smooth pavement. Few pylons. No driveways. Time to get on the throttle, right? Sure, but some of these winding curves and sweepers are deceptively long. Just make sure you leave yourself enough road to get out of them. Or at least some shoulder.

Oh, it's nice up here in the sub-alpine. It still feels remote, despite the occasional structures like the couple of cozy log cabins with stone chimneys in a roadside meadow at 16.0 mi (25.7 km). The landscape is transitioning rapidly from forest to smaller trees, exposed granite and green open spaces. How rapidly depends on you.

The pavement quality drops a touch at 17.3 mi (27.9 km), as some tar strips give the ride a little ripple. Seems the altitude has finally taken its toll on the pavement. No problem, you were getting close to the limit of your

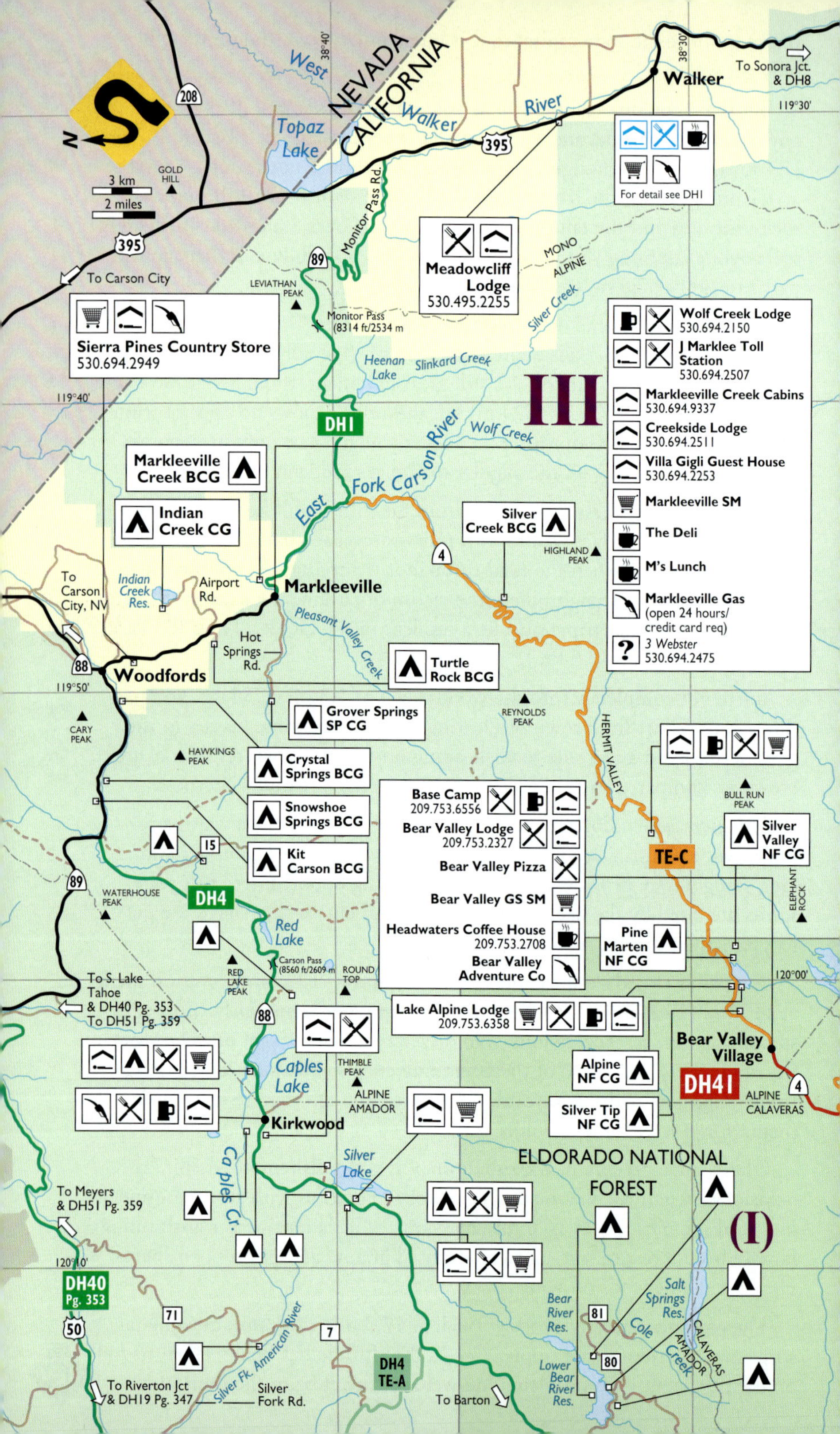

NEVADA
CALIFORNIA
Walker
To Sonora Jct. & DH8
Topaz Lake
West Walker River
For detail see DH1
Meadowcliff Lodge
530.495.2255
To Carson City
Sierra Pines Country Store
530.694.2949
Monitor Pass (8314 ft/2534 m
Monitor Pass Rd.
LEVIATHAN PEAK
GOLD HILL
MONO
ALPINE
Silver Creek
Heenan Lake
Slinkard Creek
Wolf Creek Lodge
530.694.2150
J Marklee Toll Station
530.694.2507
Markleeville Creek Cabins
530.694.9337
Creekside Lodge
530.694.2511
Villa Gigli Guest House
530.694.2253
Markleeville SM
The Deli
M's Lunch
Markleeville Gas
(open 24 hours/ credit card req)
3 Webster
530.694.2475
III
DH1
East Fork Carson River
Wolf Creek
Markleeville Creek BCG
Indian Creek CG
Silver Creek BCG
HIGHLAND PEAK
Markleeville
To Carson City, NV
Indian Creek Res.
Airport Rd.
Hot Springs Rd.
Pleasant Valley Creek
Turtle Rock BCG
Woodfords
Grover Springs SP CG
CARY PEAK
HAWKINGS PEAK
REYNOLDS PEAK
HERMIT VALLEY
Crystal Springs BCG
Snowshoe Springs BCG
Kit Carson BCG
Base Camp
209.753.6556
Bear Valley Lodge
209.753.2327
Bear Valley Pizza
Bear Valley GS SM
Headwaters Coffee House
209.753.2708
Bear Valley Adventure Co
BULL RUN PEAK
Silver Valley NF CG
TE-C
ELEPHANT ROCK
WATERHOUSE PEAK
DH4
Red Lake
Carson Pass (8560 ft/2609 m
RED LAKE PEAK
ROUND TOP
Pine Marten NF CG
To S. Lake Tahoe & DH40 Pg. 353
To DH51 Pg. 359
Lake Alpine Lodge
209.753.6358
Bear Valley Village
Caples Lake
THIMBLE PEAK
Alpine NF CG
DH41
ALPINE
AMADOR
Kirkwood
Silver Tip NF CG
ALPINE
CALAVERAS
ELDORADO NATIONAL FOREST
Silver Lake
Caples Cr.
To Meyers & DH51 Pg. 359
(I)
DH40 Pg. 353
Bear River Res.
Salt Springs Res.
Cole Creek
AMADOR
CALAVERAS
Lower Bear River Res.
Silver Fk. American River
DH4 TE-A
To Riverton Jct & DH19 Pg. 347
Silver Fork Rd.
To Barton
3 km
2 miles

mixture. No fuel adjustments needed, though, as the road descends. Wow, that was a beautiful stretch. Still is.

The beauty's not just in the road, either. There's a great vista south over Liberty Hill, as the curves start to wane at 17.9 mi (28.8 km). And another one as you come over the crest at 21.4 mi (34.4 km). But you don't need panoramic views to be impressed with the scenery up here. The stunted trees are totally cool. As are the rugged blocks of white, cappuccino-foam-streaked granite like the one past Tamarack at 22.7 mi (36.5 km).

A couple more big sweepers are all that's left in the way of curves, though. Just beyond the Alpine County line, the trees recede and expose the wide, ranching plateau of Bear Valley. The DH ends at the turnoff to the town of Bear Valley at 25.0 mi (40.2 km). Hwy 4 continues from here as **TE-C**.

Twisted Edges

TE-A Spicer Reservoir Rd (8.5 mi / 13.7 km)
The Forest Service advises that safe travel speeds average 20-30 mph (30-50 kmh) on this decently paved, scenic and very twisty road down to a waterside campsite. No official word yet from Kawasaki.

TE-B Angels Camp – Murphys (6.4 mi / 10.3 km) *Murphy's Grade Rd*
Hmm, Hwy 4 or Murphy's Grade Rd. Let's see. Though you can get jammed up in the traffic through the windier sections, the Murphy's Grade byway has less development, better valley oak scenery, equally good pavement and way more curves along the cool, forested bank of Angel's Creek.

NAVIGATION: Murphy's Main St turns into Murphy's Grade Rd.

TE-C Bear Valley Village – Hwy 4/Hwy 89 Jct (Hwy 4) (31.4 mi / 50.5 km)
Just beyond Bear Valley, Hwy 4 narrows into a one-and-a-half-lane, closed-in-winter affair through 8732 ft (2662 m) Ebbets Pass. Pavement's good – better than the tar-stripped east end of the DH, in fact – and the rugged, subalpine scenery of sparsely treed granite ridges can be gorgeous. It's the engineering that leaves a lot to be desired on a road that's either bobbing up and down in an aimlessly drifting path or switchbacking steeply with tight, off-camber curves. The westernmost 3.3 mi (5.3 km) just out of Bear Valley and easternmost 6.1 mi (9.8 km) along the east fork of Carson River are well-engineered, two-lane pieces. That still leaves 22.0 mi (35.4 km) of grinding to get to **DH1 Markleeville – Topaz Lake.** But **DH1** is worth every mile.

TE-D Copperopolis – Angels Camp (Hwy 4) (12.0 mi / 19.3 km)
Wide and sweepy at its flanks, tight in its torso, with the good pavement you'd expect from Hwy 4. this TE cuts a nice figure as it sashays up and down over the oak splattered hills west of Hwy 49.

TE-E Jamestown – Angels Camp (13.3 mi / 21.4 km) *Rawhide Rd (E 5) - Hwy 49*
Unless you're dead set on dealing with Sonoma's traffic, you'd get 'em up, move 'em out, ride 'em in, ride 'em out on the Rawhide Rd bypass every

time. A few tight turns interrupt the otherwise good engineering on this ride through fields, light forest and ranchland. The Hwy 49 section is quite similar, except it has better pavement and more pylons.

TE-F Pool Station Rd (12.6 mi / 20.3 km)
The Hwy 49 gold trail can be a trial, especially on summer weekends. Fortunately, this quiet, gently meandering bypass through the grassy, oak-cloistered hills is rarely guilty of any traffic. And it acquits itself reasonably well for pavement, too. Dive right in.

TE-G O'Byrnes Ferry Rd (E 16) (12.6 mi / 20.3 km)
This nicely paved TE hooks in neatly with **TE-D** and **TE-F** to the north and **DH70TE-B La Grange Rd** to the south. Straight at the top and bottom but there are some nice curves along the scenic Tulloch Reservoir. Rapidly being developed, though.

RIDER'S LOG: **DATE RIDDEN:** **YOUR RATING: /10**

How does this book work again? RTFM. "What is Destination Highways Northern California?" and "How to Use Our Maps" appear at the front of the book.

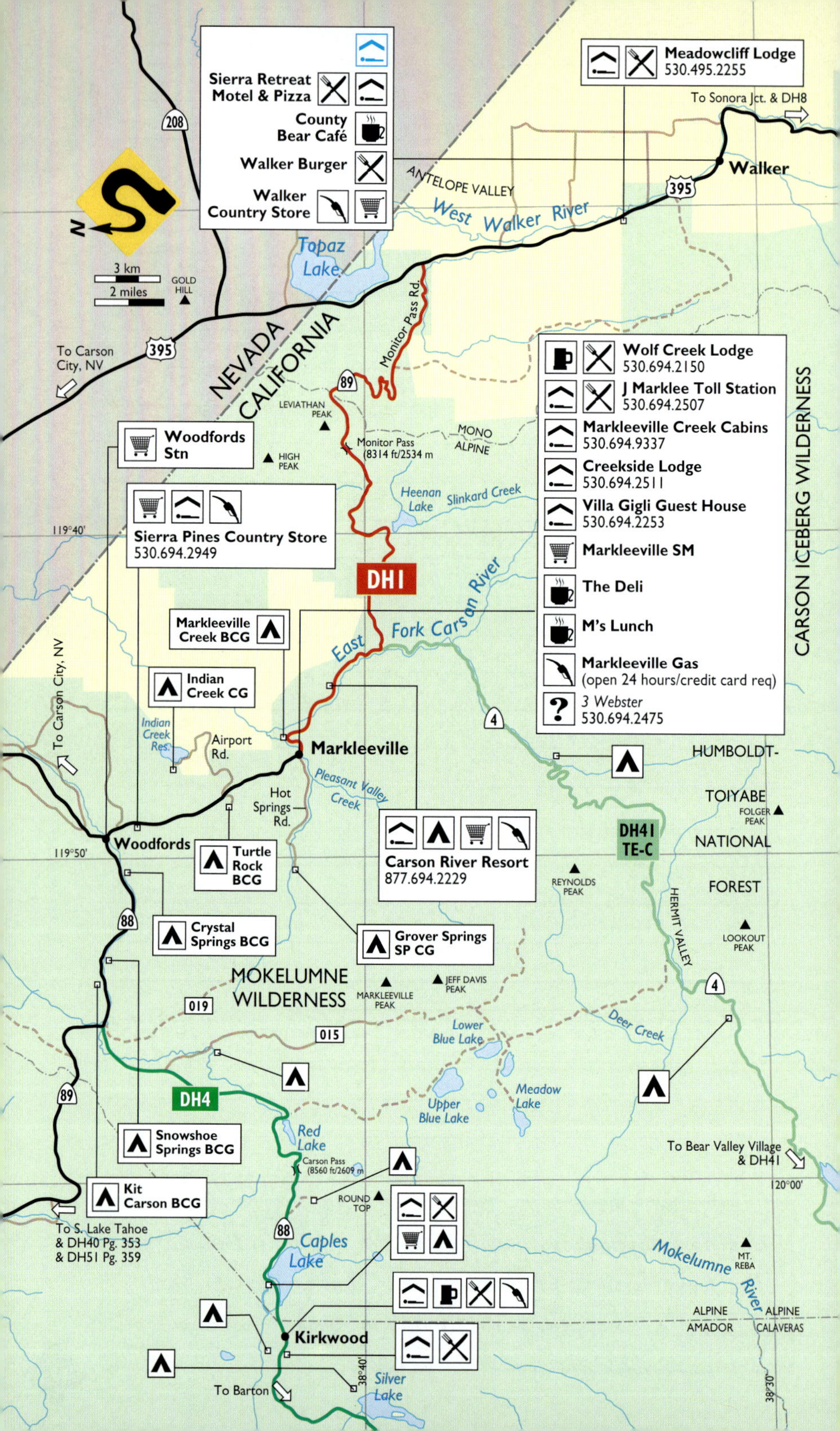

Sierra Retreat Motel & Pizza
County Bear Café
Walker Burger
Walker Country Store
Meadowcliff Lodge 530.495.2255
To Sonora Jct. & DH8
Walker
395
208
ANTELOPE VALLEY
West Walker River
Topaz Lake
Monitor Pass Rd.
3 km
2 miles
GOLD HILL
To Carson City, NV
NEVADA
CALIFORNIA
89
LEVIATHAN PEAK
Monitor Pass (8314 ft/2534 m
MONO
ALPINE
Woodfords Stn
HIGH PEAK
Sierra Pines Country Store 530.694.2949
Heenan Lake
Slinkard Creek
119°40'
DH1
East Fork Carson River
Wolf Creek Lodge 530.694.2150
J Marklee Toll Station 530.694.2507
Markleeville Creek Cabins 530.694.9337
Creekside Lodge 530.694.2511
Villa Gigli Guest House 530.694.2253
Markleeville SM
The Deli
M's Lunch
Markleeville Gas (open 24 hours/credit card req)
3 Webster 530.694.2475
CARSON ICEBERG WILDERNESS
Markleeville Creek BCG
Indian Creek CG
To Carson City, NV
Indian Creek Res.
Airport Rd.
Markleeville
4
HUMBOLDT-
TOIYABE
NATIONAL
FOREST
FOLGER PEAK
Pleasant Valley Creek
Hot Springs Rd.
Woodfords
119°50'
Turtle Rock BCG
Carson River Resort 877.694.2229
DH41 TE-C
REYNOLDS PEAK
HERMIT VALLEY
LOOKOUT PEAK
88
Crystal Springs BCG
Grover Springs SP CG
MOKELUMNE WILDERNESS
MARKLEEVILLE PEAK
JEFF DAVIS PEAK
019
015
Lower Blue Lake
Deer Creek
DH4
Upper Blue Lake
Meadow Lake
89
Red Lake
Snowshoe Springs BCG
Carson Pass (8560 ft/2609 m
To Bear Valley Village & DH41
Kit Carson BCG
ROUND TOP
120°00'
To S. Lake Tahoe & DH40 Pg. 353 & DH51 Pg. 359
Caples Lake
Mokelumne River
MT. REBA
ALPINE
AMADOR
ALPINE
CALAVERAS
Kirkwood
To Barton
38°40'
Silver Lake
38°30'

DH1 Topaz Lake – Markleeville

Monitor Pass Road (Hwy 89)

Distance:	22.3 mi / 35.9 km	Traffic:	Light

At a Glance

TIRES	
Twistiness	30.0/ 30
Pavement	17.6/ 20
Engineering	5.4/ 10
Remoteness	9.6/ 10
Scenery	13.8/ 15
Character	10.6/ 15
Total	**87.0**

No traffic lights. No movie theaters. No high school. No bank. No doctors or dentists. Welcome to Alpine County, population 1200. But who needs the basics when you've got the greatest luxury of all? Northern California's DH1, tucked away between Hwy 395 and the tiny county seat of Markleeville, is all any motorcyclist needs. Tied for tops in Twistiness. Top quarter percentile in Pavement. Ranked number three for Remoteness. And with the high, lingering views from the barren sagelands of Monitor Pass east to the peaks across Nevada's Antelope Valley and south over the forested belts to the mountains of the Carson Iceberg Wilderness, it rates first in Northern California for Scenery. The only reason it falls to 21st for Character is because it's over so fast. The Engineering, while appearing average, is outstanding when you consider that even though this road rises and falls steeply in its twisting climb over the pass, you can accelerate confidently through the curves whether you're going up or down. The only exceptions to this are some of the curves on the spectacular climb above the Antelope Valley off Hwy 395 and a few in the rocky canyon east of the Hwy 4 junction. You might be left wondering, though – if this county has no tax base, where does it get its money? Ask the county sheriff.

Access

From Hwy 89/Hwy 395 Jct

Go west on Hwy 89. You're on the road.

From Markleeville

On Hwy 89

Go south. You're on the road.

On The Road

Remoteness is high as you head off Hwy 395 and make for a cut in the rocks. Twistiness ain't bad either as a climb begins essing you up by a wall of rough-hewn rockfaces. Rows of tongue-shaped boulders stick out of the soil across the oncoming lane. Eerie silhouettes of burnt trees stand out against the dry background. The aptly named Leviathan Peak looms ahead.

You cross a cattleguard at 1.2 mi (1.9 km) and the landscape opens up like a work of art. The broad meadow on the left rises, saucer-like, to a shallow ridge. Apart from the sharp rock, the red and brown grasses and the blackened shrubs and pines, what strikes you are the many shades of green in this sage-strewn landscape. The way the rock emerges from the greenness looks more like an artist's rendering than reality. A sign at 3.2 mi (5.1 km) says "Scenic Route Begins." You don't say.

Trees multiply for an instant, both beside the road and up on the hillside. At 4.2 mi (6.8 km), the curves do too. Starting with a 25-mph (40-kmh) curve, the road rises rapidly over the view. It gets better with every foot you climb; you're now looking over a big horseshoe shaped valley surrounded by pointed rock formations that seem to tumble down to the valley's golf-course green center. In the distance beyond are Nevada's Desert Creek Peak, East Sister and the peaks of the Wassuk Range. An amazing sight.

Reaching 7000 feet (2134 m), the road sweeps in a series of long, even turns on the slope of a steep embankment. Sage, dirt, rock and dusty, stunted pines define the desert scene on both sides of the road. That is, when the side isn't a sheer dropoff. Despite the precipitous edge, the good pavement, long, even turns and terrific sightlines allow you to power through the steady curves.

The terrain feels like its flattening at 6.9 mi (11.1 km). But it isn't really. The illusion is created by the straightness of the road and unrippled fields of sage that spread out evenly now on either side. Aspens brim along the fields' edges, their bark a bright white in the constant sun. There are even some wildflowers adding a burst of color to the tapestry. Still, the earlier high views over the Antelope Valley are a tough act to follow. This looks a little like the moon would if it rained there once in a while.

You're still climbing, as evidenced by the ever-cooling temperature and the amount your throttle is opened. At 9.6 mi (15.4 km), you clear a crest and the world seems to open up. Unfolding before you is an enormous tabletop of sage spreading all the way to the line of distant, snow-topped mountains of the Sierra Nevada's Carson Iceberg Wilderness. You feel the enormity of the scene as you swoop down and then up again over the final rise, the 8314 ft (2519 m) Monitor Pass itself, at 10.0 mi (16.1 km).

The DH starts to curve again in earnest at 10.3 mi (16.6 km). Winding tightly, you descend through a grove of aspens, red-barked pine and larch. Blue mountains fill the horizon. The treed section is brief and then you're back to the sagescape at 11.5 mi (18.5 km). Despite the pitch, the road's well-engineered. And with the true pavement, you can really get into the corners. And how about this remoteness? The only sign of humanity is the rare pylon. That is, if you still consider their occupants human.

The tight turns give way to sweepers and the road even straightens briefly at 12.2 mi (19.6 km) and 12.9 mi (20.8 km). While there are few trees at roadside, there's a thick coat of forest in the bowl below to your right. The connected trees form a kind of dark green coverlet that drapes over parts of the low hills that define the roughening terrain. A sign at 13.4 mi (21.6 km) warns of a steep descent. What have you been on, you wonder.

A minor straight follows the sign, followed by a big sweeper, some middling curves and then a drop into a canyon – or "rockslide area" in CalTrans vernacular. It's quite a contrast being down deep between the steep, silver-green walls and rocky columns. With all the hooplah, you were expecting a drop in engineering. But really the road sweeps through effortlessly. Want more excitement? It's in your right hand.

It's gorgeous in here, though there are some odd sights. Like that bizarre, flat boulder off to the left at 15.8 mi (25.4 km). The corners tighten but you continue to accelerate through them, oblivious to the downward pitch. At this point, this DH is perfect and you wish it could go on forever. And not interrupt you with a stop sign at 17.8 mi (28.6 km). The DH **turns right**.

ROUTING OPTION: Turning left puts you on the mostly one-and-a-half lane ***DH41TE-C Hwy 4/Hwy 89 Jct – Bear Valley Village****. This will take you to* ***DH41 Bear Valley Village – Arnold.***

Pavement doesn't change much, but past the junction there's a feeling of being back in the real world. The East Fork of the Carson River comes into view and long sweepers continue along the riffling river, though they're not as tight as the curves in the west end of the canyon. There are even some short straights. Official river access spots and the Carson River Resort take away from the road's otherwise perfect remoteness.

There's a final jolt of great scenery, though, when you cross Hangman's Bridge at 21.1 mi (33.9 km) and take in the columns of rock on the far side of the Carson, now to your right. Looking more like eroding Egyptian sphinxes than natural phenomena, they mesmerize you, even as a wide, cow-spattered meadow opens up between you and the river and pushes them into the distance. Just make sure your eyes are back on the road for the long sweeper and pair of lesser curves that take you to Markleeville's speed zone at 22.3 mi (35.9 km). Remember, the closest hospital is in Nevada.

RIDER'S LOG: **DATE RIDDEN:** **YOUR RATING: /10**

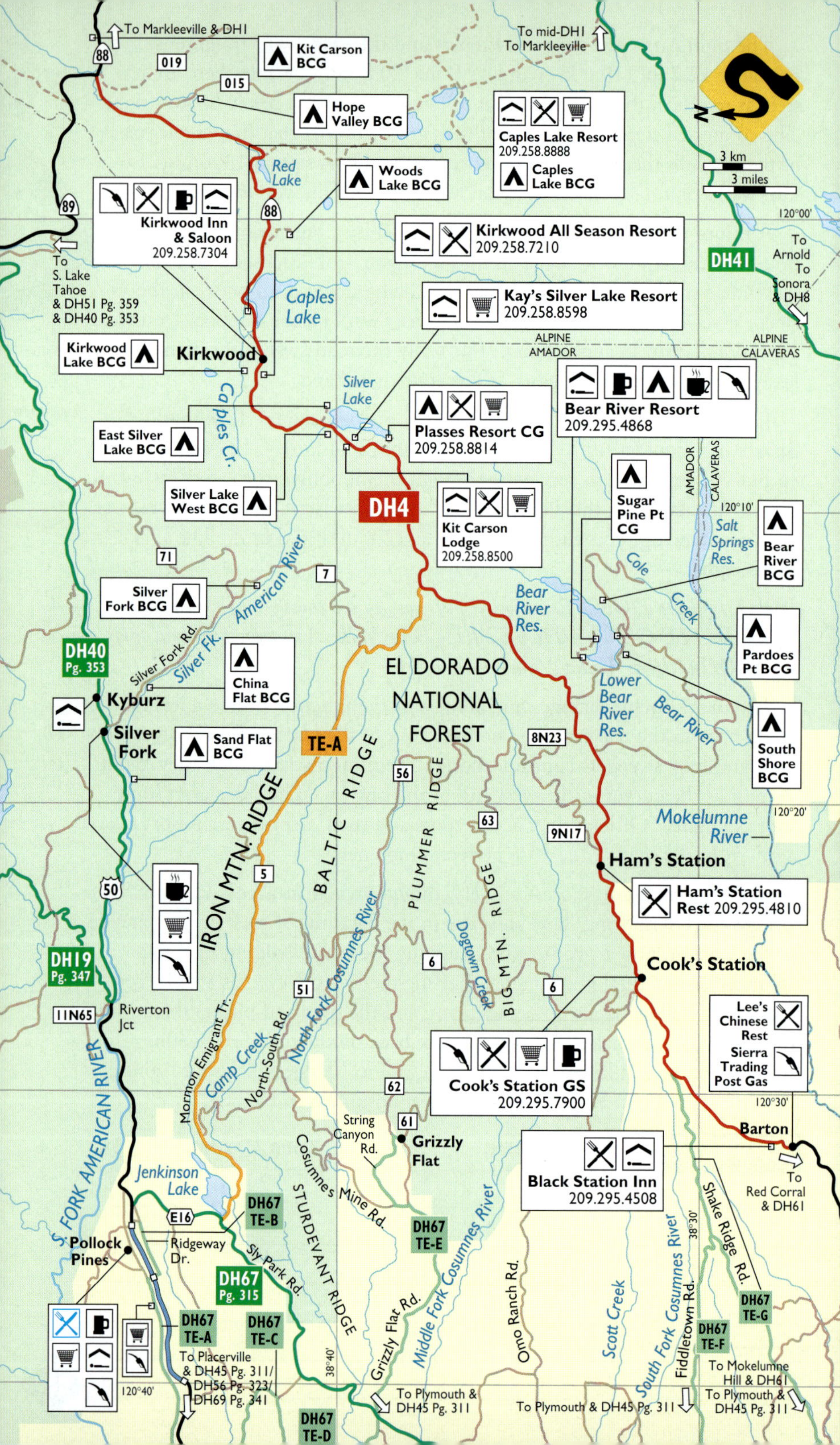

To Markleeville & DH1
Kit Carson BCG
To mid-DH1
To Markleeville
Hope Valley BCG
Caples Lake Resort
209.258.8888
Caples Lake BCG
Red Lake
Woods Lake BCG
3 km
3 miles
Kirkwood Inn & Saloon
209.258.7304
Kirkwood All Season Resort
209.258.7210
To S. Lake Tahoe & DH51 Pg. 359 & DH40 Pg. 353
Caples Lake
Kay's Silver Lake Resort
209.258.8598
To Arnold
To Sonora & DH8
DH41
120°00'
ALPINE
AMADOR
ALPINE
CALAVERAS
Kirkwood Lake BCG
Kirkwood
Silver Lake
Bear River Resort
209.295.4868
East Silver Lake BCG
Plasses Resort CG
209.258.8814
Caples Cr.
Silver Lake West BCG
DH4
Kit Carson Lodge
209.258.8500
Sugar Pine Pt CG
AMADOR
CALAVERAS
120°10'
Salt Springs Res.
Bear River BCG
Cole Creek
Silver Fork BCG
Silver Fk. American River
Bear River Res.
Pardoes Pt BCG
DH40
Pg. 353
Silver Fork Rd.
China Flat BCG
EL DORADO NATIONAL FOREST
Kyburz
Lower Bear River Res.
Bear River
Silver Fork
Sand Flat BCG
TE-A
8N23
South Shore BCG
BALTIC RIDGE
PLUMMER RIDGE
IRON MTN. RIDGE
Mokelumne River
120°20'
9N17
Ham's Station
Ham's Station Rest 209.295.4810
BIG MTN. RIDGE
Dogtown Creek
DH19
Pg. 347
Cook's Station
Riverton Jct
11N65
Lee's Chinese Rest
Sierra Trading Post Gas
North Fork Cosumnes River
North-South Rd.
Camp Creek
Mormon Emigrant Tr.
S. FORK AMERICAN RIVER
Cook's Station GS
209.295.7900
120°30'
String Canyon Rd.
Grizzly Flat
Barton
Black Station Inn
209.295.4508
To Red Corral & DH61
Jenkinson Lake
Cosumnes Mine Rd.
DH67 TE-B
DH67 TE-E
Shake Ridge Rd.
Pollock Pines
Ridgeway Dr.
E16
Sly Park Rd.
STURDEVANT RIDGE
Middle Fork Cosumnes River
DH67
Pg. 315
DH67 TE-A
DH67 TE-C
Grizzly Flat Rd.
Omo Ranch Rd.
Scott Creek
South Fork Cosumnes River
Fiddletown Rd.
38°30'
DH67 TE-G
DH67 TE-F
To Placerville & DH45 Pg. 311/ DH56 Pg. 323/ DH69 Pg. 341
120°40'
38°40'
To Plymouth & DH45 Pg. 311
To Plymouth & DH45 Pg. 311
To Mokelumne Hill & DH61
To Plymouth & DH45 Pg. 311
DH67 TE-D

DH4 Hwy 88/Hwy 89 Jct – Barton
Highway 88

Distance:	49.3 mi / 79.3 km	Traffic:	Moderate

At a Glance

TIRES	
Twistiness	23.3/ 30
Pavement	16.7/ 20
Engineering	7.9/ 10
Remoteness	9.2/ 10
Scenery	12.0/ 15
Character	14.0/ 15
Total	**83.1**

John Charles Fremont and Kit Carson would no doubt have made an award-winning television documentary had they found the Carson Pass route through the Sierra Nevada today rather than during their arduous, middle-of-winter expedition on 1844. Modern motorcycling mountain men don't have to be quite so heroic when they explore this track through great high-country mountain and lake Scenery and down into the thick, foothill forest east of the Sacramento Valley. Remoteness, which can be elusive in California, is elevated up here in the Mokelumne Wilderness, especially in the saddle between Carson Pass and Silver Lake. Pavement is coarse-grained but effortlessly smooth, apart from a little winter kill at the higher spots. Combine it with wide-open, sweeping Twistiness and better-than-average Engineering – particularly on the lots-o'-shoulder western slope – and even luxo-tourers will be on this route like starving frontiersmen on fresh game. Can you say high speed? The CHP STCs probably can. Assuming they don't explore your pocket-book, you'll enjoy a ride with more Character than our explorers had with their horses and mules. We're sure J and the Kitman would've happily exchanged their old-tech mounts for a train of video camera-equipped Wings, Kings or LTs to record their show. After all, as the song says, "You and me baby, ain't nothin' but ridin' mammals, so let's do it like they do on the Discovery Channel."

Access

From Hwy 88/Hwy 89 Jct

The DH starts at the three-way junction where 88/89 from Woodfords splits into its component parts (89 keeps going to Meyers and South Lake Tahoe.) Get west on 88 when it solos and you're on the road.

From Barton

On Hwy 88

Stay straight on 88 through miniscule Barton and you're on the road.

From Red Corral

Coming in on DH61 Mokelumne Hill – Red Corral (Hwy 26)

Turn right when the DH junctions with Hwy 88 at unsigned Red Corral. Barton is 8.1 mi (13.0 km) northeast on 88. Exit Barton and you're on the road

On The Road

The geography already has a sub-alpine look as you head west from the 88/89 junction. Ahead, you can see Waterhouse Peak, and farther to the south Stevens Peak, possibly with snow on it. Over to the left is a row of peaks connected to Hawkins Peak. The flat valley bottom you're on has scattered trees and lots of open green meadows. Good sign: the marker at the beginning says chains are required 5 mi (8 km) ahead. Let's do some 'sploring.

Smooth pavement takes you across the West Fork Carson River at 0.9 mi. (1.4 km). It's so smooth that you'd have to be crazy to give a second look to the turnoff for FSR 015 left to Lower Blue Lake and the Hope Valley BCG at 2.5 mi (4.0 km). Either crazy or a maxburner – not that there's much difference.

ROUTING OPTION: FSR 015 starts off paved but maxriders will be pleased that after two thirds of the approximately 10 mi (16 km) to Lower Blue Lake, it turns to aggregate. At the lake, loop back alongside Upper Blue Lake (also gravel) to the DH just east of Red Lake or strike out south via about 5.5 mi (8.9 km) of tenuous gravel across Deer Creek to ***DH41TE-C*** *in the Hermit Valley.*

You start to climb slightly past the turnoff. Still no real curves but Stevens and Red Lake Peaks offer some viewing recompense. As you gain altitude, the number of trees increases while the amount of meadow decreases. It's already getting cooler. Hmm, how you going to keep your engine warm?

Your first real curve, a giant sweeper at 6.4 mi (10.3 km), turns the road sharply west. It's so long, you're still leaning through it when you pass the turnoff left for Red Lake. The road gains altitude quickly and by 8.0 mi (12.9 km), you're mostly surrounded by rock. There may even be remnants of snow on surrounding mountains that are not much higher than you are. A short passing lane begins, where you get the glimpse down to your left of Red Lake. The road hooks around it, bringing more sweepers.

Riding in a shoulder season or maybe even in winter? Well, you're in a prime avalanche zone. The rockface to your right is known as Rockpile. The reason is obvious as the face gets increasingly menacing, close and vertical. But it keeps the sweepers coming. You're so high that the pavement slips a notch as a result of the weathering. At 8.8 mi (14.2 km), you reach the Carson Pass (8573 ft / 2632 m) summit and info center. Strangely enough, there is no real descent after the pass.

To the right, the mountains are rounded and even green on top as the rock faces beside you retreat and are replaced by forest. But it's not all green. Farther to the south the peaks around Round Top can still have tons of snow.

If the way ahead is clear, the sweepers are great. If you've got pylons in front groaning slowly up through the 35-mph (55-kmh) corners on the climb, all you can do is wonder where the next passing lane is. Oh, there's one. But it's on the other side. What a shame. No one's even using it....

You really don't feel like you're descending but you are, if only a little. You're technically riding through a saddle ringed by the mountains you see in the middle distance. There are a couple more curves before you see the deep blue of Caples Lake, sparkling ahead under the mountain sun. The road turns and scoots around the water's northern edge before crossing the earthen dam that holds the lake in place at 12.8 mi (20.6 km). It provides a good vantage point to view the taupe-colored, snow-capped mountains that back the lake.

You follow the western spur shoreline of Caples Lake for a little while longer and get a view of the Kirkwood ski runs. As you throttle past the lake, there's a respectable package of sweepers, although the pavement they're wrapped in ain't the best. Frankly, Kirkwood Meadows, that big green expanse out to the left at 14.2 mi (22.9 km), looks smoother.

The surface improves once the road climbs again, at least until you get to the top of the Carson Spur avalanche zone. The surroundings sure change in a short distance on this road. By 15.3 mi (24.6 km), you're up on a steep side slope, overlooking the deep gorge of the Caples Creek valley to your right. To your left a steep rockface bends the road out of shape. Just like you like it.

The road passes a viewpoint, swings away from the valley edge and sweeps into the forest on a more southerly heading. At 19.3 mi (31.1 km), you're out of the woods along Silver Lake, a body of water backed by low, rounded mountains. The much-improved asphalt pulls you away from the lake and into a rocky domain. Not much soil here but the trees somehow manage to find purchase on all this whitish sub-strata.

The curves mellow past another viewpoint. This one looks north across the nearby Silver Fork American River valley and unseen South Fork American River valley toward the Crystal Range's Mt Price and Pyramid Peak. The corners relax even more when the road gets passing lanes in both directions at 24.5 mi (39.4 km). You lose these after a mile or so, just prior to yet another vista point.

You definitely feel the downward slope, not to mention the improved pavement, by the time you reach the turnoff for the Mormon Emigrant Trail (**TE-A**) at 26.3 mi (42.3 km). Catchy name. Wouldn't mind if a few million people, regardless of their religious persuasion, used this trail to emigrate out of California. To someplace flat with no motorcycle roads.

The big, fat, juicy sweepers keep on coming. And as you descend, the forest keeps on thickening. You're on top of one of those east-west ridges so typical of the Sierra Nevada's west slope. You can't see it for the trees, but down to the north is the start of the Middle Fork Cosumnes River valley, while to the south lies the Tragedy Creek watershed. The amount of rock increases as you exit the forest suddenly and get a southerly view at 32.7 mi (52.6 km) over the Bear River Reservoir and the larger Lower Bear River Reservoir.

The forest returns just before the turnoff left for the reservoirs at 33.8 mi (54.4 km). The number of curves has been pretty consistent for a while but there are even more of them now. They're still hassle-free but as a bonus many of them are now linked. There's starting to be lots of shoulder and the pavement is sweetening. Even a couple passing lanes turn up. Gotta go.

A rockface at 38.0 mi (61.1 km) busts the road out of the trees and allows a view south down towards the North Fork Mokelumne River valley. This road just seems to go on and on. It exits the El Dorado National Forest (yes, you were in it) and blows by the Hams Station mapdot at 40.0 mi (64.4 km), reaching the collection of buildings known as Cook's Station at 42.3 mi (68.1 km). You may notice that the road surface has declined a touch. But there's still some curving through the woods to go on this DH. Unless you decide to turn onto Shake Ridge Rd (**DH67TE-G**), junctioning right at 47.2 mi (76.0 km).

The trees are a lot bigger now and crowd the ongoing curves a bit. But if you're here in high summer, you'll consider the shade a blessing. The corresponding curse is the increasing amount of development that coalesces as Barton, where the DH ends at 49.3 mi (79.3 km).

Twisted Edges

TE-A Mormon Emigrant Trail (24.7 mi / 39.7 km)

As you would expect, the pavement and engineering on this TE is above reproach. But apart from some gracefully arcing sweepers at either end, most of this remote, tall-pine-forested ridge ride is righteously straight. So here's one for the bishops: if the golden tablets don't specifically prohibit it, is it really a sin to yield to the temptation of your throttle?

Rider's Log: **Date Ridden:** **Your Rating:** **/10**

Find more information about camping in Northern California, including how to make a reservation, in the "Touring Northern California – What You Should Know" section at the front of the book.

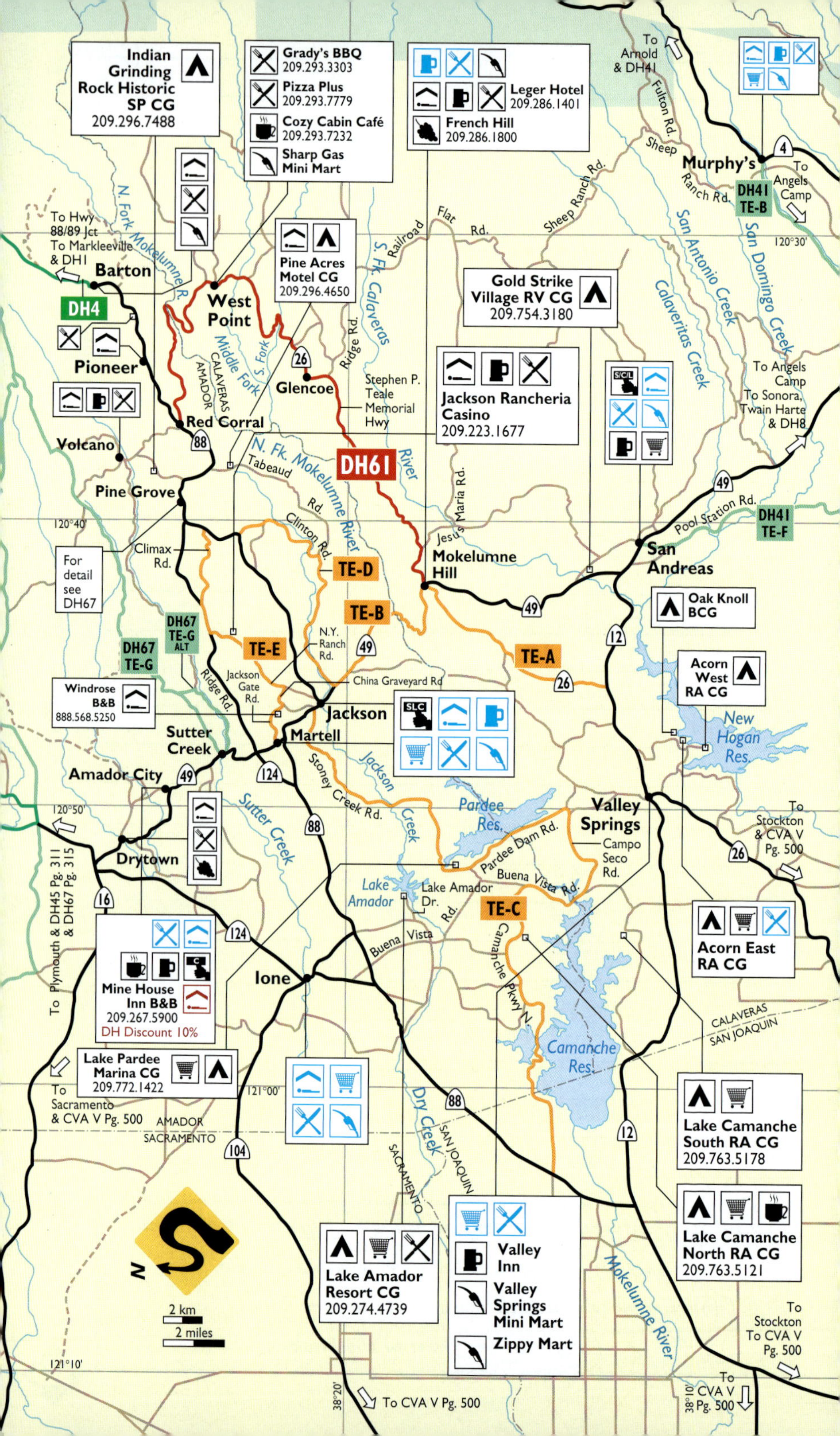

Indian Grinding Rock Historic SP CG 209.296.7488
Grady's BBQ 209.293.3303
Pizza Plus 209.293.7779
Cozy Cabin Café 209.293.7232
Sharp Gas Mini Mart
Leger Hotel 209.286.1401
French Hill 209.286.1800
To Arnold & DH41
Murphy's
DH41 TE-B
To Angels Camp
Pine Acres Motel CG 209.296.4650
Gold Strike Village RV CG 209.754.3180
Jackson Rancheria Casino 209.223.1677
To Hwy 88/89 Jct To Markleeville & DH1
Barton
DH4
West Point
Glencoe
Pioneer
Red Corral
Volcano
Pine Grove
Stephen P. Teale Memorial Hwy
DH61
To Angels Camp To Sonora, Twain Harte & DH8
DH41 TE-F
San Andreas
Mokelumne Hill
For detail see DH67
DH67 TE-G ALT
DH67 TE-G
TE-D
TE-B
TE-E
TE-A
Oak Knoll BCG
Acorn West RA CG
Windrose B&B 888.568.5250
Jackson
Martell
Sutter Creek
Amador City
Drytown
Valley Springs
New Hogan Res.
Pardee Res.
To Stockton & CVA V Pg. 500
TE-C
Acorn East RA CG
Mine House Inn B&B 209.267.5900
DH Discount 10%
Ione
Lake Amador
Camanche Res.
Lake Pardee Marina CG 209.772.1422
To Sacramento & CVA V Pg. 500
To Plymouth & DH45 Pg. 311 & DH67 Pg. 315
Lake Camanche South RA CG 209.763.5178
Lake Camanche North RA CG 209.763.5121
Lake Amador Resort CG 209.274.4739
Valley Inn
Valley Springs Mini Mart
Zippy Mart
To Stockton To CVA V Pg. 500
To CVA V Pg. 500
2 km
2 miles

DH61 Red Corral – Mokelumne Hill
Highway 26

Distance:	24.8 mi / 39.9 km	Traffic:	Very Light

At a Glance

TIRES	
Twistiness	30.0/ 30
Pavement	12.1/ 20
Engineering	4.7/ 10
Remoteness	3.9/ 10
Scenery	6.8/ 15
Character	4.0/ 15
Total	**61.5**

The Battle of the Bulge, El Guettar and Messina. Some of the great victories engineered by that soldier's soldier, General George S. Patton, Jr. But for modern two-wheeled recruits, it's the Battle of Mokelumne Hill that's really worth fighting. You can just hear the engines of the Sabres rattling as they wind above the North Fork Mokelumne River, then straighten to pass through the development quartered either side of West Point. Well-engineered volleys of curves follow, bombarding the asphalt and forcing you to ess down one side of the South Fork Mokelumne River's densely treed gorge and up the other. The eerie quiet when the road straightens through some ranchland is but a lull. The skirmish resumes in the remote, corner-riddled jungle, where you maneuver back and forth over the ridge between the Calaveras and North Mok valleys before finally dropping down the Calaveras to end the mission at Hwy 49. Just how does it feel to be in the heat of DH61? Patton himself said it best, "God help me, I do love it so."

Access

From Red Corral

Turn onto Hwy 26. When you do, you're on the road.

From Mokelumne Hill

Go northeast on Hwy 26. When you reach the end of Mok Hill's speed zone, you're on the road.

From Jackson

To Red Corral via Hwy 88, TE-D or TE-E

To access this DH from its northeast end, head past Pine Grove and look for the sign for Hwy 26. Turn right. You're on the road.

To Mokelumne Hill via TE-B

Head south on Hwy 49 and turn northeast on the well-signed Hwy 26.

On The Road

Trees are thick on either side as you split off Hwy 88 at Red Corral. The DH barrages you with a series of four connected curves at 0.7 mi (1.1 km). With all the corners to come, don't give a second thought to the piddling, housey straight at 1.3 mi (2.1 km).

It's a more sweeping rather than tight pattern of fire up to the sign at 2.0 mi (3.2 km). That's the one that warns of winding road for the next four miles. This is no drill: curves and sweepers form up together in a twisty but well engineered march through the trees and along a ridge high above the North Fork Mokelumne River. With the road's best pavement to boot, some will think it's the best part of the road. Retreat down the cutoff road back to Hwy 88 at 2.6 mi (4.2 km)? No, sir!

At 4.8 mi (7.7 km), you attack over a bridge, cross the river and penetrate Calaveras County. Climbing upward through the trees, the fine corners continue. Until you lose them, along with the fine pavement and river valley scenery at the top of a climb on the outskirts of West Point.

For a small town, West Point sure is spread out. There are lots of barracks in the trees before you actually reach duty-honor country's 35-mph (55-kmh) sign at 7.9 mi (12.7 km). Atten-hut! Slow march! Just past the town's Main St turnoff there's a fork at 8.3 mi (13.4 km). To remain on Hwy 26 and the DH, **riiight turn**!

More PMQs. It's starting to seem like you'll never get out of this quagmire. But once you're beyond the impromptu stop sign at 8.6 mi (13.8 km), things finally start to pick up. A marker describes this upcoming section of the DH as the "Stephen P. Teale Memorial Highway." Okay, Steve, let's see what your memory is worth.

Just when you think the Stevemeister's got you camouflaged in the trees and curves, 10.0 mi (16.1 km) into the battle brings a straight flat of civilian farms and lightly treed lots. The twisties finally resume at 11.2 mi (18.0 km) as you move out sharply off the flat. But the sense of remoteness you felt before West Point doesn't really parachute back in until about 12.0 mi (19.3 km), when you're charging along a side slope of esses through heavy cover above the forested canyon of the South Fork Mokelumne River.

It's not a particularly long climb; you're soon twisting down toward the river, bridging it at 13.1 mi (21.1 km). Then you march back up the other side of the canyon in yet another long series of left, right, left, right, left. This ends at 14.3 mi (23.0 km) when you briefly emerge from the forest at the top of the ascent. The road straightens out. Trees counterattack, though they're not as dense as they were in the canyon. Same could be said for the curves.

The barely curves don't last long. At 15.6 mi (25.1 km), you pass through the mapdot of Glencoe and the road starts a slow, essing rhythm. Ridge Rd, a connector to Railroad Flat Rd that comes in at 16.3 (26.2

km) hardly seems like a major artery. So it's probably just coincidence that the pavement improves once you move past the junction.

ROUTING OPTION: If you're heading over to ***DH41 Arnold – Bear Valley Village*** *and want to take a "short cut," go ahead and turn left on Ridge Rd, right on Railroad Flat and left on Sheep Ranch. Ridge is fine and Railroad Flat Rd is okay at times, but Sheep Ranch Rd is extremely rough. This road will deposit what's left of you on Hwy 4 south of Arnold at either Murphys or Avery, depending on just how you go. Just don't expect to save any time.*

Incoming! You're back in the twisties. And in heavy vegetation as the road spills into the forested valley of the Calaveras River. You don't see any water, of course, since you're flanked by trees on the left and an upward angling slope on the right. You emerge and take the cleared, brown, flattish high ground at the top of the ridge between the Calaveras and Mokelumne Rivers at 18.2 mi (29.3 km). You can take a bit of leave from the intense bombardment of curviness as well, though the S-curves soon start firing again at 19.4 mi (31.2 km).

The forest strikes again soon after. At 20.4 mi (32.8 km), you start the long final thrust to Hwy 49, dropping down again to the Calaveras side of the ridge. It's not as scenic in the heavy trees as it was atop the ridge but you're taking left and right fire so fast, you probably haven't noticed. It's hard to miss the fact the pavement's dropped one rank at 21.6 mi (34.8 km), though. But that's nothing compared to the scourged, one-lane surface of Jesus Maria Rd, left at 23.5 mi (37.8 km). Unless you're a Carthusian or Carmelite, don't even think about it.

There are more curves past Jesus Maria, but none of them are linked. In a moment of grace, the pavement improves momentarily. But by now, the S-curves have ended. And so has the DH as you reach the Mokelumne Hill speed zone and end of the battle at 24.8 mi (39.9 km). Stand… at ease! Fall out!

Twisted Edges

TE-A Mokelumne Hill – Hwy 12/Hwy 26 Jct (Hwy 26) (7.5 mi / 12.1 km)

Hwy 26 continues on from the DH. But compared to it, this TE's like being on a Mexican furlough. Pavement's about the same, maybe a touch better. The big difference is you're out of the forest and onto rolling, partly treed tank country. The curves – sweepers mainly – and valley views come from the fact the road climbs up and down a mild ridge above Chili Gulch.

TE-B Mokelumne Hill – Jackson (Hwy 49) (6.1 mi / 9.8 km)

Just so you know, going up the steep slope of Mokelumne Hill is a lot less challenging than going down. Not that either is a walk in the park. Yes, the road is wide and has great pavement. But you don't have to be going very fast on the long, tight, lingering sweepers before you're wondering how much more you can lean. Thing is, there's only one way to find out if you're man enough.

TE-C Jackson – Camanche Reservoir (24.0 mi / 38.6 km)
Stoney Creek Rd - Pardee Dam Rd - Campo Seco Rd - Buena Vista Rd - Camanche Pkwy N

The farther you get from Jackson, the flatter, drier, warmer and less treed it gets. Yet surprisingly, curves hang in for most of this varied route. Too bad some of the newish pavement is rougher than it looks, as is the case with many roads to the west of Hwy 49 in Gold Country where they just lay the black gold down on the old rough base. Still, if you're coming up from Stockton way towards Jackson, this is the one you'll want to pan first. You'll be glad they haven't closed down roads over dams in California like they have done in post-9/11 Washington State.

NAVIGATION: In Jackson, look for Hoffman St west from Hwy 49 where there is a small green sign indicating Pardee Dam is down it. Unless, of course, it's been removed to make the terrorists' job harder. Hoffman clears Jackson at 0.3 mi (0.5 km) and turns into Stoney Creek Rd at 0.9 mi (1.4 km). Make sure you slant left on Pardee Dam Rd at 9.5 mi (15.3 km). Turn right on Campo Seco Rd when you hit the T-junction at 13.8 mi (22.2 km). At 17.1 mi (27.5 km), when you see the option for Camanche Pkwy S to the left and Buena Vista Rd/Camanche Pkwy N to the right, turn right. You'll be on Buena Vista Rd. At 24.0 mi (38.6 km), make the hard left to go on Camanche Pkwy N.

TE-D Clinton Rd (8.5 mi / 13.7 km)

Avoid a busy piece of busy Hwy 88 out of Jackson by taking this back-country bypass through the woods, hills and fields north of the North Fork Mokelumne River. Snaking curves, good pavement (especially the stretch immediately west and north of the Tabeaud Rd Junction) and a lot fewer pylons make the bit of development acceptable.

NAVIGATION: Stay right off Hwy 88 to stay on the TE or else you'll be on Irishtown Rd. At the Jackson end, turn east at the Holiday Inn Express.

TE-E Jackson – Pine Grove (9.2 mi / 14.8 km) *Jackson Gate Rd - China Graveyard Rd - New York Ranch Rd - Ridge Rd - Climax Rd*

Clusters of oaks and suburban development are always in play yet you won't find much action on the brief Ridge Rd section. But this Hwy 88 bypass still pays off with curves and high-percentage pavement if you place most of your money on NY Ranch and Climax. Which you can do if you avoid a lengthy stop at the Jackson Rancheria Casino.

NAVIGATION: From the west, follow Jackson Gate Rd 1.4 mi (2.3 km) to the stop sign. Turn left onto China Graveyard Rd. At the next stop sign – a T-junction – turn left onto NY Ranch Rd. The next stop sign and T-junction is Ridge Rd at 5.3 mi (8.5 km). Turn right. When you reach a junction at 6.2 mi (10.0 km), you'll see most of the traffic turning left. You go right onto unmarked Climax Rd.

From the east, Climax Rd is well-marked off Hwy 88. From there, just keep an eye open for the road signs.

RIDER'S LOG: **DATE RIDDEN:** **YOUR RATING:** /10

Remember, you'll find video clips of all of Northern California's DHs at destination highways.com.

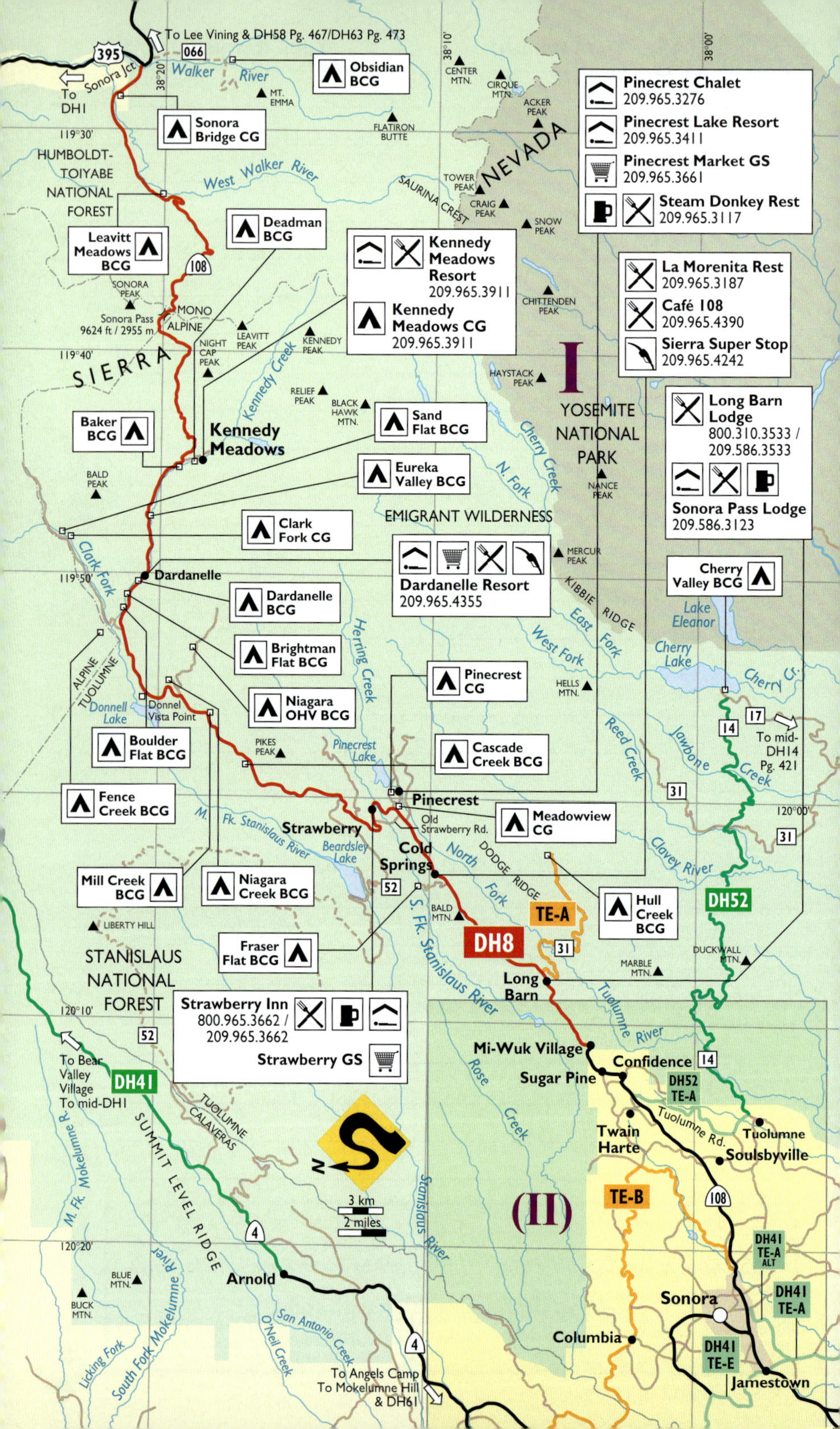

To Lee Vining & DH58 Pg. 467/DH63 Pg. 473
Obsidian BCG
Sonora Bridge CG
Leavitt Meadows BCG
Deadman BCG
Kennedy Meadows Resort 209.965.3911
Kennedy Meadows CG 209.965.3911
Pinecrest Chalet 209.965.3276
Pinecrest Lake Resort 209.965.3411
Pinecrest Market GS 209.965.3661
Steam Donkey Rest 209.965.3117
La Morenita Rest 209.965.3187
Café 108 209.965.4390
Sierra Super Stop 209.965.4242
Long Barn Lodge 800.310.3533 / 209.586.3533
Sonora Pass Lodge 209.586.3123
Baker BCG
Sand Flat BCG
Eureka Valley BCG
Clark Fork CG
Dardanelle Resort 209.965.4355
Dardanelle BCG
Brightman Flat BCG
Niagara OHV BCG
Boulder Flat BCG
Fence Creek BCG
Pinecrest CG
Cascade Creek BCG
Meadowview CG
Cherry Valley BCG
Hull Creek BCG
Mill Creek BCG
Niagara Creek BCG
Fraser Flat BCG
Strawberry Inn 800.965.3662 / 209.965.3662
Strawberry GS
HUMBOLDT-TOIYABE NATIONAL FOREST
STANISLAUS NATIONAL FOREST
YOSEMITE NATIONAL PARK
EMIGRANT WILDERNESS
NEVADA
SIERRA
Kennedy Meadows
Dardanelle
Pinecrest
Strawberry
Cold Springs
Long Barn
Mi-Wuk Village
Sugar Pine
Confidence
Twain Harte
Tuolumne
Soulsbyville
Sonora
Columbia
Jamestown
Arnold
Sonora Pass 9624 ft / 2955 m
To DH1
To Bear Valley Village To mid-DH1
To mid-DH14 Pg. 421
To Angels Camp To Mokelumne Hill & DH61
DH8
DH52
DH41
TE-A
TE-B
I
(II)
3 km
2 miles

DH8 Sonora Jct – Mi-Wuk Village (Twain Harte)

Highway 108

Distance:	64.4 mi / 103.6 km	Traffic:	Moderate

At a Glance

TIRES	
Twistiness	28.2/ 30
Pavement	15.9/ 20
Engineering	5.5/ 10
Remoteness	7.2/ 10
Scenery	11.1/ 15
Character	13.7/ 15
Total	**81.6**

"Better to have climbed and fallen than not to have climbed at all" remarked wrestling face Bret Harte when he and country-pop star Shania Twain scrapped their matrimonial plans. "It is easier to stay out than get out," replied the diva ruefully. But at least the motorcyclists among their disappointed legion of fans can find true love in the happy marriage of TIRES components that make up this fine story. Like its namesakes, DH8 has its share of fame. And no wonder. Silkily-toned, shut-in-winter Pavement and an impressive body slam of Twistiness combine with always-popular Remoteness on an entertaining climb up and down either side of Sonora Pass in the heart of the Sierra Nevada. And this crowd pleaser is suitable for cruiser audiences too. Because it bisects the Carson Iceberg and Emigrant Wildernesses, it has the kind of high-country Scenery that draws a packed house. Sure, as in many relationships, the initial excitement can ebb after a time. Especially once you get into the western foothill country west of Strawberry. There, the entertainment value is much mellower and the concert of traffic can leave you feeling like you're locked in a brutal cage match. Still, most riding aficionados would agree that it's better to stay out and climb this road rather than get out and never ride it at all. As long as you leave out the "falling" part, that is.

Access

From Sonora Jct

On Hwy 395

Head west on Hwy 108 from this ex-town. You are on the road.

From Twain Harte

On Hwy 108

Just stay on 108 east and when you leave the last of the MI-Wuk Village sprawl, you're on the road.

On The Road

The DH enters stage west from Sonora Jct (where you'll often see fully-costumed sport riders getting ready to burn up it). After darting straight

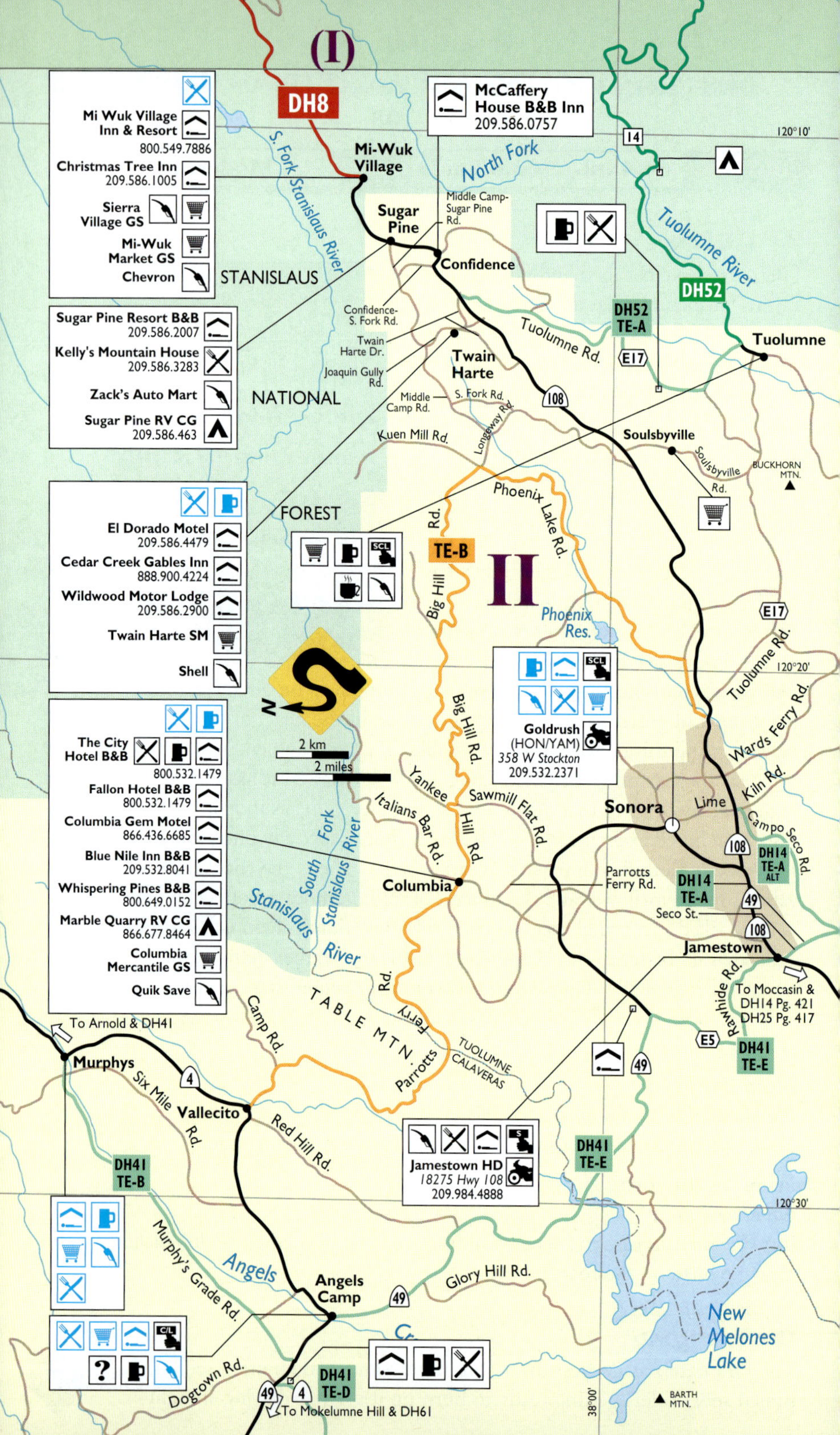
(I)
DH8
Mi Wuk Village Inn & Resort
800.549.7886
Christmas Tree Inn
209.586.1005
Sierra Village GS
Mi-Wuk Market GS
Chevron
McCaffery House B&B Inn
209.586.0757
Mi-Wuk Village
S. Fork Stanislaus River
North Fork
Sugar Pine
Middle Camp-Sugar Pine Rd.
Confidence
STANISLAUS
Tuolumne River
DH52
Sugar Pine Resort B&B
209.586.2007
Kelly's Mountain House
209.586.3283
Zack's Auto Mart
Sugar Pine RV CG
209.586.463
Confidence-S. Fork Rd.
Twain Harte Dr.
Joaquin Gully Rd.
Twain Harte
Tuolumne Rd.
DH52 TE-A
E17
Tuolumne
NATIONAL
Middle Camp Rd.
S. Fork Rd.
Longeway Rd.
108
Kuen Mill Rd.
Soulsbyville
Soulsbyville Rd.
BUCKHORN MTN.
El Dorado Motel
209.586.4479
Cedar Creek Gables Inn
888.900.4224
Wildwood Motor Lodge
209.586.2900
Twain Harte SM
Shell
FOREST
SCL
Phoenix Lake Rd.
Big Hill Rd.
TE-B
II
Phoenix Res.
E17
Tuolumne Rd.
120°20'
N
2 km
2 miles
Goldrush
(HON/YAM)
358 W Stockton
209.532.2371
Wards Ferry Rd.
Kiln Rd.
Lime
The City Hotel B&B
800.532.1479
Fallon Hotel B&B
800.532.1479
Columbia Gem Motel
866.436.6685
Blue Nile Inn B&B
209.532.8041
Whispering Pines B&B
800.649.0152
Marble Quarry RV CG
866.677.8464
Columbia Mercantile GS
Quik Save
Big Hill Rd.
Yankee Hill Rd.
Sawmill Flat Rd.
Italians Bar Rd.
Sonora
Campo Seco Rd.
South Fork Stanislaus River
Columbia
Parrotts Ferry Rd.
108
DH14 TE-A ALT
DH14 TE-A
49
Seco St.
108
Stanislaus River
Jamestown
Rawhide Rd.
To Moccasin & DH14 Pg. 421 DH25 Pg. 417
TABLE MTN.
Parrotts Ferry Rd.
Camp Rd.
TUOLUMNE
CALAVERAS
To Arnold & DH41
Murphys
4
Six Mile Rd.
Vallecito
E5
DH41 TE-E
49
Red Hill Rd.
Jamestown HD
18275 Hwy 108
209.984.4888
DH41 TE-E
DH41 TE-B
120°30'
Murphy's Grade Rd.
Angels
Angels Camp
49
Glory Hill Rd.
New Melones Lake
C/L
Cr.
Dogtown Rd.
49
4
DH41 TE-D
To Mokelumne Hill & DH61
38°00'
BARTH MTN.
14
120°10'

across the dry Little Walker River valley flat, there's a sign warning that the upcoming 26 per cent uphill grade is not suitable for trucks. Surely, it's not suitable for RVs either?

Conifers sprinkle the beige, parched terrain and the road turns gradually northward to avoid some high ground. You then turn westward around the hill and enter the narrow entrance of the West Walker River valley, crossing the river at 2.1 mi (3.4 km). The watercourse takes up a flanking position on your left as long straights linked by the odd curve move across a widening valley bottom that is soon devoid of trees. A good place to look up and check out the snow-topped Sierra Nevada ahead. Or dispose of any passing chores.

At 4.0 mi (6.4 km), you pass the entrance, right, to the USMC Mountain Warfare Training Center. With the surrounding sage and bunch-grass desert, it looks like suitable training for Iraq. Or Iran. You? It's straight here so rack it up and run.

A curve at 5.1 mi (8.2 km) fires you off the valley bottom and up into some trees. As the no-shoulder engineering drops a grade, a second sign signals good cornering opportunities in the next 24 mi (39 km). There's a platoon of them as you advance upward through the thickening woods. Assuming any enfilading pylons pull over.

The terrain's already 7000 ft (2149 m) high and it's rapidly getting cooler here in the sub-alpine. Mt Emma's across the valley to your left but you're previously engaged, too busy peeling off the continuing curves to notice. At 7.1 mi (11.4 km), the geography flattens and opens up. The pavement, good so far, improves as you flash by a viewpoint. Best of all, the twisties don't go away, they just get easier. At least till the sharp righthander tight to a rockface at 7.3 mi (11.7 km). Whoa – embarrassingly easy to blow that corner, wasn't it? Maybe it's time to wave on those un-luggaged crotchrockets nibbling at your ass.

That memorable curve has switched the road from a southwesterly to a northeasterly course and you're once more scrabbling up a steep hillside enjoying yourself far too much to read that big yellow sign that just flashed by. Probably something about risking life and limb. But then you already knew that – corner, corner, corner.

Another tight curve (do this one any better?) left at 8.1 mi (13.0 km) returns the road to its original heading. The road relaxes some and – okay, okay – it's finally straight enough to let the four rocketeers go by. At the end of the straight, there's another big yellow sign: "Road Narrows Watch For Opposing Traffic." Duh.

The ground has flattened out and the conifers struggle to find enough thin soil to remain rooted in the jumble of white rock. You're struggling to stay planted yourself on the seriously contorting gray stuff. Yeah, well, in both cases, only the fit survive.

After one more sphincter-clencher, the road briefly straightens at 12.1 mi (19.5 km) through a meadow ringed by brown mountains and dotted with, what's this…cattle? The cows face you and quietly munch roadside bunchgrass while yet another timely sign warns "Road Narrows Watch…"

Though the high country openness stays with you, the cattle and the straightness don't. By 14.2 mi (22.9 km), the road has knotted up tightly again as it threads up and down through loose forest. You might see remnants of snow to your left on the charcoal-colored, barren flanks of Night Cap Peak that you glimpse just before the road swerves drunkenly to the right and puts you, at 15.0 mi (24.1 km), in the 9624 ft (2955 m) high Sonora Pass entry point to the Stanislaus National Forest. Note the speed-checked-by-radar sign?

Out of the pass, the pavement continues its wonderfully winding ways on a gentle downslope. The vexing pylon build up ain't so wonderful, however. Particularly since the trees crowding the road and impairing the sightlines around the tight corners don't help you get by the traffic. At 17.6 mi (28.3 km), the proto-forest disappears and the grade – known here as the "Golden Stairs" – steepens considerably. The asphalt spirals tightly past a rock face and starts down into a rock-strewn moonscape overhung by the now much closer, black, brooding mass of Night Cap Peak.

You're down on the desolate valley floor amazingly fast. The road straightens briefly, just long enough for you to get by any traffic. By 19.6 mi (31.5 km) the trees have re-appeared and begun to thicken into a half decent forest. The widening valley slopes downward as you wind off its floor and begin to move steeply down its northern side. A couple of almost-hairpins introduce a sweepier stretch that blasts alongside rockfaces and gives a wide-open view across the still-spreading valley.

At 23.1 mi (37.2 km), you slice through the first of two imposing, honey-colored rock cuts. The second, sheer one is called "The Window." As the grade gets less severe, you throw open the pane on a beautiful series of esses that lasts until the turnoff left for Kennedy Meadows at 24.3 mi (39.1 km). Here the road flares out, leveling when the valley floor at last stops declining. You may not know it, but you've just drawn the curtains on the best part of the DH.

The pavement drops a grade as you make your way through a forest of stately pines. The curves, though still present, are less intense, other than in the brief bit where you're above a creek hemmed in by sheer rock walls. The road then crosses the Middle Fork Stanislaus River, cruising by the south turn for mapdot Dardanelle at 29.3 mi (47.1 km).

There are a few cabins past this mapdot before the terrain pinches in from the right and the road is forced toward the south bank of the milky green river. Gentler but still respectable curves hold sway as the valley continues to widen. You move away from the river, passing the junction for a forest service road, right at 32.3 mi (52.0 km).

CalTrans is unwilling or unable to force the Dardanelles, perhaps mindful of history having shown how difficult that task can be. Instead, CT aims the road southwest where it continues to follow the Middle Fork Stanislaus River valley. At least they keep the pavement sweet, though it slowly becomes less winding. If you're feeling a little shagged, you can take advantage of the Donnell Vista Pt rest stop, left at 35.9 mi (57.8 km). Or you can continue to blaze along on this shallow, forested descent, broken up only by sporadic, granite rockfaces and views out over the shallow vale. The only signs of civilization are the turnoffs for various campgrounds and – though it's difficult to figure where it's coming from – the increased traffic.

The DH escapes its prison of trees at 48.1 mi (77.4 km) and finds itself running along the top of a ridge between the valleys of the South Fork Stanislaus River and the North Fork Tuolumne River. At the end of a long sweeper, you can see the bald top of the ski hill on Dodge Ridge, the ridge that makes up the far boundary of the NF Tuolumne.

It's increasingly difficult to get by the traffic now. And the 45-mph (70-kph) speed limit makes things even stickier. As does Strawberry's jam, spreading out at 50.2 mi (80.8 km) on the banks of the South Fork Stanislaus River.

After Strawberry, a couple small fields of vision open over the valley to the right but they don't last forever. Soon you're back in the trees and rockcuts. Considering how small the town was, it's surprising how much more traffic there is south of it. That might have something to do with the resorty village of Pinecrest, left down Pinecrest Lake Rd at 51.7 mi (83.2 km).

Past the turnoff, there's a straight with a wide shoulder for slower pylons to use. Needless to say, few do. One of the world's great, unsolved mysteries is why pyloneers always think they are going fast enough that they don't have to use these opportunities. What, like they really think *we're* going to slow *them* down?

The fine-quality pavement remains but has straightened considerably, a situation that continues on as you flash through the village of Cold Springs at 54.4 mi (87.5 km). Then, four sweeping uphill curves land you on another ridge that overlooks the North Fork Tuolumne River valley and also offers a brief view across it to Dodge Ridge.

A straight and a few more upward curves shave up and around Bald Mtn, where at 58.0 mi (93.3 km), the highway divides into two lanes in each direction. No corners for a while on this forested stretch but you sure can pass the pylons. Mini-town Long Barn arrives the same time as the turnoff left for FSR 31 (**TE-A**), at 60.9 mi (98.0 km).

Shortly after the turnoff, the highway upgrades to a two-laner with a few long sweepers. No dotted yellow but the road has wide, helpful shoulders should you choose to maintain a rapid pace between the closely bordering trees. And should the traffic allow.

At 63.7 mi (102.5 km), you exit the Stanislaus National Forest. One last straight and the DH ends at the 35-mph (55-kmh) start of sprawling Mi-Wuk Village at 64.4 mi (103.6 km).

Twisted Edges

TE-A FSR 31 (10.0 mi / 16.0 km)

Rather camp farther east but left Sonora too late in the day to do the meatiest part of the DH in full daylight? Perhaps you can only get out of S-town for a short afternoon fix before you have to get back. Or maybe you've just ridden the DH and want a cool swim after the hot curves of its eastern section. Turn east at Long Bend and take this road down to the North Fork Tuolumne River access and then up and over Dodge Ridge. You'll get an always twisting ride that's nearly as well paved as the DH with virtually no traffic. The BCG at the end is located on an flat, open, attractive site.

NAVIGATION: Make sure you Y left at 0.1 mi (0.2 km) in order to stay on the TE.

TE-B Sonora – Vallecito (27.5 mi / 44.3 km) *Phoenix Lake Rd - Big Hill Rd - Yankee Hill Rd - Parrotts Ferry Rd*

If you like variety in your TEs, each piece of this tripartite route has a distinctly different feel. Phoenix Lake Rd is semi-urban at times but it's still a beautifully paved 35-mph (55-kmh) bypass to Hwy 108 between Sonora and Twain Harte. Big Hill Rd/Yankee Hill Rd can be rough but the tightly coiled climb up and down in the hills that attempt to constrain Greater Sonora to the south is also much more remote. Past the preserved Gold Rush town of Columbia (once the home of Amor de Cosmos and now a state historic park), Parrotts Ferry Rd turns into an excellently paved and engineered, high-speed collection of sweepers that take you down to and across the Stanislaus River and then up to junction with Hwy 4, half way between Angels Camp and Murphys.

TOUR NOTE: Big Hill Rd and Yankee Hill Rd have the unmistakable scent of venison, so consider yourself orange-alerted. One cunning, cloven-hooved terrorist attempted to take us out with a dusk suicide attack. A little later, we saw a whole cell of these woodland Al-Qaida in an adjacent field, brazenly plotting further jihadist acts. God willing, you'll be spared.

Rider's Log: **Date Ridden:** **Your Rating: /10**

Map Tip: To see the next good motorcycle road, look for the white navigation arrows at the edge of the Local maps.

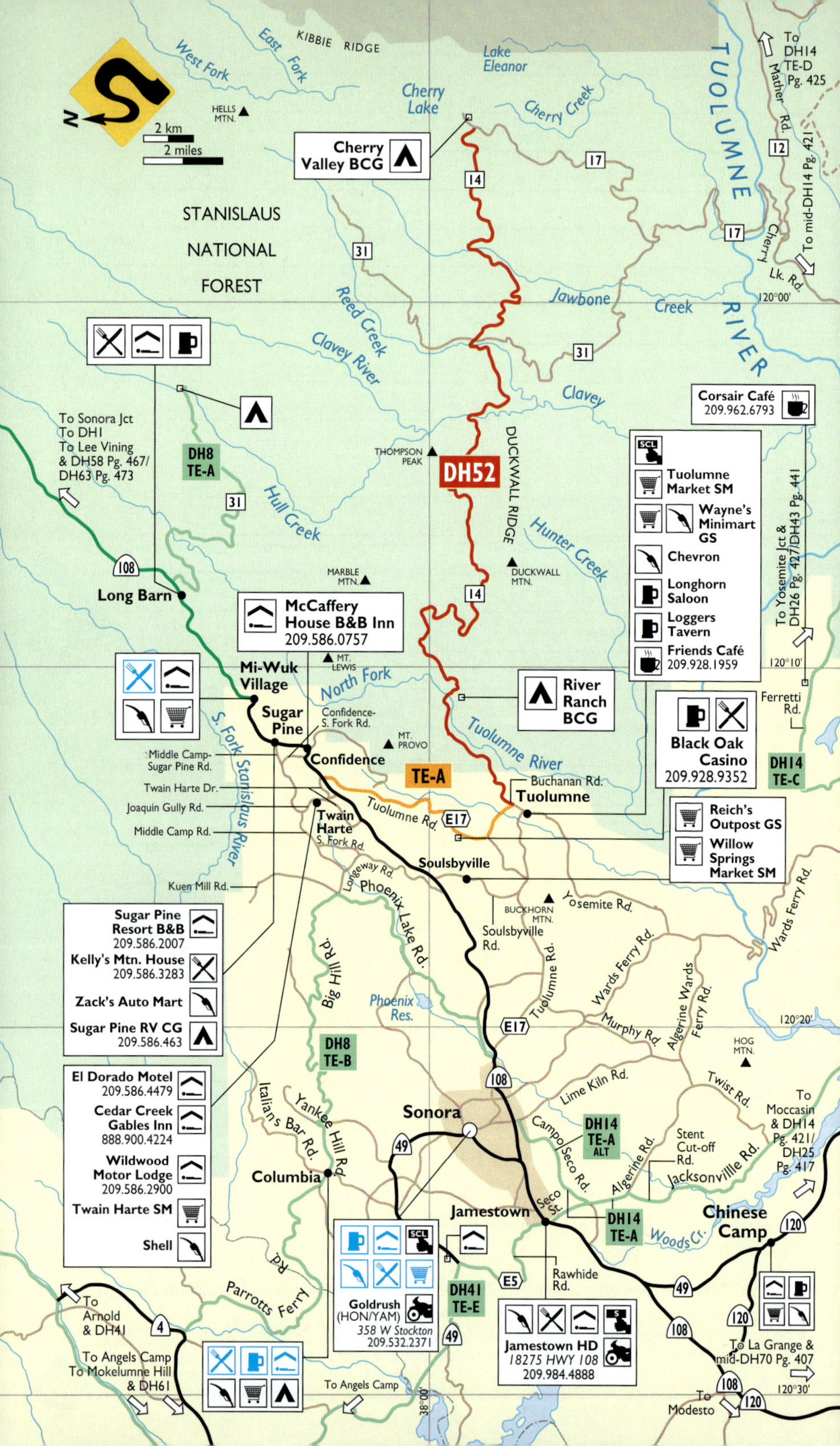

2 km
2 miles
STANISLAUS
NATIONAL
FOREST
Cherry Valley BCG
DH52
DH8 TE-A
DH8 TE-B
TE-A
DH14 TE-A ALT
DH14 TE-A
DH14 TE-C
DH41 TE-E
To Sonora Jct
To DH1
To Lee Vining
& DH58 Pg. 467/
DH63 Pg. 473
To DH14
TE-D
Pg. 425
To mid-DH14 Pg. 421
To Yosemite Jct &
DH26 Pg. 427/DH43 Pg. 441
Corsair Café
209.962.6793
Tuolumne Market SM
Wayne's Minimart GS
Chevron
Longhorn Saloon
Loggers Tavern
Friends Café
209.928.1959
Black Oak Casino
209.928.9352
Reich's Outpost GS
Willow Springs Market SM
McCaffery House B&B Inn
209.586.0757
River Ranch BCG
Sugar Pine Resort B&B
209.586.2007
Kelly's Mtn. House
209.586.3283
Zack's Auto Mart
Sugar Pine RV CG
209.586.463
El Dorado Motel
209.586.4479
Cedar Creek Gables Inn
888.900.4224
Wildwood Motor Lodge
209.586.2900
Twain Harte SM
Shell
Goldrush
(HON/YAM)
358 W Stockton
209.532.2371
Jamestown HD
18275 HWY 108
209.984.4888
To Moccasin
& DH14
Pg. 421/
DH25
Pg. 417
To La Grange &
mid-DH70 Pg. 407
To Modesto
To Arnold
& DH41
To Angels Camp
To Mokelumne Hill
& DH61
To Angels Camp
Long Barn
Mi-Wuk Village
Sugar Pine
Confidence
Twain Harte
Tuolumne
Soulsbyville
Sonora
Columbia
Jamestown
Chinese Camp
KIBBIE RIDGE
HELLS MTN.
THOMPSON PEAK
MARBLE MTN.
MT. LEWIS
MT. PROVO
DUCKWALL MTN.
DUCKWALL RIDGE
BUCKHORN MTN.
HOG MTN.
West Fork
East Fork
Cherry Lake
Lake Eleanor
Cherry Creek
TUOLUMNE RIVER
Jawbone Creek
Reed Creek
Clavey River
Clavey
Hull Creek
Hunter Creek
North Fork
Tuolumne River
S. Fork Stanislaus River
Phoenix Res.
Woods Cr.
Mather Rd.
Cherry Lk. Rd.
Ferretti Rd.
Buchanan Rd.
Confidence-S. Fork Rd.
Middle Camp-Sugar Pine Rd.
Twain Harte Dr.
Joaquin Gully Rd.
Middle Camp Rd.
Kuen Mill Rd.
Tuolumne Rd.
S. Fork Rd.
Longeway Rd.
Phoenix Lake Rd.
Big Hill Rd.
Soulsbyville Rd.
Yosemite Rd.
Tuolumne Rd.
Wards Ferry Rd.
Algerine Wards Ferry Rd.
Murphy Rd.
Lime Kiln Rd.
Twist Rd.
Campo Seco Rd.
Algerine Rd.
Stent Cut-off Rd.
Jacksonville Rd.
Seco St.
Rawhide Rd.
Italians Bar Rd.
Yankee Hill Rd.
Parrotts Ferry Rd.
120°00'
120°10'
120°20'
120°30'
38°00'

DH52 Tuolumne – Cherry Lake

Buchanan Rd / Cottonwood Rd (FSR 14)

Distance:	31.2 mi / 50.2 km	Traffic:	Light

At a Glance

Okay, okay, don't get your knickers in a knot. Sure you might be saying, "Whoa, what's with this Pavement?" about a quarter mile into this DH. Followed by "Is this piece of crap worth traveling to, to journey on?" Granted, the first 2.0 mi (3.2 km) is a little on the bumpy, patchy, narrow, unpainted and horribly engineered side. But that's only to deter curious RVs. After you endure that initial section through the canyon, the asphalt stripes up, widens and smoothes to more or less average grade over miles of well-sightlined and evenly cambered sweepers. And the only traffic you'll probably have to contend with is the weekend boaters heading to and from the lake. Sugar pines, ponderosas and white firs constitute the Scenery on most of the route, though there are some detailed rockfaces and high views as you cross and climb off the Clavey River. Once you reach the lake, you either have to backtrack or take the substandard 23.2 mi (27.1 km) run down Cherry Lake Rd (FSR 17) to mid-DH14 Moccasin – Yosemite Jct. Should you opt for FSR 17, a sheet bend or series of half-hitches should do the trick.

TIRES	
Twistiness	30.0/ 30
Pavement	9.1/ 20
Engineering	2.9/ 10
Remoteness	9.7/ 10
Scenery	9.0/ 15
Character	4.4/ 15
Total	**65.1**

Access

From Tuolumne

On Tuolumne Rd N (E 17)/Carter St

Take Tuolumne/Carter from what remains of downtown and then turn right onto Buchanan Rd. When you clear the suburbs, you're on the road.

From Mi-Wuk Village (Twain Harte)

Coming in on DH8 Sonora Jct – Mi-Wuk Village (Twain Harte) (Hwy 108) Via TE-A

Go south on Tuolumne Rd (E 17). As you enter town at the south end of the TE, turn left on Buchanan Rd. When you leave town, you're on the road.

From Sonora

On Hwy 108

Turn off Hwy 108 and take Tuolumne Rd (E 17) to Tuolumne. Continue north on Tuolumne Rd/Carter St and turn right on Buchanan Rd. When you exit town, you're on the road.

From Cherry Lake
On FSR 14
Head west. You're on the road.

On The Road

Remoteness is instant as soon as you leave Tuolumne. Twistiness and scenery get good starts, too, as the road strings along the edge of a steep, dry rock and brown grass-coated cliff mottled by bushes and dusty trees. It's the swiss cheese pavement and crummy engineering that might have you wondering if you've made a wrong turn.

Not to worry, P & E improve at 2.0 mi (3.2 km), at least enough to turn this into a motorcycle road. The faded centerline that comes with the rehab is even dotted. A nice touch since you may need to use the ascending straight to flush any pylons that may have clogged you up in the narrow drainpipe of the canyon start.

At 2.2 mi (3.5 km), the road pitches downward and begins a steady descent. Given the rough terrain, you'd expect tight curves, but these turns are consistently sweepy. The mixed con and deci forest straddling the road gets progressively thicker as you drop. Tree limbs dangle over the road in spots. But there are still openings between them where you can see the North Fork Tuolumne River effervescing below.

"End of County Maintained Road" reads the sign at 3.7 mi (6.0 km). Well, it seemed it was only maintained on a quarter-centenary basis, anyway. You hope for some change – for the better – as the county puts you in the loving hands of the Forest Service. Though you don't see a marked difference U-ing over the river and reverse-curling past the entrance to the River Ranch BCG, the truth is the pavement quality is slowly starting to improve.

Sweeper – straight – S curve – straight – sweeper. The hypnotic effect is magnified by the sameness of the surroundings. The left side slopes upwards, the right downwards toward unseen Basin Creek. Trees – principally pine now – and layers of shrubbery dab either side, sometimes relieved by a small rockfaces on the left. At 8.4 mi (13.5 km), the slope becomes less pronounced and the trees mesh into a real forest.

A speck of variety comes at 9.4 mi (15.1 km) when the right roadside plummets, opening up a near view of, well, more trees and rock. As the trees shroud the terrain again, the slope tips the opposite way, revealing similar views off the other side. Sweepers are replaced by a series of short, staccato curves. Makes little difference – with great sightlines, it doesn't take much to power through this easy slalom course.

Marble Mtn rolls across the northern horizon at 11.5 mi (18.5 km). The left side views disappear behind an arboreal wall as a big S-sweeper tilts your mirrors right then left. The road climbs and the left roadside gradually levels. Now you're into a forest of trees and shorter, tighter curves. Big painted letters on the road at 12.3 mi (19.8 km) and again at

14.2 mi (22.9 km) warn you to look out for large, small-brained bovines. Though actual speed tax collector sightings are rare.

Shifting downhill, there's an unpleasant asphalt deja-vu at 14.8 mi (23.8 km) as a bumpy right-hand sweeper signals a pavement downgrade. The "Single Lane Ahead" sign at 15.3 mi (24.6 km) brings the upcoming engineering quality into question as well. Um, like, is that for some kind of bridge or the rest of the road?

As it turns out, the one-lane road is a non event, a mild chicane that probably wouldn't even be noticeable but for a brief interruption in the centerline paint. Curiously, it's followed by a short stretch starting at 17.0 mi (27.4 km) where the road widens to three lanes – the only place on the route this happens. It's endearing, really, watching the DH compensate for its minor shortcomings.

Rounding a 20-mph (30-kmh) right-hander, you cross the bridge over the Clavey River. The striking view over the gorge from mid-span stands out on what has so far been a scenically uneventful road. As the pylons parked by the roadside suggest, there is a way to hike down to the water if you're so inclined. But then, you're already pleasantly inclined.

The scenery's better past the river. A steep rockface grapples up to your left and an equally steep one plumbs down to your right as you climb up the edge of Clavey's canyon. The road levels out at 18.9 mi (30.4 km), curving along the chasm and presenting a view of the emerald Duckwall Ridge slopes.

You've really got to wonder what kind of quack decides where signs get posted around here. Take the one at 19.8 mi (31.9 km) that says "Twisties next 2 miles." Though the landscape's different – you're now off the steep rock slope and in the woods – there's no difference in terms of curvitude between the next two miles and the two that preceded them. It's as though someone's trying to give the impression of attention to detail without actually attending to it.

With the questionable signage come a few sections of unquestionably better pavement. Noticeable, but not enough to identify a trend. The trend toward sweepers and long curves continues though, culminating in the series beginning at 22.0 mi (35.4 km).

At 24.1 mi (38.8 km), you enter the Granite Burn area, site of a 17,000-acre wildfire in 1973. According to the U.S. Forest Service, they've "invested heavily in returning the burned area to productive forest land, enhancing wildlife habitat and watershed amenities." Obviously this DH's neglected asphalt doesn't qualify as a "watershed amenity."

The woods thin and S-curves curl along an untreed cliff, allowing for some southern views. The landscape opens up further at 27.1 mi (43.6 km) where you become aware that you've gained altitude. Gone is the murky forest. Airy groves of ponderosa pines and low foliage now line the roadside. There are even some meadows as the terrain flattens. Gray shades of exposed granite add texture to the broadening plateau.

With all the space between the trees up here, one wonders why the cattle feel the need to hang out in the middle of the road. Maybe, like us, they're mysteriously drawn to wide swatches of pavement winding through the wilderness. Or maybe they're just dumb.

Assuming you've managed to dodge the livestock, at 30.2 mi (48.6 km) you're treated to your first view of Cherry Lake, lying beneath the scarred slopes of Kibbie and Cherry Ridges. At 31.2 mi (50.2 km), you reach the entrance to the Cherry Lake Campground, the official end of the DH. If you're not camping and want to take a break, there's good water access off the boat ramp a half mile or so further on. But ultimately, you'll have to make a choice: double back or endure the 23.1 mi (37.1 km) goat path down Cherry Lake Rd (FSR 17) to mid-**DH14 Moccasin – Yosemite Jct**.

Twisted Edges

TE-A Twain Harte – Tuolumne (5.6 mi / 9.0 km) *Tuolumne Rd (E 17)*
The sweepy curves are more prevalent on the more heavily forested northern end of this well-paved, fairly busy connector between **DH8** and **DH52**. Which is good since the Mi-Wuk Tribal Police are more prevalent on the south end by the Black Oak Casino. Of course, the yellow lights on the top of their cruisers might suggest they have little interest in the 45-mph (70-kmh) speed limit. But then, it might not.

Rider's Log: **Date Ridden:** **Your Rating: /10**

Don't forget to print the DH Rider Discount list of service providers from destinationhighways.com and take it with you. Then, just show 'em your book and ask for the discount.

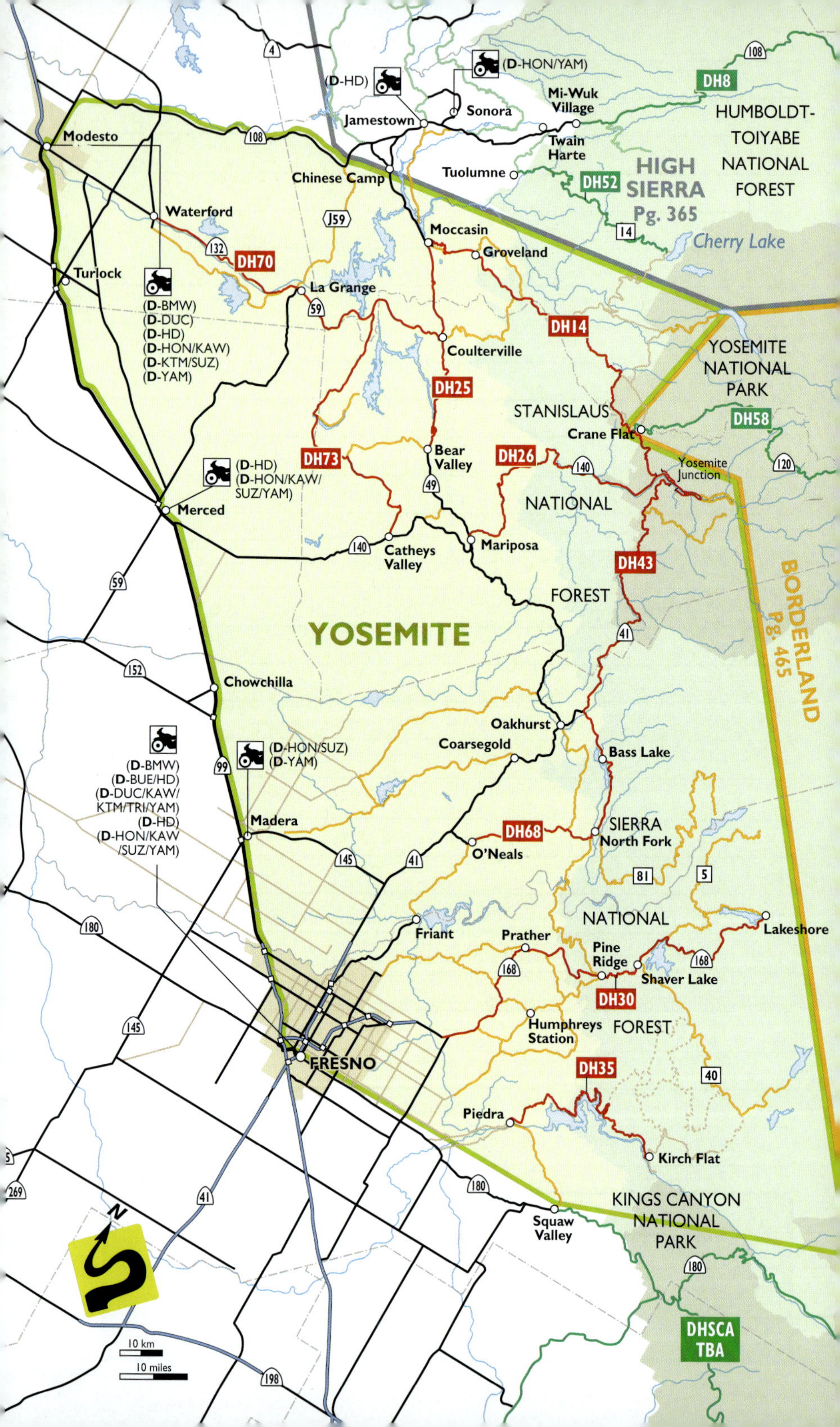

YOSEMITE
Modesto
Waterford
Turlock
Merced
Chowchilla
Madera
FRESNO
Jamestown
Sonora
Mi-Wuk Village
Twain Harte
Tuolumne
Chinese Camp
Moccasin
Groveland
La Grange
Coulterville
Bear Valley
Catheys Valley
Mariposa
Crane Flat
Yosemite Junction
Oakhurst
Coarsegold
Bass Lake
North Fork
O'Neals
Friant
Prather
Pine Ridge
Shaver Lake
Lakeshore
Humphreys Station
Piedra
Kirch Flat
Squaw Valley
Cherry Lake
HIGH SIERRA Pg. 365
HUMBOLDT-TOIYABE NATIONAL FOREST
YOSEMITE NATIONAL PARK
STANISLAUS NATIONAL FOREST
SIERRA NATIONAL FOREST
KINGS CANYON NATIONAL PARK
BORDERLAND Pg. 465
DH8
DH14
DH25
DH26
DH30
DH35
DH43
DH52
DH58
DH68
DH70
DH73
DHSCA TBA
(D-HD)
(D-HON/YAM)
(D-BMW)
(D-DUC)
(D-HD)
(D-HON/KAW)
(D-KTM/SUZ)
(D-YAM)
(D-HD)
(D-HON/KAW/SUZ/YAM)
(D-HON/SUZ)
(D-YAM)
(D-BMW)
(D-BUE/HD)
(D-DUC/KAW/KTM/TRI/YAM)
(D-HD)
(D-HON/KAW/SUZ/YAM)
10 km
10 miles

YOSEMITE

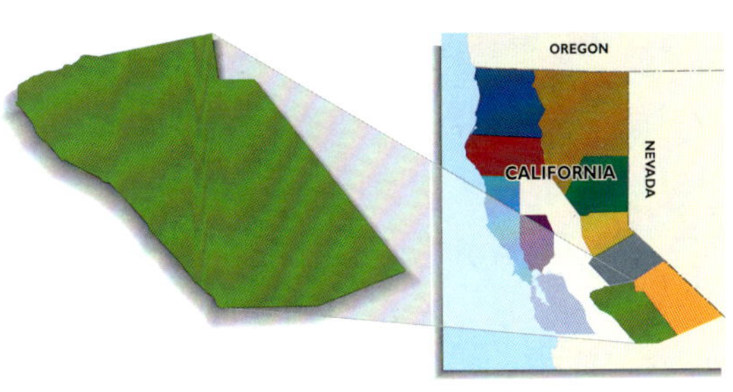

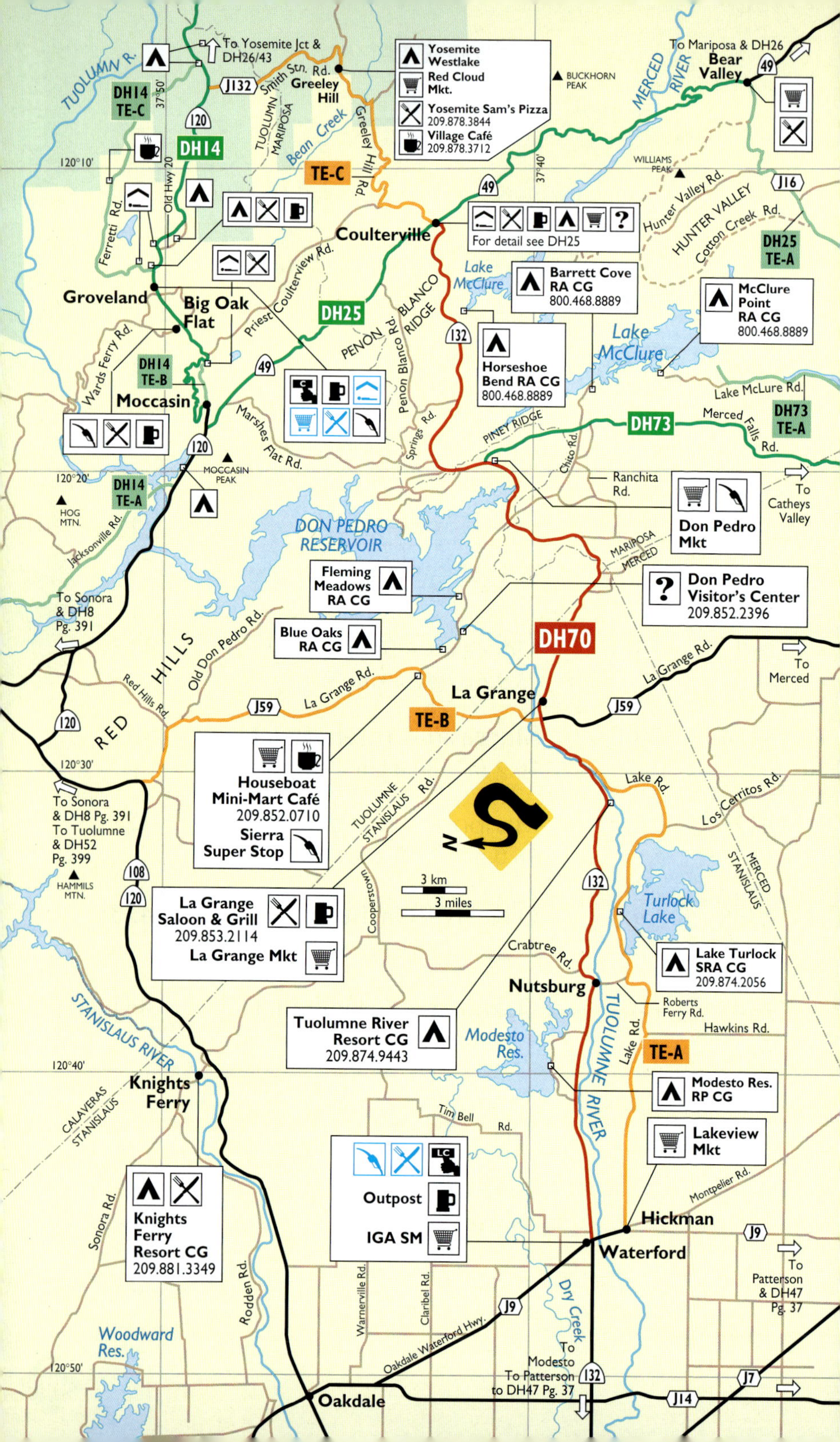

To Yosemite Jct & DH26/43
Yosemite Westlake
Red Cloud Mkt.
Yosemite Sam's Pizza 209.878.3844
Village Café 209.878.3712
Greeley Hill
Coulterville
For detail see DH25
Groveland
Big Oak Flat
Moccasin
To Mariposa & DH26
Bear Valley
Lake McClure
Barrett Cove RA CG 800.468.8889
McClure Point RA CG 800.468.8889
Horseshoe Bend RA CG 800.468.8889
Don Pedro Mkt
To Catheys Valley
DON PEDRO RESERVOIR
Fleming Meadows RA CG
Blue Oaks RA CG
Don Pedro Visitor's Center 209.852.2396
To Sonora & DH8 Pg. 391
To Merced
La Grange
Houseboat Mini-Mart Café 209.852.0710
Sierra Super Stop
To Sonora & DH8 Pg. 391 To Tuolumne & DH52 Pg. 399
La Grange Saloon & Grill 209.853.2114
La Grange Mkt
3 km
3 miles
Turlock Lake
Lake Turlock SRA CG 209.874.2056
Nutsburg
Tuolumne River Resort CG 209.874.9443
Modesto Res.
Modesto Res. RP CG
Knights Ferry
Lakeview Mkt
Outpost
IGA SM
Knights Ferry Resort CG 209.881.3349
Hickman
Waterford
To Patterson & DH47 Pg. 37
Woodward Res.
To Modesto To Patterson to DH47 Pg. 37
Oakdale
DH14
DH25
DH70
DH73
TE-A
TE-B
TE-C

DH70 Waterford – Coulterville

Highway 132

Distance:	38.8 mi / 62.4 km	Traffic:	Moderate

At a Glance

TIRES	
Twistiness	14.2/30
Pavement	14.5/20
Engineering	6.3/10
Remoteness	4.3/10
Scenery	8.7/15
Character	9.3/15
Total	**57.3**

Let's set the record straight. There's absolutely *no* connection between this Destination Highway and right-wing columnist, Ann Coulter. Seriously, how could there be? As much as she might appreciate the conservative radius of the turns on this often-straight ride – especially through the farmland west of La Grange – could Ann really swallow the gay marriage of Pavement and Engineering? Or the liberal doses of inclusive Scenery along the flat quarter-sections bordering the Tuolumne River between Waterford and La Grange, on the treeless, rolling plain west of the populated Don Pedro Reservoir and up in the wild, heather-filled mountain slopes near Coulterville? Or how about the fact that motorcyclists have the choice of terminating this ride in the middle trimester and heading south on DH73 Merced Falls Rd – Hornitos Rd? Highly unlikely. Now if Ann would only take a little affirmative action and hop aboard a bi-partisan Victory, she might find baiting speed tax collectors twice as much fun as baiting the ACLU. So, c'mon Annie. Load your tank, lock your throttle and shoot your way to Coulterville. No waiting period required.

Access

From Waterford

On Hwy 132

Head east, leave town and you're on the road.

From Coulterville (mid-DH25 Moccasin – Bear Valley)

On Hwy 49

Turn west on Hwy 132. You're on the road.

From DH73 Hornitos Rd - Merced Falls Rd

The north end of Merced Falls Rd junctions with the DH 28.3 mi (45.5 km) east of Waterville and 10.5 mi (16.9 km) west of Coulterville.

On The Road

Like many good rides, this DH starts out not being particularly recognizable as one. Thin orchards, thick power lines, commercial farm buildings and straight, straight, straight. While good pavement and engineering are always appreciated, they're not enough to keep you interested for long.

Some mini-curves – just bends really – at 2.5 mi (4.0 km) and 5.6 mi (9.0 km) relieve the early monotony. At 7.0 mi (11.3 km), you reach the junction with Roberts Ferry Rd, a link that bridges the Tuolumne River to intersect with Lake Rd (**TE-A**). Apart from the connector, there's nothing here but a store called The Nut Shop. A more appropriate STC hangout than a donut stand, when you think about it.

It gets a little curvier past Nutsburg. A trio of decent curves introduces a duet of respectable sweepers on a little rise. At 8.3 mi (13.4 km), you drop back down and the left roadside takes on a little slope. Jeez, with the cattle in fields, rolling green hills on the right, and some weave to the road, the scene's beginning to look almost bucolic.

At 9.9 mi (16.0 km), the road plateaus and loses what little intensity it was beginning to generate. Rather than really twisting, the road yawns gently left and right. Echoing the mood, the line of mature trees to the right droops lazily over the sleepy river. You could use a little wake-up of S-curves right about now.

But if anything, the road seems to be getting straighter, at least until 12.6 mi (20.4 km) where a little sweeper leads to a couple more corners. This time, there's more promise in the landscape. A band of granite escapes the grass cover to the left, a sign that you're riding the ancient bed of the river. The river with its line of trees angles across the fields toward the road ahead. The route intersects the Tuolumne River, crossing it at 15.0 mi (24.1 km), just west of the junction with the eastern end of Lake Rd (**TE-A**).

As the twisties sign suggests, life is better on this side of the river. A low, grassy shelf with exposed granite underneath lines the right side. The left is a short drop off down to the water. Oaks flourish above and below. The road winds through the twistiest and most scenic bit of this road so far before straightening to the left-right junction with La Grange Rd (**TE-B**) at 16.9 mi (27.2 km). The TE goes left. To stay on the DH, **go straight.**

Past the intersection, you enter the small town of La Grange, eyeing the bikes undoubtedly parked at the La Grange Saloon & Grill. The 30-mph (50-kmh) speed zone covers the S-curve that climbs the step at the end of town up onto the plateau. But there are more corners once the dysfunctional speed zone gets back up to normal. Not that any speed zone can really be considered "normal."

You're in one vast valley, highlighted by lonely stands of trees and sharp rocks that cut through rips in the blanket of brown and light green grass. Past the few curves just out of town, there's a straight, then a few more tighter curves and then another straight. The shoulderless thread of fine pavement rises, dips and bends as if haphazardly cast upon the rolling plain.

The road that was skinny in Merced County has broad shoulders once you cross into Mariposa at 22.3 mi (35.9 km). In fact, Engineering improves all around when the DH crosses the county line and fast, spaced sweepers blaze an even ascent. The road stays wide with another quick county change over to Tuolumne at 25.6 mi (41.2 km). The scenery and sense of remoteness suffers, though, from structures dotting the hills and roadside. Not to mention the billboard at the 25.8 mi (41.5 km) intersection blaring that the Don Pedro Market is two miles ahead.

The scenery improves when you descend past the intersection and sweep along one of the hundreds of hidden coves on the Don Pedro Reservoir. It's hillier here and trees are in abundance. The houses disappear momentarily as well, only to return with force when you emerge from the hills and flatten out by the market at 28.1 mi (45.2 km), a full 2.3 miles (3.7 km) from the billboard. So much for truth in advertising.

With all the residential side roads, it's starting to feel almost suburban as you venture past the northern junction of **DH73 Merced Falls Rd - Hornitos Rd** at 28.3 mi (45.5 km). So much so that you might regret not making that right turn. But hang in there. The road does drag a bit here, delivering only a couple of unspectacular turns through unremarkable, V-cut-obscured terrain before straightening out. The dark, newer pavement turns to a lighter grey at 29.8 mi (48.0 km) but stays smooth for the brief passing lane at 31.0 mi (49.9 km).

This DH's fine scenic finale begins officially at 32.9 mi (52.9 km). Descending, the road comes out of a V-cut and sweeps left, revealing the tall, steep, green and silver sides of Penon Blanco Ridge. The spectacular drop continues offering sweeping scenery to go with the sweeping turns. Bushy pines covering the red dirt on either side of the road add to the sea of flora. By the time you curve beneath one of the red dirt, granite, sage-covered slopes at 35.3 mi (56.8 km), it feels like a different world. And a different road.

Climbing again, the road ahead sweeps up big and fast through the remote, colorful, highland terrain. A vast canyon opens up below you. It all seems powerfully remote, at least until 37.6 mi (60.5 km) when you see the first signs of approaching civilization. At 38.8 mi (62.4 km), it's upon you as you arrive at the town of Coulterville, the western junction of J 132 (**TE-C**) and the midway point of **DH25 Moccasin – Bear Valley**. From here, it's right, left or stay the course. What's your vote?

Twisted Edges

TE-A Lake Rd (18.2 mi / 29.3 km)

Some pundits say that this TE is better than the DH it parallels. Certainly, if lack of traffic is your thing, there may be something to that. Twistiness is a toss-up. But the asphalt and engineering aren't quite as good. Nor is the scenery, though it's pleasant enough to ride past the rolling burnt-grass hills in the east, Lake Turlock in the middle and orchards in the west. But what really makes Lake Rd the TE and Hwy 132 the DH? *Destination Highways* politics, my son.

TE-B La Grange Rd (15.2 mi / 24.5 km)
Doesn't matter if you're riding an old Suzuki Farmbyke or a new V-Star Silverado, when you amble through the well-paved, easygoing curves across the dry, oak-dusted plain rolling beneath the Sierra foothills, you'll feel right at home on La Grange.

TOUR NOTE: When you hook this TE in with ***DH41TE-G O'Byrnes Rd****, a bit of* ***DH41TE-D Copperopolis – Angels Camp*** *(Hwy 4) and* ***DH41TE-F Pool Station Rd****, it's a quiet back route for those busy summer weekends. Or anytime.*

TE-C Greeley Hill Rd - Smith Station Rd (J 132) (14.0 mi / 22.5 km)
Here's another way to go if you're concerned about pylons bogging you down in the tight curves north of Coulterville on Hwy 49 (**DH25 Coulterville - Moccasin**) and up **DH14 Moccasin – Yosemite Jct's** steep Priest Grade. Fewer curves than the serpentine **DH25/14** route, to be sure, but this sweeping, scenic, often-remote backroad has far less traffic. And you don't even have to sacrifice much in pavement until you turn north onto Smith Station Rd.

NAVIGATION: Coming from Coulterville, Main St turns into Greeley Hill Rd. Make sure to turn north onto Smith Station Rd, 8.2 mi (13.2 km) from the end of Coulterville's speed zone. If you hit gravel, you missed the Smith Station Rd junction about two miles (three kilometers) back.

Coming south on Smith Station Rd from Hwy 120, turn right onto Greeley Hill Rd at 5.8 mi (9.3 km). (If you turn left this good looking road turns to gravel after a couple of miles.)

RIDER'S LOG: **DATE RIDDEN:** **YOUR RATING: /10**

What are the Top Ten Rides based on Twistiness, Pavement, Engineering, Remoteness, Scenery and Character? You'll find the answers in the TIRES Charts at the back of the book. The complete list of DHs by TIRES components is at destinationhighways.com.

Hotel Jeffery
209.878.3471
Yosemite Gold Country Motel & RV CG
800.247.9884
Coulter Cafe GS
209.878.3947
5007 Main
209.878.3074
To Cherry Lake & DH52 Pg. 399
Wards Ferry Rd.
Moccasin
Groveland
Big Oak Flat
To Sonora
To Tuolumne & DH52 Pg. 399
Buck Meadows
Harden Flat
To Yosemite Jct & DH26/43
To Yosemite Jct & DH14/43
Greeley Hill
STANISLAUS NATIONAL FOREST
Don Pedro Mkt
Coulterville
Horseshoe Bend RA CG
800.468.8889
Barrett Cove RA CG
800.468.8889
McClure Point RA CG
800.468.8889
Lake McClure
Bear Valley
Plaza Bar
Airport Inn Bar & Grill
209.377.8444
Midpines
Merced Falls
Hornitos
Mt. Bullion
Mariposa
Mormon Bar
To Oakhurst & DH43/68
To Turlock
To Waterford
To Modesto
Lake McSwath RA CG
800.468.8889
Boulder Creek B&B
800.768.4752
Simpson Trabucco Store
209.377.8424
Bon Ton Cafe
209.377.8488
Catheys Valley
Oasis Mkt
209.374.3410
The Oaks
209.966.4000
Union 76
To Hwy 99
To Merced
3 km
3 miles

DH73 Merced Falls Rd - Hornitos Rd

Distance:	32.4 mi / 52.1 km	Traffic:	Light

At a Glance

TIRES	
Twistiness	19.4/ 30
Pavement	12.2/ 20
Engineering	4.9/ 10
Remoteness	4.8/ 10
Scenery	9.2/ 15
Character	4.6/ 15
Total	55.1

"We don't need no stinkin' badges" was the motto of the Mexican 49ers who founded Hornitos. The new town quickly developed a well-earned rep as the roughest, outside-the-law gold camp in Mariposa County. Today however, with the possible exception of the bar offering "Drinks to Go", this quiet, little village is as peaceful and quiet as the mellow, law-abidin' DH that runs past it. The road, which cuts through an easy-mannered landscape of foothills, open plains and scattered oak trees does have some Twistiness, though the Pavement occasionally rocks your boat. It's proximity to the Central Valley and the buildings you see near Catheys Valley do compromise Remoteness. Nevertheless, at the end of the day, it's only the Engineering that really gets out of line on this DH – at one point, it actually moves the road more up and down than side to side. Not enough, mind you, to prevent some from being tempted to rebel against the local speed tax laws. Good thing the speed tax collectors are more likely to be keeping a lid on the numbered highway traffic nearby rather than hereabouts. Because after all, you don't need no stinkin' badges either.

Access

From mid-DH70 Waterford – Coulterville (Hwy 132)

Head south on Merced Falls Rd and you're on the road.

From Catheys Valley

On Hwy 140

Turn north on Hornitos Rd from Hwy 140 and you're on the road.

On The Road

The pavement drops a grade as you turn off **DH70**. So does the remoteness, as you find yourself in a school zone. But it's not long before you're out in open, rolling countryside again between the low, Piney Ridge to the east and some tree-scattered hills to the west. The straights along here are broken up by a short stretches of curves. You cross the Tuolumne/Mariposa County line at 2.7 mi (4.3 km).

At the end of another straight, Barrett Cove Rd accesses the Lake McClure/Exchequer Reservoir left at 3.4 mi (5.5 km). You're climbing slightly now, angling to the east as you head up into hills. At 4.7 mi (7.6 km), the road crests a mini-pass. To the southwest, you can see the flat of the Central Valley spreading out in the distance beyond your low hills. Then you descend with a mellow, welcome series of curves.

As the terrain flattens out, the corners and trees diminish in number, although at 7.8 mi (12.6 km), a 30-mph (50-kmh) corner introduces another set of easy curves. Many are quite relaxed because you're now close to the Central Valley's bottom. The countryside is so open you'll have no problem seeing around them, regardless of your speed. You'll have no trouble seeing your way past any pylons either.

You pass another low-speed advisory and cross from Mariposa into Merced County at 11.5 mi (18.5 km). It occurs to you, as you bounce along, that Merced's asphalt budget seems to be lower than Mariposa's. Or else they're just more interested in spending money on straightening rather than paving. Merced Falls Rd junctions with Hornitos Rd at 12.6 mi (20.3 km). You'll see a sign for Lake McSwain/Lake McClure. To stay on the DH, make sure you follow the sign and **turn left on Hornitos**.

A half mile later, the DH junctions with Lake McClure Rd (**TE-A**) straight ahead at 13.1 mi (21.1 km). To stay on Hornitos and the DH, **turn right onto the bridge**.

You cross the Merced River and the pavement improves. However, if you don't like blind crests, you'll be less impressed with the engineering. Or the twistiness, for that matter. These vertical undulations are a sorry substitute for the lack of curves in the now flat, almost tree-free landscape. A few corners replace the up-and-down either side of the Mariposa County line at 15.1 mi (24.3 km).

A 35-mph (55-kmh) corner at 17.8 mi (28.6 km) is the first of a bunch of tighter curves through the dry terrain that are separated by a single straight. You're still curving when the trees creep back and the road descends at 19.0 mi (30.6 km). You turn to the north, drop round a couple of more curves, enter Hornitos and junction with Bear Valley Rd (**DH25TE-A**) at 20.3 mi (32.7 km).

The number of trees increases again as you leave Hornitown, but so do the number of buildings. The curves leave momentarily but gradually represent themselves on the mostly sweet pavement. The trees flee as you bust out onto an empty flat at 23.2 mi (37.3 km). Up ahead a line of green foothills right angles your path.

The prodigal trees return by 24.8 mi (39.9 km), as you enter some subhills. So do some low-speed advisories. Buildings become more prevalent and you can probably count on this getting worse. Don't be tempted by the evocative-sounding Old Toll Rd, left in the middle of a sweeper at 26.4 mi (42.5 km). It's a miserable, pockmarked, ugly, patchwork thing that might as well be called Old Troll. Suitable only for those intent on doing every "paved" road in California.

The DH is now heading due south, splitting a couple of open fields then dodging back into the trees. Don't get too excited about the advisory signs exhibiting the usual over-caution. In fact the curves aren't overwhelming in either number or sharpness. But the increasing number of driveways and houses encourage you to watch your speed anyway. The road straightens completely toward the end, which comes at 32.4 mi (52.1 km) when you hit Hwy 140.

Twisted Edges

TE-A Lake McClure Rd (8.7 mi / 14.0 km)

Just as you start to wonder where all this sweet pavement came from, you hit the Merced Irrigation District tollbooth. Okay, now you get it. Tell 'em you're just riding to the end and back and they may let you in free. This is one dynamite little ride with decent curves complementing great pavement and engineering through forest and hill scenery. It ends with a sparkling flourish up to the Exchequer Dam viewpoint. Worth every penny.

TE-B Mt Bullion Cutoff Rd (3.1 mi / 5.0 km)

Don't let anyone try to tell you there's no gold left around here – not when you can mine this little nugget that bypasses part of Hwy 49 and Hwy 140. Amalgamates well with that twisty bit of Hwy 140 south and west of Catheys Mtn.

Rider's Log: **Date Ridden:** **Your Rating:** **/10**

Hotel Jeffery
209.878.3471
Yosemite Gold Country Motel & RV CG
800.247.9884
Coulter Cafe GS
209.878.3947
5007 Main
209.878.3074
To Cherry Lake & DH52 Pg. 399
STANISLAUS NATIONAL FOREST
17
Cherry Creek
RIVER
TUOLUMNE
M. Fk. Tuolumne R.
Cherry Lake Rd.
Wards Ferry Rd.
Ferretti Rd.
DH14 TE-A
DH14 TE-C
Groveland
Moccasin
Old Hwy 20
37°50'
120
DH14
Big Oak Flat
Buck Meadows
S. Fk. Tuolumne
Harden Flat
To Sonora
To Tuolumne & DH52 Pg. 399
J132
To Yosemite Jct & DH26/43
Marshes Flat Rd.
DH14 TE-B
Priest Coulterview Rd.
JACKASS RIDGE
TUOLUMN
MARIPOSA
Bean Creek
WAGNER RIDGE
Buck Meadows Rd.
20
Don Pedro Mkt
PENON BLANCO RIDGE
Greeley Hill
DH70 TE-C
Springs Rd.
Penon Blanco Rd.
Greeley Hill Rd.
Coulterville
Horseshoe Bend RA CG
800.468.8889
Bull Creek
To Waterford
To Modesto
DH70
132
HORSESHOE BEND MTN.
49
To Yosemite Jct. & DH14/43
PINEY RIDGE
37° 40'
Barrett Cove RA CG
800.468.8889
BUCKHORN PEAK
Chito Rd.
HUNTER VALLEY MTN.
DH25
JENKINS HILL
Ranchita Rd.
McClure Point RA CG
800.468.8889
MERCED
RIVER
DH73
Lake McClure
Hunter Valley Rd.
WILLIAMS PEAK
HUNTER VALLEY
Cotton Creek Rd.
140
MARIPOSA
MERCED
Merced Falls Rd.
Bear Valley
BULLION MTN.
Rd.
Colorado Rd.
Whitlock Rd.
Midpines
DH73 TE-A
Plaza Bar
J16
TE-A
Airport Inn Bar & Grill
209.377.8444
49
Mt. Bullion Cutoff Rd.
DH26
Lake McClure Rd.
Merced Falls
To Turlock
Hornitos
37°30'
Mt. Bullion
Old Toll Rd.
Agua Fina Rd.
Allred Rd.
INDIAN MTN.
DH73 TE-B
Mariposa
Hornitos Rd.
Indian Gulch Rd.
Slate Gulch Rd.
Hornitos Rd.
140
To Oakhurst & DH43/68
Lake McSwath RA CG
800.468.8889
CATHEYS MTN.
Mormon Bar
Yaqui Gulch Rd.
Old Hwy.
Boulder Creek B&B
800.768.4752
SHULTZ MTN.
Catheys Valley
Creek
Bear
CATHEYS VALLEY
Buckeye Rd.
LOOKOUT MTN.
Simpson Trabucco Store
209.377.8424
Bon Ton Cafe
209.377.8488
Old Highway
MOORE HILL
N
120°10'
140
Oasis Mkt
209.374.3410
The Oaks
209.966.4000
Union 76
Ben Hur Rd.
Silver Bar Rd.
3 km
3 miles
120°20'
To Hwy 99
To Merced
KNOB HILL
LUCY HILL
120°00'

DH25 Moccasin – Bear Valley

Highway 49

Distance:	25.9 mi / 41.7 km	Traffic:	Light

TIRES	
Twistiness	30.0/ 30
Pavement	14.5/ 20
Engineering	3.2/ 10
Remoteness	7.2/ 10
Scenery	10.7/ 15
Character	9.7/ 15
Total 75.3	

At a Glance

If you're thinking of "taking up serpents" (Mark 16:18), you might want to make a pilgrimage to Moccasin. Forget about the poisonous cottonmouths in the local streams. It's this DH's Twistiness and Engineering that pose a biblical challenge for any aspiring snake handler. After quietly lurking along Moccasin Creek, this road's smooth-scaled Pavement suddenly strikes up along the dry cliff of a remote and dangerous canyon. Should you survive, it backs off just as quickly, stalking you with straights and barely-curves all the way through the sleepy crossroads of Coulterville. But just past town, this viper, threatened by unspoiled mountains and steep gorges, strikes again, this time releasing its full venom. A guardrail-less road edge hisses at your tires as the road writhes along the glorious rock and shrub-studded cliffs of the steep, remote Merced River gorge. Mishandling the coils up to the celestial viewpoint just north of Bear Valley could mean certain death. But like Mark says, "They shall take up serpents; and it shall not hurt them." Just pray he meant you.

Access

From Moccasin

Coming on DH14 Yosemite Jct – Moccasin (Hwy 120)

When you reach the junction with Hwy 49, turn south. You're on the road.

From Bear Valley

On Hwy 49

Go north. You're on the road.

On The Road

The Old Moccasin Powerhouse stands across the tip of a reservoir as Hwy 49 splits off Hwy 120. No powerful curves to match, though. A few start at 1.2 mi (1.9 km) where the couple of houses that constitute suburban Moccasin flash by and the road snuggles up to an east-facing slope. Moccasin Creek crosses under the well-groomed pavement at 1.9 mi (3.1 km) and gurgles alongside. Yet the road is unaffected by the winding river, nonchalantly straightening through a shallow bowl of tree-speckled grassland.

Penon Blanco Ridge hogs the western horizon. While it sounds like the perfect name for a discount winery, there isn't a vine in sight. In fact, there's not much of anything around at all. The trees densify at 3.0 mi (4.8 km), where the terrain shifts to a westward slope. But the big change comes at 3.7 mi (6.0 km), when you see a canyon ahead with the pavement skittering through it like a dropped reel of film.

As the terrain shifts gears, you better too. Shortly after you see the chasm you're in it, sidewinding steeply up through a rocky, sage-strewn terrarium along the edge of a better-not-look-down cliff. Aside from a little breather at 5.0 mi (8.0 km), the S-curves continue all the way to 6.4 mi (10.3 km), where you reach a summit and cross the Mariposa County line.

Mariposa County advertises itself as a member of the Golden Chain Council. Which is ironic since the golden chain of esses ends precisely where that county takes over. The road went up curvy but comes down straight, turning so gradually through Mariposa's oaky landscape that you'd need a level glued across your mirrors to detect any leaning from the subtle side-to-side movements. At 10.6 mi (17.1 km), you come to Coulterville and the junction with **DH70 Coulterville – Waterford** west and J 132 (**DH70TE-C**) east. Good options, but if it's curves you seek, keep going. The DH you're on hasn't hit its stride yet.

Coming out of Coulterville, there are a couple of miles of nicely paved straightness before the 11.9 mi (19.2 km) point where a sign announces "Road Narrows" – CalTrans for "Get Ready." Sure enough. A series of tight but well-cambered sweepers starts things off, darting through the oak and grass-covered hills below Horseshoe Bend Mtn. And from 13.0 mi (20.9 km) on, you're knee-slamming through S-turns.

They're well-paved, they're decently cambered, but, boy, are these babies blind. The tightness of the turns around the cliffs of rock and red dirt combined with the steepness and daredevil dropoff that starts at 13.5 mi (21.7 km) doesn't encourage a lot of speed into the turns. As an aggressive first-timer, you'll be doing some serious shifting, dropping gears to keep the revs up as you suss out the corners and upshifting post-apex to keep from hitting your revlimiter. But we all have our problems.

Unless you're unlucky, there shouldn't be much traffic as you peg-scrape your way through a landscape that consists of nothing but silver trees, green shrubs, brown rock and black pavement. And that's a good thing. With the condensed S-curves and unending double yellow, it would be a challenge to get by an RV or tour bus here. Legally, anyway.

A descent starts at 15.1 (24.3 km) but unlike the first descent earlier, the curves in this canyon collection keep on coming. Sightlines improve with the softer grade and gentler corners. Scenery sightlines aren't bad either – just check out the views over the Merced River Gorge to Hunter Valley Mtn and Williams Peak.

The curves clench up again for a particularly precarious section starting at 19.1 mi (30.6 km), one that coincides with a particularly steep drop down to the river. Regardless of how much speed you've managed to keep up through here, slow down and take in the gorgeous crossing of the Merced River at 20.5 mi (33.0 km). If you're one of those anal types who likes to keep your eyes on the road, there's a vista point just before the bridge. Right, like you're gonna to stop now.

With the river no longer keeping the mountains at bay, the gorge to the west closes in and creates a sense of claustrophobia. The rock, shrub and tree-layered slopes seem to rise steeply above the road from all directions. Wedged somehow between all this terrain, the road climbs in its twistiest and most scenic section. The hairpins and semi-hairpins starting at 22.3 mi (35.9 km) accentuate the already challenging turns. And maxburners might even find a little gravel in 'em.

A "Site of Historical Interest" invites you off the road at 24.5 mi (39.4 km). Fitting, since the best part of this DH is now history. Apparently, this viewpoint was the site of a fort built by someone you've never heard of during the gold rush to defend his mines against claim jumpers. Interesting enough to justify the cairn, plaque and highway sign? Opinions may vary. But all will agree the top-o'-the-world panorama from the site is worth the stop.

The long series of stellar esses is over. Brush, trees and cow-splattered grassland line the level, curveless mile and a half that takes you from the viewpoint to the end of the DH in the hibernating gold rush town of Bear Valley at 25.9 mi (41.7 km). From here, your options are a straightline down 49 to Mariposa or a turn right on **TE-A Bear Valley Rd**.

Twisted Edges

TE-A Bear Valley Rd (J 16) (10.4 mi / 16.7 km)
This bear could bite if you're not careful, especially on the tightest, narrowest and least-well paved bit south of the Hunter Valley Rd junction. Initially, it prowls through forested terrain that becomes increasingly open as you near Hornitos. Riders who prefer their curves uphill may want to do it from the south end but, whichever way you take it, remember: if a bear is chasing you, you don't have to outrun the bear, just the person on the bike beside you.

Rider's Log: **Date Ridden:** **Your Rating:** **/10**

To Lee Vining
& DH63 Pg. 473
NON-FEATURED
DH SERVICES NOT
SHOWN
YOSEMITE
NATIONAL PARK
Tioga Pass Rd.
120
3 km
2 miles
N
DH43
DH43
TE-A
119°40'
DH58
Pg. 467
El Portal Rd.
Yosemite Jct
140
MERCED GORGE
Merced River
To Oakhurst & DH68
MT. GIBSON
LA CONTE POINT
GRAND CANYON OF THE TUOLUMNE R.
SMITH PEAK
HETCH HETCHY DOME
Falls Creek
Hetch Hetchy Res.
Wapama Falls
Dimond O BCG
Crane Flat GS
Big Oak Flat Rd.
Big Meadow Overlook
Mather Family Camp BCG
Mather GS
Yosemite Gatehouse Lodge
209.379.2260
Tamarack Flat BCG
El Portal
Hetch Hetchy Rd.
POOPENAUT VALLEY
Crane Flat
Carlon BCG
Crane Flat NP CG
DH26
TE-D
DH14
119°50'
Evergreen Lodge
800.935.6343
Mather
Evergreen Rd.
12
Hodgdon Meadow NP CG
Incline
Yosemite Lakes Preserve CG
800.533.1001
Big Oak Flat Entrance
Yosemite West Gate Lodge
209.962.5281
Buck Meadows Rest
209.962.5281
Exxon
Mather Rd.
S. Fk. Tuolumne River
Harden Pass Rd.
Country Store
Cherry Lake
Sweetwater BCG
17
12
M. Fk. Tuolumne R.
Harden Flat
To Mariposa To Bear Valley & DH25
14
Jawbone Creek
South Fork BCG
Yosemite Riverside Inn
800.626.7408
STANISLAUS NATIONAL FOREST
120°00'
Lumsden Bridge BCG
Cherry Lake Rd.
PILOT RIDGE
31
Lumsden BCG
17
Lost Claim BCG
Rim of the World
Corsair Café
209.962.6793
Buck Meadows Rd.
Clavey R.
Buck Meadows
20
Groveland Gas
DUCKWALL RIDGE
DH52
Pg. 399
Pine Mtn Lake Country Club CG
209.962.8615
JAWBONE RIDGE
Pines BCG
Bean Creek
DUCKWALL MTN.
MARIPOSA TUOLUMNE WAGNER RIDGE
J132
Greeley Hill
Greeley Hill Rd.
Tuolumne R.
Smith Station Rd.
To Bear Valley To Mariposa & DH26
DH70
TE-C
TE-C
Manzanita Hill B&B
209.962.4541
120
River GS
Coulterville
120°10'
BALD MTN.
DH25
Big Oak
209.962.6015
Miner's Mart
Claim Jumper
Ferretti Rd.
Berkshire Inn
209.962.6744
14
HORSESHOE BEND MTN.
To Twain Harte & DH8 Pg. 391
Old Hwy 20
JACKASS RIDGE
Coulterview Rd.
Tuolumne
Groveland
DH52
TE-A
E17
Buchanan Rd.
Big Oak Flat
132
Priest
Lake McClure
Soulsbyville
Wards Ferry Rd.
Yosemite Rd.
Old Priest Grade
49
Yosemite Pines RV CG
877.962.7690
Phoenix Lake Rd.
108
Tuolumne Rd.
TE-B
Moccasin
Merced Falls Rd.
Priest Grade
DH8
TE-B
For detail see DH41 Pg 368
Algerine Wards Ferry Rd.
Marshes Flat Rd.
PINEY RIDGE
120°20'
E17
MOCCASIN PEAK
DH73
Lime Kiln Rd.
HOG MTN.
DH70
Campo Seco Rd.
Twist Rd.
TE-A
Old Priest Station Inn
800.300.4181
Sonora
Moccasin Point RA CG
209.852.2396
Stent Cutoff Rd.
TE-A
ALT
Algerine Rd.
Jacksonville Rd.
Don Pedro Res.
(D-HON/YAM)
Jamestown
120
Kiwi Tavern & Motel
209.984.3117
Chinese Camp GS
Bonds Flat Rd.
Woods Cr.
Seco St.
49
Chinese Camp
(D-HD)
49
DH41
TE-E
To Oakdale
To Modesto
108
120
Old Don Pedro Rd.
To Waterford
To Modesto
38°00'
To Angels Camp
To Arnold & DH41 Pg. 367
37°50'
J59
La Grange Rd.
DH70
TE-B
37°40'

DH14 MOCCASIN – YOSEMITE JCT
Hwy 120 / Big Oak Flat Rd

DISTANCE:	50.2 mi / 80.8 km	TRAFFIC:	Heavy

AT A GLANCE

Handsome, colorful Major James D. Savage is best remembered for how he died, but he's also famous for three major discoveries: rich deposits of placer gold at Big Oak Flat; the magnificent Yosemite Valley during the Mariposa Indian Wars; and how to satisfy his 33 Native American wives. A tough act to follow, sure, but ride this hunky, Character-filled DH and you'll stumble on a few discoveries of your own. Like the pure vein of 24-carat curves on Priest Grade. Or the richly paved riding gold past Groveland that climbs steadily in stretched-out twisties through escalating Remoteness on the approach to the Sierra Nevada. Not to mention the increasingly rugged, foothill Scenery that climaxes when you slip into the Merced Gorge and revel in Yosemite's stunning native attractions. Just don't run afoul of the authorities like our boy Jim did. This is a heavily traveled tourist route with a CHP speed tax presence eager to put a bullet in your wallet. Could be worse, though; Jimbo ended up being shot to death by his judge.

TIRES	
Twistiness	27.0/ 30
Pavement	16.1/ 20
Engineering	7.2/ 10
Remoteness	6.5/ 10
Scenery	9.5/ 15
Character	12.5/ 15
TOTAL	**78.8**

ACCESS

From Moccasin

On Hwy 49/120

Hwy 49/120 splits at Moccasin. Stay on the 120 branch and you're on the road.

Coming in on DH25 Bear Valley – Moccasin (Hwy 49)

At the junction with Hwy 120, turn right. You're on the road.

From Yosemite Jct

Coming in on DH43 Oakhurst – Yosemite Jct

Coming in on DH26 Mariposa – Yosemite Jct (Hwy 140)

At the three-way junction, turn onto Big Oak Flat Rd. A sign also indicates Hwy 120 is in this direction. You're on the road.

ON THE ROAD

Priest Grade didn't get its name by accident. So you might want to murmur a prayer while riding that half mile or so straight over the bridge past Moccasin that you make it to the top unscathed. Old Priest Grade Rd (**TE-B**) schisms to the right at 0.7 mi (1.1 km). Holy cow, it looks good ahead.

"Curves for the next 8 mi (13 km)" shouts the yellow sign. You're climbing them fast and hard on great pavement while doubling back to the west. A hairpin-like sweeper at 1.4 mi (2.3 km) turns you abruptly back east again. The high ground ahead is Jackass Ridge. Like you care. On this twisting low ground, it's all you can do not to make an ass of yourself.

Fair-sized rock tumbles onto this road (sheesh, that mother was BIG!) and can be hard to see in late-day shadows – a particular issue here where tight corners are predominant and broken up by only the shortest of straights. At 3.0 mi (4.8 km), you've already climbed 1050 ft (322 m) up from Moccasin. And the precipitous drop-off to the right reinforces every foot.

Nice view but you ain't got the time. And if there are one or two of the frequent pylons blocking your second and third gear enjoyment of this beautiful stretch, the combination of tight twisties and steep ascent has them going so slowly that the merest crack of your throttle easily scoots you by. Unless of course, there's a tightly jacked up caravan of them.

Wonder what you missed on Old Priest Grade Rd (**TE-B**) on the far side of the gorge? Check it out mirroring your path. Hard to imagine it matching this side's smooth pavement and handy bits of occasional shoulder. Naturally, just when you're getting into a groove, you hit the top of the Grade where you merge with the east end of **TE-B** at 5.4 mi (8.9 km). That was over fast. Maybe shoot back down the TE and do it again.

Now the DH hangs a sharp left and heads directly into the hills of Jackass Ridge. Things are mellower here. Way mellower. There's even a brief shoulder pullover/passing lane thing. Of course one is always suspicious when the sheriff pulls over to let you by.

At 6.2 mi (10.0 km), you breeze through spread out Big Oak Flat. Say, this road's beginning to feel a little played out. Well, at least the sheriff pulled off… wait, the sneaky bugger pulled back in right behind. Easy….

You finally leave Big Oak behind and wind gently (and slowly) into some trees at the 3000 ft (920 m) elevation mark. They don't last though; you soon enter moderately charming Groveland at 8.0 mi (12.9 km). With its haunted hotel and California's oldest continually operating saloon (yep, another one), the place seems little changed since the Gold Rush.

You're cleanly out of town at 8.9 mi (14.3 km) just past the junction with Ferretti Rd (**TE-C**). Assuming the sheriff's no longer in your rear views, you can wick it up on those languid curves with the top-quality engineering and pavement. According to the sign, you've got 24 mi (39 km) to go before entering Yosemite. Too bad those languid curves seem to have mellowed out to nothing. Feel free to *really* wick it up.

At 12.4 mi (20.0 km), you enter the Stanislaus National Forest. The trees may be safe here but the twisties have all been harvested. The road's on a kind of open plateau, still climbing slightly. There'd be better twisties on Wagner Ridge in the distance over to your right. If only there was a road there.

Smith Station Rd (**DH70TE-C**) junctions right at 15.2 mi (24.5 km) just before the eastern end of Ferretti Rd (**TE-C**) junctions left at 16.0 mi (25.7 km). Then, at 17.3 mi (27.8 km), you leave Tuolumne and enter Mariposa County. That high country ahead is in Yosemite National Park. With every minute you climb, it gets cooler and cooler.

There are a few easygoing sweepers and moderate curves through the thickening forest as you drift through the townlet of Buck Meadows and re-enter Tuolumne County at 19.6 mi. (31.5 km). The surveyors sure had a hard time making up their minds about the county lines around here. Can't imagine they'd be much good at picking lines through the corners either.

The Rim of the World viewpoint extends from the road's north shoulder at 20.5 mi (33.0 km), offering a sweeping vista over the Tuolumne River valley and behind it, Jawbone Ridge. Unless you stop, you'll probably miss the hills of Pilot Ridge to your right. That's because the flurry of sweeping curves beginning here will have directed your attention back to the road. Where it should properly be.

You sweep down over the Tuolumne River South Fork bridge just before Cherry Lake Rd (which leads to **TE-D**) junctions left at 22.4 mi (36.0 km). After that, more curves – big, sweeping, consistent ones – take you to and past the turn off right for Harden Flat at 25.7 mi. (41.4 km). The engineering has dropped a grade and it's not that easy to get by the pylons. So it's nice when the big fellahs pull off on the other end of Harden Flat Rd at 27.2 mi (43.8 km) to head for the RV park. Hopefully, the brief dotted yellow will help you dispose of any little guys.

You cross the South Fork Tuolumne River once more at 28.4 mi (45.7 km) and bold sweepers escort you farther up through the densifying forest to the Yosemite National Park boundary. They continue to the park's money-extraction booth at 32.7 mi (52.6 km): "Ten dollars, cash only please, good for seven days. Aren't I cute in my Smokey thc Bear hat?"

In spite of the slower-traffic-use-pull-out signs past the booth, the pylons don't seem all that inclined to comply, even if they are loitering for seven days. Probably figured they paid to be on this road dammit, and they're just as entitled to use it as you are. As if. Watch for the short dotted yellow to dispense with these obstreperous folks.

That's better. Now you'll have a much more satisfying time on the increasing number of corners through the cool, dense greenery. Hopefully all the way to Crane Flat, where Hwy 120 splits off as **DH58 Crane Flat – Lee Vining** at 40.6 mi (65.3 km). From here, the DH you're on continues as mere Big Oak Flat Rd.

*TOUR NOTE: Since there's no gas in the Yosemite Valley, Crane Flat is your last chance for gas until either Wawona, 36.0 mi (57.9 km) later on **DH43***

Yosemite Jct – Oakhurst *or El Portal, 17.6 mi (28.2 km) from here on* ***DH26 Yosemite Jct – Mariposa****.*

The curves get more numerous past the DH junction but so probably does the number of pylons. Hmm… do the breaks in the double yellow at the reflectors technically make this dotted yellow in both directions? Should ask Alan Dershowitz. Whatever his advice, the safer bet might be to pull off right at the Big Meadow Overlook viewpoint at 42.8 mi (68.9 km). While you wait for a break in the proceedings, you can admire the splendid view over the Merced Gorge.

The road tightens around some rockfaces bringing poorer sightlines as you descend into the gorge. It's obvious from the number of untidy snags you see that sometime in the past, large parts of this forest were seriously swept by fire. This does allow you a better view over the Merced River's valley though, not to mention El Capitan and the magnificent cliffs on the north side of the Yosemite Valley. All momentarily visible at 47.0 mi (75.6 km).

At 47.4 mi (76.3 km), a poorly lit, nearly one-mile-long tunnel helps you get down into the Merced Gorge. There are a few pull outs at the other end of it, so watch for scenery-struck tourists wandering around gawking at the impressive vertical walls that mark the entrance to the Yosemite Valley. Two more short tunnels, steep rock faces to the left, a low rock wall and big hunks of rock right on the edge of the road all conspire with the scenery to induce you to slow down and enjoy your surroundings before the DH ends at the three-way junction with **DH43 Yosemite Jct – Oakhurst** and **DH26 Yosemite Jct – Mariposa** at 50.2 mi (80.8 km).

Twisted Edges

TE-A Moccasin – Jamestown (10.6 mi / 17.1 km) *Jacksonville Rd - Stent Cutoff Rd - Algerine Rd - Seco St*

Good pavement sweeps across Don Pedro Lake and through a blistering canyon in the south before getting rural-residential at the northern end. This quiet and easy Hwy 108/49 bypass has engineering that eliminates a lot of the challenge in the already gentle curves.

NAVIGATION: From Jamestown, Seco St turns south off Main St. At 1.1 mi (1.8 km), you'll see Jacksonville Rd go off right. Ignore it and continue straight on Algerine Rd to the Stent Cutoff Rd at 2.2 mi (3.5 km). Go right. At 2.6 mi (4.2 km), turn left onto the second part of Jacksonville Rd.

Coming from the south, be sure to turn right onto Stent Cutoff Rd at 8.0 mi (12.9 km). Then turn left onto Algerine.

TOUR NOTE: Feel free to go for a swim at the Moccasin Point Recreation Area at the south end of this TE. Only thing is, it's not really free; you gotta pay to go in.

TE-A ALT Campo Seco Rd - Lime Kiln Rd (3.2 mi / 5.2 km)
Heading east on Hwy 108 to either **DH52 Tuolumne – Cherry Lake** or

DH8 Mi-Wuk Village – Sonora Jct. This quiet stretch of good pavement through farms and residential grassland shows a better way for a couple miles.

TE-B Old Priest Grade Rd (1.9 mi / 3.1 km)
Sure, it's short but there are signs that this is our kind of road: a weight limit sign, a steep/narrow/not advisable for big pylons sign, a 15-mph (25-kmh) curve advisory sign, a twisties-for-the-next-couple-miles sign and a 25-mph (40-kmh) speed sign are all crammed in the first quarter mile. Guess they didn't have room for the great pavement and scenery signs. Mirrors the first part of the DH opposite but is a third the length and maybe a little less twisty.

ROUTING OPTION: Even if you're not riding the DH to Yosemite, you might be inclined to pull off Hwy 49 (or 120/49) at Moccasin and connect the first 5.4 mi (8.9 km) of the DH together with this TE to make a sweet little side loop.

TE-C Ferretti Rd (10.5 mi / 16.9 km)
Um, er, it's just possible that we may have mentioned this bypass to the driver of a BMW Z3 (yes, they make pylons too) while gassing up in Groveland. But it seemed somehow appropriate given that this road is named after an Italian super car. And it's not like it's the greatest TE or anything. There's lots of development around the Pine Mountain Lake Country Club and the paltry 35-mph (55-mph) speed limit is painted so large on the road, that even the world's dimmest speed tax collector won't believe you didn't see it. The curves are pretty much continuous and certainly way better than anything on the straight part of the DH it bypasses, though the camber on some of the corners is a little weird. Remoteness increases greatly as you get away from Groveland but you may find fresh cow pies (and their makers) between the cattle guards at the eastern end. And if you're one of those riders fast enough to get stuck behind a Ferretti (or four-wheeled BMW) well, ah… mea culpa.

TE-D Hetch-Hetchy Rd (8.8 mi / 14.2 km)
This well-paved twistfest along the south side rockfaces of the Poopenaut Valley down to the res is inundated with problems: you gotta pay the $10 Yosemite toll to ride it; it's got a continuous 25-mph (40-kmh) speed limit; the yellow is solid double; and you gotta ride on crappy Evergreen Rd or only-slightly-less-crappy Cherry Lake and Mather Rds to get to it. Oh, and they lock this baby up between 9 pm and 7 am nightly. But the worst part? There's a surfeit of ranger STCs keeping watch on the mucho traffic on the way to view/backpack around Wapama Falls. Ah, poop.

RIDER'S LOG: **DATE RIDDEN:** **YOUR RATING:** **/10**

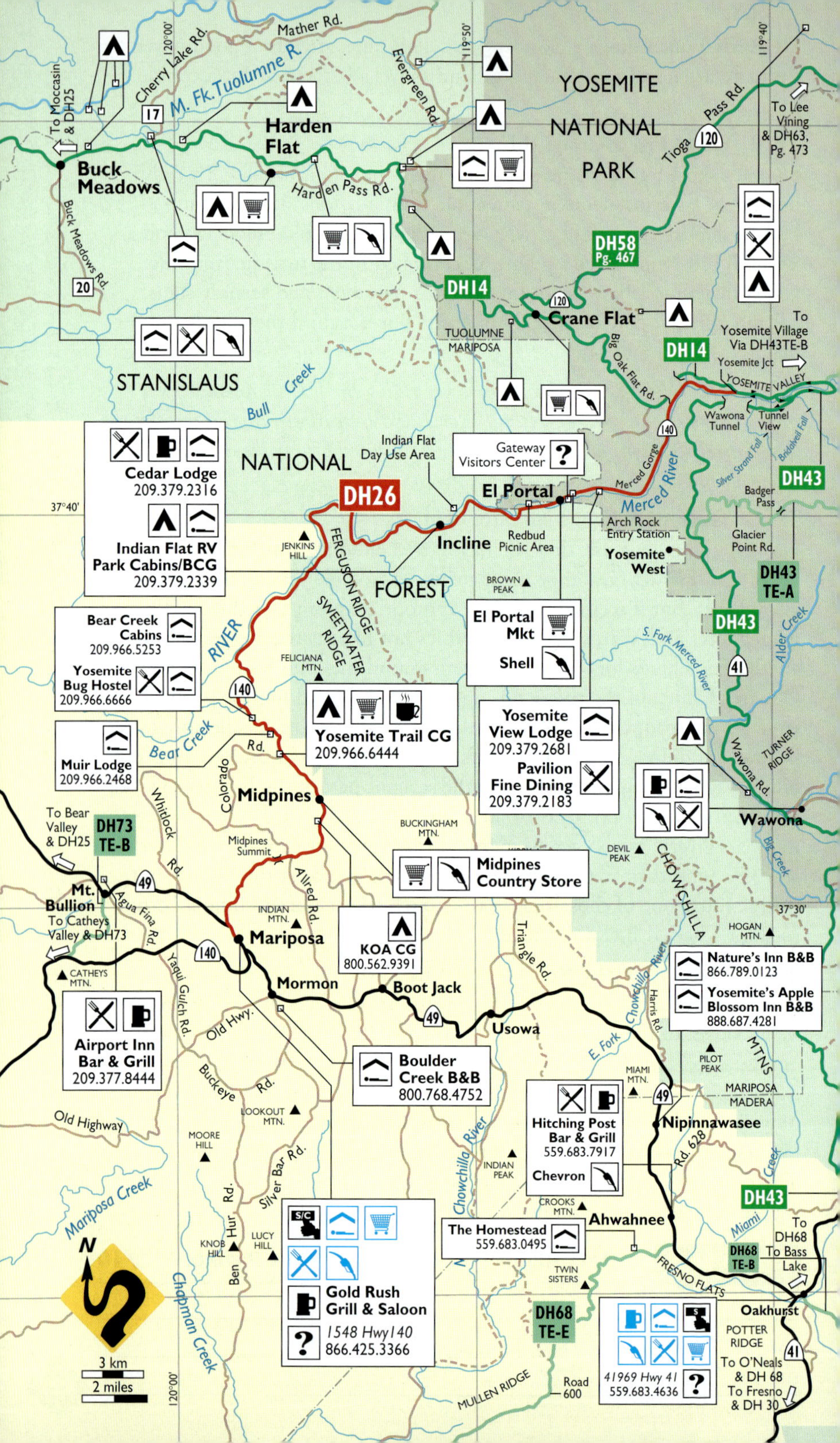

YOSEMITE NATIONAL PARK
STANISLAUS
NATIONAL
FOREST
Buck Meadows
Harden Flat
Crane Flat
El Portal
Incline
Midpines
Mariposa
Mormon
Boot Jack
Usowa
Nipinnawasee
Ahwahnee
Oakhurst
Wawona
Mt. Bullion
Yosemite West
DH14
DH58 Pg. 467
DH26
DH43
DH43 TE-A
DH73 TE-B
DH68 TE-B
DH68 TE-E
To Moccasin & DH25
To Lee Vining & DH63, Pg. 473
To Yosemite Village Via DH43TE-B
Yosemite Jct
To Bear Valley & DH25
To Catheys Valley & DH73
To DH68
To Bass Lake
To O'Neals & DH 68
To Fresno & DH 30
Cedar Lodge
209.379.2316
Indian Flat RV Park Cabins/BCG
209.379.2339
Bear Creek Cabins
209.966.5253
Yosemite Bug Hostel
209.966.6666
Muir Lodge
209.966.2468
Yosemite Trail CG
209.966.6444
Gateway Visitors Center
Indian Flat Day Use Area
Redbud Picnic Area
Arch Rock Entry Station
El Portal Mkt
Shell
Yosemite View Lodge
209.379.2681
Pavilion Fine Dining
209.379.2183
Midpines Country Store
KOA CG
800.562.9391
Airport Inn Bar & Grill
209.377.8444
Boulder Creek B&B
800.768.4752
Nature's Inn B&B
866.789.0123
Yosemite's Apple Blossom Inn B&B
888.687.4281
Hitching Post Bar & Grill
559.683.7917
Chevron
The Homestead
559.683.0495
Gold Rush Grill & Saloon
1548 Hwy140
866.425.3366
41969 Hwy 41
559.683.4636
M. Fk. Tuolumne R.
Mather Rd.
Cherry Lake Rd.
Evergreen Rd.
Harden Pass Rd.
Buck Meadows Rd.
Tioga Pass Rd.
Big Oak Flat Rd.
Merced Gorge
Merced River
Wawona Tunnel
Tunnel View
Yosemite Valley
Badger Pass
Glacier Point Rd.
Bull Creek
Bear Creek
RIVER
FERGUSON RIDGE
SWEETWATER RIDGE
Colorado Rd.
Whitlock Rd.
Allred Rd.
Midpines Summit
Agua Fina Rd.
Yaqui Gulch Rd.
Old Hwy.
Buckeye Rd.
Old Highway
Silver Bar Rd.
Ben Hur Rd.
Mariposa Creek
Chapman Creek
Chowchilla River
E. Fork Chowchilla River
Triangle Rd.
Harris Rd.
Rd. 628
Miami Creek
FRESNO FLATS
Road 600
MULLEN RIDGE
POTTER RIDGE
CHOWCHILLA MTNS
S. Fork Merced River
Alder Creek
Wawona Rd.
TURNER RIDGE
Big Creek
TUOLUMNE
MARIPOSA
MADERA
JENKINS HILL
BROWN PEAK
FELICIANA MTN.
BUCKINGHAM MTN.
DEVIL PEAK
HOGAN MTN.
INDIAN MTN.
CATHEYS MTN.
PILOT PEAK
MIAMI MTN.
INDIAN PEAK
CROOKS MTN.
TWIN SISTERS
LOOKOUT MTN.
MOORE HILL
KNOB HILL
LUCY HILL
37°40'
37°30'
120°00'
119°50'
119°40'
N
3 km
2 miles

DH26 Mariposa – Yosemite Jct

Highway 140

Distance:	36.0 mi / 57.9 km	Traffic:	Moderate

At a Glance

TIRES	
Twistiness	26.1/ 30
Pavement	14.8/ 20
Engineering	6.6/ 10
Remoteness	4.9/ 10
Scenery	11.9/ 15
Character	10.9/ 15
Total	75.2

The small town of Mariposa is named for the beautiful wildflowers that surround it. And one of the prettiest is the perennial favorite that unfolds its petals up to Yosemite National Park. Opening up from Mariposa through the oak woodlands in a series of sweeping arcs, the "Yosemite All Year Highway" clears the Midpines Summit, then intertwines with Bear Creek, climbing up its steep canyon wall before dropping sharply, crossing the creek and bedding down beside the wild Merced River. The most consistently scenic route of the three DHs into the park is also the least trafficked, though at peak times, it can be bad here too. Still its dotted-yellow straightaways and pullouts in the curvier sections usually provide enough Pylon-Killer™ to weed out the thorny vehicles. Pavement and Engineering are generally well cultivated although some of the off-camber and decreasing-radius turns along the Merced between the Briceburg Info Center and the Indian Flat Day Use Area could use some rototilling. The best part of this TIRES arrangement is arguably the last segment, beyond Arch Rock and the park toll booth. Even though the road narrows here and the speed limit drops, you can catch glimpses of Yosemite's sights while twisting through the spectacular, granite-filled Merced Canyon. Is this what they mean by flower power?

Access

From Mariposa

On Hwy 140

Head east on Hwy 140. You're on the road.

From Yosemite Jct

Coming in on DH43 Oakhurst – Yosemite Jct (Hwy 41)

Coming in on DH14 Moccasin – Yosemite Jct

Head west on Hwy 140 from the three-way junction. You're on the road.

On The Road

The DH begins right where Mariposa's 35-mph (55-kmh) speed limit ends. You're climbing immediately on fine, shouldered, sweeping pavement up a steady slope. Foothill vegetation of mixed oak and pines, brown grass and broom fill the scene. As do RVs that do not let you by. You can just hear the conversation: "Ethel, just what are these pullout things for, anyway?"

Ah, a passing lane at 2.9 mi (4.7 km). Chances are you'll need it. You reach the 2962 ft (903 m) Midpine Summit at 3.2 mi (5.1 km) then dip down into a stand of tall pines. The moderate-to-heavy tar strips that started with the passing lane continue as it ends. It's a minor matter, since the straightways and lesser curves through here hardly constitute a test of traction.

You continue to descend, passing through the one-store town of Midpines at 5.3 mi (8.5 km). Here the DH climbs again, launching into an ascending series of long, steady curves. These tighten beyond a trio of lodges when the DH esses along a steep cliff looking over Bear Creek to the green and silver undulations of Sweetwater Ridge and Feliciana Mtn. C'mon baby, light my fire.

Not too hot, though. You need to stay cool enough to handle the double apex at 9.7 mi (15.6 km). Not to mention the impressive, curling descent into Bear Creek's dry, rockface-sided canyon. The vertical, rectangular-shaped chunks fit together like they were created in some cosmic game of Tetris. And maybe they were.

But this wide, smoothly paved, beautifully engineered road was definitely the work of CalTrans. They know how to do it right when they feel like it. Continuing downward, the smell of the pylons' burning brakes finally dissipates at 11.6 mi (18.7 km), when you pass the stone Briceburg Info Center and cross Bear Creek at its confluence with the Merced River. Now you begin a level ride low along the Merced. It's still very scenic with the high, dry, sage-spotted cliffs looming above the glinting river. But wait a sec, you lose both the wide shoulder, the balanced camber and even some pavement quality. Hey CT, you know what? We take it back.

The curves ease in tightness and number as you go on but the striking scenery continues. Soft-edged splotches of green drip down onto the brown grass and rock that rises above the river. In the river, multi-colored granite is painted in shades of brown, oxidized white and shale-grey. This riverscape culminates at 15.3 mi (24.6 km), as you cross Sweetwater Creek and officially enter the Sierra National Forest.

Unofficially, you're entering a section of tighter curves separated by long, dotted-lined straightaways. Meandering along the river, not paying too much attention to your speed, you suddenly hit a blind, uncambered, 30-mph (50-kmh) corner at 17.5 mi (28.2 km). The decreasing radius one at 20.2 mi (32.5 km) is a bit of a trip, too. Especially if there's a tour bus hugging the centerline coming the other way.

There's now considerably more foliage on the riverside mountains. Where previously it was more brown than green, a solid covering of trees now sticks to the slopes like a layer of green cotton batting. The river sews a blue and white threadline through the scenic quilt and is joined by another line of stitching at 20.6 mi (33.1 km), when the south fork of Merced River ties in from the south. If you run out of material, the Savages Trading Post is located here.

There's a flurry of curves beyond the confluence. Then the road settles into the easy straights, bends and mini-curves reminiscent of the earlier ones in the first miles along the Merced. The river landscape that's been shifting from arid rock, shrubs and grass to heavy trees, then back again, strikes a balance that incorporates all facets at once. While it may not be a great place for twistiness, it's a decent place for swimming. The Indian Flat Day Use Area is at 23.5 mi (37.8 km).

At 25.6 mi (41.2 km), you pass the access to the Redbud Picnic Area and a 50-mph (80-kmh) sign announces your entry into El Portal. You may as well take advantage of the passing opportunity that follows; there are still curves to come before you cross the Merced River and actually see El Portal's store and gas station at 28.0 mi (45.1 km).

El Portal ends and you're back up to speed, admiring the river from the north side of the road. You see the first hints of Yosemite's magic in the bold monolith of Arch Rock, which comes into view ahead on the left as you pass the Gateway Visitors Center and cross the park boundary at 29.3 mi (47.1 km). Arch Rock has a smooth, aqualine slope that angles evenly down to the roadside from on high. As you pass, it's almost as if God is looking down his nose at you. That doesn't make sense, of course. He only looks down his nose at pylons.

This DH is getting special now. Just look where you are: S-curving along a low retaining wall between the shining, iron-streaked slopes that rise steeply from the fast-running, boulder-filled Merced. The rock formations in and along the river are offset by jungle-thick groves of trees plastered against the canyon wall. A myriad of shapes and sculptures protrude from the roadside rock. Like the granite wolf's head that sticks out at 30.3 mi (48.8 km). Or the hand of the stone-faced park ranger sticking his hand out of the amazingly real toll booth at 31.5 mi (50.7 km).

Slow down, you're movin' too fast. Sometimes, you're happy to ease off a bit, look up from the pavement in front of you and make the scenic moment last. It's hard to get over just how cool the well-defined and detailed rock looks in this river canyon. And how cool this road looks winding through it. This is one of those places where the 35-mph (55- kmh) speed zone is not such a big deal. That doesn't mean four-wheeled folk shouldn't do you the courtesy of using the pullouts.

Another great thing about riding through these easternmost miles of the canyon are the glimpses you catch of El Capitan and other famous Yosemite landmarks. These monsters get more monstrous as you wend your way deeper into the park amid the groves of red-barked cedars, pines and oaks that start at 34.0 mi (54.7 km). You reach the junction and DH's end at

36.0 mi (57.9 km). While a choice of **DH14 Yosemite – Moccasin** and **DH43 Yosemite – Oakhurst** awaits you here, it's the spectacular **DH43TE-B Yosemite Village Loop** that you really shouldn't miss.

RIDER'S LOG: **DATE RIDDEN:** **YOUR RATING: /10**

How do YOU rate Northern California's 74 Destination Highways? Go to destinationhighways.com, *and let other riders know.*

To Mariposa & DH26
To Yosemite Jct. & DH14/26
Nipinnawasee
Ahwahnee
DH43
41
Forks CG
N. Fk. Willow Creek
Beasone Rd.
7
Chilkoot BCG
Whiskers BCG
Soda Springs BCG
CHIQUITA RIDGE
Placer BCG
Lower Chiquito BCG
JACKASS ROCK
HELLS HALF ACRE
Sweet Water BCG
6325
Mile High Vista Point
37° 20'
TE-E
Oakhurst
Bass Lk. Rd. (Road 222)
Road 222
Rd. 432
Bass Lake
Lupine-Cedar Bluffs CG
Spring Cove CG
Wishon Pt CG
I
Rock Creek BCG
81
Fish Creek BCG
Rd. 426
TE-B
Road 223
Road 222
Willow Creek
Road 274
SOUTH FORK BLUFFS
Rd. 221
Rd. 226
Coarsegold
TE-F
Pines Resort/SM 559.642.3121
Castillo's Rest 559.683.2272
Pine's Village Bakery 559.642.3664
Chevron
Bass Fork Minute Mart 559.877.7799
South Fork
North Fork
Rd. 200
Rd. 223
Rd. 225
SIERRA NATIONAL FOREST
TE-D
San Joaquin River
CASTLE PEAK
QUARTZ MTN.
WARD MTN.
DH68
TE-C
Rd. 222/ Auberry Rd.
Italian Bar Rd.
Kerckhoff Lake
Rd. 235
41
37°10'
BLACKHAWK MTN.
Rd. (Road 200)
North Fork
MERCER MTN.
HILDRETH MTN.
O'Neals
South Fork Motel 559.877.2237
Buckhorn Rest & Lounge 559.877.8700
North Fork SM
Chevron
LONE RIDGE
San Joaquin River
GEOGRAPHIC CENTER OF CALIFORNIA
Power House Rd.
ROCK MTN.
MADERA
FRESNO
Jose Basin Rd.
(II)
TE-A
Auberry
SQUAW LEAP
DH30 TE-E
Auberry Rd.
Shaver Lake
Pine Ridge
BIG SANDY VALLEY
Lodge Rd.
DH30 TE-D
168
Prather
DH30 TE-D ALT
To Madera (Hwy 99)
Road 211
HULBERT MTN.
TICK-TACK-TOE MTN.
PINCUSHION MTN.
AUBERRY VALLEY
TABLE MTN.
Rd. 145
North Fork Rd.
Rd. 206
Millerton Rd.
Auberry Rd.
Morgan Canyon Rd.
Tollhouse
37°00'
CORLEW MTN.
Friant
DH30 TE-A
Millerton Rd.
Nicholas Rd.
Burrough Valley Rd.
DH30 TE-D
Humphreys Station
DH30 TE-A ALT
Tollhouse Rd.
DH30 TE-A
DH30 TE-C
Pittman Hill Rd.
Auberry Rd.
DH30
Maxon Rd.
Friant Rd.
OWENS MTN.
Friant Canal
Sample Rd.
Valley Rd.
Copper Ave.
Watts
168
N
DH35
Springs Rd.
Willow Ave.
Minnewawa Ave.
For detail see DH30
DH30 TE-B ALT
DH30 TE-B
Trimmer
Pine Flat Res.
Shepherd Ave.
Nees Ave.
Toll House Rd.
Dog Creek
Academy Ave.
Herndon Ave.
168
19°40'
FRESNO
19°30'
3 km
3 miles
36°50'
19°20'

DH68 O'NEALS – OAKHURST

North Fork Rd / Bass Lake Rd (Rd 200/274/222)

DISTANCE:	30.1 mi / 48.4 km	TRAFFIC:	Moderate

AT A GLANCE

TIRES	
Twistiness	22.1/ 30
Pavement	14.2/ 20
Engineering	7.8/ 10
Remoteness	3.9/ 10
Scenery	8.2/ 15
Character	3.3/ 15
TOTAL	**59.5**

Motorcyclists like to set themselves apart from the Yosemite-or-bust pylons nosing single-mindedly up to the popular national park. And what better way to make that statement than to grab your chance to turn off the straight line of Hwy 41 between Fresno and Oakhurst onto this inviting bypass route. Escaping the traffic would be reason in and of itself to take this detour. But this road offers far more than deliverance from the alphabet of RVs, SUVs and STCs. You'll enjoy mellow curves, no-surprise Engineering and average-to-good Pavement all the way from the DH's southern junction till the shoreline of Bass Lake. Here, the heavy trees and shimmering water of the Sierra National Forest's Bass Lake Recreation Area form a backdrop for a perfect synthesis of winding curves and black asphalt. At the route's northern end, just turn right and you're back on the road to… where we going again?

ACCESS

From O'Neals

Coming in on TE-A Friant – O'Neals

Rd 211 merges into North Fork Rd. Stay right. You're on the road.

From Hwy 41

South Access

Take the well-marked turnoff to North Fork. You're on the road.

From Oakhurst

Via Hwy 41

Head north on Hwy 41 approximately 3.0 mi (4.8 km) until you see the turnoff for Bass Lake Rd. Turn right. You're on the road.

Coming in on DH43 Yosemite – Oakhurst (Hwy 41)

When you reach the junction with Bass Lake Rd, turn left. You're on the road.

ON THE ROAD

The broad shoulders that characterized North Fork Rd between Hwy 41 and Road 211 narrow past the **TE-A** junction, where the DH begins.

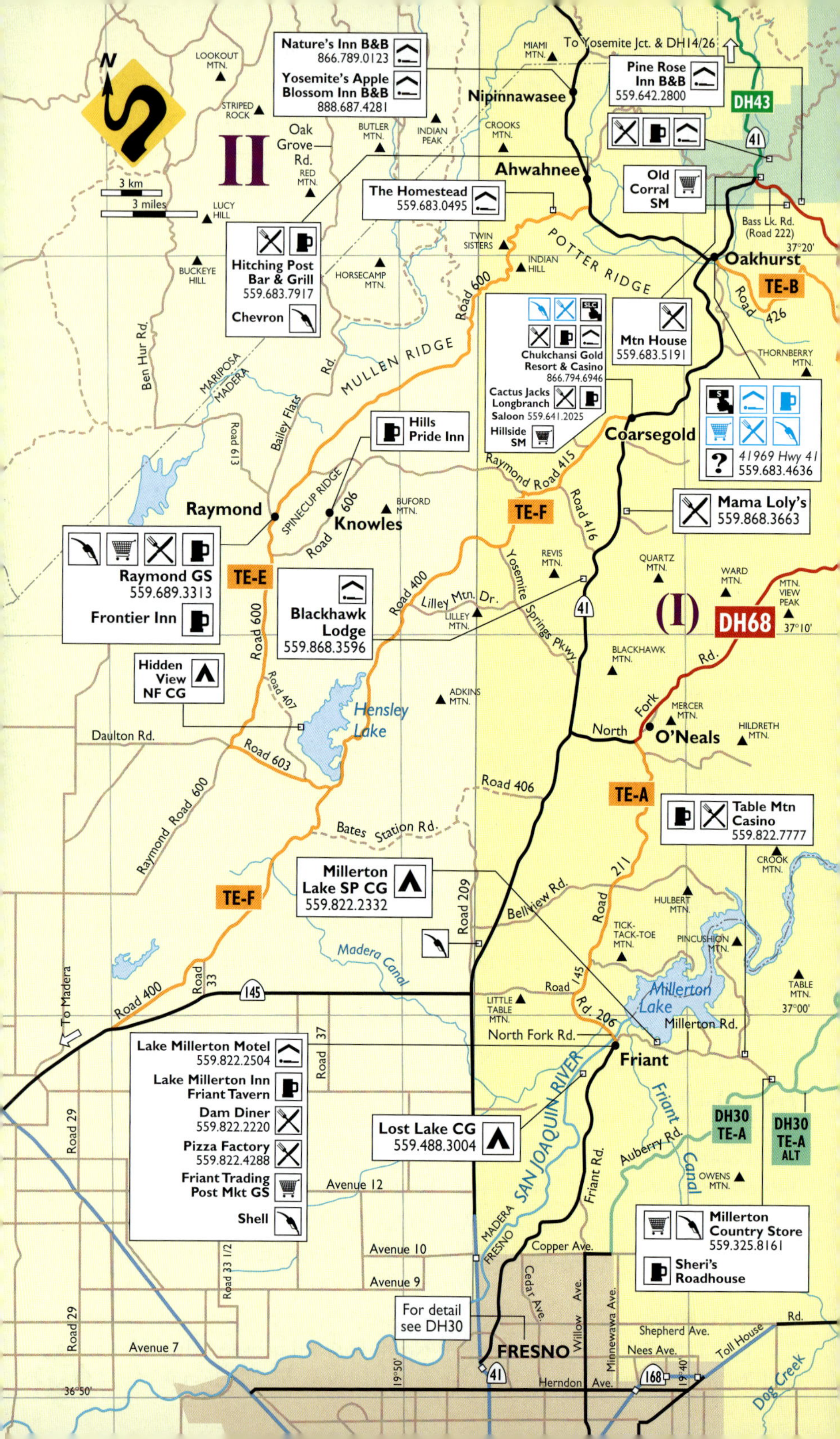

Nature's Inn B&B
866.789.0123
Yosemite's Apple Blossom Inn B&B
888.687.4281
To Yosemite Jct. & DH14/26
Pine Rose Inn B&B
559.642.2800
DH43
Nipinnawasee
Ahwahnee
Old Corral SM
The Homestead
559.683.0495
Hitching Post Bar & Grill
559.683.7917
Chevron
Oakhurst
Bass Lk. Rd. (Road 222)
TE-B
Road 426
Mtn House
559.683.5191
Chukchansi Gold Resort & Casino
866.794.6946
Cactus Jacks Longbranch Saloon 559.641.2025
Hillside SM
Coarsegold
41969 Hwy 41
559.683.4636
Hills Pride Inn
Raymond
Knowles
Mama Loly's
559.868.3663
Raymond GS
559.689.3313
Frontier Inn
TE-E
TE-F
Blackhawk Lodge
559.868.3596
Hidden View NF CG
DH68
O'Neals
North Fork Rd.
Hensley Lake
TE-A
Table Mtn Casino
559.822.7777
Millerton Lake SP CG
559.822.2332
Millerton Lake
Friant
Lake Millerton Motel
559.822.2504
Lake Millerton Inn Friant Tavern
Dam Diner
559.822.2220
Pizza Factory
559.822.4288
Friant Trading Post Mkt GS
Shell
Lost Lake CG
559.488.3004
DH30 TE-A
DH30 TE-A ALT
Millerton Country Store
559.325.8161
Sheri's Roadhouse
For detail see DH30
FRESNO
San Joaquin River
Madera Canal
Friant Canal
To Madera

This is a change that usually bodes well for twistiness, but not this time. Curves are barely in evidence as the average pavement passes a solitary elementary school and the turnoff to O'Neals so-called town center. You don't see downtown from the DH but the trailers and lean-tos that constitute its suburbs are clearly visible.

Despite the roadside clutter, it's definitely scenic as the road drifts subtly to and fro on a climb past another O'Neals access at 1.5 mi (2.4 km). Particularly at 2.1 mi (3.4 km) when a couple of moderate curves mark the beginning of a descent. The pointed peaks of Quartz and Ward Mtns along with Mountain View Peak are fronted by round hills. The soft pastel shades of the mountains contrast with the verdant, tree-textured hillsides. And such a scene would not be complete without some abandoned tin-roofed shacks rusting away at 2.7 mi (4.3 km).

The road bobs up and down through still-gentle curves. The mountains continue to poke in and out of view. Nice details such as the oak hanging over the road at 3.8 mi (6.1 km) define the foreground. At 6.0 mi (9.7 km), you cross Finegold Creek and strike higher grade pavement. You also strike a concentrated series of curves. Most are pretty mild but one or two may be cause for reflection on the clearance of your footboards. The twistiness dilutes at 9.1 mi (14.6 km). The smooth asphalt does the same. You reach the junction for Rd 221 (**TE-B**) at 11.5 mi (18.5 km).

It feels busier beyond the junction. Churches and houses cycle by like the repeating background of an inexpensively made cartoon. In fact churches and houses seem to be on about a 1:1 ratio along this not particularly curvy stretch. At least there's not much traffic. What with all the avid churchgoing, it's no wonder.

At 14.1 mi (22.7 km), the panoramic wall of the South Fork Bluffs is revealed. You descend toward the 35-mph (55-kmh) zone and North Fork – a single strip that boasts it is the geographical center of California. More significantly, it's the geographical center of this DH – if you pay attention to these directions and go the right way. Just past the turnoff right to Rd 222/Auberry Rd (**TE-C**), you reach a major intersection at 15.4 mi (24.8 km), Manzanita Rd (Rd 222) turns left from the center of town. Don't take it. Make sure you **stay right**.

You pass through town and cross over Willow Creek. At 15.8 mi (25.4 km), there's a junction with Rd 274 and a sign to Bass Lake and Yosemite. Going straight will take you to South Fork and the Mammoth Pool Reservoir (via **TE-D**). To stay on the DH, **turn left here**.

Now it's straightsville for a short bit, interrupted by a fistful of curves at 19.2 mi (30.9 km). Scenery's nice as the road runs roughly parallel to the intricate slopes of South Fork Bluffs through a lightly treed, undeveloped landscape that banks east down to the river. And it stays nice as you enter the Bass Lake National Forest Area of Sierra National Forest at 20.0 mi (32.2 km) and eye the sparkling surface of Bass Lake through the trees on your left.

You'd think on entering a national forest you'd find an even greater remoteness. Think again. This is Northern California. Where there are lakes – even fake ones – there are pylons, not to mention cottages and pedestrians. Just hope that when you ride through, the pylons will be parked at their cottages and the pedestrians will be smart enough to jump out of your way.

Fortunately, development is more or less concentrated around 20.2 and 22.3 mi (32.5 and 35.9 km). As long as the weekenders aren't commuting, you should be able to get the most out of what is undoubtedly the best part of this DH – gorgeous pavement, svelte engineering and sexy, sweeping curves, all through a forest of tall, national-forest-quality trees. If you're feeling frisky enough to rub fenders with the pylons, the turnoff to the national forest's Willow Cove day use area is at 23.8 mi (38.3 km). Of course, you'll have to interrupt a long sweeper to do it.

The turn for lakeside Bass Lake is left at 24.3 mi (39.1 km) down Rd 434, should you have an urgent need for some roadside services. You'll know you've missed the turnoff if a sweeper cuts through a white, chalky V-slope either side of the road.

At 25.7 mi (41.4 km), a curving bridge sweeps the road across the river-like North Fork Willow Creek and, at 27.6 mi (44.4 km) you leave the national forest. Hope you enjoyed it. 'Cause, at 26.3 mi (42.3 km), SLOW appears in big white letters on the pavement and the zoning changes from heavy forest to light industrial. The mini-storage bays are gone in a blink but the remote feeling is gone for good, no doubt due to the supersized slab of pavement starting at 26.9 mi (43.3 km). Its wide shoulders and extra lanes blast heavy handedly down through a vale and over the Fresno River. Development gradually increases again the further you descend through the V-shaped cut in the hills and rock. The road ends at 30.1 mi (48.4 km) when you reach the stop sign at Hwy 41. **DH43 Oakhurst –Yosemite Jct** starts here to the right.

Twisted Edges

TE-A O'Neals – Friant (11.4 mi / 18.3 km) *Rd 211 - Rd 145 - Rd 206 - North Fork Rd*

The moderate curves, adequate pavement and sometimes rolling, sometimes flat, oak-dotted grassland on the Road 211 section of this lightly trafficked TE is pretty much what you've come to expect whenever you skirt the westerly edge of the Sierra Nevada foothills. Road 145 is straighter and browner with fewer trees. Road 206 and North Fork are just plain straight and brown.

NAVIGATION: Somewhere along its course, Rd 206 changes to North Fork Rd, which is what the TE is signed as at its southern end.

TE-B Rd 221 - Rd 223 - Rd 426 (13.7 mi / 22.0 km)

If you're doing the DH from the south, this is the back way into

Oakhurst. Only thing is, you'll have to miss the best part of the DH around Bass Lake to do it. The longer 223 bit is not as well paved or as curvy as 426 and 221, but does have a lot less traffic and development.

NAVIGATION: If you're riding this road from the DH end and not Oakhurst make sure you make the hard left off Rd 221 and onto Rd 223 at 1.6 mi (2.6 km).

TOUR NOTE: Not sure what happened, but on 221, there was a Harley rider with his arm covered with road rash sitting in the back of an ambulance. Good thing he was wearing his protective T-shirt.

TE-C North Fork – Auberry (13.5 mi / 22.8 km) *Rd 222/Auberry Rd - Powerhouse Rd*

"Rd 222/Auberry Rd" reads the sign at the junction with the DH. Take it and you'll veer off the DH onto a road that winds decently enough through some higher, greener and more forested country. The Powerhouse half south of the Kerckhoff Lake/San Joaquin River has smoother pavement, better engineering, an increased number of curves and drier, more traditional Sierra foothill scenery.

TOUR NOTE: Rd 235, which junctions from the east just north of the Kerckhoff Lake/San Joaquin River crossing, can get you to the spot identified as the exact geographic center of California. You'll pay for it with narrow, punishing pavement though. That is if the UPS trucks don't turn you into grill splatter first. (Geophiles, see ***TE-D*** *for a less painful way to get to this spot.)*

TE-D South Fork – Mammoth Pool Reservoir (43.8 mi / 70.5 km) *Rd 225 - FSR 81 - FSR 6325*

Yes, you can still find remote in northern California. The third longest TE in the state takes you high into the forest beneath Whisky Ridge above the west side of the San Joaquin River canyon and almost all the way to Hells Half Acre – literally. Not the smoothest FSR TE, but it does have a surfeit of moderate cornering opportunities for your inclination. Keep in mind that unless you like prowling narrow, bumpy forest service roads or even gravel, you'll have to ride this epic puppy back out. Also keep in mind that this is high country and snow can block the roads up here quite late in the year. Or, indeed, quite early.

TOUR NOTE: Italian Bar Rd (also a continuation of Rd 225), right at 4.0 mi (6.4 km) has the exact geographic center of California on it just a couple of miles from the junction with the TE.

ROUTING OPTIONS: Like to explore or hate to come back out the same way?

(1) Take the rough, FSR 6S71 at the 35.9 mi (57.8 km) mark, north of the Soda Springs campground. Skirt around Chiquito Ridge and then take Beasore Rd back down to the DH at Bass Lake. It would be around 20 mi (32 km). Unless you have to backtrack on account of snow.

(2) Continue on FSR 81 past the turn down to Mammoth Pool Res and by Jackass Rock (hint, hint) where legend has it that you can connect to gravel

Beasore Rd. It eventually becomes paved and should take you back to the DH at Bass Lake. The length of this route is probably in the neighborhood of 35 mi (56 km), assuming you don't get lost and wander aimlessly until you run out of gas and starve to death in a snow bank. We can see you maxburners drooling already.

TE-E Ahwahnee – Hensley Lake (28.1 mi / 45.2 km)
Rd 600 - Rd 603
Combine this TE with the southern part of **TE-F** for a no-brain option to the Hwy 41 cavalcade between Oakhurst and Hwy 99. After an initial straight stretch, Hwy 49 plunges down from Fresno Flats through characteristic Sierra foothill country between the peaks of Twin Sisters and Native American Hill. The curves relax along the base of Mullen Ridge and Spinecup Ridge into Raymond. The last section down and around Hensley Lake has more hassle-free curves that thin out as the trees do.

TE-F Coarsegold – Madera (29.1 mi / 46.8 km) *Rd 415 - Rd 400*
Turn off Hwy 41 at Coarsegold for this shorter and faster alternative to **TE-E**. The Rd 415 part out of Coarsegold has some curves but can also have quite a bit of traffic. Once you turn left onto Rd 400, however, you leave most of the traffic behind. The pavement starts out great on 400 but coarsens to the south before picking up slightly for some nice lakeside cornering along Hensley Lake. The final stretch into the dry, wide-open Central Valley leaves you a couple of miles from Madera and Hwy 99.

NAVIGATION: Riding southwest from Coarsegold on Rd 415, turn left onto Rd 400 at 4.8 mi (7.7 km).

RIDER'S LOG: **DATE RIDDEN:** **YOUR RATING: /10**

Map Tip: Services on non-featured DHs and TEs are generally shown as bare icon only and sometimes no icon. For the full detail, just turn to the featured map.

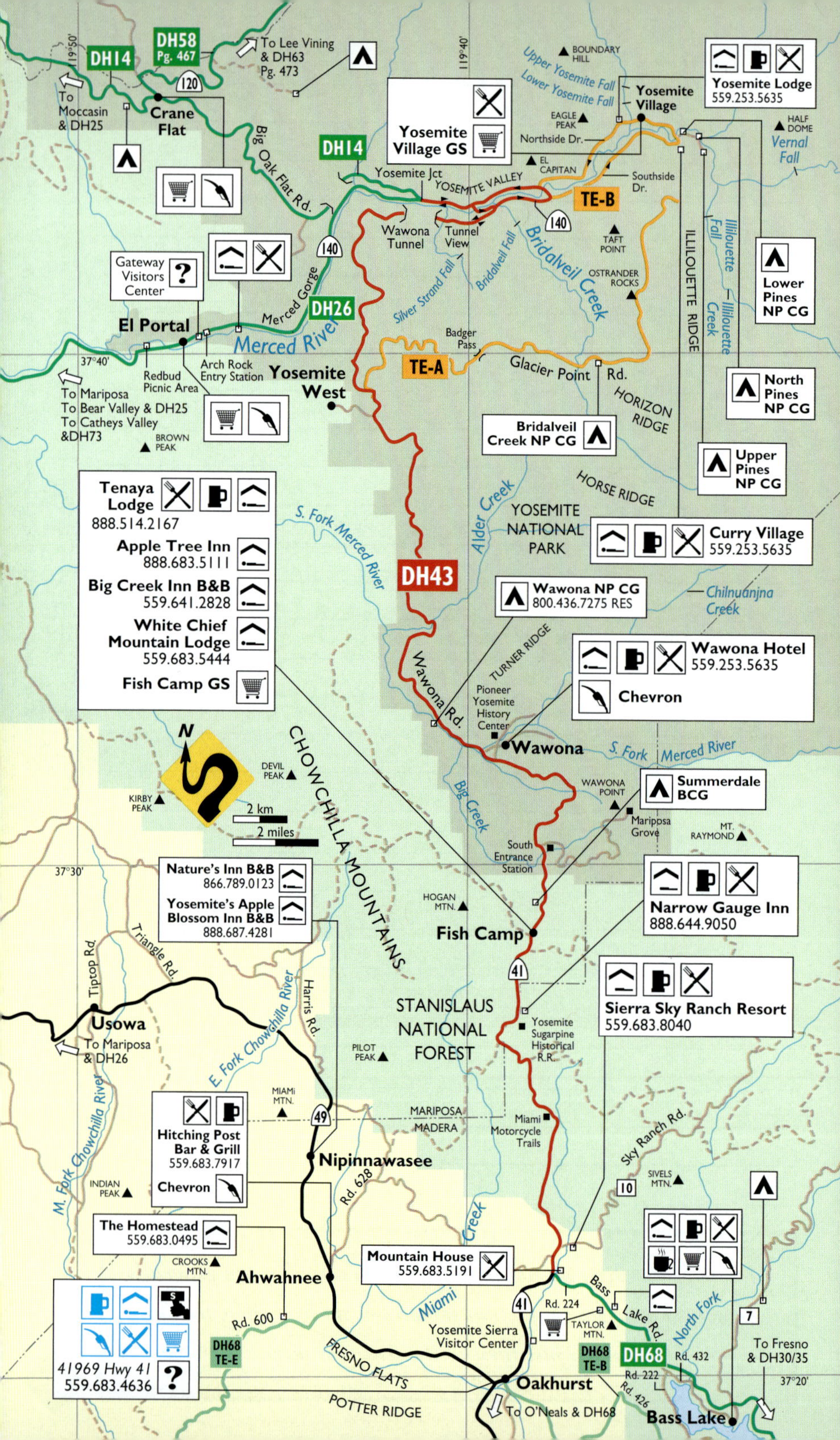

DH14
DH58
Pg. 467
To Lee Vining
& DH63
Pg. 473
119°50'
119°40'
To Moccasin
& DH25
Crane Flat
120
Big Oak Flat Rd.
BOUNDARY HILL
Upper Yosemite Fall
Lower Yosemite Fall
Yosemite Village
Yosemite Lodge
559.253.5635
Yosemite Village GS
EAGLE PEAK
Northside Dr.
HALF DOME
Vernal Fall
DH14
Yosemite Jct
YOSEMITE VALLEY
EL CAPITAN
Southside Dr.
TE-B
140
Wawona Tunnel
Tunnel View
Bridalveil Fall
Bridalveil Creek
TAFT POINT
ILLILOUETTE RIDGE
Illilouette Fall
Illilouette Creek
Lower Pines NP CG
140
Gateway Visitors Center
Merced Gorge
Silver Strand Fall
OSTRANDER ROCKS
DH26
El Portal
Merced River
Badger Pass
37°40'
Redbud Picnic Area
Arch Rock Entry Station
Yosemite West
TE-A
Glacier Point Rd.
North Pines NP CG
To Mariposa
To Bear Valley & DH25
To Catheys Valley
&DH73
BROWN PEAK
HORIZON RIDGE
Bridalveil Creek NP CG
Upper Pines NP CG
Tenaya Lodge
888.514.2167
Apple Tree Inn
888.683.5111
Big Creek Inn B&B
559.641.2828
White Chief Mountain Lodge
559.683.5444
Fish Camp GS
HORSE RIDGE
Alder Creek
YOSEMITE NATIONAL PARK
Curry Village
559.253.5635
S. Fork Merced River
DH43
Wawona NP CG
800.436.7275 RES
Chilnualna Creek
TURNER RIDGE
Wawona Hotel
559.253.5635
Chevron
Wawona Rd.
Pioneer Yosemite History Center
Wawona
S. Fork Merced River
CHOWCHILLA MOUNTAINS
DEVIL PEAK
KIRBY PEAK
WAWONA POINT
Summerdale BCG
Big Creek
Mariposa Grove
2 km
2 miles
MT. RAYMOND
South Entrance Station
37°30'
Nature's Inn B&B
866.789.0123
Yosemite's Apple Blossom Inn B&B
888.687.4281
HOGAN MTN.
Narrow Gauge Inn
888.644.9050
Fish Camp
Triangle Rd.
Tiptop Rd.
41
Sierra Sky Ranch Resort
559.683.8040
Harris Rd.
Usowa
E. Fork Chowchilla River
STANISLAUS NATIONAL FOREST
Yosemite Sugarpine Historical R.R.
To Mariposa
& DH26
PILOT PEAK
MIAMI MTN.
49
MARIPOSA
MADERA
Miami Motorcycle Trails
Sky Ranch Rd.
M. Fork Chowchilla River
Hitching Post Bar & Grill
559.683.7917
Chevron
Nipinnawasee
Rd. 628
SIVELS MTN.
10
INDIAN PEAK
The Homestead
559.683.0495
Creek
CROOKS MTN.
Mountain House
559.683.5191
Ahwahnee
Miami
Bass Lake Rd.
North Fork
Rd. 224
41
TAYLOR MTN.
7
Rd. 600
Yosemite Sierra Visitor Center
DH68
TE-E
DH68
TE-B
DH68
Rd. 432
To Fresno
& DH30/35
FRESNO FLATS
41969 Hwy 41
559.683.4636
Oakhurst
Rd. 222
37°20'
Rd. 426
POTTER RIDGE
To O'Neals & DH68
Bass Lake

DH43 Oakhurst – Yosemite Jct

Hwy 41 / Wawona Rd / Hwy 140

Distance:	43.9 mi / 70.6 km	Traffic:	Brutal

At a Glance

The UK has Marmite. Australia produces Vegemite. Yosemite (properly pronounced "Yo-se-mite") was the bear meat version developed locally by red-bearded frontiersman Samuel Yost. The American piquant is no longer made but this savory DH is a substitute to relish as it spreads its way north from Oakhurst into the heart of the spectacular Yosemite Valley. Bear in mind, you do have to take the fabled Scenery reports with more than a few grains of salt. Mostly you'll see trees; the mind-blowing stuff only appears near the very end. On the other hand, a yeasty Twistiness seasons the entire journey. Once in the national park itself, less-palatable Pavement combines with raunchier Engineering for a somewhat grittier mouth – er, tire feel. Accommodation in the park is limited, so vast numbers of pylons consume this delicacy early in the morning, then clear out in the afternoon. To go against this flow, eat this one up as a late brunch. While you can no longer savor Yost's creation, chewing on this gamey ride to Yosemite will, like the other two condiments, undoubtedly help to "ensure you and your family keep nerves, brain and digestion in proper working order." And if you wash it down with a tipple at the end, remember to raise your glass to the original Yosemite Sam.

TIRES	
Twistiness	30/30
Pavement	10.1/20
Engineering	3.8/10
Remoteness	6.7/10
Scenery	10.3/15
Character	7.3/15
Total	**68.2**

Access

From Oakhurst

On Hwy 41

Head north on Hwy 41. A few curves and a couple of miles later, you'll pass the junction with **DH68 Oakhurst – O'Neals** and be on the road.

Coming in on DH68 O'Neals – Oakhurst

At the junction with Hwy 41, turn right. You're on the road.

From Yosemite

On Northside Dr (TE-B)

From the village, head west on one-way **TE-A** for 3.4 mi (5.5 km) until you junction with the DH, 2.8 mi (4.5 km) from its Yosemite Jct end.

Coming in on DH14 Moccasin – Yosemite Jct
At the three-way DH junction, turn left. You're on the road.

Coming in on DH26 Mariposa –Yosemite Jct (Hwy 140)
At the junction, stay straight and you're on the road.

On The Road

As you leave the junction with **DH68 Oakhurst – O'Neals**, smooth pavement and gentle, consistent curves lead you away from Oakhurst's outlying development and into the Sierra National Forest at 1.9 mi. (3.1 km). Entering a national forest often produces a heightened sense of remoteness. Not here, where all the pylons can make it feel like the middle of a Sacramento rush hour.

Fortunately, if the traffic isn't completely bogged down, the move-over-for-motorcyclists rule is mostly observed at the many pull-outs. And, if it's not, isn't that why modern bikes have such bright high beams?

When the way ahead is clear, it's a nice meander through increasingly statuesque pine forest. The air cools as you climb higher into the Sierra Nevada foothills, the perfect temperature to enjoy that hot little flurry of essed curves and sweepers before and after the Madera/Mariposa County line at 6.8 mi (10.9 km). You're soon back in Madera, but just past the national forest office you're in Mariposa for good at 8.7 mi. (14.0 km). Seems the boundary boys were smoking something other than Marlboros the day they surveyed this stretch.

TOUR NOTES:
(1) If you're a keen maxburner and want to give your GS, Tiger or Caponard a bit more of a workout, Miami Motorcycle Trails consist of 60 miles of year-round roads and trails in the Sierra National Forest. There are two staging areas: Kamook is located 6.0 mi (9.7 km) north of Oakhurst, just 0.8 mi (1.2 km) off the DH. (Look for the 4000 ft (1230 m) elevation sign on the right of Hwy 41; the entrance will be on your left just a little ahead.) The other staging area, Lone Sequoia, is 8.0 mi (12.9 km) north of Oakhurst and 1.3 mi (2.0 km) off the highway. All trails are open to two-way traffic, so watch for horses, ATVs and other pylons of the dirt.

(2) If you're looking for something mellower, climb off your mount and ride the iron horses (two logging steam locomotives built in 1913 and 1928) on the sweetly restored 4.0 mi (6.4) narrow gauge railroad of the Madera Sugar Pine Lumber Company. The turnoff for it is located at the DH's 8.2 mi (13.2 km) mark. Phone 559.683.7273.

At 10.2 mi (16.4 km), you're in Fish Camp. And how about that – your favorite sign promises curves for the next 12 mi (19 km). Too bad about the pylon in front of you who won't pull over. Oh good, Fishville has reeled him in for some services. You're outta town and clear at 10.6 mi (17.1 km).

You crank it up and lean heavily into the continuing curves. But what's with the inferior asphalt quality when you exit the Sierra National

Forest and enter Yosemite National Park at 11.7 mi (18.8 km)? Well, it seems Hwy 41 ends and becomes a mere road, named "Wawona." You hit the park's south entrance booth at 12.5 mi. (20.0 km) where you get to pay $10 or so (coin of the realm only) for the drop in pavement grade. Hardly seems fair. But wait – according to the pamphlet they hand out, you're also promised speed limits that "do not exceed 45 mph (70 kmh) in Yosemite and are lower where posted." What a deal! Bet dotted yellow's an endangered species in the park as well.

TOUR NOTE: Just past the south booth on the right there is a road approximately 3.5 mi (5.6 km) long winding up to the Mariposa Grove of giant sequoias (including one 2700 year old mother of all trees) at Wawona Point. Though paved, this offshoot does have one of those "lower where posted" limits – in this case, a stately 20 mph (30 kmh).

At least the curves don't abandon you as you start out on Wawona Rd (believed to be a contraction of the "What the… whoa… nah!" reaction of pioneer riders refusing to pay for inferior pavement). In fact, the corners increase in number through the thickening forest and lots come with 25-mph (40-kph) advisories. Truth be told, the pavement's not actually all that bad. Though you can forget about the comfort of any shoulders to lean on.

Ah nature. Light green swatches of open areas on your left contrast with the landscape's dominant dark pines. Hang on, that's not meadow, it's a golf course. And at 15.9 mi. (25.6 km), you're in Wawona.

TOUR NOTES:

(1) Since there is no gas in the Yosemite Valley, Wawona is your last chance to fill up until Crane Flat, 36.0 mi (57.9 km) later on ***DH14 Yosemite Jct – Moccasin*** *or El Portal 34.2 mi (55.0 km) from here on* ***DH26 Yosemite Jct – Mariposa****.*

(2) You might want to visit the rambling and charming old Wawona Hotel, built in 1879 and still in operation. There is a Yosemite Information Station in the hotel, open from May through the summer. Wawona also has an historic covered bridge (circa 1878) at the Pioneer Yosemite History Center.

You leave town and cross the South Fork Merced River at 17.9 mi (28.8 km). It takes up station to your left but has no beneficial effect; the road's actually straighter now. The pavement's rougher as well. But at least the curves come back as you start to climb up the eastern side of the river's valley. Just hope you don't have much traffic in front of you; with no shoulder, there's no place for them to pull over. It's just you, the puttering pylons and the double yellow. And your conscience.

Check out the view over the steep drop off to the left at 20.6 mi. (33.1 km). You can see just how far you've clamored up the rock face on this side of the valley. It would be feeling pretty remote up here if it weren't for the traffic wasting a lot of the great curves.

Hey, finally a passing opportunity – though it's not a legal one. Too bad, since this well-banked series of esses would sure be a lot more fun without all the Mazdas. Especially since you're getting used to the pavement. Zoom, zoom....

Take a look left just prior to Bishop Creek at 25.5 mi (41.0 km) and you'll see the vastness of the South Fork Merced River's valley before you re-enter the forest. Also appearing: a 35-mph (55-kmh) speed zone. No matter, as long as there's no traffic in front of you, you're in your own zone.

Nice piece, huh? There's more to come beyond the junction with Glacier Point Rd (**TE-A**) at 29.7 mi (47.8 km). The next fix of S-curves never seems to end. Just like the pylons.

The geography rises higher and the trees thin, either from elevation, fire or both. The road's in more rugged and rocky terrain now and you get some glimpses of the Merced Gorge down to the left. The road turns away to the east up the subsidiary valley of Grouse Creek, crossing it at 33.2 mi (53.4 km) before doubling back west toward the gorge.

There's a good view across to the far side of the Merced before you turn to the east and approach the mouth of Yosemite Valley. At 35.7 mi. (57.4 km), you get your first look at El Capitan on the valley's far side. There is a long, open vista on the shoulder opposite, giving a very good if long-distance view of the largest exposed granite monolith in the world. Towering 3593 ft (1103 m) above the valley floor, it's twice the height of the Rock of Gibraltar.

But there are greater wonders still. Equally impressive on the far side of the valley, way down on its bottom **DH14 Yosemite Jct – Moccasin** and **DH26 Yosemite Jct – Mariposa** wind to the three-way junction with the DH you're riding.

The road is back in the trees now, slanting downhill. As the valley pinches tight, you enter the poorly lit Wawona Tunnel at 36.5 mi (58.7 km). The coolness in here is helped by occasionally dripping water. Nearly a curveless mile later, you exit right at a heavily used viewpoint overlooking the splendor of the steep walled and flat-bottomed valley. Slow down in the tunnel if you want to stop for this static view of El Capitan and the 650 ft (200 m) high Bridalveil Falls; it's easy to get distracted and blow by the turn off for it.

TOUR NOTE: Back in 1851, Lafayette Bunnell of the Mariposa Battalion captured a little of The Captain's flavor:
"Fools our fond gaze, and greatest of the great,
Defies at first our Nature's littleness,
Till, growing with its growth, we thus dilate
Our spirits to the size of that they contemplate."

Lafay could be writing ad copy for the Honda Rune. Even if you're not usually moved by great scenery, this should stagger you; everywhere you look is an Ansel Adams photograph. There are few better places than Yosemite to meditate on the meaning of "perspective" (with the exception of a top-rated DH, of course).

The road more or less straightens out as you leave the viewpoint and head down to the valley floor. That's normally a bad thing but, in this case, it's probably good, as you're paying more attention to what's around you rather than what's under your wheels. You probably won't even mind the 35-mph (55-kph) speed limit.

At 38.5 mi (62.0 km), the DH junctions with a one-way road coming across from the north side of the valley. In fact, this is also part of the DH, which you will only ride if you're doing this road from its Yosemite Jct end. That's because the section of the DH you're on becomes one way as it continues straight ahead east from this junction. You can turn right and pause for a closer look at the 65-storey high Bridalveil Falls at 38.7 mi. (62.3 km).

If you stay married to the DH, the Merced River burbles along to your immediate left. This valley bottom, now home to a thick and majestic forest, was scraped absolutely flat by glaciers eons ago, leaving the harder rock of the valley walls to soar vertically from the floor in almost perfect right angles. At 40.5 mi (65.2 km), Southside Dr (**TE-B**) continues straight on, east (one-way) to Yosemite Village (no gas). To stay on the DH, **angle left**.

After the Hwy 120/140 junction signs, the DH briefly two-ways and heads straight north at the massive, looming bulk of El Cap. Lush, green meadows to your left are backed by the valley's impressive south wall. The DH becomes one-way again and, after the junction with Northside Dr (the other end of **TE-B**) at 41.1 mi (66.1 km), heads due west back into the impressive, riverside forest.

There are a few gentle corners before the junction with the one-way cross road at 43.0 mi (69.2 km) returns of the DH to its two-way status. The road continues winding gently through the trees along the river with the scenery getting progressively less spectacular until you three-way junction with **DH14 Yosemite Jct – Moccasin** and **DH26 Yosemite Jct – Mariposa** at 43.9 mi (70.6 km). Decisions, decisions.

Twisted Edges

TE-A Glacier Point Rd (15.9 mi / 25.6 km)

The first third or so of this TE is a great horny toad of a road twisting up to Badger Pass. After that, it more or less straightens out on better pavement across a forested, sloping plateau, although there are some great curves on excellent pavement for the last mile or so. But really, the main reason to come up here is for the two Yosemite viewpoints at the end. The incredible High Sierra panorama includes Half Dome (a 8842 ft / 2715 m high, 87 million year old hunk of Plutonic rock) and four Yosemite waterfalls: Nevada, Vernal, Upper Yosemite and Lower Yosemite. A good place to get off the Corbin and onto your meditation cushion, if the tourists aren't too thick on the ground.

TOUR NOTE: This is one of the best and most easily accessed high-elevation viewpoints in the Sierra Nevada, ending as it does at the lip of the Yosemite Valley, 3,200 feet (983 m) above the valley floor. There can be snow covering the asphalt until late spring.

TE-B Yosemite Village Loop (7.9 mi / 12.7 km) *Northside Dr - Southside Dr*

Slow down and look up. Waaaay up. This is not the place for speed. Not exclusively because of the speed tax collectors, although they are one reason. No, it's more because you'll be gawking at the mind-blowing monoliths that launch skyward from the flat, grass and pined bottom of the Yosemite Valley. Not to be missed.

NAVIGATION: Although there are some two-way stretches at the eastern end, this loop is one-way going in from the DH and one-way going out. This means that you can only access it from the south side on – good guess – Southside Rd. Traveling along Southside road, you'll reach a stop sign at Sentinel Dr. Keep going straight. At the next stop sign – the one where a sign points left to "Yosemite Village and Park Exits" and straight on to Curry Village – go left on unmarked Northside Dr. The next stop sign is at of 4.5 mi (7.2 km). Keep going straight to stay on the TE (turn right to go to Yosemite Village). At 7.9 mi (12.7 km), you intersect the DH. Going straight on it (one-way, at the beginning) will take you to the three DH Yosemite Jct. Turning left on it (two-way) will take you to a T-junction where your only option is to turn left on Southside Dr and loop around on the TE again.

RIDER'S LOG: **DATE RIDDEN:** **YOUR RATING: /10**

DH70
DH73
DH25
DH14
DH26
DH68
DH43
DH30
DH35

Just what is an "STC" or "maxburner" anyway?
Check out these and other Twisted Terms in the Glossary at p.??

3 km
3 miles
Shaver Lake Village Hotel 559.841.8289
Musick Creek Inn & Chalets 559.841.3323
Primrose Inn B&B 559.841.3731
Elliot House B&B 559.841.8601
Union 76
Bass Lake
Rd. 432
Rd. 426
To Oakhurst & DH43
Road 223
Road 274
Road 222
Road 221
DH68
DH68 TE-B
DH68 TE-D
DH68 TE-C
For detail see DH68
South Fork
North Fork
N. Fork Rd.
Road 200
Road 225
Road 222/Auberry Rd.
Source Point
Castle Peak
Geographic Center of California
Road 235
Italian Bar Rd.
Redinger Lake
San Joaquin River
Lone Ridge
Jose Basin Rd.
Power House Rd
Horseshoe Bend
Smalley Rd.
Auberry
Auberry Rd.
Big Sandy Bluff
Big Sandy Valley
Prather
Auberry Rd.
TE-A
Morgan Canyon Rd.
TE-D ALT
Lodge Rd.
Black Mtn. Lookout
Tollhouse Market
Millerton Rd.
TE-A ALT
Toll House Rd.
TE-D
Humphreys Station
Pittman Hill Rd.
Sample Rd.
TE-B ALT
168
To Fresno
Shepherd Ave.
(II)
Herndon Ave.
Friant Canal
Shaw Ave.
Ashian Ave.
Academy Ave.
Watts Valley Rd.
TE-B
Riverbend Ave.
Belmont Ave.
To Sanger (SoCal)
19°30'
6325
Mammoth Pool Res.
Stump Springs Rd.
Madera
Fresno
TE-H
5
Kaiser Creek
Kaiser Wilderness
37°20'
Lakeshore Resort 559.893.3193
Rancheria Mini Mart
Kaiser Peak
Cedar Crest Resort 559-893-3233
Lakeshore
80
Crest
Black Point
Huntington Lake
Chinese Peak
Big Creek
Tamarack Creek
Huntington Lk. Rd.
TE-G
Musick Mtn.
Tamarack Mtn.
Ely Mtn.
DH30
37°10'
168
(7582ft 2328m)
I
Flume Peak
Mt. Stevenson
Huntington Lake Resort 559.893.3226
Tamarack Motor Lodge 559.893.3244
Shaver Lake
Cressman's
Bald Mtn.
TE-F
Dinkey Creek Rd.
Dinkey Creek
Providence Creek Rd.
Pine Ridge
Sierra National Forest
Auberry Rd.
TE-E
Pine Ridge
Peterson Mill Rd.
TE-D
Tollhouse
Tollhouse Rd.
Burrough Mtn.
40
McKinley Grove Rd.
Shaver Lake Lodge 559.841.3326
37°00'
Sycamore Creek
Barnes Mtn.
Dorabelle BCG
Camp Edison CG 559.841.3134
Burrough Valley Rd.
TE-C
Humphreys Station 559.299.6522
Branford Mtn.
Maxon Rd.
Big Creek
(III)
Watts Valley Rd.
Red Mtn.
Springs Rd.
Trimmer
Pine Flat Res.
Sequoia National Forest
36°50'
Pine Flat Rd.
DH35
Piedra
Elwood Rd.
Mill Creek
Trimmer Springs Rd.
Piedra Rd.
19°20'
DH35 TE-A
DHSCA TBA
To Woodlake To Visalia (SoCal)
180
19°10'

DH30 Fresno – Lakeshore
Highway 168

Distance:	52.3 mi / 84.2 km	Traffic:	Moderate

At a Glance

TIRES	
Twistiness	27.6/ 30
Pavement	15.4/ 20
Engineering	6.0/ 10
Remoteness	5.0/ 10
Scenery	8.7/ 15
Character	9.7/ 15
Total	72.4

Irritable Male Syndrome is caused by drops in testosterone. Far more serious, because it affects riders of both sexes, is Irritable Motorcyclist Syndrome – the sudden decrease in twistosterone caused by excessive exposure to speed tax collectors. And sadly, because this road is used as a training run by the CHiP motorcycle corps, you can get posses of latter-day Ponchs and Jons damping down your hormones here in a big way. And that's a shame, since this quadripartite DH has some of the best TIRES variety in NorCal. After escaping Fresnoland through the rolling, lower foothills of the Sierra Nevada, a high-speed, major-highway-like howl sweeps you up Big Sandy Bluff to cooler climes. From Pine Ridge to Shaver Lake, you get a Pavement and Engineering-challenged, tight-and-twisty romp through the thick of the Sierra National Forest. Once you are round Shaver Lake, Remoteness soars as the road stretches out and climbs into the Sierra Nevada approaches before ending at Huntington Lake. Sound good? It is – as long as you pick a good time to ride it. Problem is, since this road is also heavily patrolled by CHiP black and whites *and* monitored from the air, you really don't have a fricking clue when that might be. And that's what's *really* irritating.

Access

From Fresno

Via Hwy 168

Get on Hwy 168 heading east. Keep going. Go some more. Just after you finally leave Greater Fresno (which keeps getting greater all the time), you'll pass a junction with Academy Ave on your right. After Academy, you're in school.

Coming in on DH35 Kirch Flat – Piedra (Fresno)

Once you reach Piedra, ride 7.4 mi (11.9 km) on Trimmer Springs Rd to the junction with Belmont Ave. Go west on Belmont for about 5 mi (8 km) and you'll reach Academy Ave. Turn north on it for about 8 mi (13 km) and you'll junction with the Hwy 168 start of the DH. Turn right and you're on the road.

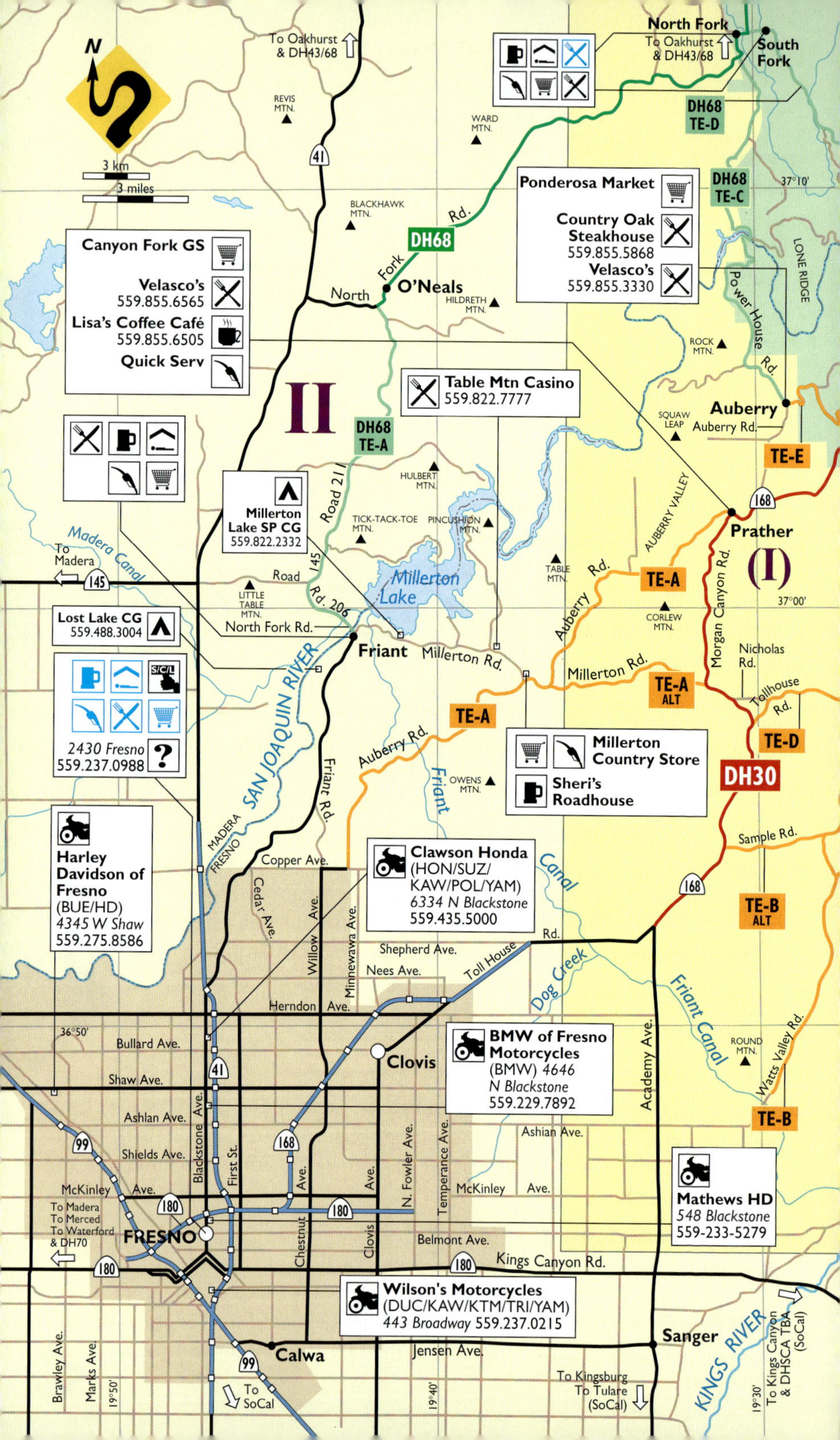

North Fork
South Fork
To Oakhurst & DH43/68
Ponderosa Market
Country Oak Steakhouse
559.855.5868
Velasco's
559.855.3330
Canyon Fork GS
Velasco's
559.855.6565
Lisa's Coffee Café
559.855.6505
Quick Serv
O'Neals
Table Mtn Casino
559.822.7777
Auberry
Millerton Lake SP CG
559.822.2332
Prather
Lost Lake CG
559.488.3004
Friant
Millerton Lake
2430 Fresno
559.237.0988
Millerton Country Store
Sheri's Roadhouse
Harley Davidson of Fresno
(BUE/HD)
4345 W Shaw
559.275.8586
Clawson Honda
(HON/SUZ/KAW/POL/YAM)
6334 N Blackstone
559.435.5000
BMW of Fresno Motorcycles
(BMW) 4646 N Blackstone
559.229.7892
Mathews HD
548 Blackstone
559-233-5279
Clovis
FRESNO
Wilson's Motorcycles
(DUC/KAW/KTM/TRI/YAM)
443 Broadway 559.237.0215
Calwa
Sanger
DH68 TE-D
DH68 TE-C
DH68 TE-A
TE-E
TE-A
TE-A ALT
TE-D
DH30
TE-B ALT
TE-B
II
(I)
SAN JOAQUIN RIVER
KINGS RIVER
To Madera
To Madera
To Merced
To Waterford & DH70
To SoCal
To Kingsburg
To Tulare (SoCal)
To Kings Canyon & DHSCA TBA (SoCal)
3 km
3 miles

From Lakeshore

At the east end of Huntington Lake, Hwy 168 begins at the three-way junction with **TE-F** and FSR 80. Get on 168 and you're on the road.

On The Road

TOUR NOTE: Apparently doing something beneficial for mankind, like writing Destination Highways, sometimes pays dividends with omniscient beings. Once, as we getting geared to go at the Academy Ave start, seven CHiPs on BMWs purred by, coming off the DH. If they'd ridden by in the other direction, we might as well have packed it in and come back another day. Giving thanks to whatever deity granted us this indulgence, we gave 'em a wave and hit the road.

You stay on the flat when you leave the junction, motoring between two dry fields towards the oak tree smattered foothills ahead. There are only a couple of curves before you're in the hills at 2.3 mi (3.7 km). The turnoff right for Sample Rd (***TE-B ALT***)is at 3.0 mi (4.8 km).

The BIG 30-mph (50-kmh) sign invites you to ride hither. But it's a bit of a tease. Initially, the hills have interspersed flat areas and it's really not until 5.0 mi (8.1 km) that you really get to experience any real curvaceousness. The cornering opportunities that do appear are rendered more challenging by the up-and-down undulations and the hillsides that sometimes crowd your sight.

By 6.0 mi (9.7 km), you're climbing and the hillsides have pinched the corners tighter. Tollhouse Rd (**TE-D**), junctions right at 7.1 mi (11.4 km). Whereas the DH technically had that moniker up till now (along with its Hwy 168 number) it now becomes Millerton Rd. That may seem silly until you remember that this is a state that doesn't number 99 per cent of its interstate exits.

You're a ways from Fresno but don't imagine there's no development around here. While the excellently paved curves continue, a fair sprinkling of large houses and other buildings mar the rolling terrain. And there'll be more to come, as Fresno and the rest of the state continue to pursue a policy of unbridled urban sprawl.

The terrain widens into a valley just before Millerton Rd leaves the DH at 9.0 mi (14.5 km) and turns left as ***TE-A ALT***. 168's name is now Morgan Canyon Rd. May sound good but everything stays pretty much the same as it was before. Except the pavement's a little rougher and the sight lines are a little poorer. The only thing canyon-like here is a mini-rockface to your left at 13.0 mi (20.9 km) where the terrain roughens briefly. You hit the townlet of Prather and then junction with the east end of the **TE-A** piece of Auberry Rd at 14.4 mi (23.2 km).

For those who care, Hwy 168 now adopts Auberry Rd as its alternate name until the non-TE part of Auberry Rd splits off north at 15.5 mi (24.9 km). Here the now-better-paved DH becomes Lodge Rd as it cruises

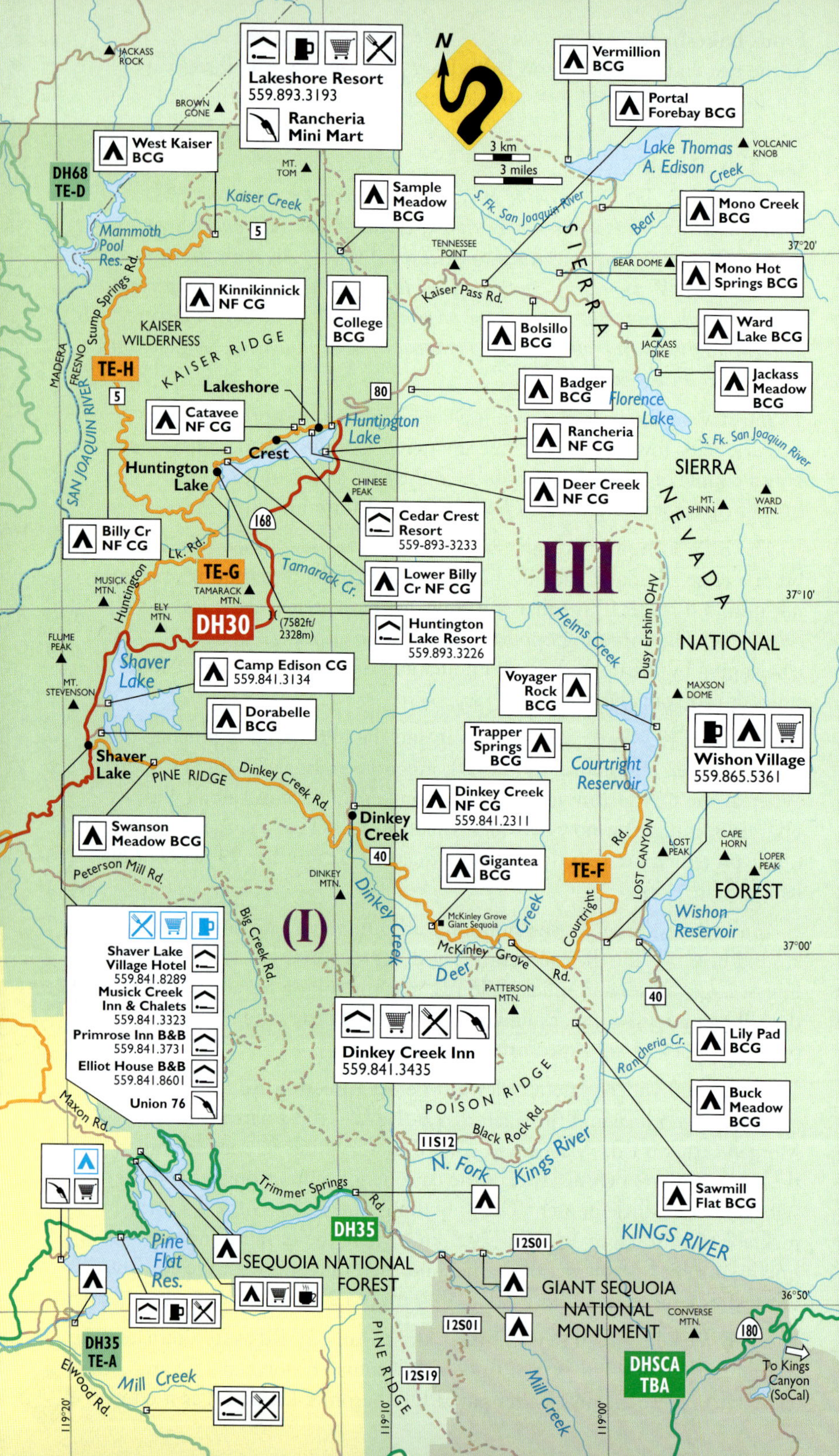

Lakeshore Resort
559.893.3193
Rancheria Mini Mart
Vermillion BCG
Portal Forebay BCG
West Kaiser BCG
DH68 TE-D
Sample Meadow BCG
Lake Thomas A. Edison
Mono Creek BCG
Mono Hot Springs BCG
Kinnikinnick NF CG
College BCG
Bolsillo BCG
Ward Lake BCG
Jackass Meadow BCG
KAISER WILDERNESS
KAISER RIDGE
TE-H
Lakeshore
Catavee NF CG
Badger BCG
Rancheria NF CG
Deer Creek NF CG
Huntington Lake
Crest
Billy Cr NF CG
Cedar Crest Resort
559-893-3233
Lower Billy Cr NF CG
TE-G
DH30
Huntington Lake Resort
559.893.3226
III
SIERRA NEVADA NATIONAL FOREST
Camp Edison CG
559.841.3134
Dorabelle BCG
Voyager Rock BCG
Trapper Springs BCG
Wishon Village
559.865.5361
Shaver Lake
Swanson Meadow BCG
Dinkey Creek NF CG
559.841.2311
Dinkey Creek
Gigantea BCG
TE-F
(I)
Shaver Lake Village Hotel
559.841.8289
Musick Creek Inn & Chalets
559.841.3323
Primrose Inn B&B
559.841.3731
Elliot House B&B
559.841.8601
Union 76
Dinkey Creek Inn
559.841.3435
Lily Pad BCG
Buck Meadow BCG
Sawmill Flat BCG
DH35
SEQUOIA NATIONAL FOREST
GIANT SEQUOIA NATIONAL MONUMENT
DH35 TE-A
DHSCA TBA
To Kings Canyon (SoCal)

through what is either farmland under threat or large housing lots, depending on how you look at it. After the stop sign at 17.1 mi (27.5 km), Lodge leaves 168 straight ahead as ***TE-D ALT***. To stay on the DH, **turn left**.

What's up next? Well, there's a sign saying this part of the road is patrolled from the air. Makes sense, since almost every other form of speed tax collector seems to be here. And you can see why, given the big jump in pavement and engineering quality. With one eye on the sky you streak, with the help of a passing lane, straight across Big Sand Valley directly at Big Sandy Bluff. Which doesn't look all that sandy. Though there's no question, it is bluffy and big. Almost as big as the sweeper that turns you up it.

The road climbs seriously on a wide-open stretch that features long, shallow sweepers, a view back over Big Sand Valley and perhaps a black and white heading down in the opposite direction. Perfect timing once more you think, as you enter the Sierra National Forest at 20.5 mi (33.0 km). You've kept your speed down but now that the local STC (Pylon Division) has gone by, you're good to go. Yes, the gods are still with you. So you twist your wrist to dive deeper and harder into those big, sweeping corners. You continue to climb back and forth, around, between and beside large white rockfaces. This is great...

What the... a *second* CHiP cruiser hoves into view and flashes past. Only it's not him going fast. Even as you hit the binders (far too late), you know you've used up all your karmic cookies for today. Sure enough, you can see the STC light show beginning in your rear-views as he easily reverses course on the four lanes of pavement. Nothing to do but close your throttle and whimper over to the shoulder, trying to remember which Greek playwright it was who said, "Whom the gods would destroy they first make mad." Oh yeah, Euripides. Well, you, for one, are certainly pissed.

TOUR NOTE: If God is on your side, perhaps your officer will turn out to be a Lead Wing rider in his real life. And you'll have an amiable discussion about riding and such before he wishes you Godspeed. If so, don't forget to nod your thanks heavenward.

Spooling back up to speed, you're probably trying to determine how fast you can safely go, given all you've seen in the way of enforcement. Fortunately, you don't have to decide. At 26.1 mi (42.0 km), the passing lane ends as Tollhouse Rd (**TE-D**) right, and Auberry Rd (**TE-E**) left, junction simultaneously. The terrain tightens up immediately afterward, plopping trees down tight on both sides of the road. The engineering drops as well and you can barely see around the compressed curves. Which might be fine if the pavement quality didn't simultaneously drop a grade. Good time for the DH to change its name again – how's "Tollhouse Rd" grab you?

The road passes Pine Ridge and opens up for a short while. But it's not long before you're back in the deep, dark forest. Alas, there's no dotted line of breadcrumbs through the woods in this fairytale. Just a solid, double-yellow line of evil. Mind you, with all these tight corners, it would be tough to get by any pylons here anyway. Besides, half of them would probably be STCs.

The road continues to climb higher and consequently the temperature cools off. The occasional building appears, a signal that you're approaching the small but surprisingly sprawly town of Shaver Lake, which you arrive in at 31.2 mi (50.2 km).

TOUR NOTE: If you're on a quest for nature's perfect sugar delivery system, the Village Restaurant in Shaver Lake serves light and fluffy pancakes that will stack up against the best you've ever had.

You leave town and the road relaxes. Especially when it gets along the west side of the fake lake itself. Then there'a a sweeping right-hander and things tighten up once more. Moving toward the north end of the water, the road begins to climb, twist and turn up through an area of exposed, whiteish-then-gray rock. The rounded igneous formations are typical of the Sierra Nevada. Less so are the dual 15-mph (25-km) hairpins.

The lake's dam abuts the right-hand side of the road at 34.0 mi (54.7 km). Then you're curving gently alongside the shoreline for the second and last time. At 35.8 mi (57.6 km), the south end of Huntington Lake Rd (**TE-G**) joins the DH left. Past this, there's a sense that you're left the last bits of civilization. Along with the heightened sense of remoteness comes good pavement, stretching out before you and climbing in regular, graceful curves. An opening in the forest on the right-hand side of the road gives you a glimpse of Pine Ridge to the south. Depending on the time of year, it may still have snow.

You continue to climb. The trees diminish in size and the rock beside your path and on the low surrounding hillsides gain more prominence. Again, depending on the month, you may see snow right by the roadside or farther off in the toolies. At 41.0 mi (66.0 km), if you glance back to your right, you can see Shaver Lake, unexpectedly far away, surrounded by its telltale, white-rock shoreline.

At 42.7 mi (68.7 km), the road crests Tamarack Ridge (7582 feet / 2328 m) and levels off among the sub-alpine forest and patches of snow. At 45.0 mi (72.4 km), after crossing Tamarack Creek, you begin to climb some more. The consistent, mellow curves continue. At 47.2 mi (76.0 km), they increase in number, though they remain predictable and ever so accommodating.

The heights of Kaiser Ridge and below that Huntington Lake, come into view at 49.8 mi (80.1 km). Past that on the right is the wide-open vertical of the Sierra Summit ski area. A few more curves and you're down at the east end of Huntington Lake where the DH ends at 52.3 mi (84.2 km).

TOUR NOTE: Be aware the services at Huntington Lake don't heat up until "late May."

Twisted Edges

TE-A Fresno – Prather (18.1 mi / 29.1 km) *Auberry Rd Part 1*
This high-speed scoot through low foothills has top-notch engineering and pavement, though not a whole lot of curves. There's some development and sometimes the traffic associated with it. Apparently, the shoulders are for bicycles. Which is fine as long as you don't need 'em.

TE-A ALT Millerton Rd (5.1 mi / 8.2 km)
More remote than **TE-A**, the *ALT* is bordered by pretty, rural countryside. Pavement is average but consistent and has enough curves to be somewhat interesting. Millerton seems to be the home of a band of extreme-sport gophers that dart back and forth across the road. The less proficient, flatter ones attract coyotes.

TE-B Fresno – Humphrey Station (13.3 mi / 21.4 km) *Watts Valley Rd Part 1 - Pittman Hill Rd*
More sweet curves though rolling, tree-sprinkled foothills on another route from the outskirts of Fresno. There's less traffic on Watts than on Pittman.

ROUTING OPTION: If the possibility of an STC-infested experience on the DH has got you down, this one combines with ***TE-D*** *from Humphrey Station for a great alternative up to Pine Ridge. And feel free to add* ***TE-C*** *into the mix.*

TE-B ALT Sample Rd (3.0 mi / 4.8 km)
More of the same, riding this well-paved little beauty allows you to sample other mix and match options.

TE-C Watts Valley Rd Part 2 - Burrough Valley Rd (15.0 mi / 24.1km)
This loop off **TE-B** offers not only some curves but less traffic and good overall pavement. The northern part of Burrough climbs up into the hills before turning straighter as you head south in the valley. The Watts Valley stretch is narrower but twistier as it climbs, dips and swirls through prettier, more rolling, less developed countryside.

ROUTING OPTION: Narrow, rough and not much fun Maxon Rd (there's a message in the first part of this road's name) provides a shortcut to mid- ***DH35 Piedra – Kirch Flat****.*

TE-D Tollhouse Rd (16.3 mi / 26.2 km)
Before they put that big, honking highway section of the DH up Big Sandy Bluff, this TE was the main road up to Shaver Lake. As a result, the lower part south of one-building Tollhouse is a well-paved-and-engineered funfest with great cornering opportunities. The narrower upper part corkscrews – at times tightly – up Burrough Mtn for about 5 mi (8 km) with some good views before flattening out and connecting with the DH. Which is great if you like to screw corks. If you don't, see the *ALT*.

TE-D ALT Lodge Rd (5.0 mi / 8.1 km)
Coming from the south on **TE-D**, and prefer to avoid the very tight northern part of Tollhouse up to Pine Ridge? Lodge not only has good pavement and a few curves, it will slant you across the bottom of Big Sand Valley so you can do the Big Sandy Bluff segment of the DH.

TE-E Pine Ridge – Auberry (12.6 mi / 20.3 km) *Auberry Rd Part 2*
Another STC avoidance route but it's much more than that. It has sweeter pavement by far than you'd expect after riding the other TEs around here. This, and a plethora of terrific curves through the hills on the ascent from Auberry to Meadow Lake make this an eminently worthy ride in its own right.

TE-F Dinkey Creek Rd - McKinley Grove Rd (FSR 40) - Courtright Rd (32.9 mi / 52.9 km)
Dinkey? With its length, this TE is anything but. Keep in mind you'll probably see lots of snow if you're up here in May and may not be able to ride it to the end. Dinkey Creek Rd has much better pavement and engineering than you would suppose along with a reasonable number of moderate curves and very little traffic. McKinley Grove (FSR 40) has tighter curves through higher, more rugged country. Courtright Rd takes you to Courtwright Res, a typical California fake lake, apparently good for fishing (as supposedly is nearby Wishon Res.) We did see a deer on this TE, although it wasn't acting in a threatening manner – other than by merely existing near a motorcycle road, of course.

NAVIGATION: Make sure to turn right onto McKinley at 11.9 mi (19.2 km) or you'll dead end in Dinkey Creek.

TOUR NOTE: There is a great swimming hole at the Dinkey Creek NF CG.

TE-G Huntington Lake Rd (15.4 mi / 24.8 km)
Hate to come back the same way you went? That's what this option is all about. The variety here kind of mimics that of the DH. Above the north side and west end of Huntington Lake, it runs quietly through the woods. From the west end of the lake, it goat paths down into the deep, scenic valley of Big Creek, which runs off the even bigger gorge of the San Joaquin River valley. There are some spectacular views here; just be careful not to wander off the road while looking. After the no-services village, it's a more relaxed but still tight concert through the forest between Tamarack Mtn and Ely Mtn to the east, and Musick Mtn to the west back to Hwy 168 at Shaver Lake.

TE-H Stump Springs Rd (FSR 5) (18.5 mi / 29.8 km)
If you like remoteness, decent pavement and lots of easy-to-manage curves, this offshoot from **TE-G** running north along the eastern heights of the San Joaquin Valley gorge may be for you. It occasionally narrows and can be littered with sand, pinecones and needles but it's very predictable. Of course, you gotta ride **TE-G** to get to it. Hint: access is easier from **TE-G**'s southern end.

TOUR NOTE: There may be more remote campgrounds in California than the West Kaiser BCG – situated on a large flat area by a burbling creek – but not many of them can be reached this easily by street bike.

ROUTING OPTION: Maxburners may be tempted to continue on the gravel past the campground. At least they may after the snow's gone, though the mad bastards probably aren't afraid of a couple of feet of that either. The road will hook up with Kaiser Pass Rd and allows you to entirely circumnavigate the heart of the Kaiser Wilderness back to Huntington Lake.

RIDER'S LOG: **DATE RIDDEN:** **YOUR RATING: /10**

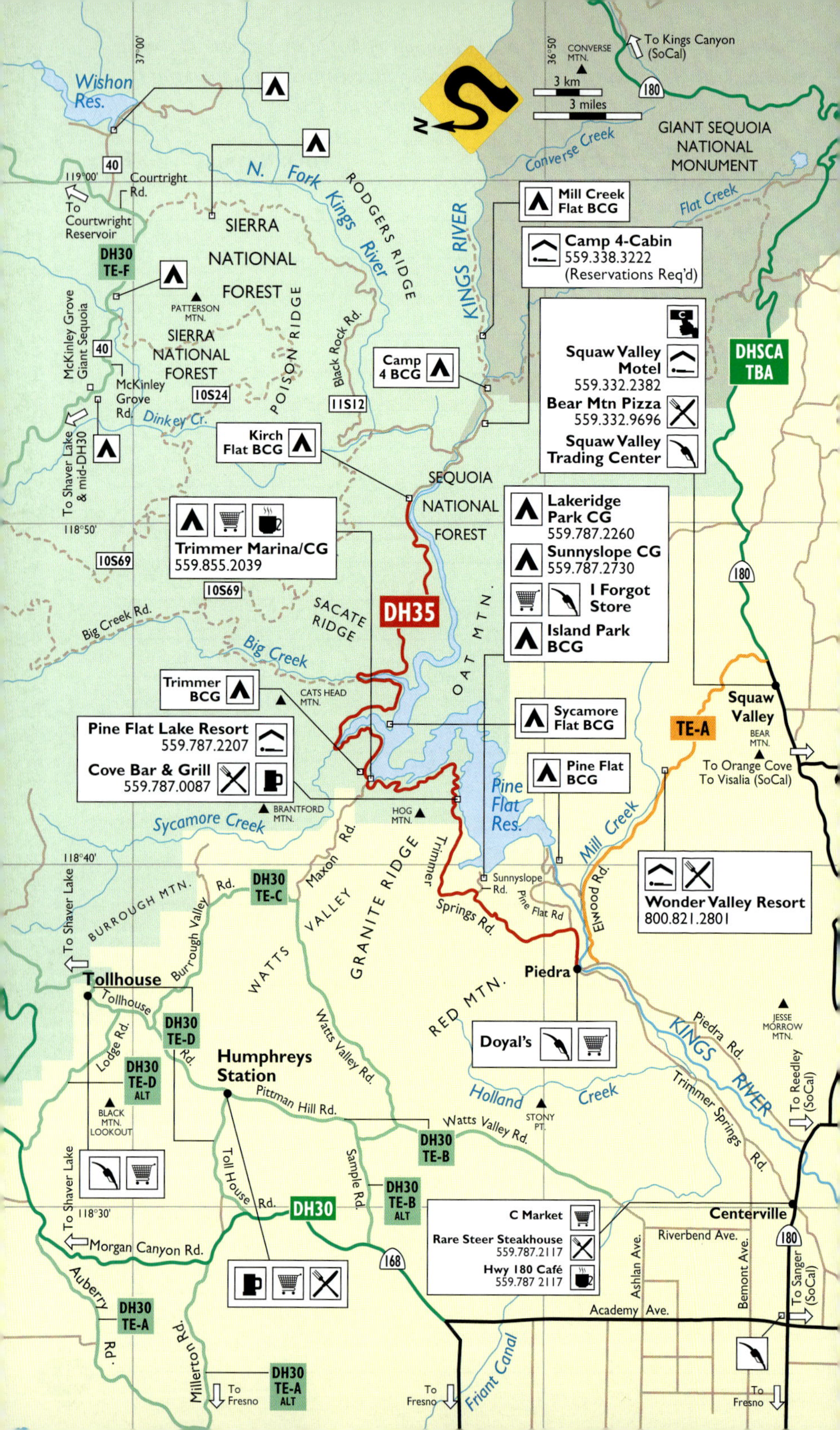

Wishon Res.
To Kings Canyon (SoCal)
CONVERSE MTN.
3 km
3 miles
GIANT SEQUOIA NATIONAL MONUMENT
Converse Creek
Flat Creek
N. Fork Kings River
RODGERS RIDGE
KINGS RIVER
Courtright Rd.
To Courtwright Reservoir
SIERRA NATIONAL FOREST
Mill Creek Flat BCG
Camp 4-Cabin
559.338.3222
(Reservations Req'd)
DH30 TE-F
PATTERSON MTN.
POISON RIDGE
Black Rock Rd.
McKinley Grove Giant Sequoia
McKinley Grove Rd.
10S24
11S12
Camp 4 BCG
Squaw Valley Motel
559.332.2382
Bear Mtn Pizza
559.332.9696
Squaw Valley Trading Center
DHSCA TBA
Dinkey Cr.
To Shaver Lake & mid-DH30
Kirch Flat BCG
SEQUOIA NATIONAL FOREST
Trimmer Marina/CG
559.855.2039
10S69
Lakeridge Park CG
559.787.2260
Sunnyslope CG
559.787.2730
I Forgot Store
Island Park BCG
DH35
SACATE RIDGE
OAT MTN.
Big Creek Rd.
Big Creek
Trimmer BCG
CATS HEAD MTN.
Squaw Valley
BEAR MTN.
TE-A
To Orange Cove
To Visalia (SoCal)
Sycamore Flat BCG
Pine Flat Lake Resort
559.787.2207
Cove Bar & Grill
559.787.0087
Pine Flat BCG
Pine Flat Res.
BRANTFORD MTN.
HOG MTN.
Sycamore Creek
Mill Creek
Maxon Rd.
GRANITE RIDGE
Trimmer Springs Rd.
Sunnyslope Rd.
Pine Flat Rd
Elwood Rd.
Wonder Valley Resort
800.821.2801
To Shaver Lake
BURROUGH MTN. Rd.
DH30 TE-C
VALLEY
WATTS
Burrough Valley
Tollhouse
Tollhouse Rd.
Piedra
RED MTN.
Lodge Rd.
DH30 TE-D
Watts Valley Rd.
Doyal's
Piedra Rd.
KINGS RIVER
JESSE MORROW MTN.
DH30 TE-D ALT
Humphreys Station
Pittman Hill Rd.
Holland Creek
STONY PT.
Trimmer Springs Rd.
To Reedley (SoCal)
BLACK MTN. LOOKOUT
Watts Valley Rd.
DH30 TE-B
Toll House Rd.
Sample Rd.
DH30 TE-B ALT
DH30
C Market
Rare Steer Steakhouse
559.787.2117
Hwy 180 Café
559.787 2117
Centerville
Riverbend Ave.
To Shaver Lake
Morgan Canyon Rd.
Auberry Rd.
DH30 TE-A
Ashlan Ave.
Bemont Ave.
Academy Ave.
To Sanger (SoCal)
Millerton Rd.
To Fresno
DH30 TE-A ALT
To Fresno
Friant Canal
To Fresno

DH35 Piedra (Fresno) – Kirch Flat

Trimmer Springs Road

Distance:	30.8 mi / 49.6 km	Traffic:	Light

At a Glance

Come on baby let's do the twist

TIRES	
Twistiness	30.0/ 30
Pavement	11.3/ 20
Engineering	3.3/ 10
Remoteness	7.2/ 10
Scenery	11.5/ 15
Character	7.5/ 15
Total	70.8

The King of the Twist lost 30 pounds over three weeks demonstrating his new dance. We're not suggesting you'll lose any weight, but if you like doin' the two-wheeled twist, this DH is the greatest thing to hit Northern California since the Mosquito (DH16). Trimmer Springs Rd is no one hit wonder either. For sure, it's the never-ending melody of S-turns that hooks you. But dig that three-part scenic harmony. Panoramic views over Pine Flat Lake to mountains in the south and east resonate for much of the ride as the road edges high along steep, grass and granite-sided ridges, coming down to water level only in the canyon at the very end. The mixed Pavement won't win any Grammys, but the Remoteness of this gravel-outer makes it an instant classic, even with the distortion of pleasure boats on the reservoir and power lines at the end. So as you're rockin' and rollin' lookin' out for the rollin' rocks, just remember who thought of it first. Take it away, Chubby…

Twist baby twist
Take your throttle in your hand
And go like this

Access

From Fresno

Via Hwy 180 and Trimmer Springs Rd

Head east on Hwy 180 to Centerville. Turn north on the quiet Trimmer Springs Rd. This road is east of the Centerville's sparse service strip and west of the Kings River. When you reach Belmont Ave, turn right (Belmont Ave becomes Trimmer Springs Rd at this point) and ride through the developed farmland and then along the river. You'll reach the mapdot of Piedra at 9.5 mi (15.3 km). You're on the road.

Coming in on DH30 Lakeshore – Fresno (Hwy 168)

DH30 ends at Academy Ave. Turn south on it for about 8 mi (13 km) to Belmont Ave. Go east on Belmont for about 5 mi (8 km) and you'll reach

Trimmer Springs Rd. Turn left and ride the 7.4 mi (11.9 km) to Piedra. Once past it, you're on the road.

Coming in on DH30TE-B Humphrey Station – Fresno (Watts Valley Rd - Pittman Hill Rd)
At the Fresno end of Watts Valley Rd, turn south on Riverbend Ave for a few miles and then go east on Belmont for another few miles to reach Trimmer Springs Rd. Turn left and ride the 7.4 mi (11.9 km) to Piedra. Once past it, you're on the road.

From Squaw Valley
Via TE-A Elwood Rd
At the end of Elwood Rd, turn right on Piedra Rd and right again on Trimmer Springs. You're on the road.

On The Road

TOUR NOTE: If you've come from Fresno, you might be thinking these guys at Destination Highways are little confused. After all, those were some rockin' S-curves along the Kings River west of Piedra. And yet according to them, the DH starts when Trimmer Springs Rd leaves the river and straightens out. Got news for you – considering the number and quality of curves coming up, those weren't even worth counting.

For a road with a top Twistiness rating, corners are pretty rare in the flat, early going out of Piedra. But that's not going to last long. Look ahead and you'll see the oak-mottled, brown-grass hillsides on either side heighten and converge in the near distance. It's actually rather picturesque, but it's not what you came for.

The road runs along a dry creek bed. It's been dry so long, the only evidence of running water is a shallow depression, then a bridge at 2.5 mi (4.0 km). The road crosses the non-creek and starts to rise. The left roadside drops off, a little at first and then more steeply, giving birth to a tight sweeper at 3.5 mi (5.6 km). It esses handily into another. Then more S-curves grapple up the steepening slope. Stuck behind a boat-hauling pylon on its way to the lake? Well, despite the blind corners, the yellow line's still dotted, doubling up only as you pass the junction with Sunnyslope Rd at 4.6 mi (7.4 km).

The terrain flattens, providing room for some light development. But at 6.0 mi (9.7 km), you descend through some sparse trees, curving and sweeping as you go. At 7.1 mi (11.4 km), the terrain to left shifts upward, the road feints right and there's your first view over the Pine Flat Reservoir to the pointed, tree-covered hills that line its southern shore.

This looks good. The road stays high, winding above the water. And though you see signs for services and accommodation on side roads dropping off to the right, buildings themselves largely remain invisible in the increasingly arid landscape. The contrast between the aqua blue and the barren grass and rock slope is startling. So is the contrast between the great pavement and the rough cattleguards.

S-curve after s-curve, the DH twists relentlessly. You sense trouble at 9.8 mi (15.8 km) when the road pulls away from the lake. But it's back almost immediately, essing on the high, dry bank above the water in long, drawn-out curves that are so predictable the more blind left-handers don't really slow you down. Unlike those dang cattleguards.

The perspectives on the lake change as you curl along its shore. There's a particularly intricate scene at 12.9 mi (20.8 km) where the waterway narrows and the toe of Oat Mtn threatens to step across it. Clumps of grass, trees and individual rocks detail the landscape on the other side. The nothingtown of Trimmer is around the corner at 23.1 mi (13.6 km).

*ROUTING OPTION: Just past Trimmer is a turnoff marked to Tollhouse and Shaver Lake. For those who aren't into reversing course all the way back to Piedra but want to stay on pavement, this narrow, bumpy connection will take you to mid-**DH30 Fresno – Lakeshore**.*

The road's a touch straighter beyond Trimmer's short speed zone. Perhaps "straighter" isn't quite the word given that the road continues to curve, now on a southwest tack. It's just that you've come to expect you'll be constantly down on one knee or the other. Maybe a touch more throttle will do it….

But not too much. At 15.6 mi (25.1 km), the DH shifts north to follow Sycamore Creek through a steep-sided canyon. With a line of trees to the right, you lose sight of the water. But no matter, you should be watching the road anyway. At 17.3 mi (27.8 km), you cross a high bridge over what should be a creek. But hang on, you can't see any water. No wonder – there isn't any.

Well, it's official. The pavement is definitely getting rougher. And if experience is any guide, gravel-outers like this generally don't get better once they get worse. Scenery's not the greatest in this section either, since trees continue to obscure whatever you would see if they weren't there. At least there's no traffic. Unless you count the ground squirrels darting across the road.

At 19.7 mi (31.7 km), the great lake vistas come back but the pavement's still struggling. The road seems to be narrowing a bit as well, tracing that finger of the lake that becomes Big Creek. At 21.8 mi (35.1 km), you bridge the creek/lake and turn sharply south along the long, thin bay. The curves take on a sweepier tone as the road esses along the steep, grass and rock-covered slope of Sacate Ridge. There's some cool detail in the ridge. Like the fractured, volcanic rock face at 23.1 mi (37.2 km).

*ROUTING NOTE: Rather than cross the creek, maxburners can head up the gravel Big Creek Rd to make connections with the top end of **DH30TE-D Tollhouse Rd** or a couple of points along **DH30TE-F Dinkey Creek Rd - McKinley Grove Rd - Courtright Rd.***

Turning due east again, you gain more altitude. The road stretches out and at 23.6 mi (38.0 km), you actually ride a full 100 feet (30 m) without curving. This anomaly barely registers before the road resumes its essing pattern. Still the DH has definitely lost some of its intensity. The curves aren't quite as tight and the side slope is much gentler. Even though you're high up, you're more inland from the water. Trees find room to grow on the right and you often lose the lake. In consolation, it's the most remote part of the ride – just you, the road and the constellation of mountains and ridges across the sky.

At 26.5 mi (42.6 km), a descent begins with a couple of short straightaways. Pitching downward through a slide area, you're able to see more and more of the mottled mountains both to the east and on the south side of the river-width eastern tip of the reservoir. What should be a great scenic stretch is tarnished, however, by the thick power lines and towers that hopscotch up out of the canyon and over the road. But you'll be glad you came to play when you hit the piece of smooth, just-out-of-the-box pavement at 28.2 mi (45.4 km).

The DH is essing tight and steep now. As the terrain sharpens, the grass and trees on the left-side slope erode at times to bare slate and granite. The scenery gets a further shot in the arm when the river below comes into view at 29.7 mi (47.8 km). Could do without the power lines and station, but they're at your back by 30.2 mi (48.6 km), leaving a picture-perfect runout to the DH's terminus, Kirch Flat BCG and picnic area, at 30.8 mi (49.6 km).

TOUR NOTE: If you're the planning type, and you've got your own sleeping bags or linen, the otherwise furbished Camp 4 Cabin (full kitchen, bathroom, electricity and appliances) is located just a stone's throw beyond the campground. Immediately past Kirch Flat, you will cross the Kings River bridge, putting you on the south side of the Kings River. You will be on FSR 12S01. Approximately 1.0 mi (1.6 km) further, when the pavement turns to dirt, don't cross the Bailey Bridge back over the river but stay on the south side. The cabin is 0.7 mi (1.1 km) down the road. To reserve: 559.338.3222.

ROUTING OPTIONS: If you're not a gravelphobe, you can turn this DH into a loop either by heading south on FSR 12S01 to Hwy 180 or crossing the Bailey Bridge back to the north side of the river and following the steep, gravel Black Rock Rd (FSR 11S12) up to the paved eastern end of ***DH30TE-F*** *and on to Shaver Lake (mid-**DH30 Fresno – Lakeshore**. If you go this way, be sure to stop at McKinley Grove to check out the giant Sequoias.*

Twisted Edges

TE-A Elwood Rd (11.9 mi / 19.1 km)

It's 2100 miles to Chicago, we've got a full tank of gas, half a pack of cigarettes, smooth, shoulderless pavement winding north of Wonder Valley, rough, even narrower pavement tightly twisting south, varied, rolling grass and treed terrain throughout, barely any development blues, it's dark and we're wearing sunglasses. Hit it.

RIDER'S LOG: **DATE RIDDEN:** **YOUR RATING:** /10

How does this book work again? RTFM. "What is Destination Highways Northern California?" and "How to Use Our Maps" appear at the front of the book.

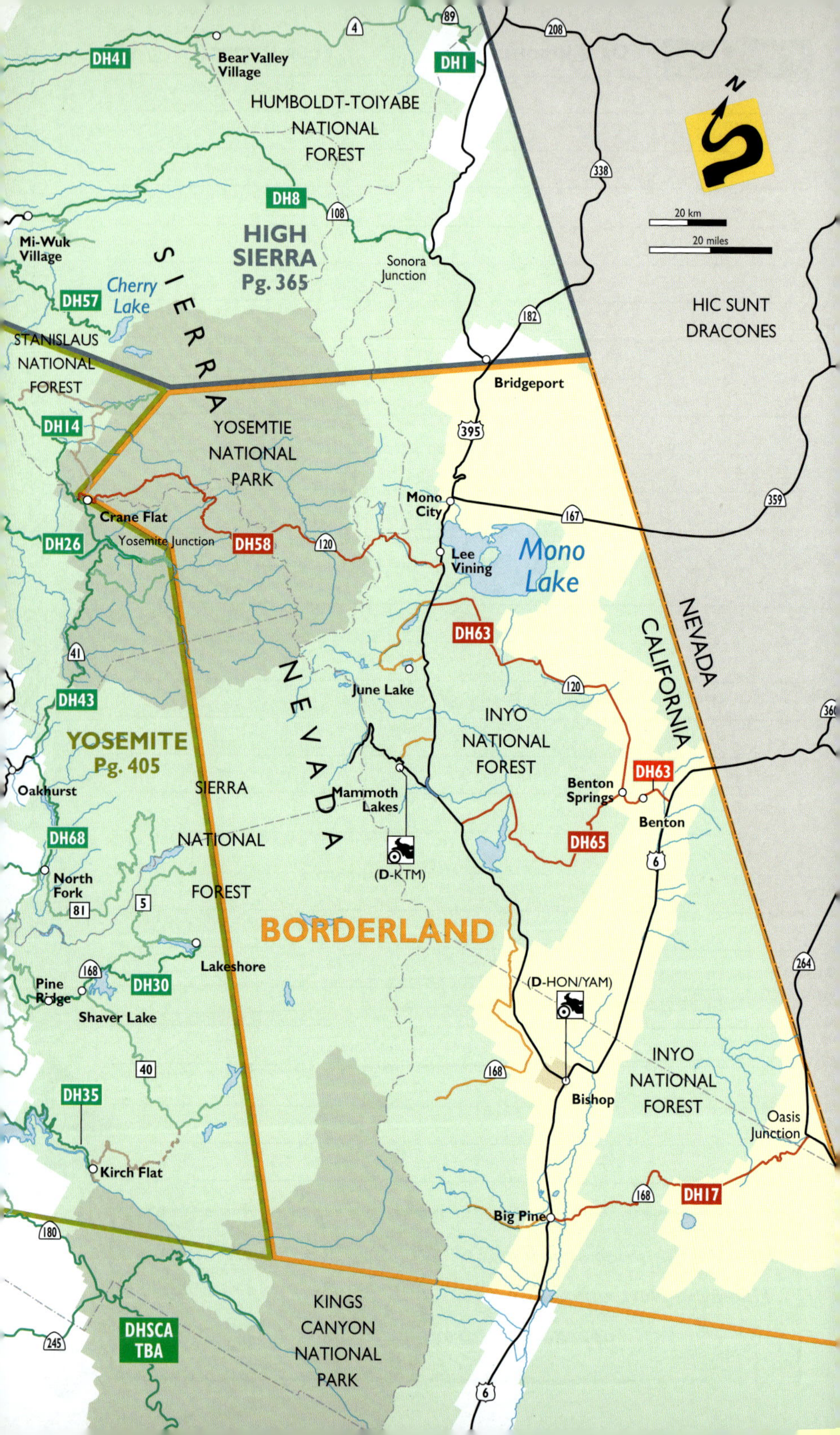

Bear Valley Village
HUMBOLDT-TOIYABE NATIONAL FOREST
DH41
DH1
DH8
HIGH SIERRA Pg. 365
Mi-Wuk Village
Cherry Lake
DH57
Sonora Junction
SIERRA
STANISLAUS NATIONAL FOREST
HIC SUNT DRACONES
20 km
20 miles
Bridgeport
DH14
YOSEMTIE NATIONAL PARK
Mono City
Crane Flat
Yosemite Junction
DH58
DH26
Lee Vining
Mono Lake
DH63
NEVADA
CALIFORNIA
June Lake
INYO NATIONAL FOREST
DH43
YOSEMITE Pg. 405
Oakhurst
SIERRA NATIONAL FOREST
Mammoth Lakes
Benton Springs
Benton
DH65
DH68
North Fork
(D-KTM)
BORDERLAND
Lakeshore
Pine Ridge
DH30
Shaver Lake
(D-HON/YAM)
Bishop
DH35
Oasis Junction
Kirch Flat
DH17
Big Pine
KINGS CANYON NATIONAL PARK
DHSCA TBA

Borderland

RANK DH#/74	TIRES Total/100	DESTINATION HIGHWAY	PAGE
DH58	62.4	Crane Flat – Lee Vining 58.8 mi / 94.6 km	467
DH63	61.4	Lee Vining – Benton 45.6 mi / 73.4 km	473
DH65	60.6	Benton Crossing Road 30.6 mi / 49.2 km	479
DH17	78.2	Big Pine – Oasis Jct 38.1 mi / 61.3 km	485

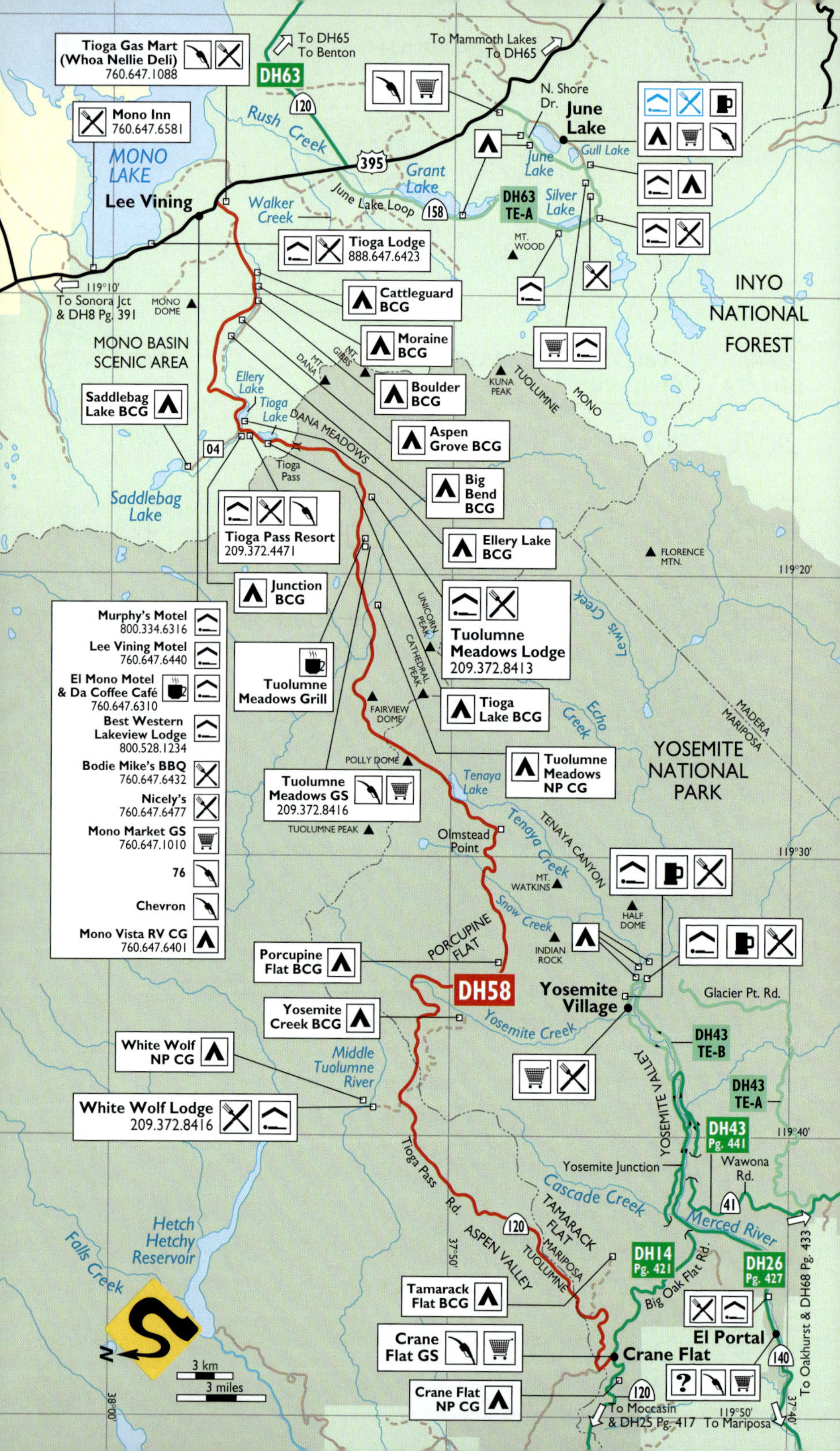
Tioga Gas Mart
(Whoa Nellie Deli)
760.647.1088
Mono Inn
760.647.6581
MONO LAKE
Lee Vining
To DH65
To Benton
DH63
120
Rush Creek
395
To Mammoth Lakes
To DH65
N. Shore Dr.
June Lake
Gull Lake
June Lake
Grant Lake
June Lake Loop
158
DH63 TE-A
Silver Lake
Walker Creek
MT. WOOD
Tioga Lodge
888.647.6423
119°10'
To Sonora Jct
& DH8 Pg. 391
MONO DOME
Cattleguard BCG
Moraine BCG
MONO BASIN SCENIC AREA
INYO NATIONAL FOREST
MT. GIBBS
MT. DANA
Boulder BCG
KUNA PEAK
TUOLUMNE
MONO
Ellery Lake
Tioga Lake
Saddlebag Lake BCG
Aspen Grove BCG
DANA MEADOWS
04
Tioga Pass
Big Bend BCG
Saddlebag Lake
Tioga Pass Resort
209.372.4471
Ellery Lake BCG
FLORENCE MTN.
119°20'
Junction BCG
Murphy's Motel
800.334.6316
Lee Vining Motel
760.647.6440
El Mono Motel
& Da Coffee Café
760.647.6310
Best Western
Lakeview Lodge
800.528.1234
Bodie Mike's BBQ
760.647.6432
Nicely's
760.647.6477
Mono Market GS
760.647.1010
76
Chevron
Mono Vista RV CG
760.647.6401
Tuolumne Meadows Grill
UNICORN PEAK
CATHEDRAL PEAK
Tuolumne Meadows Lodge
209.372.8413
Lewis Creek
Tioga Lake BCG
FAIRVIEW DOME
Echo Creek
MADERA
MARIPOSA
YOSEMITE NATIONAL PARK
POLLY DOME
Tuolumne Meadows NP CG
Tuolumne Meadows GS
209.372.8416
Tenaya Lake
TUOLUMNE PEAK
Olmstead Point
TENAYA CANYON
119°30'
Tenaya Creek
MT. WATKINS
HALF DOME
Snow Creek
INDIAN ROCK
PORCUPINE FLAT
Porcupine Flat BCG
DH58
Yosemite Village
Glacier Pt. Rd.
Yosemite Creek BCG
Yosemite Creek
DH43 TE-B
White Wolf NP CG
Middle Tuolumne River
DH43 TE-A
YOSEMITE VALLEY
White Wolf Lodge
209.372.8416
DH43 Pg. 441
119°40'
Wawona Rd.
Yosemite Junction
Tioga Pass Rd.
Cascade Creek
41
Merced River
Hetch Hetchy Reservoir
120
TAMARACK FLAT
MARIPOSA
TUOLUMNE
ASPEN VALLEY
37°50'
DH14 Pg. 421
Big Oak Flat Rd.
DH26 Pg. 427
To Oakhurst & DH68 Pg. 433
Falls Creek
Tamarack Flat BCG
El Portal
Crane Flat GS
Crane Flat
140
N
3 km
3 miles
Crane Flat NP CG
120
To Moccasin
& DH25 Pg. 417
119°50'
To Mariposa
37°40'
38°00'

DH58 CRANE FLAT – LEE VINING

Tioga Pass Road (Hwy 120)

DISTANCE:	58.8 mi / 94.6 km	TRAFFIC:	Can Be Heavy

AT A GLANCE

TIRES	
Twistiness	10.6/ 30
Pavement	12.6/ 20
Engineering	6.3/10
Remoteness	7.6/10
Scenery	12.1/15
Character	13.2/15
TOTAL	62.4

At 9945 ft (3030 m), Tioga Pass is California's highest paved pass, so it's no surprise that the DH that traverses through the heart of the Sierra Nevada rates so highly for Scenery. Striking rock formations and airy pine forests prevail for the often-straight climb from Crane Flat to Tioga Pass where domes, horned peaks, granite monoliths and ridges of rocky debris crafted by the last ice age circle its vast meadows. You'd think these grand spectacles would create a sense of high Remoteness. It would, but for the pylon-driving multitudes picnicking amid the Indian paintbrush and cinquefoil. There are more wonders after you leave the populated meadows, ride along a small lake chain and enter one of the road's few good sections of sweepers. Here, the highway drops steeply through an enormous, pure rock gorge down into the dry sagelands of the Mono Basin. While it may seem odd that such dramatic terrain can produce a road that scores so dismally for Twistiness, sometimes you have to give up a few curves to experience this kind of natural beauty. Guess that's why they call it sport-*touring*.

ACCESS

From mid-DH14 Moccasin – Yosemite Jct

Tioga Pass Rd turns off this route 40.5 mi (65.2 km) from Moccasin and 9.6 mi (15.4 km) from Yosemite Jct.

From Lee Vining

Via Hwy 395

Go south on Hwy 395 about a quarter mile (0.4 km) and turn west on Hwy 120. You're on the road.

Coming in on DH63 Benton – Lee Vining (Hwy 120)

When you reach Hwy 395, go north about 5.0 mi (8.0 km) and turn west on the continuation of Hwy 120. You're on the road.

ON THE ROAD

Leaving the junction with **DH14 Moccasin – Yosemite Jct** and stealing the Hwy 120 designation, the DH curves gingerly through a short 25-mph

(40-kmh) zone of buildings and parking lots among the trees. At 0.8 mi (1.3 km), the limit increases to 35 mph (55 kmh), the development decreases to nothing and the DH starts winding steadily along a slope. See that rugged landscape of carved boulders, sloping granite and tall pines? Get used to it.

The road straightens at 3.3 mi (5.3 km) as it passes through the strewn boulders and tall, spaced pines of Tamarack Flat. The burnt red of diseased firs add an ironic spark of color to the grey and green. But it's the feeling of altitude that's really striking. Look to the northwest and you'll notice that the road is already higher than the mountains across the Aspen Valley.

The right roadside slope rises and the blackened burn of Big Oak Flat disappears at 6.2 mi (10.0 km). Towering, thick-trunked lodgepole pines shoot straight up beside the road, showing off the rich texture of their reddish, contoured bark. A short bridge over the south fork of the Tuolumne River gives another flash of view to the left over the Aspen. Then at 8.0 mi (12.9 km), there's a view again to the left, albeit more closed in this time, across a gorge to a round-domed rockface. A 45-mph (70-kmh) sign appears amid the nature at 8.3 mi (13.4 km).

The sign's followed by the first flurry of curves you've seen in a while. This is invariably where you'll catch up to the RV with mountain bikes hanging off the back. It's also where the landscape changes. The trees thin out as they try to dig their roots into what looks like solid granite. At 9.7 mi (15.6 km), you see the most dramatic example of this as a broad, flat surface of striped rock angles gently upward to the left. Boulders that look as if they've rolled down gather at the bottom. If Mother Nature could just time it right, maybe she could bowl down a rock and take out that number seven pin of an RV.

A dotted yellow line comes at 10.2 mi (16.4 km), coinciding with another brief section where you're back among the close-in trees. But overall it's the granite that dominates the scene. A sign at 11.5 mi (18.5 km) tells you to "Watch for Rocks". You've been watching rocks for the last ten miles. It's not like there's been a lot of curves to look at.

At 12.2 mi (19.6 km), you hit the 8000 ft (2438 m) level. Almost immediately, you lose a little of that altitude on a straightaway that drops down to a little alpine lake at 13.5 mi (21.7 km). Tongues of rock flick out of a broad boulderscape. Feel like hanging out around here for a day or two? The turnoff to the rustic White Wolf Lodge is at 14.4 mi (23.2 km).

All right, enough already. The granite and tall pine forest held your attention for awhile. And the first real sight of sweeping, glaciated Sierra Nevada slopes visible from 15.9 mi (25.6 km) is worthy of note. But a motorcycle road needs a different kind of sweeping as well, you know.

As if on cue, the pitch of the descent steepens and there's a hint of curvitude beginning at 17.5 mi (28.2 km). At 17.8 mi (28.6 km), a tidbit of shoulder widens into a nice viewpoint. Flat, angling slabs of rock spread away from the road and open up more panoramic, rocky mountain views. The curves aren't too tight but they're definitely there. As always, how far you have to lean is a function of how fast you're traveling.

You cross Yosemite Creek at 19.7 mi (31.7 km), site of a picnic ground and trailhead. Actually, you don't need to stop to relax as the DH straightens out for titch before launching into a series of sweepers at 21.8 mi (35.1 km). They take you back into a flatter, more forested section. "Porcupine Flat" says the sign. Too bad – where there's a flat, there's inevitably a straightaway.

The flat ends at 25.3 mi (40.7 km) when the rugged terrain returns. But the straight continues through chunks of granite that litter the roadside, dotted by patches of trees and shadowed by smallish domes. A few curves and then a sweeper at 27.8 mi (44.7 km) takes you into a vast bowl, the southern side of which is Mt. Watkins, a sheer-sided granite monolith with a distinctive swirling pattern. The immediate left side of the road has its attractions as well. Look for the rockface at 28.8 mi (46.3 km) that resembles a frozen granite waterfall.

You see no soil here. This now sub-alpine landscape is nothing but rock and a few struggling trees. Fields of granite tilt up slightly on the left. Small knobs rise against the backdrop as if in a painting. But if you really want to see a masterpiece, get off the bike at Olmstead Point at 29.3 mi (47.1 km) and stroll a quarter mile for a look down Tenaya Canyon at Half Dome, the world-famous granite monolith rising nearly a mile above Yosemite Valley's floor. Or just keep riding.

The incredible, top-of-the-world feeling continues. Tenaya Lake fills the shallow valley on the right. At 31.6 mi (50.8 km), you run along the lake for a spell. Pylons pile up in the parking lots and along the roadside so their occupants can picnic and sunbathe on the lake's easy-access mile long sandy beach. You don't want to get sand in your chain now. Shaft drive? Okay, fine.

The scenery is truly spectacular. And it gets even more impressive as you leave the lake and enter another granitescape, this one dominated by Cathedral Peak and the conical Fairview Dome. The boulder-strewn terrain is punctuated by the deep green of a large alpine meadow on the right. Almost makes you forget there are no curves. Almost.

You begin a descent at 34.8 mi (56.0 km). There's a stint in the trees where you lose much of the landscape's effect, but the drama resumes at 37.1 mi (59.7 km), where Unicorn Peak marks the entrance to Tuolumne Meadows. This enormous field of deep green spreads out beside the DH and into the distance. Anyone bring a frisbee?

Tuolumne Meadows is a beautiful place. Trouble is, a lot of people know it. The wide expanse of green ringed by granite foothills is dotted with hikers and picknickers. The roadside is filled with parked pylons. The gas station, grill and visitors center are handy. Unlike the 25-mph (35-kmh) speed zone.

The speed zone goes on and on, finally ending at 39.8 mi (64.0 km) at the foot of Lembert Dome. Then you're back up to speed and into an airy, dwarfed pine forest on smoother, but barely bending pavement. "Elevation 9000 Feet" (2743 m) says the sign at 41.3 mi (66.5 km). Another thousand feet to go.

The ensuing trip through the trees is interrupted by a nice view of the Tuolumne River. Then at 43.6 mi (70.2 km), you enter Dana Meadows, a green blanket spreading out below Mts Dana and Gibbs. These mountains are a study in contrast with one a dry heap of crumbling moraine and the other colorful and vibrant with trees climbing its flanks. Yes, despite the lack of curves, you gotta love riding at this altitude. There's just something about the crisp mountain air. Even if it's sometimes filtered through the exhaust pipe of the pylon in front of you.

There's a brief spell in the trees and then an even grander part of the meadows opens up. Granite peaks with tiny pockets of snow rise behind. Ahead, a stop sign at 46.5 mi (74.8 km) marks the exit gate of Yosemite and your entrance into the Inyo National Forest. Where the scenery's "inyo face".

It doesn't take long for Inyo to pick up the scenery where Yosemite left off. Tioga Lake lies right of the road, nestled beneath a red cliff at its far end, a thick band of trees on its east side and a little alpine meadow beside the shore nearest to you. Past the historic Tioga Pass Resort and turnoff for Saddlebag Lake at 49.0 mi (78.8 km), a gigantic, yet minutely detailed cliff face rises behind another alpine lake, Ellery. Little glaciers at the top of the cliff fill the gaps between enormous rods of vertical rock. It is magnificent.

And there's more. The right roadside steepens to rockface as you ride past the far end of Ellery Lake. You sweep around a corner and…wow, the bottom drops out of the terrain. Where there was a roadside lake a moment ago, there is now a deep, wide gorge cut through the landscape of sharp, metallic rock. It's almost asteroid like, with the only vegetation being a few short, thick-trunked oaks to the left and some trickles of green on the higher slopes ahead and across the gorge.

The road tumbles into the view, hairpinning along a slope of sliding rock, then steadily sweeping its way steeply down out of the alpine into more temperate climes. The scene is so awe-inspiring, it may not occur to you that you're in the midst of some of the best corners on the entire road. It certainly doesn't seem to have occurred to the crawling, pullout-oblivious pylons.

The drop in elevation is rapid. Your temperature rounds up almost as fast as your tach as you drop pass the elevation milestones and settle toward the bottom of the gorge. You reach 8000 feet (2438 m) at 53.7 mi

(86.4 km) and are met with a stretch of fresher pavement. By 55.3 mi (89.0 km), the dramatic rockscape is gone and you're riding straight and level on a wide-shouldered slab of asphalt across a shallow bowl of sage.

This is the Mono Basin Scenic Area. Frankly, after what you've just witnessed, it seems a little monotonous. That impression changes somewhat at 57.9 mi (93.2 km) when you get your first view of the turquoise, green, brown and red coloration of Mono Lake and its surrounding environs. The DH ends at 58.8 mi (94.6 km) where it junctions with Hwy 395, a quarter mile (0.4 km) south of Lee Vining.

RIDER'S LOG: **DATE RIDDEN:** **YOUR RATING: /10**

Find more information about camping in Northern California, including how to make a reservation, in the "Touring Northern California – What You Should Know" section at the front of the book.

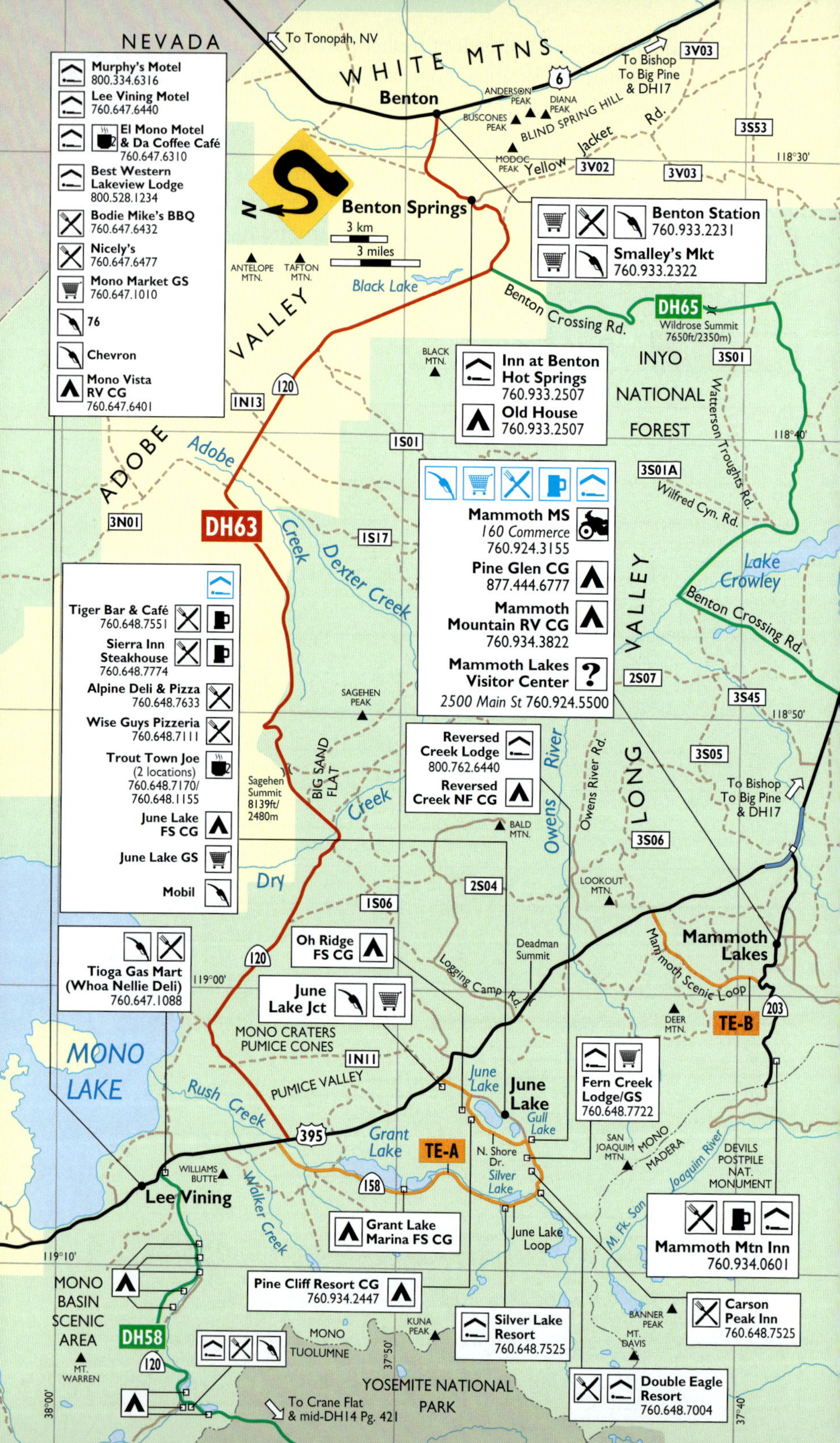

NEVADA
To Tonopah, NV
WHITE MTNS.
To Bishop
To Big Pine
& DH17
3V03
6
Benton
ANDERSON PEAK
DIANA PEAK
BUSCONES PEAK
MODOC PEAK
BLIND SPRING HILL Rd.
Yellow Jacket
3V02
3V03
3S53
118°30'
Murphy's Motel
800.334.6316
Lee Vining Motel
760.647.6440
El Mono Motel
& Da Coffee Café
760.647.6310
Best Western
Lakeview Lodge
800.528.1234
Bodie Mike's BBQ
760.647.6432
Nicely's
760.647.6477
Mono Market GS
760.647.1010
76
Chevron
Mono Vista
RV CG
760.647.6401
N
Benton Springs
3 km
3 miles
ANTELOPE MTN.
TAFTON MTN.
Black Lake
Benton Station
760.933.2231
Smalley's Mkt
760.933.2322
Benton Crossing Rd.
DH65
Wildrose Summit
7650ft/2350m)
VALLEY
BLACK MTN.
Inn at Benton
Hot Springs
760.933.2507
Old House
760.933.2507
INYO
NATIONAL
FOREST
3S01
Watterson Troughs Rd.
118°40'
120
1N13
1S01
ADOBE
Adobe
3N01
DH63
Creek
Dexter Creek
1S17
3S01A
Wilfred Cyn. Rd.
Mammoth MS
160 Commerce
760.924.3155
Pine Glen CG
877.444.6777
Mammoth
Mountain RV CG
760.934.3822
Mammoth Lakes
Visitor Center
2500 Main St 760.924.5500
Lake
Crowley
Benton Crossing Rd.
VALLEY
2S07
3S45
118°50'
Tiger Bar & Café
760.648.7551
Sierra Inn
Steakhouse
760.648.7774
Alpine Deli & Pizza
760.648.7633
Wise Guys Pizzeria
760.648.7111
Trout Town Joe
(2 locations)
760.648.7170/
760.648.1155
June Lake
FS CG
June Lake GS
Mobil
SAGEHEN PEAK
Sagehen
Summit
8139ft/
2480m
BIG SAND FLAT
Creek
Reversed
Creek Lodge
800.762.6440
Reversed
Creek NF CG
River
Owens
Owens River Rd.
LONG
3S05
To Bishop
To Big Pine
& DH17
BALD MTN.
3S06
Dry
2S04
1S06
LOOKOUT MTN.
Tioga Gas Mart
(Whoa Nellie Deli)
760.647.1088
120
Oh Ridge
FS CG
Deadman
Summit
Logging Camp Rd.
Mammoth
Lakes
Mammoth Scenic Loop
119°00'
June
Lake Jct
MONO CRATERS
PUMICE CONES
DEER MTN.
TE-B
203
1N11
MONO
LAKE
PUMICE VALLEY
Rush Creek
June
Lake
June
Lake
Gull
Lake
Fern Creek
Lodge/GS
760.648.7722
395
Grant
Lake
TE-A
N. Shore
Dr.
Silver
Lake
SAN JOAQUIN MTN.
MONO
MADERA
Joaquin River
DEVILS
POSTPILE
NAT.
MONUMENT
WILLIAMS BUTTE
Lee Vining
Walker Creek
158
Grant Lake
Marina FS CG
June Lake
Loop
M. Fk. San
Mammoth Mtn Inn
760.934.0601
119°10'
MONO
BASIN
SCENIC
AREA
Pine Cliff Resort CG
760.934.2447
BANNER PEAK
Carson
Peak Inn
760.648.7525
DH58
MONO
TUOLUMNE
KUNA PEAK
Silver Lake
Resort
760.648.7525
MT. DAVIS
120
MT. WARREN
37°50'
YOSEMITE NATIONAL
PARK
Double Eagle
Resort
760.648.7004
38°00'
To Crane Flat
& mid-DH14 Pg. 421
37°40'

DH63 LEE VINING – BENTON

Highway 120

DISTANCE:	45.6 mi / 73.4 km	TRAFFIC:	Light

AT A GLANCE

TIRES	
Twistiness	9.8/30
Pavement	15.2/20
Engineering	6.1/10
Remoteness	9.5/10
Scenery	12.6/15
Character	8.2/15
TOTAL	**61.4**

If you're particular about curves, this may not be your ride. But if you just want to get away from it all while staying on decent asphalt, the badlands east of the Sierra Nevada are a good place to be. Fortunately, the eastern-most leg of Hwy 120 offers enough scenic variety and drifting sweepers to make it more than just a place to hide from traffic. From its junction with Hwy 395 south of Lee Vining, this remote DH starts out straight across the Pumice Valley toward the south shore of Mono Lake. Then it rounds the ancient Mono Craters and angles southwest on a climb through rock, sand, sage and pine forest to the Sagehen Summit. The lee side of the summit is mostly flat desert-scape, but presents bizarre rock formations, lingering views of the White Mtns to the east and even a couple of twisty sections. The only development on this hot and sweaty ride is the surviving ghost town of Benton Hot Springs where you can strip off your leathers and soak in an outdoor, spring-fed wooden tub before carrying on. Didn't bring your bathing suit? Don't worry. Out here, they're not too particular, either.

ACCESS

From Lee Vining

Coming in on DH58 Crane Flat – Lee Vining (Hwy 120)

Hwy 120 jogs south on Hwy 395 before continuing east. Go south on Hwy 395 and turn left onto Hwy 120. You're on the road.

From Benton

Go west on Hwy 120. You're on the road.

ON THE ROAD

Off Hwy 395 and into the barrens, the DH begins on a northeast tack. The dusty, broom-covered flat sweeps all the way to the multi-shaded Pumice Cones in the distance. The road is scenic, remote and, apart from some tar strips, smoothly paved. All that's missing are some curves.

There are some minor undulations, both back and forth and up and down as you draw nearer the cones. Over a rise, Mono Lake appears to the left, shimmering against the intense dryness. A mirror-tilting pair of 35-mph (55-kmh) curves guides you past the cones and on a downward drift toward the wind-whipped water. Rings around the lake show its slow process of evaporation. There's nothing slow about the curve evaporation, though – they dry up completely at 4.8 mi (7.7 km) when the road shifts to the southeast.

You figure you're in for miles of sage but at 5.5 mi (8.9 km), you enter a pine forest. Spaced over the pebbly ground, the trees somehow flourish beneath eroding edges of extinct volcanoes. The pines dissipate at 6.8 mi (10.9 km), creating a wide, sandy stretch that looks like a large beach. And maybe it is one. Even though you'd have to run at least three miles to jump in the lake.

It's easy to forget how high it is here in the desert, though you're reminded when you reach the 7000 ft (2134 m) elevation mark at 7.6 mi (12.2 km). The pines return, resting on a carpet of sagebrush. A handful of spaced, meandering curves commence at 9.4 mi (15.1 km). The steady rise and fall of the road creates a lot of blind crests that tend to keep your speed down. Think of them as natural speed tax collectors.

At 11.8 mi (19.0 km), the trees disappear and the road empties into the broad, sage-filled saucer of Big Sand Flat, a plateau that spreads out beneath a band of trees and some low peaks. "Cattle Next 34 Miles" says the sign. Well, at least something lives around here.

There's a curve just beyond the cow sign but it's followed by a long looking straight across the flat. It's not complete desolation, however. At 14.4 mi (23.2 km), you pass some low dunes to the left and a shallow curve points the road toward a smattering of lonely, silhouetted trees. At 15.4 mi (24.8 km), you crest the 8139 ft (2480 m) Sagehen Summit although it hardly feels like one. Hope it's curvier going down than coming up. That wouldn't take much.

Small rock tetons stick out of the dry earth like partially uncovered dinosaur bones as you descend off the summit. By 16.8 mi (27.0 km), the landscape is much rougher and the road responds with a few of its sharper corners. As you drop into North Canyon and take aim at the Black and White Mtns, you hope that some serious twisties are about to evolve. But, no, the Curvaceous Era ends at 17.6 mi (28.3 km) where you're on another straight.

The scene opening up before you on the mild descent is impressive, though. The road slowly bends west and slightly north while the sea of sage is punctuated by islands of rock and a long ridge topping a broad plateau. In the distance, you can see the outlines of Antelope and Trafton Mtns brushed on the sky.

A rare curve at 21.0 mi (33.8 km) points the road southeast on another straight along the edge of what is now the Adobe Valley. Broad pines stick up like feathers from the rows of pointed, rocky vertebra that poke out of the sage-covered earth. The bright red rock takes on some strange shapes, like the sphinx head at 24.1 mi (38.8 km). But it's nothing compared to the canyon at 25.1 mi (40.4 km).

It's positively surreal in the canyon. Holes in the sharp red rock make it look like coral. Small trees and shrubs jut out of it, like plants on the sea bottom. A 30-mph (50-kmh) curve marks the exit from the canyon at 26.2 mi (42.2 km) and you have to tilt your bike. If you remember how.

Now comes the really fun part. At 27.8 mi (44.7 km), a sign warns of "Dips Next 5 Miles". The first few are a curiosity and at least take away from the monotony of a long straightaway. But after awhile, the blind rises begin to feel more like speed bumps. If you've got the stomach of a teenager, you'll be fine. The rest of us might want to slow down.

The roller coaster is over by 33.1 mi (53.3 km). The landscape continues to enthrall, however, as painted mountains provide a backdrop for mottled green and milk-chocolate-colored mounds. A white layer of salt rings the edge of Black Lake, off to the left. At 38.4 mi (61.8 km), you curve past the lonely junction with **DH65 Benton Crossing Road**.

Despite its lack of curves, this road's got some cool stuff going on. But nothing cooler than the shar-pei rocks that greet you just beyond the **DH65** junction. Light brown with detailed wrinkles, they look like an artist's rendering of nature, rather than nature itself. Beyond them, the slow descent steepens toward the White Mtns, now squarely in your face. The long, steady curves wind easily downward, gradually tightening into the S-curves that zig-zag into the treed oasis of historic Benton Hot Springs.

TOUR NOTE: As long as it's not 100 degrees, you might want to stop at Benton Hot Springs' Old House (760-933-2507), which offers clean and sanitary baths in antique redwood tubs in an outdoor setting for $6 per person (or $15 per tub) per hour. Baths are drained and cleaned after each use. The Inn at Benton Hot Springs also has spring-fed pools.

There's a rare twisties sign when you leave Benton Hot Springs. The mild curves that follow barely seem to warrant it, though, in context, they probably qualify. They steer you toward the grove of trees that surround the burnt-out little town of Benton. The DH ends when you T-junction with Hwy 6, beneath the White Mtns, at 45.6 mi (73.4 km)

Twisted Edges

TE-A June Lake Loop (Hwy 158) - North Shore Dr (16.6 mi / 26.7 km)
Finely contoured, perfectly paved sweepers above the lake on North Shore Dr give way to a twisty, but busy canyon below the fantastic Ansel Adams cliffs back on the main loop. As you venture further north, the tight corners stretch out into straights and long curves through an empty landscape along the shores of Silver and Grant Lakes.

NAVIGATION: Note that this TE does not go through the town of June Lake but turns off Hwy 158 to go around the lake's north shore. From the south end, turn right onto North Shore Dr 0.9 mi (1.4 km) off Hwy 395. From the TE's northern junction with Hwy 395, your left turn is at 12.0 mi (19.3 km).

TE-B Mammoth Scenic Loop (5.9 mi / 9.5 km)
Arguably, this quiet peaceful and slightly tar-strippy back road into Mammoth Lakes is misnamed. It's not really a loop, since you have to head back to Hwy 395 on a busy section of Hwy 203 to make it one. It's not really that scenic, either, since most of it meanders through a sage-based pine forest, with only a couple token views of Mammoth Mtn. A more fitting name? How about **DH63TE-B**?

ROUTING OPTION: If the traffic's light, turn right on Hwy 203 at the south end of this TE and enjoy tight, exquisitely paved and engineered handful of curves that twist another 3.0 mi (4.8 km) up to the base of the ski area, or 4.4 mi (7.1 km) to the National Park Service gate. Beyond that, as long as it's before 7am or after 7:30pm, you can pay a $7 toll to ride the one-lane scenic road down to Agnew Meadows, Reds Meadow, Devils Postpile National Monument and Rainbow Falls. Between those hours, you have to take a shuttle bus. Pretty, but tends to take the thrill out of biking.

RIDER'S LOG: **DATE RIDDEN:** **YOUR RATING:** **/10**

***Remember, you'll find video clips of all of Northern California's DHs at* destination highways.com.**

To Lee Vining & DH58
To Nevada
Black Lake
Benton Springs
Benton
DH63
DH65
Benton Station
760.933.2231
Smalley's Mkt
760.933.2322
Brown's Owens River CG
760.920.0975
GLASS MTN. RIDGE
LONG VALLEY
INYO NATIONAL FOREST
BENTON RANGE
BANNER RIDGE
BLIND SPRING HILL
HAMMIL VALLEY
WHITE MTNS.
Wildrose Summit 7650ft/2350m
To Mammoth Lakes
To DH63
To Lee Vining &DH58
Whitmore Hot Springs
WATTERSON CANYON
Benton Crossing Rd.
WATTERSON DIVIDE
Inn at Benton Hot Springs
760.933.2507
Old House
760.933.2507
CHALFANT VALLEY
Lake Crowley
Owens Gorge Rd
Round Mtn. Rd.
Tom's Place
Tuff NF CG
Crowley Creek Rd.
French Camp NF CG
Holiday NF CG
Paradise Resort CG
760.387.2370
Owens River
Rock Creek
Iris Meadow NF CG
TE-A
Paradise
VOLCANIC TABLELAND
Big Meadow NF CG
East Fork NF CG
Rock Creek Rd.
WHEELER RIDGE
Palisade NF CG
Tom's Place Resort
760.935.4239
Pine Grove NF CG
Lower Rock Creek Rd.
ROUND VALLEY
Pine Creek Rd.
Pleasant Valley BCG
Upper Pine Grove NF CG
TE-B
Owens River
INYO NATIONAL FOREST
Mosquito Flat BCG
Pine Creek
Round Valley Rd.
Sawmill Rd.
Dixon Ln.
Big Trees NF CG
TUNGSTEN HILLS
Bishop
E. Line St.
W. Line St.
Horton Creek BCG
Brown's Millpond CG
760.873.5342
Forks NF CG
McGee Crk.
Ed Powers Rd.
Creek
Four Jeffrey BCG
Intake 2 NF CG
Starlite Dr.
TE-C
Browns Town CG
760.873.8522
Creekside RV CG
760.873.4483
690 N Main
760.873.8405
W. Fork Coyote Creek
Bishop
Cardinal Village Resort
760.873.4789
Bishop Park NF CG
Golden State Cycle
(HON/YAM)
174 S Main
760.872.1570
Aspendel
North Lake BCG
Mtn Glen BCG
South Lake Rd.
To Big Pine & DH17
Willow Camp BCG
Bishop Creek Lodge
760.873.4484
Sabrina BCG
Lake Sabrina
Lake Sabrina Cafe
760.873.7425
Parchers Resort
760.873.4177

DH65 BENTON CROSSING ROAD

DH58 DH63 DH65 DH17

DISTANCE:	30.6 mi / 49.2 km	TRAFFIC:	Light

AT A GLANCE

TIRES	
Twistiness	7.3/30
Pavement	16.8/20
Engineering	8.4/10
Remoteness	9.6/10
Scenery	12.1/15
Character	6.4/15
TOTAL	**60.6**

California Inline Skating's MISRA (**M**odest **I**nline **S**kating **R**oad **A**ssessment) gives this transition between DH63 Lee Vining – Benton and Hwy 395 four skate wheels for its smooth Pavement, light traffic and surrounding mountain Scenery, recommending it to beginning fruitbooters who have mastered "basic stroking." Great. Bad enough that bicycle websites tout this DH, now you have to watch for sessions of bladerunners from nearby Mammoth Lakes clogging up the scene. The sketchy MISRAble system confirms a few things but 'core riders obviously need TIRES to get completely up to speed. For example, Twistiness is so low even panicking am motorcyclists won't try and use their heels to brake. What curvitude does exist is almost entirely located in the first half transfer from the Adobe Valley up into the rasta-mellow Benton Range. There are only a few corners down the Watterson Canyon tranny and virtually zippo around both fake Lake Crowley and through the volcanic, flat bottom Long Valley Caldera. As you'd expect then, Character's a bit of a poseur, though Engineering's pretty rad with only one potential sack-it disaster spot on the tightest piece up to Banner Ridge. Remoteness is gnarly since the only development consists of a campground/store/cafe and low-key Whitmore Hot Springs. That's probably why speed tax po-pos spend so little time here – that and the fact dildobladers can't stroke fast enough to exceed the 55-mph (90-kmh) limit. As for those rodneykingesque "Share the Road" signs, well, why can't we all just get along? After all, we do share a common belief in wheels in line.

ACCESS

From Mammoth Lakes

Via Hwy 395

Benton Crossing Rd junctions north off 395 just south of Mammoth's airport, about 5.5 mi (8.9 km) southeast of the Mammoth Lakes turn off. Take it. You're on the road.

From mid-DH62 Lee Vining – Benton (Hwy 120)
The east end of Benton Crossing Rd turns south off Hwy 120 6.2 mi (10.0 km) west of Benton and 3.7 mi (5.6 km) west of Benton Hot Springs.

On The Road

Shake out your Canadian Passport, strap your helmet over it and roll. And man, at the beginning you can really rip it straight south through the sage up this canyonlike offshoot of the Adobe Valley.

Dead ahead across the flat lie the low, brown mounds of the Benton Range. But you don't get your first curve until 1.9 mi (3.1 km) and, even then, it's not much. There's a few more climbing slightly through a small grouping of trees and then you're back on a straight flat bisecting sage. Gradually, the trees take over as the incline continues and you begin to carve big, fast sweepers. At 4.0 mi (6.4 km), the canyon ends, at least as far as the road goes. Whereupon a fat corner doubles you back on a roll-in transition northeast up and into the Benton Range.

An exposed, buckskin colored rock slope appears on your right as you climb. To your left, there's a view out over the canyon. The low guardrail close to the far road edge looks like a good spot for tech dogs to trick but a bad spot for you to slam. Into, that is.

The road swings southeast and you level out at 6.0 mi (9.7 km) on a sage-covered plateau that angles toward the Benton Range. Over to the northeast across a desolate field, the striking, bald, taupe White Mountains that mark the Nevada border can be seen through a gap in the Bentons.

The forest stays on your right until a big sweeper aims the road in a southerly direction to parallel the base of Banner Ridge. Then, the silviculture retreats to the west. That high ground far in the distance? It's the eastern edge of the Sierra Nevada.

The modest Wildrose Summit (7650 ft / 2350 m) is signposted at 6.9 mi (11.1 km). Reaching Wildrose after the climb is supposedly an impressive feat for bicyclists. For motorcyclists, of course, it's no sweat, particularly due to the lack of curves. At least it feels remote, apart from the occasional perspiring pedaler.

Banner Ridge moves in on the road, forcing it to angle even more toward the south to circumnavigate the ridge's base. Except for the one gentle curve that turns the road slightly eastward, it's still straight. Finally, at 11.0 mi (17.7 km), a legitimate sweeper reorients the DH sharply west. Don't get excited, it's only one. The small, directional shift doesn't count.

Things gets a little better when the landscape undulates into low, tree-scattered hills at 12.4 mi (20.0 km). As you wander through a few desultory sweepers, the eastern escarpment of the Sierra Nevada comes and goes behind the hills. You reach the Watterson Divide (7525 ft / 2350 m) at 15.1 mi (24.3 km).

You won't be getting any air on the slight crests in the road as you pump it down a mild descent through drying terrain. Gradually, the topography tightens up to form the shallow Watterson Canyon. It throws a few more corners down for you but unless you're totally wound out, you won't likely be utilizing the outside edge of your rubber busting any fancy soul grind tricks.

The Sierra Nevada looms large on the horizon as you continue west. Roadside cattle may loom even larger. Fabulous: bicyclists, roadrunners and now ruminants. At least there's not herds of pylons.

You hop a cattle guard and, at 18.7 mi (30.1 km), get your first glimpse of Lake Crowley glinting in the late day sun down in the flat Long Valley Caldera. By 19.0 mi (30.6 km), you've transitioned down onto this tableau where the large lake forces you to the northeast.

TOUR NOTE: According to the US Geological Survey the Caldera is still an active volcanic area. So you should be aware that "common precursory indicators of volcanic activity include increased seismicity, ground deformation, and variations in the nature and rate of gas emissions." Hard to tell if you're on a hardtail, though.

The Caldera is a large, flat-bottomed, sage-covered bowl that spreads out beneath a cerulean blue, high country sky. As *CA Inline Skating* observes, you can "...admire the craggy snow-capped peaks towering over the perimeter of Long Valley. Mammoth Mountain dominates the view of the Sierras to the west and south, the Glass Mountain range is close by to the north, and the White Mountains decorate the eastern horizon. After a particularly wet winter, the high peaks will still wear their brilliant white crowns for several months." Couldn't have said it better ourselves.

Apparently skaters here are "spoiled by the option of skating road-width slaloms at will" through this bowl. Yeah, well, not when we're around, bladeboys. Sharing the road cuts two ways, right? Try not to flatten any of the slalomers as they scatter in front of you like startled deer. Remember, skater road kill ain't purty. It's also hell on the suspension.

Snick it up to top if you're not already there, crack the throttle and liberate some carbon. You'll scream by the campground and quickly come to the big sweeper in the road across the Owens River (the actual Benton Crossing) at 23.9 mi (38.5 km).

From here, the road heads straight at the Sierra Nevada massif. Sage, some grassland, a few cows, the Whitmore Hot Springs and one or two slight curves lie across the Caldera between you and the Hwy 395 end of the DH at 30.6 mi (49.2 km). Want a more vivid picture? Check out our website sponsor-me video footie.

Twisted Edges

TE-A Lower Rock Creek Rd (10.9 mi / 17.5 km)

Paradise? Well, not quite. But at times this terrific Hwy 395 bypass sports great pavement, tons of curves and varied scenery. It climbs up close to the Sierras running in and out of a steep walled valley and passing through the old gold rush town that bears the overused name.

TE-B Pine Creek Rd - Round Valley Rd - Sawmill Rd - Ed Powers Rd (11.8 mi / 19.0 km)

Round Valley spreads out below Wheeler Ridge. Sounds like a good place for a quiet, bypass route that connects **TE-A** and **TE-C**. Mostly straight with some farmland 90s, this so-so paved ride across the sage plain is a remote and scenic way to avoid the buzz of Hwy 395 for a spell. It's much more scenic riding it north.

NAVIGATION: From the north, ride west on Pine Creek. Turn left down Round Valley Rd at 1.6 mi (2.6 km), right on Sawmill Rd at 8.0 mi (12.9 km) and right again on Ed Powers Rd at 9.7 mi (15.6 km).

From the south, Ed Powers Rd turns north off Hwy 168. At 2.1 mi (3.4 km), turn left on Sawmill Rd. At 3.8 mi (6.1 km), turn left on S. Round Valley Rd. The right onto Pine Creek Rd is at 10.2 mi (16.4 km).

TE-C Bishop – Lake Sabrina (Hwy 168) (15.2 mi / 24.5 km)

Forget about eating breakfast in Bishop. With the painted canvass of the eastern Sierra slope directly in your face, illuminated by the sun behind you, morning is the perfect time to take a run up Hwy 168 to one of the restaurants near Sabrina Lake. The fine engineering on this straight and sometimes sweepy road make it an easy, pre-latté ride to boot.

TOUR NOTE: To get to the Lake Sabrina Boat Landing Café, carry on down the one- lane road past the Sabrina Lake CG entrance to the boat launch. Even if you're not hungry, the extra mile is worth the view.

RIDER'S LOG: **DATE RIDDEN:** **YOUR RATING: /10**

Map Tip: To see the next good motorcycle road, look for the white navigation arrows at the edge of the Local maps.

Bristlecone Manor Motel 800.263-3927
Starlight Motel 760.938.2011
Big Pine Motel 888.524.7787
Rossi's 760.938.2308
E J's Hitchin' Rail Tavern
Carroll's Market
Country Kitchen 760.938.2402
Uncle Bud's 760.938.2500
126 South Main 866.938.2114
Grandview BCG
Glacier View BCG
Baker Creek BCG
Tinnemaha BCG
Taboose Creek BCG
Glacier Lodge 760.938.2312
Goodale Creek BCG
Upper Sage Flat BCG
Sage Flat BCG
Big Pine Creek BCG
DH17
TE-A
Big Pine
Westgard Pass Rd.
Westgard Pass 7271 ft/2232 m
Gilbert Summit 6374 ft/1956 m
Oasis Junction
To Death Valley
To Benton & DH65
To Bishop
To Lone Pine
CALIFORNIA
NEVADA
FISH LAKE VALLEY
ANCIENT BRISTLECONE PINE FOREST
WHITE MOUNTAINS
INYO NATIONAL FOREST
PIPER MOUNTAIN WILDERNESS
OWENS VALLEY
DEEP SPRING VALLEY
EUREKA VALLEY
INYO MTNS.
Deep Springs Lake
Deep Springs Ranch
Schulman Grove & Visitor Center
Sierra View Overlook
Patriarch Grove
UC Barcroft Research Lab
Death Valley Rd.
Glacier Lodge Rd.
Crocker St.
3 km
3 miles

DH17 Big Pine – Oasis Jct

Highway 168

Distance:	38.1 mi / 61.3 km	Traffic:	Light

DH58 DH63 DH65 DH17

At a Glance

TIRES	
Twistiness	25.9/ 30
Pavement	16.3/ 20
Engineering	5.0/ 10
Remoteness	9.0/ 10
Scenery	12.2/ 15
Character	9.8/ 15
Total	**78.2**

You're a very nosy fellow, kitty cat, huh? Kinda' like Jack Nicholson's character in *Chinatown*. 'Cept you're sniffing around the Owens Valley looking for curves rather than wondering what happened to the water that once made this area rich and green. You know what happens to nosy fellows on a bike? Huh? No? Wanna guess? Okay. They find DHs. Like this one that knifes east into the White Mtns, slices down into Deep Springs Valley, cuts sweetly up round the base of Chocolate Mt and finally noses you almost to Nevada. The abundant swirls of Twistiness produced by the light and dark mountains are bracketed by warm up/cool down straights either end and a very long, plain ol' vanilla stretch in the middle. The melt-in-your-mouth Pavement permeates most of the road except either side of Westgard Pass, where the generally good Engineering can drain away faster than water. On the other hand, no H_2O means no development. So Remoteness is excellent and lets you breathe in the desolate badlands Scenery the entire way. And with so little traffic, you don't have to worry much about a speed tax collector sticking a switchblade up your nostril. Sure, it's a shame that in the early 1900s all the water was stole… er, brought from this area to Los Angeles. But today, Big Pine should attract a rich torrent of riders bringing green from LA. If it doesn't bring you, well as Jake would say, you're dumber than you think we think you are.

Access

From Big Pine

On Hwy 395

Turn east on Hwy 168 at the northern edge of town. You're on the road.

From Oasis Jct

On Hwy 266

Hwy 266 junctions from the north and the south with Hwy 168. Head west on 168 and you're on the road.

On The Road

TOUR NOTE: The next services are 97 mi (156 km) away, in Nevada. There are none at the Oasis Jct end of the DH.

The "big pine" of local namesake is long gone but a majestic lone sequoia on Hwy 168 stands as a beacon for the DH's junction with Hwy 395. (Apparently, the town is considering a change in name to Pretty Big Sequoia.) The Sierra Nevada towers behind as you razor straight east through the sage of Owens Valley toward the White Mtns on the left and the Inyo Mtns on the right. The not-particularly-big tree on the left is the last one you'll see for awhile.

You cross the Owens River at 1.5 mi (2.4 km) and if it's dry, well you know why. You may be able to see remnants of former irrigation canals and once-cleared lands in this area. Speaking of dry, Death Valley Rd, an isolated back way into Death Valley, junctions right at 2.3 mi (3.7 km)

ROUTING OPTION: It's about 72 mi (116 km) via Death Valley Rd to the junction with Hwy 267 at the north end of Death Valley. The first 25 mi (40 km) or so are on so-so pavement through the Inyo Mtns and the Little Cowhorn Valley. Then, there's approximately 8 mi (13 km) of gravel that crosses the Eureka Valley, followed by another 4 mi (6 km) of asphalt through the Last Chance Range's Hanging Rock Canyon before a final 36 mi (58 km) of aggregate takes you more or less straight to Hwy 26. Problem is, all this gravel is subject to wash-outs that close the road, so maxburners should check locally. For the rest of us, just note the cool names.

The DH swings to the north on a banked curve that has a sign promising more of the same for the next 16 mi (25 km). With no immediate follow up, it seems more like a politician's promise at first. But then the pavement smoothes out at 3.1 mi (5.0 km) just in time for four moderate curves, the last three essed together.

There's more good but low-key cornering before you enter a shallow draw at 4.6 mi (7.4 km). As this gully tightens up, the road moves first to the left side of it and then to the right. The odd, lazy curve takes some advantage of the excellent pavement on a gradual climb. By 7.5 mi (12.1 km), the narrowing valley has guided you out of the foothills and into the barren, low White Mtns proper. More curves start to hook up. And as the passage continues to close in, even more connect. It's a nice piece, Jack.

The White Mtns, squatting in the rain shadow of the Sierra Nevada, have a semi-arid climate. Even so, hardy trees begin to sprinkle the terrain, more on the low mountains to the south than those to the north. But you're probably more interested in the sprinkle of curves beneath your wheels as the geography grips the road even tighter. At 10.0 mi (16.1 km), you start to get low-speed advisories. Too bad the pavement, undulating a bit now, drops a grade in concert with the engineering.

A road-narrows-watch-for-opposing-traffic sign suddenly pops up. Can it get any narrower? Sure, just remove the painted line in the middle and turn the road to one lane. Which is precisely what happens at 10.1 mi (16.2 km). Riding here takes a certain amount of finesse. Rough and threatening, volcanic Cenozoic rock Vs down on both sides of the road. But the trip back in geological time is over by 10.4 mi (16.7 km) where the gorge spits the road out into the open and the paint returns. The timeless curves, however, continue unperturbed.

You enter another little gorge. But before the paint can disappear and the road narrow again, you exit at 11.7 mi (18.8 km), reoriented northward. The asphalt straightens and White Mountain Rd junctions left at 13.0 mi (20.9 km).

TOUR NOTE: White Mountain Rd, after 11.1 mi (17.9 km) of coarse asphalt, leads to the Schulman Grove of bristlecone pines, the world's oldest living things, at an elevation of 10,000 ft (3070 m). There are also some panoramic views up here of the White Mtns around you and to the west across Owens Valley, the Sierra Nevada. The Patriarch Grove lies north of Schulman Grove after 12 mi (19 km) more of gravel. It's the home of the world's largest bristlecone, the Patriarch Tree, some 4200 years old.

The DH is so dead straight past the bristlecone turnoff, you wonder if they forgot to replace the signs up here when the 55 era ended. Surely, it can't still be the double nickel (loonie less a dime) you see posted.

But sometimes signs are necessary. For example, the only reason you're aware you've arrived at unimpressive Westgard Pass (7271 ft / 2232 m) is that it's sign-posted. You sure don't need the next three signs to tell you where you are, though: the steep grade, 35-mph (55 kmh) advisory and twisties for the next 5 mi (8 km) all indicate good times are coming. And true enough, by 14.1 mi (22.7 km), you're descending and everything is as promised. Though the advisory's maybe a *little* cautious.

The scattered trees quickly thin out to nothing on the left side as you head down into a gorge. The sage that replaces them makes for great sightlines through the continuing curves. Improved asphalt hits at 15.0 mi (24.1 km) as does a bit of hard shoulder outside the white lines. The only nit to pick with this great, velvety smooth stretch is the occasional pavement dip.

You proceed down the ravine. Rubbly looking but sharply angled rock, almost as striking as the stuff on the ascent to Westgard Pass, appears either side of the road. As the canyon widens at 17.6 mi (28.3 km), you can see the big, broad Deep Springs Valley backed by the arid peaks of the Piper Mountain Wilderness. FYI, that dry white patch over to the right in the valley is Deep Springs "Lake".

The road continues to descend but the curves mellow, disappearing completely by the time you slant onto the lowest part of the valley floor at 20.0 mi (32.2 km). As the road straightens, you get an opportunity to take in the impressive remoteness of this bowl-like valley. Ringed by parched, golden-brown mountains, it's so dry and barren it's difficult to believe they ranch cattle down here. At 22.8 mi (36.7 km), a barely perceptible shift in the road's path turns you toward the northeast lip of the basin. It can be hot down here. Maybe it would feel cooler if you went a little… bit… faster….

A look in your rear-views shows the Sierra Nevada peeking above the pale brown slopes of the receding Whites. At 27.5 mi (44.3 km), a few buildings appear inexplicably among the few trees on the left-hand side of the road, along with one slight curve. These structures must be connected to nearby Deep Springs Ranch. By now you'd almost forgotten what buildings looked like.

Wakey, wakey. The curve at 29.9 mi (48.1 km) and the sign saying more for the next 6 mi (10 km) announce the end of your break. Back to work, you rapidly climb out of the valley and enter a tight series of corners below the massive chunk of Chocolate Mtn. The road swings north and suddenly you're winding high on the west side of a dry gulch. Your speed's low here, so your knees are unlikely to be, even given the tightness of the corners.

There's a brief glimpse to the left down into Fish Lake Valley before a large hook in the road gives you your last view back down Deep Springs Valley. Above that is the Sierra Nevada, far in the distance. It's easier to see this great view coming in the other direction – one more reason to make the return trip.

You've climbed high in a hurry. Gilbert Summit (6374 ft / 1956 m), apparently not good enough to be considered a pass, is at 32.9 mi (52.9 km). Frankly, because of the twisties, scenery and the up-and-down feel, it's much more pass-like than Westgard. Go figure.

The tight curves are almost uninterrupted through the treeless but hilly terrain and lots are essed together. The pavement even widens a little bit on the sharper corners, which is always helpful. That brief flash of green in the gap between two hills ahead indicates your destination, Fish Lake Valley. You sense the final descent is near.

And it is. You shift downwards and the edges of the road thrust upwards, degrading the sightlines and forcing you to keep your speed modest. At least until 35.2 mi (56.6 km), where the geography relaxes and the road straightens as it enters the valley. You exit Inyo and enter Mono County at 36.5 mi (58.7 km). After that, it's straight as a blade until you junction with Hwy 266 at the end of the DH. Your tripmeter reads 38.1 mi (61.3 km). Your satisfaction meter reads even higher.

ROUTING OPTION: You can either motor on to uncharted Nevada or return whence you came.

Twisted Edges

TE-A Glacier Lodge Rd (10.6 mi / 17.1 km)

Even though this road is very twisty on the early treeless part from Big

Pine, it straightens out the higher you go. Dotted yellow all the way helps you get by any traffic heading to the Inyo National Forest campgrounds in the cooler Sierra Nevada below Mt Alice.

NAVIGATION: This TE starts out off Hwy 395 in the middle of Big Pine as Crocker St West.

TOUR NOTE: Although the main lodge building referred to in the road's name burned down a few years ago, it's supposedly going to be rebuilt.

RIDER'S LOG: **DATE RIDDEN:** **YOUR RATING: /10**

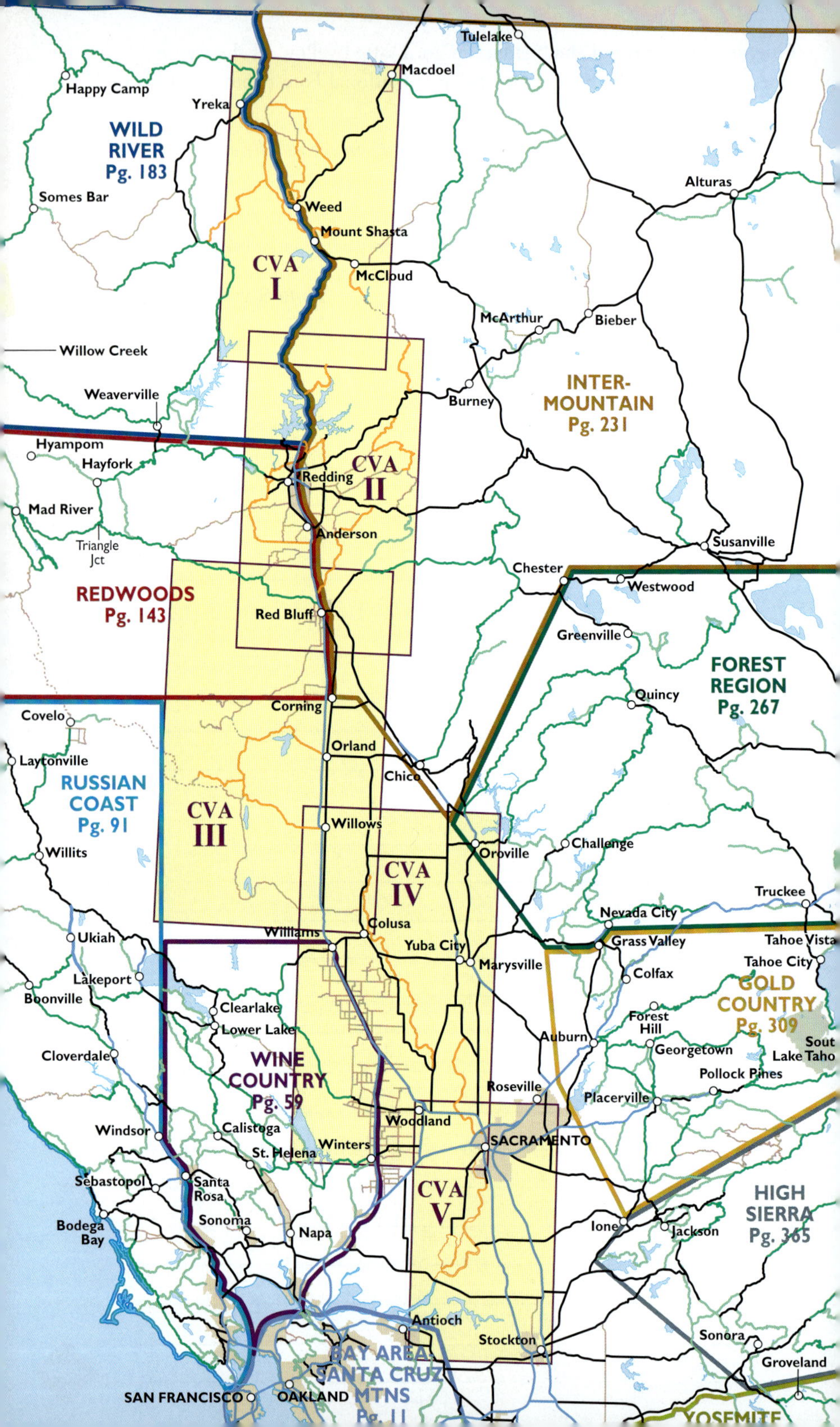
Tulelake
Macdoel
Happy Camp
Yreka
WILD RIVER Pg. 183
Somes Bar
Weed
Mount Shasta
CVA I
McCloud
Alturas
McArthur
Bieber
Willow Creek
Weaverville
Burney
INTER-MOUNTAIN Pg. 231
Hyampom
Hayfork
Redding
CVA II
Mad River
Anderson
Triangle Jct
Susanville
Chester
Westwood
REDWOODS Pg. 143
Red Bluff
Greenville
FOREST REGION Pg. 267
Quincy
Corning
Covelo
Laytonville
Orland
Chico
RUSSIAN COAST Pg. 91
CVA III
Willows
Willits
Oroville
Challenge
CVA IV
Truckee
Nevada City
Colusa
Williams
Ukiah
Yuba City
Grass Valley
Tahoe Vista
Marysville
Tahoe City
Lakeport
Colfax
GOLD COUNTRY Pg. 309
Boonville
Clearlake
Forest Hill
Lower Lake
Auburn
Cloverdale
Georgetown
WINE COUNTRY Pg. 59
Pollock Pines
Roseville
Placerville
Woodland
Windsor
Calistoga
SACRAMENTO
St. Helena
Winters
Sebastopol
Santa Rosa
CVA V
HIGH SIERRA Pg. 365
Bodega Bay
Sonoma
Napa
Ione
Jackson
Antioch
Stockton
Sonora
BAY AREA SANTA CRUZ MTNS
Groveland
SAN FRANCISCO
OAKLAND

Central Valley TEs

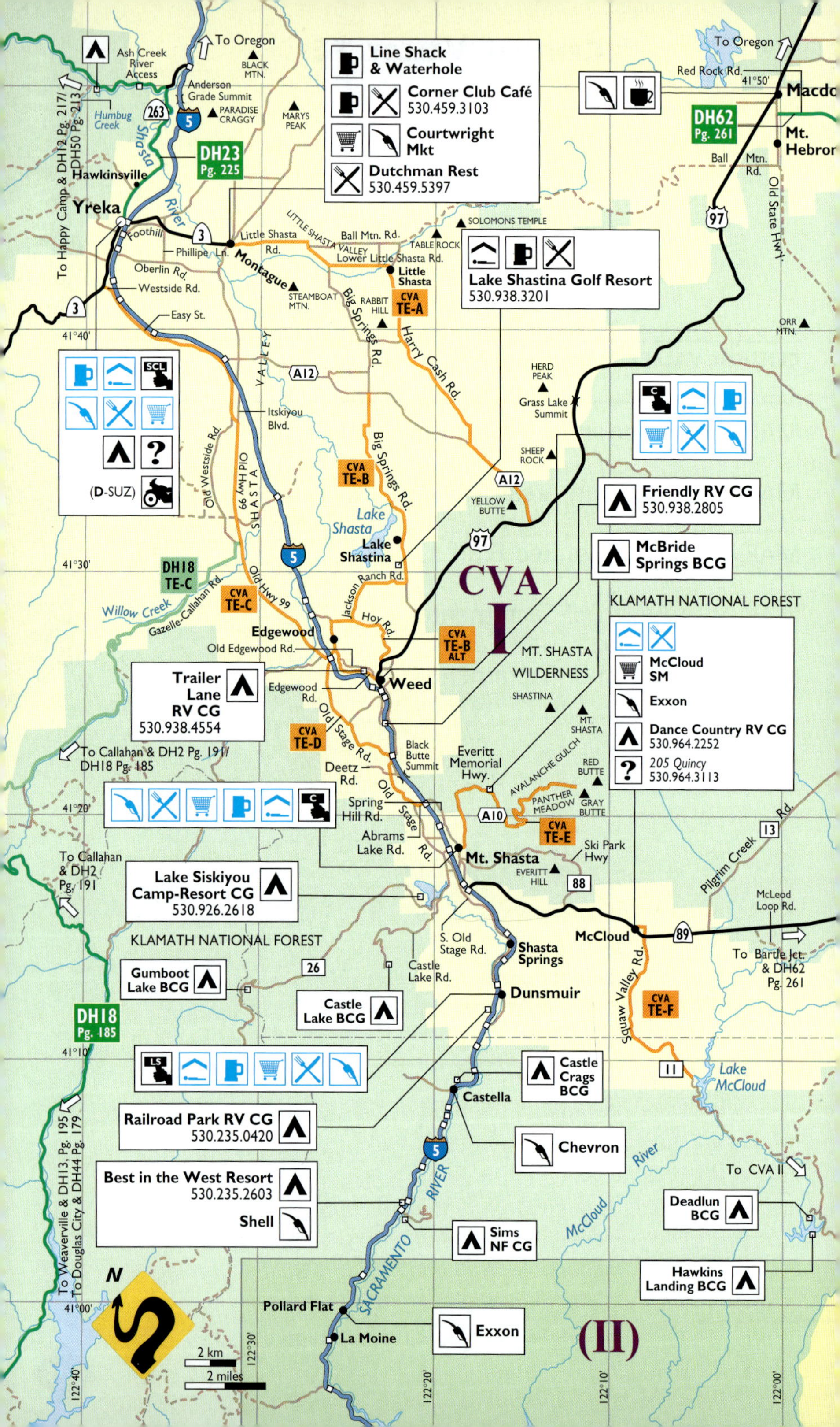

Line Shack & Waterhole
Corner Club Café 530.459.3103
Courtwright Mkt
Dutchman Rest 530.459.5397
Lake Shastina Golf Resort 530.938.3201
Friendly RV CG 530.938.2805
McBride Springs BCG
KLAMATH NATIONAL FOREST
McCloud SM
Exxon
Dance Country RV CG 530.964.2252
205 Quincy 530.964.3113
Trailer Lane RV CG 530.938.4554
Lake Siskiyou Camp-Resort CG 530.926.2618
Gumboot Lake BCG
Castle Lake BCG
Castle Crags BCG
Chevron
Railroad Park RV CG 530.235.0420
Best in the West Resort 530.235.2603
Shell
Sims NF CG
Deadlun BCG
Hawkins Landing BCG
Exxon
CVA I
(II)
MT. SHASTA WILDERNESS
To Oregon
Yreka
Weed
Mt. Shasta
McCloud
Dunsmuir
Castella
Shasta Springs
Edgewood
Montague
Little Shasta
Lake Shastina
Hawkinsville
Pollard Flat
La Moine
Macdo
Mt. Hebron
DH23 Pg. 225
DH62 Pg. 261
DH18 TE-C
DH18 Pg. 185
CVA TE-A
CVA TE-B
CVA TE-C
CVA TE-D
CVA TE-E
CVA TE-F
CVA TE-B ALT
To Happy Camp & DH12 Pg. 217/ DH50 Pg. 213
To Callahan & DH2 Pg. 191/ DH18 Pg. 185
To Callahan & DH2 Pg. 191
To Weaverville & DH13, Pg. 195 To Douglas City & DH44 Pg. 179
To Bartle Jct. & DH62 Pg. 261
To CVA II
Ash Creek River Access
Anderson Grade Summit
Black Butte Summit
Grass Lake Summit
Everitt Memorial Hwy.
Ski Park Hwy
Squaw Valley Rd.
Pilgrim Creek Rd.
McLeod Loop Rd.
Old Stage Rd.
S. Old Stage Rd.
Castle Lake Rd.
Abrams Lake Rd.
Spring Hill Rd.
Deetz Rd.
Edgewood Rd.
Old Edgewood Rd.
Old Hwy 99
Old Westside Rd.
Gazelle-Callahan Rd.
Itskiyou Blvd.
Big Springs Rd.
Harry Cash Rd.
Hoy Rd.
Jackson Ranch Rd.
Ball Mtn. Rd.
Lower Little Shasta Rd.
Little Shasta Rd.
Phillipe Ln.
Oberlin Rd.
Westside Rd.
Easy St.
Foothill
Red Rock Rd.
Old State Hwy.
Lake Shasta
Lake McCloud
Willow Creek
Humbug Creek
Shasta River
Sacramento River
McCloud River
SHASTA VALLEY
KLAMATH NATIONAL FOREST
2 km
2 miles
N

MAP I
Oregon To Mt. Shasta

CVA TE-A Little Shasta Rd – Lower Little Shasta Rd – Harry Cash Rd (16.9 mi / 27.2 km)

MAP I Mostly straight at the top and even when you get some curves south of Little Shasta, they're poorly paved and engineered. So why pay the price for this ride through the farmland, range and sage east of the I-5? The in-your-face views of Mt Shasta at the remote south end are money, baby, money.

CVA TE-B Big Springs Rd – Jackson Ranch Rd – Hoy Rd Part 1 – Edgewood Rd (24.0 mi / 38.6 km)

MAP I This TE picks up where **CVA TE-A** left off with Big Springs Rd taking aim at Mt. Shasta with a much better paved and engineered series of straights and shallow sweepers through pine-peppered rangeland. Jackson Ranch is straight at first, and then gets a little bendy as it enters a wide but lovely valley blocked by the Scott Mtns on the other side of the I-5. The quality of the pavement and engineering drops as you turn down through Edgewood, then wind through the pine forest, paralleling the interstate, into the town of Weed.

NAVIGATION: From Weed, take N Weed Blvd and follow the directions north of town to Edgewood.

CVA TE-B ALT Hoy Rd Part 2 (3.6 mi / 5.8 km)

MAP I If you want more views and a slightly different perspective of Mt. Shasta and are prepared to endure some bumpy pavement for it, this lazy rural back way through some roadside farms may be worth it. The peacocks on the road pale in comparison to Shasta's display.

CVA TE-C Yreka – Mt Shasta (23.3 mi / 37.5 km) *Westside Rd – Easy Street - Old Hwy 99*

MAP I Great pavement and surrounding mountain scenery are the draws here, and the fact you get to avoid the speed tax collectors on the I-5 for a spell. It sure ain't the long straightaways.

CVA TE-D Weed – Mt Shasta (9.9 mi / 15.9 km) *Old Stage Rd - Abrams Lake Rd*

MAP I Not as well engineered as Old Hwy 99 to the north but unlike 99, it actually has some curves in its pretty pine woods. The road's climbing and dipping offers some captivating views of the surrounding mountains. Pavement varies, but is generally good.

NAVIGATION: From Mt Shasta, head north on N Mt Shasta Blvd. This will turn into Spring Hill Dr. Turn left on Abrams Lake Rd and cross the I-5 interchange.

ROUTING OPTION: If you're coming south from Weed, you can continue south on Old Hwy 99 past Abrams Lake Rd, and take a later cut off back to Mt Shasta, but it gets straighter and housier down here. If you carry on long enough, the road narrows to a cracked, one-lane sullivan that connects to the I-5 south of Mt Shasta.

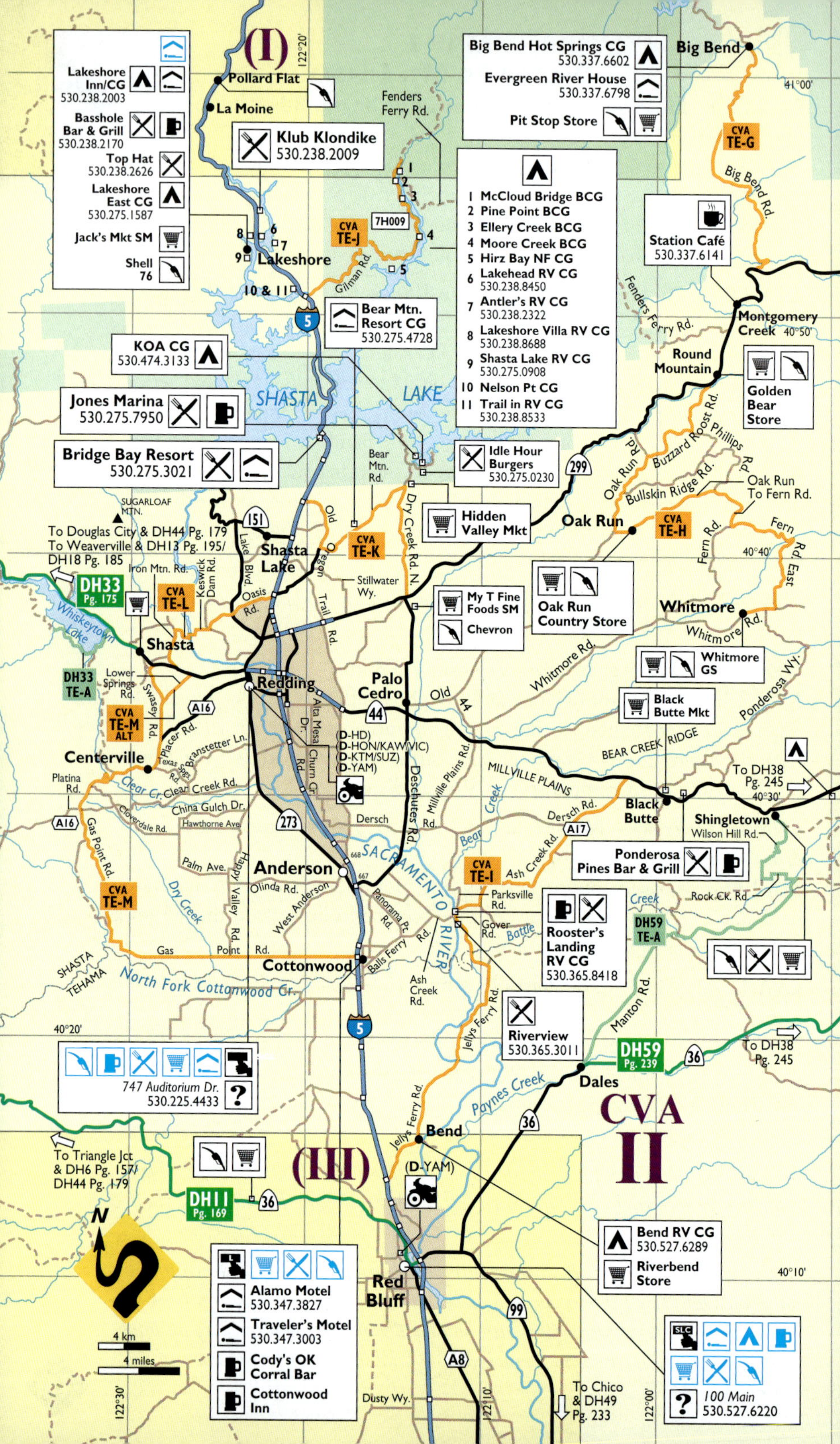
(I)
Pollard Flat
La Moine
Lakeshore Inn/CG 530.238.2003
Basshole Bar & Grill 530.238.2170
Top Hat 530.238.2626
Lakeshore East CG 530.275.1587
Jack's Mkt SM
Shell 76
Klub Klondike 530.238.2009
Fenders Ferry Rd.
Big Bend Hot Springs CG 530.337.6602
Evergreen River House 530.337.6798
Pit Stop Store
Big Bend
CVA TE-G
Big Bend Rd.
1 McCloud Bridge BCG
2 Pine Point BCG
3 Ellery Creek BCG
4 Moore Creek BCG
5 Hirz Bay NF CG
6 Lakehead RV CG 530.238.8450
7 Antler's RV CG 530.238.2322
8 Lakeshore Villa RV CG 530.238.8688
9 Shasta Lake RV CG 530.275.0908
10 Nelson Pt CG
11 Trail in RV CG 530.238.8533
Station Café 530.337.6141
7H009
CVA TE-J
Gilman Rd.
Lakeshore
10 & 11
Bear Mtn. Resort CG 530.275.4728
KOA CG 530.474.3133
Jones Marina 530.275.7950
Bridge Bay Resort 530.275.3021
SHASTA LAKE
Fenders Ferry Rd.
Montgomery Creek
Round Mountain
Golden Bear Store
Idle Hour Burgers 530.275.0230
Bear Mtn. Rd.
Hidden Valley Mkt
SUGARLOAF MTN.
To Douglas City & DH44 Pg. 179
To Weaverville & DH13 Pg. 195/ DH18 Pg. 185
DH33 Pg. 175
Iron Mtn. Rd.
Keswick Dam Rd.
CVA TE-L
Whiskeytown Lake
Shasta
Lake Blvd.
Shasta Lake
Oasis Rd.
Old Oregon Trail Rd.
CVA TE-K
Stillwater Wy.
Dry Creek Rd. N.
My T Fine Foods SM
Chevron
Oak Run
Oak Run Rd.
Buzzard Roost Rd.
Phillips Rd.
Bullskin Ridge Rd.
Oak Run To Fern Rd.
CVA TE-H
Fern Rd.
Fern Rd. East
Oak Run Country Store
Whitmore
Whitmore Rd.
Whitmore GS
DH33 TE-A
Lower Springs Rd.
Swasey Rd.
Redding
Palo Cedro
Old 44
CVA TE-M ALT
Placer Rd.
Branstetter Ln.
Centerville
Texas Spgs Rd.
Platina Rd.
Clear Cr.
Clear Creek Rd.
China Gulch Dr.
Cloverdale Rd.
Hawthorne Ave.
Alta Mesa Dr.
Churn Cr. Rd.
(D-HD)
(D-HON/KAW/VIC)
(D-KTM/SUZ)
(D-YAM)
Deschutes Rd.
Millville Plains Rd.
MILLVILLE PLAINS
BEAR CREEK RIDGE
Black Butte Mkt
Ponderosa Wy.
To DH38 Pg. 245
Black Butte
Shingletown
Wilson Hill Rd.
Gas Point Rd.
Palm Ave.
Happy Valley Rd.
Dersch
Anderson
SACRAMENTO RIVER
Bear Creek
Dersch Rd.
Ash Creek Rd.
CVA TE-I
Ponderosa Pines Bar & Grill
CVA TE-M
Dry Creek
Olinda Rd.
West Anderson
Panorama Pt. Rd.
Parksville Rd.
Gover Rd.
Battle Creek
Rooster's Landing RV CG 530.365.8418
Rock Ck. Rd.
DH59 TE-A
Gas Point Rd.
SHASTA TEHAMA
North Fork Cottonwood Cr.
Cottonwood
Balls Ferry Rd.
Ash Creek Rd.
Jellys Ferry Rd.
Riverview 530.365.3011
Manton Rd.
40°20'
747 Auditorium Dr. 530.225.4433
DH59 Pg. 239
To DH38 Pg. 245
Dales
Paynes Creek
CVA II
To Triangle Jct & DH6 Pg. 157/ DH44 Pg. 179
DH11 Pg. 169
(III)
Jellys Ferry Rd.
Bend
(D-YAM)
Bend RV CG 530.527.6289
Riverbend Store
Alamo Motel 530.347.3827
Traveler's Motel 530.347.3003
Cody's OK Corral Bar
Cottonwood Inn
Red Bluff
4 km
4 miles
Dusty Wy.
To Chico & DH49 Pg. 233
100 Main 530.527.6220
122°20'
41°00'
40°50'
40°40'
40°30'
40°10'
122°30'
122°10'
122°00'
5
299
151
44
A16
273
A17
36
99
A8
668
667

CVA TE-E Everitt Memorial Hwy (9.0 mi / 14.5 km)
MAP I Decent pavement, lots of twisties and tremendous views of Mt Shasta await you on this memorable dead ender up to Panther Meadow.

NAVIGATION: Taking the main exit from the I-5 for the town of Mt Shasta puts you on Lake St. Lake turns into the Everitt Memorial Hwy.

CVA TE-F McCloud – McCloud Lake (9.0 mi / 14.6 km) *Squaw Valley Rd*
MAP I Lightly traveled, excellently paved, mostly straight through the fields of Native American Woman Valley and mainly curvy when you get into the forest closer to the lake. The views of Mt Shasta coming back are sure better than the sightlines around the corners in the trees. Couldn't see an Olympic ski hill either.

*ROUTING OPTION: Maxburners can punch ahead on poor asphalt around Lake McCloud and then ride about 5 mi (8 km) of their preferred road surface along Hawkin Creek before returning to a kind of pavement at the Iron Canyon Reservoir. About 10 mi (16 km) later they can soak their punished bodies in the hot springs at Big Bend. After that, they can take **CVA TE-G** out to Hwy 299 and head south to **CVA TE-H**.*

MAP II
Redding Area

CVA TE-G Hillcrest – Big Bend (13.0 mi / 20.9 km) *Big Bend Rd*
MAP II Maybe the pavement's not the best in the world but this quiet meander through the higher land just west of the Pit River valley does have some curves. And you may see more curves in Big Bend; the hot springs are clothing optional.

TOUR NOTE: Apparently, motorcyclists are not the "type of customer the Big Bend Hot Springs Resort prefers." All the more reason to check it out.

*ROUTING OPTION: If you're not filled with naked fear at the thought of about 5 mi (8 km) of gravel in the middle, FSR 11 will take you about 15 mi (24 km) west from Big Bend to McCloud Lake. A couple more miles of inferior pavement around the lake and you'll be on **CVA TE-F**'s great stuff.*

CVA TE-H Round Mountain – Whitmore (29.7 mi / 47.8 km) *Buzzard Roost Rd - Oak Run Rd - Oak Run To Fern Rd - Fern Rd E - Whitmore Rd*
MAP II This one puts together the best pavement and curves of all the options wandering the rolling upslopes east of Redding. If you choose to take the other roads up here and end up bored or buzzard pickins, you only have yourself to blame. No bull.

NAVIGATION: Stay right at 2.8 mi (4.5 km) on Buzzard Roost. Go left on Oak Run at 6.0 mi (9.7 km). Turn left on Oak Run To Fern Rd at 11.1 mi (17.9 km). Turn left onto (unmarked) Fern Rd E at 19.9 mi (32.0 km). At 27.6 mi (44.4 km), turn right on Whitmore.

ROUTING OPTION: If you've done the TE north to south, you have two options once you reach Whitmore. You can continue on Whitmore Rd west down to Hwy 44 or head back east on the TE for a mile and take bumpy

Ponderosa Way down to the same 44. The Cartwrights recommend the former unless your tolerance for rough stuff is very high.

CVA TE-I Black Butte – Red Bluff (A 17) (28.5 mi / 45.9 km) *Dersch Rd - Ash Creek Rd - Gover Rd - Jellys Ferry Rd*
MAP II The first half runs on mostly flat ground either side of the Sacramento River before it heads into higher, drier country. There are almost no curves but if you like quiet you'll find that here along with a variety of terrain. Pavement is not great but it's serviceable enough. A good place to just relax and enjoy the rural ambience.

*NAVIGATION: From Red Bluff take the Jellys Ferry Rd I-5 Exit, three exits north of town (it's the second exit north of **DH11**'s east end.)*

CVA TE-J Gilman Rd (16.9 mi / 27.2 km)
MAP II This one's for the purists. If it's all about tight, but well-engineered and predictable curves on smooth pavement – which of course it is – this road out to and along the McCloud River Arm of Shasta Lake ranks as one of Northern California's great TEs. Apart from the rockfaces that keep this local gem twisting from start to finish, don't expect to see much scenery when you're this deep in the forest. But don't expect to see much traffic either. There's little to attract the pylons but a campground and an inviting day use spot at the end.

*ROUTING OPTION: Beyond the pavement, Maxburners can travel the gravel about 30 miles (50 km) on Fenders Ferry Rd (FSR 27) and come out on Hwy 299, halfway between **CVA TE-G** and **H**, just west of Montgomery Creek. Too bad for the rest of us – we have to turn around and ride the TE again.*

CVA TE-K Dry Creek Rd N - Bear Mtn Rd - Old Oregon Trail (13.6 mi / 21.9 km)
MAP II This pleasant, meandering trip through airy pine forest and a touch of farmland is not only a clever way to bypass Redding, but a place where you'll find some great pavement and some smart curves here and there, especially near Shasta Lake.

TOUR NOTE: It's a nice extension to ride up to Shasta Lake where the road splits. The east arm, which goes up to a boat ramp, has more good riding, with a dock at the end you can swim off. Then again, the bumpy west arm has the bar.

CVA TE-L Oasis Rd - Lake Blvd - Keswick Dam Rd - Iron Mountain Rd (6.0 mi / 9.7 km)
MAP II This eclectic bypass gets you away from the homogenous pylons and onto a quieter, curvier mixture of trees, concrete, shrubs and powerlines.

NAVIGATION: Coming from the I-5, take Oasis Rd to its T-junction with Lake Blvd. Turn left and then quickly right onto Keswick Dam Rd. Your other option is to take the next exit north onto Shasta Dam Blvd (Hwy 151) and then go left on Lake Blvd and down to Keswick Dam Rd.

CVA TE-M Shasta – Cottonwood (28.4 mi / 45.7 km) *Swasey Dr - Placer Rd - Gas Point Rd*

MAP II A long way round, but it's faster than slogging through Redding. A lot curvier and more remote, too. The top part of Swasey twists tightly through a light pine forest but the best section is Placer Rd between Centerville and Igo where the road makes a contorted crossing of the Clear Creek canyon. Gas Point is neither as well paved nor as twisty but is much quieter as it drifts through the oak and pine-filled rangeland and heads into the long straightaway at the south end.

CVA TE-M ALT Lower Springs Rd (1.9 mi / 3.1 km)
MAP II Pavement and engineering aren't not quite as good, but this piece of road is otherwise similar to the northern part of Swasey. The way to go if you're heading to Redding.

MAP III
South of Red Bluff

CVA TE-N Orlando – Elk Creek (35.6 mi / 57.3 km) *Newville Rd (Road 200) - Road 306 - Hwy 162*
MAP III Makes a nice loop off I-5 and around Black Butte Lake when combined with **CVA TE-P**. It's not the same kind of road, though – more curves and grittier pavement make the road feel like it could have been imported from New Zealand. And when the countryside around here is greened up in the spring, it's even more reminiscent of Aotearoa, right down to the sheep.

ROUTING OPTIONS: North of this TE, there are more side roads that can keep you off I-5 all the way up to Red Bluff. But only hard-core remoteness fans will bother with these roads due to their poor pavement and boring nature.

TOUR NOTE: If you're an olive fan, you'll want to check out the Olive Pit in Corning, the next I-5 town north of Orland.

CVA TE-O Alder Springs Rd (FH 7) (15.6 mi / 25.1 km)
MAP III Anytime's a good time to visit your cousin Clem at the Alder Springs Corrections Camp. And surely it's just coincidence the road up there's the best motorcycling road around. After winding 3.6 miles (5.8 km) through uninteresting farmland, you cross into the Mendocino National Forest and twist upwards on a wide ribbon of smooth pavement through the shrub-covered slopes and tall stands of pine. Look at the bright side, cuz. By the time you get out, maybe they'll pave it all the way to Covelo.

*ROUTING OPTION: For dramatic mountain scenery, old-growth forest and flamboyant wildflowers, continue west after the pavement ends. You'll have to maxburns approximately 26.5 mi (42.5 km) before the pavement resumes at Eel River as **DH15TE-A Mendocino Pass Rd**, 8.4 mi (13.5 km) east of Covelo.*

CVA TE-P Willows – Elk Creek (Hwy 162) (20.1 mi / 32.3 km)
MAP III It's a bit of a drag strip across the plain when you first leave I-5, but this TE turns into a well-banked, easy-sweeping road through some bare and tree-checkered foothills just beyond the Thunderhill Park Raceway. Don't go getting any ideas.

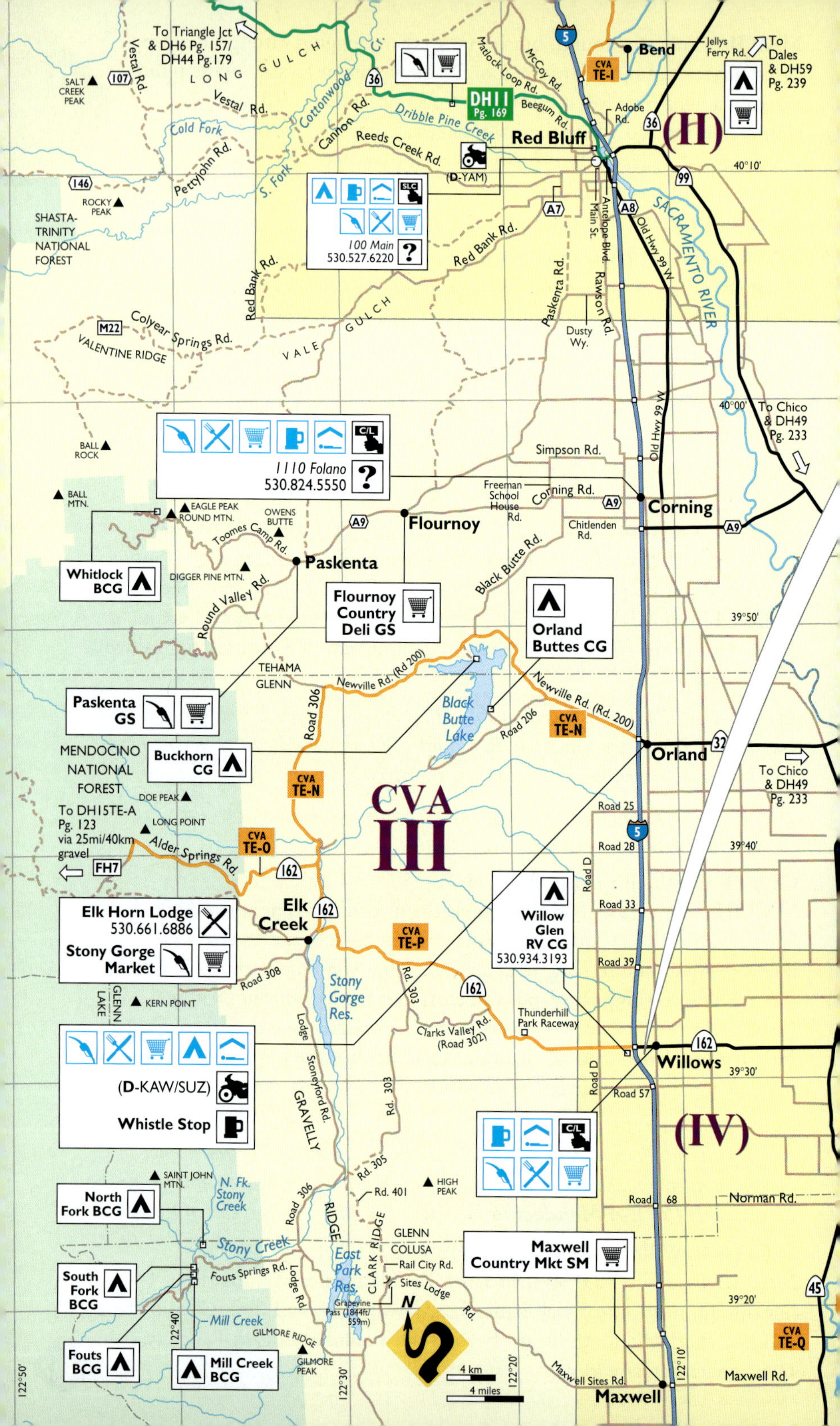

To Triangle Jct & DH6 Pg. 157/ DH44 Pg.179
LONG GULCH
SALT CREEK PEAK
Vestal Rd.
Cold Fork
Pettyjohn Rd.
S. Fork Cottonwood Cr.
Cannon Rd.
Dribble Pine Creek
Reeds Creek Rd.
DH11 Pg. 169
Matlock Loop Rd.
McCoy Rd.
Beegum Rd.
Red Bluff
(D-YAM)
100 Main 530.527.6220
Bend
Jellys Ferry Rd.
To Dales & DH59 Pg. 239
CVA TE-I
Adobe Rd.
(II)
40°10'
ROCKY PEAK
SHASTA-TRINITY NATIONAL FOREST
Red Bank Rd.
Antelope Blvd.
Main St.
Old Hwy 99 W
SACRAMENTO RIVER
Paskenta Rd.
Rawson Rd.
Dusty Wy.
Colyear Springs Rd.
VALENTINE RIDGE
VALE GULCH
40°00'
To Chico & DH49 Pg. 233
BALL ROCK
1110 Folano 530.824.5550
Simpson Rd.
Freeman School House Rd.
Corning Rd.
Corning
Chitlenden Rd.
BALL MTN.
EAGLE PEAK
ROUND MTN.
OWENS BUTTE
Toomes Camp Rd.
Flournoy
Paskenta
DIGGER PINE MTN.
Whitlock BCG
Round Valley Rd.
Flournoy Country Deli GS
Black Butte Rd.
Orland Buttes CG
39°50'
TEHAMA
GLENN
Newville Rd. (Rd 200)
Black Butte Lake
Newville Rd. (Rd. 200)
Road 206
CVA TE-N
Paskenta GS
Road 306
Orland
To Chico & DH49 Pg. 233
MENDOCINO NATIONAL FOREST
Buckhorn CG
CVA TE-N
CVA III
DOE PEAK
Road 25
To DH15TE-A Pg. 123 via 25mi/40km gravel
LONG POINT
Road 28
39°40'
Alder Springs Rd.
CVA TE-O
Road D
Road 33
Elk Creek
Elk Horn Lodge 530.661.6886
Stony Gorge Market
CVA TE-P
Willow Glen RV CG 530.934.3193
Road 39
Road 308
Rd. 303
GLENN LAKE
KERN POINT
Stony Gorge Res.
Thunderhill Park Raceway
Clarks Valley Rd. (Road 302)
Willows
39°30'
(D-KAW/SUZ)
Whistle Stop
Lodge Stoneyford Rd.
GRAVELLY
Road 57
Rd. 303
(IV)
Rd. 305
SAINT JOHN MTN.
N. Fk. Stony Creek
North Fork BCG
Road 306
Rd. 401
HIGH PEAK
Road 68
Norman Rd.
RIDGE
CLARK RIDGE
GLENN
COLUSA
Maxwell Country Mkt SM
Stony Creek
South Fork BCG
Fouts Springs Rd.
Lodge Rd.
East Park Res.
Rail City Rd.
Sites Lodge Rd.
Grapevine Pass (1,844ft/559m)
39°20'
Mill Creek
GILMORE RIDGE
GILMORE PEAK
CVA TE-Q
Fouts BCG
Mill Creek BCG
122°40'
122°30'
122°20'
122°10'
122°50'
4 km
4 miles
Maxwell Sites Rd.
Maxwell Rd.
Maxwell

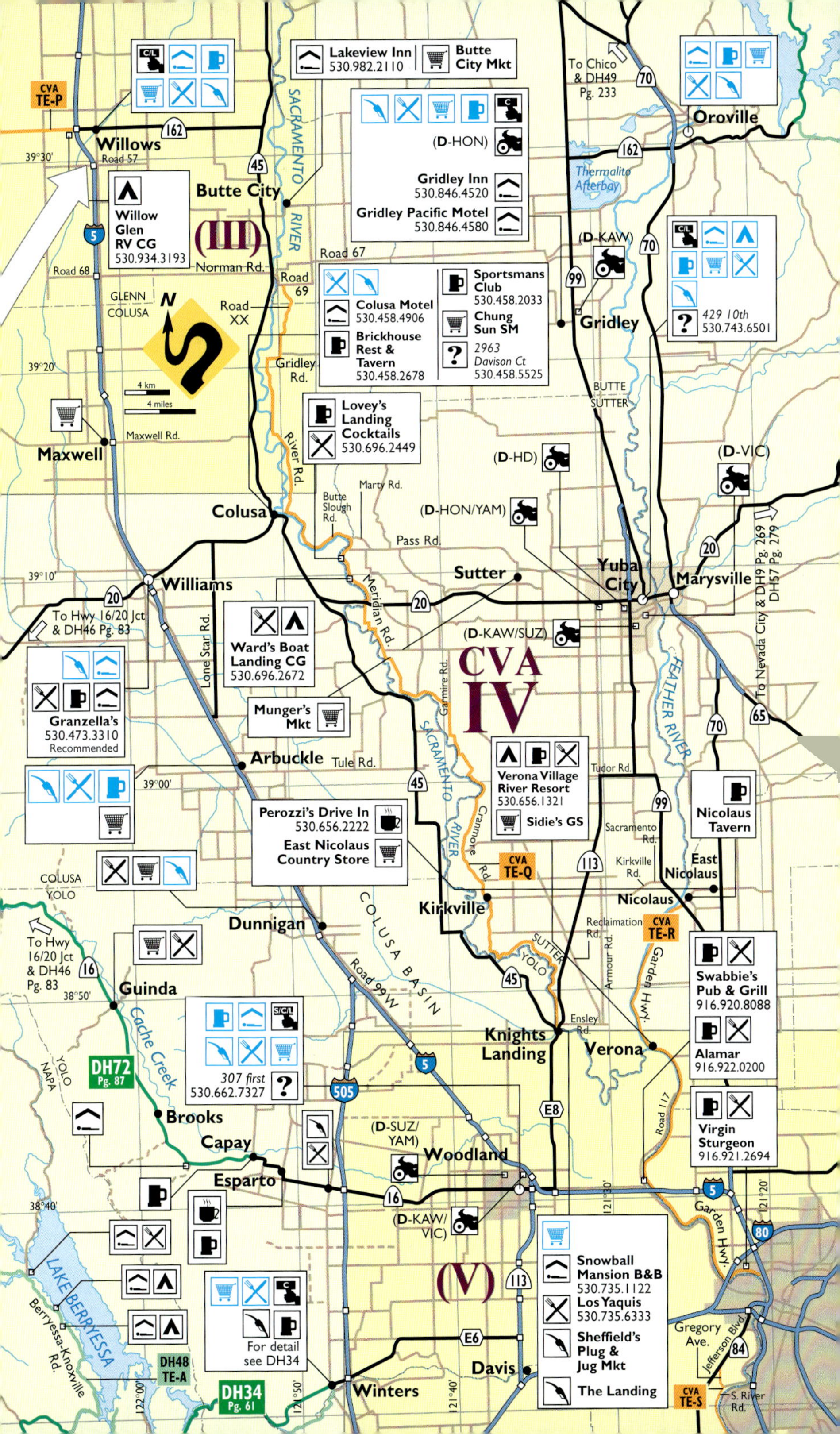

Lakeview Inn 530.982.2110
Butte City Mkt
Willows
Willow Glen RV CG 530.934.3193
Butte City
(III)
Gridley Inn 530.846.4520
Gridley Pacific Motel 530.846.4580
Oroville
To Chico & DH49 Pg. 233
Colusa Motel 530.458.4906
Brickhouse Rest & Tavern 530.458.2678
Sportsmans Club 530.458.2033
Chung Sun SM
2963 Davison Ct 530.458.5525
Gridley
429 10th 530.743.6501
Lovey's Landing Cocktails 530.696.2449
Maxwell
Colusa
Williams
Sutter
Yuba City
Marysville
To Hwy 16/20 Jct & DH46 Pg. 83
Ward's Boat Landing CG 530.696.2672
Granzella's 530.473.3310 Recommended
CVA IV
Munger's Mkt
Arbuckle
Verona Village River Resort 530.656.1321
Sidie's GS
Perozzi's Drive In 530.656.2222
East Nicolaus Country Store
Nicolaus Tavern
East Nicolaus
Nicolaus
Kirkville
Dunnigan
Swabbie's Pub & Grill 916.920.8088
Alamar 916.922.0200
Virgin Sturgeon 916.921.2694
Guinda
Knights Landing
Verona
307 first 530.662.7327
Brooks
Capay
Esparto
Woodland
(V)
Snowball Mansion B&B 530.735.1122
Los Yaquis 530.735.6333
Sheffield's Plug & Jug Mkt
The Landing
For detail see DH34
Davis
Winters
To Nevada City & DH19 Pg. 269 DH57 Pg. 279
Sacramento River
Feather River
Colusa Basin
Cache Creek
Lake Berryessa

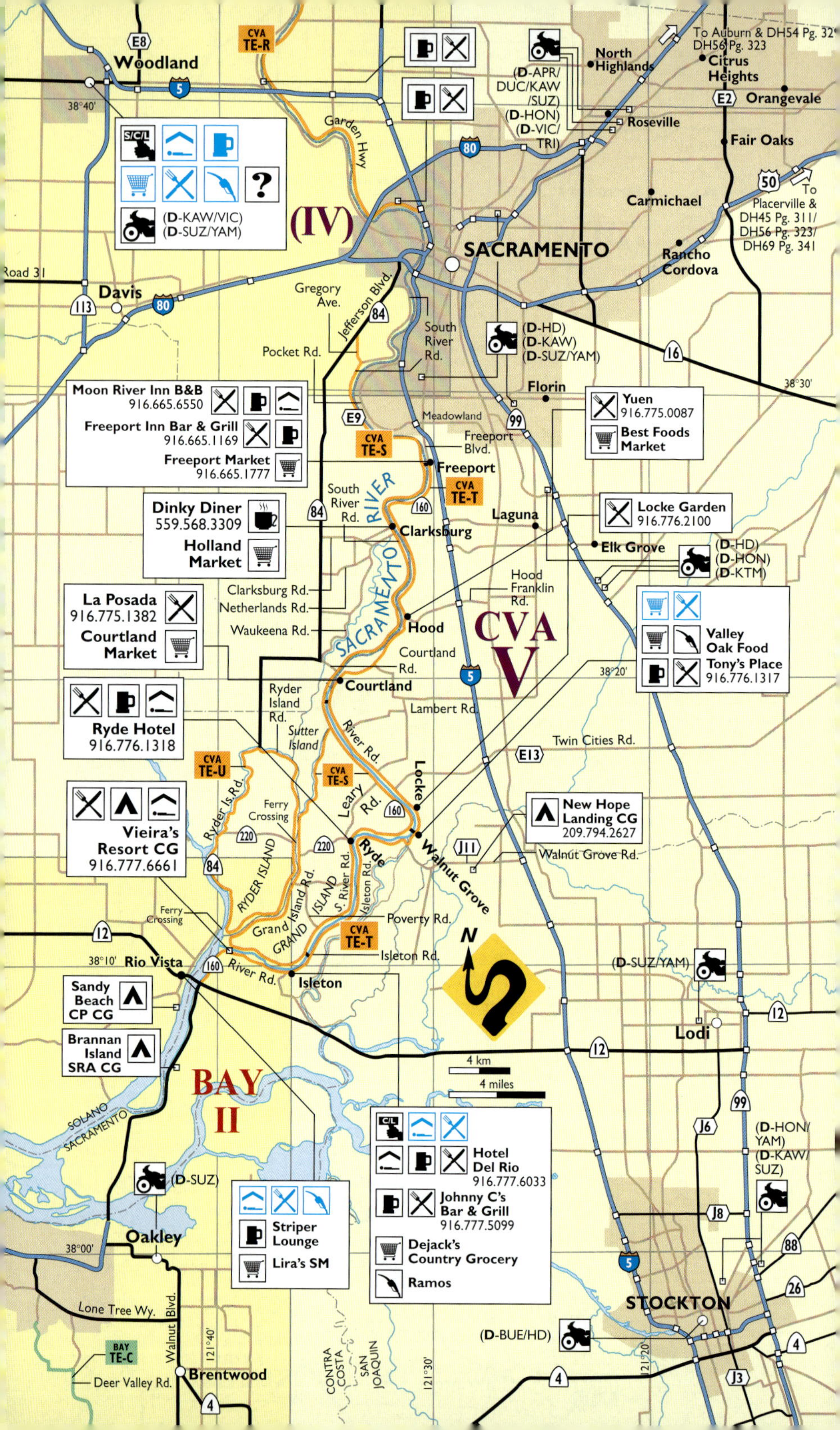

Woodland
Davis
SACRAMENTO
North Highlands
Citrus Heights
Orangevale
Roseville
Fair Oaks
Carmichael
Rancho Cordova
Florin
Laguna
Elk Grove
Freeport
Clarksburg
Hood
Courtland
Locke
Ryde
Walnut Grove
Isleton
Rio Vista
Lodi
Oakley
Brentwood
STOCKTON
To Auburn & DH54 Pg. 321/ DH56 Pg. 323
To Placerville & DH45 Pg. 311/ DH56 Pg. 323/ DH69 Pg. 341
(IV)
CVA V
BAY II
CVA TE-R
CVA TE-S
CVA TE-T
CVA TE-U
BAY TE-C
(D-KAW/VIC) (D-SUZ/YAM)
(D-APR/ DUC/KAW /SUZ) (D-HON) (D-VIC/ TRI)
(D-HD) (D-KAW) (D-SUZ/YAM)
(D-HD) (D-HON) (D-KTM)
(D-SUZ/YAM)
(D-HON/ YAM) (D-KAW/ SUZ)
(D-BUE/HD)
(D-SUZ)
Moon River Inn B&B 916.665.6550
Freeport Inn Bar & Grill 916.665.1169
Freeport Market 916.665.1777
Dinky Diner 559.568.3309
Holland Market
La Posada 916.775.1382
Courtland Market
Ryde Hotel 916.776.1318
Vieira's Resort CG 916.777.6661
Sandy Beach CP CG
Brannan Island SRA CG
Yuen 916.775.0087
Best Foods Market
Locke Garden 916.776.2100
Valley Oak Food
Tony's Place 916.776.1317
New Hope Landing CG 209.794.2627
Hotel Del Rio 916.777.6033
Johnny C's Bar & Grill 916.777.5099
Dejack's Country Grocery
Ramos
Striper Lounge
Lira's SM
Garden Hwy
Gregory Ave.
Jefferson Blvd.
South River Rd.
Pocket Rd.
Meadowland
Freeport Blvd.
South River Rd.
Clarksburg Rd.
Netherlands Rd.
Waukeena Rd.
Hood Franklin Rd.
Courtland Rd.
Ryder Island Rd.
Lambert Rd.
Sutter Island
River Rd.
Twin Cities Rd.
Leary Rd.
Ryder Is.Rd.
Ferry Crossing
RYDER ISLAND
Grand Island Rd.
GRAND ISLAND
S. River Rd.
Isleton Rd.
Poverty Rd.
Walnut Grove Rd.
River Rd.
SACRAMENTO RIVER
SOLANO
SACRAMENTO
CONTRA COSTA
SAN JOAQUIN
Lone Tree Wy.
Walnut Blvd.
Deer Valley Rd.
Road 31
38°40'
38°30'
38°20'
38°10'
38°00'
121°40'
121°30'
121°20'
4 km
4 miles
N

MAP IV

North of Sacramento

CVA TE-Q Afton – Knight's Landing (58.4 mi / 94.0 km) *Road XX - River Rd - Butte Slough Rd - Marty Rd - Meridian Rd - Garmire Rd - Cranmore Rd*

MAP IV You never quite know what's coming next on this quiet sequence of off-the-beaten paths that track the Sacramento River. Not always scenic but old wooden bridges and trips on and off the levee add character to a revolving scene of marshland, farmland and orchards. So much so that you don't really mind the short sections of jarring pavement and awkward engineering.

NAVIGATION: Heading south, turn left onto Butte Slough Rd (14.8 mi / 23.8 km) just before the bridge over the river into Colusa. When you reach the T-intersection at Pass Rd just past Ward's Landing, turn right. When you reach the T-jct at Garmire Rd, also turn right.

From Knight's Landing, cross the Sacramento and immediately turn left onto Cranmore Rd. Further north, make sure to turn left onto Marty Rd just past Lovee's Landing.

If you're coming from the north end of ***CVA TE-R****, Ensley Rd, Armour Rd, Kirkville Rd and Sacramento Rd provide a good connection to Knights Landing.*

CVA TE-R Nicolaus – West Sacramento (28.0 mi / 45.1 km) *Garden Hwy*

MAP IV Sometimes you're up on the river levee and sometimes you're not on this quiet, non-taxing option to part of Hwy 99 along the Feather and Sacramento Rivers. Few curves and poorer pavement on the half north of Verona. If you happen to be "fly and riding" into the Sacramento International Airport, this is your closest TE.

NAVIGATION: In West Sacramento you want the I-5 Garden Hwy Exit between the two arms of I-80. Once off I-5, make sure you head west on Garden and not east. You escape Sacramento quickly once you ride under the west arm of I-80.

In Sacramento, the best way to hook this together with similar but longer ***CVA TE-S*** *is to use I-5 and I-80 as described in* ***CVA TE-S****'s NAVIGATION.*

From the north end, Sacramento Rd, Kirkville Rd, Armour Rd and Ensley Rd provide a convenient connector between Hwy 99 just north of Nicolaus and the Knights Landing end of ***CVA TE-Q****.*

MAP V

South of Sacramento

CVA TE-S West Sacramento – Grand Island Loop (50.8 mi / 81.8 km) *Gregory Ave - S River Rd (E 9) - S River Rd (Hwy 160) - Grand Island Rd*

MAP V This TE runs down the Sacramento River and loops around Grand Island before tying back into itself at the Grand Island Bridge. It has no more curves than **CVA TE-R** but it's longer and, except for the Grand

Island Rd part, better paved. It's also more remote and has prettier countryside and more services. It also has companion **CVA TE-T** on the other side of the river to vary your return trip.

NAVIGATION: Coming from Sacramento, get on I-80 (across I-5) as if you're heading for San Francisco. Cross the Sacramento River and take the first exit (3) for S River Rd/Jefferson Blvd in West Sacramento. Turn south on Jefferson Blvd/Hwy 84. Stay south on Jefferson across the Sacramento River Deep Water Ship Channel. When you are 4.0 mi (6.4 km) south of I-80, take Gregory Ave slanting southeast off Jefferson/84.

TOUR NOTE: The funky Ryde Hotel is a nice place for a refreshment/lunch stop. Just the bar may be open.

CVA TE-T Freeport (Sacramento) – Rio Vista (20.4 mi / 32.8 km)
River Rd Part 1 (Hwy 160) - Isleton Rd - River Rd Part 3 (Hwy 160)
MAP V This run on the east side of the Sacramento River is similar to **CVA TE-S**. Except more of Hwy 160 runs on the east side so the pavement overall is a bit better. The towns are also bigger and more numerous. Plus there is a lot more traffic. Oh yeah, and you might see STCs on this side.

NAVIGATION: From the Sacramento end, take the Pocket Rd/Meadowland Rd exit east off I-5. A couple of blocks later, turn south on Freeport Blvd.

Heading south through Walnut Grove, make sure to turn right and take the second bridge (just south of town) and then right again on the other side to stay on the TE.

If you're doing the TE south to north, turn left over this bridge and then left again on the other side when you get to Walnut Grove.

CVA TE-U Ryder Island Rd - Hwy 84 (20.4 mi / 32.8 km)
MAP V If you don't have the same kind of time or budget as Ewan MacGregor, this bit of circumnavigation around the perimeter of quiet Ryer Island might just do you. The section of Hwy 84 north of Hwy 220 has some actual curves to go along with its better pavement. How rare – CalTrans actually saved the best asphalt for the curves!

*NAVIGATION: The mid-Ryer Island ferry from **CVA TE-S** runs continuously 24 hours except: 12pm – 12:20pm & 8pm – 8:20pm.*

Some maps show that Hwy 84 can get you on and off Ryer Island. In fact, at the southern end of the island you have to take a ferry off (same hours as the mid-island one).

DHNZ32 Whakatangihangakoa - Maungahoronukupokai

Appendices

List of Destination Highways and Twisted Edges

PAGE

CVA TE-L Oasis Rd - Lake Blvd - Keswick Dam Rd - Iron Mountain Rd
CVA TE-M Swasey Dr - Placer Rd - Gas Point Rd
M ALT Lower Springs Rd
CVA TE-N Newville Rd (Rd 200) - Rd 306 - Hwy 162
CVA TE-O Alder Springs Rd (FH 7)
CVA TE-P Willows - Elk Creek (Hwy 162)
CVA TE-Q Road XX - River Rd - Butte Slough Rd - Marty Rd - Meridian Rd - Garmire Rd - Cranmore Rd
CVA TE-R Garden Hwy
CVA TE-S Gregory Ave - S River Rd (E 9) - S River Rd (Hwy 160) - Grand Island Rd
CVA TE-T River Rd Part 1 (Hwy 160 - Isleton Rd - River Rd Part 3 (Hwy 160)
CVA TE-U Ryder Island Rd - Hwy 84

DH No.	Total /100	Road Name	Length
		BAY AREA - SANTA CRUZ MOUNTAINS	
28	72.9	Woodside - San Gregorio	19.4 mi / 31.2 km
39	70.0	Boulder Creek - Saratoga (San Jose)	20.6 mi / 33.2 km
47	67.1	Livermore - Patterson	52.9 mi / 85.1 km
55	63.3	Saratoga Gap - Hwy 35/Hwy 92 Jct	26.2 mi / 42.2 km
74	55.0	Santa Cruz - Jamison Cr. Rd/Hwy 236 Jct	17.9 mi / 28.8 km
		WINE COUNTRY	
34	71.2	Winters - Rutherford/Napa	35.0 mi / 56.3 km 30.0 mi / 48.3 km
46	67.2	Clearlake - Hwy 16/Hwy 20 Jct	18.4 mi / 29.6 km
48	66.4	Lake Hennessey - Middleton	30.8 mi / 49.6 km
53	65.0	Calistoga - Kelseyville	36.0 mi / 57.9 km
72	55.2	Capay - Hwy 16/Hwy 20 Jct	32.8 mi / 52.8 km
		RUSSIAN COAST	
5	82.5	Cleone (Ft Bragg) - Leggett	39.8 mi / 64.1 km
10	80.3	Dry Creek Rd - Skaggs Springs Rd	22.4 mi / 36.1 km
15	78.7	Longvale Jct - Covelo	28.9 mi / 46.5 km
22	76.4	Ukiah - Boonville	17.1 mi / 27.5 km
24	76.0	Old Hopland - Lakeport	16.5 mi / 26.6 km
27	73.8	Cloverdale - Boonville	26.1 mi / 42.0 km
29	72.6	Jenner - Albion (Mendocino)	76.0 mi / 122.3 km
32	72.3	Ft Bragg - Willits	31.0 mi / 49.9 km
37	70.7	Tamalpais Valley - Tomales	43.2 mi / 69.5 km
		REDWOODS	
6	82.2	Carlotta (Fortuna) - Triangle Jct	65.3 mi / 105.1 km
11	79.6	Triangle Jct - Red Bluff	65.3 mi / 105.1 km
33	71.7	Shasta (Redding) - Douglas City	31.9 mi / 51.3 km
36	70.8	Mad River Loop	44.3 mi / 71.3 km
44	67.5	Douglas City - Triangle Jct	35.3 mi / 56.8 km
64	61.2	Lost Coast	66.6 mi / 107.2 km
66	60.6	Avenue of the Giants	31.6 mi / 50.9 km

Traffic	Twistiness	Pavement	Engineering	Remoteness	Scenery	Character
Moderate	29.4	17.0	6.3	3.7	8.5	8.0
Moderate	30.0	15.4	5.4	4	7.1	8.1
Light	30.0	10.6	3.8	5.8	9.6	7.3
Light	24.7	14.9	6.0	4.3	9.2	4.2
Moderate	22.5	11.5	5.5	3.8	7.8	3.9
Moderate to Heavy	30.0	11.6	5.3	4.0	9.9	10.4
Heavy	21.7	16.6	9.6	6.0	10.4	2.9
Light	26.5	14.3	6.1	5.1	9.4	5.0
Heavy	26.3	17.3	6.0	2.6	7.0	5.8
Moderate	14.3	14.0	6.8	4.7	10.1	5.3
Moderate	30.0	19.0	4.9	6.7	10.2	11.7
Moderate	26.9	19.0	8.6	5.6	10.9	9.3
Light	29.5	15.9	5.7	7.5	10.0	10.1
Moderate	30.0	16.1	5.7	5.1	11.6	7.9
Light	30.0	15.9	4.8	6.2	10.9	8.2
Moderate	29.2	16.3	5.9	3.7	9.7	9.0
Moderate	24.0	17.0	5.5	4.0	11.0	11.1
Heavy	30.0	18.0	5.5	4.6	8.2	6.0
Moderate	27.5	15.1	5.4	4.2	9.6	8.9
Light	30.0	15.9	6.4	6.4	9.7	13.8
Light	28.1	17.9	5.7	7.6	8.9	11.4
Heavy	25.3	17.2	8.6	5.5	9.9	5.2
Light	26.3	16.6	5.2	6.6	9.1	7.0
Moderate	26.7	14.9	5.9	5.3	9.0	5.7
Light	28.8	6.2	2.6	7.1	11.1	5.4
Light	19.7	16.0	5.6	3.7	10.5	5.1

DH No.	Total /100	Road Name	Length
		WILD RIVER	
2	85.0	Callahan - Cecilville	29.8 mi / 48.0 km
12	79.3	Happy Camp - Willow Creek	82.0 mi / 132.0 km
13	79.2	Weaverville - Willow Creek	54.9 mi / 88.3 km
18	78.2	Weaverville - Callahan	61.7 mi / 99.3 km
20	77.0	Crescent City - O'Brien, OR	41.4 mi / 66.6 km
23	76.2	Yreka - Happy Camp	70.5 mi / 113.5 km
31	72.4	Willow Creek - Blue Lake (Arcata)	32.3 mi / 52.0 km
50	65.6	O'Brien, OR - Happy Camp	37.3 mi / 60.0 km
		INTER-MOUNTAIN	
38	70.7	Lassen Park Road	34.3 mi / 55.2 km
49	66.2	Chico - Hwy 32/Hwy 36/89 Jct	51.4 mi / 82.7 km
59	62.2	Dales (Red Bluff) - Hwy 32/Hwy 36/89 Jct	45.1 mi / 72.6 km
60	61.6	Eagle Lake Road	35.2 mi / 56.6 km
62	61.4	Bartle - McDoel Jct	59.1 mi / 95.1 km
71	57.2	Alturas - Cedarville	24.4 mi / 39.3 km
		FOREST REGION	
3	83.4	Oroville - Greenville/Quincy	71.2 mi / 114.6 km 67.6 mi / 108.8 km
7	81.9	Quincy - Oroville	58.5 mi / 94.1 km
9	81.0	Nevada City - Sattley	73.4 mi / 117.6 km
21	76.5	Challenge - East Quincy (Quincy)	51.8 mi / 83.4 km
42	69.5	Taylorsville - Janesville (Susanville)	41.0 mi / 66.0 km
57	62.5	Nevada City - Hwy 20/I-80 Jct	26.6 mi / 42.8 km
		GOLD COUNTRY	
16	78.6	Mosquito Ridge Road	41.3 mi / 66.5 km
19	77.8	Georgetown - Riverton Jct	54.0 mi / 86.9 km
40	69.8	Riverton Jct - Meyers (South Lake Tahoe)	30.8 mi / 49.6 km
45	67.4	Plymouth - El Dorado (Placerville)	14.3 mi / 23.0 km
51	65.3	Camp Richardson (South Lake Tahoe) - Tahoma	15.0 mi / 24.1 km
54	64.4	Auburn - Foresthill	17.0 mi / 27.4 km
56	63.2	Placerville - Auburn	23.6 mi / 38.0 km
67	60.2	Pollock Pines - Plymouth	32.9 mi / 52.9 km
69	59.0	Cool - Placerville	26.8 mi / 43.1 km

Traffic	Twistiness	Pavement	Engineering	Remoteness	Scenery	Character
Very Light	30.0	19.4	5.8	9.0	9.7	11.1
Light	28.9	13.6	6.7	7.0	10.3	12.8
Moderate	26.8	17.5	6.8	5.3	10.2	12.6
Light	26.3	18.2	6.6	8.1	10.2	8.8
Moderate	24.7	20.0	8.1	5.5	9.6	9.1
Light	23.7	18.1	6.5	4.5	10.0	13.4
Moderate	24.0	17.9	9.3	5.8	10.2	5.2
Very Light	30.0	9.0	4.9	7.8	9.0	4.9
Moderate	26.0	15.1	5.2	6.1	12.7	5.6
Moderate	23.5	13.6	7.2	7.0	8.8	6.1
Moderate	14.6	19.9	8.4	6.0	9.7	3.6
Light	20.8	11.2	5.8	7.6	9.8	6.4
Very Light	14.0	13.8	7.0	8.0	10.0	8.6
Light	12.2	14.8	6.8	6.1	11.4	5.9
Can be Heavy	26.8	17.8	7.0	6.1	11.5	14.2
Light	30.0	17.4	6.3	6.4	8.6	13.2
Moderate	30.0	15.6	5.8	6.2	9.0	14.4
Light	30.0	13.6	4.7	6.9	8.6	12.7
Light	30.0	11.9	4.3	7.2	9.4	6.7
Moderate	16.7	20.0	7.3	5.4	8.8	4.3
Light	30.0	12.2	4.1	9.8	10.0	12.5
Light	27.2	16.0	6.1	7.5	8.1	12.9
Brutal	24.0	18.6	7.8	4.1	10.3	5.0
Moderate	25.1	15.6	5.7	4.5	9.4	7.1
Almost Always Brutal	26.7	17.8	5.7	2.0	10.7	2.4
Heavy	22.5	18.5	9.7	3.1	7.9	2.7
Brutal	26.6	16.4	5.8	2.3	8.2	3.9
Moderate	25.2	12.6	6.2	3.8	7.1	5.3
Moderate	25.0	12.7	4.4	3.8	7.8	5.3

DH No.	Total /100	Road Name	Length
		HIGH SIERRA	
1	87.0	Topaz Lake - Markleeville	22.3 mi / 35.9 km
4	83.1	Hwy 88/Hwy 89 Jct - Barton	49.3 mi / 79.3 km
8	81.6	Sonora Jct - Mi-Wuk Village (Twain Harte)	64.4 mi / 103.6 km
41	69.8	Arnold - Bear Valley Village	25.0 mi / 40.2 km
52	65.1	Tuolumne - Cherry Lake	31.2 mi / 50.2 km
61	61.5	Red Corral - Mokelumne Hill	24.8 mi / 39.9 km
		YOSEMITE	
14	78.8	Moccasin - Yosemite Jct	50.2 mi / 80.8 km
25	75.3	Moccasin - Bear Valley	25.9 mi / 41.7 km
26	75.2	Mariposa - Yosemite Jct	36.0 mi / 57.9 km
30	72.4	Fresno - Lakeshore	52.3 mi / 84.2 km
35	70.8	Piedra (Fresno) - Kirch Flat	30.8 mi / 49.6 km
43	68.2	Oakhurst - Yosemite Jct	43.9 mi / 70.6 km
68	59.5	O'Neals - Oakhurst	30.1 mi / 48.4 km
70	57.3	Waterford - Coulterville	38.8 mi / 62.4 km
73	55.1	Merced Falls Road - Hornitos Road	32.4 mi / 52.1 km
		BORDERLAND	
17	78.2	Big Pine - Oasis Jct	38.1 mi / 61.3 km
58	62.4	Crane Flat - Lee Vining	58.8 mi / 94.6 km
63	61.4	Lee Vining - Benton	45.6 mi / 73.4 km
65	60.6	Benton Crossing Road	30.6 mi / 49.2 km

Traffic	Twistiness	Pavement	Engineering	Remoteness	Scenery	Character
Light	30.0	17.6	5.4	9.6	13.8	10.6
Moderate	23.3	16.7	7.9	9.2	12.0	14.0
Moderate	28.2	15.9	5.5	7.2	11.1	13.7
LIght	23.4	16.5	8.2	6.2	9.5	6.0
Light	30.0	9.1	2.9	9.7	9.0	4.4
Very Light	30.0	12.1	4.7	3.9	6.8	4.0
Heavy	27.0	16.1	7.2	6.5	9.5	12.5
Light	30.0	14.5	3.2	7.2	10.7	9.7
Moderate	26.1	14.8	6.6	4.9	11.9	10.9
Moderate	27.6	15.4	6.0	5.0	8.7	9.7
Light	30.0	11.3	3.3	7.2	11.5	7.5
Brutal	30.0	10.1	3.8	6.7	10.3	7.3
Moderate	22.1	14.2	7.8	3.9	8.2	3.3
Moderate	14.2	14.5	6.3	4.3	8.7	9.3
Light	19.4	12.2	4.9	4.8	9.2	4.6
Light	25.9	16.3	5.0	9.0	12.2	9.8
Can be Heavy	10.6	12.6	6.3	7.6	12.1	13.2
Light	9.8	15.2	6.1	9.5	12.6	8.2
Light	7.3	16.8	8.4	9.6	12.1	6.4

Tires By Total Rating

DH No.	Total /100	Road Name	Pg No.	Length
1	87.0	Topaz Lake - Markleeville	375	22.3 mi / 35.9 km
2	85.0	Callahan - Cecilville	191	29.8 mi / 48.0 km
3	83.4	Oroville - Greenville/Quincy	295	71.2 mi / 114.6 km 67.6 mi / 108.8 km
4	83.1	Hwy 88/Hwy 89 Jct - Barton	379	49.3 mi / 79.3 km
5	82.5	Cleone (Ft Bragg) - Leggett	115	39.8 mi / 64.1 km
6	82.2	Carlotta (Fortuna) - Triangle Jct	157	65.3 mi / 105.1 km
7	81.9	Quincy - Oroville	289	58.5 mi / 94.1 km
8	81.6	Sonora Jct - Mi-Wuk Village (Twain Harte)	391	64.4 mi / 103.6 km
9	81.0	Nevada City - Sattley	269	73.4 mi / 117.6 km
10	80.3	Dry Creek Rd - Skaggs Springs Rd	137	22.4 mi / 36.1 km
11	79.6	Triangle Jct - Red Bluff	169	65.3 mi / 105.1 km
12	79.3	Happy Camp - Willow Creek	217	82.0 mi / 132.0 km
13	79.2	Weaverville - Willow Creek	195	54.9 mi / 88.3 km
14	78.8	Moccasin - Yosemite Jct	421	50.2 mi / 80.8 km
15	78.7	Longvale Jct - Covelo	121	28.9 mi / 46.5 km
16	78.6	Mosquito Ridge Road	335	41.3 mi / 66.5 km
17	78.2	Big Pine - Oasis Jct	485	38.1 mi / 61.3 km
18	78.2	Weaverville - Callahan	185	61.7 mi / 99.3 km
19	77.8	Georgetown - Riverton Jct	347	54.0 mi / 86.9 km
20	77.0	Crescent City - O'Brien, OR	207	41.4 mi / 66.6 km
21	76.5	Challenge - East Quincy (Quincy)	283	51.8 mi / 83.4 km
22	76.4	Ukiah - Boonville	125	17.1 mi / 27.5 km
23	76.2	Yreka - Happy Camp	225	70.5 mi / 113.5 km
24	76.0	Old Hopland - Lakeport	133	16.5 mi / 26.6 km
25	75.3	Moccasin - Bear Valley	417	25.9 mi / 41.7 km
26	75.2	Mariposa - Yosemite Jct	427	36.0 mi / 57.9 km
27	73.8	Cloverdale - Boonville	129	26.1 mi / 42.0 km
28	72.9	Woodside - San Gregorio	19	19.4 mi / 31.2 km
29	72.6	Jenner - Albion (Mendocino)	103	76.0 mi / 122.3 km
30	72.4	Fresno - Lakeshore	449	52.3 mi / 84.2 km
31	72.4	Willow Creek - Blue Lake (Arcata)	201	32.3 mi / 52.0 km
32	72.3	Ft Bragg - Willits	111	31.0 mi / 49.9 km
33	71.7	Shasta (Redding) - Douglas City	175	31.9 mi / 51.3 km

Traffic	Twistiness	Pavement	Engineering	Remoteness	Scenery	Character
Light	30.0	17.6	5.4	9.6	13.8	10.6
Very Light	30.0	19.4	5.8	9.0	9.7	11.1
Can be Heavy	26.8	17.8	7.0	6.1	11.5	14.2
Moderate	23.3	16.7	7.9	9.2	12.0	14.0
Moderate	30.0	19.0	4.9	6.7	10.2	11.7
Light	30.0	15.9	6.4	6.4	9.7	13.8
Light	30.0	17.4	6.3	6.4	8.6	13.2
Moderate	28.2	15.9	5.5	7.2	11.1	13.7
Moderate	30.0	15.6	5.8	6.2	9.0	14.4
Moderate	26.9	19.0	8.6	5.6	10.9	9.3
Light	28.1	17.9	5.7	7.6	8.9	11.4
Light	28.9	13.6	6.7	7.0	10.3	12.8
Moderate	26.8	17.5	6.8	5.3	10.2	12.6
Heavy	27.0	16.1	7.2	6.5	9.5	12.5
Light	29.5	15.9	5.7	7.5	10.0	10.1
Light	30.0	12.2	4.1	9.8	10.0	12.5
Light	25.9	16.3	5.0	9.0	12.2	9.8
Light	26.3	18.2	6.6	8.1	10.2	8.8
Light	27.2	16.0	6.1	7.5	8.1	12.9
Moderate	24.7	20.0	8.1	5.5	9.6	9.1
Light	30.0	13.6	4.7	6.9	8.6	12.7
Moderate	30.0	16.1	5.7	5.1	11.6	7.9
Light	23.7	18.1	6.5	4.5	10.0	13.4
Light	30.0	15.9	4.8	6.2	10.9	8.2
Light	30.0	14.5	3.2	7.2	10.7	9.7
Moderate	26.1	14.8	6.6	4.9	11.9	10.9
Moderate	29.2	16.3	5.9	3.7	9.7	9.0
Moderate	29.4	17.0	6.3	3.7	8.5	8.0
Moderate	24.0	17.0	5.5	4.0	11.0	11.1
Moderate	27.6	15.4	6.0	5.0	8.7	9.7
Moderate	24.0	17.9	9.3	5.8	10.2	5.2
Heavy	30.0	18.0	5.5	4.6	8.2	6.0
Heavy	25.3	17.2	8.6	5.5	9.9	5.2

Tires By Total Rating

DH No.	Total /100	Road Name	Pg No.	Length
34	71.2	Winters - Rutherford/Napa	61	35.0 mi / 56.3 km* 30.0 mi / 48.3 km*
35	70.8	Piedra (Fresno) - Kirch Flat	459	30.8 mi / 49.6 km
36	70.8	Mad River Loop	163	44.3 mi / 71.3 km
37	70.7	Tamalpais Valley - Tomales	93	43.2 mi / 69.5 km
38	70.7	Lassen Park Road	245	34.3 mi / 55.2 km
39	70.0	Boulder Creek - Saratoga (San Jose)	25	20.6 mi / 33.2 km
40	69.8	Riverton Jct - Meyers (S Lake Tahoe)	353	30.8 mi / 49.6 km
41	69.8	Arnold - Bear Valley Village	367	25.0 mi / 40.2 km
42	69.5	Taylorsville - Janesville (Susanville)	303	41.0 mi / 66.0 km
43	68.2	Oakhurst - Yosemite Jct	441	43.9 mi / 70.6 km
44	67.5	Douglas City - Triangle Jct	179	35.3 mi / 56.8 km
45	67.4	Plymouth - El Dorado (Placerville)	311	14.3 mi / 23.0 km
46	67.2	Clearlake - Hwy 16/Hwy 20 Jct	83	18.4 mi / 29.6 km
47	67.1	Livermore - Patterson	37	52.9 mi / 85.1 km
48	66.4	Lake Hennessey - Middleton	69	30.8 mi / 49.6 km
49	66.2	Chico - Hwy 32/Hwy 36/89 Jct	233	51.4 mi / 82.7 km
50	65.6	O'Brien, OR - Happy Camp	213	37.3 mi / 60.0 km
51	65.3	Camp Richardson (S Lake Tahoe) - Tahoma	359	15.0 mi / 24.1 km
52	65.1	Tuolumne - Cherry Lake	399	31.2 mi / 50.2 km
53	65.0	Calistoga - Kelseyville	73	36.0 mi / 57.9 km
54	64.4	Auburn - Foresthill	329	17.0 mi / 27.4 km
55	63.3	Saratoga Gap - Hwy 35/Hwy 92 Jct	13	26.2 mi / 42.2 km
56	63.2	Placerville - Auburn	323	23.6 mi / 38.0 km
57	62.5	Nevada City - Hwy 20/I-80 Jct	279	26.6 mi / 42.8 km
58	62.4	Crane Flat - Lee Vining	467	58.8 mi / 94.6 km
59	62.2	Dales (Red Bluff) - Hwy 32/Hwy 36/89 Jct	239	45.1 mi / 72.6 km
60	61.6	Eagle Lake Road	251	35.2 mi / 56.6 km
61	61.5	Red Corral - Mokelumne Hill	385	24.8 mi / 39.9 km
62	61.4	Bartle - McDoel Jct	261	59.1 mi / 95.1 km
63	61.4	Lee Vining - Benton	473	45.6 mi / 73.4 km
64	61.2	Lost Coast	151	66.6 mi / 107.2 km
65	60.6	Benton Crossing Road	479	30.6 mi / 49.2 km
66	60.6	Avenue of the Giants	145	31.6 mi / 50.9 km

Traffic	Twistiness	Pavement	Engineering	Remoteness	Scenery	Character
Moderate/ Heavy	30.0	11.6	5.3	4.0	9.9	10.4
Light	30.0	11.3	3.3	7.2	11.5	7.5
Light	26.3	16.6	5.2	6.6	9.1	7.0
Moderate	27.5	15.1	5.4	4.2	9.6	8.9
Moderate	26.0	15.1	5.2	6.1	12.7	5.6
Moderate	30.0	15.4	5.4	4	7.1	8.1
Brutal	24.0	18.6	7.8	4.1	10.3	5.0
LIght	23.4	16.5	8.2	6.2	9.5	6.0
Light	30.0	11.9	4.3	7.2	9.4	6.7
Brutal	30.0	10.1	3.8	6.7	10.3	7.3
Moderate	26.7	14.9	5.9	5.3	9.0	5.7
Moderate	25.1	15.6	5.7	4.5	9.4	7.1
Heavy	21.7	16.6	9.6	6.0	10.4	2.9
Light	30.0	10.6	3.8	5.8	9.6	7.3
Light	26.5	14.3	6.1	5.1	9.4	5.0
Moderate	23.5	13.6	7.2	7.0	8.8	6.1
Very Light	30.0	9.0	4.9	7.8	9.0	4.9
Almost Always Brutal	26.7	17.8	5.7	2.0	10.7	2.4
Light	30.0	9.1	2.9	9.7	9.0	4.4
Heavy	26.3	17.3	6.0	2.6	7.0	5.8
Heavy	22.5	18.5	9.7	3.1	7.9	2.7
Light	24.7	14.9	6.0	4.3	9.2	4.2
Brutal	26.6	16.4	5.8	2.3	8.2	3.9
Moderate	16.7	20.0	7.3	5.4	8.8	4.3
Can be Heavy	10.6	12.6	6.3	7.6	12.1	13.2
Moderate	14.6	19.9	8.4	6.0	9.7	3.6
Light	20.8	11.2	5.8	7.6	9.8	6.4
Very Light	30.0	12.1	4.7	3.9	6.8	4.0
Very Light	14.0	13.8	7.0	8.0	10.0	8.6
Light	9.8	15.2	6.1	9.5	12.6	8.2
Light	28.8	6.2	2.6	7.1	11.1	5.4
Light	7.3	16.8	8.4	9.6	12.1	6.4
Light	19.7	16.0	5.6	3.7	10.5	5.1

Tires By Total Rating

DH No.	Total /100	Road Name	Pg No.	Length
67	60.2	Pollock Pines - Plymouth	315	32.9 mi / 52.9 km
68	59.5	O'Neals - Oakhurst	433	30.1 mi / 48.4 km
69	59.0	Cool - Placerville	341	26.8 mi / 43.1 km
70	57.3	Waterford - Coulterville	407	38.8 mi / 62.4 km
71	57.2	Alturas - Cedarville	255	24.4 mi / 39.3 km
72	55.2	Capay - Hwy 16/Hwy 20 Jct	87	32.8 mi / 52.8 km
73	55.1	Merced Falls Road - Hornitos Road	413	32.4 mi / 52.1 km
74	55.0	Santa Cruz - Jamison Cr. Road/Hwy 236 Jct	31	17.9 mi / 28.8 km

Traffic	Twistiness	Pavement	Engineering	Remoteness	Scenery	Character
Moderate	25.2	12.6	6.2	3.8	7.1	5.3
Moderate	22.1	14.2	7.8	3.9	8.2	3.3
Moderate	25.0	12.7	4.4	3.8	7.8	5.3
Moderate	14.2	14.5	6.3	4.3	8.7	9.3
Light	12.2	14.8	6.8	6.1	11.4	5.9
Moderate	14.3	14.0	6.8	4.7	10.1	5.3
Light	19.4	12.2	4.9	4.8	9.2	4.6
Moderate	22.5	11.5	5.5	3.8	7.8	3.9

Tires - Top Ten

By Twistiness

DH No.	Total /100	Road Name	Length
24	76.0	Old Hopland - Lakeport	16.5 mi / 26.6 km
52	65.1	Tuolumne - Cherry Lake	31.2 mi / 50.2 km
35	70.8	Piedra (Fresno) - Kirch Flat	30.8 mi / 49.6 km
16	78.6	Mosquito Ridge Road	41.3 mi / 66.5 km
39	70.0	Boulder Creek - Saratoga (San Jose)	20.6 mi / 33.2 km
47	67.1	Livermore - Patterson	52.9 mi / 85.1 km
61	61.5	Red Corral - Mokelumne Hill	24.8 mi / 39.9 km
25	75.3	Moccasin - Bear Valley	25.9 mi / 41.7 km
5	82.5	Cleone (Ft Bragg) - Leggett	39.8 mi / 64.1 km
42	69.5	Taylorsville - Janesville (Susanville)	41.0 mi / 66.0 km

By Pavement

DH No.	Total /100	Road Name	Length
20	77.0	Crescent City - O'Brien, OR	41.4 mi / 66.6 km
57	62.5	Nevada City - Hwy 20/I-80 Jct	26.6 mi / 42.8 km
59	62.2	Dales (Red Bluff) - Hwy 32/Hwy 36/89 Jct	45.1 mi / 72.6 km
2	85.0	Callahan - Cecilville	29.8 mi / 48.0 km
5	82.5	Cleone (Ft Bragg) - Leggett	39.8 mi / 64.1 km
10	80.3	Dry Creek Road - Skaggs Springs Road	22.4 mi / 36.1 km
40	69.8	Riverton Jct - Meyers (South Lake Tahoe)	30.8 mi / 49.6 km
54	64.4	Auburn - Foresthill	17.0 mi / 27.4 km
18	78.2	Weaverville - Callahan	61.7 mi / 99.3 km
23	76.2	Yreka - Happy Camp	70.5 mi / 113.5 km

By Engineering

DH No.	Total /100	Road Name	Length
54	64.4	Auburn - Foresthill	17.0 mi / 27.4 km
46	67.2	Clearlake - Hwy 16/Hwy 20 Jct	18.4 mi / 29.6 km
31	72.4	Willow Creek - Blue Lake (Arcata)	32.3 mi / 52.0 km
10	80.3	Dry Creek Road - Skaggs Springs Road	22.4 mi / 36.1 km
33	71.7	Shasta (Redding) - Douglas City	31.9 mi / 51.3 km
59	62.2	Dales (Red Bluff) - Hwy 32/Hwy 36/89 Jct	45.1 mi / 72.6 km
65	60.6	Benton Crossing Road	30.6 mi / 49.2 km
41	69.8	Arnold - Bear Valley Village	25.0 mi / 40.2 km
20	77.0	Crescent City - O'Brien, OR	41.4 mi / 66.6 km
4	83.1	Hwy 88/Hwy 89 Jct - Barton	49.3 mi / /79.3 km

Traffic	Twistiness	Pavement	Engineering	Remoteness	Scenery	Character
Light	30.0	15.9	4.8	6.2	10.9	8.2
Light	30.0	9.1	2.9	9.7	9.0	4.4
Light	30.0	11.3	3.3	7.2	11.5	7.5
Light	30.0	12.2	4.1	9.8	10.0	12.5
Moderate	30.0	15.4	5.4	4	7.1	8.1
Light	30.0	10.6	3.8	5.8	9.6	7.3
Very Light	30.0	12.1	4.7	3.9	6.8	4.0
Light	30.0	14.5	3.2	7.2	10.7	9.7
Moderate	30.0	19.0	4.9	6.7	10.2	11.7
Light	30.0	11.9	4.3	7.2	9.4	6.7
Moderate	24.7	20.0	8.1	5.5	9.6	9.1
Moderate	16.7	20.0	7.3	5.4	8.8	4.3
Moderate	14.6	19.9	8.4	6.0	9.7	3.6
Very Light	30.0	19.4	5.8	9.0	9.7	11.1
Moderate	30.0	19.0	4.9	6.7	10.2	11.7
Moderate	26.9	19.0	8.6	5.6	10.9	9.3
Brutal	24.0	18.6	7.8	4.1	10.3	5.0
Heavy	22.5	18.5	9.7	3.1	7.9	2.7
Light	26.3	18.2	6.6	8.1	10.2	8.8
Light	23.7	18.1	6.5	4.5	10.0	13.4
Heavy	22.5	18.5	9.7	3.1	7.9	2.7
Heavy	21.7	16.6	9.6	6.0	10.4	2.9
Moderate	24.0	17.9	9.3	5.8	10.2	5.2
Moderate	26.9	19.0	8.6	5.6	10.9	9.3
Heavy	25.3	17.2	8.6	5.5	9.9	5.2
Moderate	14.6	19.9	8.4	6.0	9.7	3.6
Light	7.3	16.8	8.4	9.6	12.1	6.4
LIght	23.4	16.5	8.2	6.2	9.5	6.0
Moderate	24.7	20.0	8.1	5.5	9.6	9.1
Moderate	23.3	16.7	7.9	9.2	12.0	14.0

Tires - Top Ten

By Remoteness

DH No.	Total /100	Road Name	Length
16	78.6	Mosquito Ridge Road	41.3 mi / 66.5 km
52	65.1	Tuolumne - Cherry Lake	31.2 mi / 50.2 km
65	60.6	Benton Crossing Road	30.6 mi / 49.2 km
1	87.0	Topaz Lake - Markleeville	22.3 mi / 35.9 km
63	61.4	Lee Vining - Benton	45.6 mi / 73.4 km
4	83.1	Hwy 88/Hwy 89 Jct - Barton	49.3 mi / 79.3 km
2	85.0	Callahan - Cecilville	29.8 mi / 48.0 km
17	78.2	Big Pine - Oasis Jct, NV	38.1 mi / 61.3 km
18	78.2	Weaverville - Callahan	61.7 mi / 99.3 km
62	61.4	Bartle - McDoel Jct	59.1 mi / 95.1 km

By Scenery

DH No.	Total /100	Road Name	Length
1	87.0	Topaz Lake - Markleeville	22.3 mi / 35.9 km
38	70.7	Lassen Park Road	34.3 mi / 55.2 km
63	61.4	Lee Vining - Benton	45.6 mi / 73.4 km
17	78.2	Big Pine - Oasis Jct	38.1 mi / 61.3 km
65	60.6	Benton Crossing Road	30.6 mi / 49.2 km
58	62.4	Crane Flat - Lee Vining	58.8 mi / 94.6 km
4	83.1	Hwy 88/Hwy 89 Jct - Barton	49.3 mi / 79.3 km
26	75.2	Mariposa - Yosemite Jct	36.0 mi / 57.9 km
22	76.4	Ukiah - Boonville	17.1 mi / 27.5 km
35	70.8	Piedra (Fresno) - Kirch Flat	30.8 mi / 49.6 km

By Character

DH No.	Total /100	Road Name	Length
9	81.0	Nevada City - Sattley	73.4 mi / 117.6 km
3	83.4	Oroville - Greenville/Quincy	71.2 mi / 114.6 km 67.6 mi / 108.8 km
4	83.1	Hwy 88/Hwy 89 Jct - Barton	49.3 mi / 79.3 km
6	82.2	Carlotta (Fortuna) - Triangle Jct	65.3 mi / 105.1 km
8	81.6	Sonora Jct - Mi-Wuk Village (Twain Harte)	64.4 mi / 103.6 km
23	76.2	Yreka - Happy Camp	70.5 mi / 113.5 km
58	62.4	Crane Flat - Lee Vining	58.8 mi / 94.6 km
7	81.9	Quincy - Oroville	58.5 mi / 94.1 km
19	77.8	Georgetown - Riverton Jct	54.0 mi / 86.9 km
12	79.3	Happy Camp - Willow Creek	82.0 mi / 132.0 km

Traffic	Twistiness	Pavement	Engineering	Remoteness	Scenery	Character
Light	30.0	12.2	4.1	9.8	10.0	12.5
Light	30.0	9.1	2.9	9.7	9.0	4.4
Light	7.3	16.8	8.4	9.6	12.1	6.4
Light	30.0	17.6	5.4	9.6	13.8	10.6
Light	9.8	15.2	6.1	9.5	12.6	8.2
Moderate	23.3	16.7	7.9	9.2	12.0	14.0
Very Light	30.0	19.4	5.8	9.0	9.7	11.1
Light	25.9	16.3	5.0	9.0	12.2	9.8
Light	26.3	18.2	6.6	8.1	10.2	8.8
Very Light	14.0	13.8	7.0	8.0	10.0	8.6

Traffic	Twistiness	Pavement	Engineering	Remoteness	Scenery	Character
Light	30.0	17.6	5.4	9.6	13.8	10.6
Moderate	26.0	15.1	5.2	6.1	12.7	5.6
Light	9.8	15.2	6.1	9.5	12.6	8.2
Light	25.9	16.3	5.0	9.0	12.2	9.8
Light	7.3	16.8	8.4	9.6	12.1	6.4
Can be Heavy	10.6	12.6	6.3	7.6	12.1	13.2
Moderate	23.3	16.7	7.9	9.2	12.0	14.0
Moderate	26.1	14.8	6.6	4.9	11.9	10.9
Moderate	30.0	16.1	5.7	5.1	11.6	7.9
Light	30.0	11.3	3.3	7.2	11.5	7.5

Traffic	Twistiness	Pavement	Engineering	Remoteness	Scenery	Character
Moderate	30.0	15.6	5.8	6.2	9.0	14.4
Can be Heavy	26.8	17.8	7.0	6.1	11.5	14.2
Moderate	23.3	16.7	7.9	9.2	12.0	14.0
Light	30.0	15.9	6.4	6.4	9.7	13.8
Moderate	28.2	15.9	5.5	7.2	11.1	13.7
Light	23.7	18.1	6.5	4.5	10.0	13.4
Can be Heavy	10.6	12.6	6.3	7.6	12.1	13.2
Light	30.0	17.4	6.3	6.4	8.6	13.2
Light	27.2	16.0	6.1	7.5	8.1	12.9
Light	28.9	13.6	6.7	7.0	10.3	12.8

DEALER	APRILIA	BMW	BUELL	DUCATI	HARLEY-DAVIDSON	HONDA	KAWASAKI	KTM	MOTO GUZZI	SUZUKI	TRIUMPH	VICTORY	YAMAHA
BAY AREA – SANTA CRUZ MOUNTAINS													
Berkeley Honda 735 Gilman **Berkeley (Oakland)** 510.525.5525						●							●
Bay Area Yamaha 1601 Adrian **Burlingame (San Mateo)** 650.697.9750													●
Moto Italiano of Santa Cruz 200 Kennedy **Capitola (Santa Cruz)** 831.476.3663	●			●					●				
Concord Kawasaki Yamaha 1395 Galindo **Concord** 925.689.5770							●						●
Concord Motorsports 1651 Concord **Concord** 925.687.7742						●				●			
Mission Motorcycles 6232 Mission **Daly City (San Francisco)** 650.992.1234						●	●						●
Ankar Cycle Center 41315 Albrae **Fremont** 510.657.7200			●		●								
Fremont Honda Kawasaki 41545 Albrae **Fremont** 510.661.0100						●	●						
High Gear Powersports 7661 Monterey **Gilroy** 408.842.9955						●	●			●			●
Indian Victory Motorcycle 7191 Monterey **Gilroy** 408.848.2262												●	

DEALER	APRILIA	BMW	BUELL	DUCATI	HARLEY-DAVIDSON	HONDA	KAWASAKI	KTM	MOTO GUZZI	SUZUKI	TRIUMPH	VICTORY	YAMAHA
BAY AREA – SANTA CRUZ MOUNTAINS (Continued...)													
East Bay Motorsports 21756 Foothill **Hayward** 510.889.7900						●	●			●			●
Hollister Motor Sports 396 4th St **Hollister** 831.635.9323							●						
California Speed Sports 2310 Nissen **Livermore** 925.606.1998	●							●	●				
Livermore Buell HD 7576 Southfront **Livermore** 925.606.0100			●		●								
Milpitas Motorsports 620 S Main **Milpitas (San Jose)** 408.263.6060						●							
House of Thunder HD 16175 Condit **Morgan Hill** 408.776.1900					●								
Cal Moto 2490 Old Middlefield **Mountain View (San Jose)** 650.966.1183		●									●		
Oakland: *Also see Berkeley, San Leandro*													
Rockridge Two Wheels 5291 College **Oakland** 510.594.0789	●												
Oakley Sport 3765 Main **Oakley** 925.625.4390										●			
Devil Mountain Buell Harley Shop 2240 Loveridge **Pittsburg** 510.276.3525			●		●								

DEALER	APRILIA	BMW	BUELL	DUCATI	HARLEY-DAVIDSON	HONDA	KAWASAKI	KTM	MOTO GUZZI	SUZUKI	TRIUMPH	VICTORY	YAMAHA
BAY AREA – SANTA CRUZ MOUNTAINS (Continued...)													
Penninsula Buell HD 380 Convention **Redwood City** 650.568.0800			●		●								
Redwood City Hon Kaw 890 2nd Ave **Redwood City** 650.364.1104						●	●	●		●			
San Francisco: *Also see Daly City*													
BMW of San Francisco 1675 Howard **San Francisco** 415.551.4207		●											
Dudley Perkins Co. 66 Page **San Francisco** 415.703.9494			●		●								
Golden Gate Cycles 1540 Pine **San Francisco** 415.771.4535						●	●			●			●
Munroe Motors (**D-MV AUG**) 412 Valencia **San Francisco** 415.626.3496				●					●		●		
Scuderia West (**D-BIM**) 69 Duboce **San Francisco** 415.621.7223	●							●				●	
San Jose: *Also see Milpitas, Moutain View, Santa Clara, Sunnyvale*													
GP Sports 2020 Camden **San Jose** 408.377.8780						●				●			●
Moto Italiano 1425 W San Carlos **San Jose** 408.287.6680	●								●		●		
San Jose BMW 1886 W San Carlos **San Jose** 408.295.0205		●											

DEALER	APRILIA	BMW	BUELL	DUCATI	HARLEY-DAVIDSON	HONDA	KAWASAKI	KTM	MOTO GUZZI	SUZUKI	TRIUMPH	VICTORY	YAMAHA
BAY AREA – SANTA CRUZ MOUNTAINS **(Continued...)**													
San Jose Harley-Davidson 1551 Parkmoor **San Jose** 408.998.1464					●								
San Jose Yamaha 776 N 13th St **San Jose** 408.287.2946													●
Bay Area Motorsports 10550 International **San Leandro (Oakland)** 510.635.6300						●	●						
Bob Dron Harley-Davidson 200 Hegenberger **San Leandro (Oakland)** 510.635.0100					●								
Munroe Motors East Bay 15296 E 14th St **San Leandro (Oakland)** 510.276.3525				●				●			●		
Rockridge Two Wheels 5291 College **San Leandro (Oakland)** 510.594.0789	●												
Suzuki of Oakland 6601 San Leandro **San Leandro (Oakland)** 510.569.4767										●			
San Mateo: *Also see Burlingame*													
Honda Suzuki of San Mateo 101 E 25th Ave **San Mateo** 650.341.5867						●				●			
Mcquire HD Shop 2000 San Ramon Valley **San Ramon** 925.838.4647					●								
GP Sports 2360 El Camino Real **Santa Clara (San Jose)** 408.246.7323							●			●			●

DEALER	APRILIA	BMW	BUELL	DUCATI	HARLEY-DAVIDSON	HONDA	KAWASAKI	KTM	MOTO GUZZI	SUZUKI	TRIUMPH	VICTORY	YAMAHA
BAY AREA – SANTA CRUZ MOUNTAINS (Continued...)													
Santa Cruz: *Also see Capitola*													
All American Hon Suz 6990 Soquel **Santa Cruz** 831.476.8100						●	●			●			
Moore & Sons Motorcycles 2-1431 E Cliff **Santa Cruz** 831.475.3619								●					
Santa Cruz Buell HD 1148 Soquel **Santa Cruz** 831.421.9600			●		●								
Bike World 953 W El Camino Real **Sunnyvale (San Jose)** 408.245.4888							●			●			
Honda Penninsula 1289 W El Camino Real **Sunnyvale (San Jose)** 650.967.1539				●		●							
Diablo Kawasaki BMW 1255 Parkside **Walnut Creek** 925.938.8373		●					●						
McGuire Buell HD 1425 Parkside **Walnut Creek** 925.945.6500			●		●								
BMW Yamaha of Santa Cruz County 1875 Main **Watsonville** 831.722.6262		●											●
Green Valley Buell HD 1059 S Green Valley **Watsonville** 831.768.9500			●		●								

DEALER	APRILIA	BMW	BUELL	DUCATI	HARLEY-DAVIDSON	HONDA	KAWASAKI	KTM	MOTO GUZZI	SUZUKI	TRIUMPH	VICTORY	YAMAHA
WINE COUNTRY													
Michael's Harley-Davidson 7601 Redwood **Cotati (Rohnert Park)** 707.793.9180					●								
Fairfield Cycle Center 1800 West Texas **Fairfield** 707.432.1660						●				●			
Yamaha of Napa 459 Soscol **Napa** 707.254.7432													●
Santa Rosa: *Also see Windsor (Russian Coast Region)*													
Jim & Jim's of Santa Rosa 910 Santa Rosa **Santa Rosa** 707.545.1672										●			●
Moto Mechanica 1111 Petaluma Hill **Santa Rosa** 707.578.6686	●			●					●		●		
Northbay Motorsport 2875 Santa Rosa **Santa Rosa** 707.542.5355						●	●	●					
Revolution Moto 301 D St **Santa Rosa** 707.523.2371	●												
Santa Rosa Vee Twin 1240 Petaluma Hill **Santa Rosa** 707.523.9696												●	
Parriott Motors 1027 Pope **St Helena** 707.963.3190						●							
Vacaville Harley-Davidson 100 Auto Center **Vacaville** 707.455.7000					●								

DEALER	APRILIA	BMW	BUELL	DUCATI	HARLEY-DAVIDSON	HONDA	KAWASAKI	KTM	MOTO GUZZI	SUZUKI	TRIUMPH	VICTORY	YAMAHA
WINE COUNTRY (Continued...)													
Vacaville Motorsports 1385 E Monte Vista **Vacaville** 707.469.7195							●						●
Buell HD of Vallejo 1600 Sonoma **Vallejo** 707.643.1413			●		●								
Mach1 Motorsports 510 Couch **Vallejo** 707.643.2548						●		●					●
Suz Powersports of Vallejo 33 Tennessee **Vallejo** 707.644.3756							●			●			
RUSSIAN COAST													
Golden Gate HD Buell 13 San Clemente **Corte Madera** 415.927.4464			●		●								
Marin Cycleworks 5776 Paradise **Corte Madera** 415.924.0327						●	●			●			
Hillside Honda 460 S Main **Lakeport** 707.263.9000						●							●
Golden Gate HD Buell 7077 Redwood **Novato** 415.878.4988			●		●								
Cycle West Honda Suzuki 1375 Industrial **Petaluma** 707.769.5240						●				●			
G&B Kawasaki Yamaha 326 Petaluma **Petaluma** 707.763.4658							●						●

DEALER	APRILIA	BMW	BUELL	DUCATI	HARLEY-DAVIDSON	HONDA	KAWASAKI	KTM	MOTO GUZZI	SUZUKI	TRIUMPH	VICTORY	YAMAHA
RUSSIAN COAST (Continued...)													
Hattar Motorsports 601 East Francisco **San Rafael** 415.456.3345				●							●		●
Marin BMW Motorcycles 30 Castro **San Rafael** 415.454.2041		●											
Buell HD of Ukiah 2501 N State **Ukiah** 707.462.1672			●		●								
Lost Coast Motorcycles of Ukiah 1125 S State **Ukiah** 707.462.5160										●			●
Motosports of Ukiah 1850 N State **Ukiah** 707.462.8653						●	●						
Ukiah Cycle Center 1420 S State **Ukiah** 707.463.2424								●					
Santa Rosa BMW 800 American **Windsor (Santa Rosa)** 707.838.9100		●											
REDWOODS													
S & K Yamaha 1156 Monroe **Red Bluff (Santa Rosa)** 530.527.1466													●
Redding: *Also see Shasta Lake*													
Fator's Motorcycle Sales 682 Grove **Redding** 530.221.6612								●		●			
Lee's Honda Kawasaki 2230 Larkspur **Redding** 530.221.6788						●	●					●	

DEALER	APRILIA	BMW	BUELL	DUCATI	HARLEY-DAVIDSON	HONDA	KAWASAKI	KTM	MOTO GUZZI	SUZUKI	TRIUMPH	VICTORY	YAMAHA
REDWOODS (Continued...)													
Redding Harley-Davidson 1268 Twin View **Redding** 530.241.7117					●								
Dazey's Motorsports 591 Briceland **Redway** 707.923.4332													●
Redding Yamaha 3119 Twin View **Shasta Lake (Redding)** 530.275.7300													●
WILD RIVER													
Eureka Motorsports 1601 Broadway **Eureka** 707.445.3093							●	●		●			
Redwood HD Buell 21 West 4th St **Eureka** 707.444.0111			●		●								
Richard Miller Motorcycles 1725 Tomlinson **Eureka** 707.443.8031						●							●
Yreka Motorsports 1409 S Main **Yreka** 530.842.0706										●			
INTER MOUNTAIN													
Chico Honda Motorcycles 11096 Midway **Chico** 530.342.4216						●							
Chico Motorsports 1538 Park **Chico** 530.345.5247							●			●			
Glende Polaris 2838 Highway 32 **Chico** 530.345.2886												●	

DEALER	APRILIA	BMW	BUELL	DUCATI	HARLEY-DAVIDSON	HONDA	KAWASAKI	KTM	MOTO GUZZI	SUZUKI	TRIUMPH	VICTORY	YAMAHA
INTER MOUNTAIN (Continued...)													
Hall's HD & Buell 1501 Mangrove **Chico** 530.893.1918			●		●								
Ozzie's BMW Center 2438 Cohasset **Chico** 530.345.4462		●											
Yamaha of Chico 1341 Mangrove **Chico** 530.343.2192				●				●					●
FOREST REGION													
Motor Services JCT Hwy 89 & 36 **Chester** 530.258.3856								●					●
Sierra Yamaha 94601 Hwy 70 **Chilcoot** 530.993.4310													●
GOLD COUNTRY													
Apex Honda Suzuki Yamaha 536 Grass Valley (Hwy 49) **Auburn** 530.885.7105						●				●			●
Auburn HD Buell 12075 Locksley **Auburn** 530.885.7161			●		●								
Auburn Power Sports 1460 Canal **Auburn** 530.823.5768							●					●	
HD Buell of Folsom 115 Woodmere **Folsom** 916.608.9922			●		●								
Folsom Cycle & ATV 82 Clarksville **Folsom** 916.984.5600							●			●			

DEALER	APRILIA	BMW	BUELL	DUCATI	HARLEY-DAVIDSON	HONDA	KAWASAKI	KTM	MOTO GUZZI	SUZUKI	TRIUMPH	VICTORY	YAMAHA
GOLD COUNTRY (Continued...)													
Folsom Lake Yamaha 291 Iron Point **Folsom** 916.294.0000													●
Sierra Motor Sports 12121 Nevada City **Grass Valley** 530.273.1384						●		●		●			
Hangtown HD Buell 629 Main **Placerville** 530.344.0401			●		●								
Mike's Cycle of Placerville 291 Placerville **Placerville** 530.622.0209							●						
RPS Motor Sports 4516 Missouri Flat **Placerville** 530.295.8286										●			
Buell HD of Rocklin 4425 Granite **Rocklin** 916.624.9211			●		●								
HIGH SIERRA													
HD of Jamestown 18275 Highway 108 **Jamestown** 209.984.4888					●								
Gold Rush Honda Yamaha 358 W Stockton **Sonora** 209.532.2371						●							●
YOSEMITE													
BMW of Fresno Motorcycles 4646 N Blackstone **Fresno** 559.229.7892		●											
Clawson Motorsports 6334 N Blackstone **Fresno** 559.435.5020						●	●			●			●

DEALER	APRILIA	BMW	BUELL	DUCATI	HARLEY-DAVIDSON	HONDA	KAWASAKI	KTM	MOTO GUZZI	SUZUKI	TRIUMPH	VICTORY	YAMAHA
YOSEMITE (Continued...)													
HD Buell of Fresno 4345 W Shaw **Fresno** 559.275.8586			●		●								
Mathews Harley-Davidson 548 Blackstone **Fresno** 559.233.5279					●								
Wilson's Motorcycles 443 Broadway #1467 **Fresno** 559.237.0215				●			●	●			●		●
Honda Suzuki of Madera 124 South East st **Madera** 559.674.0041						●				●			
Yamaha 99 28615 Green Court **Madera** 559.645.4545													●
Merced Power Sports 265 W 15th St **Merced** 209.722.8055						●	●			●			●
Yosemite Harley-Davidson 1645 W Hwy 140 **Merced** 209.723.9702					●								
Cycle Specialities BMW 307 Maze **Modesto** 209.524.2955		●											
DH Cycles 531 Kansas **Modesto** 209.524.1588								●		●			
Honda of Modesto 1120 N Carpenter **Modesto** 209.529.5424						●	●						
Mitchell's Modesto HD 500 N Carpenter **Modesto** 209.522.1061					●								

DEALER	APRILIA	BMW	BUELL	DUCATI	HARLEY-DAVIDSON	HONDA	KAWASAKI	KTM	MOTO GUZZI	SUZUKI	TRIUMPH	VICTORY	YAMAHA
YOSEMITE (Continued...)													
Modesto Ducati 1408 N Carpenter **Modesto** 209.578.1330				●									
Yamaha of Modesto 1302 9th St **Modesto** 209.527.5603													●
BORDERLAND													
Golden State Cycle 174 S Main **Bishop** 760.872.1570						●							●
Mammoth Motorsports 160 Commerce **Mammoth Lakes** 760.924.3155								●					
CENTRAL VALLEY													
CVA MAP I													
Yreka Suzuki 1409 S Main **Yreka** 530.841.0861										●			
CVA MAP II													
Fator's Motorcycle Sales 682 Grove **Redding** 530.221.6612								●		●			
Lee's Honda Kawasaki 2230 Larkspur **Redding** 530.221.6788						●	●						
Redding Harley-Davidson 1268 Twin View **Redding** 530.241.7117					●								
Redding Yamaha 3119 Twin View **Shasta Lake (Redding)** 530.275.7300													●

DEALER	APRILIA	BMW	BUELL	DUCATI	HARLEY-DAVIDSON	HONDA	KAWASAKI	KTM	MOTO GUZZI	SUZUKI	TRIUMPH	VICTORY	YAMAHA
CENTRAL VALLEY (Continued...)													
CVA MAP III													
Peterich Cycle and Engineering 212 E Walker **Orland** 530.865.9433							●			●			
S & K Yamaha 1156 Monroe **Red Bluff** 530.527.1466													●
CVA MAP IV													
Guidera's Harley-Davidson 720 Onstott Frontage W **Yuba City** 530.673.3548					●								
Honda Yamaha Sports Center 2530 Colusa **Yuba City** 530.673.5676						●							●
Riverfront Kawasaki Suzuki 437 N Palora **Yuba City** 530.673.3744							●			●			
Twin Rivers Polaris 501 Plumas **Yuba City** 530.673.2525												●	
Dow Lewis Motors 1722 Highway 99 **Gridley** 530.846.6700							●						
Gridley Growers 700 Hazel **Gridley** 530.846.5666						●							
CVA MAP V													
Carmichael Honda 7829 Fair Oaks **Carmichael (Sacramento)** 916.944.1318						●							
Elk Grove Cycle Center 8672 W Stockton **Elk Grove** 916.525.2444						●							

DEALER	APRILIA	BMW	BUELL	DUCATI	HARLEY-DAVIDSON	HONDA	KAWASAKI	KTM	MOTO GUZZI	SUZUKI	TRIUMPH	VICTORY	YAMAHA
CENTRAL VALLEY (Continued...)													
Harley-Davidson of Elk Grove Shop 10291 E Stockton **Elk Grove** 916.714.6952					●								
Nor-Cal Motorsports 9175 Union Park Way **Elk Grove** 916.714.1350								●					
Wright Motors 214 N Sacremento **Lodi** 209.368.1139										●			●
Oakley Sport 3765 Main **Oakley** 925.625.4390										●			
A & S BMW Motorcycles 1125 Orlando **Roseville (Sacramento)** 916.726.7334		●											
Motorcycle Performance Center 100 Louis **Roseville (Sacramento)** 916.722.2300								●					
Roseville Cycle Center 900 Riverside **Roseville (Sacramento)** 916.782.2171						●	●			●			
Roseville Yamaha 2014 Taylor, # I-80 **Roseville (Sacramento)** 916.784.2444													●
Sacramento: Also see Carmichael, Roseville													
Capitol Yamaha 4622 Auburn **Sacramento** 916.485.9200													●
Good Times Motorsports 4727 Auburn **Sacramento** 916.344.8835	●			●			●			●			

DEALER	APRILIA	BMW	BUELL	DUCATI	HARLEY-DAVIDSON	HONDA	KAWASAKI	KTM	MOTO GUZZI	SUZUKI	TRIUMPH	VICTORY	YAMAHA
CENTRAL VALLEY (Continued...)													
HD of Sacramento 1000 Arden **Sacramento** 916.929.4680					●								
Kawasaki of Sacramento 5830 Florin **Sacramento** 916.290.8555							●						
P.C.P. Motorsports 6500 Freeport **Sacramento** 916.428.4040										●			●
Performance Cycle 5201 Auburn **Sacramento** 916.344.7911											●	●	
Jorgy's Suzuki Recreational Center 2955 N Wilson **Stockton** 209.463.2912							●			●			
Stockton Honda Yamaha 3295 N Ad Art **Stockton** 209.931.7940						●							●
Valley HD Buell 711 E Miner **Stockton** 209.941.0420			●		●								
Schroeder Motor Sports 460 North East **Woodland** 530.406.8706							●					●	
Woodland Cycle & Saw 32 Kentucky **Woodland** 530.666.5349										●			●
CENTRAL VALLEY DONUT HOLE													
Dixon Polaris 1150 N First **Dixon** 707.693.8166												●	

DEALER	APRILIA	BMW	BUELL	DUCATI	HARLEY-DAVIDSON	HONDA	KAWASAKI	KTM	MOTO GUZZI	SUZUKI	TRIUMPH	VICTORY	YAMAHA
CENTRAL VALLEY (Continued...)													
CENTRAL VALLEY DONUT HOLE													
Golden Valley HD Shop 1415 Badger Flat **Los Banos** 209.827.5900					●								
Pacheco Power Centre 1560 W Pacheco **Los Banos** 209.826.2575												●	
Malott's Honda 1780 E Yosemite **Manteca** 209.823.7181						●							●

See Index for page references

ACLU	*(org)* organization steadfastly committed to the protection of your civil liberties. Unless you insist on not wearing a helmet
Accelero Tributum Exactor	*(lat)* see speed tax collector
Alice's Restaurant	*(n)* place where you can get anything you want
Aotearoa	*(maori)* aka Land of the Long White Dotted Line. Non-colonial name for New Zealand
Bayatopolis	*(n)* Bay Area
Belly-shover	*(n)* sport rider
Berkeley Free Ride Movement	*(n)* 1960's predecessor to Greypeace
Bond, James	*(n)* Sean Connery. Period.
Bonds, Barry	(1964-) misunderstood San Francisco Giants left fielder
boomer	*(n)* person born between 1945 and 1963
Brent, David	*(n)* fictional boss who's all too real
Byronic	*(adj)* as relating to Scottish romantic poet Lord Byron (1788-1824)
California Highway Patrol	*(org)* state operated speed tax collecting organization
CalTrans	*(org)* California Department of Transportation
Canadian Passport	*(n)* hairstyle indistinguishable from the classic mullet
Carmelite	*(n)* serious Catholic
Carthusian	*(n) very* serious Catholic
Cenozoic Era	*(n)* period in history when all roads were gravel
Chapman, Brent	(1959-) husband of Kerry-Lynne Findlay
CHP	*(abb)* see California Highway Patrol
CHiP	*(n)* endearing term for CHP member. Never used by native Californians.
Class M Licence	*(n)* a Californian's ticket to ride
COG	(abb) Concours Owners Group. Not to be confused with HOG. Or maybe it is.
Constable, John	(1776-1837) English landscape artist whose paintings score 10/10 for Scenery

Crowe, Russell	(1964-) actor, musician, heartthrob and Heritage Softail enthusiast
Cruise, Tom	(1962-) OT VII who rides in the missionary position
Dali, Salvador	(1904-1989) artist, founder of surrealism and constant source of inspiration for Orange County Choppers
de Cosmos, Amor	(1825-1897) Flaky Placerville photographer who became premier of British Columbia in 1872, thus forging a link between *Destination Highways NorCal* and *Destination Highways BC*
Destination Highways Oregon	*(n)* mythical motorcycle tour guide book
Dershowitz, Alan	*(n)* guy you hire when you really, really need to beat that ticket.
dueling banjoes	*(n)* Ned Beatty's favorite tune
Ekland, Britt	(1942-) Airhead with diminishing valve lift clearance
ER	*(n)* TV show that reminds you to dress for the crash
Far Side	*(n)* apolitical cartoon strip that makes dumb animals seem human
Ford, Henry J.	(1863-1947) American pylonmaker and rabid anti-motorcyclist
GLBT	*(abbr)* easy way to say Gay Lesbian Bisexual Transgendered without tripping over your tongue, startling grandma or leaving anyone out. Often confused with a sandwich involving bacon
Golden Tablets	*(n)* after-market product for the GWRRA member who has everything
Grammys	*(n)* famously lame American music awards
Grasshopper	*(n)* Beaver Cleaver with an oriental twist
Greypeace	*(n)* international nonprofit society dedicated to the preservation and development of twisty paved roads
Grimm's Fairy Tales	*(n)* politically incorrect 19th century stories for kids
Harte, Bret	(1836-) writer/wrestler
Hayden, Nicky	(1981-) young gun of the AMA Superbike
Homer's Odyssey	*(n)* antiquated piece of fiction loosely based on fact. Rather like the California Vehicle Code
illegitimus non carborundum	*(lat)* "don't let the bastards grind you down"

ilico via	*(lat)* "on the road"
Impressionist	*(n)* artistic movement from the latter part of the 19th century. Exquisitely captured how the world looks after too many Amstels in the sun
Johnson, Jimmie	(1975-) perennial NASCAR title contender
Jon	*(n)* cute, non-threatening speed tax collector
keystone cop	*(n)* speed tax collector in sepia
Knowles, Beyonce	(1981-) one of Destiny's Children
Knox, John	(1505-1572) father of the Scottish Protestant Reformation
Lavalife	*(n)* dating and relationship site your friends use
Lazio	*(n)* region of Italy
Lincoln, Abraham	(1809-1865) *(n)* sixteenth president of the United States and inventor of the cruiser riding position
Linnaeus' *System Naturae*	*(lat)* system for classifying natural phenomena developed by the Swedish doctor, Carlos Linnaeus in 1758. Despite 250 years of revision, experts still can't decide where to fit scooters
Llewellyn, Richard	(1906-1983) author who inspired the forthcoming *Destination Highways South Wales*
Loch Ness	*(gael)* large, deep, freshwater lake in the Scottish Highlands 175 mi (280 km) from Glasgow Ducati
MacAdam, John Loudon	(1756-1836) inventor of modern pavement. And dedicatee of *Destination Highways BC*
McCovey, Willie	(1938-) former baseball great. Now purveyor of the McCoveyburger
MacGregor, Ewan	(1971-) Scottish actor with motorcycling cred
maxburns	*(v)* to ride on gravel. Derived from Max Burns (1904-), renowned Canadian motorcycle writer and dirt afficianado. maxburner *(n)* maxburning *(adv)*
Maxburnism	*(n)* gravel-based belief system
Mayhew, Tim	(c.1970-) creator of pashnit.com, website featuring a comprehensive collection of bumpy, poorly engineered, one-lane California roads
Mays, Willie	(1931-) Say Hey Kid and tea totaling godfather of Barry Bonds
Mecca	*(n)* Sturgis for Muslims
Mona Lisa	(1479-?) Pre-Vespa Italian chick
Mladin, Mat	(1972-) Four time American Superbike Champion

APPENDICES

Musee d'Orsay	*(fr)* Orsay Museum
natural nine	*(n)* winning baccarat hand
Nicholson, Jack	(1937-) Easy Riding Hell's Angel on Wheels
PMQs	*(abb/mil)* private married quarters
Pollock, Jackson	(1912–1956) Abstract Expressionist who missed the wrong corner
Ponch	*(n)* agnostic incarnation of Erik Estrada
Post-Impressionist	*(n)* pre-airbrush
pucks	*(n)* footboards for sportbike riders
pylon	*(n)* any vehicle not a motorcycle
pyloneer	*(n)* one who operates a pylon
Reese, Kyle	*(n)* character who took on Schwarzenneger and won. Fictional
Rock of Gilbraltar	*(n)* extremely large rock overlooking the strait that links the Atlantic to the Mediterranean. Even bigger than the one in the middle of the road that time…
Sacramauburnville	*(n)* what Sacramento, Auburn and Placerville are becoming
Santana, Carlos	(1947-) legendary guitarist sometimes confused with George Santayana (1863-1952). Better axeman but not quite as deep a thinker
Seeger, Pete	(1919-) iconic American folk singer who looks at life from both sides
Serengetis	*(n)* sunglasses for people too cheap to buy Revos but sensible enough to avoid the cheap plastic gas-station crap that Bosworth wears
serofa domesticus	*(n)* domestic pig
show-and-shine	*(n)* motorcycle event where form overwhelms function
siren	*(n)* femme fatale
soul grind	*(n)* X-speak for a grind where the leading skate is parallel with an obstacle and the rear is perpendicular to it
speed tax collector	*(n)* police officer
STC	*(abb)* see speed tax collector
Sullivan	*(n)* twisty, poorly paved, one-lane road. Named for Dan Sullivan, SF Bay Area COG member from Napa who seeks out twisty, poorly paved one-lane roads – and then highsides on them

Syracusean	*(n)* citizen of the ancient city of Syracuse, Utah
TIRES	*(abb)* Total Integrated Road Evaluation System.
Tetris	*(n)* Russian Pong
Theron, Charlize	(1975-) the other naked Monster
Tin Lizzie	*(n)* nickname for the Ford Model T, mass produced between 1908 and 1927
trailer-queening	*(v)* when "Live to Ride" becomes "Drive to Ride"
Twain, Mark	(1835-1910) American humorist and author. No relation to…
Twain, Shania	(1965-) Canadian recording artist and digital motorcyclist
UPS	*(abb)* United Parcel Service. Renowned for being everywhere you don't want them to be.
Via Destinatum	*(lat)* Destination Highway
Via eram brevis tamen dulcis	*(lat)* "The road is short however sweet"
Victor Foxtrot Roger	*(mil)* Military-speak for Honda VFR
Voltaire	(1694-1778) French philosopher and satirist
Wallenda	*(n)* trapeze artist who rides without a net
"Who'll ride the road? I, said the motorcyclist."	*(quot)* Variation on motorcycling poem from the early 1800's, Who Killed Cock Robin?
Webster, Noah	(1758-1843) American lexicographer who saw money in reversing "re" and dropping the "u" in perfectly good words
Woleesenbet, Daniel	(c.1962-) Alameda County's Director of Public Works
Women on Wheels	*(n)* National Female MC. Inventors of several "If you can read this…" T-shirt variations.
Yin and Yang	*(n)* ancient Chinese logo
Zamboni	*(n)* dream machine that repaves the road before every ride

INDEX

Contact Information:

Twisted Edge Publishing Inc.
Suite 194 - 1857 West 4th Avenue
Vancouver, BC, Canada
V6J 1M4

Phone: 604.721.5001 (toll free: 877.655.5006)
Fax: 604.721.5002 (toll free: 877.655.5007)
Website: destinationhighways.com
Email: info@destinationhighways.com

Get all three Destination Highways books

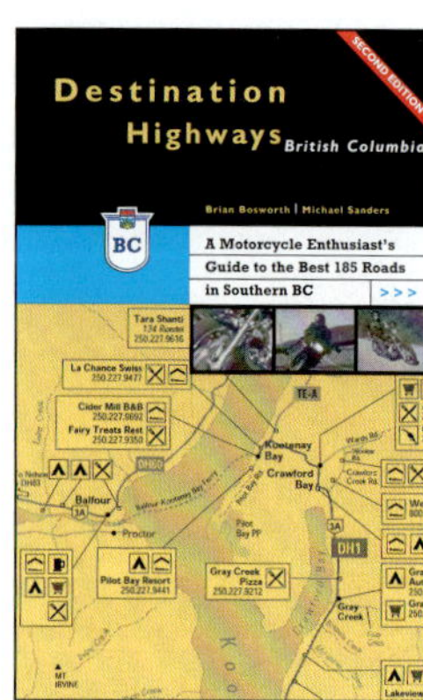

DH BC

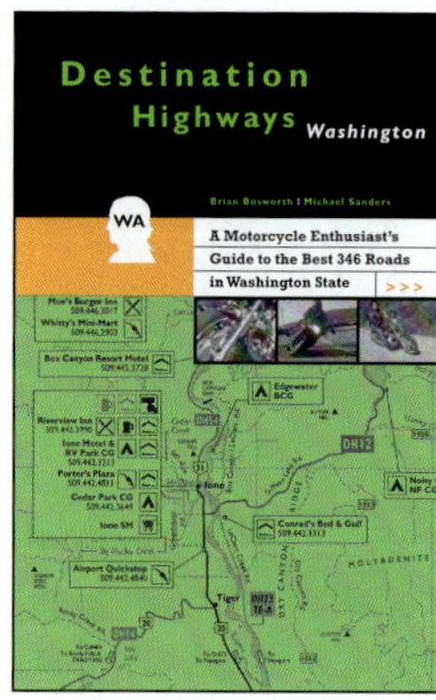

DH Washington

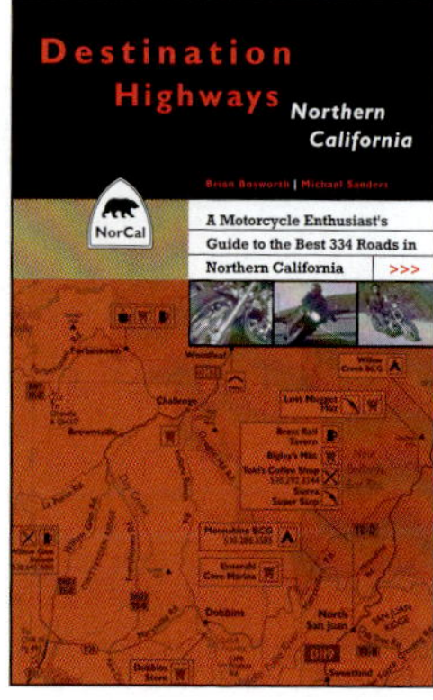

DH NorCal

Dealer inquiries welcome

Hundreds of businesses displaying this sticker offer a discount to riders upon presentation of any Destination Highways book. Most are not in listed in our books and are listed only at *DH Rider Discounts* on destinationhighways.com. For the latest additions, print the list off just before you leave.

Use just a few *DH Rider Discounts* and basically, you get all the information in the book for free. Plus, you'll be patronizing motorcycle-friendly places, some of which are run by fellow riders, who will offer you a warm and friendly reception.

If you have a business and want to offer a *DH Rider Discount* to enthusiasts who own a Destination Highways book, go to destinationhighways.com, click on the *DH Rider Discounts* link at the top of the main menu, and fill out the form at the bottom of the page.

Contact Information:

Twisted Edge Publishing Inc.
Suite 194 - 1857 West 4th Avenue
Vancouver, BC, Canada
V6J 1M4

Phone: 604.721.5001 (toll free: 877.655.5006)
Fax: 604.721.5002 (toll free: 877.655.5007)
Website: destinationhighways.com
Email: info@destinationhighways.com

Get all three Destination Highways books

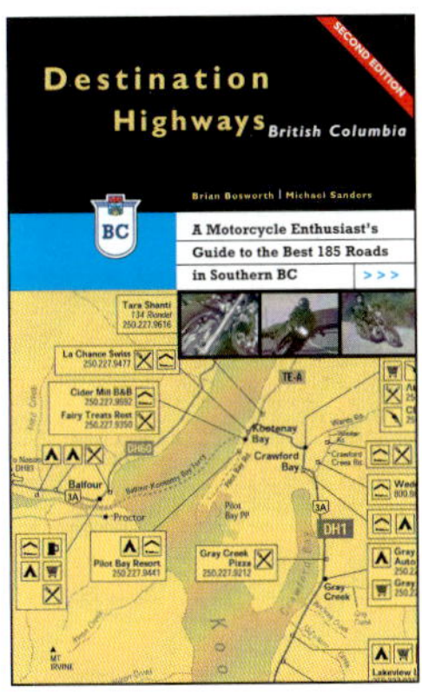

DH BC

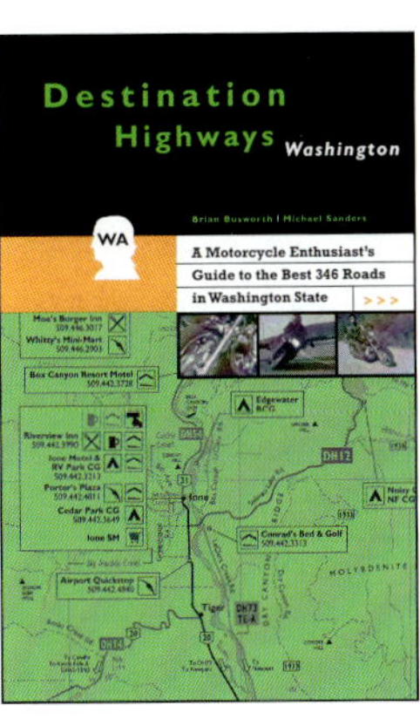

DH Washington

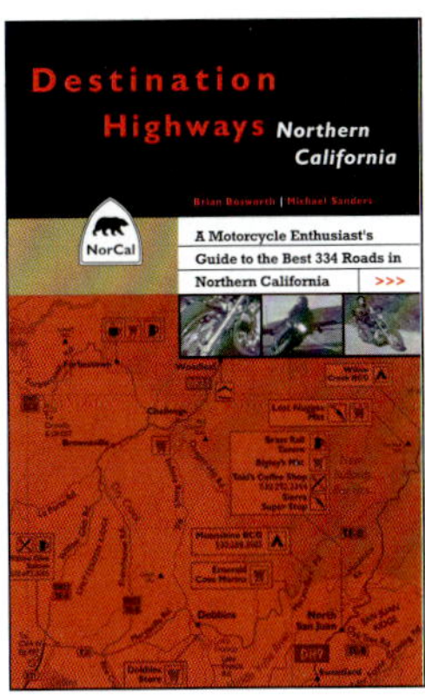

DH NorCal

Dealer inquiries welcome

TEAR OUT

Contact Information:

Twisted Edge Publishing Inc.
Suite 194 - 1857 West 4th Avenue
Vancouver, BC, Canada
V6J 1M4

Phone: 604.721.5001 (toll free: 877.655.5006)
Fax: 604.721.5002 (toll free: 877.655.5007)
Website: destinationhighways.com
Email: info@destinationhighways.com

Get all three Destination Highways books

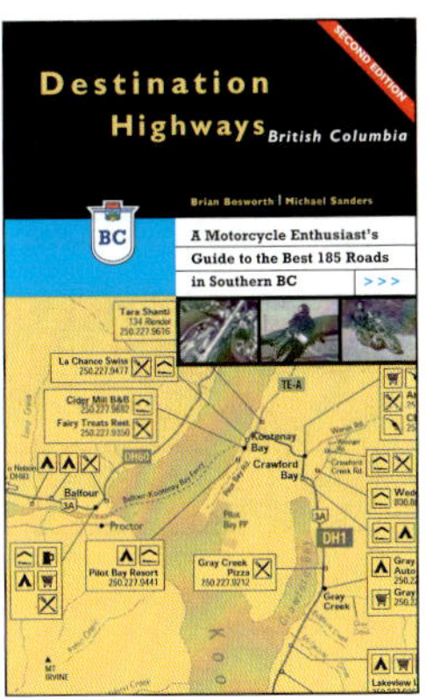

DH BC

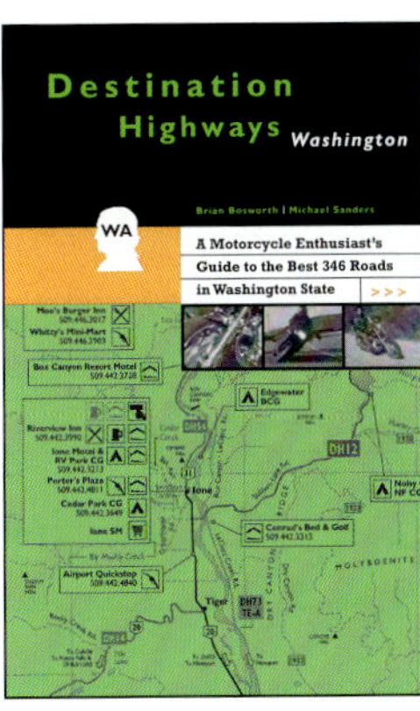

DH Washington

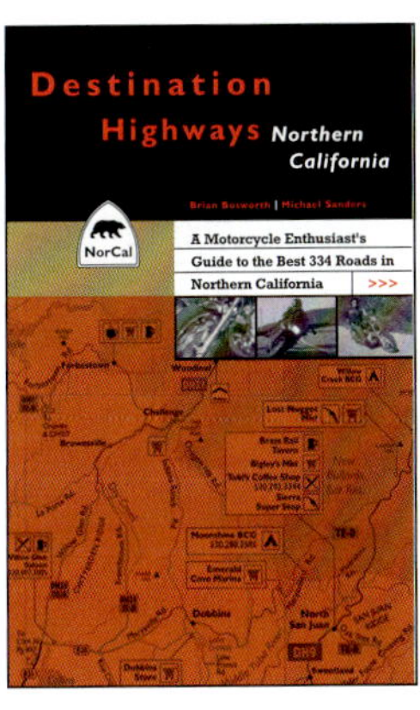

DH NorCal

Dealer inquiries welcome

Contact Information:

Twisted Edge Publishing Inc.
Suite 194 - 1857 West 4th Avenue
Vancouver, BC, Canada
V6J 1M4

Phone: 604.721.5001 (toll free: 877.655.5006)
Fax: 604.721.5002 (toll free: 877.655.5007)
Website: destinationhighways.com
Email: info@destinationhighways.com

Get all three Destination Highways books

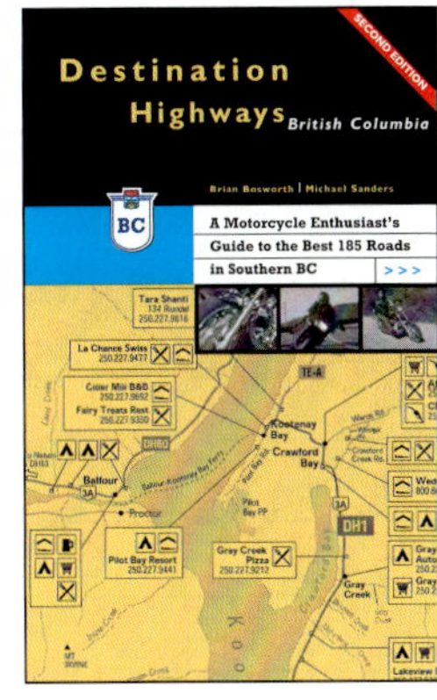

DH BC

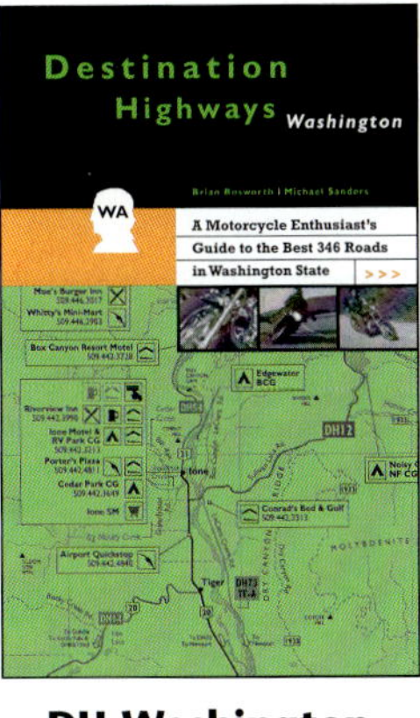

DH Washington

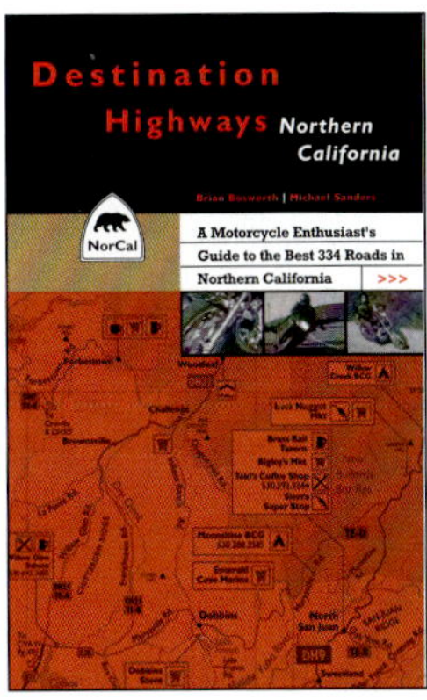

DH NorCal

Dealer inquiries welcome

CONTACT INFORMATION:

Twisted Edge Publishing Inc.
Suite 194 - 1857 West 4th Avenue
Vancouver, BC, Canada
V6J 1M4

Phone: 604.721.5001 (toll free: 877.655.5006)
Fax: 604.721.5002 (toll free: 877.655.5007)
Website: destinationhighways.com
Email: info@destinationhighways.com

Get all three Destination Highways books

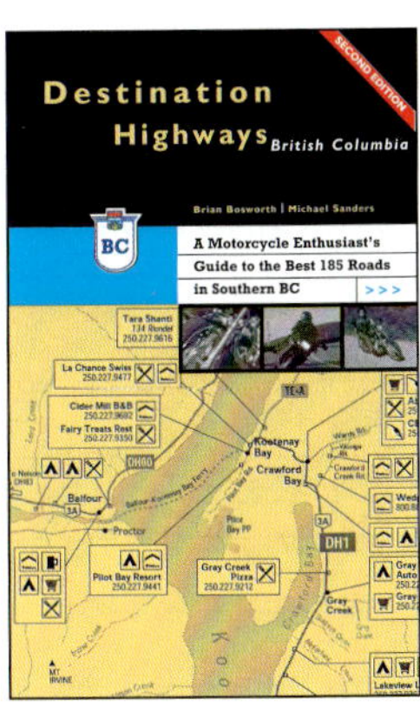

DH BC

DH Washington

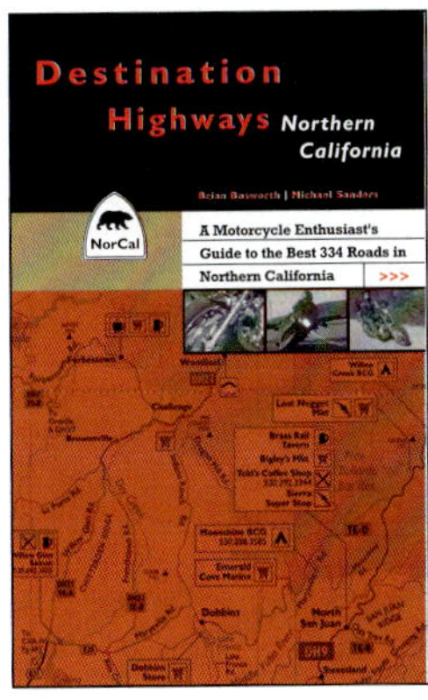

DH NorCal

Dealer inquiries welcome

TEAR OUT TEAR OUT TEAR OUT TEAR OUT